Patronage by Maria Edgeworth

Maria Edgeworth was born at Black Bourton, Oxfordshire on January 1st 1768. Her early years were with her mother's family in England. Sadly, her mother died when Maria was five.

Maria was educated at Mrs Lattafière's school in Derby in 1775. There she studied dancing, French and other subjects. Maria transferred to Mrs Devis's school in Upper Wimpole Street, London. Her father began to focus more attention on Maria in 1781 when she nearly lost her sight to an eye infection.

She returned home to Ireland at 14 and took charge of her younger siblings. She herself was home-tutored by her father in Irish economics and politics, science, literature and law. Despite her youth literature was in her blood. Maria also became her father's assistant in managing the family's large Edgeworthstown estate.

Maria first published 1795 with 'Letters for Literary Ladies'. That same year 'An Essay on the Noble Science of Self-Justification', written for a female audience, advised women on how to obtain better rights in general and specifically from their husbands.

'Practical Education' (1798) is a progressive work on education. Maria's ambition was to create an independent thinker who understands the consequences of his or her actions.

Her first novel, 'Castle Rackrent' was published anonymously in 1800 without her father's knowledge. It was an immediate success and firmly established Maria's appeal to the public.

Her father married four times and the last of these to Frances, a year younger and a confidante of Maria, who pushed them to travel more widely: London, Britain and Europe were all now visited.

The second series of 'Tales of Fashionable Life' (1812) did so well that she was now the most commercially successful novelist of her age.

She particularly worked hard to improve the living standards of the poor in Edgeworthstown and to provide schools for the local children of all and any denomination.

After a visit to see her relations Maria had severe chest pains and died suddenly of a heart attack in Edgeworthstown on 22nd May 1849. She was 81.

Index of Contents

PATRONAGE

"Above a patron—though I condescend
Sometimes to call a minister my friend."

TO THE READER

My daughter again applies to me for my paternal imprimatur; and I hope that I am not swayed by partiality, when I give the sanction which she requires.

To excite the rising generation to depend upon their own exertions for success in life is surely a laudable endeavour; but, while the young mind is cautioned against dependence on the patronage of the great, and of office, it is encouraged to rely upon such friends as may be acquired by personal merit, good manners, and good conduct.

RICHARD LOVELL EDGEWORTH.
Edgeworthstown,

Oct. 6, 1813.

PREFACE TO THE THIRD EDITION

The public has called for a third impression of this book; it was, therefore, the duty of the author to take advantage of the corrections which have been communicated to her by private friends and public censors. Whatever she has thought liable to just censure has in the present edition been amended, as far as is consistent with the identity of the story. It is remarkable that several incidents which have been objected to as impossible or improbable were true. For instance, the medical case, in Chapter XIX.

A bishop was really saved from suffocation by a clergyman in his diocese (no matter where or when), in the manner represented in Chapter X. The bishop died long ago; and he never was an epicure. A considerable estate was about seventy years ago regained, as described in Chapter XLII., by the discovery of a sixpence under the seal of a deed, which had been coined later than the date of the deed. Whether it be advantageous or prudent to introduce such singular facts in a fictitious history is a separate consideration, which might lead to a discussion too long for the present occasion.

On some other points of more importance to the writer, it is necessary here to add a few words. It has been supposed that some parts of PATRONAGE were not written by Miss Edgeworth. This is not fact: the whole of these volumes were written by her, the opinions they contain are her own, and she is answerable for all the faults which may be found in them. Of ignorance of law, and medicine, and of diplomacy, she pleads guilty; and of making any vain or absurd pretensions to legal or medical learning, she hopes, by candid judges, to be acquitted. If in the letters and history of her lawyer and physician she has sometimes introduced technical phrases, it was done merely to give, as far as she could, the colour of reality to her fictitious personages. To fulfil the main purpose of her story it was essential only to show how some lawyers and physicians may be pushed forward for a time, without much knowledge either of law or medicine; or how, on the contrary, others may, independently of patronage, advance themselves permanently by their own merit. If this principal object of the fiction be accomplished, the author's ignorance on professional subjects is of little consequence to the moral or interest of the tale.

As to the charge of having drawn satirical portraits, she has already disclaimed all personality, and all intention of satirizing any profession; and she is grieved to find it necessary to repel such a charge. The author of a slight work of fiction may, however, be consoled for any unjust imputation of personal satire, by reflecting, that even the grave and impartial historian cannot always escape similar suspicion. Tacitus says that "there must always be men, who, from congenial manners, and sympathy in vice, will think the fidelity of history a satire on themselves; and even the praise due to virtue is sure to give umbrage."

August 1, 1815.

PATRONAGE

CHAPTER I

"How the wind is rising!" said Rosamond.—"God help the poor people at sea to-night!"

Her brother Godfrey smiled.—"One would think," said he, "that she had an argosy of lovers at sea, uninsured."

"You gentlemen," replied Rosamond, "imagine that ladies are always thinking of lovers."

"Not always," said Godfrey; "only when they show themselves particularly disposed to humanity."

"My humanity, on the present occasion, cannot even be suspected," said Rosamond; "for you know, alas! that I have no lover at sea or land."

"But a shipwreck might bless the lucky shore with some rich waif," said Godfrey.

"Waifs and strays belong to the lady of the manor," said Rosamond; "and I have no claim to them."

"My mother would, I dare say, make over her right to you," said Godfrey.

"But that would do me no good," said Rosamond; "for here is Caroline, with superior claims of every sort, and with that most undisputed of all the rights of woman—beauty."

"True: but Caroline would never accept of stray hearts," said Godfrey. "See how her lip curls with pride at the bare imagination!"

"Pride never curled Caroline's lip," cried Rosamond: "besides, pride is very becoming to a woman. No woman can be good for much without it, can she, mother?"

"Before you fly off, Rosamond, to my mother as to an ally, whom you are sure I cannot resist," said Godfrey, "settle first whether you mean to defend Caroline upon the ground of her having or not having pride."

A fresh gust of wind rose at this moment, and Rosamond listened to it anxiously.

"Seriously, Godfrey," said she, "do you remember the ship-wrecks last winter?"

As she spoke, Rosamond went to one of the windows, and opened the shutter. Her sister Caroline followed, and they looked out in silence.

"I see a light to the left of the beacon," said Caroline.—"I never saw a light there before—What can it mean?"

"Only some fishermen," said Godfrey.

"But, brother, it is quite a storm," persisted Rosamond.

"Only equinoctial gales, my dear."

"Only equinoctial gales! But to drowning people it would be no comfort that they were shipwrecked only by equinoctial gales. There! there! what do you think of that blast?" cried Rosamond; "is not there some danger now?"

"Godfrey will not allow it," said Mrs. Percy: "he is a soldier, and it is his trade not to know fear."

"Show him a certain danger," cried Mr. Percy, looking up from a letter he was writing,—"show him a certain danger, and he will feel fear as much as the greatest coward of you all. Ha! upon my word, it is an ugly night," continued he, going to the window.

"Oh, my dear father!" cried Rosamond, "did you see that light—out at sea?—There! there!—to the left."

"To the east—I see it."

"Hark! did you hear?"

"Minute guns!" said Caroline.

There was a dead silence instantly.—Every body listened.—Guns were heard again.—The signal of some vessel in distress. The sound seemed near the shore.—Mr. Percy and Godfrey hastened immediately to the coast.—Their servants and some people from the neighbouring village, whom they summoned, quickly followed. They found that a vessel had struck upon a rock, and from the redoubled signals it appeared that the danger must be imminent.

The boatmen, who were just wakened, were surly, and swore that they would not stir; that whoever she was, she might weather out the night, for that, till daybreak, they couldn't get alongside of her. Godfrey instantly jumped into a boat, declaring he would go out directly at all hazards.—Mr. Percy with as much intrepidity, but, as became his age, with more prudence, provided whatever assistance was necessary from the villagers, who declared they would go any where with him; the boatmen, then ashamed, or afraid of losing the offered reward, pushed aside the land lubbers, and were ready to put out to sea.

Out they rowed—and they were soon so near the vessel, that they could hear the cries and voices of the crew. The boats hailed her, and she answered that she was Dutch, homeward bound—had mistaken the lights upon the coast—had struck on a rock—was filling with water—and must go down in half an hour.

The moment the boats came alongside of her, the crew crowded into them so fast, and with such disorder and precipitation, that they were in great danger of being overset, which, Mr. Percy seeing, called out in a loud and commanding voice to stop several who were in the act of coming down the ship's side, and promised to return for them if they would wait. But just as he gave the order for his boatmen to push off, a French voice called out "Monsieur!—Monsieur l'Anglois!—one moment."

Mr. Percy looked back and saw, as the moon shone full upon the wreck, a figure standing at the poop, leaning over with out-stretched arms.

"I am Monsieur de Tourville, monsieur—a chargé d'affaires—with papers of the greatest importance—despatches."

"I will return for you, sir—it is impossible for me to take you now—our boat is loaded as much as it can bear," cried Mr. Percy; and he repeated his order to the boatmen to push off.

Whilst Godfrey and Mr. Percy were trimming the boat, M. de Tourville made an effort to jump into it.

"Oh! don't do it, sir!" cried a woman with a child in her arms; "the gentleman will come back for us: for God's sake, don't jump into it!"

"Don't attempt it, sir," cried Mr. Percy, looking up, "or you'll sink us all."

M. de Tourville threw down the poor woman who tried to stop him, and he leaped from the side of the ship. At the same moment Mr. Percy, seizing an oar, pushed the boat off, and saved it from being overset, as it must have been if M. de Tourville had scrambled into it. He fell into the water. Mr. Percy, without waiting to see the event, went off as fast as possible, justly considering that the lives of the number he had under his protection, including his son's and his own, were not to be sacrificed for one man, whatever his name or office might be, especially when that man had persisted against all warning in his rash selfishness.

At imminent danger to themselves, Mr. Percy and Godfrey, after landing those in the boat, returned once more to the wreck; and though they both declared that their consciences would be at ease even if they found that M. de Tourville was drowned, yet it was evident that they rejoiced to see him safe on board. This time the boat held him, and all the rest of his fellow sufferers; and Mr. Percy and his son had the satisfaction of bringing every soul safely to shore.—M. de Tourville, as soon as he found himself on terra firma, joined with all around him in warm thanks to Mr. Percy and his son, by whom their lives had been saved.—Godfrey undertook to find lodgings for some of the passengers and for the ship's crew in the village, and Mr. Percy invited the captain, M. de Tourville, and the rest of the passengers, to Percy-hall, where Mrs. Percy and her daughters had prepared every thing for their hospitable reception. When they had warmed, dried, and refreshed themselves, they were left to enjoy what they wanted most—repose. The Percy family, nearly as much fatigued as their guests, were also glad to rest—all but Rosamond, who was wide awake, and so much excited by what had happened, that she continued talking to her sister, who slept in the same room with her, of every circumstance, and filling her imagination with all that might come to pass from the adventures of the night, whilst Caroline, too sleepy to be able to answer judiciously, or even plausibly, said, "Yes," "No," and "Very true," in the wrong place; and at length, incapable of uttering even a monosyllable, was reduced to inarticulate sounds in sign of attention. These grew fainter and fainter, and after long intervals absolutely failing, Rosamond with some surprise and indignation, exclaimed, "I do believe, Caroline, you are asleep!" And, in despair, Rosamond, for want of an auditor, was compelled to compose herself to rest.

In the course of a few hours the storm abated, and in the morning, when the family and their shipwrecked guests assembled at breakfast, all was calm and serene. Much to Rosamond's dissatisfaction, M. de Tourville did not make his appearance. Of the other strangers she had seen only a glimpse the preceding night, and had not settled her curiosity concerning what sort of beings they were. On a clear view by daylight of the personages who now sat at the breakfast-table, there did not appear much to interest her romantic imagination, or to excite her benevolent sympathy. They had the appearance of careful money-making men, thick, square-built Dutch merchants, who said little and eat much—butter especially. With one accord, as soon as they had breakfasted, they rose, and begged permission to go down to the wreck to look after their property. Mr. Percy and Godfrey offered immediately to accompany them to the coast.

Mr. Percy had taken the precaution to set guards to watch all night, from the time he left the vessel, that no depredations might be committed. They found that some of the cargo had been damaged by the sea-water, but excepting this loss there was no other of any consequence; the best part of the goods was perfectly safe. As it was found that it would take some time to repair the wreck, the Prussian and Hamburgh passengers determined to go on board a vessel which was to sail from a neighbouring port with the first fair wind. They came, previously to their departure, to thank the Percy family, and to assure them that their hospitality would never be forgotten.—Mr. Percy pressed them to stay at Percy-hall till the vessel should sail, and till the captain should send notice of the first change of wind.—This offer, however, was declined, and the Dutch merchants, with due acknowledgments, said, by their speaking partner, that "they considered it safest and best to go with the goods, and so wished Mr. Percy a good morning, and that he might prosper in all his dealings; and, sir," concluded he, "in any of the changes of fortune, which happen to men by land as well as by sea, please to remember the names of Grinderweld, Groensvelt, and Slidderchild of Amsterdam, or our correspondents, Panton and Co., London."

So having said, they walked away, keeping an eye upon the goods.

When Mr. Percy returned home it was near dinner-time, yet M. de Tourville had not made his appearance. He was all this while indulging in a comfortable sleep. He had no goods on board the wreck except his clothes, and as these were in certain trunks and portmanteaus in which Comtois, his valet, had a joint concern, M. de Tourville securely trusted that they would be obtained without his taking any trouble.

Comtois and the trunks again appeared, and a few minutes before dinner M. de Tourville made his entrance into the drawing-room, no longer in the plight of a shipwrecked mariner, but in gallant trim, wafting gales of momentary bliss as he went round the room paying his compliments to the ladies, bowing, smiling, apologizing,—the very pink of courtesy!—The gentlemen of the family, who had seen him the preceding night in his frightened, angry, drenched, and miserable state, could scarcely believe him to be the same person.

A Frenchman, it will be allowed, can contrive to say more, and to tell more of his private history in a given time, than could be accomplished by a person of any other nation. In the few minutes before dinner he found means to inform the company, that he was private secretary and favourite of the minister of a certain German court. To account for his having taken his passage in a Dutch merchant vessel, and for his appearing without a suitable suite, he whispered that he had been instructed to preserve a strict incognito, from which, indeed, nothing but the horrors of the preceding night could have drawn him.

Dinner was served, and at dinner M. de Tourville was seen, according to the polished forms of society, humbling himself in all the hypocrisy of politeness; with ascetic good-breeding, preferring every creature's ease and convenience to his own, practising a continual system of self-denial, such as almost implied a total annihilation of self-interest and self-love. All this was strikingly contrasted with the selfishness which he had recently betrayed, when he was in personal danger. Yet the influence of polite manners prevailed so far as to make his former conduct be forgotten by most of the family.

After dinner, when the ladies retired, in the female privy council held to discuss the merits of the absent gentlemen, Rosamond spoke first, and during the course of five minutes pronounced as many contradictory opinions of M. de Tourville, as could well be enunciated in the same space of time.—At last she paused, and her mother smiled.

"I understand your smile, mother," said Rosamond; "but the reason I appear a little to contradict myself sometimes in my judgment of character is, because I speak my thoughts just as they rise in my mind, while persons who have a character for judgment to support always keep the changes of their opinion snug to themselves, never showing the items of the account on either side, and let you see nothing but their balance.—This is very grand, and, if their balance be right, very glorious.—But ignominious as my mode of proceeding may seem, exposing me to the rebukes, derision, uplifted hands and eyes of my auditors, yet exactly because I am checked at every little mistake I make in my accounts, the chance is in my favour that my totals should at last be right, and my balance perfectly accurate."

"Very true, my dear: as long as you choose for your auditors only your friends, you are wise; but you sometimes lay your accounts open to strangers; and as they see only your errors, without ever coming to your conclusion, they form no favourable opinion of your accuracy."

"I don't mind what strangers think of me—much," said Rosamond.—"At least you will allow, mamma, that I have reason to be satisfied, if only those who do not know me should form an unfavourable opinion of my judgment—and, after all, ma'am, of the two classes of people, those who 'never said a foolish thing, and never did a wise one,' and those who never did a foolish thing, and never said a wise one, would not you rather that I should belong to the latter class?"

"Certainly, if I were reduced to the cruel alternative: but is there an unavoidable necessity for your belonging to either class?"

"I will consider of it, ma'am," said Rosamond: "in the meantime, Caroline, you will allow that M. de Tourville is very agreeable?"

"Agreeable!" repeated Caroline; "such a selfish being? Have you forgotten his attempting to jump into the boat, at the hazard of oversetting it, and of drowning my father and Godfrey, who went out to save him—and when my father warned him—and promised to return for him—selfish, cowardly creature!"

"Oh! poor man, he was so frightened, that he did not know what he was doing—he was not himself."

"You mean he was himself," said Caroline.

"You are very ungrateful, Caroline," cried Rosamond; "for I am sure M. de Tourville admires you extremely—yes, in spite of that provoking, incredulous smile, I say he does admire you exceedingly."

"And if he did," replied Caroline, "that would make no difference in my opinion of him."

"I doubt that," said Rosamond: "I know a person's admiring me would make a great difference in my opinion of his taste and judgment—and how much more if he had sense enough to admire you!"

Rosamond paused, and stood for some minutes silent in reverie.

"It will never do, my dear," said Mrs. Percy, looking up at her; "trust me it will never do; turn him which way you will in your imagination, you will never make a hero of him—nor yet a brother-in-law."

"My dear mother, how could you guess what I was thinking of?" said Rosamond, colouring a little, and laughing; "but I assure you—now let me explain to you, ma'am, in one word, what I think of M. de Tourville."

"Hush! my dear, he is here."

The gentlemen came into the room to tea.—M. de Tourville walked to the table at which Mrs. Percy was sitting; and, after various compliments on the beauty of the views from the windows, on the richness of the foliage in the park, and the superiority of English verdure, he next turned to look at the pictures in the saloon, distinguished a portrait by Sir Joshua Reynolds, then passing to a table on which lay several books—"Is it permitted?" said he, taking up one of them—the Life of Lord Nelson.

M. de Tourville did not miss the opportunity of paying a just and what to English ears he knew must be a delightful, tribute of praise to our naval hero. Then opening several other books, he made a rash attempt to pronounce in English their titles, and with the happy facility of a Frenchman, he touched upon various subjects, dwelt upon none, but found means on all to say something to raise himself and his country in the opinion of the company, and at the same time to make all his auditors pleased with themselves. Presently, taking a seat between Rosamond and Caroline, he applied himself to draw out their talents for conversation. Nor did he labour in vain. They did not shut themselves up in stupid and provoking silence, nor did they make any ostentatious display of their knowledge or abilities.—M. de Tourville, as Rosamond had justly observed, seemed to be particularly struck with Miss Caroline Percy.— She was beautiful, and of an uncommon style of beauty. Ingenuous, unaffected, and with all the simplicity of youth, there was a certain dignity and graceful self-possession in her manner, which gave the idea of a superior character. She had, perhaps, less of what the French call esprit than M. de Tourville had been accustomed to meet with in young persons on the continent, but he was the more surprised by the strength and justness of thought which appeared in her plain replies to the finesse of some of his questions.

The morning of the second day that he was at Percy-hall, M. de Tourville was admiring the Miss Percys' drawings, especially some miniatures of Caroline's, and he produced his snuff-box, to show Mr. Percy a beautiful miniature on its lid.

It was exquisitely painted. M. de Tourville offered it to Caroline to copy, and Mrs. Percy urged her to make the attempt.

"It is the celebrated Euphrosyne," said he, "who from the stage was very near mounting a throne."

M. de Tourville left the miniature in the hands of the ladies to be admired, and, addressing himself to Mr. Percy, began to tell with much mystery the story of Euphrosyne. She was an actress of whom the prince, heir apparent at the German court where he resided, had become violently enamoured. One of the prince's young confidants had assisted his royal highness in carrying on a secret correspondence with Euphrosyne, which she managed so artfully that the prince was on the point of giving her a written promise of marriage, when the intrigue was discovered, and prevented from proceeding farther, by a certain Count Albert Altenberg, a young nobleman who had till that moment been one of the prince's favourites, but who by thus opposing his passion lost entirely his prince's favour. The story was a common story of an intrigue, such as happens every day in every country where there is a young prince; but there was something uncommon in the conduct of Count Altenberg. Mr. Percy expressed his admiration of it; but M. de Tourville, though he acknowledged, as in morality bound, that the count's conduct had been admirable, just what it ought to be upon this occasion, yet spoke of him altogether as une tête exaltée, a young man of a romantic Quixotic enthusiasm, to which he had sacrificed the interests of his family, and his own hopes of advancement at court. In support of this opinion, M. de Tourville related several anecdotes, and on each of these anecdotes Mr. Percy and M. de Tourville differed in opinion. All that was produced to prove that the young count had no judgment or discretion appeared to Mr. Percy proofs of his independence of character and greatness of soul. Mr. Percy repeated the anecdotes to Mrs. Percy and his daughters; and M. de Tourville, as soon as he saw that the ladies, and especially Caroline, differed from him, immediately endeavoured to slide round to their opinion, and assured Caroline, with many asseverations, and with his hand upon his heart, that he had merely been speaking of the light in which these things appeared to the generality of men of the world; that for his own particular feelings they were all in favour of the frankness and generosity of character evinced by these imprudences—he only lamented that certain qualities should expose their possessor to the censure and ridicule of those who were like half the world, incapable of being moved by any motive but interest, and unable to reach to the idea of the moral sublime.

The more M. de Tourville said upon the subject, and the more gesture and emphasis he used to impress the belief in his truth, the less Caroline believed him, and the more dislike and contempt she felt for the duplicity and pitiful meanness of a character, which was always endeavouring to seem, instead of to be.—He understood and felt the expression of her countenance, and mortified by that dignified silence, which said more than words could express, he turned away, and never afterwards addressed to her any of his confidential conversation.

From this moment Rosamond's opinion of M. de Tourville changed. She gave him up altogether, and denied, or at least gave him grudgingly, that praise, which he eminently deserved for agreeable manners and conversational talents. Not a foible of his now escaped her quick observation and her lively perception of ridicule.

Whether from accident, or from some suspicion that he had lost ground with the ladies, M. de Tourville the next day directed the principal part of his conversation to the gentlemen of the family: comforting himself with the importance of his political and official character, he talked grandly of politics and diplomacy. Rosamond, who listened with an air of arch attention, from time to time, with a tone of ironical simplicity, asked explanations on certain points relative to the diplomatic code of morality, and professed herself much edified and enlightened by the answers she received.

She wished, as she told Caroline, that some one would write Advice to Diplomatists, in the manner of Swift's advice to Servants; and she observed that M. de Tourville, chargé d'affaires, &c., might supply anecdotes illustrative, and might embellish the work with a portrait of a finished diplomatist. Unfortunately for the public, on the third morning of the diplomatist's visit, a circumstance occurred, which prevented the farther development of his character, stopped his flow of anecdote, and snatched him from the company of his hospitable hosts. In looking over his papers, in order to show Mr. Percy a complimentary letter from some crowned head, M. de Tourville discovered that an important packet of papers belonging to his despatches was missing. He had in the moment of danger and terror stuffed all his despatches into his great-coat pocket; in getting out of the boat he had given his coat to Comtois to carry, and, strange to tell, this chargé d'affaires had taken it upon trust, from the assertion of his valet, that all his papers were safe. He once, indeed, had looked them over, but so carelessly that he never had missed the packet. His dismay was great when he discovered his loss. He repeated at least a thousand times that he was an undone man, unless the packet could be found.—Search was made for it, in the boat, on the shore, in every probable and improbable place—but all in vain; and in the midst of the search a messenger came to announce that the wind was fair, that the ship would sail in one hour, and that the captain could wait for no man. M. de Tourville was obliged to take his departure without this precious packet.

Mrs. Percy was the only person in the family who had the humanity to pity him. He was too little of a soldier for Godfrey's taste, too much of a courtier for Mr. Percy, too frivolous for Caroline, and too little romantic for Rosamond.

"So," said Rosamond, "here was a fine beginning of a romance with a shipwreck, that ends only in five square merchants, who do not lose even a guilder of their property, and a diplomatist, with whom we are sure of nothing but that he has lost a bundle of papers for which nobody cares!"

In a few days the remembrance of the whole adventure began to fade from her fancy. M. de Tourville, and his snuff-box, and his essences, and his flattery, and his diplomacy, and his lost packet, and all the circumstances of the shipwreck, would have appeared as a dream, if they had not been maintained in the rank of realities by the daily sight of the wreck, and by the actual presence of the Dutch sailors, who were repairing the vessel.

CHAPTER II

A few days after the departure of M. de Tourville, Commissioner Falconer, a friend, or at least a relation of Mr. Percy's, came to pay him a visit. As the commissioner looked out of the window and observed the Dutch carpenter, who was passing by with tools under his arm, he began to talk of the late shipwreck. Mr. Falconer said he had heard much of the successful exertions and hospitality of the Percy family on that occasion—regretted that he had himself been called to town just at that time—asked many questions about the passengers on board the vessel, and when M. de Tourville was described to him, deplored that Mr. Percy had never thought of trying to detain this foreigner a few days longer.

For, argued the commissioner, though M. de Tourville might not be an accredited chargé d'affaires, yet, since he was a person in some degree in an official capacity, and intrusted with secret negotiations, government might have wished to know something about him. "And at all events," added the commissioner, with a shrewd smile, "it would have been a fine way of paying our court to a certain great man."

"So, commissioner, you still put your trust in great men?" said Mr. Percy.

"Not in all great men, but in some," replied the commissioner; "for instance, in your old friend, Lord Oldborough, who, I'm happy to inform you, is just come into our neighbourhood to Clermont-park, of which he has at last completed the purchase, and has sent down his plate and pictures.—Who knows but he may make Clermont-park his summer residence, instead of his place in Essex? and if he should, there's no saying of what advantage it might be, for I have it from the very best authority, that his lordship's influence in a certain quarter is greater than ever. Of course, Mr. Percy, you will wait upon Lord Oldborough, when he comes to this part of the country?"

"No, I believe not," said Mr. Percy: "I have no connexion with him now."

"But you were so intimate with him abroad," expostulated Mr. Falconer.

"It is five-and-twenty years since I knew him abroad," said Mr. Percy; "and from all I have heard, he is an altered man. When I was intimate with Lord Oldborough, he was a generous, open-hearted youth: he has since become a politician, and I fear he has sold himself for a riband to the demon of ambition."

"No matter to whom he has sold himself, or for what," replied the commissioner; "that is his affair, not ours. We must not be too nice. He is well disposed towards you; and, my dear sir, I should take it as a very particular favour if you would introduce me to his lordship."

"With great pleasure," said Mr. Percy, "the very first opportunity."

"We must make opportunities—not wait for them," said the commissioner, smiling. "Let me entreat that you will pay your respects to his lordship as soon as he comes into the country. It really is but civil—and take me in your hand."

"With all my heart," said Mr. Percy; "but mine shall only be a visit of civility."

Well satisfied with having obtained this promise, Commissioner Falconer departed.

Besides his general desire to be acquainted with the great, the commissioner had particular reasons for wishing to be introduced at this time to Lord Oldborough, and he had a peculiar cause for being curious about M. de Tourville.—Mr. Falconer was in possession of the packet which that diplomatist had lost. It had been found by one of the commissioner's sons, Mr. John Falconer; or rather by Mr. John Falconer's dog, Neptune, who brought it to his master when he was bathing in the sea the day after the shipwreck. It had been thrown by the tide among some sea-weed, where it was entangled, and where it lay hid till it was discovered by the dog. Mr. John Falconer had carried it home, and boasting of his dog's sagacity, had produced it rather as a proof of the capital manner in which he had taught Neptune to fetch and carry, than from any idea or care for the value of the packet; John Falconer being one of those men who care for very little in this world,

"Whilst they have their dog and their gun."

Not so the commissioner, who immediately began to examine the papers with serious curiosity, to discover whether they could by any means be productive of advantage to him or his family. The sea-water had injured only the outer pages; but though the inner were not in the least damaged, it was difficult to make out their contents, for they were written in cipher. Commissioner Falconer, however, was skilled in the art of deciphering, and possessed all the ingenuity and patience necessary for the business. The title, superscription, and signature of the paper were obliterated, so that he could not guess from whom they came, or to whom they were addressed; he perceived that they were political; but of what degree of importance they might be he could not decide, till he heard of M. de Tourville the diplomatist, and of his distress at the loss of this packet. The commissioner then resolved to devote the evening, ensuing day, and night, if requisite, to the business, that he might have it in readiness to carry with him when he went to pay his respects to Lord Oldborough. Foreseeing that something might be made of this intercepted despatch, and fearing that if he mentioned it to Mr. Percy, that gentleman might object to opening the papers, Mr. Falconer left Percy-hall without giving the most remote hint of the treasure which he possessed, or of the use that he intended to make of his discovery.

Early in the ensuing week Mr. Percy went to pay his visit of civility, and Mr. Falconer his visit of policy, to Lord Oldborough. His lordship was so much altered, that it was with difficulty Mr. Percy recollected in him any traces of the same person. The Lord Oldborough he had formerly known was gay, gallant, and rather dissipated; of a frank, joyous air and manner. The Lord Oldborough whom he now saw was a serious, reserved-looking personage, with a face in which the lines of thought and care were deeply marked; large eyebrows, vigilant eyes, with an expression of ability and decision in his whole countenance, but not of tranquillity or of happiness. His manner was well-bred, but rather cold and formal: his conversation circumspect, calculated to draw forth the opinions, and to benefit by the information of others, rather than to assert or display his own. He seemed to converse, to think, to live, not with any enjoyment of the present, but with a view to some future object, about which he was constantly anxious.

Mr. Percy and Mr. Falconer both observed Lord Oldborough attentively during this visit: Mr. Percy studied him with philosophical curiosity, to discover what changes had been made in his lordship's character by the operation of ambition, and to determine how far that passion had contributed to his happiness; Mr. Falconer studied him with the interested eye of a man of the world, eager to discern what advantage could be made by ministering to that ambition, and to decide whether there was about his lordship the making of a good patron.

There was, he thought, the right twist, if he had but skill to follow, and humour it in the working; but this was a task of much nicety. Lord Oldborough appeared to be aware of the commissioner's views, and was not disposed to burden himself with new friends. It seemed easy to go to a certain point with his lordship, but difficult to get farther; easy to obtain his attention, but impossible to gain his confidence.

The commissioner, however, had many resources ready; many small means of fastening himself both on his lordship's private and public interests. He determined to begin first with the despatch which he had been deciphering. With this view he led Mr. Percy to speak of the shipwreck, and of M. de Tourville.

Lord Oldborough's attention was immediately awakened; and when Mr. Falconer perceived that the regret for not having seen M. de Tourville, and the curiosity to know the nature of his secret negotiations had been sufficiently excited, the commissioner quitted the subject, as he could go no farther whilst restrained by Mr. Percy's presence. He took the first opportunity of leaving the room with his lordship's nephew, Col. Hauton, to look at some horses, which were to run at the ensuing races.

Left alone with Mr. Percy, Lord Oldborough looked less reserved, for he plainly saw, indeed Mr. Percy plainly showed, that he had nothing to ask from the great man, but that he came only to see his friend.

"Many years since we met, Mr. Percy," said his lordship, sitting down and placing his chair for the first time without considering whether his face or his back were to the light.—"A great many years since we met, Mr. Percy; and yet I should not think so from your appearance; you do not look as if—shall I say it?—five-and-twenty years had passed since that time. But you have been leading an easy life in the country—the happiest life: I envy you."

Mr. Percy, thinking that these were words of course, the mere polite cant of a courtier to a country gentleman, smiled, and replied, that few who were acquainted with their different situations in the world would imagine that Mr. Percy could be an object of envy to Lord Oldborough, a statesman at the summit of favour and fortune.

"Not the summit," said Lord Oldborough, sighing; "and if I were even at the summit, it is, you know, a dangerous situation. Fortune's wheel never stands still—the highest point is therefore the most perilous." His lordship sighed again as deeply as before; then spoke, or rather led to the subject of general politics, of which Mr. Percy gave his opinions with freedom and openness, yet without ever forgetting the respect due to Lord Oldborough's situation. His lordship seemed sensible of this attention, sometimes nodded, and sometimes smiled, as Mr. Percy spoke of public men or measures; but when he expressed any sentiment of patriotism, or of public virtue, Lord Oldborough took to his snuff-box, shook and levelled the snuff; and if he listened, listened as to words superfluous and irrelevant. When Mr. Percy uttered any principle favourable to the liberty of the press, or of the people, his lordship would take several pinches of snuff rapidly, to hide the expression of his countenance; if the topics were continued, his averted eyes and compressed lips showed disapprobation, and the difficulty he felt in refraining from reply. From reply, however, he did absolutely refrain; and after a pause of a few moments, with a smile, in a softer and lower voice than his usual tone, he asked Mr. Percy some questions about his family, and turned the conversation again to domestic affairs;—expressed surprise, that a man of Mr. Percy's talents should live in such absolute retirement; and seeming to forget what he had said himself but half an hour before, of the pains and dangers of ambition, and all that Mr. Percy had said of his love of domestic life, appeared to take it for granted that Mr. Percy would be glad to shine in public, if opportunity were not wanting. Upon this supposition, his lordship dexterously pointed out ways by which he might distinguish himself; threw out assurances of his own good wishes, compliments to his talents; and, in short, sounded his heart, still expecting to find corruption or ambition at the bottom. But none was to be found. Lord Oldborough was convinced of it—and surprised. Perhaps his esteem for Mr. Percy's understanding fell some degrees—he considered him as an eccentric person, acting from unaccountable motives; but still he respected him as that rarest of all things in a politician's eye—a really honest independent man. He believed also that Mr. Percy had some regard for him; and whatever portion it might be, it was valuable and extraordinary—for it was disinterested: besides, they could never cross in their objects—and as Mr. Percy lived out of the world, and had no connexion with any party, he was a perfectly safe man. All these thoughts acted so powerfully upon Lord Oldborough, that he threw aside his reserve, in a manner which would have astonished and delighted Mr. Falconer. Mr. Percy was astonished, but not delighted—he saw a noble mind corroded and debased by ambition—virtuous principle, generous feeling, stifled—a powerful, capacious understanding distorted—a soul, once expatiating and full of high thoughts, now confined to a span—bent down to low concerns—imprisoned in the precincts of a court.

"You pity me," said Lord Oldborough, who seemed to understand Mr. Percy's thoughts; "you pity me—I pity myself. But such is ambition, and I cannot live without it—once and always its slave."

"A person of such a strong mind as Lord Oldborough could emancipate himself from any slavery—even that of habit."

"Yes, if he wished to break through it—but he does not."

"Can he have utterly—"

"Lost his taste for freedom? you would say. Yes—utterly. I see you pity me," said his lordship with a bitter smile; "and," added he, rising proudly, "I am unused to be pitied, and I am awkward, I fear, under the obligation." Resuming his friendly aspect, however, in a moment or two, he followed Mr. Percy, who had turned to examine a fine picture.

"Yes; a Corregio. You are not aware, my dear sir," continued he, "that between the youth you knew at Paris, and the man who has now the honour to speak to you, there is nothing in common—absolutely nothing—except regard for Mr. Percy. You had always great knowledge of character, I remember; but with respect to my own, you will recollect that I have the advantage of possessing la carte du pays. You are grown quite a philosopher, I find; and so am I, in my own way. In short, to put the question between us at rest for ever, there is nothing left for me in life but ambition. Now let us go to Corregio, or what you please."

Mr. Percy followed his lordship's lead immediately to Italy, to France, to Paris, and talking over old times and youthful days, the conversation grew gay and familiar. Lord Oldborough seemed enlivened and pleased, and yet, as if it were a reminiscence of a former state of existence, he often repeated, "Ah! those were young days—very young: I was a boy then—quite a boy." At last Mr. Percy touched upon love and women, and, by accident, mentioned an Italian lady whom they had known abroad.—A flash of pale anger, almost of frenzy, passed across Lord Oldborough's countenance: he turned short, darted full on Mr. Percy a penetrating, imperious, interrogative look.—Answered by the innocence, the steady openness of Mr. Percy's countenance, Lord Oldborough grew red instantly, and, conscious of his unusual change of colour, stood actually abashed. A moment afterward, commanding his agitation, he forced his whole person to an air of tranquillity—took up the red book which lay upon his table, walked deliberately to a window, and, looking earnestly through his glass, asked if Mr. Percy could recollect who was member for some borough in the neighbourhood? The conversation after this languished; and though some efforts were made, it never recovered the tone of ease and confidence. Both parties felt relieved from an indefinable sort of constraint by the return of the other gentlemen. Mr. Falconer begged Mr. Percy to go and look at a carriage of a new construction, which the colonel had just brought from town; and the colonel accompanying Mr. Percy, the stage was thus left clear for the commissioner to open his business about M. de Tourville's packet. He did it with so much address, and with so little circumlocution, that Lord Oldborough immediately comprehended how important the papers might be to him, and how necessary it was to secure the decipherer. When Mr. Percy returned, he found the commissioner and his lordship in earnest and seemingly confidential conversation. Both Mr. Falconer and Mr. Percy were now pressed to stay to dine and to sleep at Clermont-park; an invitation which Mr. Percy declined, but which the commissioner accepted.

In the evening, when the company who had dined at Clermont-park were settled to cards and music, Lord Oldborough, after walking up and down the room with the commissioner in silence for some minutes, retired with him into his study, rang, and gave orders that they should not be interrupted on any account till supper. The servant informed his lordship that such and such persons, whom he had appointed, were waiting.—"I cannot possibly see them till to-morrow," naming the hour. The servant laid on the table before his lordship a huge parcel of letters. Lord Oldborough, with an air of repressed impatience, bid the man send his secretary, Mr. Drakelow,—looked over the letters, wrote with a pencil, and with great despatch, a few words on the back of each—met Mr. Drakelow as he entered the room— put the unfolded letters all together into his hands—"The answers on the back—to be made out in form—ready for signature at six to-morrow."

"Yes, my lord. May I ask—"

"Ask nothing, sir, if you please—I am busy—you have your directions."

Mr. Drakelow bowed submissive, and made his exit with great celerity.

"Now to our business, my dear sir," said his lordship, seating himself at the table with Mr. Falconer, who immediately produced M. de Tourville's papers.

It is not at this period of our story necessary to state precisely their contents; it is sufficient to say, that they opened to Lord Oldborough a scene of diplomatic treachery abroad, and of ungrateful duplicity at home. From some of the intercepted letters he discovered that certain of his colleagues, who appeared to be acting along with him with the utmost cordiality, were secretly combined against him; and were carrying on an underplot, to deprive him at once of popularity, favour, place, and power. The strength, firmness, hardness of mind, which Lord Oldborough exhibited at the moment of this discovery, perfectly amazed Mr. Falconer. His lordship gave no sign of astonishment, uttered no indignant exclamation, nor betrayed any symptoms of alarm; but he listened with motionless attention, when Mr. Falconer from time to time interrupted his reading, and put himself to great expense of face and lungs to express his abhorrence of "such inconceivable treachery." Lord Oldborough maintained an absolute silence, and waiting till the commissioner had exhausted himself in invective, would point with his pencil to the line in the paper where he had left off, and calmly say—"Have the goodness to go on—Let us proceed, sir, if you please."

The commissioner went on till he came to the most important and interesting point, and then glancing his eye on his intended patron's profile, which was towards him, he suddenly stopped. Lord Oldborough, raising his head from the hand on which it leaned, turned his full front face upon Mr. Falconer.

"Let me hear the whole, if you please, sir.—To form a judgment upon any business, it is necessary to have the whole before us.—You need not fear to shock my feelings, sir. I wish always to see men and things as they are." Mr. Falconer still hesitating, and turning over the leaves—"As my friend in this business, Mr. Falconer," continued his lordship, "you will comprehend that the essential point is to put me as soon as possible in possession of the facts—then I can decide, and act. If it will not fatigue you too much, I wish to go through these papers before I sleep."

"Fatigue! Oh, my lord, I am not in the least—cannot be fatigued! But the fact is, I cannot go on; for the next pages I have not yet deciphered—the cipher changes here."

Lord Oldborough looked much disappointed and provoked; but, after a few minutes' pause, calmly said, "What time will it take, sir, to decipher the remainder?"

The commissioner protested he did not know—could not form an idea—he and his son had spent many hours of intense labour on the first papers before he could make out the first cipher—now this was a new one, probably more difficult, and whether he could make it out at all, or in what time, he was utterly unable to say. Lord Oldborough replied, "Let us understand one another at once, Commissioner Falconer, if you please. My maxim, and the maxim of every man in public life is, or ought to be—Serve me, and I will serve you. I have no pretensions to Mr. Falconer's friendship on any other grounds, I am sensible; nor on any other terms can he have a claim to whatever power of patronage I possess. But I neither serve nor will be served by halves: my first object is to make myself master, as soon as possible, of the contents of the papers in your hands; my next to secure your inviolable secrecy on the whole transaction."

The commissioner was going to make vows of secrecy and protestations of zeal, but Lord Oldborough cut all that short with "Of course—of course," pronounced in the driest accent, and went on with, "Now, sir, you know my object; will you do me the honour to state yours?—you will excuse my abruptness— time in some circumstances is every thing—Do me and yourself the justice to say at once what return I can make for the service you have done or may do me and government."

"My only hesitation in speaking, my lord, was—"

"Have no hesitation in speaking, I beseech you, sir."

I beseech, in tone, was in effect, I command you, sir;—and Mr. Falconer, under the influence of an imperious and superior mind, came at once to that point, which he had not intended to come to for a month, or to approach till after infinite precaution and circumlocution.

"My object is to push my son Cunningham in the diplomatic line, my lord—and I wish to make him one of your secretaries."

The commissioner stopped short, astonished to find that the truth, and the whole truth, had absolutely passed his lips, and in such plain words; but they could not be recalled: he gasped for breath—and began an apologetical sentence about poor Mr. Drakelow, whom he should be sorry to injure or displace.

"Never mind that now—time enough to think of Drakelow," said Lord Oldborough, walking up and down the room—then stopping short, "I must see your son, sir."

"I will bring him here to-morrow, if your lordship pleases."

"As soon as possible! But he can come surely without your going for him—write, and beg that we may see him at breakfast—at nine, if you please."

The letter was written, and despatched immediately. Lord Oldborough, whilst the commissioner was writing, noted down the heads of what he had learned from M. de Tourville's packet: then locked up those of the papers which had been deciphered, put the others into Mr. Falconer's charge, and recommended it to him to use all possible despatch in deciphering the remainder.—The commissioner declared he would sit up all night at the task; this did not appear to be more than was expected.—His lordship rung, and ordered candles in Mr. Falconer's room, then returned to the company in the saloon, without saying another word. None could guess by his countenance or deportment that any unusual circumstance had happened, or that his mind was in the least perturbed. Mrs. Drakelow thought he was wholly absorbed in a rubber of whist, and Miss Drakelow at the same time was persuaded that he was listening to her music.

Punctual to the appointed hour—for ambition is as punctual to appointments as love—Mr. Cunningham Falconer made his appearance at nine, and was presented by his father to Lord Oldborough, who received him, not with any show of gracious kindness, but as one who had been forced upon him by circumstances, and whom, for valuable considerations, he had bargained to take into his service. To try the young diplomatist's talents, Lord Oldborough led him first to speak on the subject of the Tourville papers, then urged him on to the affairs of Germany, and the general interests and policy of the different courts of Europe. Trembling, and in agony for his son, the commissioner stood aware of the danger of the youth's venturing out of his depth, aware also of the danger of showing that he dared not venture, and incapable of deciding between these equal fears: but soon he was re-assured by the calmness of his son. Cunningham, who had not so much information or capacity, but who had less sensibility than his father, often succeeded where his father's timidity prognosticated failure. Indeed, on the present occasion, the care which the young diplomatist took not to commit himself, the dexterity with which he "helped himself by countenance and gesture," and "was judicious by signs," proved that he was well skilled in all those arts of seeming wise, which have been so well noted for use by "the greatest, wisest, meanest of mankind." Young though he was, Cunningham was quite sufficiently slow, circumspect, and solemn, to deserve to be ranked among those whom Bacon calls Formalists, "who do nothing, or little, very solemnly—who seem always to keep back somewhat; and when they know within themselves that they speak of what they do not know, would, nevertheless, seem to others to know that of which they may not well speak."

Lord Oldborough listened to whatever he said, and marked all that he did not say with an air of attentive composure, which, as Mr. Falconer thought, augured well for his son; but now and then there was, for scarcely a definable portion of time, an expression of humour in his lordship's eye, a sarcastic smile, which escaped the commissioner's observation, and which, even if he had observed, he could not, with his limited knowledge of Lord Oldborough's character, have rightly interpreted. If his lordship had expressed his thoughts, perhaps, they might have been, though in words less quaint, nearly the same as those of the philosophic statesman, who says, "It is a ridiculous thing, and fit for a satire to persons of judgment, to see what shifts these formalists have, and what prospectives to make superficies to seem body that hath depth and bulk."

But Lord Oldborough philosophizing, and Lord Oldborough acting, were two different people. His perception of the ridicule of the young secretary's solemnity, and of the insufficiency of his information and capacity, made no alteration in the minister's determination. The question was not whether the individual was fit for this place, or that employment, but whether it was expedient he should have it for the security of political power. Waiving all delicacy, Lord Oldborough now, as in most other cases, made it his chief object to be understood and obeyed; therefore he applied directly to the universal motive, and spoke the universal language of interest.

"Mr. Falconer," said he, "if you put me in possession of the remainder of M. de Tourville's papers this night, I will to-morrow morning put this young gentleman into the hands of my present secretary, Mr. Drakelow, who will prepare him for the situation you desire. Mr. Drakelow himself will, probably, soon leave me, to be employed more advantageously for his majesty's service, in some other manner."

The decipherers, father and son, shut themselves up directly, and set to work with all imaginable zeal. The whole packet was nearly expounded before night, and the next morning Lord Oldborough performed his part of the agreement. He sent for Mr. Drakelow, and said, "Mr. Drakelow, I beg that, upon your return to town, you will be so good as to take this young gentleman, Mr. Cunningham Falconer, to your office. Endeavour to prepare him to supply your place with me whenever it may be proper for his majesty's service, and for your interest, to send you to Constantinople, or elsewhere."

Mr. Drakelow, though infinitely surprised and displeased, bowed all submission. Nothing else he knew was to be done with Lord Oldborough. His lordship, as soon as his secretary had left the room, turned to Cunningham, and said, "You will not mention anything concerning M. de Tourville's intercepted papers to Mr. Drakelow, or to any other person. Affairs call me to town immediately: to-morrow morning at six, I set off. You will, if you please, sir, be ready to accompany me. I will not detain you longer from any preparations you may have to make for your journey."

No sooner had the father and son quitted Lord Oldborough's presence than Mr. Falconer exclaimed with exultation, "I long to see our good cousin Percy, that I may tell him how I have provided already for one of my sons."

"But remember, sir," said Cunningham, "that Mr. Percy is to know nothing of the Tourville packet."

"To be sure not," said Mr. Falconer; "he is to know nothing of the means, he is to see only the end—the successful end. Ha! cousin Percy, I think we know rather better than you do how to make something of every thing—even of a shipwreck."

"To prevent his having any suspicions," continued Cunningham, "it will be best to give Mr. Percy some probable reason for Lord Oldborough's taking to us so suddenly. It will be well to hint that you have opportunities of obliging about the borough, or about the address at the county-meeting, or—"

"No, no; no particulars; never go to particulars," said old Falconer: "stick to generals, and you are safe. Say, in general, that I had an opportunity of obliging government. Percy is not curious, especially about jobbing. He will ask no questions; or, if he should, I can easily put him upon a wrong scent. Now, Cunningham, listen to me: I have done my best, and have pushed you into a fine situation: but remember, you cannot get on in the diplomatic line without a certain degree of diplomatic information. I have pointed this out to you often; you have neglected to make yourself master of these things, and, for want of them in office, you will come, I fear, some day or other to shame."

"Do not be afraid of that—no danger of my coming to shame any more than a thousand other people in office, who never trouble themselves about diplomatic information, and all that. There is always some clerk who knows the forms, and with those, and looking for what one wants upon the spur of the occasion in books and pamphlets, and so forth, one may go on very well—if one does but know how to keep one's own counsel. You see I got through with Lord Oldborough to-day—"

"Ay—but I assure you I trembled for you, and I could have squeezed myself into an auger-hole once, when you blundered about that treaty of which I knew that you knew nothing."

"Oh! sir, I assure you I had turned over the leaves. I was correct enough as to the dates; and, suppose I blundered, as my brother Buckhurst says, half the world never know what they are saying, and the other half never find it out.—Why, sir, you were telling me the other night such a blunder of Prince Potemkin's—"

"Very true," interrupted the commissioner; "but you are not Prince Potemkin, nor yet a prime minister; if you were, no matter how little you knew—you might get other people to supply your deficiencies. But now, in your place, and in the course of making your way upwards, you will be called upon to supply others with the information they may want. And you know I shall not be always at your elbow; therefore I really am afraid—"

"Dear sir, fear nothing," said Cunningham: "I shall do as well as others do—the greatest difficulty is over. I have taken the first step, and it has cost nothing."

"Well, get on, my boy—honestly, if you can—but get on."

CHAPTER III

With the true genius of a political castle-builder, Mr. Falconer began to add story after story to the edifice, of which he had thus promptly and successfully laid the foundation. Having by a lucky hit provided for one of his sons, that is to say, put him in a fair way of being provided for, the industrious father began to form plans for the advancement of his two other sons, Buckhurst and John: Buckhurst was destined by his father for the church; John for the army. The commissioner, notwithstanding he had been closeted for some hours with Lord Oldborough, and notwithstanding his son Cunningham was to be one of his lordship's secretaries, was well aware that little or no progress had been made in Lord Oldborough's real favour or confidence. Mr. Falconer knew that he had been literally paid by the job, that he was considered and treated accordingly; yet, upon the whole, he was well pleased that it should be so, for he foresaw the possibility of his doing for his lordship many more jobs, public and private. He lost no time in preparing for the continuity of his secret services, and in creating a political necessity for his being employed in future, in a manner that might ensure the advancement of the rest of his family. In the first place, he knew that Lord Oldborough was desirous, for the enlargement of the grounds at Clermont-park, to purchase certain adjoining lands, which, from some ancient pique, the owner was unwilling to sell. The proprietor was a tenant of Mr. Falconer's: he undertook to negotiate the business, and to use his influence to bring his tenant to reason. This offer, made through Cunningham, was accepted by Lord Oldborough, and the negotiation led to fresh communications.—There was soon to be a county meeting, and an address was to be procured in favour of certain measures of government, which it was expected would be violently opposed. In the commissioner's letters to his son, the private secretary, he could say and suggest whatever he pleased; he pointed out the gentlemen of the county who ought to be conciliated, and he offered his services to represent things properly to some with whom he was intimate. The sheriff and the under-sheriff also should know, without being informed directly from ministry, what course in conducting the meeting would be agreeable in a certain quarter— who so proper to say and do all that might be expedient as Mr. Falconer, who was on the spot, and well acquainted with the county?—The commissioner was informed by the private secretary, that his services would be acceptable. There happened also, at this time, to be some disputes and grievances in that part of the country about tax-gatherers. Mr. Falconer hinted, that he could soften and accommodate matters, if he were empowered to do so—and he was so empowered. Besides all this, there was a borough in that county, in which the interest of government had been declining; attempts were made to open the borough—Mr. Falconer could be of use in keeping it close—and he was commissioned to do every thing in his power in the business. In a short time Mr. Falconer was acting on all these points as an agent and partizan of Lord Oldborough's. But there was one thing which made him uneasy; he was acting here, as in many former instances, merely upon vague hopes of future reward.

Whilst his mind was full of these thoughts, a new prospect of advantage opened to him in another direction. Colonel Hauton, Lord Oldborough's nephew, stayed, during his uncle's absence, at Clermont-park, to be in readiness for the races, which, this year, were expected to be uncommonly fine. Buckhurst Falconer had been at school and at the university with the colonel, and had frequently helped him in his Latin exercises. The colonel having been always deficient in scholarship, he had early contracted an aversion to literature, which at last amounted to an antipathy even to the very sight of books, in consequence, perhaps, of his uncle's ardent and precipitate desire to make him apply to them whilst his head was full of tops and balls, kites and ponies. Be this as it may, Commissioner Falconer thought his son Buckhurst might benefit by his school friendship, and might now renew and improve the connexion. Accordingly, Buckhurst waited upon the colonel,—was immediately recognized, and received with promising demonstrations of joy.

It would be difficult, indeed impossible, to describe Colonel Hauton, so as to distinguish him from a thousand other young men of the same class, except, perhaps, that he might be characterized by having more exclusive and inveterate selfishness. Yet this was so far from appearing or being suspected on a first acquaintance, that he was generally thought a sociable, good-natured fellow. It was his absolute dependence upon others for daily amusement and ideas, or, rather, for knowing what to do with himself, that gave him this semblance of being sociable; the total want of proper pride and dignity in his whole deportment, a certain slang and familiarity of tone, gave superficial observers the notion that he was good-natured. It was Colonel Hauton's great ambition to look like his own coachman; he succeeded only so far as to look like his groom: but though he kept company with jockeys and coachmen, grooms and stable-boys, yet not the stiffest, haughtiest, flat-backed Don of Spain, in Spain's proudest days, could be more completely aristocratic in his principles, or more despotic in his habits. This could not break out to his equals, and his equals cared little how he treated his inferiors. His present pleasure, or rather his present business, for no man made more a business of pleasure than Colonel Hauton, was the turf. Buckhurst Falconer could not here assist him as much as in making Latin verses—but he could admire and sympathize; and the colonel, proud of being now the superior, proud of his knowing style and his capital stud, enjoyed Buckhurst's company particularly, pressed him to stay at Clermont-park, and to accompany him to the races. There was to be a famous match between Colonel Hauton's High-Blood and Squire Burton's Wildfire; and the preparations of the horses and of their riders occupied the intervening days. With all imaginable care, anxiety, and solemnity, these important preparations were conducted. At stated hours, Colonel Hauton, and with him Buckhurst, went to see High-Blood rubbed down, and fed, and watered, and exercised, and minuted, and rubbed down, and littered. Next to the horse, the rider, Jack Giles, was to be attended to with the greatest solicitude; he was to be weighed—and starved—and watched—and drammed—and sweated—and weighed again—and so on in daily succession; and harder still, through this whole course he was to be kept in humour: "None that ever sarved man or beast," as the stable-boy declared, "ever worked harder for their bread than his master and master's companion did this week for their pleasure." At last the great, the important day arrived, and Jack Giles was weighed for the last time in public, and so was Tom Hand, Squire Burton's rider—and

High-Blood and Wildfire were brought out; and the spectators assembled in the stand, and about the scales, were all impatience, especially those who had betted on either of the horses. And, Now, Hauton!—Now, Burton!—Now, High-Blood!—Now, Wildfire!—Now, Jack Giles!—and Now, Tom Hand! resounded on all sides. The gentlemen on the race-ground were all on tiptoe in their stirrups. The ladies in the stand stretched their necks of snow, and nobody looked at them.—Two men were run over, and nobody took them up.—Two ladies fainted, and two gentlemen betted across them. This was no time for nice observances—Jack Giles's spirit began to flag—and Tom Hand's judgment to tell—High-Blood, on the full stretch, was within view of the winning-post, when Wildfire, quite in wind, was put to his speed by the judicious Tom Hand—he sprang forward, came up with High-Blood—passed him—Jack Giles strove in vain to regain his ground—High-Blood was blown, beyond the power of whip or spur—Wildfire reached the post, and Squire Burton won the match hollow.

His friends congratulated him and themselves loudly, and extolled Tom Hand and Wildfire to the skies. In the moment of disappointment, Colonel Hauton, out of humour, said something that implied a suspicion of unfairness on the part of Burton or Tom Hand, which the honest squire could not brook either for self or rider. He swore that his Tom Hand was as honest a fellow as any in England, and he would back him for such. The colonel, depending on his own and his uncle's importance, on his party and his flatterers, treated the squire with some of the haughtiness of rank, which the squire retorted with some rustic English humour. The colonel, who had not wit at will to put down his antagonist, became still more provoked to see that such a low-born fellow as the squire should and could laugh and make others laugh. For the lack of wit the colonel had recourse to insolence, and went on from one impertinence to another, till the squire, enraged, declared that he would not be browbeat by any lord's nephew or jackanapes colonel that ever wore a head; and as he spoke, tremendous in his ire, Squire Burton brandished high the British horsewhip. At this critical moment, as it has been asserted by some of the bystanders, the colonel quailed and backed a few paces; but others pretend that Buckhurst Falconer pushed before him. It is certain that Buckhurst stopped the blow—wrested the horsewhip from the squire—was challenged by him on the spot—accepted the challenge—fought the squire—winged him—appeared on the race ground afterwards, and was admired by the ladies in public, and by his father in private, who looked upon the duel and horsewhipping, from which he thus saved his patron's nephew, as the most fortunate circumstance that could have happened to his son upon his entrance into life.

"Such an advantage as this gives us such a claim upon the colonel—and, indeed, upon the whole family. Lord Oldborough, having no children of his own, looks to the nephew as his heir; and though he may be vexed now and then by the colonel's extravagance, and angry that he could not give this nephew more of a political turn, yet such as he is, depend upon it he can do what he pleases with Lord Oldborough. Whoever has the nephew's ear, has the uncle's heart; or I should say, whoever has the nephew's heart, has the uncle's ear."

"Mayn't we as well put hearts out of the question on all sides, sir?" said Buckhurst.

"With all my heart," said his father, laughing, "provided we don't put a good living out of the question on our side."

Buckhurst looked averse, and said he did not know there was any such thing in question.

"No!" said his father: "was it then from the pure and abstract love of being horsewhipped, or shot at, that you took this quarrel off his hands?"

"Faith! I did it from spirit, pure spirit," said Buckhurst: "I could not stand by, and see one who had been my schoolfellow horsewhipped—if he did not stand by himself, yet I could not but stand by him, for you know I was there as one of his party—and as I backed his bets on High-Blood, I could do no less than back his cause altogether.—Oh! I could not stand by and see a chum of my own horsewhipped."

"Well, that was all very spirited and generous; but now, as you are something too old for mere schoolboy notions," said the commissioner, "let us look a little farther, and see what we can make of it. It's only a silly boyish thing as you consider it; but I hope we can turn it to good account."

"I never thought of turning it to account, sir."

"Think of it now," said the father, a little provoked by the careless disinterestedness of the son. "In plain English, here is a colonel in his majesty's service saved from a horsewhipping—a whole noble family saved from disgrace: these are things not to be forgotten; that is, not to be forgotten, if you force people to remember them: otherwise—my word for it—I know the great—the whole would be forgotten in a week. Therefore, leave me to follow the thing up properly with the uncle, and do you never let it sleep with the nephew: sometimes a bold stroke, sometimes a delicate touch, just as the occasion serves, or as may suit the company present—all that I trust to your own address and judgment."

"Trust nothing, sir, to my address or judgment; for in these things I have neither. I always act just from impulse and feeling, right or wrong—I have no talents for finesse—leave them all to Cunningham—that's his trade, and he likes it, luckily: and you should be content with having one such genius in your family—no family could bear two."

"Come, come, pray be serious, Buckhurst. If you have not or will not use any common sense and address to advance yourself, leave that to me. You see how I have pushed up Cunningham already, and all I ask of you is to be quiet, and let me push you up."

"Oh! dear sir, I am very much obliged to you: if that is all, I will be quite quiet—so that I am not to do any thing shabby or dirty for it. I should be vastly glad to get a good place, and be provided for handsomely."

"No doubt; and let me tell you that many I could name have, with inferior claims, and without any natural connexion or relationship, from the mere favour of proper friends, obtained church benefices of much greater value than the living we have in our eye: you know—"

"I do not know, indeed," said Buckhurst; "I protest I have no living in my eye."

"What! not know that the living of Chipping-Friars is in the gift of Colonel Hauton—and the present incumbent has had one paralytic stroke already. There's a prospect for you, Buckhurst!"

"To be frank with you, sir, I have no taste for the church."

"No taste for nine hundred a year, Buckhurst? No desire for fortune, Mr. Philosopher?"

"Pardon me, a very strong taste for that, sir—not a bit of a philosopher—as much in love with fortune as any man, young or old: is there no way to fortune but through the church?"

"None for you so sure and so easy, all circumstances considered," said his father. "I have planned and settled it, and you have nothing to do but to get yourself ordained as soon as possible. I shall write to my friend the bishop for that purpose this very night."

"Let me beg; father, that you will not be so precipitate. Upon my word, sir, I cannot go into orders. I am not—in short, I am not fit for the church."

The father stared with an expression between anger and astonishment.

"Have not you gone through the university?"

"Yes, sir:—but—but I am scarcely sober, and staid, and moral enough for the church. Such a wild fellow as I am, I really could not in conscience—I would not upon any account, for any living upon earth, or any emolument, go into the church, unless I thought I should do credit to it."

"And why should not you do credit to the church? I don't see that you are wilder than your neighbours, and need not be more scrupulous. There is G—, who at your age was wild enough, but he took up in time, and is now a plump dean. Then there is the bishop that is just made: I remember him such a youth as you are. Come, come, these are idle scruples. Let me hear no more, my dear Buckhurst, of your conscience."

"Dear sir, I never pleaded my conscience on any occasion before—you know that I am no puritan—but really on this point I have some conscience, and I beg you not to press me farther. You have other sons; and if you cannot spare Cunningham, that treasure of diplomacy!—there's John; surely you might contrive to spare him for the church."

"Spare him I would, and welcome. But you know I could never get John into orders."

"Why not, sir? John, I'll swear, would have no objection to the church, provided you could get him a good fat living."

"But I am not talking of his objections. To be sure he would make no objection to a good fat living, nor would any body in his senses, except yourself. But I ask you how I could possibly get your brother John into the church? John's a dunce,—and you know it."

"Nobody better, sir: but are there no dunces in the church?—And as you are so good as to think that I'm no wilder than my neighbours, you surely will not say that my brother is more a dunce than his neighbours. Put him into the hands of a clever grinder or crammer, and they would soon cram the necessary portion of Latin and Greek into him, and they would get him through the university for us readily enough; and a degree once obtained, he might snap his fingers at Latin and Greek all the rest of his life. Once in orders, and he might sit down upon his fat living, or lie down content, all his days, only taking care to have some poor devil of a curate up and about, doing duty for him."

"So I find you have no great scruples for your brother, whatever you may have for yourself?"

"Sir, I am not the keeper of my brother's conscience—Indeed, if I were, you might congratulate me in the words of Sir B. R. upon the possession of a sinecure place."

"It is a pity, Buckhurst, that you cannot use your wit for yourself as well as for other people. Ah! Buckhurst! Buckhurst! you will, I fear, do worse in the world than any of your brothers; for wits are always unlucky: sharp-sighted enough to every thing else, but blind, stone blind to their own interest. Wit is folly, when one is talking of serious business."

"Well, my dear father, be agreeable, and I will not be witty.—In fact, in downright earnest, the sum total of the business is, that I have a great desire to go into the army, and I entreat you to procure me a commission."

"Then the sum total of the business is, that I will not; for I cannot afford to purchase you a commission, and to maintain you in the army—"

"But by using interest, perhaps, sir," said Buckhurst.

"My interest must be all for your brother John; for I tell you I can do nothing else for him but put him into the army.—He's a dunce.—I must get him a commission, and then I have done with him."

"I wish I were a dunce," said Buckhurst, sighing; "for then I might go into the army—instead of being forced into the church."

"There's no force upon your inclinations, Buckhurst," said his father in a soft tone; "I only show you that it is impossible I should maintain you in the army, and, therefore, beg you to put the army out of your head. And I don't well see what else you could do. You have not application enough for the bar, nor have I any friends among the attorneys except Sharpe, who, between you and me, might take your dinners, and leave you without a brief afterwards. You have talents, I grant," continued the commissioner, "and if you had but application, and if your uncle the judge had not died last year—"

"Oh, sir, he is dead, and we can't help it," interrupted Buckhurst. "And as for me, I never had, and never shall have, any application: so pray put the bar out of your mind."

"Very cavalier, indeed!—but I will make you serious at once, Buckhurst. You have nothing to expect from my death—I have not a farthing to leave you—my place, you know, is only for life—your mother's fortune is all in annuity, and two girls to be provided for—and to live as we must live—up to and beyond my income—shall have nothing to leave. Though you are my eldest son, you see it is in vain to look to my death—so into the church you must go, or be a beggar—and get a living or starve. Now I have done," concluded the commissioner, quitting his son; "and I leave you to think of what has been said."

Buckhurst thought and thought; but still his interest and his conscience were at variance, and he could not bring himself either to be virtuous or vicious enough to comply with his father's wishes. He could not decide to go into the church merely from interested motives—from that his conscience revolted; he could not determine to make himself fit to do credit to the sacred profession—against this his habits and his love of pleasure revolted. He went to his brother John, to try what could be done with him. Latin and Greek were insuperable objections with John; besides, though he had a dull imagination in general, John's fancy had been smitten with one bright idea of an epaulette, from which no considerations, fraternal, political, moral, or religious, could distract his attention.—His genius, he said, was for the army, and into the army he would go.—So to his genius, Buckhurst, in despair, was obliged to leave him.—The commissioner neglected not to push the claim which he had on Colonel Hauton, and he chose his time so well, when proper people were by, and when the colonel did not wish to have the squire, and the horse-whip, and the duel, brought before the public, that he obtained, if not a full acknowledgment of obligation, a promise of doing any thing and every thing in his power for his friend Buckhurst. Any thing and every thing were indefinite, unsatisfactory terms; and the commissioner, bold in dealing with the timid temper of the colonel, though he had been cautious with the determined character of the uncle, pressed his point—named the living of Chipping-Friars—showed how well he would be satisfied, and how well he could represent matters, if the promise were given; and at the same time made it understood how loudly he could complain, and how disgraceful his complaints might prove to the Oldborough family, if his son were treated with ingratitude. The colonel particularly dreaded that he should be suspected of want of spirit, and that his uncle should have the transaction laid before him in this improper point of view. He pondered for a few moments, and the promise for the living of Chipping-Friars was given. The commissioner, secure of this, next returned to the point with his son, and absolutely insisted upon his—going into orders. Buckhurst, who had tried wit and raillery in vain, now tried persuasion and earnest entreaties; but these were equally fruitless: his father, though an easy, good-natured man, except where his favourite plans were crossed, was peremptory, and, without using harsh words, he employed the harshest measures to force his son's compliance. Buckhurst had contracted some debts at the university, none of any great consequence, but such as he could not pay immediately.—The bets he had laid and lost upon High-Blood were also to be provided for; debts of honour claimed precedency, and must be directly discharged. His father positively refused to assist him, except upon condition of his compliance with his wishes; and so far from affording him any means of settling with his creditors, it has been proved, from the commissioner's private answers to some of their applications, that he not only refused to pay a farthing for his son, but encouraged the creditors to threaten him in the strongest manner with the terrors of law and arrest. Thus pressed and embarrassed, this young man, who had many honourable and religious sentiments and genuine feelings, but no power of adhering to principle or reason, was miserable beyond expression one hour—and the next he became totally forgetful that there was any thing to be thought of but the amusement of the moment. Incapable of coming to any serious decision, he walked up and down his room talking, partly to himself, and partly, for want of a better companion, to his brother John.

"So I must pay Wallis to-morrow, or he'll arrest me; and I must give my father an answer about the church to-night—for he writes to the bishop, and will wait no longer. Oh! hang it.' hang it, John! what the devil shall I do? My father won't pay a farthing for me, unless I go into the church!"

"Well, then, why can't you go into the church!" said John: "since you are through the university, the worst is over."

"But I think it so wrong, so base—for money—for emolument! I cannot do it. I am not fit for the church—I know I shall disgrace it," said Buckhurst, striking his forehead: "I cannot do it—I can not—it is against my conscience."

John stopped, as he was filling his shooting-pouch, and looked at Buckhurst (his mouth half open) with an expression of surprise at these demonstrations of sensibility. He had some sympathy for the external symptoms of pain which he saw in his brother, but no clear conception of the internal cause.

"Why, Buckhurst," said he, "if you cannot do it, you can't, you know, Buckhurst: but I don't see why you should be a disgrace to the church more than another, as my father says. If I were but through the university, I had as lieve go into the church as not—that's all I can say. And if my genius were not for the military line, there's nothing I should relish better than the living of Chipping-Friars, I'm sure. The only thing that I see against it is, that that paralytic incumbent may live many a year: but, then, you get your debts paid now by only going into orders, and that's a great point. But if it goes against your conscience—you know best—if you can't, you can't."

"After all, I can't go to jail—I can't let myself be arrested—I can't starve—I can't be a beggar," said Buckhurst; "and, as you say, I should be so easy if these cursed debts were paid—and if I got this living of nine hundred a year, how comfortable I should be! Then I could marry, by Jove! and I'd propose directly for Caroline Percy, for I'm confoundedly in love with her—such a sweet tempered, good creature!—not a girl so much admired! Colonel Hauton, and G—, and P—, and D—, asked me, 'Who is that pretty girl?'—She certainly is a very pretty girl."

"She certainly is," repeated John. "This devil of a fellow never cleans my gun."

"Not regularly handsome, neither," pursued Buckhurst; "but, as Hauton says, fascinating and new; and a new face in public is a great matter. Such a fashionable-looking figure, too—though she has not come out yet; dances charmingly—would dance divinely, if she would let herself out; and she sings and plays like an angel, fifty times better than our two precious sisters, who have been at it from their cradles, with all the Signor Squalicis at their elbows. Caroline Percy never exhibits in public: the mother does not like it, I suppose."

"So I suppose," said John. "Curse this flint!—flints are growing worse and worse every day—I wonder what in the world are become of all the good flints there used to be!"

"Very unlike our mother, I am sure," continued Buckhurst. "There are Georgiana and Bell at all the parties and concerts as regularly as any of the professors, standing up in the midst of the singing men and women, favouring the public in as fine a bravura style, and making as ugly faces as the best of them. Do you remember the Italian's compliment to Miss —?—I vish, miss, I had your assurance.'"

"Very good, ha!—very fair, faith!" said John. "Do you know what I've done with my powder horn?"

"Not I—put it in the oven, may be, to dry," said Buckhurst. "But as I was saying of my dear Caroline—My Caroline! she is not mine yet."

"Very true," said John.

"Very true! Why, John, you are enough to provoke a saint!"

"I was agreeing with you, I thought," said John.

"But nothing is so provoking as always agreeing with one—and I can tell you, Mr. Verytrue, that though Caroline Percy is not mine yet, I have nevertheless a little suspicion, that, such even as I am, she might readily be brought to love, honour, and obey me."

"I don't doubt it, for I never yet knew a woman that was not ready enough to be married," quoth John. "But this is not the right ramrod, after all."

"There you are wrong, John, on the other side," said Buckhurst; "for I can assure you, Miss Caroline Percy is not one of your young ladies who would marry any body. And even though she might like me, I am not at all sure that she would marry me—for obedience to the best of fathers might interfere."

"There's the point," said John; "for thereby hangs the fortune; and it would be a deuced thing to have the girl without the fortune."

"Not so deuced a thing to me as you think," said Buckhurst, laughing; "for, poor as I am, I can assure you the fortune is not my object—I am not a mercenary dog."

"By-the-bye," cried John, "now you talk of dogs, I wish to Heaven above, you had not given away that fine puppy of mine to that foolish old man, who never was out a shooting in his days—the dog's just as much thrown away as if you had drowned him. Now, do you know, if I had had the making of that puppy—"

"Puppy!" exclaimed Buckhurst: "is it possible you can be thinking of a puppy, John, when I am talking to you of what is of so much consequence?—when the whole happiness of my life is at stake?"

"Stake!—Well, but what can I do more!" said John: "have not I been standing here this half hour with my gun in my hand this fine day, listening to you prosing about I don't know what?"

"That's the very thing I complain of—that you do not know what: a pretty brother!" said Buckhurst.

John made no further reply, but left the room sullenly, whistling as he went.

Left to his own cogitations, Buckhurst fell into a reverie upon the charms of Caroline Percy, and upon the probable pleasure of dancing with her at the race-ball; after this, he recurred to the bitter recollection, that he must decide about his debts, and the church. A bright idea came into his mind, that he might have recourse to Mr. Percy, and, perhaps, prevail upon him to persuade his father not to force him to a step which he could not reconcile either to his conscience or his inclination.—No sooner thought than done.—He called for his horse and rode as hard as he could to Percy-hall.—When a boy he had been intimate in the Percy family; but he had been long absent at school and at the university; they had seen him only during the vacations, and since his late return to the country. Though Mr. Percy could not entirely approve of his character, yet he thought there were many good points about Buckhurst; the frankness and candour with which he now laid his whole mind and all his affairs open to him—debts—love—fears—hopes—follies—faults—without reserve or extenuation, interested Mr. Percy in his favour.—Pitying his distress, and admiring the motives from which he acted, Mr. Percy said, that though he had no right to interfere in Mr. Falconer's family affairs, yet that he could, and would, so far assist Buckhurst, as to lend him the money for which he was immediately pressed, that he might not be driven by necessity to go into that profession, which ought to be embraced only from the highest and purest motives. Buckhurst thanked him with transports of gratitude for this generous kindness, which was far beyond his expectations, and which, indeed, had never entered into his hopes. Mr. Percy seized the moment when the young man's mind was warmed with good feelings, to endeavour to bring him to serious thoughts and rational determinations about his future life. He represented, that it was unreasonable to expect that his father should let him go into the army, when he had received an education to prepare himself for a profession, in which his literary talents might be of advantage both to himself and his family; that Mr. Falconer was not rich enough to forward two of his sons in the army; that if Buckhurst, from conscientious motives, declined the provision which his father had in view for him in the church, he was bound to exert himself to obtain an independent maintenance in another line of life; that he had talents which would succeed at the bar, if he had application and perseverance sufficient to go through the necessary drudgery at the commencement of the study of the law.

Here Buckhurst groaned.—But Mr. Percy observed that there was no other way of proving that he acted from conscientious motives respecting the church; for otherwise it would appear that he preferred the army only because he fancied it would afford a life of idleness and pleasure.—That this would also be his only chance of winning the approbation of the object of his affections, and of placing himself in a situation in which he could marry.—Buckhurst, who was capable of being strongly influenced by good motives, especially from one who had obliged him, instantly, and in the most handsome manner, acknowledged the truth and justice of Mr. Percy's arguments, and declared that he was ready to begin the study of the law directly, if his father would consent to it; and that he would submit to any drudgery rather than do what he felt to be base and wrong. Mr. Percy, at his earnest request, applied to Mr. Falconer, and with all the delicacy that was becoming, claimed the right of relationship to speak of Mr. Falconer's family affairs, and told him what he had ventured to do about Buckhurst's debts; and what the young man now wished for himself.—The commissioner looked much disappointed and vexed.

"The bar!" cried he: "Mr. Percy, you don't know him as well as I do. I will answer for it, he will never go through with it—and then he is to change his profession again!—and all the expense and all the trouble is to fall on me!—and I am to provide for him at last!—In all probability, by the time Buckhurst knows his own mind, the paralytic incumbent will be dead, and the living of Chipping-Friars given away.—And where am I to find nine hundred a year, I pray you, at a minute's notice, for this conscientious youth, who, by that time, will tell me his scruples were all nonsense, and that I should have known better than to listen to them? Nine hundred a year does not come in a man's way at every turn of his life; and if he gives it up now, it is not my fault—let him look to it."

Mr. Percy replied, "that Buckhurst had declared himself ready to abide by the consequences, and that he promised he would never complain of the lot he had chosen for himself, much less reproach his father for his compliance, and that he was resolute to maintain himself at the bar."

"Yes: very fine.—And how long will it be before he makes nine hundred a year at the bar?"

Mr. Percy, who knew that none but worldly considerations made any impression upon this father, suggested that he would have to maintain his son during the life of the paralytic incumbent, and the expense of Buckhurst's being at the bar would not probably be greater; and though it might be several years before he could make nine hundred, or, perhaps, one hundred a year at the bar, yet that if he succeeded, which, with Buckhurst's talents, nothing but the want of perseverance could prevent, he might make nine thousand a year by the profession of the law—more than in the scope of human probability, and with all the patronage his father's address could procure, he could hope to obtain in the church.

"Well, let him try—let him try," repeated the commissioner, who, vexed as he was, did not choose to run the risk of disobliging Mr. Percy, losing a good match for him, or undergoing the scandal of its being known that he forced his son into the church.

For obtaining this consent, however reluctantly granted by the commissioner, Buckhurst warmly thanked Mr. Percy, who made one condition with him, that he would go up to town immediately to commence his studies.

This Buckhurst faithfully promised to do, and only implored permission to declare his attachment to Caroline.—Caroline was at this time not quite eighteen, too young, her father said, to think of forming any serious engagement, even were it with a person suited to her in fortune and in every other respect.

Buckhurst declared that he had no idea of endeavouring even to obtain from Miss Caroline Percy any promise or engagement.—He had been treated, he said, too generously by her father, to attempt to take any step without his entire approbation.

He knew he was not, and could not for many years, be in circumstances that would enable him to support a daughter of Mr. Percy's in the station to which she was, by her birth and fortune, entitled.— All he asked, he repeated, was to be permitted to declare to her his passion.

Mr. Percy thought it was more prudent to let it be declared openly than to have it secretly suspected; therefore he consented to this request, trusting much to Buckhurst's honour and to Caroline's prudence.

To this first declaration of love Caroline listened with a degree of composure which astonished and mortified her lover. He had flattered himself that, at least, her vanity or pride would have been apparently gratified by her conquest.—But there was none of the flutter of vanity in her manner, nor any of the repressed satisfaction of pride. There were in her looks and words only simplicity and dignity.—She said that she was at present occupied happily in various ways, endeavouring to improve herself, and that she should be sorry to have her mind turned from these pursuits; she desired to secure time to compare and judge of her own tastes, and of the characters of others, before she should make any engagement, or form an attachment on which the happiness of her life must depend. She said she was equally desirous to keep herself free, and to avoid injuring the happiness of the man who had honoured her by his preference; therefore she requested he would discontinue a pursuit, which she could not encourage him to hope would ever be successful.—Long before the time when she should think it prudent to marry, even if she were to meet with a character perfectly suited to hers, she hoped that her cousin Buckhurst would be united to some woman who would be able to return his affection.

The manner in which all this was said convinced Buckhurst that she spoke the plain and exact truth. From the ease and frankness with which she had hitherto conversed with him, he had flattered himself that it would not be difficult to prepossess her heart in his favour; but now, when he saw the same ease and simplicity unchanged in her manner, he was convinced that he had been mistaken. He had still hopes that in time he might make an impression upon her, and he urged that she was not yet sufficiently acquainted with his character to be able to judge whether or not it would suit hers. She frankly told him all she thought of him, and in doing so impressed him with the conviction that she had both discerned the merits and discovered the defects of his character: she gave him back a representation of himself, which he felt to be exactly just, and yet which struck him with all the force of novelty.

"It is myself," he exclaimed: "but I never knew myself till now."

He had such pleasure in hearing Caroline speak of him, that he wished even to hear her speak of his faults—of these he would, however, have been better pleased, if she had spoken with less calmness and indulgence.

"She is a great way from love as yet," thought Buckhurst. "It is astonishing, that with powers and knowledge on all other subjects so far above her age, she should know so little even of the common language of sentiment; very extraordinary, that with so much kindness, and such an amiable disposition, she should have so little sensibility."

The novelty of this insensibility, and of this perfect simplicity, so unlike all he had observed in the manners and minds of other young ladies to whom he had been accustomed, had, however, a great effect upon her lover. The openness and unaffected serenity of Caroline's countenance at this moment appeared to him more charming than any other thing he had ever beheld in the most finished coquette, or the most fashionable beauty.

What a divine creature she will be a few years hence! thought he. The time will come, when Love may waken this Psyche!—And what glory it would be to me to produce to the world such perfection!

With these mixed ideas of love and glory, Buckhurst took leave of Caroline; still he retained hope in spite of her calm and decided refusal. He knew the power of constant attention, and the display of ardent passion, to win the female heart. He trusted also in no slight degree to the reputation he had already acquired of being a favourite with the fair sex.

CHAPTER IV

Buckhurst Falconer returned to Percy-hall.

He came provided with something like an excuse—he had business—his father had desired him to ask Mr. Percy to take charge of a box of family papers for him, as he apprehended that, when he was absent from the country, his steward had not been as careful of them as he ought to have been.

Mr. Percy willingly consented to take charge of the papers, but he desired that, before they were left with him, Buckhurst should take a list of them.

Buckhurst was unprepared for this task.

His head was intent on a ball and on Caroline. However, he was obliged to undergo this labour; and when he had finished it, Mr. Percy, who happened to be preparing some new leases of considerable farms, was so busy, in the midst of his papers, that there was no such thing as touching upon the subject of the ball. At length the ladies of the family appeared, and all the parchments were at last out of the way—Buckhurst began upon his real business, and said he meant to delay going to town a few days longer, because there was to be a ball early in the ensuing week.—"Nothing more natural," said Mr. Percy, "than to wish to go to a ball; yet," added he, gravely, "when a man of honour gives his promise that nothing shall prevent him from commencing his studies immediately, I did not expect that the first temptation—"

"Oh! my dear Mr. Percy," said Buckhurst, endeavouring to laugh away the displeasure, or rather the disappointment which he saw in Mr. Percy's countenance, "a few days can make no difference."

"Only the difference of a term," said Mr. Percy; "and the difference between promising and performing. You thought me unjust yesterday, when I told you that I feared you would prefer present amusement to future happiness."

"Amusement!" exclaimed Buckhurst, turning suddenly towards Caroline; "do you imagine that is my object?" Then approaching her, he said in a low voice, "It is a natural mistake for you to make, Miss Caroline Percy—for you—who know nothing of love. Amusement! It is not amusement that detains me—can you think I would stay for a ball, unless I expected to meet you there?"

"Then I will not go," said Caroline: "it would be coquetry to meet you there, when, as I thought, I had distinctly explained to you yesterday—"

"Oh! don't repeat that," interrupted Buckhurst: "a lady is never bound to remember what she said yesterday—especially if it were a cruel sentence; I hope hereafter you will change your mind—let me live upon hope."

"I will never give any false hopes," said Caroline; "and since I cannot add to your happiness, I will take care not to diminish it. I will not be the cause of your breaking your promise to my father: I will not be the means of tempting you to lower yourself in his opinion—I will not go to this ball."

Buckhurst smiled, went on with some commonplace raillery about cruelty, and took his leave, fancying that Caroline could not be in earnest in her threat, as he called it.—As his disobedience would have the excuse of love, he thought he might venture to transgress the letter of the promise.

When the time came, he went to the ball, almost certain that Caroline would break her resolution, as he knew that she had never yet been at a public assembly, and it was natural that one so sure of being admired would be anxious to be seen. His surprise and disappointment were great when no Caroline appeared.

He asked Rosamond if her sister was not well?

"Perfectly well."

"Then why is not she here?"

"Don't you recollect her telling you that she would not come?"

"Yes: but I did not think she was in earnest."

"How little you know of Caroline," replied Rosamond, "if you imagine that either in trifles, or in matters of consequence, she would say one thing and do another."

"I feel," said Buckhurst, colouring, "what that emphasis on she means. But I did not think you would have reproached me so severely. I thought my cousin Rosamond was my friend."

"So I am—but not a friend to your faults."

"Surely it is no great crime in a young man to like going to a ball better than going to the Temple! But I am really concerned," continued Buckhurst, "that I have deprived Miss Caroline Percy of the pleasure of being here to-night—and this was to have been her first appearance in public—I am quite sorry."

"Caroline is not at all impatient to appear in public; and as to the pleasure of being at a ball, it costs her little to sacrifice that, or any pleasure of her own, for the advantage of others."

"When Miss Caroline Percy said something about my falling in her father's opinion for such a trifle, I could not guess that she was serious."

"She does not," replied Rosamond, "think it a trifle to break a promise."

Buckhurst looked at his watch. "The mail-coach will pass through this town in an hour. It shall take me to London—Good bye—I will not stay another moment—I am gone. I wish I had gone yesterday—pray, my dear, good Rosamond, say so for me to Caroline."

At this moment a beautiful young lady, attended by a large party, entered the ball-room. Buckhurst stopped to inquire who she was.

"Did you never see my sister before?" replied Colonel Hauton—"Oh! I must introduce you, and you shall dance with her."

"You do me a great deal of honour—I shall be very happy—that is, I should be extremely happy—only unfortunately I am under a necessity of setting off immediately for London—I'm afraid I shall be late for the mail—Good night."

Buckhurst made an effort, as he spoke, to pass on; but Colonel Hauton bursting into one of his horse laughs, held him fast by the arm, swore he must be drunk, for that he did not know what he was saying or doing.

Commissioner Falconer, who now came up, whispered to Buckhurst, "Are you mad? You can't refuse— you'll affront for ever!"

"I can't help it," said Buckhurst: "I'm sorry for it—I cannot help it."

He still kept on his way towards the door.

"But," expostulated the commissioner, following him out, "you can surely stay, be introduced, and pay your compliments to the young lady—you are time enough for the mail. Don't affront people for nothing, who may be of the greatest use to you."

"But, my dear father, I don't want people to be of use to me."

"Well, at any rate turn back just to see what a charming creature Miss Hauton is. Such an entrée! So much the air of a woman of fashion! every eye riveted—the whole room in admiration of her!"

"I did not see any thing remarkable about her," said Buckhurst, turning back to look at her again. "If you think I should affront—I would not really affront Hauton, who has always been so civil to me—I'll go and be introduced and pay my compliments, since you say it is necessary; but I shall not stay five minutes."

Buckhurst returned to be introduced to Miss Hauton. This young lady was so beautiful that she would, in all probability, have attracted general attention, even if she had not been the sister of a man of Colonel Hauton's fortune, and the niece of a nobleman of Lord Oldborough's political consequence; but undoubtedly these circumstances much increased the power of her charms over the imaginations of her admirers. All the gentlemen at this hall were unanimous in declaring that she was a most fascinating creature. Buckhurst Falconer and Godfrey Percy were introduced to her nearly at the same time. Godfrey asked her to dance—and Buckhurst could not help staying to see her. She danced so gracefully, that while he thought he had stayed only five minutes, he delayed a quarter of an hour. Many gentlemen were ambitious of the honour of Miss Hauton's hand; but, to their disappointment, she declined dancing any more; and though Buckhurst Falconer had determined not to have stayed, nor to dance with her, yet an undefinable perverse curiosity induced him to delay a few minutes to determine whether she conversed as well as she danced. The sound of her voice was sweet and soft, and there was an air of languor in her whole person and manner, with an apparent indifference to general admiration, which charmed Godfrey Percy, especially as he perceived, that she could be animated by his conversation. To Buckhurst's wit she listened with politeness, but obviously without interest. Buckhurst looked at his watch again—but it was now too late for the mail. Rosamond was surprised to see him still in the ball-room. He laid all the blame on his father, and pleaded that he was detained by parental orders which he could not disobey. He sat beside Rosamond at supper, and used much eloquence to convince her that he had obeyed against his will.

In the mean time Godfrey, seated next to his fair partner, became every moment more and more sensible of the advantages of his situation. Towards the end of supper, when the buzz of general conversation increased, it happened that somebody near Miss Hauton spoke of a marriage that was likely to take place in the fashionable world, and all who thought themselves, or who wished to be thought good authorities, began to settle how it would be, and when it would be: but a gentleman of Godfrey's acquaintance, who sat next to him, said, in a low voice, "It will never be."—"Why?" said Godfrey.—The gentleman answered in a whisper, "There is an insuperable objection: the mother—don't you recollect?—the mother was a divorcée; and no man of sense would venture to marry the daughter—"

"No, certainly," said Godfrey; "I did not know the fact."

He turned, as he finished speaking, to ask Miss Hauton if she would permit him to help her to something that stood before him; but to his surprise and alarm he perceived that she was pale, trembling, and scarcely able to support herself.—He, for the first moment, thought only that she was taken suddenly ill, and he was going to call Lady Oldborough's attention to her indisposition—but Miss Hauton stopped him, and said in a low, tremulous voice—"Take no notice." He then poured out a glass of water, put it within her reach, turned away in obedience to her wishes, and sat in such a manner as to screen her from observation. A confused recollection now came across his mind of his having heard many years ago, when he was a child, of the divorce of some Lady Anne Hauton, and the truth occurred to him, that this was Miss Hauton's mother, and that Miss Hauton had overheard the whisper.

In a few moments, anxious to see whether she had recovered, and yet afraid to distress her by his attention, he half turned his head, and looking down at her plate, asked if she was better.

"Quite well, thank you."

He then raised his eyes, and looking as unconcernedly as he could, resumed his former attitude, and began some trifling conversation; but whatever effort he made to appear the same as before, there was some constraint, or some difference in his voice and manner, which the young lady perceived—her voice immediately changed and faltered—he spoke quickly—both spoke at the same time, without knowing what either said or what they said themselves—their eyes met, and both were silent—Miss Hauton blushed deeply. He saw that his conjecture was right, and she saw, by Godfrey's countenance, that her secret was discovered: her eyes fell, she grew pale, and instantly fainted. Lady Oldborough came to her assistance, but she was too helpless a fine lady to be of the least use: she could only say that it must be the heat of the room, and that she should faint herself in another moment.

Godfrey whispered to his mother—and Miss Hauton was carried into the open air. Lady Oldborough and her smelling-bottle followed. Godfrey, leaving the young lady with them, returned quickly to the supper-room, to prevent any one from intruding upon her. He met Buckhurst Falconer and Colonel Hauton at the door, and stopped them with assurances that Miss Hauton had all the assistance she could want.

"I'll tell you what she wants," cried the Colonel to Buckhurst; "a jaunt to Cheltenham, which would do her and me, too, a d—d deal of good; for now the races are over, what the devil shall we do with ourselves here? I'll rattle Maria off the day after to-morrow in my phaeton. No—Buckhurst, my good fellow, I'll drive you in the phaeton, and I'll make Lady Oldborough take Maria in the coach."

Godfrey Percy, who, as he passed, could not avoid hearing this invitation, did not stay to learn Buckhurst's answer, but went instantly into the room. No one, not even the gentleman whose whisper had occasioned it, had the least suspicion of the real cause of Miss Hauton's indisposition. Lady Oldborough had assigned as the occasion of the young lady's illness "the heat of the room," and an old medical dowager was eager to establish that "it was owing to some strawberry ice, as, to her certain knowledge, ice, in some shape or other, was the cause of most of the mischief in the world."

Whilst the partizans of heat and ice were still battling, and whilst the dancers had quite forgotten Miss Hauton, and every thing but themselves, the young lady returned to the room. Godfrey went to order Mrs. Percy's carriage, and the Percy family left the ball.

When Godfrey found himself in the carriage with his own family, he began eagerly to talk of Miss Hauton; he was anxious to know what all and each thought of her, in general, and in particular: he talked so much of her, and seemed so much surprised that any body could wish to talk or think of any thing else, that Mrs. Percy could not help smiling. Mr. Percy, leaning back in the carriage, said that he felt inclined to sleep.

"To sleep!" repeated Godfrey: "is it possible that you can be sleepy, sir?"

"Very possible, my dear son—it is past four o'clock, I believe."

Godfrey was silent for some minutes, and he began to think over every word and look that had passed between him and Miss Hauton. He had been only amused with her conversation, and charmed by her grace and beauty in the beginning of the evening; but the sensibility she had afterwards shown had touched him so much, that he was extremely anxious to interest his father in her favour. He explained the cause of her fainting, and asked whether she was not much to be pitied. All pitied her—and Godfrey, encouraged by this pity, went on to prove that she ought not to be blamed for her mother's faults; that nothing could be more unjust and cruel than to think ill of the innocent daughter, because her mother had been imprudent.

"But, Godfrey," said Rosamond, "you seem to be answering some one who has attacked Miss Hauton— whom are you contending with?"

"With himself," said Mr. Percy. "His prudence tells him that the gentleman was quite right in saying that no man of sense would marry the daughter of a woman who had conducted herself ill, and yet he wishes to make an exception to the general rule in favour of pretty Miss Hauton."

"Pretty! My dear father, she is a great deal more than pretty: if she were only pretty, I should not be so much interested about her. But putting her quite out of the question, I do not agree with the general principle that a man should not marry the daughter of a woman who has conducted herself ill."

"I think you did agree with it till you knew that it applied to Miss Hauton's case," said Mr. Percy: "as well as I remember, Godfrey, I heard you once answer on a similar occasion, 'No, no—I will have nothing to do with any of the daughters of that mother—black cats have black kittens'—or 'black dogs have black puppies'—I forget which you said."

"Whichever it was, I am ashamed of having quoted such a vulgar proverb," said Godfrey.

"It may be a vulgar proverb, but I doubt whether it be a vulgar error," said Mr. Percy: "I have great faith in the wisdom of nations. So much so in the present instance, that I own I would rather a son of mine were to marry a well-conducted farmer's daughter of honest parentage, than the daughter of an ill-conducted lady of rank or fashion. The farmer's daughter might be trained into a gentlewoman, and might make my son at least a faithful wife, which is more than he could expect, or than I should expect, from the young lady, who had early seen the example of what was bad, and whose predispositions would be provided with the excuse of the old song."

Godfrey took fire at this, and exclaimed against the injustice of a doctrine which would render wretched for life many young women who might possess every amiable and estimable quality, and who could never remedy the misfortune of their birth. Godfrey urged, that whilst this would render the good miserable, it would be the most probable means of driving the weak from despair into vice.

Rosamond eagerly joined her brother's side of the question. Mr. Percy, though he knew, he said, that he must appear one of the "fathers with flinty hearts," protested that he felt great compassion for the unfortunate individuals, as much as a man who was not in love with any of them could reasonably be expected to feel.

"But now," continued he, "granting that all the consequences which Godfrey has predicted were to follow from my doctrine, yet I am inclined to believe that society would, upon the whole, be the gainer by such severity, or, as I am willing to allow it to be, such apparent injustice. The adherence to this principle would be the misery, perhaps the ruin, of a few; but would, I think, tend to the safety and happiness of so many, that the evil would be nothing in comparison to the good. The certainty of shame descending to the daughters would be a powerful means of deterring mothers from ill-conduct; and might probably operate more effectually to restrain licentiousness in high life than heavy damages, or the now transient disgrace of public trial and divorce. As to the apparent injustice of punishing children for the faults of their parents, it should be considered that in most other cases children suffer discredit more or less for the faults of their parents of whatever kind; and that, on the other hand, they enjoy the advantage of the good characters which their parents establish. This must be so from the necessary effect of experience, and from the nature of human belief, except in cases where passion operates to destroy or suspend the power of reason—"

"That is not my case, I assure you, sir," interrupted Godfrey.

Mr. Percy smiled, and continued:—"It appears to me highly advantageous, that character, in general, should descend to posterity as well as riches or honours, which are, in fact, often the representations, or consequences, in other forms, of different parts of character—industry, talents, courage. For instance, in the lower ranks of life, it is a common saying, that a good name is the richest legacy a woman can leave her daughter. This idea should be impressed more fully than it is upon the higher classes. At present, money too frequently forms a compensation for every thing in high life. It is not uncommon to see the natural daughters of men of rank, or of large fortune, portioned so magnificently, either with solid gold, or promised family protection, that their origin by the mother's side, and the character of the mother, are quite forgotten. Can this be advantageous to good morals? Surely a mother living in open defiance of the virtue of her sex should not see her illegitimate offspring, instead of being her shame, become her glory.—On the contrary, nothing could tend more to prevent the ill conduct of women in high life than the certainty that men who, from their fortune, birth, and character, might be deemed the most desirable matches, would shun alliances with the daughters of women of tainted reputation."

Godfrey eagerly declared his contempt for those men who married for money or ambition either illegitimate or legitimate daughters. He should be sorry, he said, to do any thing that would countenance vice, which ought to be put out of countenance by all means—if possible. But he was not the guardian of public morals; and even if he were, he should still think it unjust that the innocent should suffer for the guilty. That for his own part, if he could put his father's disapprobation out of the question, he should easily settle his mind, and overcome all objections in a prudential point of view to marrying an amiable woman who had had the misfortune to have a worthless mother.

Mrs. Percy had not yet given her opinion—all eyes turned towards her. As usual, she spoke with persuasive gentleness and good sense; she marked where each had, in the warmth of argument, said more than they intended, and she seized the just medium by which all might be conciliated. She said that she thought the important point to be considered was, what the education of the daughter had been; on this a prudent man would form his opinion, not on the mere accident of her birth. He would inquire whether the girl had lived with the ill-conducted mother—had been in situations to be influenced by her example, or by that of the company which she kept. If such had been the case, Mrs. Percy declared she thought it would be imprudent and wrong to marry the daughter. But if the daughter had been separated in early childhood from the mother, had never been exposed to the influence of her example, had, on the contrary, been educated carefully in strict moral and religious principles, it would be cruel, because unnecessary, to object to an alliance with such a woman. The objection would appear inconsistent, as well as unjust, if made by, those who professed to believe in the unlimited power of education.

Godfrey rubbed his hands with delight—Mr. Percy smiled, and acknowledged that he was compelled to admit the truth and justice of this statement.

"Pray do you know, Godfrey," said Rosamond, "whether Miss Hauton lived with her mother, or was educated by her?"

"I cannot tell," said Godfrey; "but I will make it my business to find out. At all events, my dear mother," continued he, "a child cannot decide by whom she will be educated. It is not her fault if her childhood be passed with a mother who is no fit guardian for her."

"I acknowledge," said Mrs. Percy, "that is her misfortune."

"And would you make it an irreparable misfortune?" said Godfrey, in an expostulatory tone: "my dear mother—only consider."

"My dear son, I do consider," said Mrs. Percy; "but I cannot give up the point of education. I should be very sorry to see a son of mine married to a woman who had been in this unfortunate predicament. But," added Mrs. Percy, after a few minutes' silence, "if from the time her own will and judgment could be supposed to act, she had chosen for her companions respectable and amiable persons, and had conducted herself with uniform propriety and discretion, I think I might be brought to allow of an exception to my general principle." She looked at Mr. Percy.

"Undoubtedly," said Mr. Percy; "exceptions must not merely be allowed, but will force themselves in favour of superior merit, of extraordinary excellence, which will rise above every unfavourable circumstance in any class, in any condition of life in which it may exist, which will throw off any stigma, however disgraceful, counteract all prepossessions, however potent, rise against all power of depression—redeem a family—redeem a race."

"Now, father, you speak like yourself!" cried Godfrey: "this is all I ask—all I wish."

"And here," continued Mr. Percy, "is an adequate motive for a good and great mind—yes, great—for I believe there are great minds in the female as well as in the male part of the creation; I say, here is an adequate motive to excite a woman of a good and great mind to exert herself to struggle against the misfortunes of her birth."

"For instance," said Rosamond, "my sister Caroline is just the kind of woman, who, if she had been one of these unfortunate daughters, would have made herself an exception."

"Very likely," said Mr. Percy, laughing; "but why you should go so far out of your way to make an unfortunate daughter of poor Caroline, and why you should picture to yourself, as Dr. Johnson would say, what would be probable in an impossible situation, I cannot conceive, except for the pleasure of exercising, as you do upon most occasions, a fine romantic imagination."

"At all events I am perfectly satisfied," said Godfrey. "Since you admit of exceptions, sir, I agree with you entirely."

"No, not entirely. I am sure you cannot agree with me entirely, until I admit Miss Hauton to be one of my exceptions."

"That will come in time, if she deserve it," said Mrs. Percy.

Godfrey thanked his mother with great warmth, and observed, that she was always the most indulgent of friends.

"But remember my if," said Mrs. Percy: "I know nothing of Miss Hauton at present, except that she is very pretty, and that she has engaging manners—Do you, my dear Godfrey?"

"Yes, indeed, ma'am, I know a great deal more of her."

"Did you ever see her before this night?"

"Never," said Godfrey.

"And at a ball!" said Mrs. Percy: "you must have wonderful penetration into character.—But Cupid, though blindfold, can see more at a single glance than a philosophic eye can discover with the most minute examination."

"But, Cupid out of the question, let me ask you, mother," said Godfrey, "whether you do not think Miss Hauton has a great deal of sensibility? You saw that there was no affectation in her fainting."

"None, none," said Mrs. Percy.

"There, father!" cried Godfrey, in an exulting tone; "and sensibility is the foundation of every thing that is most amiable and charming, of every grace, of every virtue in woman."

"Yes," said Mr. Percy, "and perhaps of some of their errors and vices. It depends upon how it is governed, whether sensibility be a curse or a blessing to its possessor, and to society."

"A curse!" cried Godfrey; "yes, if a woman be doomed—"

"Come, come, my dear Godfrey," interrupted Mr. Percy, "do not let us talk any more upon the subject just now, because you are too much interested to reason coolly."

Rosamond then took her turn to talk of what was uppermost in her thoughts—Buckhurst Falconer, whom she alternately blamed and pitied, accused and defended; sometimes rejoicing that Caroline had rejected his suit, sometimes pitying him for his disappointment, and repeating that with such talents, frankness, and generosity of disposition, it was much to be regretted that he had not that rectitude of principle, and steadiness of character, which alone could render him worthy of Caroline. Then passing from compassion for the son to indignation against the father, she observed, "that Commissioner Falconer seemed determined to counteract all that was good in his son's disposition, that he actually did every thing in his power to encourage Buckhurst in a taste for dissipation, as it seemed on purpose to keep him in a state of dependence, and to enslave him to the great.

"I hope, with all my heart, I hope," continued Rosamond, "that Buckhurst will have sense and steadiness enough to refuse; but I heard his father supporting that foolish Colonel Hauton's persuasions, and urging his poor son to go with those people to Cheltenham. Now, if once he gets into that extravagant, dissipated set, he will be ruined for ever!—Adieu to all hopes of him. He will no more go to the bar than I shall—he will think of nothing but pleasure; he will run in debt again, and then farewell principle, and with principle, farewell all hopes of him. But I think he will have sense and steadiness enough to resist his father, and to refuse to accompany this profligate patron, Colonel Hauton.—Godfrey, what is your opinion? Do you think Buckhurst will go?"

"I do not know," replied Godfrey: "in his place I should find it very easy, but in my own case, I confess, I should feel it difficult, to refuse, if I were pressed to join a party of pleasure with Miss Hauton."

CHAPTER V

Godfrey Percy went in the morning to inquire after the health of his fair partner: this was only a common civility. On his way thither he overtook and joined a party of gentlemen, who were also going to Clermont-park. They entered into conversation, and talked of the preceding night—one of the gentlemen, an elderly man, who had not been at the ball, happened to be acquainted with Miss Hauton, and with her family. Godfrey heard from him all the particulars respecting Lady Anne Hauton, and was thrown into a melancholy reverie by learning that Miss Hauton had been educated by this mother, and had always lived with her till her ladyship's death, which happened about two years before this time.— After receiving this intelligence, Godfrey heard little more of the conversation that passed till he reached Clermont-park.—A number of young people were assembled in the music-room practising for a concert.—Miss Hauton was at the piano-forte when he entered the room: she was sitting with her back to the door, surrounded by a crowd of amateurs; she did not see him—he stood behind listening to her singing. Her voice was delightful; but he was surprised, and not pleased, by the choice of her songs: she was singing, with some other high-bred young ladies, songs which, to use the gentlest expression, were rather too anacreontic—songs which, though sanctioned by fashion, were not such as a young lady of taste would prefer, or such as a man of delicacy would like to hear from his sister or his wife. They were nevertheless highly applauded by all the audience, except by Godfrey, who remained silent behind the young lady. In the fluctuation of the crowd he was pressed nearer and nearer to her chair. As she finished singing a fashionable air, she heard a sigh from the person behind her.

"That's your favourite, I think?" said she, turning round, and looking up. "Mr. Percy! I—I thought it was Mr. Falconer." Face, neck, hands, suddenly blushed: she stooped for a music-book, and searched for some time in that attitude for she knew not what, whilst all the gentlemen officiously offered their services, and begged only to know for what book she was looking.

"Come, come, Maria," cried Colonel Hauton, "what the d— are you about?—Can't you give us another of these? You can't be better. Come, you're keeping Miss Drakelow."

"Go on, Miss Drakelow, if you please, without me."

"Impossible. Come, come, Maria, what the deuce are you at?"

Miss Hauton, afraid to refuse her brother, afraid to provoke the comments of the company, began to sing, or rather to attempt to sing—her voice faltered; she cleared her throat, and began again—worse still, she was out of tune: she affected to laugh. Then, pushing back her chair, she rose, drew her veil over her face, and said, "I have sung till I have no voice left.—Does nobody walk this morning?"

"No, no," said Colonel Hauton; "who the deuce would be bored with being broiled at this time of day? Miss Drakelow—Miss Chatterton, give us some more music, I beseech you; for I like music better in a morning than at night—the mornings, when one can't go out, are so confoundedly long and heavy."

The young ladies played, and Miss Hauton seated herself apart from the group of musicians, upon a bergère, leaning on her hand, in a melancholy attitude. Buckhurst Falconer followed and sat down beside her, endeavouring to entertain her with some witty anecdote.

She smiled with effort, listened with painful attention, and the moment the anecdote was ended, her eyes wandered out of the window. Buckhurst rose, vacated his seat, and before any of the other gentlemen who had gathered round could avail themselves of that envied place, Miss Hauton, complaining of the intolerable heat, removed nearer to the window, to an ottoman, one half of which was already so fully occupied by a large dog of her brother's, that she was in no danger from any other intruder. Some of the gentlemen, who were not blessed with much sagacity, followed, to talk to her of the beauty of the dog which she was stroking; but to an eulogium upon its long ears, and even to a quotation from Shakspeare about dewlaps, she listened with so vacant an air, that her followers gave up the point, and successively retired, leaving her to her meditations. Godfrey, who had kept aloof, had in the mean time been looking at some books that lay on a reading table.—Maria Hauton was written in the first page of several of them.—All were novels—some French, and some German, of a sort which he did not like.

"What have you there, Mr. Percy?" said Miss Hauton.—"Nothing worth your notice, I am afraid. I dare say you do not like novels."

"Pardon me, I like some novels very much."

"Which?" said Miss Hauton, rising and approaching the table.

"All that are just representations of life and manners, or of the human heart," said Godfrey, "provided they are—"

"Ah! the human heart!" interrupted Miss Hauton: "the heart only can understand the heart—who, in modern times, can describe the human heart?"

"Not to speak of foreigners—Miss Burney—Mrs. Inchbald—Mrs. Opie," said Godfrey.

"True; and yet I—and yet—" said Miss Hauton, pausing and sighing.

"And yet that was not what I was thinking of," she should have said, had she finished her sentence with the truth; but this not being convenient, she left it unfinished, and began a new one, with "Some of these novels are sad trash—I hope Mr. Godfrey Percy will not judge of my taste by them: that would be condemning me for the crimes of my bookseller, who will send us down everything new that comes out."

Godfrey disclaimed the idea of condemning or blaming Miss Hauton's taste: "he could not," he said, "be so presumptuous, so impertinent."

"So then," said she, "Mr. Godfrey Percy is like all the rest of his sex, and I must not expect to hear the truth from him."—She paused—and looked at a print which he was examining.—"I would, however, rather have him speak severely than think hardly of me."

"He has no right to speak, and certainly no inclination to think hardly of Miss Hauton," replied Godfrey gravely, but with an emotion which he in vain endeavoured to suppress. To change the conversation, he asked her opinion about a figure in the print. She took out her glass, and stooped to look quite closely at it.—"Before you utterly condemn me," continued she, speaking in a low voice, "consider how fashion silences one's better taste and feelings, and how difficult it is when all around one—"

Miss Chatterton, Miss Drakelow, and some officers of their suite came up at this instant; a deputation, they said, to bring Miss Hauton back, to favour them with another song, as she must now have recovered her voice.

"No—no—excuse me," said she, smiling languidly; "I beg not to be pressed any more. I am really not well—I absolutely cannot sing any more this morning. I have already sung so much—too much," added she, when the deputation had retired, so that the last words could be heard only by him for whom they were intended.

Though Miss Hauton's apologizing thus for her conduct, and making a young gentleman, with whom she was but just acquainted, the judge of her actions, might be deemed a still farther proof of her indiscretion, yet the condescension was so flattering, and it appeared such an instance of ingenuous disposition, that Godfrey was sensibly touched by it. He followed the fair Maria to her ottoman, from which she banished Pompey the Great, to make room for him. The recollection of his father's warning words, however, came across Godfrey's mind; he bowed an answer to a motion that invited him to the dangerous seat, and continued standing with an air of safe respect.

"I hope you will have the goodness to express to Mrs. Percy how much I felt her kindness to me last night, when—when I wanted it so much. There is something so soothing, so gentle, so indulgent about Mrs. Percy, so loveable!"

"She is very good, very indulgent, indeed," said Godfrey, in a tone of strong affection,—"very loveable—that is the exact word."

"I fear it is not English," said Miss Hauton.

"Il mérite bien de l'être," said Godfrey.

A profound silence ensued.—Colonel Hauton came up to this pair, while they were still silent, and with their eyes fixed upon the ground.

"D—d agreeable you two seem," cried the colonel.—"Buckhurst, you have always so much to say for yourself, do help your cousin here: I'm sure I know how to pity him, for many a time the morning after a ball, I've been with my partner in just as bad a quandary—without a word to throw to a dog."

"Impossible, surely, colonel, when you had such a fine animal as this," said Godfrey, caressing Pompey, who lay at his feet. "Where did you get this handsome dog?"

The colonel then entered into the history of Pompey the Great. "I was speaking," said Miss Hauton, "to Mr. Godfrey Percy of his family—relations of yours, Mr. Falconer, are not they? He has another sister, I think, some one told me, a beautiful sister, Caroline, who was not at the ball last night?"

"Yes," said Buckhurst, who looked at this instant also to the dog for assistance—"Pompey!—Pompey!—poor fellow!"

"Is Miss Caroline Percy like her mother?"

"No."

"Like her father—or her brother?"

"Not particularly—Will you honour me with any commands for town?—Colonel, have you any?—I'm just going off with Major Clay," said Buckhurst.

"Not you, indeed," cried the colonel; "your father has made you over to me, and I won't give you leave of absence, my good fellow.—You're under orders for Cheltenham to-morrow, my boy—No reply, sir—no arguing with your commanding officer. You've no more to do, but to tell Clay to go without you."

"And now," continued the colonel, returning to Godfrey Percy, after Buckhurst had left the room, "what hinders you from making one of our party? You can't do better. There's Maria and Lady Oldborough were both wishing it at breakfast—Maria, can't you say something?"

Maria's eyes said more than the colonel could have said, if he had spoken for ever.

"But perhaps Mr. Godfrey Percy may have other engagements," said she, with a timid persuasive tone, which Godfrey found it extremely difficult to resist.

"Bellamy! where the d—l do you come from?—Very glad to see you, faith!" cried the colonel, going forward to shake hands with a very handsome man, who had just then entered the room. "Maria," said Colonel Hauton, turning to his sister, "don't you know Bellamy?—Bellamy," repeated he, coming close to her, whilst the gentleman was paying his compliments to Lady Oldborough, "Captain Bellamy, with whom you used to waltz every night, you know, at—what's the name of the woman's?"

"I never waltzed with him but once—or twice, that I remember," said Miss Hauton, "and then because you insisted upon it."

"I!—Well, I did very right if I did, because you were keeping all the world waiting, and I knew you intended to do it at last—so I thought you might as well do it at first. But I don't know what's the matter with you this morning—we must drive a little spirit into you at Cheltenham."

Captain Bellamy came up to pay his respects, or rather his compliments, to Miss Hauton: there was no respect in his manner, but the confidence of one who had been accustomed to be well received.

"She has not been well—fainted last night at a ball—is hipped this morning; but we'll get her spirits up again when we have her at Cheltenham—We shall be a famous dashing party! I have been beating up for recruits all day—here's one," said Colonel Hauton, turning to Godfrey Percy.

"Excuse me," said Godfrey, "I am engaged—I am obliged to join my regiment immediately." He bowed gravely to Miss Hauton—wished her a good morning; and, without trusting himself to another look, retreated, saying to himself,

"Sir, she's yours—You have brushed from the grape its soft blue;
From the rosebud you've shaken its tremulous dew:
What you've touched you may take.—Pretty waltzer, adieu!"

From this moment he mentioned Miss Hauton's name no more in his own family. His whole mind now seemed, and not only seemed, but was, full of military thoughts. So quickly in youth do different and opposite trains of ideas and emotions succeed to each other; and so easy it is, by a timely exercise of reason and self-command, to prevent a fancy from becoming a passion. Perhaps, if his own happiness alone had been in question, Godfrey might not have shown precisely the same prudence; but on this occasion his generosity and honour assisted his discretion. He plainly saw that Miss Hauton was not exactly a woman whom he could wish to make his wife—and he was too honourable to trifle with her affections. He was not such a coxcomb as to imagine that, in the course of so slight an acquaintance, he could have made any serious impression on this young lady's heart: yet he could not but perceive that she had distinguished him from the first hour he was introduced to her; and he was aware that, with her extreme sensibility, and an unoccupied imagination, she might rapidly form for him an attachment that might lead to mutual misery.

Mr. Percy rejoiced in his son's honourable conduct, and he was particularly pleased by Godfrey's determining to join his regiment immediately. Mr. Percy thought it advantageous for the eldest son of a man of fortune to be absent for some years from his home, from his father's estate, tenants, and dependents, to see something of the world, to learn to estimate himself and others, and thus to have means of becoming a really respectable, enlightened, and useful country gentleman—not one of those booby squires, born only to consume the fruits of the earth, who spend their lives in coursing, shooting, hunting, carousing [Footnote: See an eloquent address to country gentlemen, in Young's Annals of Agriculture, vol. i., last page.], "who eat, drink, sleep, die, and rot in oblivion." He thought it in these times the duty of every young heir to serve a few years, that he might be as able, as willing, to join in the defence of his country, if necessary. Godfrey went, perhaps, beyond his father's ideas upon this subject, for he had an ardent desire to go into the army as a profession, and almost regretted that his being an eldest son might induce him to forego it after a few campaigns.

Godfrey did not enter into the army from the puerile vanity of wearing a red coat and an epaulette; nor to save himself the trouble of pursuing his studies; nor because he thought the army a good lounge, or a happy escape from parental control; nor yet did he consider the military profession as a mercenary speculation, in which he was to calculate the chance of getting into the shoes, or over the head, of Lieutenant A— or Captain B—. He had higher objects; he had a noble ambition to distinguish himself. Not in mere technical phrase, or to grace a bumper toast, but in truth, and as a governing principle of action, he felt zeal for the interests of the service. Yet Godfrey was not without faults; and of these his parents, fond as they were of him, were well aware.

Mrs. Percy, in particular, felt much anxiety, when the moment fixed for his departure approached; when she considered that he was now to mix with companions very different from those with whom he had hitherto associated, and to be placed in a situation where calmness of temper and prudence would be more requisite than military courage or generosity of disposition.

"Well, my dear mother," cried Godfrey, when he came to take leave, "fare you well: if I live, I hope I shall distinguish myself; and if I fall—

'How sleep the brave, who sink to rest!'"

"God bless you, my dear son!" said his mother. She seemed to have much more to say, but, unable at that moment to express it, she turned to her husband, who knew all she thought and felt.

"My dear Godfrey," said his father, "I have never troubled you with much advice; but now you are going from me, let me advise you to take care that the same enthusiasm which makes you think your own country the best country upon earth, your own family the best family in that country, and your own regiment the best regiment in the service, all which is becoming a good patriot, a good son, and a good soldier, should go a step—a dangerous step farther, and should degenerate into party spirit, or what the French call esprit-de-corps."

"The French!" cried Godfrey. "Oh! hang the French! Never mind what the French call it, sir."

"And degenerating into party-spirit, or what is called esprit-de-corps," resumed Mr. Percy, smiling, "should, in spite of your more enlarged views of the military art and science, and your knowledge of all that Alexander and Cæsar, and Marshal Saxe and Turenne, and the Duke of Marlborough and Lord Peterborough, ever said or did, persuade you to believe that your brother officers, whoever they may be, are the greatest men that ever existed, and that their opinions should rule the world, or at least should govern you."

"More than all the rest, I fear, my dear Godfrey," interposed Mrs. Percy, "that, when you do not find the world so good as you imagine it to be, you will, by quarrelling with it directly, make it worse to you than it really is. But if you discover that merit is not always immediately rewarded or promoted, do not let your indignation, and—shall I say it—impatience of spirit, excite you to offend your superiors in station, and, by these means, retard your own advancement."

"Surely, if I should be treated with injustice, you would not have me bear it patiently?" cried Godfrey, turning quickly.

"In the first place, stay till it happens before you take fire," said his father; "and, in the next place, remember that patience, and deference to his superiors, form an indispensable part of a young soldier's merit."

"Ah! my dear," said Mrs. Percy, looking up at her son anxiously, "if, even at this instant, even with us, even at the bare imagination of injustice, you take offence, I fear—I very much fear—" said she, laying her hand upon his arm.

"My dearest mother," said Godfrey, in a softened tone, taking his mother's hand in the most respectful and tender manner, "fear nothing for me. I will be as patient as a lamb, rather than be a source of anxiety to you."

"And now, my good friends, fare ye well!" said Godfrey, turning to take leave of his sisters.

The young soldier departed. His last words, as he got upon his horse, were to Caroline. "Caroline, you will be married before I return."

But to descend to the common affairs of life. Whilst all these visits and balls, coquettings and separations, had been going on, the Dutch carpenters had been repairing the wreck; and, from time to time, complaints had been made of them by Mr. Percy's old steward. The careful steward's indignation was first excited by their forgetting every night to lock a certain gate, with the key of which they had been entrusted. Then they had wasted his master's timber, and various tools were missing—they had been twice as long as they ought to have been in finishing their work, and now, when the wind was fair, the whole ship's crew impatient to sail, and not above half a day's work wanting, the carpenters were smoking and drinking, instead of putting their hands to the business. The Dutch carpenter, who was at this moment more than half intoxicated, answered the steward's just reproaches with much insolence. Mr. Percy, feeling that his hospitality and good-nature were encroached upon and abused, declared that he would no longer permit the Dutchmen to have the use of his house, and ordered his steward to see that they quitted it immediately.

These men, and all belonging to them, consequently left the place in a few hours; whatever remained to be done to the vessel was finished that evening, and she sailed, to the great joy of her whole crew, and of Mr. Percy's steward, who, when he brought the news of this event to his master, protested that he was as glad as if any body had given him twenty golden guineas, that he had at last got safely rid of these ill-mannered drunken fellows, who, after all his master had done for them, never so much as said, "thank you," and who had wasted and spoiled more by their carelessness than their heads were worth.

Alas! he little knew at that moment how much more his master was to lose by their carelessness, and he rejoiced too soon at having got rid of them.

In the middle of the night the family were alarmed by the cry of fire!—A fire had broken out in the outhouse, which had been lent to the Dutchmen; before it was discovered, the roof was in a blaze; the wind unfortunately blew towards a hay-rick, which was soon in flames, and the burning hay spread the fire to a considerable distance, till it caught the veranda at the east wing of the dwelling-house. One of the servants, who slept in that part of the house, was awakened by the light from the burning veranda, but by the time the alarm was given, and before the family could get out of their rooms, the flames had reached Mr. Percy's study, which contained his most valuable papers. Mr. Percy, whose voice all his family, in the midst of their terror and confusion, obeyed, directed with great presence of mind what should be done by each. He sent one to open a cistern of water at the top of the house, and to let it flow over the roof, another to tear down the trellis next the part that was on fire; others he despatched for barrows-full of wet mortar from a heap which was in a back yard near the house; others he stationed in readiness to throw the mortar where it was most needful to extinguish the flames, or to prevent their communicating with the rest of the building. He went himself to the place where the fire raged with the greatest violence, whilst his wife and daughters were giving out from the study the valuable papers, which, as he directed, were thrown in one heap on the lawn, at a sufficient distance from the house to prevent any danger of their being burnt—most of them were in tin cases that were easily removed—the loose papers and books were put into baskets, and covered with wet blankets, so that the pieces of the burning trellis, which fell upon them as they were carried out, did them no injury. It was wonderful with what silence, order, and despatch, this went on whilst three females, instead of shrieking and fainting, combined to do what was useful and prudent. In spite of all Mr. Percy's exertions, however, the flames burst in from the burning trellis through one of the windows of the study, before the men could tear down the shutters and architraves, as he had ordered. The fire caught the wood-work, and ran along the book-shelves on one side of the wall with terrible rapidity, so that the whole room was, in a few minutes, in a blaze—they were forced to leave it before they had carried out many of the books. Some old papers remained in the presses, supposed to be duplicates, and of no consequence. This whole wing of the house they were obliged to abandon to the flames, but the fire was stopped in its progress at last, and the principal part of the mansion was preserved by wet mortar, according to Mr. Percy's judicious order, by the prompt obedience, and by the unanimity, of all who assisted.

The next morning the family saw the melancholy spectacle of a heap of ruins in the place of that library which they all loved so much. However, it was their disposition to make the best of misfortunes; instead of deploring what they had lost, they rejoiced in having suffered so little and saved so much. They particularly rejoiced that no lives had been sacrificed;—Mr. Percy declared, that for his own part, he would willingly undergo much greater pecuniary loss, to have had the satisfaction of seeing in all his family so much presence of mind, and so much freedom from selfishness, as they had shown upon this occasion.

When he said something of this sort before his servants, who were all assembled, it was observed that one of them, a very old nurse, looked immediately at Caroline, then lifted up her hands and eyes to heaven, in silent gratitude. Upon inquiry it appeared, that in the confusion and terror, when the alarm had first been raised, the nurse had been forgotten, or it had been taken for granted that she had gone home to her own cottage the preceding evening.

Caroline, however, recollected her, and ran to her room, which was in the attic story over the library.

When Caroline opened the door she could scarcely see the bed.—She made her way to it, however, got old Martha out of the room, and with great difficulty brought the bewildered, decrepit creature, safely down a small staircase, which the flames had not then reached.—Nothing could exceed her gratitude; with eyes streaming with tears, and a head shaking with strong emotion, she delighted in relating all these circumstances, and declared that none but Miss Caroline could have persuaded her to go down that staircase, when she saw all below in flames.

Mr. Percy's first care was to look over his papers, to see whether any were missing.—To his consternation, one valuable deed, a deed by which he held the whole Percy estate, was nowhere to be found. He had particular reason for being alarmed by the loss of this paper.—The heir-at-law to this estate had long been lying in wait to make an attack upon him.—Aware of this, Mr. Percy took all prudent means to conceal the loss of this paper, and he cautioned his whole family never to mention it.

It happened about this time, that a poor old man, to whom Buckhurst Falconer had given that puppy which his brother John had so bitterly regretted, came to Mr. Percy to complain that the dog had brought him into great trouble. The puppy had grown into a dog, and of this the old man had forgotten to give notice to the tax-gatherer. Mr. Percy perceiving clearly that the man had no design to defraud, and pitying him for having thus, by his ignorance or carelessness, subjected himself to the heavy penalty of ten pounds, which, without selling his only cow, he was unable to pay, advised him to state the simple fact in a petition, and Mr. Percy promised to transmit this petition to government, with a memorial against the tax-gatherer, who had been accused, in many instances, of oppressive and corrupt conduct. He had hitherto defied all complainants, because he was armed strong in law by an attorney who was his near relation—an attorney of the name of Sharpe, whose cunning and skill in the doubles and mazes of his profession, and whose active and vindictive temper had rendered him the terror of the neighbourhood. Not only the poor but the rich feared him, for he never failed to devise means of revenging himself wherever he was offended. He one morning waited on Mr. Percy, to speak to him about the memorial, which, he understood, Mr. Percy was drawing up against Mr. Bates, the tax-gatherer.

"Perhaps, Mr. Percy," said he, "you don't know that Mr. Bates is my near relation?"

Mr. Percy replied, that he had not known it; but that now that he did, he could not perceive how that altered the business; as he interfered, not from any private motive, but from a sense of public justice, which made him desire to remove a person from a situation for which he had shown himself utterly unfit.

Mr. Sharpe smiled a malicious smile, and declared that, for his part, he did not pretend to be a reformer of abuses: he thought, in the present times, that gentlemen who wished well to their king and the peace of the country ought not to be forward to lend their names to popular discontents, and should not embarrass government with petty complaints. Gentlemen could never foresee where such things would end, and therefore, in the existing circumstances, they ought surely to endeavour to strengthen, instead of weakening, the hands of government.

To this commonplace cant, by which all sorts of corruption and all public delinquents might be screened, and by which selfishness and fraud hope to pass for loyalty and love of the peace of the country, Mr. Percy did not attempt, or rather did not deign, any reply.

Mr. Sharpe then insinuated that Lord Oldborough, who had put Bates into his present situation, would be displeased by a complaint against him. Mr. Sharpe observed, that Lord Oldborough was remarkable for standing steadily by all the persons whom he appointed, and that, if Mr. Percy persisted in this attack, he would probably not find himself thanked by his own relations, the Falconers.

This hint produced no effect: so at last Mr. Sharpe concluded, by saying, with an air of prodigious legal assurance, that for his own part he was quite at ease about the result of the affair, for he was confident that, when the matter came to be properly inquired into, and the witnesses to be cross-examined, no malpractices could be brought home to his relation.

Then Mr. Percy observed, that a memorial, praying to have the circumstances inquired into, could be no disadvantage to Mr. Bates, but the contrary, as it would tend to prove his innocence publicly, and to remove the prejudice which now subsisted against him.—Mr. Percy, who had the memorial at this time in his hand, deliberately folded it up, and directed it.

"Then, sir," cried Mr. Sharpe, put off his guard by anger, "since you are determined to throw away the scabbard, you cannot be surprised if I do the same."

Mr. Percy, smiling, said that he feared no sword but the sword of justice, which could not fall on his head, while he was doing what was just. As he spoke, he prepared to seal the memorial.

Mr. Sharpe's habitual caution recurring in the space of a second or two, he begged pardon if zeal for his relation had hurried him into any unbecoming warmth of expression, and stretching out his hand eagerly to stop Mr. Percy, as he was going to press down the seal, "Give me leave, sir," said he, "give me leave to run my eye over that memorial—may I beg? before you seal it."

"And welcome," said Mr. Percy, putting the paper into his hand: "all that I do shall be done openly and fairly."

The attorney took possession of the memorial, and began to con it over. As he was reading it, he happened to stand in a recessed window, so that he could not easily be seen by any person who entered the room: at this moment Rosamond came in suddenly, exclaiming, as she held up a huge unfolded parchment, "I've found it!—I've found it, my dear father!—I do believe this is Sir John Percy's deed that was lost!—I always said it was not burned.—What's the matter?—What do you mean?—Nobody can hear me? the outer door is shut—Perhaps this is only a copy.—It is not signed or sealed, but I suppose—"

Here she stopped short, for she saw Mr. Sharpe—She looked so much astounded, that even if he had not heard all she had said, her countenance would have excited his curiosity. The attorney had heard every syllable she had uttered, and he knew enough of Mr. Percy's affairs to comprehend the full extent of the advantage that might be made of this discovery. He coolly returned the memorial, acknowledging that it was drawn up with much moderation and ability, but regretting that Mr. Percy should think it necessary to send it; and concluding with a few general expressions of the regard he had always felt for the family, he took his leave.

"All is safe!" cried Rosamond, as soon as she heard the house door shut after he was gone. "All is safe, thank Heaven!—for that man's head was luckily so full of this memorial, that he never heard one word I said."

Mr. Percy was of a different opinion: he was persuaded that the attorney would not neglect so fine an opportunity of revenge. Sharpe had formerly been employed in suits of Sir Robert Percy, the heir-at-law. Here was now the promise of a lawsuit, that would at all events put a great deal of money into the pockets of the lawyers, and a considerable gratuity would be ensured to the person who should first inform Sir Robert of the loss of the important conveyance.

Mr. Percy's opinion of the revengeful nature of Sharpe, and his perception that he was in the solicitor's power, did not, however, make any change in his resolution about the memorial.—It was sent, and Bates was turned out of his office. For some time nothing more was heard of Mr. Sharpe.—Mr. Percy, for many months afterward, was busied in rebuilding that part of his house which had been destroyed by the fire; and as he was naturally of a sanguine temper, little inclined to occupy himself with cabals and quarrels, the transaction concerning Bates, and even the attorney's threat of throwing away the scabbard, passed from his mind. The family pursued the happy tenour of their lives, without remembering that there was such a being as Mr. Solicitor Sharpe.

CHAPTER VI

At the time of the fire at Percy-hall, a painted glass window in the passage—we should say the gallery—leading to the study had been destroyed.—Old Martha, whose life Caroline had saved, had a son, who possessed some talents as a painter, and who had learnt the art of painting on glass. He had been early in his life assisted by the Percy family, and, desirous to offer some small testimony of his gratitude, he begged permission to paint a new window for the gallery.—He chose for his subject the fire, and the moment when Caroline was assisting his decrepit mother down the dangerous staircase.—The painting was finished unknown to Caroline, and put up on her birthday, when she had just attained her eighteenth year. This was the only circumstance worth recording which the biographer can find noted in the family annals at this period. In this dearth of events, may we take the liberty of introducing, according to the fashion of modern biography, a few private letters? They are written by persons of whom the reader as yet knows nothing—Mr. Percy's second and third sons, Alfred and Erasmus. Alfred was a barrister; Erasmus a physician: they were both at this time in London, just commencing their professional career. Their characters—but let their characters speak for themselves in their letters, else neither their letters nor their characters can be worth attention.

ALFRED PERCY TO HIS FATHER.

"MY DEAR FATHER,

"Thank you for the books—I have been reading hard lately, for I have still, alas! leisure enough to read. I cannot expect to be employed, or to have fees for some time to come. I am armed with patience—I am told that I have got through the worst part of my profession, the reading of dry law. This is tiresome enough, to be sure; but I think the courting of attorneys and solicitors is the worst part of the beginning of my profession: for this I was not, and I believe I never shall be, sufficiently prepared. I give them no dinners, and they neglect me; yet I hope I pay them proper attention. To make amends, however, I have been so fortunate as to form acquaintance with some gentlemen of the bar, who possess enlarged minds and general knowledge: their conversation is of the greatest use and pleasure to me. But many barristers here are men who live entirely among themselves, with their heads in their green bags, and their souls narrowed to a point: mere machines for drawing pleas and rejoinders.

"I remember Burke asserts (and I was once, with true professional party-spirit, angry with him for the assertion) that the study of the law has a contractile power on the mind; I am now convinced it has, from what I see, and what I feel; therefore I will do all I can to counteract this contraction by the expansive force of literature. I lose no opportunity of making acquaintance with literary men, and cultivating their society. The other day, at Hookham's library, I met with a man of considerable talents—a Mr. Temple: he was looking for a passage in the life of the lord-keeper Guildford, which I happened to know. This brought us into a conversation, with which we were mutually so well pleased, that we agreed to dine together, for further information—and we soon knew all that was to be known of each other's history.

"Temple is of a very good family, though the younger son of a younger brother. He was brought up by his grandfather, with whom he was a favourite. Accustomed, from his childhood, to live with the rich and great, to see a grand establishment, to be waited upon, to have servants, horses, carriages at his command, and always to consider himself as a part of a family who possessed every thing they could wish for in life; he says, he almost forgot, or rather never thought of the time when he was to have nothing, and when he should be obliged to provide entirely for himself. Fortunately for him, his grandfather having early discerned that he had considerable talents, determined that he should have all the advantages of education, which he thought would prepare him to shine in parliament.—His grandfather, however, died when Temple was yet scarcely eighteen.—He had put off writing a codicil to his will, by which Temple lost the provision intended for him.—All hopes of being brought into parliament were over. His uncle, who succeeded to the estate, had sons of his own. There were family jealousies, and young Temple, as having been a favourite, was disliked.—Promises were made by other relations, and by former friends, and by these he was amused and misled for some time; but he found he was only wasting his life, attending upon these great relations. The unkindness and falsehood of some, and the haughty neglect of others, hurt his high spirit, and roused his strong indignation. He, in his turn, neglected and offended, was cast off at last, or forgotten by most of the fine promisers.—At which, he says, he has had reason to rejoice, for this threw him upon his own resources, and made him exert his own mind.—He applied, in earnest, to prepare himself for the profession for which he was best fitted, and went to the bar.—Now comes the part of his history for which he, with reason, blames himself. He was disgusted, not so much by the labour, as by the many disagreeable circumstances, which necessarily occur in the beginning of a barrister's course.—He could not bear the waiting in the courts, or on circuit, without business, without notice. He thought his merit would never make its way, and was provoked by seeing two or three stupid fellows pushed on by solicitors, or helped up by judges.—He had so much knowledge, talent, and eloquence, that he must in time have made a great figure, and would, undoubtedly, have risen to the first dignities, had he persevered; but he sacrificed himself to pique and impatience. He quitted the bar, and the very summer after he had left it, the illness of a senior counsel on that circuit afforded an opportunity where Temple would have been called upon, and where he could fully have displayed his talents. Once known, such a man would have been always distinguished.—He now bitterly regrets that he abandoned his profession.—This imprudence gave his friends a fair excuse for casting him off; but, he says, their neglect grieves him not, for he had resolved never more to trust to their promises, or to stoop to apply to them for patronage. He has been these last two years in an obscure garret writing for bread. He says, however, that he is sure he is happier, even in this situation, than are some of his cousins at this instant, who are struggling in poverty to be genteel, or to keep up a family name, and he would not change places with those who are in a state of idle and opprobrious dependence. I understand (remember, this is a secret between ourselves)—I understand that Secretary Cunningham Falconer has found him out, and makes good use of his pen, but pays him shabbily. Temple is too much of a man of honour to peach. So Lord Oldborough knows nothing of the matter; and Cunningham gets half his business done, and supplies all his deficiencies, by means of this poor drudging genius. Perhaps I have tired you with this history of my new friend; but he has interested me extremely:—he has faults certainly, perhaps too high a spirit, too much sensibility; but he has such strict integrity, so much generosity of mind, and something so engaging in his manners, that I cannot help loving, admiring, and pitying him—that last sentiment, however, I am obliged to conceal, for he would not bear it.

"I see very little of Erasmus. He has been in the country this fortnight with some patient. I long for his return.—I will make the inquiries you desire about Buckhurst Falconer.

"Your affectionate son,

"ALFRED PERCY.

"P.S. Yes, my dear Rosamond, I shall be obliged to you for the flower-roots for my landlady's daughter."

LETTER FROM ERASMUS TO HIS FATHER.

"MY DEAR FATHER,

"Pray do not feel disappointed when I tell you that I am not getting on quite so fast as I expected. I assure you, however, that I have not neglected any honourable means of bringing myself into notice. But it is very difficult for a young man to rise without puffing, or using low means.

"I met Lady Jane Granville a few days ago. She gave me a note to Sir Amyas Courtney, a fashionable physician and a great favourite of hers.—She told me that he had formerly been acquainted with some of my family, and she so strongly urged me to wait upon him, that to avoid offending her ladyship, I promised to avail myself of her introduction.

"I called several times before I found Sir Amyas at home. At last, by appointment, I went to breakfast with him one morning when he was confined to the house by an influenza. He received me in the most courteous manner—recollected to have danced with my mother years ago, at a ball at Lord Somebody's—professed the greatest respect for the name of Percy—asked me various questions about my grandfather, which I could not answer, and paid you more compliments than I can remember. Sir Amyas is certainly the prettiest behaved physician breathing, with the sweetest assortment of tittle-tattle, with an inexhaustible fund of anecdotes and compliments for the great, and an intimate acquaintance with the fair and fashionable. He has also the happiest art of speaking a vast deal, and yet saying nothing; seeming to give an opinion, without ever committing himself.—The address with which he avoids contested points of science, and the art with which he displays his superficial knowledge, and conceals his want of depth, is truly amusing. He slid away from science as soon as he could, to politics, where he kept safe in commonplace newspaper-phrases; and in the happy persuasion that every thing is for the best, and that every man in power, let him be of what party he may, can do no wrong. He did not seem quite satisfied with my countenance as he spoke, and once or twice paused for my acquiescence—in vain.

"We were interrupted by the entrance of a Mr. Gresham, a rich merchant, who came to look at a picture which Sir Amyas shows as a true Titian. Mr. Gresham spoke, as I thought, with much good sense and taste about it, and Sir Amyas talked a great deal of amateur-nonsense. Still in the same namby-pamby style, and with the same soft voice and sweet smile, Sir Amyas talked on of pictures and battles, and carnage and levees, and drawing-rooms and balls, and butterflies.—He has a museum for the ladies, and he took me to look at it.—Sad was the hour and luckless was the day!—Among his shells was one upon which he peculiarly prided himself, and which he showed me as an unique. I was, I assure you, prudently silent till he pressed for my opinion, and then I could not avoid confessing that I suspected it to be a made shell—made, Caroline knows how, by the application of acids. The countenance of Sir Amyas clouded over, and I saw that I at this moment lost all chance of his future favour. He made me some fine speeches, when I was going away, and dwelt upon his great desire to oblige any friend of Lady Jane Granville's.

"A few days afterwards, I saw her ladyship again, and found, by her manner, that she had not been satisfied by Sir Amyas Courtney's report of me. She pressed me to tell her all that had passed between us. She was provoked by my imprudence, as she called it, about the shell, and exhorted me to repair it by future attentions and complaisance. When I declined paying court to Sir Amyas, as inconsistent with my ideas and feelings of independence, her ladyship grew angry—said that my father had inspired all his sons with absurd notions of independence, which would prevent their rising in the world, or succeeding in any profession. I believe I then grew warm in defence of my father and myself. The conclusion of the whole was, that we remained of our own opinions, and that her ladyship protested she would never more attempt to serve us. Alfred has called since on Lady Jane, but has not been admitted. I am sorry that I too have offended her, for I really like her, and am grateful for her kindness, but I cannot court her patronage, nor bend to her idol, Sir Amyas.—

"Your affectionate son,

"ERASMUS PERCY."

LETTER FROM ERASMUS PERCY TO HIS FATHER.

"MY DEAR FATHER,

"I told you in my last how I lost all hopes of favour from Sir Amyas Courtney, and how determined I was not to bend to him.—On some occasion soon afterwards this determination appeared, and recommended me immediately to the notice of a certain Dr. Frumpton, who is the antagonist and sworn foe to Sir Amyas.—Do you know who Dr. Frumpton is—and who he was—and how he has risen to his present height?

"He was a farrier in a remote county: he began by persuading the country people in his neighbourhood that he had a specific for the bite of a mad dog.

"It happened that he cured an old dowager's favourite waiting-maid who had been bitten by a cross lap-dog, which her servants pronounced to be mad, that they might have an excuse for hanging it.

"The fame of this cure was spread by the dowager among her numerous acquaintance in town and country.

"Then he took agues—and afterwards scrofula—under his protection; patronized by his old dowager, and lucky in some of his desperate quackery, Dr. Frumpton's reputation rapidly increased, and from different counties fools came to consult him. His manners were bearish even to persons of quality who resorted to his den; but these brutal manners imposed upon many, heightened the idea of his confidence in himself, and commanded the submission of the timid.—His tone grew higher and higher, and he more and more easily bullied the credulity of man and woman-kind.—It seems that either extreme of soft and polished, or of rough and brutal manner, can succeed with certain physicians.—Dr. Frumpton's name, and Dr. Frumpton's wonderful cures, were in every newspaper, and in every shop-window. No man ever puffed himself better even in this puffing age.—His success was viewed with scornful yet with jealous eyes by the regularly bred physicians, and they did all they could to keep him down—Sir Amyas Courtney, in particular, who would never call him any thing but that farrier, making what noise he could about Frumpton's practising without a diploma. In pure spite, Frumpton took to learning—late as it was, he put himself to school—with virulent zeal he read and crammed till, Heaven knows how! he accomplished getting a diploma—stood all prescribed examinations, and has grinned defiance ever since at Sir Amyas.

"Frumpton, delighted with the story of the made shell, and conceiving me to be the enemy of his enemy, resolved, as he declared, to take me by the hand; and, such is the magical deception of self-love, that his apparent friendliness towards me made him appear quite agreeable, and notwithstanding all that I had heard and known of him, I fancied his brutality was frankness, and his presumption strength of character.—I gave him credit especially for a happy instinct for true merit, and an honourable antipathy to flattery and meanness.—The manner in which he pronounced the words, fawning puppy! applied to Sir Amyas Courtney, pleased me peculiarly—and I had just exalted Frumpton into a great man, and an original genius, when he fell flat to the level, and below the level of common mortals.

"It happened, as I was walking home with him, we were stopped in the street by a crowd, which had gathered round a poor man, who had fallen from a scaffold, and had broken his leg. Dr. Frumpton immediately said, 'Send for Bland, the surgeon, who lives at the corner of the street.' The poor man was carried into a shop; we followed him. I found that his leg, besides being broken, was terribly bruised and cut. The surgeon in a few minutes arrived. Mr. Bland, it seems, is a protégé of Frumpton's, who formerly practised human farriery under him.

"Mr. Bland, after slightly looking at it, said, 'the leg must come off, the sooner the better.' The man, perceiving that I pitied him, cast such a beseeching look at me, as made me interpose, impertinently perhaps, but I could not resist it. I forget what I said; but I know the sense of it was, that I thought the poor fellow's leg could and ought to be saved.—I remember Dr. Frumpton glared upon me instantly with eyes of fury, and asked how I dared to interfere in a surgical case; and to contradict his friend, Mr. Bland, a surgeon!

"They prepared for the operation—the surgeon whipped on his mittens—the poor man, who was almost fainting with loss of blood, cast another piteous look at me, and said, in an Irish accent, 'Long life to you, dear!—and don't let'm—for what will I be without a leg? And my wife and children!'

"He fell back in a swoon, and I sprung between the surgeon and him; insisting that, as he had appealed to me, he should be left to me; and declared that I would have him carried to St. George's Hospital, where I knew he would be taken care of properly.

"Frumpton stamped, and scarcely articulate with rage, bade me—'stir the man at your peril!' adding expressions injurious to the hospital, with the governors of which he had some quarrel. I made a sign to the workmen who had brought in the wounded man; they lifted him instantly, and carried him out before me; and one of them, being his countryman, followed, crying aloud, 'Success to your honour! and may you never want a friend!'

"Frumpton seized him by both shoulders, and pushing him out of the house, exclaimed, 'Success, by G—, he shall never have, if I can help it! He has lost a friend such as he can never get again—By G—, I'll make him repent this!'

"Unmoved by these denunciations, I pursued my way to the hospital. You know in what an admirable manner the London hospitals are conducted.—At St. George's this poor man was received, and attended with the greatest care and skill. The surgeon who has taken charge of him assures me that his leg will, a month hence, be as useful as any leg in London.

"Dr. Frumpton and Mr. Bland have, I find, loudly complained of my interference, as contrary to all medical etiquette—Etiquette!—from Frumpton!—The story has been told with many exaggerations, and always to my disadvantage.—I cannot, however, repent.—Let me lose what I may, I am satisfied with the pleasure of seeing the poor man in a way to do well. Pray let me hear from you, my dear father, and say, if you can, that you think me right—Thank Caroline for her letter.

"Your affectionate

"ERASMUS PERCY."

LETTER FROM ALFRED.

"My dear father, I have made all possible inquiries about Buckhurst Falconer. He stayed at Cheltenham till about a month ago with the Hautons, and I hear attended Miss Hauton every where: but I do not think there is any reason to believe the report of his paying his addresses to her. The public attention he showed her was, in my opinion, designed only to pique Caroline, whom, I'm persuaded, he thinks (between the fits of half-a-dozen other fancies) the first of women—as he always calls her. Rosamond need not waste much pity on him. He is an out-of-sight-out-of-mind man. The pleasure of the present moment is all in all with him.—He has many good points in his disposition; but Caroline had penetration enough to see that his character would never suit hers; and I rejoice that she gave him a decided refusal.

"Since he came to town, he has, by his convivial powers, his good stories, good songs, and knack of mimicry, made himself so famous, that he has more invitations to dinner than he can accept. He has wit and talents fit for more than being the buffoon or mocking-bird of a good dinner and a pleasant party; but he seems so well contented with this réputation de salon, that I am afraid his ambition will not rise to any thing higher. After leading this idle life, and enjoying this cheap-earned praise, he will never submit to the seclusion and application necessary for the attainment of the great prizes of professional excellence. I doubt whether he will even persevere so far as to be called to the bar; though the other day when I met him in Bond-street, he assured me, and bid me assure you, that he is getting on famously, and eating his terms with a prodigious appetite. He seemed heartily glad to see me, and expressed warm gratitude for your having saved his conscience, and having prevented his father from forcing him, as he said, to be a disgrace to the church.

"Rosamond asks what sort of girls the Miss Falconers are, and whether the Falconers have been civil to me since I settled in town?—Yes; pretty well. The girls are mere show girls—like a myriad of others— sing, play, dance, dress, flirt, and all that. Georgiana is beautiful sometimes; Arabella, ugly always. I don't like either of them, and they don't like me, for I am not an eldest son. The mother was prodigiously pleased with me at first, because she mistook me for Godfrey, or rather she mistook me for the heir of our branch of the Percys. I hear that Mrs. Falconer has infinite address, both as a political and hymeneal intrigante: but I have not time to study her. Altogether, the family, though they live in constant gaiety, do not give me the idea of being happy among one another. I have no particular reason for saying this. I judge only from the tact on this subject which I have acquired from my own happy experience.

"Love to Rosamond—I am afraid she will think I have been too severe upon Buckhurst Falconer. I know he is a favourite, at least a protégé of hers and of Godfrey. Bid her remember I have acknowledged that he has talents and generosity; but that which interests Rosamond in his favour inclines ill-natured me against him—his being one of Caroline's suitors. I think he has great assurance to continue, in spite of all repulse, to hope, especially as he does nothing to render himself more worthy of encouragement. Thank Caroline for her letter; and assure Rosamond, that, though I have never noticed it, I was grateful for her entertaining account of M. de Tourville's vis: I confess, I am rather late with my acknowledgments; but the fire at Percy-hall, and many events which rapidly succeeded, put that whole affair out of my head. Moreover, the story of Euphrosyne and Count Albert was so squeezed under the seal, that I must beg notes of explanation in her next. Who the deuce is Euphrosyne? and what does the letter P—for the rest of the word was torn out—stand for? and is Count Albert a hero in a novel, or a real live man?

"I saw a live man yesterday, whom I did not at all like to see—Sharpe, walking with our good cousin, Sir Robert Percy, in close conversation. This conjunction, I fear, bodes us no good.—Pray, do pray make another search for the deed.

"Your affectionate son,

"ALFRED PERCY."

Soon after this letter had been received, and while the picture of his life, and the portraits of his worthy companions were yet fresh in her view, Buckhurst Falconer took the unhappy moment to write to renew his declaration of passionate attachment to Caroline, and to beg to be permitted to wait upon her once more.

From the indignant blush which mounted in Caroline's face on reading his letter, Rosamond saw how unlikely it was that this request should be granted. It came, indeed, at an unlucky time. Rosamond could not refrain from a few words of apology, and looks of commiseration for Buckhurst; yet she entirely approved of Caroline's answer to his letter, and the steady repetition of her refusal, and even of the strengthened terms in which it was now expressed. Rosamond was always prudent for her friends, when it came to any serious point where their interests or happiness were concerned. Her affection for her friends, and her fear of doing wrong on such occasions, awakened her judgment, and so controlled her imagination, that she then proved herself uncommonly judicious and discreet.—Prudence had not, it is true, been a part of Rosamond's character in childhood; but, in the course of her education, a considerable portion of it had been infused by a very careful and skilful hand. Perhaps it had never completely assimilated with the original composition: sometimes the prudence fell to the bottom, sometimes was shaken to the top, according to the agitation or tranquillity of her mind; sometimes it was so faintly visible, that its existence might be doubted by the hasty observer; but when put to a proper test, it never failed to reappear in full force.—After any effort of discretion in conduct, Rosamond, however, often relieved and amused herself by talking in favour of the imprudent side of the question.

"You have decided prudently, my dear Caroline, I acknowledge," said she. "But now your letter is fairly gone; now that it is all over, and that we are safe, I begin to think you are a little too prudent for your age.—Bless me, Caroline, if you are so prudent at eighteen, what will you be at thirty? Beware!—and in the mean time you will never be a heroine—what a stupid uninteresting heroine you will make! You will never get into any entanglements, never have any adventures; or if kind fate should, propitious to my prayer, bring you into some charming difficulties, even then we could not tremble for you, or enjoy all the luxury of pity, because we should always know that you would be so well able to extricate yourself—so certain to conquer, or—not die—but endure.—Recollect that Doctor Johnson, when his learned sock was off, confessed that he could never be thoroughly interested for Clarissa, because he knew that her prudence would always be equal to every occasion."

Mrs. Percy began to question whether Johnson had ever expressed this sentiment seriously: she reprobated the cruelty of friendly biographers, who publish every light expression that escapes from celebrated lips in private conversation; she was going to have added a word or two about the injury done to the public, to young people especially, by the spreading such rash dogmas under the sanction of a great name.

But Rosamond did not give her mother time to enforce this moral; she went on rapidly with her own thoughts.

"Caroline, my dear," continued she, "you shall not be my heroine; you are too well proportioned for a heroine—in mind, I mean: a heroine may—must have a finely-proportioned person, but never a well-proportioned mind. All her virtues must be larger than the life; all her passions those of a tragedy queen.

Produce—only dare to produce—one of your reasonable wives, mothers, daughters, or sisters on the theatre, and you would see them hissed off the stage. Good people are acknowledged to be the bane of the drama and the novel—I never wish to see a reasonable woman on the stage, or an unreasonable woman off it. I have the greatest sympathy and admiration for your true heroine in a book; but I grant you, that in real life, in a private room, the tragedy queen would be too much for me; and the novel heroine would be the most useless, troublesome, affected, haranguing, egotistical, insufferable being imaginable! So, my dear Caroline, I am content, that you are my sister, and my friend, though I give you up as a heroine."

CHAPTER VII

LETTER FROM GODFREY PERCY TO MRS. PERCY.

"London, the British Hotel.

"You will be surprised, my dear mother, to find that I am in London, instead of being, as I had hoped I should have been by this time, with the army on the continent. Just as we were going to embark, we were countermanded, and ordered to stay at our quarters. Conceive our disappointment—to remain in garrison at the most stupid, idle country town in England.

"You ask how I like my brother officers, and what sort of men they are?—Major Gascoigne, son to my father's friend, I like extremely; he is a man of a liberal spirit, much information, and zeal for the army. But what I particularly admire in him is his candour. He says it is his own fault that he is not higher in the army—that when he was a very young man, he was of too unbending a temper—mistook bluntness for sincerity—did not treat his superior officer with proper deference—lost a good friend by it.

"A fine lesson for me! and the better, because not intended.

"Next to Gascoigne I like Captain Henry: a young man of my own age, uncommonly handsome, but quite free from conceit. There is something in his manners so gentlemanlike, and he is of so frank a disposition, that I was immediately prepossessed in his favour.—I don't like him the worse for having a tinge of proper pride, especially in the circumstances in which he is placed. I understand that it is suspected he is not of a good family; but I am not impertinent enough to inquire into particulars. I have been told, that when he first came into the regiment, some of the officers wanted to make out what family he belongs to, and whether he is, or is not, one of the Irish Henrys. They showed their curiosity in an unwarrantable manner; and Henry, who has great feeling, and a spirit as quick to resent injury as to be won by kindness, was going to call one of these gentlemen to account for his impertinence. He would have had half a dozen duels upon his hands, if Gascoigne had not settled them. I have not time to tell you the whole story—but it is enough to say, that Major Gascoigne showed great address and prudence, as well as steadiness, and you would all love Captain Henry for his gratitude—he thinks Gascoigne a demi-god.

"The rest of my brother-officers are nothing supernatural—just what you may call mere red coats; some of them fond of high play, others fond of drinking: so I have formed no intimacy but with Gascoigne and Henry. My father will see that I do not yet think that the officers of my own mess must all be the first men in the universe.

"Love to all at home. I hope we shall sail soon, and I hope Rosamond will give me credit for the length of this letter.—She cannot say, with all her malice, that my lines are at shooting distance, or that my words are stretched out like a lawyer's—two good pages, count which way you will!—and from Godfrey, who is not a letter-writer, as Alfred is!—Two good pages, did I say? why, here's the best part of a third for you, if you allow me to be,

"My dear mother,
  with much respect,
 "Your dutiful, obedient,
   and affectionate son,
    "GODFREY PERCY."

Whilst Godfrey remained in quarters at this most idle and stupid of country towns, some circumstances occurred in the regiment which put his prudence to trial, and, sooner than he expected, called upon him for the exercise of that spirit of forbearance and temper which he had promised his mother he would show.—It was the more difficult to him to keep his temper, because it was an affair which touched the interest of his friend Major Gascoigne. The lieutenant-colonel of the regiment having been promoted, Major Gascoigne had reasonable expectations of succeeding him; but, to his disappointment, a younger man than himself, and a stranger to the regiment, was put over his head. It was said that this appointment was made in consequence of the new colonel being a nephew of Lord Skreene, and of his also having it in his power to command two votes in parliament.

For the truth of this story we cannot pretend to vouch. But the credit the report gained in the regiment created great discontents, which the behaviour of the new lieutenant-colonel unfortunately was not calculated to dissipate.—He certainly did not bear his honours meekly, but, on the contrary, gave himself airs of authority, and played the martinet to a useless and ridiculous degree. This, from a mere parade officer, who had never been out of London, to a man like the major—who had seen service and could show wounds—was, to use the mildest expression, ill-judged. Captain Henry said it was intolerable—and Godfrey thought so.

Every parade day something unpleasant occurred, and, when it was talked over, some of the officers took part with Gascoigne, and some with the lieutenant-colonel—very few, however, with the latter— only those who wanted to keep in favour: officers in quarters as these were, had not much to do; therefore they had the more time for disputes, which became of more and more consequence every hour. Major Gascoigne behaved incomparably well, never failing in respect towards his superior officer when he was present, and when he was absent doing all that was possible to restrain the imprudent zeal and indignation of his young friends.

One day, when Godfrey, Captain Henry, and Major Gascoigne were together, the major actually knelt down to Henry, to prevail upon him to give up a mad design of challenging his colonel.

That very day, not an hour afterwards, the lieutenant-colonel took occasion to thwart the major about some circumstance of no consequence. Godfrey's blood boiled in his veins—his promise to his mother, that he would be as gentle as a lamb, he recollected at this instant—with difficulty he restrained himself—still his blood boiled. Major Gascoigne's fear that Godfrey and Henry should embroil themselves for his sake increased, for he saw what passed in their hearts, and he had no peace of mind by day, or rest by night.

Generous people are, of all others, the most touched by generosity, either of feeling or action. In this state of irritation, it was not possible that things should long go on without coming to a crisis. Major Gascoigne proposed, as the measure that would be most likely to restore and preserve peace, to quit the regiment.—It was a great sacrifice on his part, and, at first, none of his friends would consent to his making it; but, at last, he brought them all to acknowledge that it was, upon the whole, the best thing that could be done. Gascoigne had a friend, a major in another regiment then in England, who was willing to make an exchange with him, and he thought that the business could be arranged without much difficulty. However, from caprice, the love of showing his power, or from some unknown reason, the lieutenant-colonel made it his pleasure to oppose the exchange, and said that it could not be done; though, as Captain Henry said, every body knew, that by his writing a line to Lord Skreene it would have been accomplished directly. It now recurred to Godfrey, that Cunningham Falconer, being secretary to Lord Oldborough, might be of use in this affair. Cunningham had always professed the greatest regard for Godfrey, and he was determined, at least, to make this trial of his sincerity.

The secretary sent a civil answer in an official style, explaining that his office was not the War Office; concluding by an assurance, that if Captain Percy could point out how he could do so with propriety, nothing could give Mr. C. Falconer greater pleasure than to have an opportunity of obliging him.

Now Captain Percy, having a sort of generous good faith about him, believed this last assurance; fancied that as he was no great writer he had not explained himself well by letter, and that he should make Cunningham understand him better viva voce. Keeping his own counsel, and telling only Major Gascoigne and Captain Henry his object, he asked for a fortnight's leave of absence, and, with some difficulty obtained it. He went to London, waited on Secretary Falconer, and found him ten times more official in his style of conversation than in his letters. Godfrey recollected that his cousin Cunningham had always been solemnly inclined, but now he found him grown so mysterious, that he could scarcely obtain a plain answer to the simplest question. "The whole man, head and heart, seemed," as Godfrey said, "to be diplomatically closed." It was clear, from the little that Cunningham did articulate, that he would do nothing in furthering the exchange desired for Major Gascoigne; but whether this arose from his having no influence with Lord Oldborough, or from his fear of wearing it out, our young officer could not determine. He left the secretary in disgust and despair, and went to wait on Commissioner Falconer, who gave him a polite invitation to dinner, and overwhelmed him with professions of friendship; but, as soon as Godfrey explained his business, the commissioner protested that he could not venture to speak to Lord Oldborough on such an affair, and he earnestly advised him not to interest himself so much for Major Gascoigne, who, though doubtless a very deserving officer, was, in fact, nothing more. He next had recourse to Buckhurst Falconer, and asked him to persuade Colonel Hauton to speak to his uncle upon the subject. This Buckhurst immediately promised to do, and kept his promise. But Colonel Hauton swore that his uncle never, on any occasion, listened to his representations; therefore it was quite useless to speak to him. After wandering from office to office, wasting hour after hour, and day after day, waiting for people who did him no good when he did see them, Godfrey at last determined to do what he should have done at first—apply to Lord Oldborough. It is always better to deal with principals than with secondaries. Lord Oldborough had the reputation of being inaccessible, haughty, and peremptory in the extreme; the secretaries, clerks, and under-clerks, "trembled at his name, each under each, through all their ranks of venality." But to Captain Percy's surprise, the moment his name was announced, the minister immediately recognized him, and received him most graciously. His lordship inquired after his old friend, Mr. Percy—said that Mr. Percy was one of the few really independent men he had ever known. "Mr. Percy is an excellent country gentleman, and, for England's sake, I wish there were many, many more such. Now, sir, how can I serve his son?"

With frankness and brevity which suited the minister and the man, Godfrey told his business, and Lord Oldborough, with laconic decision, equally pleasing to the young soldier, replied, "that if it was possible, the thing should be done for Major Gascoigne"—inquired how long Captain Percy purposed to stay in town—desired to see him the day before he should leave London, and named the hour.

All the diplomacy of Cunningham Falconer's face could not disguise his astonishment when he saw the manner in which his master treated Godfrey.—The next day the commissioner invited Captain Percy in a pressing manner to dine with him: "We shall have a very pleasant party," said Mr. Falconer, "and Mrs. Falconer insists upon the pleasure of your company—you have never seen my girls since they were children—your own near relations!—you must be better acquainted: come—I will take no denial."

Godfrey willingly accepted the invitation: he would, perhaps, have found means to have excused himself, had he known whom he was to meet at this dinner—Miss Hauton—the dangerous fair one, whom he had resolved to avoid. But he was in the room with her, and beyond all power of receding, before he knew his peril. The young lady looked more beautiful than ever, and more melancholy. One of the Miss Falconers took an opportunity of telling him, in confidence, the cause of her poor friend's dejection. "Her uncle, Lord Oldborough, wants to marry her to the Marquis of Twickenham, the eldest son of the Duke of Greenwich, and Miss Hauton can't endure him."

The marquis was also at this dinner—Godfrey did not much wonder at the lady's dislike; for he was a mean, peevish-looking man, had no conversation, and appeared to be fond of drinking.

"But Lord Oldborough, who is all for ambition," whispered Miss Falconer, "and who maintains that there is no such thing as love, except in novels, says, that his niece may read foolish novels after marriage as well as before, if she pleases, but that she must marry like a reasonable woman."

Godfrey pitied her; and, whilst he was pitying, Mrs. Falconer arranged a party for the opera for this night, in which Godfrey found himself included. Perhaps he was imprudent; but he was a young man, and human nature is—human nature.

At the opera Godfrey felt his danger increase every moment. Miss Hauton was particularly engaging, and many circumstances conspired to flatter his vanity, and to interest him for this fair victim of ambition. Her marquis was in the box, smelling of claret, and paying his devoirs to his intended bride, apparently very little to her satisfaction. Commissioner Falconer, leaning forward, complimented Miss Hauton upon her appearance this night, and observed that though it was a new opera, all fashionable eyes were turned from the stage to Lady Oldborough's box.

Miss Hauton smiled civilly upon the commissioner, then turning to Godfrey, in a low soft voice, repeated,

"And ev'n when fashion's brightest arts decoy,
The heart distrusting asks, if this be joy?"

Godfrey was touched—she saw it, and sighed. A short time afterwards her marquis left the box. Miss Hauton recovered from her languor, and became animated in conversation with Godfrey. He felt the whole power of her charms, the immediate force of the temptation; but he recollected who she was—he recollected that she had not shown any instances of discretion which could redeem her from the consequences of a mother's disgrace: the songs he had heard from Miss Hauton's lips, Captain Bellamy and the waltzing, came full upon his mind.

"No," said he to himself, "as a wife I cannot think of her: were the Marquis of Twickenham out of the question, my wife she cannot be. Then honour forbids me to trifle with her affections merely to gratify my vanity or the feelings of the moment."

Captain Percy well knew that some men can satisfy their consciences by calling a certain sort of treachery by the soft name of gallantry. He was aware that he could, like many others in similar circumstances, deceive by equivocal looks and expressions, and then throw the blame from themselves, by asking why the woman was such a fool as to believe, protesting that they never had a thought of her, and swearing that they had not the least idea she had ever understood them to mean any thing serious; but Godfrey had too much good feeling and good principle to follow such examples.

Miss Hauton had a copy of the new opera before her, and as she turned over the leaves, she pointed out to him the passages that she liked. Some were peculiarly applicable to her own situation, representing a heroine forced to marry a man she hates, whilst she tenderly loves another. Godfrey could not, or would not, understand the Italian. It was perfectly well explained to him; and then, perceiving the applications made of certain lines by Miss Hauton's voice and eyes, he had no resource but in a new singer, to whom he became suddenly so attentive that nothing could distract him from the stage. When the actress ceased to sing, he found means to engage the Miss Falconers in a discussion of her merits, which, with all the nonsense and compliments to their taste the occasion required, filled up the dangerous interval till the opera was over; then—more dangerous still—waiting for carriages in the crush room; but through all these perils, Godfrey passed so dexterously, as to leave Miss Hauton in doubt whether she had been understood or not. Thus he hoped that her conscience would in future, if she should ever after her marriage reflect on the opera of this night, be as much at ease as his own—though perhaps not with so good reason.

After this night, Godfrey would not expose himself to a repetition of similar danger; and that he might avoid meeting this fair lady again, he refused two invitations from Mrs. Falconer to a ball at her house, and to a musical party.—This deserves to be recorded to his credit, because he was very fond both of music and dancing.

The day before he was to leave town, at the hour and minute appointed, Godfrey waited upon Lord Oldborough; but not such his reception now as it had been on his first visit to this minister: he was kept two hours waiting alone in an antechamber. At last the cabinet door opened, and Lord Oldborough appeared with a dark cold countenance, and a haughty stiffness in his whole frame. His lordship walked deliberately forward, till he came within a yard of our young officer, and then, without speaking, bent his head and body slowly, and so remained, as if waiting to be informed who Captain Percy was, and what his business might be. Astonishment, and offended pride, flashed successively in Godfrey's countenance. Lord Oldborough, after fixing his interrogating eyes upon him ineffectually, receiving no explanation, seemed to come a little to his recollection, and condescended to say, "Captain Percy, I believe!—your commands with me, Captain Percy."

"My lord, I have the honour to be here by your lordship's appointment on Major Gascoigne's business."

"Sir, you had a note from me yesterday, I believe, which contained all that I have it in my power to say on Major Gascoigne's business."

"Pardon me, my lord—I never had the honour of receiving any note from your lordship."

"Very extraordinary! I sent it by my own man. You are at Batts' hotel, sir?"

"No, my lord, at the British hotel."

"Ha!—that is the cause of the mistake. You will find my note, sir, at Batts'."

Captain Percy bowed—Lord Oldborough bowed—not a word more passed. Lord Oldborough walked on to his carriage, which rolled him away with glorious rapidity, whilst Godfrey, his face flushed with resentment, looked after him for an instant, then putting on his hat, which the porter held to him, he walked off as fast as possible to Batts' hotel, impatient to see the note which was to explain the meaning of this extraordinary conduct. The note he found; but it threw little light upon the business. It was written in Secretary Cunningham Falconer's hand, and was as follows:

"Lord Oldborough will inform Captain Percy when any thing shall be decided upon relative to the business on which Captain Percy spoke to Lord Oldborough: and as communication by letter will answer every purpose, his lordship hopes that he shall not be the means of detaining Captain Percy longer from his regiment.

"Tuesday, —."

A civil dismission!—After three attempts Godfrey obtained a sight of Secretary Cunningham, who, as he thought, was at the bottom of the affair; but this suspicion was at first dissipated by the unusual openness with which the secretary looked and spoke. Apparently without fear of committing himself, he said at once that it was a very extraordinary proceeding—that he could no way account for it, but by supposing that the lieutenant-colonel in question had, through his relation, Lord Skreene, influenced his Grace of Greenwich, and that Lord Oldborough could not, in the present conjuncture, make any movement in direct opposition to the duke.

"In all these things, in all transactions with politicians," said Godfrey, "there are wheels within wheels, which we simple people never suspect; and by awkwardly interfering with them when they are in motion, we are hurt, we know not how or why."

Cunningham smiled significantly, but was silent—his air of frankness vanished, and his solemn reserve returned. "Cunningham will never be hurt in that way," thought Godfrey; "I never saw a fellow so careful of himself. I am convinced he would not hazard his little finger to save the whole British empire, much less to serve a private friend like me, or a poor honest man like Gascoigne."

Godfrey was too proud to make any further attempts to interest his diplomatic cousin in the affair. He rose, and bade the secretary adieu, who, with proper smiles and bows, attended him to the very door.

"Thank Heaven!" thought Godfrey, as he left the secretary's office, "I am not forced to dance attendance upon any great man, or any great man's secretary. I am—like my father—independent, and will keep myself so; and if ever I live upon a smile for years, it shall not be upon the smiles of a minister, but on those of a fair lady."

Godfrey left town immediately, and returned to his regiment.

CHAPTER VIII

Little versed in the ways of courts or courtiers, Godfrey had been easily deceived by the apparent candour of Cunningham Falconer. The fact was, that Cunningham, not directly from himself, but by means of persons of whom Lord Oldborough could have no suspicion, had insinuated to his lordship that Godfrey Percy was the secret cause of the aversion Miss Hauton showed to the proposed match with the Marquis of Twickenham. This idea once suggested was easily confirmed by the account of the young lady's behaviour at the opera, which was reported to Lord Oldborough with proper exaggerations, and with a total misrepresentation of Godfrey's conduct. The fainting at the ball was also recollected, and many other little circumstances combined to bring conviction to Lord Oldborough's mind. He was now persuaded that Major Gascoigne's business was merely a pretence for Godfrey's coming to town: apprehension of being disappointed in completing an alliance essential to his ambitious views, pique at the idea of being deceived, and nearly duped by a boy and girl, a rooted hatred and utter contempt for love and love affairs, altogether produced that change in Lord Oldborough's manner towards Captain Percy which had appeared so extraordinary.—Had Captain Percy delayed to leave town, he would next day have received orders from his commanding officer to join his regiment. As to Major Gascoigne's business, it had made so little impression upon Lord Oldborough, that he had totally forgotten the poor major's name till Godfrey repeated it to him. Indeed, Godfrey himself could scarcely have blamed his lordship for this, had he known how much business, how many cares pressed at this time upon the mind of the unhappy statesman.—Besides a load of public business, and all the open and violent attacks of opposition, which he had usually to sustain, he was now under great and increasing anxiety from the discovery of that plot against him, among his immediate associates in office, which the Tourville papers, deciphered by Commissioner Falconer and Cunningham, had but partially revealed. Lord Oldborough was in the condition of a person apprised that he is standing upon ground that is undermined, but who does not know exactly by what hand or at what moment the train that may destroy him is to be set on fire. One word frequently recurred in the Tourville papers, which puzzled Commissioner Falconer extremely, and of which he was never able to make out the meaning; the word was Gassoc. It was used thus: "We are sorry to find that the Gassoc has not agreed to our proposal."—"No answer has been given to question No. 2 by the Gassoc."—"With regard to the subsidy, of which 35,000l. have not been sent or received, the Gassoc has never explained; in consequence, great discontents here."—"If the Gassoc be finally determined against the Eagle, means must be taken to accomplish the purposes alluded to in paragraph 4, in green (of the 7th ult.), also those in No. B. in lemon juice (of September last)."—"The Gassoc will take notes of the mining tools forgotten—also bullets too large, and no flints (as per No. 9, in sympathetic ink)—also the sea charts, sent instead of maps—consequent delay in march of troops—loss of fortress—to be attributed to the Eagle."

The Eagle, which at first had been taken for granted to be the Austrian eagle, was discovered to be Lord Oldborough. An eagle was his lordship's crest, and the sea-charts, and the mining-tools, brought the sense home to him conclusively. It was plain that the Gassoc stood for some person who was inimical to Lord Oldborough, but who it could be was the question. Commissioner Falconer suggested, that for Gassoc, you should read Gosshawk; then, said he, "by finding what nobleman or gentleman has a gosshawk in his arms, you have the family name, and the individual is afterwards easily ascertained." To the Heralds'-office the commissioner went a gosshawking, but after spending a whole day with the assistance of Garter king at arms, he could make nothing of his gosshawks, and he gave them up.

He next presumed that there might be a mistake of one letter in the foreign spelling of the word, and that Gassoc should be Cassock, and might then mean a certain bishop, who was known to be a particular enemy of Lord Oldborough. But still there were things ascribed to the Gassoc, which could not come within the jurisdiction or cognizance of the Cassock—and the commissioner was reluctantly obliged to give up the church. He next suggested, that not only one letter, but every letter in the word might be mistaken in the foreign spelling, and that Gassoc might be the French or German written imitation of the oral sound of some English proper name. The commissioner supported this opinion very plausibly by citing many instances of the barbarous spelling of English names by foreigners: Bassompierre writes Jorchaux for York-house, Innimthort for Kensington; even in the polite memoirs of le Comte de Grammont, we have Soutkask for Southesk, and Warméstre for some English name not yet deciphered. Upon this hint the commissioner and Cunningham made anagrams of half the noble names in England, but in vain.

Afterwards, recollecting that it was the fashion at one time even to pun in the coats of arms of the nobility, and in the choice of their mottos, he went to work again at the Heralds'-office, and tried a course of puns, but to no purpose: the commissioner was mortified to find all his ingenuity at fault.

Cunningham took care not to suggest anything, therefore he could never be convicted of mistake. Nor was he in the least vexed by his father's or his own fruitless labour, because he thought it might tend to his future advancement.

Lord Oldborough had thrown out a hint that it would soon be necessary to recall the present and send a new envoy or resident to the German court in question; Cunningham nourished a hope of being chosen for this purpose, as the Tourville papers were already known to him, and he could, under private instructions, negotiate with M. de Tourville, and draw from him an explanation. He did not, however, trust even his father with the hope he had conceived, but relied on his own address, and continually strove, by oblique hints, to magnify the danger of leaving any part of the plot unravelled.

What effect these suggestions produced, or whether they produced any, Cunningham was unable to judge from the minister's impenetrable countenance. Lord Oldborough lost not a moment in repairing the mistake about sea-charts, and the omission of mining tools, which he had discovered from a paragraph in the Tourville papers; he stayed not to inquire whether the error had been wilful or unintentional—that he left for future investigation. His next object was the subsidy. This day the Duke of Greenwich gave a cabinet dinner. After dinner, when the servants had retired, and when none of the company were prepared for such a stroke, Lord Oldborough, in his decided, but very calm manner, began with, "My lords, I must call your attention to an affair of some importance—the subsidy from the secret service to our German ally."

All who had within them sins unwhipped of justice trembled.

"I have learned, no matter how," continued Lord Oldborough, "that, by some strange mistake, 35,000l of that subsidy were not remitted at the time appointed by us, and that discontents, likely to be prejudicial to his majesty's service, have arisen in consequence of this delay."

His lordship paused, and appeared to take no notice of the faces of feigned astonishment and real consciousness by which he was surrounded. Each looked at the other to inquire by what means this secret was divulged, and to discover, if possible, how much more was known. Lord Skreene began at the same moment with the Duke of Greenwich to suggest that some clerk or agent must certainly be much to blame. Lord Oldborough, in his decided tone, replied that it was indifferent to him what clerk, agent, or principal was to blame in the business; but that if the money were not bonâ fide remitted, and acknowledged by the court to which it was promised, and before any disagreeable consequences should ensue, he must be under the necessity of stating the affair to his majesty—of resigning his office, and bringing the whole before parliament.

The terror of his voice, and lightning of his eye, the dread of his determined spirit, operated powerfully. The subsidy was remitted the next day, though at the expense of a service of plate which Lord Skreene had bespoken for his mistress, and though Secretary Cope was compelled to sell at some disadvantage a few of the very few remaining acres of his paternal estate, to make good what had been borrowed from the secret service money.

At the cabinet dinner, the keen eye of Lord Oldborough had discerned some displeasure lurking in the mind of the Duke of Greenwich—a man of considerable political consequence from his rank and connexions, and from the number of voices he could command or influence. Lord Oldborough knew that, if he could regain the duke, he could keep in awe his other enemies. His grace was a puzzle-headed, pompous fool, whom Heaven had cursed with the desire to be a statesman. He had not more than four ideas; but to those four, which he conceived to be his own, he was exclusively attached.—Yet a person of address and cunning could put things into his head, which after a time he would find there, believe to be his own, and which he would then propose as new with great solemnity, and support with much zeal. Lord Oldborough, however, was neither able nor willing to manage his grace in this manner; he was too imperious; his pride of character was at continual variance with the duke's pride of rank. The duke's was a sort of pride which Lord Oldborough did not always understand, and which, when he did, he despised—it was a species of pride that was perpetually taking offence at trifling failures in etiquette, of which Lord Oldborough, intent upon great objects, was sometimes guilty. There is a class of politicians who err by looking for causes in too high a sphere, and by attributing the changes which perplex states and monarchs to great passions and large motives. Lord Oldborough was one of this class, and with all his talents would have failed in every attempt to comprehend and conciliate the Duke of Greenwich, had he not been assisted by the inferior genius of Commissioner Falconer. While his lordship was thus searching far and wide among the reasonable and probable causes for the duke's coldness, examining and re-examining the bearings of every political measure, as it could affect his grace's interest immediately or remotely, Commissioner Falconer sought for the cause, and found it in the lowest scale of trifles—he made the discovery by means which Lord Oldborough could not have devised, and would not have used. The duke had a favourite under-clerk, who, for a valuable consideration, disclosed the secret to the commissioner. Lord Oldborough had sent his grace a note, written in his own hand, sealed with a wafer. The clerk, who was present when the note was received, said that the duke's face flushed violently, and that he flung the note immediately to his secretary, exclaiming, "Open that, if you please, sir—I wonder how any man can have the impertinence to send me his spittle!"

This nice offence, which bore so coarse a comment, had alienated the mind of the Duke of Greenwich. When Commissioner Falconer had thus sagaciously discovered the cause of the noble duke's displeasure, he with great address applied a remedy. Without ever hinting that he knew of the offensive circumstance, having some business to transact with the duke, he contrived, as if undesignedly, to turn the conversation upon his friend Lord Oldborough's strange and unaccountable negligence of common forms and etiquette; as a proof of which he told the duke in confidence, and in a very low voice, an anecdote, which he heard from his son Cunningham, from Lord Oldborough's own secretary, or the commissioner protested that he would not, he could not have believed it—his lordship had been once actually upon the point of sealing a note with a wafer to one of the royal dukes!—had the wafer absolutely on his lips, when Cunningham felt it his duty to take the liberty of remonstrating. Upon which, Lord Oldborough, as Commissioner Falconer said, looked with the utmost surprise, and replied, "I have sealed with a wafer to the Duke of Greenwich, and he was not offended."

This anecdote, the truth of which it fortunately never occurred to the duke to doubt, had an immediate and powerful effect upon his mind, as the commissioner saw by the complacent smile that played on his countenance, and still further by the condescending pity with which his grace observed, that "Great geniuses never understand common things—but do every thing awkwardly, whether they cut open a book, or seal a note."

Mr. Falconer having thus brought the duke into fine temper, left him in the best dispositions possible towards Lord Oldborough, went to his lordship to report progress, and to boast of his success; but he told only as much of what had passed as he thought would suit the statesman's character, and ensure his approbation.—The Duke of Greenwich was as much pleased by this reconciliation as Lord Oldborough; for, though in a fit of offended pride he had been so rash as to join his lordship's enemies, yet he had always dreaded coming to open war with such an adversary. His grace felt infinitely more safe and comfortable when he was leaning upon Lord Oldborough than when he stood opposed to him, even in secret. There were points in politics in which he and Lord Oldborough coincided, though they had arrived at these by far different roads. They agreed in an overweening love of aristocracy, and in an inclination towards arbitrary power; they agreed in a hatred of innovation; they agreed in the principle that free discussion should be discouraged, and that the country should be governed with a high and strong hand. On these principles Lord Oldborough always acted, but seldom spoke, and the Duke of Greenwich continually talked, but seldom acted: in fact, his grace, "though he roared so loud, and looked so wondrous grim," was, in action, afraid of every shadow. Right glad was he to have his political vaunts made good by a coadjutor of commanding talents, resource, and civil courage. Yet, as Lord Oldborough observed, with a man of such wayward pride and weak understanding, there was no security from day to day for the permanence of his attachment. It was then that Commissioner Falconer, ever ready at expedients, suggested that an alliance between his grace's family and his lordship's would be the best possible security; and that the alliance might be easily effected, since it was evident of late that the Marquis of Twickenham was much disposed to admire the charms of his lordship's niece, Miss Hauton. Lord Oldborough had not remarked that the marquis admired any thing but good wine; his lordship's attention was not turned to these things, nor had he, in general, much faith in friendships founded on family alliances; but he observed that the duke was peculiarly tenacious of connexions and relationships, and, therefore, this might be the best method of holding him.

From the moment Lord Oldborough decided in favour of this scheme, Mr. and Mrs. Falconer had done all in their power, with the utmost zeal and address, to forward it, by contriving continual dancing-parties and musical meetings, at their house, for the young people. Lady Oldborough, who was sickly, whose manners were not popular, and who could not bear to be put out of her way, was quite unsuited to this sort of business, and rejoiced that the Falconers took it off her hands. Things were just in this state, and Lord Oldborough had fixed his mind upon the match, when Godfrey Percy's arrival in town had threatened disappointment. In consequence of this fear, Lord Oldborough not only despatched Godfrey directly to his regiment, but, to put an end to the danger at once, to banish the idea of seeing him again completely out of the young lady's head, the cruel uncle and decided politician had Godfrey's regiment ordered immediately to the West Indies.

LETTER FROM GODFREY PERCY TO HIS FATHER.

"My dear father,

"We have a new lieutenant-colonel. Lord Skreene has removed his precious nephew to another regiment, and to punish us for not liking the pretty boy, has ordered us all off to the West Indies: so ends our croaking. Our new King Log we cannot complain of as too young, or too much on the qui vive: he looks as if he were far gone in a lethargy, can hardly keep himself awake while he is giving the word of command, and, instead of being a martinet, I am sure he would not care if the whole corps wore their regimentals the wrong side outwards.—Gascoigne will have all the regimental business on his shoulders, and no man can do it better.—He is now at my elbow, supplying four hundred men and forty officers with heads. The noise of questions and commands, and the notes of preparation, are so loud and dissonant, that I hardly know what I write. Gascoigne, though not benefited, was obliged to me for my wrong-head-journey to London. Henry was very angry with Lord Oldborough for jilting me—Gascoigne with much ado kept him in proper manners towards the lieutenant-colonel, and I, in admiration of Gascoigne, kept my temper miraculously. But there was an impertinent puppy of an ensign, a partisan of the lieutenant-colonel, who wanted, I'm convinced, to have the credit of fighting a duel for the colonel, and he one day said, in Captain Henry's hearing, that 'it was no wonder some men should rail against ministerial influence, who had no friends to look to, and were men of no family.'—'Do you mean that for me, sir?' said Henry. 'Judge for yourself, sir.' Poor Henry judged ill, and challenged the ensign.—They fought, and the ensign was slightly wounded. This duel has wakened curiosity again about Captain Henry's birth, and he is in danger of being exposed continually to things he could not like, and could not well resent. He consulted Gascoigne and me, and has told us all he knows of his history.—Read what follows to yourself, for I have permission to speak of his affairs only to you. Captain Henry assured us that he really does not know to what family he belongs, nor who his father and mother were; but he has reason to believe that they were Irish. He was bred up in a merchant's house in Dublin. The merchant broke, and went off with his family to America. Henry was at that time fifteen or sixteen. The merchant then said, that Henry was not his nephew, nor any relation to him, but hinted that he was the son of a Mr. Henry, who had taken an unfortunate part in the troubles of Ireland, and who had suffered—that his mother had been a servant-maid, and that she was dead. The merchant added, that he had taken care of Henry from regard to his father, but that, obliged by his own failure in business to quit the country, he must thenceforward resign the charge.—He farther observed, that the army was now the young man's only resource, and, on taking leave, he put into Henry's hands a 50l. note, and an ensign's commission.—With his commission he joined his regiment, which was at Cork. A few days after his arrival, a Cork banker called upon him, and inquired whether he was Ensign Charles Henry; and upon his answering in the affirmative, informed him that he had orders to pay him 400l. a year in quarterly payments. The order came from a house in Dublin, and this was all the banker knew. On Henry's application in Dublin, he was told that they had direction to stop payment of the annuity if any questions were asked.—Of course, Henry asked no more.—The annuity has been regularly paid to him ever since—When he was scarcely seventeen, he was pillaged of a couple of hundred pounds one night by a set of sharpers at the gaming-table: this loss roused his prudence, and he has never played since. He has for many years lived within his pay; for he prudently considered, that the extraordinary supply might suddenly fail, and then he might be left in debt and distress, and at the same time with habits of extravagance.—Instead of which, he has laid up money every year, and has a considerable sum. He wishes to quit the army, and to go into a mercantile house, for which his early education has fitted him. He has a particular talent for languages: speaks French and Italian accurately—Spanish and Dutch well enough for all the purposes of commerce. So any mercantile house, who wants a partner, agent, or clerk for foreign affairs (perhaps I am not correct in the technical terms), could not do better than to take Charles Henry. For his integrity and honour I would answer with my life. Now, my dear father, could you have the goodness to assist us so far as to write and inquire about the partner in London of those Dutch merchants, whom you had an opportunity of obliging at the time of the shipwreck?—I cannot recollect their strange names, but if I am not mistaken, they left you their address, and that of their London correspondent.—If this partner should be a substantial man, perhaps our best plan would be to try to get Henry into his house. You have certainly some claim there, and the Dutchmen desired we would apply to them if ever they could do any thing to serve us—we can but try. I am afraid you will say, 'This is like one of Godfrey's wild schemes.' I am still more afraid that you should think Henry's romantic story is against him—but such things are—that is all I can say. Here is no motive for deception; and if you were to see the young man, his countenance and manner would immediately persuade you of his perfect truth and ingenuousness. I am aware that his romantic history would not do for the Dutch merchants, or the London partner; they would probably set him down directly for an adventurer, and refuse to have any thing to do with him: so I see no necessity for beginning by stating it. I know you hate, and I am sure so do I, all novel-like concealments and mysteries; but because a man makes a bargain with another, he is not obliged to tell him his whole history—because he takes him for his partner or his master, he is not called upon to make him his confidant. All that the merchants can want or have a right to know is forthcoming and clear—character and money.

"My affectionate love and old-fashioned duty to my dear mother—pray assure her and my sisters that they shall hear from me, though I am going to have 'one foot on sea and one on land.'

"Tell dear Caroline the portfolio she made for me shall go with me to the world's end; and Rosamond's Tippoo Saib shall see the West Indies—Gascoigne has been in the West Indies before now, and he says and proves, that temperance and spice are the best preservatives in that climate; so you need not fear for me, for you know I love pepper better than port. I am called away, and can only add that the yellow fever there has subsided, as an officer who arrived last week tells me. Our regiment is just going to embark in high spirits.—God bless you all.

"Your affectionate son,

"G. Percy.

"P. S. Don't let my mother or Rosamond trust to newspaper reports—trust to nothing but my letters;—Caroline, I know, is fit to be the sister, and I hope will some time be the mother, of heroes."

CHAPTER IX

Lord Oldborough expected that the prompt measure of despatching the dangerous Godfrey to the West Indies would restore things to their former train. For a week after Godfrey Percy's departure, Miss Hauton seemed much affected by it, and was from morning till night languid or in the sullens: of all which Lord Oldborough took not the slightest notice. In the course of a fortnight Miss Falconer, who became inseparable from Miss Hauton, flattering, pitying, and humouring her, contrived to recover the young lady from this fit of despondency, and produced her again at musical parties. She was passionately fond of music; the Miss Falconers played on the piano-forte and sung, their brother John accompanied exquisitely on the flute, and the Marquis of Twickenham, who was dull as "the fat weed that grows on Lethe's brink," stood by—admiring. His proposal was made in form—and in form the young lady evaded it—in form her uncle, Lord Oldborough, told her that the thing must be, and proceeded directly to decide upon the settlements with the Duke of Greenwich, and set the lawyers to work. In the mean time, the bride elect wept, and deplored, and refused to eat, drink, or speak, except to the Miss Falconers, with whom she was closeted for hours, and to whom the task of managing her was consigned by common consent. The marquis, who, though he was, as he said, much in love, was not very delicate as to the possession of the lady's affections, wondered that any one going to be married to the Marquis of Twickenham could be so shy and so melancholy; but her confidantes assured him that it was all uncommon refinement and sensibility, which was their sweetest Maria's only fault. Excellent claret, and a moderately good opinion of himself, persuaded the marquis of the truth of all which the Miss Falconers pleased to say, and her uncle graciously granted the delays, which the young lady prayed for week after week—till, at last, striking his hand upon the table, Lord Oldborough said, "There must be an end of this—the papers must be signed this day se'nnight—Maria Hauton shall be married this day fortnight."—Maria Hauton was sent for to her uncle's study; heard her doom in sullen silence; but she made no show of resistance, and Lord Oldborough was satisfied. An hour afterwards Commissioner Falconer begged admission, and presented himself with a face of consternation—Lord Oldborough, not easily surprised or alarmed, waited, however, with some anxiety, till he should speak.

"My lord, I beg pardon for this intrusion: I know, at this time, you are much occupied; but it is absolutely necessary I should communicate—I feel it to be my duty immediately—and I cannot hesitate—though I really do not know how to bring myself—"

There was something in the apparent embarrassment and distress of Mr. Falconer, which Lord Oldborough's penetrating eye instantly discerned to be affected.—His lordship turned a chair towards him, but said not a word.—The commissioner sat down like a man acting despair; but looking for a moment in Lord Oldborough's face, he saw what his lordship was thinking of, and immediately his affected embarrassment became real and great.

"Well, commissioner, what is the difficulty?"

"My lord, I have within this quarter of an hour heard what will ruin me for ever in your lordship's opinion, unless your lordship does me the justice to believe that I never heard or suspected it before—I have only to trust to your magnanimity—and I do."

Lord Oldborough bowed slightly—"The fact, if you please, my dear sir."

"The fact, my lord, is, that Captain Bellamy, whose eyes, I suppose, have been quickened by jealousy, has discovered what has escaped us all—what never would have occurred to me—what never could have entered into my mind to suspect—what I still hope—"

"The fact, sir, let me beg."

The urgency of Lord Oldborough's look and voice admitted of no delay.

"Miss Hauton is in love with my son John."

"Indeed!"

This "Indeed!" was pronounced in a tone which left the commissioner in doubt what it expressed, whether pure surprise, indignation, or contempt—most of the last, perhaps: he longed to hear it repeated, but he had not that satisfaction. Lord Oldborough turned abruptly—walked up and down the room with such a firm tread as sounded ominously to the commissioner's ear.

"So then, sir, Miss Hauton, I think you tell me, is in love with Cornet Falconer?"

"Captain Bellamy says so, my lord."

"Sir, I care not what Captain Bellamy says—nor do I well know who or what he is—much less what he can have to do with my family affairs—I ask, sir, what reason you have to believe that my niece is in love, as it is called, with your son? You certainly would not make such a report to me without good reason for believing it—what are your reasons?"

"Excuse me, my lord, my reasons are founded on information which I do not think myself at liberty to repeat: but upon hearing the report from—" The commissioner, in the hurry and confusion of his mind, and in his new situation, totally lost his tact, and at this moment was upon the point of again saying from Captain Bellamy; but the flash of Lord Oldborough's eye warned him of his danger—he dropped the name.

"I immediately went to sound my son John, and, as far as I can judge, he has not yet any suspicion of the truth."

Lord Oldborough's countenance cleared. The commissioner recovered his presence of mind, for he thought he saw his way before him. "I thought it my duty to let your lordship know the first hint I had of such a nature; for how soon it might be surmised, or what steps might be taken, I must leave it to your lordship to judge—I can only assure you, that as yet, to the best of my belief, John has not any suspicion: fortunately, he is very slow—and not very bright."

Lord Oldborough stood with compressed lips, seeming to listen, but deep in thought.

"Mr. Commissioner Falconer, let us understand one another well now—as we have done hitherto. If your son, Cornet Falconer, were to marry Maria Hauton, she would no longer be my niece, he would have a portionless, friendless, and, in my opinion, a very silly wife. He is, I think you say, not very bright himself—he would probably remain a cornet the rest of his days—all idea of assistance being of course out of the question in that case, from me or mine, to him or his."

The awful pause which Lord Oldborough made, and his determined look, gave the commissioner opportunity to reflect much in a few seconds.

"On the contrary," resumed his lordship, "if your son John, my dear sir, show the same desire to comply with my wishes, and to serve my interests, which I have found in the rest of his family, he shall find me willing and able to advance him as well as his brother Cunningham."

"Your lordship's wishes will, I can answer for it, be laws to him, as well as to the rest of his family."

"In one word then—let Cornet Falconer be married elsewhere, within a fortnight, and I prophesy that within a year he shall be a field-officer—within two years, a lieutenant-colonel."

Commissioner Falconer bowed twice—low to the field-officer—lower to the lieutenant-colonel.

"I have long had a match in my eye for John," said the father; "but a fortnight, my gracious lord—that is so very short a time! Your lordship will consider there are delicacies in these cases—no young lady—it is impossible—your lordship must be sensible that it is really impossible, with a young lady of any family."

"I am aware that it is difficult, but not impossible," replied Lord Oldborough, rising deliberately.

The commissioner took his leave, stammering somewhat of "nothing being impossible for a friend," courtier, he should have said.

The commissioner set to work in earnest about the match he had in view for John. Not one, but several fair visions flitted before the eye of his politic mind. The Miss Chattertons—any one of whom would, he knew, come readily within the terms prescribed, but then they had neither fortune nor connexions. A relation of Lady Jane Granville's—excellent connexion, and reasonable fortune; but there all the decorum of regular approaches and time would be necessary: luckily, a certain Miss Petcalf was just arrived from India with a large fortune. The general, her father, was anxious to introduce his daughter to the fashionable world, and to marry her for connexion—fortune no object to him—delicacies he would waive. The commissioner saw—counted—and decided—(there was a brother Petcalf, too, who might do for Georgiana—but for that no hurry)—John was asked by his father if he would like to be a major in a year, and a lieutenant-colonel in two years?

To be sure he would—was he a fool?

Then he must be married in a fortnight.

John did not see how this conclusion followed immediately from the premises, for John was not quite a fool; so he answered "Indeed!" An indeed so unlike Lord Oldborough's, that the commissioner, struck with the contrast, could scarcely maintain the gravity the occasion required, and he could only pronounce the words, "General Petcalf has a daughter."

"Ay, Miss Petcalf—ay, he is a general; true—now I see it all: well, I'm their man—I have no objection—But Miss Petcalf!—is not that the Indian girl? Is not there a drop of black blood?—No, no, father," cried John, drawing himself up, "I'll be d—d...."

"Hear me first, my own John," cried his father, much and justly alarmed, for this motion was the precursor of an obstinate fit, which, if John took, perish father, mother, the whole human race, he could not be moved from the settled purpose of his soul. "Hear me, my beloved John—for you are a man of sense," said his unblushing father: "do you think I'd have a drop of black blood for my daughter-in-law, much less let my favourite son—But there's none—it is climate—all climate—as you may see by only looking at Mrs. Governor Carneguy, how she figures every where; and Miss Petcalf is nothing near so dark as Mrs. Carneguy, surely."

"Surely," said John.

"And her father, the general, gives her an Indian fortune to suit an Indian complexion."

"That's good, at any rate," quoth John.

"Yes, my dear major—yes, my lieutenant-colonel—to be sure that's good. So to secure the good the gods provide us, go you this minute, dress, and away to your fair Indian! I'll undertake the business with the general."

"But a fortnight, my dear father," said John, looking into the glass: "how can that be?"

"Look again, and tell me how it can not be? Pray don't put that difficulty into Miss Petcalf's head—into her heart I am sure it would never come."

John yielded his shoulder to the push his father gave him towards the door, but suddenly turning back, "Zounds! father, a fortnight!" he exclaimed: "why there won't be time to buy even boots!"

"And what are even boots," replied his father, "to such a man as you? Go, go, man; your legs are better than all the boots in the world."

Flattery can find her way to soothe the dullest, coldest ear alive. John looked in the glass again—dressed—and went to flatter Miss Petcalf. The proposal was graciously accepted, for the commissioner stated, as he was permitted in confidence to the general, that his son was under the special patronage of Lord Oldborough, who would make him a lieutenant-colonel in two years. The general, who looked only for connexion and genteel family, was satisfied. The young lady started at the first mention of an early day; but there was an absolute necessity for pressing that point, since the young officer was ordered to go abroad in a fortnight, and could not bear to leave England without completing his union with Miss Petcalf. These reasons, as no other were to be had, proved sufficient with father and daughter.

John was presented with a captain's commission. He, before the end of the fortnight, looked again and again in the glass to take leave of himself, hung up his flute, and—was married. The bride and bridegroom were presented to Lord and Lady Oldborough, and went immediately abroad.

Thus the forms of homage and the rights of vassalage are altered; the competition for favour having succeeded to the dependence for protection, the feudal lord of ancient times could ill compete in power with the influence of the modern political patron.

Pending the negotiation of this marriage, and during the whole of this eventful fortnight, Cunningham Falconer had been in the utmost anxiety that can be conceived—not for a brother's interests, but for his own: his own advancement he judged would depend upon the result, and he could not rest day or night till the marriage was happily completed—though, at the same time, he secretly cursed all the loves and marriages, which had drawn Lord Oldborough's attention away from that embassy on which his own heart was fixed.

Buckhurst, the while, though not admitted behind the scenes, said he was sufficiently amused by what he saw on the stage, enjoyed the comedy of the whole, and pretty well made out for himself the double plot. The confidante, Miss Falconer, played her part to admiration, and prevailed on Miss Hauton to appear on the appointed day in the character of a reasonable woman; and accordingly she suffered herself to be led, in fashionable style, to the hymeneal altar by the Marquis of Twickenham. This dénouement satisfied Lord Oldborough.

CHAPTER X

The day after his niece's marriage was happily effected, Lord Oldborough said to his secretary, "Now, Mr. Cunningham Falconer, I have leisure to turn my mind again to the Tourville papers."

"I was in hopes, my lord," said the secretary (se composant le visage), "I was in hopes that this happy alliance, which secures the Duke of Greenwich, would have put your lordship's mind completely at ease, and that you would not have felt it necessary to examine farther into that mystery."

"Weak men never foresee adversity during prosperity, nor prosperity during adversity," replied Lord Oldborough. "His majesty has decided immediately to recall his present envoy at that German court; a new one will be sent, and the choice of that envoy his majesty is graciously pleased to leave to me.—You are a very young man, Mr. Cunningham Falconer, but you have given me such written irrefragable proofs of your ability and information, that I have no scruple in recommending you to his majesty as a person to whom his interests may be intrusted, and the zeal and attachment your family have shown me in actions, not in words only, have convinced me that I cannot choose better for my private affairs. Therefore, if the appointment be agreeable to you, you cannot too soon make what preparations may be necessary."

Cunningham, delighted, made his acknowledgments and thanks for the honour and the favour conferred upon him with all the eloquence in his power.

"I endeavour not to do any thing hastily, Mr. Cunningham Falconer," said his lordship. "I frankly tell you, that I was not at first prepossessed in your favour, nor did I feel inclined to do more for you than that to which I had been induced by peculiar circumstances. Under this prepossession, I perhaps did not for some time do justice to your talents; but I should be without judgment or without candour, if I did not feel and acknowledge the merit of the performance which I hold in my hand."

The performance was a pamphlet in support of Lord Oldborough's administration, published in Cunningham's name, but the greater part of it was written by his good genius in the garret.

"On this," said Lord Oldborough, putting his hand upon it as it lay on the table, "on this found your just title, sir, to my esteem and confidence."

Would not the truth have burst from any man of common generosity, honour, or honesty?—Would not a man who had any feeling, conscience, or shame, supposing he could have resolved to keep his secret, at this instant, have been ready to sink into the earth with confusion, under this unmerited praise?—In availing himself falsely of a title to esteem and confidence, then fraudulently of another's talents to obtain favour, honour, and emolument, would not a blush, or silence, some awkwardness, or some hesitation, have betrayed him to eyes far less penetrating than those of Lord Oldborough? Yet nothing of this was felt by Cunningham: he made, with a good grace, all the disqualifying speeches of a modest author, repeated his thanks and assurances of grateful attachment, and retired triumphant.—It must be acknowledged that he was fit for a diplomatist. His credentials were forthwith made out in form, and his instructions, public and private, furnished. No expense was spared in fitting him out for his embassy— his preparations made, his suite appointed, his liveries finished, his carriage at the door, he departed in grand style; and all Commissioner Falconer's friends, of which, at this time, he could not fail to have many, poured in with congratulations on the rapid advancement of his sons, and on all sides exclamations were heard in favour of friends in power.

"True—very true, indeed. And see what it is," said Commissioner Falconer, turning to Buckhurst, "see what it is to have a son so perverse, that he will not make use of a good friend when he has one, and who will not accept the promise of an excellent living when he can get it!"

All his friends and acquaintance now joining in one chorus told Buckhurst, in courtly terms, that he was a fool, and Buckhurst began to think they must be right.—"For here," said he to himself, "are my two precious brothers finely provided for, one an envoy, the other a major in esse, and a lieutenant-colonel in posse—and I, in esse and in posse, what?—Nothing but a good fellow—one day with the four in hand club, the next in my chambers, studying the law, by which I shall never make a penny. And there's Miss Caroline Percy, who has declined the honour of my hand, no doubt, merely because I have indulged a little in good company, instead of immuring myself with Coke and Blackstone, Viner and Saunders, Bosanquet and Puller, or chaining myself to a special-pleader's desk, like cousin Alfred, that galley-slave of the law!—No, no, I'll not make a galley-slave of myself. Besides, at my mother's, in all that set, and in the higher circles with Hauton and the Clays, and those people, whenever I appear in the character of a poor barrister, I am scouted—should never have got on at all, but for my being a wit—a wit!—and have not I wit enough to make my fortune? As my father says, What hinders me?—My conscience only. And why should my conscience be so cursedly delicate, so unlike other men's consciences?"

In this humour, Buckhurst was easily persuaded by his father to take orders. The paralytic incumbent of Chipping-Friars had just at this time another stroke of the palsy, on which Colonel Hauton congratulated the young deacon; and, to keep him in patience while waiting for the third stroke, made him chaplain to his regiment.—The Clays also introduced him to their uncle, Bishop Clay, who had, as they told him, taken a prodigious fancy to him; for he observed, that in carving a partridge, Buckhurst never touched the wing with a knife, but after nicking the joint, tore it off, so as to leave adhering to the bone that muscle obnoxious to all good eaters.—The bishop pronounced him to be "a capital carver."

Fortune at this time threw into Buckhurst's hands unasked, unlooked-for, and in the oddest way imaginable, a gift of no small value in itself, and an earnest of her future favours. At some high festival, Buckhurst was invited to dine with the bishop. Now Bishop Clay was a rubicund, full-blown, short-necked prelate, with the fear of apoplexy continually before him, except when dinner was on the table; and at this time a dinner was on the table, rich with every dainty of the season, that earth, air, and sea, could provide. Grace being first said by the chaplain, the bishop sat down "richly to enjoy;" but it happened in the first onset, that a morsel too large for his lordship's swallow stuck in his throat. The bishop grew crimson—purple—black in the face; the chaplain started up, and untied his neckcloth. The guests crowded round, one offering water, another advising bread, another calling for a raw egg, another thumping his lordship on the back. Buckhurst Falconer, with more presence of mind than was shown by any other person, saved his patron's life. He blew with force in the bishop's ear, and thus produced such a salutary convulsion in the throat, as relieved his lordship from the danger of suffocation [Footnote: Some learned persons assert that this could not have happened. We can only aver that it did happen. The assertions against the possibility of the fact remind us of the physician in Zadig, who, as the fable tells us, wrote a book to prove that Zadig should have gone blind, though he had actually recovered the use of his eye.—Zadig never read the book.]. The bishop, recovering his breath and vital functions, sat up, restored to life and dinner—he ate again, and drank to Mr. Buckhurst Falconer's health, with thanks for this good service to the church, to which he prophesied the reverend young gentleman would, in good time, prove an honour. And that he might be, in some measure, the means of accomplishing his own prophecy, Bishop Clay did, before he slept, which was immediately after dinner, present Mr. Buckhurst Falconer with a living worth 400l. a year; a living which had not fallen into the bishop's gift above half a day, and which, as there were six worthy clergymen in waiting for it, would necessarily have been disposed of the next morning.

"Oh! star of patronage, shine ever thus upon the Falconers!" cried Buckhurst, when, elevated with wine in honour of the church, he gave an account to his father at night of the success of the day.—"Oh! thou, whose influence has, for us, arrested Fortune at the top of her wheel, be ever thus propitious!—Only make me a dean. Have you not made my brother, the dunce, a colonel? and my brother, the knave, an envoy?—I only pray to be a dean—I ask not yet to be a bishop—you see I have some conscience left."

"True," said his father, laughing. "Now go to bed, Buckhurst; you may, for your fortune is up."

"Ha! my good cousin Percys, where are you now?—Education, merit, male and female, where are you now?—Planting cabbages, and presiding at a day-school: one son plodding in a pleader's office—another cast in an election for an hospital physician—a third encountering a plague in the West Indies. I give you joy!"

No wonder the commissioner exulted, for he had not only provided thus rapidly for his sons, but he had besides happy expectations for himself.—With Lord Oldborough he was now in higher favour and confidence than he had ever hoped to be. Lord Oldborough, who was a man little prone to promise, and who always did more than he said, had, since the marriage of his niece, thrown out a hint that he was aware of the expense it must have been to Commissioner and Mrs. Falconer to give entertainments continually, and to keep open house, as they had done this winter, for his political friends—no instance of zeal in his majesty's service, his lordship said, he hoped was ever lost upon him, and, if he continued in power, he trusted he should find occasion to show his gratitude. This from another minister might mean nothing but to pay with words; from Lord Oldborough the commissioner justly deemed it as good as a promissory note for a lucrative place. Accordingly he put it in circulation directly among his creditors, and he no longer trembled at the expense at which he had lived and was living. Both Mrs. Falconer and he had ever considered a good cook, and an agreeable house, as indispensably necessary to those who would rise in the world; and they laid it down as a maxim, that, if people wished to grow rich, they must begin by appearing so. Upon this plan every thing in their establishment, table, servants, equipage, dress, were far more splendid than their fortune could afford. The immediate gratification which resulted from this display, combining with their maxims of policy, encouraged the whole family to continue this desperate game. Whenever the timidity of the commissioner had started; when, pressed by his creditors, he had backed, and had wished to stop in this course of extravagance; his lady, of a more intrepid character, urged him forward, pleading that he had gone too far to recede—that the poorer they were, the more necessary to keep up the brilliant appearance of affluence. How else could her daughters, after all the sums that had been risked upon them, hope to be advantageously established? How otherwise could they preserve what her friend Lady Jane Granville so justly styled the patronage of fashion?

When success proved Mrs. Falconer to be right, "Now, Commissioner Falconer! Now!" How she triumphed, and how she talked! Her sons all in such favour—her daughters in such fashion! No party without the Miss Falconers!—Miss Falconers must sing—Miss Falconers must play—Miss Falconers must dance, or no lady of a house could feel herself happy, or could think she had done her duty—no piano, no harp could draw such crowds as the Miss Falconers. It was the ambition among the fashionable men to dance with the Miss Falconers, to flirt with the Miss Falconers. "Not merely flirting, ma'am," as Mrs.

Falconer said, and took proper pains should be heard, "but several serious proposals from very respectable quarters:" however, none yet exactly what she could resolve to accept for the girls—she looked high for them, she owned—she thought she had a right to look high. Girls in fashion should not take the first offers—they should hold up their heads: why should they not aspire to rank, why not to title, as well as to fortune?

Poor Petcalf! General Petcalf's son had been for some time, as it was well known, desperately in love with Miss Georgiana Falconer; but what chance had he now? However, he was to be managed: he was useful sometimes, as a partner, "to whom one may say one is engaged when a person one does not choose to dance with asks for the honour of one's hand—useful sometimes to turn over the leaves of the music-book—useful always as an attendant in public places—useful, in short, to be exhibited as a captive; for one captive leads to another conquest." And Miss Arabella Falconer, too, could boast her conquests, though nobody merely by looking at her would have guessed it: but she was a striking exemplification of the truth of Lady Jane Granville's maxim, that fashion, like Venus's girdle, can beautify any girl, let her be ever so ugly.

And now the Falconer family having risen and succeeded beyond their most sanguine hopes by a combination of lucky circumstances, and by adherence to their favourite system, we leave them fortified in their principles, and at the height of prosperity.

CHAPTER XI

Fortune, as if she had been piqued by Mr. Percy's disdain, and jealous of his professed reliance upon the superior power of her rival, Prudence, seemed now determined to humble him and all his family, to try if she could not force him to make some of the customary sacrifices of principle to propitiate her favour.

Unsuspicious of the designs that were carrying forward against him in secret, Mr. Percy had quite forgotten his fears that his wicked relation Sir Robert Percy, and Solicitor Sharpe, might take advantage of the loss of that deed which had never been found since the night of the fire at Percy-hall. It was nearly two years afterwards that Mr. Percy received a letter from his cousin, Sir Robert, informing him that he had been advised to dispute the title to the Percy estate, that he had the opinion of the first lawyers in England in his favour, and that he had given directions to his solicitor, Mr. Sharpe, to commence a suit to reinstate the lawful heir in the property of his ancestors.—Sir Robert Percy added something about his reluctance to go to law, and a vast deal about candour, justice, and family friendship, which it would be needless and unreasonable to repeat.

Fresh search was now made for the lost deed, but in vain; and in vain Rosamond reproached herself with having betrayed the secret of that loss to the revengeful attorney.—The ensuing post brought notice from Mr. Sharpe that proceedings were commenced.—In Sir Robert's letter, though not in the attorney's, there was obviously left an opening for an offer to compromise; this was done either with intent to lure Mr. Percy on to make an offer, which might afterwards appear against him, or it was done in the hope that, intimidated by the fear of an expensive and hazardous suit, Mr. Percy might give up half his estate, to secure the quiet possession of the remainder. But they knew little of Mr. Percy who argued in this manner: he was neither to be lured nor intimidated from his right—all compromise, "all terms of commerce he disdained." He sent no answer, but prepared to make a vigorous defence. For this purpose he wrote to his son Alfred, desiring him to spare no pains or expense, to engage the best counsel, and to put them in full possession of the cause. Alfred regretted that he was not of sufficient standing at the bar to take the lead in conducting his father's cause: he, however, prepared all the documents with great care and ability. From time to time, as the business went on, he wrote to his father in good spirits, saying that he had excellent hopes they should succeed, notwithstanding the unfortunate loss of the deed; that the more he considered the case, the more clearly the justice of their cause and the solidity of their right appeared. Alas! Alfred showed himself to be but a young lawyer, in depending so much upon right and justice, while a point of law was against him. It is unnecessary, and would be equally tedious and unintelligible to most readers, to dwell upon the details of this suit. Contrary to the usual complaints of the law's delay, this cause went through the courts in a short time, because Mr. Percy did not make use of any subterfuge to protract the business. A decree was given in favour of Sir Robert Percy, and he became the legal possessor of the great Percy estate in Hampshire, which had been so long the object of his machinations.

Thus, at one stroke, the Percy family fell from the station and affluence which they had so long, and, in the opinion of all who knew them, so well enjoyed. Great was the regret among the higher classes, and great, indeed, the lamentations of the poor in the neighbourhood, when the decree was made known. It seemed as if the change in their situation was deplored as a general misfortune, and as if it were felt by all more than by the sufferers themselves, who were never seen to give way to weak complaints, or heard to utter an invective against their adversary. This magnanimity increased the public sympathy, and pity for them was soon converted into indignation against Sir Robert Percy. Naturally insolent, and now elated with success, he wrote post after post to express his impatience to come and take possession of his estate, and to hasten the departure of his relations from the family seat. This was as cruel as it was unnecessary, for from the moment when they learnt the event of the trial, they had been occupied with the preparations for their departure; for the resignation of all the conveniences and luxuries they possessed, all the pleasures associated with the idea of home; for parting with all the animate and inanimate objects to which they had long and early habits of affection and attachment. This family had never been proud in prosperity, nor were they abject in adversity: they submitted with fortitude to their fate; yet they could not, without regret, leave the place where they had spent so many happy years.

It had been settled that the improvements which Mr. Percy had made on the estate, the expense of the buildings and furniture at Percy-hall, of which a valuation had been made, should be taken in lieu of all arrears of rent to which Sir Robert might lay claim. In consequence of this award, Mr. Percy and his family were anxious to leave every thing about the house and place in perfect order, that they might fulfil punctually their part of the agreement. The evening before they were to quit Percy-hall, they went into every room, to take a review of the whole. The house was peculiarly convenient and well arranged. Mr. Percy had spared nothing to render it in every respect agreeable, not only to his guests, but to his family, to make his children happy in their home. His daughters' apartments he had fitted up for them in the neatest manner, and they had taken pleasure in ornamenting them with their own work and drawings. They felt very melancholy the evening they were to take leave of these for ever. They took down some of their drawings, and all the little trophies preserved from childhood, memorials of early ingenuity or taste, which could be of no use or value to any one except to themselves; every thing else they agreed to leave as usual, to show how kind their father had been to them—a sentiment well suited to their good and innocent minds. They opened their writing-tables and their drawing-boxes for the last time; for the last time they put fresh flowers into their flower-pots, and, with a sigh, left their little apartments.

All the family then went out to walk in the park and through the shrubberies. It was a delightful summer's evening; the birds were singing—"Caring little," as Rosamond said, "for our going away." The sun was just setting, and they thought they had never seen the place look so beautiful. Indeed Mr. and Mrs. Percy had, for many years, delighted in cultivating the natural beauties of this picturesque situation, and their improvements were now beginning to appear to advantage. But they were never to enjoy the success of their labours! The old steward followed the family in this walk. He stopped every now and then to deplore over each fine tree or shrub as they passed, and could scarcely refrain from bursting into invectives against him that was coming after them into possession.

"The whole country cries shame upon the villain," John began; but Mr. Percy, with a smile, stopped him.

"Let us bear our misfortunes, John, with a good grace; let us be thankful for the happiness which we have enjoyed, and submit ourselves to the will of Providence. Without any hypocrisy or affected resignation, I say, at this instant, what with my whole heart I feel, that I submit, without repining, to the will of God, and firmly believe that all is for the best."

"And so I strive to do," said John. "But only, I say, if it had pleased God to order it otherwise, it's a pity the wicked should come just after us to enjoy themselves, when they have robbed us of all."

"Not of all," said Mr. Percy.

"What is it they have not robbed us of?" cried John: "not a thing but they must have from us."

"No; the best of all things we keep for ourselves—it cannot be taken from us—a good conscience."

"Worth all the rest—that's true," said John; "and that is what he will never have who is coming here to-morrow—never—never! They say he don't sleep at nights. But I'll say no more about him, only—he's not a good man."

"I am sure, John, you are not a good courtier," said Mrs. Percy, smiling: "you ought to prepare to pay your court to your new master."

"My new master!" cried John, growing red: "the longest day ever I live, I'll never have a new master! All that I have in the world came from you, and I'll never have another master. Sure you will let me follow you? I will be no trouble: though but little, may be I can do something still. Surely, madam—surely, sir—young ladies, you'll speak for me—I shall be let to follow the fortunes of the family, and go along with you into banishment."

"My good John," said Mr. Percy, "since you desire to follow us into banishment, as you call it, you shall; and as long as we have any thing upon earth, you shall never want. You must stay here to-morrow, after we are gone, to give up possession." (John could not stand this, but turned away to hide his face.) "When your business is done," continued Mr. Percy, "you may set out and follow us as soon as you please."

"I thank you, sir, kindly," said John, with a most grateful bow, that took in all the family, "that's new life to me."

He said not a word more during the rest of the walk, except just as he passed near the beach where the ship was wrecked, he exclaimed, "There was the first beginning of all our misfortune: who would have thought that when we gave them shelter we should be turned out so soon ourselves? 'twas that drunken rascal of a Dutch carpenter was the cause of all!"

The next morning the whole family set out in an open carriage, which had been made for the purpose of carrying as many of the young people as possible upon excursions of pleasure. It was a large sociable, which they used to call their caravan.

At the great gate of the park old John stopped the carriage, and leaning over to his master, whispered, "I beg your pardon, sir, but God bless you, and don't drive through the village: if you please, take the back road; for I've just learned that he is on the great road, and as near hand as the turn at the school-house, and they say he wants to be driving in his coach and four through the village as you are all going out— now I wouldn't for any thing he had that triumph over us."

"Thank you, good John," said Mr. Percy, "but such triumphs cannot mortify us."

Poor John reluctantly opened the gate and let the carriage pass—they drove on—they cast a lingering look behind as they quitted the park—

—"Must I then leave thee, Paradise?"—

As they passed through the village the poor people came out of their houses to take leave of their excellent landlord; they flocked round the carriage, and hung upon it till it stopped, and then, with one voice, they poured forth praises, and blessings, and prayers for better days. Just at this moment Sir Robert Percy made his appearance. His equipage was splendid; his coachman drove his four fine horses down the street, the middle of which was cleared in an instant. The crowd gazed at the show as it passed—Sir Robert gave a signal to his coachman to drive slower, that he might longer enjoy the triumph—he put his head out of the coach window, but no one cried, "God bless him!" His insolence was obviously mortified as he passed the Percy family, for Mr. Percy bowed with an air of dignity and cheerfulness which seemed to say, "My fortune is yours—but I am still myself." Some of the spectators clapped their hands, and some wept.

Mr. Percy seemed to have prepared his mind for every circumstance of his departure, and to be perfectly composed, or at least master of his feelings; but a small incident, which had not been foreseen, suddenly moved him almost to tears: as they crossed the bridge, which was at the farthest end of the village, they heard the muffled bells of the church toll as if for a public calamity [Footnote: On Mr. Morris's departure from Piercefield the same circumstance happened.]. Instantly recollecting the resentment to which these poor people were exposing themselves, by this mark of their affection and regret, Mr. Percy went by a short path to the church as quickly as possible, and had the bells unmuffled.

CHAPTER XII

Mr. Percy fortunately possessed, independently of the Percy estate, a farm worth about seven or eight hundred a year, which he had purchased with part of his wife's fortune; on which he had built a lodge, that he had intended for the future residence of one of his sons. The Hills was the name of this lodge, to which all the family now retired. Though it was in the same county with Percy-hall, Clermont-park, Falconer-court, Hungerford-castle, and within reach of several other gentlemen's seats, yet from its being in a hilly part of the country, through which no regular road had been made, it was little frequented, and gave the idea not only of complete retirement, but of remoteness. Though a lonely situation, it was, however, a beautiful one. The house stood on the brow of a hill, and looked into a deep glen, through the steep descent of which ran a clear and copious rivulet rolling over a stony bed; the rocks were covered with mountain flowers, and wild shrubs—But nothing is more tiresome than a picture in prose: we shall, therefore, beg our readers to recall to their imagination some of the views they may have seen in Wales, and they will probably have a better idea of this place than any that we could give by the most laboured description, amplified with all the epithets in the English language.

The house at the Hills, though finished, was yet but scantily furnished, and was so small that it could hardly hold the family, who were now obliged to take refuge in it. However, they were well disposed to accommodate each other: they had habits of order, and had so little accustomed themselves to be waited upon, that this sudden change in their fortune and way of life did not appear terrible, as it would to many in the same rank. Undoubtedly they felt the loss of real conveniences, but they were not tormented with ideal wants, or with the pangs of mortified vanity. Evils they had to bear, but they were not the most dreadful of all evils—those of the imagination.

Mr. Percy, to whom his whole family looked for counsel and support, now showed all the energy and decision of his character. What he knew must be done sooner or later he did decidedly at first. The superfluities to which his family had been accustomed, were instantly abandoned. The great torment of decayed gentry is the remembrance of their former station, and a weak desire still to appear what their fortune no longer allows them to be. This folly Mr. Percy had not to combat in his family, where all were eager to resign even more of their own comforts than the occasion required. It was the object now for the family who were at home to live as frugally as possible, that they might save as much of their small income as they could, to assist and forward the sons in their professions.

The eldest son, Godfrey, could not yet have heard of the change in his father's fortune, and in his own expectations; but from a passage in his last letter, it was evident that he had some idea of the possibility of such a reverse, and that he was preparing himself to live with economy. From Alfred and Erasmus Mr. Percy had at this trying time the satisfaction of receiving at once the kindest and the most manly letters, containing strong expressions of gratitude to their father for having given them such an education as would enable them, notwithstanding the loss of hereditary fortune, to become independent and respectable. What would have been the difference of their fate and of their feelings, had they been suffered to grow up into mere idle lounging gentlemen, or four-in-hand coachmen! In different words, but with the same spirit, both brothers declared that this change in the circumstances of their family did not depress their minds, but, on the contrary, gave them new and powerful motives for exertion. It seemed to be the first wish of their souls to fulfil the fond hopes and predictions of their father, and to make some return for the care their parents had taken of their education.

Their father, pleased by the sanguine hopes and ardent spirit expressed in their letters, was, however, sensible that a considerable time must elapse before they could make any thing by law or medicine. They were as yet only in the outset of their professions, the difficult beginning, when men must toil often without reward, be subject to crosses and losses, and rebukes and rebuffs, when their rivals push them back, and when they want the assistance of friends to help them forward, whilst with scarcely the means to live they must appear like gentlemen.

Besides the faithful steward, two servants, who were much attached to the family, accompanied them to their retirement. One was Mrs. Harte, who had lived with Mrs. Percy above thirty years; and who, from being a housekeeper with handsome wages and plenary power over a numerous household at Percy-hall, now served with increased zeal at the Hills, doing a great part of the work of the house herself, with the assistance only of a stout country girl newly hired, whose awkwardness and ignorance, or, as Mrs. Harte expressed it, whose comical ways, she bore with a patience that cost her more than all the rest. The other servant who followed the altered fortunes of the Percy family was a young man of the name of Johnson, whom Mr. Percy had bred up from a boy, and who was so creditable a servant that he could readily have obtained a place with high wages in any opulent family, either in the country or in London; but he chose to abide by his master, who could now only afford to give him very little. Indeed, Mr. Percy would not have kept any man-servant in his present circumstances, but out of regard for this young man, who seemed miserable at the thoughts of leaving him, and who undertook to make himself useful in the farm as well as in the house.

Very different was Johnson from the present race of fine town servants, who follow with no unequal steps the follies and vices of their betters; and who, by their insolence and extravagance, become the just torments of their masters. Very different was Johnson from some country servants, who with gross selfishness look solely to their own eating and drinking, and whose only thought is how to swallow as much and do as little as possible.

As soon as he had settled his home, Mr. Percy looked abroad to a tract of improveable ground, on which he might employ his agricultural skill. He had reason to rejoice in having really led the life of a country gentleman. He understood country business, and he was ably assisted in all the details of farming and management. Never, in the most prosperous days, did the old steward seem so fully interested in his master's affairs, so punctual and active in executing his commands, and, above all, so respectful in his manner to his master, as now in his fallen fortunes.

It would be uninteresting to readers who are not farmers to enter into a detail of Mr. Percy's probable improvements. It is enough to say, that his hopes were founded upon experience, and that he was a man capable of calculating. He had been long in the habit of keeping accurate accounts, not such as gentlemen display when they are pleased to prove that their farm, produces more than ever farm produced before. All the tradesmen with whom he had dealt were, notwithstanding his change of fortune, ready to trust him; and those who were strangers, finding themselves regularly paid, soon acquired confidence in his punctuality. So that, far from being terrified at having so little, he felt surprised at having still so much money at his command.—The enjoyment of high credit must surely give more pleasurable feelings than the mere possession of wealth.

Often, during the first year after he had been deprived of the Percy estate, Mr. Percy declared, that, as to himself, he had actually lost nothing; for he had never been expensive or luxurious, his personal enjoyments were nearly the same, and his active pursuits were not very different from what they had always been. He had, it is true, less time than he wished to give to literature, or to indulge in the company and conversation of his wife and daughters; but even the pain of this privation was compensated by the pleasure he felt in observing the excellences in their characters which adversity developed.—It has by some persons been thought, that women who have been suffered to acquire literary tastes, whose understandings have been cultivated and refined, are apt to disdain or to become unfit for the useful minutiæ of domestic duties. In the education of her daughters Mrs. Percy had guarded against this danger, and she now experienced the happy effects of her prudence. At first they had felt it somewhat irksome, in their change of circumstances, to be forced to spend a considerable portion of their time in preparations for the mere business of living, but they perceived that this constraint gave a new spring to their minds, and a higher relish to their favourite employments. After the domestic business of the day was done, they enjoyed, with fresh delight, the pleasures of which it is not in the power of fortune to deprive us.

Soon after the family were settled at the Hills, they were surprised by a visit from Commissioner Falconer—surprised, because, though they knew that he had a certain degree of commonplace friendship for them as relations, yet they were aware that his regard was not independent of fortune, and they had never supposed that he would come to seek them in their retirement. After some general expressions of condolence on their losses, their change of situation, and the inconveniences to which a large family, bred up, as they had been, in affluence, must suffer in their present abode, he went out to walk with Mr. Percy, and he then began to talk over his own family affairs. With polite acknowledgment to Mr. Percy of the advantage he had derived from his introduction to Lord Oldborough, and with modestly implied compliments to his own address in turning that introduction to the best possible account, Mr. Falconer led to the subject on which he wanted to dilate.

"You see, my dear Mr. Percy," said he, "without vanity I may now venture to say, my plans for advancing my family have all succeeded; my sons have risen in the world, or rather have been pushed up, beyond my most sanguine hopes."

"I give you joy with all my heart," said Mr. Percy.

"But, my good sir, listen to me; your sons might have been in as advantageous situations, if you had not been too proud to benefit by the evidently favourable dispositions which Lord Oldborough shewed towards you and yours."

"Too proud! No, my friend, I assure you, pride never influenced my conduct—I acted from principle."

"So you are pleased to call it.—But we will not go back to the past—no man likes to acknowledge he has been wrong. Let us, if you please, look to the future. You know that you are now in a different situation from what you were formerly, when you could afford to follow your principles or your systems. Now, my dear sir, give me leave to tell you that it is your duty, absolutely your duty, to make use of your interest for your sons. There is not a man in England, who, if he chose it, might secure for his sons a better patron than you could."

"I trust," replied Mr. Percy, "that I have secured for my sons what is better than a good patron—a good education."

"Both are best," said Mr. Falconer. "Proud as you are, cousin Percy, you must allow this, when you look round and see who rises, and how.—And now we are by ourselves, let me ask you, frankly and seriously, why do not you try to establish your sons by patronage?"

"Frankly and seriously, then, because I detest and despise the whole system of patronage."

"That's very strong," said Mr. Falconer. "And I am glad for your sake, and for the sake of your family, that nobody heard it but myself."

"If the whole world heard me," pursued Mr. Percy, "I should say just the same. Strong—very strong!—I am glad of it; for (excuse me, you are my relation, and we are on terms of familiarity) the delicate, guarded, qualifying, trimming, mincing, pouncet-box, gentleman-usher mode of speaking truth, makes no sort of impression. Truth should always be strong—speaking or acting."

"Well, well, I beg your pardon; as strong let it be as you please, only let it be cool, and then we cannot fail to understand one another. I think you were going to explain to me why you detest and despise what you call the system of patronage."

"Because I believe it to be ruinous to my country. Whenever the honours of professions, civil, military, or ecclesiastical, are bestowed by favour, not earned by merit—whenever the places of trust and dignity in a state are to be gained by intrigue and solicitation—there is an end of generous emulation, and consequently of exertion. Talents and integrity, in losing their reward of glory, lose their vigour, and often their very existence. If the affairs of this nation were guided, and if her battles were fought by the corrupt, imbecile creatures of patronage, how would they be guided?—how fought?—Woe be to the country that trusts to such rulers and such defenders! Woe has been to every country that has so trusted!—May such never be the fate of England!—And that it never may, let every honest independent Englishman set his face, his hand, his heart against this base, this ruinous system!—I will for one."

"For one!—alas!" said Mr. Falconer, with a sigh meant to be heard, and a smile not intended to be seen, "what can one do in such a desperate case?—I am afraid certain things will go on in the world for ever, whether we benefit by them or not.—And if I grant that patronage is sometimes a public evil, you must allow that it is often a private benefit."

"I doubt even that," said Mr. Percy; "for those young men who are brought up to expect patronage in any profession—But," said Mr. Percy, checking himself, "I forgot whom I am speaking to: I don't wish to say any thing that can hurt your feelings, especially when you are so kind to come to see me in adversity, and when you show so much interest in my affairs."

"Oh! pray go on, go on," said the commissioner, smiling, "you will not hurt me, I assure you: consider I am too firm in the success of my system to be easily offended on that point—go on!—Those young men who are brought up to expect patronage in any profession—"

"Are apt to depend upon it too much," continued Mr. Percy, "and consequently neglect to acquire knowledge. They know that things will be passed over for them, and they think that they need not be assiduous, because they are secure of being provided for, independently of their own exertions; and if they have a turn for extravagance, they may indulge it, because a place will set all to rights."

"And if they are provided for, and if they do get good places, are they not well enough off?" said Mr. Falconer: "I'll answer for it, your sons would think so."

Mr. Percy, with a look of proud humility, replied, "I am inclined to believe that my sons would not think themselves well off, unless they were distinguished by their own merit."

"To be sure," said Mr. Falconer, correcting himself; "of course I mean that too: but a young man can never distinguish himself, you know, so well as when his merit is raised to a conspicuous situation."

"Or disgrace himself so effectually, as when he is raised to a situation for which he is unprepared and unfit."

The commissioner's brow clouded—some unpleasant reflection or apprehension seemed to cross his mind. Mr. Percy had no intention of raising any; he meant no allusion to the commissioner's sons—he hastened to turn what he had said more decidedly upon his own.

"I have chosen for my sons, or rather they have chosen for themselves," continued he, "professions which are independent of influence, and in which it could be of little use to them. Patrons can be of little advantage to a lawyer or a physician. No judge, no attorney, can push a lawyer up, beyond a certain point—he may rise like a rocket, but he will fall like the stick, if he be not supported by his own inherent powers. Where property or life is at stake, men will not compliment or even be influenced by great recommendations—they will consult the best lawyer, and the best physician, whoever he may be. I have endeavoured to give my Alfred and Erasmus such an education as shall enable them honestly to work their own way to eminence."

"A friend's helping hand is no bad thing," said Mr. Falconer, "in that hard and slippery ascent."

"As many friends, as many helping hands, in a fair way, as you please," said Mr. Percy: "I by no means would inculcate the anti-social, absurd, impossible doctrine, that young men, or any men, can or ought to be independent of the world. Let my sons make friends for themselves, and enjoy the advantage of mine. I object only to their becoming dependent, wasting the best years of their lives in a miserable, debasing servitude to patrons—to patrons, who at last may perhaps capriciously desert them at their utmost need."

Again, without designing it, Mr. Percy wakened unpleasant recollections in the mind of the commissioner.

"Ah! there you touch a tender string with me," said Mr. Falconer, sighing. "I have known something of that in my life. Lord N— and Mr. G— did indeed use me shamefully ill. But I was young then, and did not choose my friends well. I know more of the world now, and have done better for my sons—and shall do better, I trust, for myself. In the mean time, my dear Mr. Percy, let us think of your affairs. Such a man as you should not be lost here on a farm amongst turnips and carrots. So Lord Oldborough says and thinks—and, in short, to come to the point at once, I was not sounding you from idle curiosity respecting patronage, or from any impertinent desire to interfere with your concerns; but I come, commissioned by Lord Oldborough, to make an offer, which, I am persuaded, whatever theoretical objections might occur," said the commissioner, with a significant smile, "Mr. Percy is too much a man of practical sense to reject. Lord Oldborough empowers me to say, that it is his wish to see his government supported and strengthened by men of Mr. Percy's talents and character; that he is persuaded that Mr. Percy would speak well in parliament; that if Mr. Percy will join us, his lordship will bring him into parliament, and give him thus an opportunity of at once distinguishing himself, advancing his family, repairing the injustice of fortune, and serving his country."

Commissioner Falconer made this offer with much pomposity, with the air of a person sure that he is saying something infinitely flattering, and at the same time with a lurking smile on his countenance, at the idea of the ease and certainty with which this offer would induce Mr. Percy to recant all he had said against patrons and patronage. He was curious to hear how the philosopher would change his tone; but, to his surprise, Mr. Percy did not alter it in the least.

He returned his respectful and grateful acknowledgments to Lord Oldborough, but begged leave totally to decline the honour intended him; he could not, he said, accept it consistently with his principles—he could not go into parliament with a view to advance himself or to provide for his family.

The commissioner interrupted to qualify, for he was afraid he had spoken too broadly, and observed that what he had said was quite confidential.

Mr. Percy understood it so, and assured him there was no danger that it should be repeated. The commissioner was then in a state to listen again quietly.

Mr. Percy said, that when he was rich, he had preferred domestic happiness to ambition, therefore he had never stood for the county to which he belonged; that now he was poor, he felt an additional reason for keeping out of parliament, that he might not put himself in a situation to be tempted—a situation where he must spend more than he could afford, and could only pay his expenses by selling his conscience.

The commissioner was silent with astonishment for some moments after Mr. Percy ceased speaking. He had always thought his good cousin a singular man, but he had never thought him a wrongheaded fool till this moment. At first he was somewhat vexed, for Mr. Percy's sake and for the sake of his sons, that he refused such an offer; for the commissioner had some of the feelings of a relation, but more of the habits of a politician, and these last, in a few moments, reconciled him to what he thought the ruin of his cousin's prospects in life. Mr. Falconer considered, that if Mr. Percy were to go into parliament to join their party, and to get near Lord Oldborough, he might become a dangerous rival. He pressed the matter, therefore, no longer with urgency, but only just sufficient to enable him to report to Lord Oldborough that he had executed his commission, but had found Mr. Percy impracticable.

CHAPTER XIII

However sincere the general pity and esteem for the Percy family, they did not escape the common lot of mortality; they had their share of blame, as well as of condolence, from their friends and acquaintance. Some discovered that all the misfortunes of the family might have been avoided, if they had listened to good advice; others were quite clear that the lawsuit would have been decided in Mr. Percy's favour, if he had employed their solicitor or their barrister; or, in short, if every step of the suit had been directed differently.

Commissioner Falconer now joined the band of reproaching friends. He did not blame Mr. Percy, however, for the conduct of the lawsuit, for of that he confessed himself to be no judge, but he thought he understood the right way of advancing a family in the world; and on this subject he now took a higher tone than he had formerly felt himself entitled to assume. Success gives such rights—especially over the unfortunate. The commissioner said loudly in all companies, that he had hoped his relation, Mr. Percy, who certainly was a man of talents, and he was convinced well-intentioned, would not have shown himself so obstinately attached to his peculiar opinions—especially to his strange notions of independence, which must disgust, ultimately, friends whom it was most the interest of his family to please; that he doubted not that the young men of the Percy family bitterly regretted that their father would not avail himself of the advantages of his connexions, of the favourable dispositions, and, to his knowledge, most condescending offers that had been made to him—offers which, the commissioner said, he must term really condescending, when he considered that Mr. Percy had never paid the common court that was expected by a minister. Other circumstances, too, enhanced the favour: offence had undoubtedly been given by the ill-timed, injudicious interference of Captain Godfrey Percy about regimental business—some Major Gascoigne—yet, notwithstanding this, a certain person, whose steadiness in his friendships the commissioner declared he could never sufficiently admire, had not, for the son's errors, changed his favourable opinion or disposition towards the father.

Mr. Falconer concluded, with a sigh, "There are some men whom the best of friends cannot serve—and such we can only leave to their fate."

The commissioner now considering Mr. Percy as a person so obstinately odd that it was unsafe for a rising man to have any thing more to do with him, it was agreed in the Falconer family, that it was necessary to let the Percys drop—gently, without making any noise. Mrs. Falconer and her daughters having always resided in London during the winter, and at some watering place in summer, knew scarcely any thing of the female part of the Percy family. Mrs. Falconer had occasionally met Mrs. Percy, but the young ladies, who had not yet been in town, she had never seen since they were children. Mrs. Falconer now considered this as a peculiarly fortunate circumstance, because she should not be blamed for cutting them, and should escape all the unpleasantness of breaking off an intimacy with relations.

The commissioner acceded to all his lady's observations, and easily shook off that attachment, which he had professed for so many years, perhaps felt, for his good cousin Percy—perhaps felt, we say: because we really believe that he was attached to Mr. Percy while that gentleman was in prosperity. There are persons who have an exclusive sympathy with the prosperous.

There was one, however, who, in this respect, felt differently from the rest of the family. Buckhurst Falconer, with a generous impulse of affection and gratitude, declared that he would not desert Mr. Percy or any of the family in adversity; he could never forget how kind they had been to him when he was in distress. Buckhurst's resentment against Caroline for her repeated refusals suddenly subsided; his attachment revived with redoubled force. He protested that he loved her the better for having lost her fortune, and he reiterated this protestation more loudly, because his father declared it was absurd and ridiculous. The son persisted, till the father, though not subject to make violent resolutions, was wrought to such a pitch as to swear, that if Buckhurst should be fool enough to think seriously of a girl who was now a beggar, he would absolutely refuse his consent to the match, and would never give his son a shilling.

Buckhurst immediately wrote to Caroline a passionate declaration of the constancy and ardour of his attachment, and entreated her permission to wait upon her immediately.

"Do not sacrifice me," said Buckhurst, "to idle niceties. That I have many faults, I am conscious; but none, I trust, for which you ought utterly to condemn me—none but what you can cure. I am ready to be every thing which you approve. Give me but leave to hope. There is no sacrifice I will not make to facilitate, to expedite our union. I have been ordained, one living I possess, and that which Colonel Hauton has promised me will soon come into my possession. Believe me, I was decided to go into the church by my attachment—to my passion for you, every scruple, every consideration gave way. As to the rest, I shall never be deterred from following the dictates of my heart by the opposition of ambitious parents. Caroline, do not sacrifice me to idle niceties—I know I have the misfortune not to please your brother Alfred: to do him justice, he has fairly told me that he does not think me worthy of his sister

Caroline. I forgive him, I admire him for the pride with which he pronounces the words, my sister Caroline. But though she may easily find a more faultless character, she will never find a warmer heart, or one more truly—more ardently attached."

There was something frank, warm, and generous in this letter, which pleased Rosamond, and which, she said, justified her good opinion of Buckhurst. Indeed, the great merit of being ardently attached to her sister Caroline was sufficient, in Rosamond's eyes, to cover a multitude of sins: and the contrast between his warmth at this moment, and the coldness of the rest of his family, struck her forcibly. Rosamond thought that Alfred had been too severe in his judgment, and observed, that it was in vain to look with a lantern all over the world for a faultless character—a monster. It was quite sufficient if a woman could find an honest man—that She was sure Buckhurst had no faults but what love would cure.

"But love has not cured him of any yet," said Caroline.

"Try marriage," said Rosamond, laughing.

Caroline shook her head. "Consider at what expense that trial must be made."

At the first reading of Buckhurst's letter Caroline had been pleased with it; but on a second perusal, she was dissatisfied with the passage about his parents, nor could she approve of his giving up what he now called his scruples, to obtain a competence for the woman he professed to adore. She knew that he had been leading a dissipated life in town; that he must, therefore, be less fit than he formerly was to make a good husband, and still less likely to make a respectable clergyman. He had some right feeling, but no steady principle, as Caroline observed. She was grateful for the constancy of his attachment, and for the generosity he showed in his whole conduct towards her; nor was she insensible to the urgency with which Rosamond pleaded in his favour: but she was firm in her own judgment; and her refusal, though expressed in the terms that could best soften the pain it must give, was as decided as possible.

Soon after her letter had been sent, she and Rosamond had taken a longer walk one evening than usual, and, eager in conversation, went on so far in this wild unfrequented part of the country, that when they saw the sun setting, they began to fear they should not reach home before it was dark. They wished to find a shorter way than that by which they went, and they looked about in hopes of seeing some labourer (some swinked hedger) returning from his work, or a cottage where they could meet with a guide.—But there was no person or house within sight. At last Caroline, who had climbed upon a high bank in the lane where they were walking, saw a smoke rising between some trees at a little distance; and toward this spot they made their way through another lane, the entrance to which had been stopped up with furze bushes. They soon came within sight of a poor-looking cottage, and saw a young woman walking very slowly with a child in her arms. She was going towards the house, and did not perceive the young ladies till they were close to her. She turned suddenly when they spoke—started—looked frightened and confused; the infant began to cry, and hushing it as well as she could, she answered to their questions with a bewildered look, "I don't know indeed—I can't tell—I don't know any thing, ladies—ask at the cottage, yonder." Then she quickened her pace, and walked so fast to the house, that they could hardly keep up with her. She pushed open the hatch door, and called "Dorothy! Dorothy, come out." But no Dorothy answered.—The young woman seemed at a loss what to do; and as she stood hesitating, her face, which had at first appeared pale and emaciated, flushed up to her temples. She looked very handsome, but in ill-health.

"Be pleased, ladies," said she, with diffidence, and trembling from head to foot, "be pleased to sit down and rest, ladies. One will be in directly who knows the ways—I am a stranger in these parts."

As soon as she had set the chairs, she was retiring to an inner room, but her child, who was pleased with Caroline's face as she smiled and nodded at him, stretched out his little hands towards her.

"Oh! let my sister give him a kiss," said Rosamond. The mother stopped, yet appeared unwilling. The child patted Caroline's cheek, played with her hair, and laughed aloud. Caroline offered to take the child in her arms, but the mother held him fast, and escaped into the inner room, where they heard her sobbing violently. Caroline and Rosamond looked at one another in silence, and left the cottage by tacit consent, sorry that they had given pain, and feeling that they had no right to intrude further. "We can go home the same way that we came," said Caroline, "and that is better than to trouble any body."

"Certainly," said Rosamond: "yet I should like to know something more about this poor woman if I could, without—If we happened to meet Dorothy, whoever she is."

At this instant they saw an old woman come from a copse near the cottage, with a bundle of sticks on her back and a tin can in her hand: this was Dorothy. She saved them all the trouble and delicacy of asking questions, for there was not a more communicative creature breathing. She in the first place threw down her faggots, and offered her service to guide the young ladies home; she guessed they belonged to the family that was newly come to settle at the Hills, which she described, though she could not tell the name. She would not be denied the pleasure of showing them the shortest and safest way, and the only way by which they could get home before it was night-fall. So they accepted her kind offer, and she trudged on, talking as she went.

"It is a weary thing, ladies, to live in this lone place, where one does not see a soul to speak to from one month's end to another—especially to me that has lived afore now in my younger days in Lon'on. But it's as God pleases! and I wish none had greater troubles in this world than I—You were up at the house, ladies? There within at my little place—ay—then you saw the greatest and the only great trouble I have, or ever had in this life.—Did not you, ladies, see the young woman with the child in her arms?—But may be you did not mind Kate, and she's nothing now to look at, quite faded and gone, though she's only one month past nineteen years of age. I am sure I ought to know, for I was at her christening, and nursed her mother. She's of very good parentage, that is, of a farmer's family, that has, as well as his neighbours, that lives a great way off, quite on the other side of the country. And not a year, at least not a year and a half ago, I remember Kate Robinson dancing on the green at Squire Burton's there with the rest of the girls of the village, and without compare the prettiest and freshest, and most blithsome and innocent of them all. Ay, she was innocent then, none ever more so, and she had no care, but all looking kind upon her in this world, and fond parents taking pride in her—and now look at her what she is! Cast off by all, shamed, and forgotten, and broken-hearted, and lost as much as if she was in her grave. And better she was in her grave than as she is."

The old woman now really felt so much that she stopped speaking, and she was silent for several minutes.

"Ah! dear ladies," said she, looking up at Rosamond and Caroline, "I see you have kind hearts within you, and I thank you for pitying poor Kate."

"I wish we could do any thing to serve her," said Caroline.

"Ah! miss, that I am afraid you can't—that's what I am afraid none can now." The good woman paused and looked as if she expected to be questioned. Caroline was silent, and the old woman looked disappointed.

"We do not like to question you," said Rosamond, "lest we should ask what you might not like to answer, or what the young woman would be sorry that you should answer."

"Why, miss, that's very considerate in you, and only that I know it would be for her benefit, I am sure I would not have said a word—but here I have so very little to give her, and that little so coarse fare to what she been used to, both when she was at service, and when she was with her own people, that I be afraid, weak as she be grown now, she won't do. And though I have been a good nurse in my day, I think she wants now a bit better doctor than I be—and then if she could see the minister, to take the weight off her heart, to make her not fret so, to bid her look up above for comfort, and to raise her with the hope and trust that God will have more mercy upon her than her father and mother do have; and to make her—hardest of all!—forget him that has forsaken her and her little one, and been so cruel—Oh! ladies, to do all that, needs a person that can speak to her better and with more authority than I can."

The poor woman stopped again for some minutes, and then recollecting that she had not told what she had intended to tell, she said, "I suppose, ladies, you guess now how it be, and I ought to beg pardon for speaking of such a thing, or such a one, as—as poor Kate is now, to you, young ladies; but though she is fallen so low, and an outcast, she is not hardened; and if it had been so that it had pleased Heaven that she had been a wife to one in her own condition—Oh! what a wife, and what a mother there was lost in her! The man that wronged her has a deal to answer for. But he has no thought of that, nor care for her, or his child; but he is a fine man about London, they say, driving about with colonels, and lords, and dancing with ladies. Oh! if they saw Kate, one would guess they would not think so much of him: but yet, may be, they'd think more—there's no saying how the quality ladies judge on these matters. But this I know, that though he was very free of his money, and generous to Kate at the first, and even for some months after he quit the country, till I suppose he forgot her, yet he has not sent her a guinea for self or child these four months, nor a line of a letter of any kind, which she pined for more, and we kept thinking the letters she did write did not get to him by the post, so we sent one by a grandson of my own, that we knowed would put the letter safe into his hands, and did, just as the young gentleman was, as my grandson told me, coming out of a fine house in London, and going, with a long whip in his hand, to get upon the coach-box of a coach, with four horses too—and he looks at the letter, and puts it in his pocket, and calls to my boy, 'No answer now, my good friend—but I'll write by post to her.' Those were the very words; and then that colonel that was with him laughing and making game like, went to snatch the letter out of the pocket, saying, 'Show us that love-letter, Buckhurst'—Lord forgive me! what have I done now?" said the old woman, stopping short, struck by the sudden change in the countenance of both her auditors.

"Mr. Buckhurst Falconer is a relation of ours," said Rosamond.

"Dear ladies, how could I think you knew him even?" interrupted the old woman. "I beg your pardon. Kate says he's not so cruel as he seems, and that if he were here this minute, he'd be as kind and generous to her as ever.—It's all forgetfulness just, and giddiness, she says—or, may be, as to the money, that he has it not to spare."

"To spare!" repeated Caroline, indignantly.

"Lord love her! what a colour she has now—and what a spirit spoke there! But, ladies, I'd be sorry to hurt the young gentleman; for Kate would be angry at me for that worse than at any thing. And as to all that has happened, you know it's nothing extraordinary, but what happens every day, by all accounts; and young gentlemen, such as he be, thinks nothing of it; and the great ladies, I know, by what I noticed when I was in sarvice once in Lon'on myself, the great ladies thinks the better of them for such things."

"I am not a great lady," said Caroline.

"Nor I, thank God!" said Rosamond.

"Well, for certain, if you are not great, you're good ladies," said the old woman.

As they were now within sight of their own house, they thanked and dismissed their loquacious but kind-hearted guide, putting into her hand some money for poor Kate, Caroline promising to make further inquiries—Rosamond, without restriction, promising all manner of assistance, pecuniary, medical, and spiritual.

The result of the inquiries that were made confirmed the truth of all that old Dorothy had related, and brought to light other circumstances relative to the seduction and desertion of this poor girl, which so shocked Rosamond, that in proportion to her former prepossession in Buckhurst's favour was now her abhorrence; and as if to repair the imprudence with which she had formerly used her influence over her sister's mind in his favour, she now went as far on the opposite side, abjuring him with the strongest expressions of indignation, and wishing that Caroline's last letter had not gone to Buckhurst, that she might have given her refusal on this special account, in the most severe and indignant terms the English language could supply.

Mrs. Percy, however, on the contrary, rejoiced that Caroline's letter had been sent before they knew any thing of this affair.

"But, ma'am," cried Rosamond, "surely it would have been right for Caroline to have given this reason for her refusal, and to have declared that this had proved to her beyond a possibility of doubt that her former objections to Mr. Buckhurst Falconer's principles were too well founded; and it would have become Caroline to have written with strong indignation. I am persuaded," continued Rosamond, "that if women would reprobate young men for such instances of profligacy and cruelty, instead of suffering such conduct to go under the fine plausible general names of gallantry and wildness, it would make a greater impression than all the sermons that could be preached. And Caroline, who has beauty and eloquence, can do this with effect. I remember Godfrey once said, that the peculiar characteristic of Caroline, that in which she differed most from the common herd of young ladies, is in her power of feeling and expressing virtuous indignation. I am sure that Godfrey, partial as he is to Mr. Buckhurst Falconer, would think that Caroline ought, on such an occasion, to set an example of that proper spirit, which, superior to the fear of ridicule and fashion, dares to speak the indignation it feels."

"Very well spoken, and better felt, my dear daughter," said Mrs. Percy. "And Heaven forbid I should lower the tone of your mind, or your honest indignation against vice; but, Rosamond, my dear, let us be just.—I must do even those, whom Godfrey calls the common herd of young ladies, the justice to believe that there are many among them who have good feeling enough to be angry, very angry, with a lover upon such an occasion—angry enough to write him a most indignant, and, perhaps, very eloquent letter.—You may recollect more than one heroine of a novel, who discards her lover upon such a discovery as was made by you last night. It is a common novel incident, and, of course, from novels every young lady, even, who might not have felt without a precedent, knows how she ought to express herself in such circumstances. But you will observe, my dear, that both in novels and in real life, young ladies generally like and encourage men of feeling in contradistinction to men of principle, and too often men of gallantry in preference to men of correct morals: in short, that such a character as that of Mr. Buckhurst Falconer is just the kind of person with whom many women would fall in love. By suffering this to be thought the taste of our sex, ladies encourage libertinism in general, more than they can possibly discourage it by the loudest display of indignation against particular instances.—If, like your sister Caroline, young ladies would show that they really do not prefer such men, it would do essential service. And observe, my dear Rosamond, this can be done by every young woman with perfect delicacy: but I do not see how she can, with propriety or good effect, do more. It is a subject ladies cannot well discuss; a subject upon which the manners and customs of the world are so much at variance with religion and morality, that entering upon the discussion would lead to greater difficulties than you are aware of. It is, therefore, best for our sex to show their disapprobation of vice, and to prove their sense of virtue and religion by their conduct, rather than to proclaim it to the world in words. Had Caroline in her letter expressed her indignation in the most severe terms that the English language could supply, she would only have exposed herself to the ridicule of Mr. Buckhurst Falconer's fashionable companions, as a prating, preaching prude, without doing the least good to him, or to any one living."

Rosamond reluctantly acknowledged that perhaps her mother was right.

"But, Caroline, how quietly you sit by, while we are talking of you and your lover!" cried Rosamond; "I do not know whether to be provoked with you, or to admire you."

"Admire me, pray," said Caroline, "if you can."

"I do not believe you will ever be in love," said Rosamond. "I confess I should admire, or, at least, love you better, if you had more feeling," added Rosamond, hastily.

"By what do you judge that I want feeling?" said Caroline, colouring deeply, and with a look and tone that expressed her keen sense of injustice. "What proof have I ever given you of my want of feeling?"

"No proof, that I can recollect," said Rosamond, laughing; "no proof, but that you have never been in love."

"Is it a proof I am incapable of feeling, that I have not been in love with one who has proved himself utterly unworthy of my esteem—against whose conduct my sister cannot find words sufficiently severe to express her indignation? Rosamond, my mind inclined towards him at the first reading of his last letter; but if I had ever given him any encouragement, if I had loved him, what would have been my misery at this moment!"

"All! my dear, but then if you had been very miserable, I should have pitied you so much, and loved you so heartily for being in love," said Rosamond, still laughing—

"Oh! Rosamond," continued Caroline, whose mind was now too highly wrought for raillery, "is love to be trifled with? No, only by trifling minds or by rash characters, by those who do not conceive its power— its danger. Recollect what we have just seen: a young, beautiful woman sinking into the grave with shame—deserted by her parents—wishing her child unborn. Do you remember her look of agony when we praised that child? the strongest charm of nature reversed—the strongest ties dissolved; and love brought her to this! She is only a poor servant girl. But the highest and the fairest, those of the most cultivated understandings, of the tenderest hearts, cannot love bring them down to the same level—to the same fate?—And not only our weak sex, but over the stronger sex, and the strongest of the strong, and the wisest of the wise, what is, what has ever been the power, the delusions of that passion, which can cast a spell over the greatest hero, throw a blot on the brightest glory, blast in a moment a life of fame!—What must be the power of that passion, which can inspire genius in the dullest and the coldest, waken heroism in the most timid of creatures, exalt to the highest point, or to the lowest degrade our nature—the bitterest curse, or the sweetest blessing Heaven bestows on us in this life!—Oh! sister, is love to be trifled with?"

Caroline paused, and Rosamond, for some instants, looked at her and at her mother in silence; then exclaimed, "All this from Caroline! Are not you astonished, mother?"

"No," said Mrs. Percy; "I was aware that this was in Caroline's mind."

"I was not," said Rosamond. "She who never spoke of love!—I little imagined that she thought of it so highly, so seriously."

"Yes, I do think of it seriously, highly may Heaven grant!" cried Caroline, looking fervently upwards as she spoke with an illuminated countenance. "May Heaven grant that love be a blessing and not a curse to me! Heaven grant that I may never, in any moment of selfish vanity, try to excite a passion which I cannot return! Heaven grant that I never may feel the passion of love but for one whom I shall entirely esteem, who shall be worthy to fill my whole soul!"

"Mother," continued Caroline, turning eagerly, and seizing her mother's hand, "my guide, my guardian, whenever you see me in any, the slightest inclination to coquetry, warn me—as you wish to save me from that which I should most dread, the reproaches of my own conscience—in the first, the very first instance, reprove me, mother, if you can—with severity. And you, my sister, my bosom friend, do not use your influence to soften, to open my mind to love; but if ever you perceive me yielding my heart to the first tenderness of the passion, watch over me, if the object be not every way worthy of me, my equal, my superior.—Oh! as you would wish to snatch me from the grave, rouse me from the delusion—save me from disappointment, regret, remorse, which I know that I could not bear, and live."

Her mother, into whose arms she threw herself, pressed Caroline close to her heart, while Rosamond, to whom she had given her hand, held it fast, and stood motionless between surprise and sympathy. Caroline, to whose usual manners and disposition every thing theatrical or romantic was so foreign, seemed, as soon as she recollected herself, to be ashamed of the excessive emotion and enthusiasm she had shown; withdrawing her hand from her sister, she turned away, and left the room.

Her mother and sister both remained silent for a considerable time, fully occupied with their own thoughts and feelings. The mother's reverie looked to the future prospects of her daughter;—confident in Caroline's character, yet uncertain of her fate, she felt a pleasing yet painful solicitude.

Rosamond's thoughts turned rather to the past than to the future: she recollected and compared words and looks, yet found insuperable difficulty in connecting all she had ever before known or fancied of Caroline with what she had just seen and heard. Rosamond did not fairly recover from her surprise, and from her look of perplexity, during a full hour that she remained absolutely silent, poring upon a screen, upon which she saw nothing.

She then went in search of Caroline, in hopes of renewing the conversation; but she found her busied in some of the common affairs of life, and apparently a different person.

Rosamond, though she made divers attempts, could not lead Caroline back again to the same train of thought, or tone of expression. Indeed, Rosamond did not attempt it very skilfully, but rather with the awkward impatience of one not accustomed to use address. Caroline, intent upon the means of assisting the poor young woman whom they had seen at the cottage, went there again as soon as she could, to warn old Dorothy, in the first place, to be less communicative, and not on any account to mention to any one else the names and circumstances which she had told them with so little reserve. Caroline next applied to Dr. Leicester, the vicar of their former parish, a most amiable and respectable clergyman, who had come from his vicarage, near Percy-hall, to spend what time he could spare from his duties with his favourite parishioners; at Caroline's request he willingly went to see this unhappy young woman, and succeeded in his endeavours to soothe and tranquillize her mind by speaking to her words of peace. His mild piety raised and comforted the trembling penitent; and while all prospect of forgiveness from her parents, or of happiness in this world, was at an end, he fixed her thoughts on those better hopes and promises which religion only can afford. Her health appeared suddenly to mend when her mind was more at ease: but this was only transient, and Dr. Percy, to whom Caroline applied for his medical opinion, gave little hopes of her recovery. All that could be done by medicine and proper kindness to assuage her sufferings during her decline was done in the best manner by Mrs. Percy and her daughters, especially by Caroline: the young woman, nevertheless, died in six weeks, and was buried without Buckhurst Falconer's making any inquiry concerning her, probably without his knowing of her death. A few days after she was no more, a letter came to her from him, which was returned unopened by Dorothy, who could just write well enough to make these words intelligible in the cover:

"SIR,

"Kate Robinson is dead—this four days—your child is with me still, and well.—She bid me tell you, if ever you asked more concerning her—she left you her forgiveness on her death-bed, and hopes you will be happy, sir.—

"Your humble servant,

"DOROTHY WHITE."

A bank note of ten pounds was received by Dorothy soon afterwards for the use of the child, and deep regret was expressed by the father for the death of its mother. But, as Dorothy said, "that came too late to be of any good to her."

CHAPTER XIV

Soon after the death of poor Kate, the attention of the Percy family was taken up by a succession of different visits; some from their old neighbours and really affectionate friends, some from among the band of reproaching condolers. The first we shall mention, who partook of the nature of both these classes, was Lady Jane Granville: she was a sincere and warm friend, but a tormenting family adviser and director.

Her ladyship was nearly related to Mr. Percy, which gave her, on this occasion, rights of which she knew how to avail herself.

To do her justice, she was better qualified to be an adviser and protector than many who assume a familiar tone and character.

Lady Jane Granville was of high birth and fortune, had always lived in good company, had seen a great deal of the world, both abroad and at home; she had a complete knowledge of all that makes people well received in society, had generalized her observations, and had formed them into maxims of prudence and politeness, which redounded the more to her credit in conversation, as they were never committed to writing, and could, therefore, never be brought to the dangerous test of being printed and published. Her ladyship valued her own traditional wisdom, and oral instruction, beyond any thing that can be learned from books. She had acquired a tact, which, disclaiming and disdaining every regular process of reasoning, led her with admirable certainty to right conclusions in her own concerns, and thus, in some degree, justified the peremptory tone she assumed in advising others.

Though by no means pleased with Mr. and Mrs. Percy's answer to several of her letters of counsel, yet she thought it her duty, as a friend and relation, to persevere. She invited herself to the Hills, where, with great difficulty, through scarcely practicable cross roads, she arrived. She was so much fatigued and exhausted, in body and mind, that during the first evening she could talk of nothing but her hair-breadth escapes. The next morning after breakfast, she began with, "My dear Mr. Percy, now I have a moment's ease, I have a thousand things to say to you. I am very much surprised that you have thought fit to settle here quite out of the world. Will you give me leave to speak my mind freely to you on the subject?"

"As freely as you please, my dear Lady Jane, upon any subject, if you will only promise not to be offended, if we should not coincide in opinion."

"Certainly, certainly; I am sure I never expect or wish any body to submit to my opinion, though I have had opportunities of seeing something of the world: but I assure you, that nothing but very particular regard would induce me to offer my advice. It is a maxim of mine, that family interference begins in ill-breeding and ends in impertinence, and accordingly it is a thing I have ever particularly avoided. But with a particular friend and near relation like you, my dear Mr. Percy, I think there ought to be an exception. Now, my dear sir, the young people have just left the room—I can take this opportunity of speaking freely: your daughters—what will you do with them?"

"Do with them! I beg pardon for repeating your ladyship's words, but I don't precisely understand your question."

"Well, precise sir, then, in other words, how do you mean to dispose of them?"

"I don't mean to dispose of them at all," said Mr. Percy.

"Then let me tell you, my good friend," said Lady Jane, with a most prophetic tone, "let me tell you, that you will live to repent that.—You know I have seen something of the world—you ought to bring them forward, and make the most of their birth, family, and connexions, put them in a way of showing their accomplishments, make proper acquaintance, and obtain for your girls what I call the patronage of fashion."

"Patronage!" repeated Mr. Percy: "it seems to be my doom to hear of nothing but patronage, whichever way I turn. What! patronage for my daughters as well as for my sons!"

"Yes," said Lady Jane, "and look to it; for your daughters will never go on without it. Upon their first coming out, you should—" Here her ladyship stopped short, for Caroline and Rosamond returned. "Oh! go on, go on, let me beg of your ladyship," said Mr. Percy: "why should not my daughters have the advantage of hearing what you are saying?"

"Well, then, I will tell them candidly that upon their first coming out, it will be an inconceivable advantage, whatever you may think of it, to have the patronage of fashion! Every day we see many an ugly face, many a mere simpleton, many a girl who had nothing upon earth but her dress, become quite charming, when the radiance of fashion is upon them. And there are some people who can throw this radiance where and on whom they please, just as easily," said Lady Jane, playing with a spoon she held in her hand, "just as easily as I throw the sunshine now upon this object and now upon that, now upon Caroline and now upon Rosamond. And, observe, no eye turns upon the beauteous Caroline now, because she is left in the shade."

It was Mr. Percy's policy to allow Lady Jane full liberty to finish all she wished to say without interruption; for when people are interrupted, they imagine they have much more to add. Let them go on, and they come to the end of their sense, and even of their words, sooner than they or you could probably expect.

"Now," continued her ladyship, "to apply to living examples; you know Mrs. Paul Cotterel?"

"No."

"Well!—Lady Peppercorn?"

"No."

"Nor the Miss Blissets?"

"No."

"That is the misfortune of living so much out of the world!—But there are the Falconers, we all know them at least—now look at the Miss Falconers."

"Alas! we have not the honour of knowing even the Miss Falconers," said Mr. Percy, "though they are our cousins."

"Is it possible that you don't know the Miss Falconers?"

"Very possible," replied Mr. Percy: "they live always in town, and we have never seen them since they were children: except a visit or two which passed between us just after Mrs. Falconer's marriage, we know nothing even of her, though we are all acquainted with the commissioner, who comes from time to time to this part of the country."

"A very clever man is the commissioner in his way," said Lady Jane, "but nothing to his wife. I can assure you, Mrs. Falconer is particularly well worth your knowing; for unless maternal rivalship should interfere, I know few people in the world who could be more useful to your girls when you bring them out. She has a vast deal of address. And for a proof, as I was going to point out to you, there are the Miss Falconers in the first circles—asked every where—yet without fortunes, and with no pretensions beyond, or equal to, what your daughters have—not with half Rosamond's wit and information— nothing comparable in point of beauty and accomplishments, to Caroline; yet how they have got on! See what fashion can do! Come, come, we must court her patronage—leave that to me: I assure you I understand the ways and means."

"I have no doubt of that," said Mr. Percy. "All that your ladyship has said is excellent sense, and incontrovertible as far as—"

"Oh! I knew you would think so: I knew we should understand one another as soon as you had heard all I had to say."

"Excellent sense, and incontrovertible, as far as it relates to the means, but perhaps we may not agree as to the ends; and if these are different, you know your means, though the best adapted for gaining your objects, may be quite useless or unfit for the attainment of mine."

"At once, then, we can't differ as to our objects, for it is my object to see your daughters happily married; now tell me," said Lady Jane, appealing alternately to Mr. and Mrs. Percy, "honestly tell me, is not this your object—and yours?"

"Honestly, it is," said Mr. and Mrs. Percy.

"That's right—I knew we must agree there."

"But," said Mrs. Percy, "allow me to ask what you mean by happily married?"

"What do I mean? Just what you mean—what every body means at the bottom of their hearts: in the first place married to men who have some fortune."

"What does your ladyship mean by some fortune?"

"Why—you have such a strange way of not understanding! We who live in the world must speak as the world speaks—we cannot recur continually to a philosophical dictionary, and if we had recourse to it, we should only be sent from a to z, and from z back again to a; see affluence, see competence, see luxury, see philosophy, and see at last that you see nothing, and that you knew as much before you opened the book as when you shut it—which indeed is what I find to be the case with most books I read."

Triumphant from the consciousness of having hitherto had all the wit on her side, Lady Jane looked round, and continued: "Though I don't pretend to draw my maxims from books, yet this much I do know, that in matrimony, let people have ever so much sense, and merit, and love, and all that, they must have bread and butter into the bargain, or it won't do."

"Certainly," said Mrs. Percy: "under that head I suppose you include all the necessaries of life."

"And some of the luxuries, if you please; for in these days luxuries are become necessaries."

"A barouche and four, for instance?" said Mrs. Percy.

"Oh! no, no—my dear madam, I speak within bounds; you cannot expect a barouche and four for girls who have nothing."

"I expect it as little as I wish it for them," said Mrs. Percy, smiling; "and as little as my daughters, I believe, desire it."

"But if such a thing should offer, I presume you would not wish that Rosamond or Caroline should refuse?"

"That depends upon who offers it," said Mrs. Percy. "But whatever my wishes might be, I should, as I believe I safely may, leave my daughters entirely at liberty to judge and decide for themselves."

"Yes, I believe you safely may," said Lady Jane, "as long as you keep them here. You might as well talk of leaving them at liberty in the deserts of Arabia. You don't expect that knights and squires should come hither in quest of your damsels?"

"Then you would have the damsels sally forth in quest of the knights and squires?" said Mr. Percy.

"Let them sally forth at any rate," said Lady Jane, laughing; "nobody has a right to ask in quest of what. We are not now in the times of ancient romance, when young ladies were to sit straight-laced at their looms, or never to stir farther than to their bower windows."

"Young ladies must now go a great deal farther," said Mr. Percy, "before the discourteous knights will deign to take any notice of them."

"Ay, indeed, it is shameful!" said Lady Jane sighing. "I declare it is shameful!" repeated she, indignantly. "Do you know, that last winter at Bath the ladies were forced to ask the gentlemen to dance?"

"Forced?" said Mr. Percy.

"Yes, forced!" said Lady Jane, "or else they must have sat still all night like so many simpletons."

"Sad alternative!" said Mr. Percy; "and what is worse, I understand that partners for life are scarcely to be had on easier terms; at least so I am informed by one of your excellent modern mothers, Mrs. Chatterton, who has been leading her three gawky graces about from one watering-place to another these six years, fishing, and hunting, and hawking for husbands. 'There now! I have carried my girls to Bath, and to London, and to Tunbridge, and to Weymouth, and to Cheltenham, and every where; I am sure I can do no more for them.' I assure you," continued Mr. Percy, "I have heard Mrs. Chatterton say these very words in a room full of company."

"In a room full of company? Shocking!" said Lady Jane. "But then poor Mrs. Chatterton is a fool, you know; and, what is worse, not well mannered,—how should she? But I flatter myself, if you will trust me with your daughter Caroline, we should manage matters rather better. Now let me tell you my plan. My plan is to take Caroline with me immediately to Tunbridge, previous to her London campaign. Nothing can be a greater mistake than to keep a young lady up, and prevent her being seen till the moment when she is to be brought out: it is of incalculable advantage that, previously to her appearance in the great world, she should have been seen by certain fashionable prôneurs. It is essential that certain reports respecting her accomplishments and connexions should have had time to circulate properly."

All this Mr. and Mrs. Percy acknowledged, in as unqualified a manner as Lady Jane could desire, was fit and necessary to secure what is called a young lady's success in the fashionable world; but they said that it was not their object to dispose of their daughters, as it is called, to the best advantage. The arts which are commonly practised for this purpose they thought not only indelicate, but ultimately impolitic and absurd; for men in general are now so well aware of them, that they avoid the snares, and ridicule and detest those by whom they are contrived. If, now and then, a dupe be found, still the chance is, that the match so made turns out unhappily; at best, attachments formed in public places, and in the hurry of a town life, can seldom be founded on any real knowledge of character, or suitableness of taste and temper. "It is much more probable," added Mrs. Percy, "that happy marriages should be made where people have leisure and opportunities of becoming really and intimately acquainted with each other's dispositions."

"Vastly well!" said Lady Jane: "so you mean to bury your daughters in the country—to shut them up, at least—all the days of their unfortunate lives?"

Mr. and Mrs. Percy, both at the same moment, eagerly declared that they had no such absurd or cruel intention towards their daughters. "On the contrary," said Mr. Percy, "we shall take every proper occasion, that our present fortune and situation will allow, of letting them see agreeable and sensible persons."

"Are they to spring out of the ground, these agreeable and sensible persons?" said Lady Jane. "Whom do you see in this desert, or expect to see?"

"We see your ladyship, in the first place," said Mr. Percy: "you cannot therefore wonder if we are proud enough to expect to see sometimes good company, persons of merit, and even of fashion, though we have lost our station and fortune."

"That is very politely turned by you, Mr. Percy. Much more polite than my desert. But I could not bear the thoughts of your sweet pretty Caroline's blushing unseen."

"Nor could we," said Mr. Percy, "bear the thoughts of her ceasing to blush from being too much seen. We could not bear the thoughts of fitting our daughters out, and sending them to the London market, with the portionless class of matrimonial adventurers, of whom even the few that succeed are often doomed but to splendid misery in marriage; and the numbers who fail in their venture are, after a certain time, consigned to neglect and contempt in single wretchedness. Here, on the contrary, in the bosom of their own families, without seeking to entice or entrap, they can at all events never be disappointed or degraded; and, whether married or single, will be respected and respectable, in youth and age—secure of friends, and of a happy home."

"Happy nonsense! begging your pardon, my dear coz. Shall I tell you what the end of all this living in the bosom of their own families will be?—that they will die old maids. For mercy's sake, my dear Mrs. Percy, do not let Mr. Percy be philosophical for your daughters, whatever he may be for himself. You, I am sure, cannot wish your poor daughters to be old maids," said her ladyship, with a tremendous accent upon the word.

"No, I should wish them to marry, if I could ensure for them good husbands, not merely good fortunes. The warmest wish of my heart," cried Mrs. Percy, "is to see my daughters as happy as I am myself, married to men of their own choice, whom they can entirely esteem, and fondly love. But I would rather see my daughters in their graves than see them throw themselves away upon men unworthy of them, or sell themselves to husbands unsuited to them, merely for the sake of being established, for the vulgar notion of getting married, or to avoid the imaginary and unjust ridicule of being old maids."

The warmth and energy with which these last words were spoken, by so gentle a person as Mrs. Percy, surprised Lady Jane so much, that she was silent; all her ideas being suddenly at a stand, and her sagacity at fault. Mr. Percy proposed a walk to show her the Hills; as her ladyship rose to accompany him, she said to herself, "Who could have guessed that Mrs. Percy was so romantic?—But she has caught it from her husband.—What a strange father and mother!—But for the sake of the poor girls, I will not give up the point. I will have Caroline with me to Tunbridge, and to town, in spite of their wise heads."

She renewed her attack in the evening after tea. Rising, and walking towards the window, "A word with you, Mr. Percy, if you please. The young people are going to walk, and now we can talk the matter over by ourselves."

"Why should not we talk it over before the young people?" said Mr. Percy. "We always speak of every thing openly in this family," continued he, turning to Lady Jane; "and I think that is one reason why we live so happily together. I let my children know all my views for them, all my affairs, and my opinions, I may say all my thoughts, or how could I expect them to trust me with theirs?"

"As to that, children are bound by gratitude to treat their parents with perfect openness," said Lady Jane; "and it is the duty of children, you know, to make their parents their confidants upon all occasions."

"Duty and gratitude are excellent things," said Mr. Percy, "but somewhat more is necessary between parent and child to produce friendship. Recollect the Duc d'Epernon's reply to his king, who reproached him with want of affection. 'Sire, you may command my services, my life; but your majesty knows, friendship is to be won only by friendship.'"

"Very true," said Lady Jane; "but friendship is not, properly speaking, the connexion that subsists between parents and children."

"I am sorry you think so," said Mr. Percy, smiling: "pray do not teach my children that doctrine."

"Nay," said Lady Jane, "no matter whether we call it friendship or not; I will answer for it, that without any refined notions about perfect openness and confidence, your children will be fond of you, if you are indulgent to them in certain points. Caroline, my dear," said she, turning to Caroline, who was at the farthest end of the room, "don't look so unconscious, for you are a party concerned; so come and kneel at the feet of this perverse father of yours, to plead your cause and mine—I must take you with me to Tunbridge. You must let me have her a summer and winter, and I will answer for Caroline's success."

"What does your ladyship mean by my success?" said Caroline.

"Why, child—Now don't play your father's philosophic airs upon me! We people who live in the world, and not with philosophers, are not prepared for such entrapping interrogatories. But come, I mean in plain English, my dear, though I am afraid it will shock your ears, that you will be" (speaking loud) "pretty well admired, pretty well abused, and—oh, shocking!—pretty well married."

"Pretty well married!" repeated Mrs. Percy, in a scornful tone: "but neither Caroline nor I should be satisfied unless she be very well married."

"Heyday! There is no knowing where to have you lady philosophers. This morning you did not desire a coach and four for your daughters, not you; now you quarrel with me on the other side of the question. Really, for a lady of moderation, you are a little exorbitant. Pretty well married, you know, implies 2000l. a-year; and very well married, nothing under 10,000l."

"Is that the language of the market? I did not understand the exact meaning of very well married—did you, Caroline? I own I expect something more than 10,000l. a-year."

"More!—you unconscionable wretch! how much more?" said Lady Jane.

"Infinitely more," said Mr. Percy: "I expect a man of sense, temper, and virtue, who would love my daughter as she deserves to be loved."

"Let me advise you," said Lady Jane, in her very gravest tone, "not to puff up Caroline's imagination with a parcel of romantic notions.—I never yet knew any good done by it. Depend on it you will be disappointed, if you expect a genius to descend from the clouds express for your daughters. Let them do as other people do, and they may have a chance of meeting with some good sort of men, who will make them as happy as—as happy as their neighbours."

"And how happy is that?" said Caroline: "as happy as we are now?"

"As you are now!" said Lady Jane: "a vastly pretty maidenly speech! But young ladies, nevertheless, usually think that the saffron robe of Hymen would not be the most unbecoming dress in the world; and whether it be in compliance with their daughters' taste, or their own convenience, most parents are in a hurry to purchase it."

"Sometimes at the expense of their daughters' happiness for life," said Mrs. Percy.

"Well, lest we should go over the same ground, and get into the same labyrinth, where we lost ourselves this morning, let me come to the point at once.—May I hope, Mr. and Mrs. Percy, to have the pleasure of Caroline's company at Tunbridge next week, and in town next winter, or not?—That is the question."

"That is a question which your ladyship will be so good as to ask Caroline, if you please," said Mr. Percy; "both her mother and I wish that she should decide for herself."

"Indeed?" cried Lady Jane: "then, my dear Caroline, if you please, come with me this minute to my dressing-room, and we'll settle it all at my toilette de nuit. I have a notion," added her ladyship, as she drew Caroline's arm within hers, and led her out of the room, "I have a notion that I shall not find you quite so impracticable as your father has shown himself."

"You may leave us, Keppel," said Lady Jane to her maid, as she went into her dressing-room—"I will ring when I want you.—My love," said she to Caroline, who stood beside her dressing-table, "why did not you let Keppel dress your hair to-day?—But no matter—when I once get you to town, we'll manage it all our own way. I have a notion that you are not of a positive temper."

Caroline coloured at this speech.

"I see what are you thinking of," said Lady Jane, mistaking her countenance; "and to tell you the truth, I also am sadly afraid, by what I see, that we shall hardly gain our point. I know your father—some difficulty will be started, and ten to one he will not allow me to have you at last, unless you try and persuade him yourself."

"I never try to persuade my father to do any thing."

"What, then, he is not a man to be persuaded?"

"No," said Caroline, smiling; "but what is much better, he is a man to be convinced."

"Better!" exclaimed Lady Jane: "Why surely you had not rather live with a man you were to convince than one you could persuade?"

"Would it not be safer?" said Caroline: "the arts of persuasion might be turned against us by others, but the power of conviction never could."

"Now, my dear, you are too deep for me," replied Lady Jane. "You said very little in our long debate this morning, and I'm afraid I said too much; but I own I could not help speaking candidly. Between ourselves, your father has some notions, which, you know, are a little odd."

"My father!" exclaimed Caroline.

"Yes, my dear, though he is your father, and my relation too, you know one cannot be quite blinded by partiality—and I never would give up my judgment."

"Nor would I," said Caroline. "Nor I am sure would my father ever desire it. You see how freely he permits, he encourages us all to converse with him. He is never displeased with any of us for being of a different opinion from him."

"He may not show displeasure," said Lady Jane.

"Oh! he does not feel it, ma'am—I assure you," said Caroline, with emotion. "You do not know my father, indeed you do not."

"My dear," said Lady Jane, retracting, "I know he is an excellent father, and I am sure I would have you think so—it is your duty; but, at the same time, you know he is not infallible, and you must not insist," added she, sharply, "upon all the world being of one way of thinking.—My dear, you are his favourite, and it is no wonder you defend him."

"Indeed, ma'am," said Caroline, "if I am his favourite, I do not know it."

"My dear, don't mistake me. It is no wonder that you are. You must be a favourite with every body; and yet," said Lady Jane, and she paused, "as you hinted, perhaps I am mistaken; I think Rosamond seems— hey?—Now tell me candidly—which is the favourite?"

"I would if I knew," said Caroline.

"Oh! but there must be some favourite in a family—I know there must; and since you will not speak, I guess how it is. Perhaps, if I had asked your sister Rosamond to go to town with me next winter, your father would have been better pleased, and would have consented more readily."

"To lose her company if she were his favourite?" said Caroline, smiling.

"But you know, my dear," continued Lady Jane, without hearing or attending to this, "you know, my dear, that Rosamond, though a very good girl and very sensible, I am sure, yet she has not your personal advantages, and I could do nothing for her in town, except, perhaps, introduce her at Mrs. Cator's, and Lady Spilsbury's, or Lady Angelica Headingham's conversazione—Rosamond has a mixture of naïveté and sprightliness that is new, and might take. If she had more courage, and would hazard more in conversation, if she had, in short, l'art de se faire valoir, one could hand her verses about, and get her forward in the bel-esprit line. But she must stay till we have brought you into fashion, my dear, and another winter, perhaps—Well, my love, I will not keep you up longer. On Monday, if you please, we shall go—since you say you are sure your father is in earnest, in giving you leave to decide for yourself."

What was Lady Jane Granville's astonishment, when she heard Caroline decline, with polite thanks, her kind invitation!

Her ladyship stood silent with suspended indignation.

"This cannot be your own determination, child?"

"I beg your ladyship's pardon—it is entirely my own. When a person is convinced by good reasons, those reasons surely become their own. But independently of all the arguments which I have heard from my father and mother, my own feelings must prevent me from leaving home in our present circumstances. I cannot quit my parents and my sister, now they are, comparatively speaking, in distress. Neither in prosperity nor in adversity do I wish to leave my family, but certainly not in adversity."

"High-flown notions! Your family is not in any great distress, that I see: there is a change, to be sure, in the style of life; but a daughter more, you know only increases the—the difficulties."

"I believe my father and mother do not think so," said Caroline; "and till they do, I wish to stay with them, and share their fortune, whatever it may be."

"I have done—as you please—you are to decide for yourself, Miss Caroline Percy: this is your final determination?"

"It is," said Caroline; "but permit me," added she, taking Lady Jane's hand, and endeavouring by the kindest tone of gratitude to avert the displeasure which she saw gathering, "permit me to assure you, that I am truly grateful for your kindness, and I hope—I am sure, that I never shall forget it."

Lady Jane drew away her hand haughtily. "Permit me to assure you, Miss Caroline Percy, that there are few, very few young ladies indeed, even among my own nearest relations, to whom I would have undertaken to be chaperon. I do not know another young lady in England to whom I would have made the offer I have made to you, nor would that offer ever have been made could I reasonably have foreseen the possibility of its being refused. Let us say no more, ma'am, if you please—we understand one another now—and I wish you a good night."

Caroline retired, sorry to have displeased one who had shown so much friendly eagerness to serve her, yet not in the least disposed to change her determination. The next day Lady Jane's morning face boded no good. Mr. and Mrs. Percy in vain endeavoured by all the kind attentions in their power to assuage her feelings, but nothing restored her to that sweet temper in which she had begun the chapter of advice. She soon announced that she had received letters which called her immediately to Tunbridge, and her ladyship quitted the Hills, resolving never more to visit relations who would not be guided by her opinion.

The next persons who came to visit the Percy family in their retirement were Mrs. Hungerford and her daughter, Mrs. Mortimer, who had been friends and near neighbours whilst they resided at Percy-hall, and whose society they had particularly regretted. The distance at which they now lived from Hungerford Castle was such, that they had little hope that any intercourse could be kept up with its inhabitants, especially as Mrs. Hungerford had arrived at that time of life when she was exempted from the ceremony of visiting, and she seldom stirred from home except when she went to town annually to see her daughter Mortimer.

"So," said Mrs. Hungerford, as Mr. Percy helped her out of her carriage, "my good friend, you are surprised at seeing me, are you?—Ah! you thought I was too old or too lazy to come; but I am happy to be able to convince you that you are mistaken. See what motive will do! You know Mr. Percy says, that people can do any thing they please, and it is certain that it pleased me to do this."

When she was seated, and Mrs. Percy spoke of the distance from which she had kindly come to see them, she answered, "I hear people talk of a visiting distance; and I understand perfectly well what it means when acquaintance are in question, but for friends there is no visiting distance. Remove to the Land's End, and, old as I am, I will pursue and overtake you too, tortoise as I seem; and don't depend upon dark nights, for every night is full moon to me, when I am bent upon a visit to a friend; and don't depend upon hills—there are no Pyrenees between us."

These sound, perhaps, like mere civil speeches, but they came from one who always spoke sincerely, and who was no common person. Mrs. Hungerford was, by those who did not know her, thought proud; those who did, knew that she had reason to be proud. She was of noble descent, dignified appearance, polite manners, strong understanding, and high character. Her fortune, connexions, various knowledge, and extraordinary merit, had, during a long life, given her means of becoming acquainted with most of the persons of any celebrity or worth in her own or in foreign countries. No new candidate for fame appeared in any line of life, without desiring to be noticed by Mrs. Hungerford; no traveller of distinction or of literature visited England without providing himself with letters of introduction to Mrs. Hungerford, and to her accomplished daughter, the wife of Admiral Mortimer. In her early youth she had passed some years abroad, and had the vivacity, ease, polish, tact, and esprit de société of a Frenchwoman, with the solidity of understanding, amiable qualities, domestic tastes, and virtues of an Englishwoman. The mutual affection of this mother and daughter not only secured their own happiness, but diffused an additional charm over their manners, and increased the interest which they otherwise inspired. Mrs. Mortimer's house in London was the resort of the best company, in the best sense of the word: it was not that dull, dismal, unnatural thing, an English conversazione, where people are set, against their will and their nature, to talk wit; or reduced, against their pride and their conscience, to worship idols. This society partook of the nature of the best English and the best French society, judiciously combined: the French mixture of persons of talents and of rank, men of literature and of the world; the French habit of mingling feminine and masculine subjects of conversation, instead of separating the sexes, far as the confines of their prison-room will allow, into hostile parties, dooming one sex to politics, argument, and eternal sense, the other to scandal, dress, and eternal nonsense. Yet with these French manners there were English morals; with this French ease, gaiety, and politeness, English sincerity, confidence, and safety: no simagrée, no espionnage; no intrigue, political or gallant; none of that profligacy, which not only disgraced, but destroyed the reality of pleasure in Parisian society, at its most brilliant era. The persons of whom Mrs. Mortimer's society was formed were, in their habits and good sense, so thoroughly English, that, even had it been possible for them to put morality and religion out of the question, they would still have thought it quite as convenient and agreeable to love their own husbands and wives as to play at cross-purposes in gallanting their neighbours'. Of consequence, Mrs. Mortimer, in the bloom of youth and height of fashion, instead of being a coquette, "hunting after men with her eyes," was beloved, almost to adoration, as a daughter, a wife, a mother, a friend. Mrs. Hungerford, at an advanced age, was not a wretched, selfish Madame du Deffand, exacting hommage and attentions, yet disbelieving in the existence of friendship; complaining in the midst of all the luxuries of life, mental and corporeal, of being oppressed by ennui, unable to find any one to love and esteem, or incapable of loving and esteeming any one; Mrs. Hungerford, surrounded

"With all that should accompany old age,
As honour, love, obedience, troops of friends."

was, as she often declared, with gratitude to Providence, happier in age than she had been even in youth. With warm affections, and benevolence guided and governed in its objects by reason and religion; indulgent to human nature in general, and loving it, but not with German cosmopolitism—first and best, loving her daughter, her family, comprising a wide and happy extent of relations and connexions, sons and nephews in the army and navy, or in different employments in the state: many of these young men already distinguished, others wanting only opportunity to do equal honour to their name.

During the summer, Mrs. Mortimer usually spent some months at Hungerford Castle, and generally took with her from town some friends whose company she thought would peculiarly suit her mother's taste. Mrs. Hungerford had always been in the habit of inviting the Percy family, whenever she had any body with her whom she thought they would wish to see or hear; and thus the young people, though living retired in the country, had enjoyed the advantages of becoming early acquainted with many celebrated literary and public characters, and of living in the best society; these were advantages which they obtained from their education and their merit; for assuredly Mrs. Hungerford would never have troubled herself with them merely because they were her neighbours, possessing so many thousand pounds a year, and representatives of the Percy interest in the county.—A proof of which, if any were wanting, is, that she never took the least notice of those who now held their place at Percy-hall; and the first visit she paid when she came to the country, the first visit she had been known to pay for years, was to her friends the Percys, after they had lost their thousands per annum. So completely was it themselves and not their fortune which she had always considered, that she never condoled with them, and scarcely seemed to advert to any change in their circumstances. She perceived, to be sure, that she was not at Percy-hall; she discovered, probably, that she was in a small instead of a large room; the change of prospect from the windows struck her eye, and she remarked that this part of the country was more beautiful than that to which she had been accustomed.—As to the more or less of show, of dress, or equipage, these things did not merely make no difference in Mrs. Hungerford's estimation of persons, but in fact scarcely made any impression upon her senses or attention. She had been so much accustomed to magnificence upon a large scale, that the different subordinate degrees were lost upon her; and she had seen so many changes of fashion and of fortune, that she attached little importance to these. Regardless of the drapery of objects, she saw at once what was substantial and essential. It might, she thought, be one man's taste to visit her in a barouche and four, with half-a-dozen servants, and another person's pleasure to come without parade or attendants—this was indifferent to her. It was their conversation, their characters, their merit, she looked to; and many a lord and lady of showy dress and equipage, and vast importance in their own opinions, shrunk into insignificance in the company of Mrs. Hungerford; and, though in the room with her, passed before her eyes without making a sufficient sensation upon her organs to attract her notice, or to change the course of her thoughts.

All these peculiarities in this lady's character rendered her particularly agreeable to the Percy family in their present circumstances. She pressed them to pay her a long visit.

"You see," said Mrs. Hungerford, "that I had the grace to forbear asking this favour till I had possession of my daughter Mortimer, and could bring her with me to entice you.—And my dear young friends, you shall find young friends too, as well as old ones, at my house: my nieces, the Lady Pembrokes, are to be with me; and Lady Angelica Headingham, who will entertain you, though, perhaps, you will sometimes be tired for her, she works so hard aux galères de bel-esprit. I acknowledge she has a little too much affectation. But we must have charity for affectation and its multitude of foibles; for, you know, Locke says that it is only a mistaken desire to please. Angelica will find out her mistakes in time, and after trying all manners, will hold fast by the best—that is, the most natural: in the mean time, do you, my dear young friends, come and admire her as an inimitable actress. Then, Mr. Percy, I have for you three temptations—a man of letters, a man of science, and a man of sense. And, for the climax of my eloquence, I have reserved," continued she turning to Mrs. Percy, "my appeal to the mother's feelings. Know, then, that my son, my eldest hope, my colonel, has arrived from the continent—landed last night—I expect him home in a few days, and you must come and flatter me that he is prodigiously improved by the service he has seen, and the wounds which he can show, and assure me that, next to your own Godfrey, you would name my Gustavus, of all the officers in the army, as most deserving to be our commander-in-chief."

An invitation, which there were so many good and kind reasons for accepting, could not be refused. But before we go to Hungerford Castle, and before we see Colonel Hungerford—upon whom, doubtless, many a one at this instant, as well as Rosamond Percy, has formed designs or prognostics in favour of Caroline—we must read the following letter, and bring up the affairs of Alfred and Erasmus.

CHAPTER XV

LETTER FROM ALFRED PERCY TO HIS MOTHER.

"My Dear Mother,

"I am shocked by your story of Kate Robinson. I agree with you in rejoicing that Caroline had sufficient penetration to see the faults of Buckhurst Falconer's character, and steadiness enough, notwithstanding his agreeable talents, never to give him any encouragement. I agree with you, also, that it was fortunate that her last letter to him was written and sent before this affair came to her knowledge. It was much better that she should abide by her objection to his general principles than to have had explanations and discussions on a subject into which she could not enter with propriety.

"I will, as you desire, keep Buckhurst's secret. Indeed, in a worldly point of view, it behoves him that it should be carefully kept, because Bishop Clay, the prelate, who gave him his present living, though he tolerates gormandizing to excess, is extremely strict with his clergy in other matters; and, as I once heard Buckhurst say,

'Compounds for sins he is inclin'd to,
By damning those he has no mind to.'"

"Buckhurst had, I believe, hopes that Caroline would have relented, in consequence of his last overture; he was thrown into despair by her answer, containing, as he told me, such a calm and civil repetition of her refusal—that he swears he will never trouble her again. For a fortnight after, he protests he was ready to hang himself. About that time, I suppose, when he heard of Kate Robinson's death, he shut himself up in his rooms for several days—said he was not well, and could not see any body. When he came out again, he looked wretchedly ill, and unhappy: I pitied him—I felt the truth of what Rosamond said, 'that there is such a mixture of good and bad in his character, as makes me change my opinion of him every half hour.'

"He has just done me an essential service. He learnt the other day from one of his sisters the secret reason why Lord Oldborough was displeased with Godfrey, and why Godfrey was despatched to the West Indies.—Lord Oldborough had been told, either by Cunningham, or by one of his sisters, that Godfrey made love to Miss Hauton, and that when he came to town ostensibly on some regimental business, and was pleading for a brother officer, his concealed motive was to break off the marriage of his lordship's niece. Buckhurst had been at the opera in the same box with Miss Hauton and with my brother Godfrey one night. Godfrey's conduct had been misrepresented, and as soon as Buckhurst found that Lord Oldborough had been deceived, he was determined that he should know the truth; or, at least, that he should know that my brother was not to blame. Godfrey never mentioned the subject to me; but, from what I can understand, the lady showed him distinguished attention. How Buckhurst Falconer managed to right my brother in Lord Oldborough's opinion without involving the young lady, I do not know.—He said that he had fortunately had an opportunity one evening at his father's, when he was playing at chess with Lord Oldborough, of speaking to him on that subject, when none of his family was watching him. He told me that Lord Oldborough desires to see me, and has appointed his hour to-morrow morning. Now, Rosamond, my dear, set your imagination to work; I must go and draw a replication, which will keep mine fast bound.

"Yours truly,

"Alfred Percy."

At the appointed hour, Alfred waited upon the minister, and was received graciously. Not one word of Godfrey, however, or of any thing leading to that subject. Lord Oldborough spoke to Alfred as to the son of his old friend. He began by lamenting the misfortunes which had deprived Mr. Percy of that estate and station to which he had done honour. His lordship went on to say that he was sorry that Mr. Percy's love of retirement, or pride of independence, precluded all idea of seeing him in parliament; but he hoped that Mr. Percy's sons were, in this extravagant notion of independence, and in this only, unlike their father.

With all due deference, Alfred took the liberty of replying to the word extravagant, and endeavoured to explain that his father's ideas of independence did not go beyond just bounds: Lord Oldborough, contrary to his usual custom when he met with any thing like contradiction, did not look displeased; on the contrary, he complimented Alfred on his being a good advocate. Alfred was going to fall into a commonplace, about a good cause; but from that he was happily saved by Lord Oldborough's changing the conversation.

He took up a pamphlet which lay upon his table. It was Cunningham Falconer's, that is to say, the pamphlet which was published in Cunningham's name, and for which he was mean enough to take the credit from the poor starving genius in the garret. Lord Oldborough turned over the leaves. "Here is a passage that was quoted yesterday at dinner at Commissioner Falconer's, but I don't think that any of the company, or the commissioner himself, though he is, or was, a reading man, could recollect to what author it alludes."

Lord Oldborough pointed to the passage: "Thus the fame of heroes is at last neglected by their worshippers, and left to the care of the birds of heaven, or abandoned to the serpents of the earth."

Alfred fortunately recollected that this alluded to a description in Arrian of the island of Achilles, the present Isle of Serpents, where there is that temple of the hero, of which, as the historian says, "the care is left to the birds alone, who every morning repair to the sea, wet their wings, and sprinkle the temple, afterwards sweeping with their plumage its sacred pavement."

Lord Oldborough smiled, and said, "The author—the reputed author of this pamphlet, sir, is obliged to you for throwing light upon a passage which he could not himself elucidate."

This speech of Lord Oldborough's alluded to something that had passed at a dinner at Lord Skreene's, the day before Cunningham had set out on his embassy. Cunningham had been posed by this passage, for which Secretary Cope, who hated him, had maliciously complimented him, and besought him to explain it. Secretary Cope, who was a poet, made an epigram on Cunningham the diplomatist. The lines we do not remember. The points of it were, that Cunningham was so complete a diplomatist, that he would not commit himself by giving up his authority, even for a quotation, and that when he knew the author of an excellent thing, he, with admirable good faith, kept it to himself. This epigram remained at the time a profound secret to Lord Oldborough. Whilst Cunningham was going with a prosperous gale, it was not heard of; but it worked round, according to the manoeuvres of courts, just by the time the tide of favour began to ebb. Lord Oldborough, dissatisfied with one of Cunningham's despatches, was heard to say, as he folded it up, "A slovenly performance!"

Then, at the happy moment, stepped in the rival Secretary Cope, and put into his lordship's hands the epigram and the anecdote.

All this the reader is to take as a note explanatory upon Lord Oldborough's last speech to Alfred, and now to go on with the conversation—at the word elucidate.

"I suspect," continued his lordship, "that Mr. Alfred Percy knows more of this pamphlet altogether than the reputed author ever did."

Alfred felt himself change colour, and the genius in the garret rushed upon his mind; at the same instant he recollected that he was not at liberty to name Mr. Temple, and that he must not betray Cunningham. Alfred answered that it was not surprising he should know the pamphlet well, as he probably admired it more, and had read it oftener, than the author himself had ever done.

"Very well parried, young gentleman. You will not allow, then, that you had any hand in writing it?"

"No, my lord," said Alfred, "I had none whatever; I never saw it till it was published."

"I have not a right, in politeness, to press the question. Permit me, however, to say, that it is a performance of which any man might be proud."

"I should, my lord, be proud—very proud, if I had written it; but I am incapable of assuming a merit that is not mine, and I trust the manner in which I now disclaim it does not appear like the affected modesty of an author who wishes to have that believed which he denies. I hope I convince your lordship of the truth."

"I cannot have any doubt of what you assert in this serious manner, sir. May I ask if you can tell me the name of the real author?"

"Excuse me, my lord—I cannot. I have answered your lordship with perfect openness, as far as I am concerned."

"Sir," said Lord Oldborough, "I confess that I began this conversation with the prepossession that you were equal to a performance of which I think highly, but you have succeeded in convincing me that I was mistaken—that you are not equal—but superior to it."

Upon this compliment, Alfred, as he thought the force of politeness could no farther go, rose, bowed, and prepared to retire.

"Are you in a hurry to leave me, Mr. Percy?"

"Quite the contrary, but I was afraid of encroaching upon your lordship's goodness; I know that your time is most valuable, and that your lordship has so much business of importance."

"Perhaps Mr. Alfred Percy may assist me in saving time hereafter."

Alfred sat down again, as his lordship's eye desired it.—Lord Oldborough remained for a few moments silent, leaning upon his arm on the table, deep in thought.

"Yes, sir," said he, "I certainly have, as you say, much business upon my hands. But that is not the difficulty; with hands and heads business is easily arranged and expedited. I have hands and heads enough at my command. Talents of all sorts can be obtained for their price, but that which is above all price, integrity, cannot—there's the difficulty—there is my difficulty. I have not a single man about me whom I can trust—many who understand my views, but none who feel them—'Des ames de boue et de fange!' Wretches who care not if the throne and the country perish, if their little interests—Young gentleman," said he, recollecting himself, and turning to Alfred, "I feel as if I were speaking to a part of your father when I am speaking to you."

Alfred felt this, and Lord Oldborough saw that he felt it strongly.

"Then, my dear sir," said he, "you understand me—I see we understand and shall suit one another. I am in want of a secretary to supply the place of Mr. Cunningham Falconer. Mr. Drakelow is going to Constantinople; but he shall first initiate his successor in the business of his office—a routine, which little minds would make great minds believe is a mystery above ordinary comprehension. But, sir, I have no doubt that you will be expert in a very short time in the technical part—in the routine of office; and if it suits your views, in one word, I should be happy to have you for my private secretary. Take time to consider, if you do not wish to give an answer immediately; but I beg that you will consult no one but yourself—not even your father. And as soon as your mind is made up, let me know your decision."

After returning thanks to the minister, who had, by this time, risen to a prodigious height in Alfred's opinion; after having reiterated his thanks with a warmth which was not displeasing, he retired. The account of his feelings on this occasion is given with much truth in his own letter, from which we extract the passage:

"I believe I felt a little like Gil Blas after his first visit at court. Vapours of ambition certainly mounted into my head, and made me a little giddy; that night I did not sleep quite so well as usual. The bar and the court, Lord Oldborough and my special pleader, were continually before my eyes balancing in my imagination all the pros and cons. I fatigued myself, but could neither rest nor decide. Seven years of famine at the bar—horrible! but then independence and liberty of conscience—and in time, success—the certain reward of industry—well-earned wealth—perhaps honours—why not the highest professional honours? The life of a party-man and a politician, agreed by all who have tried, even by this very Lord Oldborough himself, agreed to be an unhappy life—obliged to live with people I despise—might be tempted, like others, to do things for which I should despise myself—subject to caprice—at best, my fortune quite dependent on my patron's continuance in power—power and favour uncertain.

"It was long before I got my pros and cons even into this rude preparation for comparison, and longer still before the logical process of giving to each good and evil its just value, and drawing clear deductions from distinct premises, could be accomplished. However, in four-and-twenty hours I solved the problem.

"I waited upon Lord Oldborough to tell him my conclusion. With professions of gratitude, respect, and attachment, more sincere, I fancy, than those he usually hears, I began; and ended by telling him, in the best manner I could, that I thought my trade was more honest than his, and that, hard as a lawyer's life was, I preferred it to a politician's.—You don't suspect me of saying all this—no, I was not quite so brutal; but, perhaps, it was implied by my declining the honour of the secretaryship, and preferring to abide by my profession. Lord Oldborough looked—or my vanity fancied that he looked—disappointed.

After a pause of silent displeasure, he said, 'Well, sir, upon the whole I believe you have decided wisely. I am sorry that you cannot serve me, and that I cannot serve you in the manner which I had proposed. Yours is a profession in which ministerial support can be of little use, but in which talents, perseverance, and integrity, are secure, sooner or later, of success. I have, therefore, only to wish you opportunity: and if any means in my power should occur of accelerating that opportunity, you may depend upon it, sir.' said his lordship, holding out his hand to me, 'I shall not forget you—even if you were not the son of my old friend, you have made an interest for yourself in my mind.'

"Thus satisfactorily we parted—no—just as I reached the door, his lordship added, 'Your brother, Captain Percy—have you heard from him lately?'

"'Yes, my lord, from Plymouth, where they were driven back by contrary winds.'

"'Ha!—he was well, I hope?'

"'Very well, I thank your lordship.'

"'That's well—he is a temperate man, I think. So he will stand the climate of the West Indies—and, probably, it will not be necessary for his majesty's service that he should remain there long.'

"I bowed—was again retiring and was again recalled.

"'There was a major in your brother's regiment about whom Captain Percy spoke to me—Major—'

"'Gascoigne, I believe, my lord.'

"'Gascoigne—true—Gascoigne.' His lordship wrote the name down in a note-book.

"Bows for the last time—not a word more on either side.

"And now that I have written all this to you, my dear mother, I am almost ashamed to send it—because it is so full of egotism. But Rosamond, the excuser general, will apologize for me, by pleading that I was obliged to tell the truth, and the whole truth.

"Love to Caroline, and thanks for her letter.—Love to Rosamond, upon condition that she will write to me from Hungerford Castle, and cheer my solitude in London with news from the country, and from home.

"Your affectionate son,

"ALFRED PERCY.

"P.S. I hope you all like O'Brien."

We hope the reader will recollect the poor Irishman, whose leg the surgeon had condemned to be cut off, but which was saved by Erasmus. A considerable time afterwards, one morning, when Erasmus was just getting up, he heard a loud knock at his door, and in one and the same instant pushing past his servant into his bedchamber, and to the foot of his bed, rushed this Irishman O'Brien, breathless, and with a face perspiring joy. "I axe your honour's pardon, master, but it's what you're wanting down street in all haste—here's an elegant case for ye, doctor dear!—That painter-jantleman down in the square there beyond that is not expicted."

"Not expected!" said Erasmus.

"Ay, not expected: so put on ye with the speed of light—Where's his waistcoat," continued he, turning to Dr. Percy's astonished servant, "and coat?—the top coat, and the wig—has he one?—Well! boots or shoes give him any way."

"But I don't clearly understand—Pray did this gentleman send for me?" said Dr. Percy.

"Send for your honour! Troth he never thought of it—no, nor couldn't—how could he? and he in the way he was and is. But God bless ye! and never mind shaving, or another might get it afore we'd be back. Though there was none in it but myself when I left it—but still keep on buttoning for the life."

Erasmus dressed as quickly as he could, not understanding, however, above one word in ten that had been said to him. His servant, who did not comprehend even one word, endeavoured in vain to obtain an explanation; but O'Brien, paying no regard to his solemn face of curiosity, put him aside with his hand, and continuing to address Dr. Percy, followed him about the room.

"Master! you mind my mintioning to you last time I seen your honour, that my leg was weak by times, no fault though to the doctor that cured it—so I could not be after carrying the weighty loads I used up and down the ladders at every call, so I quit sarving the masons, and sought for lighter work, and found an employ that shuted me with a 'jantleman painter', grinding of his colours, and that was what I was at this morning, so I was, and standing as close to him as I am this minute to your honour, thinking of nothing at all just now, please your honour, forenent him—asy grinding, whin he took some sort or kind of a fit."

"A fit! Why did you not tell me that sooner?"

"Sure I tould you he was not expicted,—that is, if you don't know in England, not expicted to live; and sure I tould your honour so from the first," said O'Brien. "But then the jantleman was as well as I am this minute, that minute afore—and the nixt fell his length on the floor entirely. Well! I set and up again, and, for want of better, filled out a thimble-full, say, of the spirits of wine as they call it, which he got by good luck for the varnish, and made him take it down, and he come to, and I axed him how was he after it?—Better, says he. That's well, says I; and who will I send for to ye, sir? says I. But afore he could make answer, I bethought me of your own honour; and for fear he would say another, I never troubled him, putting the question to him again, but just set the spirits nigh hand him, and away with me here; I come off without letting on a word to nobody, good or bad, in dread your honour would miss the job."

"Job!" said Dr. Percy's servant: "do you think my master wants a job?"

"Oh! Lord love ye, and just give his hat. Would you have us be standing on ceremony now in a case of life and death?"

Dr. Percy was, as far as he understood it, of the Irishman's way of thinking. He followed as fast as he could to the painter's—found that he had had a slight paralytic stroke, from which he had recovered.

We need not detail the particulars. Nature and Dr. Percy brought him through. He was satisfied with his physician; for Erasmus would not take any fee, because he went unsent for by the patient. The painter, after his recovery, was one day complimenting Dr. Percy on the inestimable service he had done the arts in restoring him to his pencil, in proof of which the artist showed many master-pieces that wanted only the finishing touch, in particular a huge, long-limbed, fantastic, allegorical piece of his own design, which he assured Dr. Percy was the finest example of the beau idéal, ancient or modern, that human genius had ever produced upon canvas. "And what do you think, doctor," said the painter, "tell me what you can think of a connoisseur, a patron, sir, who could stop my hand, and force me from that immortal work to a portrait? A portrait! Barbarian! He fit to encourage genius! He set up to be a Mecænas! Mere vanity! Gives pensions to four sign-post daubers, not fit to grind my colours! Knows no more of the art than that fellow," pointing to the Irishman, who was at that instant grinding the colours—asy as he described himself.

"And lets me languish here in obscurity!" continued the enraged painter. "Now I'll never put another stroke to his Dutch beauty's portrait, if I starve—if I rot for it in jail! He a Mecænas!"

The changes upon this abuse were rung repeatedly by this irritated genius, his voice and palsied hand trembling with rage while he spoke, till he was interrupted by a carriage stopping at the door.

"Here's the patron!" cried the Irishman, with an arch look. "Ay, it's the patron, sure enough!"

Dr. Percy was going away, but O'Brien got between him and the door, menacing his coat with his pallet-knife covered with oil—Erasmus stopped.

"I axe your pardon, but don't go," whispered he: "I wouldn't for the best coat nor waistcoat ever I seen you went this minute, dear!"

Mr. Gresham was announced—a gentleman of a most respectable, benevolent, prepossessing appearance, whom Erasmus had some recollection of having seen before. Mr. Gresham recognized him instantly: he was the merchant whom Erasmus had met at Sir Amyas Courtney's the morning when he offended Sir Amyas about the made shell. After having spoken a few words to the painter about the portrait, Mr. Gresham turned to Dr. Percy, and said, "I am afraid, sir, that you lost a friend at court by your sincerity about a shell."

Before Erasmus could answer—in less time than he could have thought it possible to take off a stocking, a great bare leg—O'Brien's leg, came between Mr. Gresham and Dr. Percy. "There's what lost him a rich friend any way, and gained him a poor one, if that would do any good. There it is now! This leg! God for ever bless him and reward him for it!"

Then with eloquence, emphasis, and action, which came from the heart, and went to the heart, the poor fellow told how his leg had been saved, and spoke of what Dr. Percy had done for him, in terms which Erasmus would have been ashamed to hear, but that he really was so much affected with O'Brien's gratitude, and thought it did so much honour to human nature, that he could not stop him.—Mr. Gresham was touched also; and upon observing this, Erasmus's friend, with his odd mixture of comedy and pathos, ended with this exhortation, "And God bless you, sir! you're a great man, and have many to my knowledge under a compliment to you, and if you've any friends that are lying, or sick, if you'd recommend them to send for him in preference to any other of the doctors, it would be a charity to themselves and to me; for I will never have peace else, thinking how I have been a hinderance to him.

And a charity it would be to themselves, for what does the sick want but to be cured? and there's the man will do that for them, as two witnesses here present can prove—that jantleman, if he would spake, and myself."

Erasmus now peremptorily stopped this scene, for he began to feel for himself, and to be ashamed of the ridicule which his puffing friend, in his zeal, was throwing upon him. Erasmus said that he had done nothing for O'Brien except placing him in St. George's Hospital, where he had been admirably well attended. Mr. Gresham, however, at once relieved his wounded delicacy, and dispelled all fears and anxiety, by the manner in which he spoke and looked. He concluded by inviting Dr. Percy to his house, expressing with much cordiality a wish to be more intimately acquainted with a young gentleman, of whose character he had accidentally learned more good than his modesty seemed willing to allow should be known.

O'Brien's eyes sparkled; he rubbed his hands, but restrained himself lest Dr. Percy should be displeased. When Erasmus went away, O'Brien followed him down stairs, begging his honour's pardon—if he had said any thing wrong or unbecoming, it was through ignorance.

It was impossible to be angry with him.

We extract from Erasmus's letter to his mother the following account of his first visit to Mr. Gresham.

"When I went to see Mr. Gresham, I was directed to an unfashionable part of the town, to one of the dark old streets of the city; and from all appearance I thought I was going to grope my way into some strange dismal den, like many of the ancient houses in that quarter of the town. But, to my surprise, after passing through a court, and up an unpromising staircase, I found myself in a spacious apartment. The darkness changed to light, the smoke and din of the city to retirement and fresh air. A near view of the Thames appeared through large windows down to the floor, balconies filled with flowers and sweet shrubs!—It was an Arabian scene in London. Rosamond, how you would have been delighted! But I have not yet told you that there was a young and beautiful lady sitting near the balcony, and her name is Constance: that is all I shall tell you about the young lady at present. I must go on with Mr. Gresham, who was in his picture-gallery—yes, picture-gallery—and a very fine one it is. Mr. Gresham, whose fortune is one of those of which only English merchants can form any adequate idea, makes use of it in a manner which does honour to his profession and to his country: he has patronized the arts with a munificence not unworthy of the Medici.

"My complaining genius, the painter, who had abused his patron so much, was there with his portrait, which, notwithstanding his vow never to touch it again, he had finished, and brought home, and with it the sprawling Venus: he was now extremely angry with Mr. Gresham for declining to purchase this chef-d'oeuvre. With the painter was a poet equally vain and dissatisfied.

"I admired the mildness with which Mr. Gresham bore with their ill-humour and vanity.—After the painter and poet, to my satisfaction, had departed, I said something expressive of my pity for patrons who had to deal with the irritable race. He mildly replied, that he thought that a man, surrounded as he was with all the comforts and luxuries of life, should have compassion, and should make allowance for genius struggling with poverty, disease, and disappointment. He acknowledged that he had met with much ingratitude, and had been plagued by the pretensions, expectations, and quarrels of his tribe of poets and painters. 'For a man's own happiness,' said he, 'the trade of a patron is the most dreadful he can follow—gathering samphire were nothing to it.'

"Pray tell my father this, because it opens a new view, and new confirmation of his opinions—I never spent a more agreeable day than this with Mr. Gresham. He converses well, and has a variety of information, which he pours forth liberally, and yet without the slightest ostentation: his only wish seems to be to entertain and inform those to whom he speaks—he has no desire to shine. In a few hours we went over a world of literature. I was proud to follow him, and he seemed pleased that I could sometimes anticipate—I happened to know as well as he did the history of the two Flamels, and several particulars of the Jesuits in Paraguay.

"My father often told us, when we were boys, that there is no knowledge, however distant it seems from our profession, that may not, some time or other, be useful; and Mr. Gresham, after he had conversed sufficiently with me both on literature and science, to discover that I was not an ignorant pretender, grew warm in his desire to serve me. But he had the politeness to refrain from saying any thing directly about medicine; he expressed only an increased desire to cultivate my acquaintance, and begged that I would call upon him at any hour, and give him the pleasure of my conversation, whenever I had time.

"The next morning he called upon me, and told me that he was desired to ask my advice for a sick partner of his, to whom, if I would accompany him, he would immediately introduce me. Who and what this partner is, and of what disease he is dying, if you have any curiosity to know, you shall hear in my next, this frank will hold no more—except love, light as air, to all at home.

"Dear mother, affectionately yours,

"E. PERCY"

CHAPTER XVI

Now for the visit to Hungerford Castle—a fine old place in a beautiful park, which excelled many parks of greater extent by the uncommon size of its venerable oaks. In the castle, which was sufficiently spacious to accommodate with ease and perfect comfort the troops of friends which its owner's beneficent character drew round her, there were apartments that usually bore the name of some of those persons who were considered as the most intimate friends of the family. The Percys were of this number. They found their own rooms ready, the old servants of the house rejoicing to see them again, and eager in offering their services. Many things showed that they had been thought of, and expected; yet there was nothing that could remind them that any change had taken place in their fortune: no formal or peculiar civilities from the mistress of the house, from her daughter, or nieces—neither more nor less attention than usual; but by every thing that marked old habits of intimacy and confidence, the Percys were, as if undesignedly and necessarily, distinguished from other guests.

Of these the most conspicuous was the Lady Angelica Headingham.—Her ladyship had lately come to a large estate, and had consequently produced a great sensation in the fashionable world. During the early part of her life she had been much and injudiciously restrained. The moment the pressure was taken off, the spirit boiled with surprising rapidity: immediately Lady Angelica Headingham shone forth a beauty, a bel-esprit, and a patroness; and though she appeared as it were impromptu in these characters, yet, to do her justice, she supported them with as much spirit, truth, and confidence, as if she had been in the habit of playing them all her life, and as if she had trod the fashionable stage from her teens. There was only one point in which, perhaps, she erred: from not having been early accustomed to flattery, she did not receive it with quite sufficient nonchalance. The adoration paid to her in her triple capacity by crowds of worshippers only increased the avidity of her taste for incense, to receive which she would now and then stoop lower than became a goddess. She had not yet been suspected of a real partiality for any of her admirers, though she was accused of giving each just as much encouragement as was necessary to turn his head. Of these admirers, two, the most eager and earnest in the pursuit, had followed her ladyship to the country, and were now at Hungerford Castle— Sir James Harcourt and Mr. Barclay.

Sir James Harcourt was remarkably handsome and fashionable—completely a man of the world, and a courtier: who, after having ruined his fortune by standing for government two contested county elections, had dangled year after year at court, living upon the hope and promise of a pension or a place, till his creditors warning him that they could wait no longer, he had fallen in love with Lady Angelica Headingham. Her ladyship's other admirer, Mr. Barclay, was a man of considerable fortune, of good family, and of excellent sense and character. He had arrived at that time of life when he wished to settle to the quiet enjoyment of domestic happiness; but he had seen so much misery arise from unfortunate marriages among some of his particular friends, that he had been afraid of forming any attachment, or, at least, engagement. His acquaintance with fashionable life had still further rendered him averse from matrimony; and from love he had defended himself with infinite caution, and escaped, till in an unlucky moment he had met with Lady Angelica. Against his better judgment, he had been captivated by her charms and talents: his reason, however, still struggled with his passion—he had never actually declared his love; but the lady knew it probably better than he did, and her caprice and coquetry cost him many an agonizing hour. All which he bore with the silence and patience of a martyr.

When the Percy family saw Lady Angelica for the first time, she was in all her glory—fresh from a successful toilette, conscious of renovated powers, with an accumulated spirit of animation, and inspired by the ambition to charm a new audience. Though past the bloom of youth, she was a handsome showy woman, with the air of one who requires and receives admiration. Her attitudes, her action, and the varied expression she threw into her countenance, were more than the occasion required, and rather too evidently designed to interest or to fascinate. She was surrounded by a group of gentlemen; Sir James Harcourt, Mr. Barclay, Mr. Seebright, a young poet; Mr. Grey, a man of science; and others—personnages muets. Arduous as was the task, Lady Angelica's various powers and indefatigable exertion proved capable of keeping each of these different minds in full play, and in high admiration.

Beauties are always curious about beauties, and wits about wits. Lady Angelica had heard that one of the Miss Percys was uncommonly handsome. Quick as eye could glance, her ladyship's passed by Mrs. Percy and Rosamond as they entered the room, fixed upon Caroline, and was satisfied. There was beauty enough to alarm, but simplicity sufficient to remove all fears of rivalship. Caroline entered, without any prepared grace or practised smile, but merely as if she were coming into a room. Her two friends, the Lady Pembrokes, instantly placed her between them, her countenance expressing just what she felt, affectionate pleasure at seeing them.

"A sweet pretty creature, really!" whispered Lady Angelica, to her admirer in waiting, Sir James Harcourt.

"Ye—ye—yes; but nothing marquante," replied Sir James.

Mr. Barclay's eye followed, and fixed upon Caroline, with a degree of interest. The room was so large, and they were at such a distance from Caroline, who was now occupied in listening to her friends, that Lady Angelica could continue her observations without fear of being overheard.

"There is something so interesting in that air of simplicity!" pursued her ladyship, addressing herself to Mr. Barclay. "Don't you think there is a wonderful charm in simplicity? 'Tis a pity it can't last: it is like those delicate colours which always catch the eye the moment they are seen, by which I've been taken in a hundred times, and have now forsworn for ever—treacherous colours that fade, and fly even while you look at them."

"That is a pity," said Mr. Barclay, withdrawing his eyes from Caroline.

"A thousand pities," said Lady Angelica. "Perhaps, in the country, this delicate charm might possibly, and with infinite care and caution, last a few years, but in town it would not last a season."

"True—too true," said Mr. Barclay.

"For which reason," pursued Lady Angelica, "give me something a little more durable, something that can stand what it must meet with in the world: fashion, for instance, though not half so charming till we are used to it; or knowledge, though often dearly bought; or genius, though doubly taxed with censure; or wit, though so hard to be had genuine—any thing is better than a faded charm, a has-been-pretty simplicity."

"When it comes to that, it is lamentable, indeed," said Mr. Barclay. He seemed to wish to say something more in favour of simplicity, but to be overpowered by wit.

Sir James shrugged his shoulders, and protested that simplicity had something too fade in it, to suit his taste.

All this time, where was Colonel Hungerford? He had been expected to arrive this day; but a letter came to tell his mother, that he was detained by indispensable military business, and that, he feared, he could not for some weeks have the pleasure of being at home. Every one looked and felt disappointed.

"So," thought Rosamond, "we shall be gone before he comes, and he will not see Caroline!"

"So!" said Lady Angelica, to herself, "he will not see me."

Rosamond was somewhat comforted for her disappointment, by observing that Caroline was not quite lost upon Mr. Barclay, pre-occupied though he was with his brilliant mistress. She thought he seemed to notice the marked difference there was in their manner of passing the day.

Lady Angelica, though she would sometimes handle a pencil, touch the harp, or take up a book, yet never was really employed. Caroline was continually occupied. In the morning, she usually sat with Rosamond and the two Lady Pembrokes, in a little room called the Oriel, which opened into the great library. Here in happy retirement Caroline and Rosamond looked over Mrs. Hungerford's select library, and delighted to read the passages which had been marked with approbation. At other times, without disturbing the rest of the company, or being disturbed by them, Caroline enjoyed the opportunity of cultivating her talents for music and painting, with the assistance of her two friends, who eminently excelled in these accomplishments.

All this time Lady Angelica spent in talking to show her wit, or lounging to show her grace. Now and then her ladyship condescended to join the young people, when they went out to walk, but never unless they were attended by gentlemen. The beauties of nature have come into fashion of late, and Lady Angelica Headingham could talk of bold outlines, and sublime mountains, the charming effects of light and shade, fine accidents, and rich foliage, spring verdure and autumnal tints,—whilst Caroline could enjoy all these things, without expecting to be admired for admiring them. Mrs. Mortimer was planting a new shrubbery, and laying out a ride through the park. Caroline took an unaffected interest in all her plans, whilst Lady Angelica was interested only in showing how much she remembered of Price, and Repton, and Knight. She became too hot or too cold, or she was tired to death, the moment she ceased to be the principal object of attention. But though her ladyship was thus idle by day, she sometimes worked hard by night—hard as Butler is said to have toiled in secret, to support the character of an idle universal genius, who knows every thing without studying any thing. From dictionaries and extracts, abridgments and beauties of various authors, here, and there, and every where, she picked up shining scraps, and often by an ostentation of superficial knowledge succeeded in appearing in conversation to possess a vast extent of literature, and to be deeply skilled in matters of science, of which she knew nothing, and for which she had no taste.

Mr. Seebright, the poet, was easily duped by this display: he expressed the most flattering astonishment, and pronounced her ladyship to be an universal genius. He looked up to Lady Angelica for patronage. He was so weak, or so ignorant of the world, as to imagine that the patronage of a fashionable literary lady of high rank would immediately guide the opinion of the public, and bring a poet forward to fortune and fame. With these hopes he performed his daily, hourly duty of admiration to his fair patroness, with all possible zeal and assiduity; but it was observed by Rosamond that, in conversation, whenever Mr. Seebright had a new idea or a favourite allusion to produce, his eye involuntarily turned first to Caroline; and though he professed, on all points of taste and criticism, to be implicitly governed by Lady Angelica Headingham, there was "a small still voice" to which he more anxiously listened.

As to Mr. Grey, the roan of science—he soon detected Lady Angelica's ignorance; smiled in silence at her blunders, and despised her for her arts of pretence. In vain, to win his suffrage, she produced the letters of various men of note and talent with whom she was in correspondence; in vain she talked of all the persons of rank who were her relations or dear friends:—she should be so happy to introduce him to this great man, or to mention him to that great lady; she should be so proud, on her return to town, to have Mr. Grey at her esprit parties; she would have such and such celebrated characters to meet him, and would have the pleasure and honour of introducing him to every person worth knowing in town.

With all due civility Mr. Grey declined these offers. There were few persons the pleasure or honour of whose company could compensate to him for the loss of his time, or equal the enjoyment he had in his own occupations; and those few he was so happy to have for his friends, he did not wish to form new acquaintance—he never went to conversaziones—he was much obliged to her ladyship, but he did not want to be mentioned to great men or great women. The nature of his fame was quite independent of fashion.—In this respect men of science have much the advantage of men of taste. Works of taste may, to a certain degree, be cried up or cried down by fashion. The full-fledged bard soars superior, and looks down at once upon the great and little world; but the young poet, in his first attempts to rise, is often obliged, or thinks himself obliged, to have his wing impelled by patronage.

With all her resources, however, both of patronage and of bel-esprit, Lady Angelica was equally surprised and mortified to find herself foiled at her own arms, by a girl whom nobody knew. She changed her manoeuvres—she thought she could show Miss Caroline Percy, that, whatever might be her abilities, her knowledge, or her charms, these must all submit to the superior power of fashion. Caroline having lived in the country, could not know much of the world of fashion. This was a world from which she thought she could move every other at pleasure. Her conversation was no longer of books, of which all of equal talents were competent to form a judgment; but her talk was now of persons, with whom no one who had not lived in the great world could pretend to be acquainted, of whom they could not presume to judge. Her ladyship tried in vain to draw Mrs. Hungerford and Mrs. Mortimer to her aid; they were too well-bred to encourage this exclusive and unprofitable conversation. But her ladyship knew that she could be sufficiently supported by Sir James Harcourt! He prided himself upon knowing and being known to every body, that is, any body, in London; he had an inexhaustible fund of town and court anecdote. What an auxiliary for Lady Angelica! But though their combined operations were carried on with consummate skill, and though the league offensive was strictly kept with every demonstration of mutual amity that could excite jealousy or express contempt for rival powers; yet the ultimate purpose was not gained—Caroline was not mortified, and Mr. Barclay was not jealous; at least, he was not sufficiently jealous to afford a clear triumph.

One morning, when she had been playing off all her graces, while Sir James admired her in every Proteus form of affectation, Mr. Barclay, as she thought, evidently pained by her coquetry, retired from the sofa, where she sat, and went to Mrs. Hungerford's table, where he took up a book and began to read. Lady Angelica spared no art to distract his attention: she contrived for herself an employment, which called forth continual exclamations of admiration, joy, despair, which at first made Mr. Barclay turn to see by what they could be caused; but when he found that they were occasioned only by the rise or fall of a house of cards which she was building, he internally said, "Pshaw!" and afterwards kept his eyes fixed upon his book. Sir James continued to serve the fair architect with the frail materials for her building— her Folly, as she called it—and for his services he received much encouragement of smiles, and many marked commendations. Mrs. Hungerford called upon Mr. Barclay to read a favourite poem.

Mr. Barclay read remarkably well, and soon fixed the attention of all the company, except that of Lady Angelica and her knight, Sir James Harcourt, whom she detained in her service. She could not be so flagrantly rude as to interrupt the reader by audible exclamations, but by dumb-show, by a variety of gestures and pretty looks of delight at every fresh story added to her card edifice, and at every motion of terror lest her tower should fall, her ladyship showed Mr. Barclay that she was not listening to that which she knew he was particularly desirous that she should hear.

The moment the reader's voice ceased, Lady Angelica approached the table. "Ten millions of pardons!" said she, drawing some cards from beneath Miss Caroline Percy's elbow, which rested on them. "Unpardonable wretch that I am, to have disturbed such a reverie—and such an attitude! Mr. Barclay," continued her ladyship, "now if you have leisure to think of me, may I trouble you for some of your little cards for the attic of my dear Folly?"

Mr. Barclay coolly presented the cards to her ladyship: then looked out of the window, observed that his horse was at the door, and was following Mr. Percy out of the room, when Lady Angelica, just as Mr. Barclay passed, blew down her tower, and exclaimed, "There's an end of my folly—of one of my follies, I mean: I wish I could blow them all away so easily."

The sigh and look of penitence with which she pronounced these words were accepted as expiation—Mr. Barclay stopped and returned; while sweeping the wreck of her tower from the table, she repeated,

"Easy, as when ashore an infant stands,
And draws imagined houses on the sands,
The sportive wanton, pleased with some new play,
Sweeps the slight works and fancied domes away:
Thus vanish at thy touch the tow'rs and walls,
The toil of mornings in a moment falls."

"Beautiful lines!" said Mr. Barclay.

"And charmingly repeated," said Sir James Harcourt: "are they your ladyship's own?"

"No; Homer's," said she, smiling; "Pope's Homer's, I mean."

To cover his blunder as fast as possible, Sir James went on to something else, and asked what her ladyship thought of Flaxman's sketches from the Iliad and Odyssey? He had seen the book lying on the library table yesterday: indeed, his eye had been caught, as it lay open, by a striking resemblance—he knew it was very rude to talk of likenesses—but, really, the resemblance was striking between a lady he had in his view, and one of the figures in Flaxman, of Venus, or Penelope, he could not say which, but he would look for the book and see in a moment.

The book was not to be found on the library table; Mrs. Hungerford said she believed it was in the Oriel: Sir James went to look—Miss Caroline Percy was drawing from it—that was unlucky, for Mr. Barclay followed, stayed to admire Miss Percy's drawings, which he had never seen before, and in looking over these sketches of hers from Flaxman's Homer, and from Euripides and Æschylus, which the Lady Pembrokes showed him, and in speaking of these, he discovered so much of Caroline's taste, literature, and feeling, that he could not quit the Oriel. Lady Angelica had followed to prevent mischief, and Mrs. Hungerford had followed to enjoy the pleasure of seeing Caroline's modest merit appreciated. Whilst Mr. Barclay admired in silence, Sir James Harcourt, not with his usual politeness, exclaimed, "I protest I had no notion that Miss Caroline Percy drew in this style!"

"That's possible," cried Lady Mary Pembroke, colouring with that prompt indignation which she was prone to feel when any thing was said that seemed derogatory to her friends, "that's possible, Sir James; and yet you find Miss Caroline Percy does draw in this very superior style—yes, and it is the perfection of her accomplishments, that they are never exhibited."

"You have always the pleasure of discovering them," said Mrs. Hungerford; "they are as a woman's accomplishments and acquirements ought to be, more retiring than obtrusive; or as my old friend, Dr. South, quaintly but aptly expresses it—more in intaglio than in cameo."

At this instant a sudden scream was heard from Lady Angelica Headingham, who caught hold of Mr. Barclay's arm, and writhed as if in agony.

"Good Heavens! What is the matter?" cried Mr. Barclay.

"Oh! cramp! cramp! horrid cramp! in my foot—in my leg!"

"Rest upon me," said Mr. Barclay, "and stretch your foot out."

"Torture!—I can't." It was impossible that she could stand without the support of both gentlemen.

"Carry me to the sofa—there!"

When they had carried her out of the Oriel to the sofa in the library, and when her ladyship found that she had excited sufficient interest, and drawn the attention of Mr. Barclay away from Caroline, her ladyship began to grow a little better, and by graceful degrees recovered the use of her pretty limbs. And now, as she had reason to be satisfied with the degree of feeling which Mr. Barclay had involuntarily shown for her when he thought she was suffering, if her vanity had had any touch of gratitude or affection mixed with it, she would not have taken this moment to torment the heart of the man—the only man who ever really loved her; but all in her was vanity: she began to coquet with Sir James Harcourt—she let him put on her sandal and tie its strings—she sent him for her shawl, for she had a mind to walk in the park—and when Mr. Barclay offered to attend her, and when she found that Caroline and the Lady Pembrokes were going, she had a mind not to go, and she resolved to detain them all in admiration of her. She took her shawl from Sir James, and throwing it round her in graceful drapery, she asked him if he had ever seen any of Lady Hamilton's attitudes, or rather scenic representations with shawl drapery.

Yes, he had; but he should be charmed to see them in perfection from her ladyship.

Notwithstanding the hint Mrs. Hungerford had given about exhibiting, and notwithstanding Mr. Barclay's grave looks, Lady Angelica, avowedly to please Sir James Harcourt, consented to give the exhibition of the passions. She ran into the Oriel—attired herself in a most appropriate manner, and appeared first in the character of Fear—then of Hope: she acted admirably, but just as

"Hope enchanted, smiled, and waved her golden hair,"

her ladyship's auburn tresses caught on some ornament in the room. The whole fabric was raised a little from the fair head on which it seemed to grow—Caroline sprang forward instantly, and dexterously disentangling the accomplished actress, relieved her from this imminent and awkward peril.

"I am sure I'm exceedingly obliged to Miss Caroline Percy," said her ladyship, adjusting her head-dress. "There, now, all's right again—thank you, Miss Percy—don't trouble yourself, pray."

The heartless manner of these thanks, and her ladyship's preparing to go on again with her exhibition, so displeased and disgusted Mr. Barclay, that he left her to the flattery of Sir James Harcourt, and, sighing deeply, quitted the room.

Lady Angelica, proud of showing her power of tormenting a man of his sense, smiled victorious; and, in a half whisper, said to Mrs. Hungerford, "Exit Mr. Barclay, jealous, because he thinks I did the shawl attitudes for Sir James, and not for him—Poor man! he's very angry; but he'll ride it off—or I'll smile it off."

Mrs. Hungerford shook her head. When her ladyship's exhibition had finished, and when Sir James had continued repeating, either with his words or his looks, "Charming! Is not she charming?" till the time of dressing, an hour to which he was always punctual, he retired to his toilette, and Lady Angelica found herself alone with Mrs. Hungerford.

"Oh! how tired I am!" cried her ladyship, throwing herself on a sofa beside her. "My spirits do so wear me out! I am sure I'm too much for you, Mrs. Hungerford; I am afraid you think me a strange wild creature: but, dear madam, why do you look so grave?"

"My dear Lady Angelica Headingham," said Mrs. Hungerford, in a serious but affectionate tone, laying her hand upon Lady Angelica's as she spoke, "I was, you know, your mother's most intimate friend—I wish to be yours. Considering this and my age, I think I may venture to speak to you with more freedom than any one else now living could with propriety—it grieves me to see such a woman as you are, being spoiled by adulation."

"Thank you, my dear Mrs. Hungerford! and now do tell me all my faults," said Lady Angelica: "only first let me just say, that if you are going to tell me that I am a coquette, and a fool, I know I am—both—and I can't help it; and I know I am what some people call odd—but I would not for the world be a common character."

"Then you must not be a coquette," said Mrs. Hungerford, "for that is common character—the hackneyed character of every play, of every novel. And whatever is common is vulgar, you know: airs and affectation are common and paltry—throw them aside, my dear Lady Angelica; disdain flattery, prove that you value your own esteem above vulgar admiration, and then, with such beauty and talents as you possess, you may be what you admire, an uncommon character."

"Maybe!" repeated Lady Angelica in a voice of vexation. "Well, I know I have a hundred faults; but I never before heard any body, friend or enemy, deny that I am an uncommon character. Now, Mrs. Hungerford, do you know any one of a more uncommon character?"

"Yes," said Mrs. Hungerford, smiling, "I know the thing that's most uncommon,

'I know a reasonable woman,
Handsome and witty, yet a friend.'"

"Oh! your friend, Miss Caroline Percy, I suppose. Well! though she is so great a favourite of yours, I must say that, to my fancy, she is as little of an uncommon character as any girl I ever saw—uncommon beauty, I acknowledge, she has, though not the style of face I like."

"And an uncommonly good understanding, without one grain of envy, affectation, or vanity," said Mrs. Hungerford.

"Vanity!—Stay till you see her tried," said Lady Angelica; "stay till she has gone through one winter's campaign in London; stay till she has as many admirers as—"

"As you have," said Mrs. Hungerford, smiling. "She seems to be in a fair way of soon trying that experiment to your satisfaction."

A considerable pause ensued; during which many conflicting passions appeared in Lady Angelica's countenance.

"After all, Mrs. Hungerford," resumed she, "do you think Mr. Barclay is really attached to me?"

"I think he was really attached to you, and strongly: but you have been doing all you can to weaken and destroy his attachment, I fear."

"Fear nothing! I fear nothing," exclaimed Lady Angelica, "now you tell me, dear Mrs. Hungerford, that you do not doubt the reality of his love: all the rest I will answer for—trust to me, I know my game."

Mrs. Hungerford sighed; and replied, "I am old, have stood by, and seen this game played and lost so often, and by as able players as Lady Angelica Headingham—take care—remember I warn you."

Miss Caroline Percy came into the room at this instant—Lady Angelica went to her toilette to repair her charms.

CHAPTER XVII

While Mrs. Hungerford was wasting her good advice upon Lady Angelica, Sir James Harcourt at his toilette received this day's letters, which he read, as usual, while his hair was dressing. Some of these letters were from creditors, who were impatient to hear when his advantageous marriage would be concluded, or when he would obtain that place which had been so long promised. The place at court, as he was by this post informed by a private, very confidential letter, under a government cover and huge seal, from his intimate friend, my Lord Skreene, ministers had found themselves under the unfortunate necessity of giving away, to secure three votes on a certain cabinet question.

Sir James threw the letter from him, without reading the rest of his dear friend's official apologies: "So, the place at court is out of the question—a wife must be my last resource," thought he, "but how to bring her to the point?"

Sir James knew that though he was now in high favour, he might, at some sudden turn of caprice, be discarded or deserted by his fair one, as had been the fate of so many of his predecessors. The ruling passion, vanity, must be touched, and the obvious means of awakening jealousy were in his power. He determined to pay attentions to Miss Caroline Percy: his experience in the tactics of gallantry supplying the place of knowledge of the human heart, he counterfeited the symptoms of a new passion, and acted "The Inconstant" so well, that Lady Angelica had no doubt of his being what be appeared. She was not prepared for this turn of fate, well as she thought she knew her game, and at this unlucky moment, just when she wanted to play off Sir James against Mr. Barclay—and in an old castle in the country too, where no substitute was to be had!

Her ladyship was the more vexed, because Mrs. Hungerford must see her distress. Unused to any thing that opposed her wishes, she lost all temper, and every word and look manifested resentment and disdain towards her innocent and generous rival. In this jealousy, as there was no mixture of love to colour and conceal its nature, it could not pass for refinement of sentiment—it bore no resemblance to any thing noble—it must have been detected, even by a less penetrating and less interested observer than Mr. Barclay. His eyes were now completely opened.

In the mean time, Caroline's character, the more it was brought into light, the more its value, goodness, and purity appeared. In the education of a beauty, as of a prince, it is essential early to inspire an utter contempt of flattery, and to give the habit of observing, and consequently the power of judging, of character.

Caroline, on this occasion, when, perhaps, some little temptation might have been felt by some ladies, remembered her own prayer against coquetry—her manner towards Sir James was free from all possibility of reproach or misconstruction: and by simply and steadily adhering to the truth, and going the straight road, she avoided all the difficulties in which she would have been involved, had she deviated but for a moment into any crooked path.

But to return to Lady Angelica Headingham. She was pleased to see Sir James Harcourt disconcerted, and delighted to see him mortified. Her ladyship's disdainful manner towards Caroline was thrown aside,

"And all the cruel language of the eye"

changed at once. Lady Angelica acknowledged that no one could show more magnanimity than Miss Caroline Percy had displayed in her conduct to Sir James Harcourt. This speech was made of course to be repeated, and when Caroline heard it she could not help smiling at the word magnanimity, which sounded to her rather too grand for the occasion.

Sir James Harcourt finding himself completely foiled in his schemes, and perceiving that the parties were closing and combining in a manner which his knowledge of the world had not taught him to foresee, endeavoured with all possible address and expedition to make his separate peace with Lady Angelica. Her ladyship, however, was proud to show that she had too much sense and spirit to accept again the homage of this recreant knight. He had not time to sue for pardon—his adventure might have ended in a jail; so forthwith he took his departure from Hungerford Castle, undetermined whether he should again haste to court to beg a place, or bend his course to the city, there to barter his fashion against the solid gold of some merchant, rolling in his majesty's coin, who might be silly enough to give his daughter, for a bow, to a courtier without a shilling. On one point, however, Sir James was decided— betide him weal, betide him woe—that his next mistress should neither be a wit, nor a beauty, nor yet a patroness.

After the departure of the baronet, the Lady Angelica expected to find her remaining lover at her feet, in transports of joy and gratitude for this haughty dismissal of his rival. No such thing: Mr. Barclay seemed disposed to throw himself at the feet of another, and of the last person in the world at whose feet her ladyship could bear to think of seeing him. Yet if she had even now taken Mrs. Hungerford's friendly warning, she might still have saved herself from mortification; but she was hurried on by her evil genius—the spirit of coquetry.

She had promised to pay a visit this summer to an aunt of Mr. Barclay, Lady B—, who lived in Leicestershire. And now, when every thing was arranged for her reception, Lady Angelica changed her mind, and told Mr. Barclay that she could not go, that she had just received letters from town, from several of her fashionable friends, who were setting out for Weymouth, and who insisted upon her meeting them there—and there was a delightful Miss Kew, a protégée of hers, who was gone to Weymouth in the hope and trust that her ladyship would produce her and her new novel at the reading parties which Lady Angelica had projected. She declared that she could not possibly disappoint Miss

Kew; besides, she had promised to carry Mr. Seebright to Weymouth, to introduce him and his poem to her friends—his subscription and the success of his poem entirely depended upon her going to Weymouth—she could not possibly disappoint him.

Mr. Barclay thought more of his own disappointment—and said so: at which her ladyship rejoiced, for she wished to make this a trial of her power; and she desired rather that her reasons should not appear valid, and that her excuses should not be reasonable, on purpose that she might compel Mr. Barclay to submit to her caprice, and carry him off in triumph in her train.

She carelessly repeated that Leicestershire was out of the question at this time, but that Mr. Barclay might attend her, if he pleased.

But it did not please him: he did not think that his aunt was properly treated, and he preferred her to all the bel-esprits and fine ladies who were going to Weymouth—her charming self excepted.

She depended too much on the power of that charming self. Mr. Barclay, whose bands she had gradually loosened, now made one resolute effort, asserted and recovered his liberty. He declared that to Weymouth he could not have the honour of attending her: if her ladyship thought the claims and feelings of her protégées of greater consequence than his, if she held herself more bound by the promises she had given to Mr. Seebright, Miss Kew, or any of her bel-esprit friends, than by those with which she had honoured his aunt, he could not presume to dispute her pleasure, or further to press Lady B.'s request; he could only lament—and submit.

Lady Angelica flattered herself that this was only a bravado, or a temporary ebullition of courage, but, to her surprise and dismay, Mr. Barclay continued firm, calm, and civil. His heart now turned to the object on which his understanding had long since told him it should fix. He saw that Miss Caroline Percy was all that could make him happy for life, if he could win her affections; but of the possibility of succeeding he had great doubts. He had, to be sure, some circumstances in his favour: he was of a good family, and had a considerable fortune; in a worldly point of view he was a most advantageous match for Caroline Percy, but he knew that an establishment was not the first object, either with her, or with her parents; neither could he wish that any motives of interest should operate in his favour. His character, his principles, were good, and he had reason to believe that Mr. Percy was impressed with a highly favourable opinion of his good sense and general understanding. Caroline talked to him always as if she liked his conversation, and felt esteem for his character; but the very freedom and ease of her manner showed that she had no thoughts of him. He was many years older than Caroline: it did not amount to an absolute disparity, but it was an alarming difference. Mr. Barclay, who estimated himself with perfect impartiality and candour, was sensible that though his temper was good, yet that he was somewhat fastidious, and though his manners were polite, yet they were reserved—they wanted that amenity, gaiety, and frankness, which might be essential to win and keep a lady's heart. The more his love, the more doubts of his own deserts increased; but at last he determined to try his fate. He caught a glimpse of Caroline one morning as she was drawing in the Oriel. Her sister and the two Lady Pembrokes were in the library, and he thought he was secure of finding her alone.

"May I beg the favour of a few minutes?"—he began with a voice of much emotion as he entered the room; but he stopped short at the sight of Lady Angelica.

In spite of all the rouge she wore, her ladyship's change of colour was striking. Her lips trembled and grew pale. Mr. Barclay's eyes fixed upon her for one moment with astonishment, then turning calmly away, he addressed himself to Caroline, his emotion recurring, though he merely spoke to her of a drawing which she was examining, and though he only said, "Is this yours?"

"Yes, Lady Angelica has just given it to me; it is one of her drawings—a view of Weymouth."

"Very beautiful," said Mr. Barclay, coldly—"a view of Weymouth."

"Where I hope to be the day after to-morrow," cried Lady Angelica, speaking in a hurried, piqued, and haughty voice—"I am dying to get to Weymouth. Mr. Barclay, if you have any letters for your friends there, I shall be happy to carry them. Only let them be given to my woman in time," added her ladyship, rising; "and now I must go and say vivace! presto! prestissimo! to her preparations. Well, have you any commands?"

"No commands—but my best wishes for your ladyship's health and happiness, whenever and wherever you go."

Lady Angelica sunk down upon her seat—made a strong effort to rise again—but was unable. Caroline, without appearing to take any notice of this, turned to Mr. Barclay, and said, "Will you have the goodness now to give me the book which you were so kind as to promise me?"

Mr. Barclay went in search of it. Caroline proceeded with her drawing, gave Lady Angelica time to recover, and left her the hope that her perturbation had not been noticed. Her ladyship, as soon as she could, left the room, repeating that she had some orders to give for her departure. Caroline waited some time in vain for Mr. Barclay and his book. Afterwards, as she was going up stairs, she was met by Rosamond, who, with a face full of mystery, whispered, "Caroline, my father wants you this instant in my mother's dressing-room—Mr. Barclay," added she, in a low voice, and nodding her head, "Oh! I see you know what I mean—I knew how it would be—I said so last night. Now go to my father, and you will hear all the particulars."

Caroline heard from her father the confirmation of Rosamond's intelligence, and she received from him and from her mother the kind assurance that they would leave her entirely at liberty to accept or refuse Mr. Barclay, according as her own judgment and feelings might dictate. They said, that though it might be, in point of fortune, a highly advantageous match, and though they saw nothing to which they could object in his character, understanding, and temper, yet they should not attempt to influence her in his favour. They begged her to decide entirely for herself, and to consult only her own happiness.

"All I insist upon, my dear daughter, is, that you should, without any idle or unjust generosity, consider first and solely what is for your own happiness."

"And for Mr. Barclay's," said Caroline.

"And for Mr. Barclay's, as far as you are concerned: but, remember, the question he asks you is, whether you can love him, whether you will marry him, not whether you would advise him to love or marry somebody else? Don't I know all that passes in your mind?"

"Not all, perhaps," said Caroline, "nor can I tell it you, because it is another person's secret; therefore, I am sure you will not question me further: but since you are so kind as to trust to my judgment, trust to it entirely, when I assure you that I will, without any idle or unjust generosity, consider, principally, what is for my own happiness."

"I am satisfied," said Mr. Percy, "no—one thing more: without meaning or wishing to penetrate into any other person's affairs, I have a full right to say to my daughter all that may be necessary to assist her in deciding on a point the most material to her happiness. Now, Caroline," continued her father, looking away from her, "observe, I do not endeavour, from my knowledge of your countenance, even to guess whether what I imagine is fact; but I state to you this supposition—suppose you had been told that another lady is attached to Mr. Barclay?"

"I never was told so," interrupted Caroline, "but I have discovered it by accident—No, I have said too much—I do not think that person is attached to him, but that she might easily have become attached, if this proposal had been made to her instead of to me; and I think that their two characters are exactly suited to each other—much better suited than mine could be to Mr. Barclay, or his to me: she has wit and imagination, and great vivacity; he has judgment, prudence, and solid sense: in each there is what would compensate for what is wanting in the other, and both together would make a happy union."

"My dear Caroline," said her father, "I must put you upon your guard against the too easy faith of a sincere affectionate heart. I am really surprised that you, who have always shown such good judgment of character, should now be so totally mistaken as to think a woman capable of a real love who is merely acting a part from vanity and coquetry."

"Vanity! coquetry!" repeated Caroline: "nobody upon earth is more free from vanity and coquetry than—Surely you do not imagine I am thinking of Lady Angelica Headingham?—Oh! no; I have no compassion for her. I know that if she suffers from losing Mr. Barclay, it will be only from losing 'the dear delight of giving pain,' and I should be very sorry she ever again enjoyed that delight at Mr. Barclay's expense. I assure you, I am not thinking of Lady Angelica."

Both Mr. and Mrs. Percy were in doubt whether Caroline was thinking of her sister Rosamond or of her friend Lady Mary Pembroke; but without attempting to discover, they only repeated that, whoever the person in question might be, or however amiable or dear to Caroline, she ought not to let this idea interfere with her own happiness, or influence her in giving an answer to Mr. Barclay's proposal, which she ought either to accept or decline, according as her own feelings and judgment should decide.—"If you wish to take time to decide, your father and I will make Mr. Barclay clearly understand that he is not to consider this as any encouragement; and as to the rest," added Mrs. Percy, "when you are sure that you mean right, and that you do right, you will not, my dear Caroline, I hope, be deterred from determining upon what is best for your own happiness, merely by the weak fear of what idle foolish people will say about an affair in which they have no concern."

Caroline assured her mother that no such weak fear acted upon her mind; and that in any case where she had the least doubt whether she could like a person as a husband or not, she should certainly ask for time to consider, before she would give an answer; but that, with respect to Mr. Barclay, she had had sufficient opportunities of seeing and judging of him in the character of a lover, whilst he had been the admirer of Lady Angelica; that she fully appreciated his good qualities, and was grateful for his favourable opinion; but that she felt perfectly certain that she did not and could not love him; and therefore she desired, as soon as possible, to put him out of the pain of suspense, to prevent him from having the mortification of showing himself the admirer of one by whom he must ultimately be refused;

and to leave him at liberty to turn his thoughts elsewhere, to some person to whom he was better suited, and who was better suited to him.

Mr. Barclay had made Mrs. Hungerford alone his confidant. As to Lady Angelica Headingham, he thought that her ladyship could not be in any doubt of the state of his affections as far as she was concerned, and that was all she had a right to know. He never had actually declared his passion for her, and his attentions had completely ceased since the determination she had made to break her engagement with his aunt; but Lady Angelica had still imagined that he would not be able to bring himself to part with her for ever, and she trusted that, even at the moment of getting into her carriage, she might prevail upon him to forget his wrongs, and might at last carry him off. These hopes had been checked, and for a moment overthrown, by Mr. Barclay's appearance this morning in the Oriel; the emotion with which she saw him speak to Caroline, and the indifference with which she heard him wish her ladyship health and happiness at Weymouth, or wherever she went, for an instant convinced her of the truth. But obstinate vanity recurred to the hope that he was not yet irreclaimable, and under this persuasion she hurried on the preparations for her departure, impatient for the moment of crisis—of triumph.

The moment of crisis arrived—but not of triumph. Lady Angelica Headingham's landau came to the door. But trunks packed and corded gave no pang to her former lover—Mrs. Hungerford did not press her to stay—Mr. Barclay handed her into the carriage—she stooped to conquer, so far as to tell him that, as she had only Mr. Seebright and her maid, she could give him a seat in her carriage, if he would come to Weymouth, and that she would thence, in a fortnight at farthest, go to his aunt, dear Lady B—, in Leicestershire. But all in vain—she saw it would not do—bid her servant shut the carriage-door— desired Mr. Seebright to draw up the glass, and, with a look of angry contempt towards Mr. Barclay, threw herself back on the seat to conceal the vexation which she could not control, and drove away for ever from irreclaimable lovers and lost friends. We do not envy Mr. Seebright his trip to Weymouth with his patroness in this humour; but without troubling ourselves further to inquire what became of her, we leave her

"To flaunt, and go down a disregarded thing."

Rosamond seemed to think that if Caroline married Mr. Barclay, the dénouement would be too near, too clear, and commonplace: she said that in this case Caroline would just be married, like any body else, to a man with a good fortune, good character, good sense, and every thing very good, but nothing extraordinary, and she would be settled at Mr. Barclay's seat in Leicestershire, and she would be Mrs. Barclay, and, perhaps, happy enough, but nothing extraordinary.

This plain view of things, and this positive termination of all hope of romance, did not please Rosamond's imagination. She was relieved, when at last Caroline surprised her with the assurance that there was no probability of Mr. Barclay's succeeding in his suit. "And yet," said Caroline, "if I were compelled at this moment to marry, of all men I have ever yet seen, Mr. Barclay is the person to whom I could engage myself with the least reluctance—the person with whom I think I should have the best security for happiness."

Rosamond's face again lengthened. "If that is the case," said she, "though you have no intention of marrying him at present, you will, I suppose, be reasoned into marrying him in time."

"No," said Caroline, "for I cannot be reasoned into loving him."

"There's my own dear Caroline," cried Rosamond: "I was horribly afraid that this man of sense would have convinced you that esteem was quite sufficient without love."

"Impossible!" said Caroline. "There must be some very powerful motive that could induce me to quit my family: I can conceive no motive sufficiently powerful, except love."

Rosamond was delighted.

"For what else could I marry?" continued Caroline: "I, who am left by the kindest of parents freely to my own choice—could I marry for a house in Leicestershire? or for a barouche and four? on Lady Jane Granville's principles for an establishment? or on the missy notion of being married, and having a house of my own, and ordering my own dinner?—Was this your notion of me?" said Caroline, with a look of such surprise, that Rosamond was obliged to fall immediately to protestations, and appeals to common sense. "How was it possible she could have formed such ideas!"

"Then why were you so much surprised and transported just now, when I told you that no motive but love could induce me to marry?"

"I don't recollect being surprised—I was only delighted. I never suspected that you could marry without love, but I thought that you and I might differ as to the quantity—the degree."

"No common degree of love, and no common love, would be sufficient to induce me to marry," said Caroline.

"Once, and but once, before in your life, you gave me the idea of your having such an exalted opinion of love," replied Rosamond.

"But to return to Mr. Barclay," said Caroline. "I have, as I promised my father that I would, consulted in the first place my own heart, and considered my own happiness. He appears to me incapable of that enthusiasm which rises either to the moral or intellectual sublime. I respect his understanding, and esteem his principles; but in conversing with him, I always feel—and in passing my life with him, how much more should I feel!—that there is a want of the higher qualities of the mind. He shows no invention, no genius, no magnanimity—nothing heroic, nothing great, nothing which could waken sympathy, or excite that strong attachment, which I think that I am capable of feeling for a superior character—for a character at once good and great."

"And where upon earth are you to find such a man? Who is romantic now?" cried Rosamond. "But I am very glad that you are a little romantic; I am glad that you have in you a touch of human absurdity, else how could you be my sister, or how could I love you as I do?"

"I am heartily glad that you love me, but I am not sensible of my present immediate claim to your love by my touch of human absurdity," said Caroline, smiling. "What did I say, that was absurd or romantic?"

"My dear, people never think their own romance absurd. Well! granted that you are not romantic, since that is a point which I find I must grant before we can go on,—now, tell me, was Mr. Barclay very sorry when you refused him?" said Rosamond.

"I dare not tell you that there is yet no danger of his breaking his heart," said Caroline.

"So I thought," cried Rosamond, with a look of ineffable contempt. "I thought he was not a man to break his heart for love. With all his sense, I dare say he will go back to his Lady Angelica Headingham. I should not be surprised if he went after her to Weymouth to-morrow."

"I should," said Caroline; "especially as he has just ordered his carriage to take him to his aunt, Lady B—, in Leicestershire."

"Oh! poor man!" said Rosamond, "now I do pity him."

"Because he is going to his aunt?"

"No; Caroline—you are very cruel—because I am sure he is very much touched and disappointed by your refusal. He cannot bear to see you again. Poor! poor Mr. Barclay! I have been shamefully ill-natured. I hope I did not prejudice your mind against him—I'll go directly and take leave of him—poor Mr. Barclay!"

Rosamond, however, returned a few minutes afterwards, to complain that Mr. Barclay had not made efforts enough to persuade Caroline to listen to him.

"If he had been warmly in love, he would not so easily have given up hope.

'None, without hope, e'er loved the brightest fair;
But love can hope, where Reason should despair.'"

"That, I think, is perfectly true," said Rosamond.

Never—begging Rosamond and the poet's pardon—never—except where reason is very weak, or where the brightest fair has some touch of the equivocating fiend. Love, let poets and lovers say what they will to the contrary, can no more subsist without hope than flame can exist without fuel. In all the cases cited to prove the contrary, we suspect that there has been some inaccuracy in the experiment, and that by mistake a little, a very little hope has been admitted. The slightest portion, a quantity imperceptible to common observation, is known to be quite sufficient to maintain the passion; but a total exclusion of hope secures its extinction.

Mr. Barclay's departure was much regretted by all at Hungerford Castle, most, perhaps, by the person who expressed that regret the least, Lady Mary Pembroke—who now silently enjoyed the full chorus of praise that was poured forth in honour of the departed. Lady Mary's common mode of enjoying the praise of her friends was not in silence; all she thought and felt usually came to her lips with the ingenuous vivacity of youth and innocence. Caroline had managed so well by not managing at all, that Lady Mary, far from guessing the real cause of Mr. Barclay's sudden departure, repeatedly expressed surprise that her aunt Hungerford did not press him to stay a little longer; and once said she wondered how Mr. Barclay could leave Hungerford Castle whilst Caroline was there; that she had begun to think he had formed an attachment which would do him more honour than his passion for Lady Angelica Headingham, but that she feared he would have a relapse of that fit of folly, and that it would at last end fatally in marriage.

Mrs. Hungerford smiled at the openness with which her niece told her conjectures, and at the steadiness with which Caroline kept Mr. Barclay's secret, by saying no more than just the thing she ought. "The power of keeping a secret is very different from the habit of dissimulation. You would convince me of this, if I had doubted it," said Mrs. Hungerford, to Caroline. "Now that the affair is settled, my dear, I must insist upon your praising me, as I have praised you for discretion. I hope I never influenced your decision by word or look, but I will now own to you that I was very anxious that you should decide precisely as you have done. Mr. Barclay is a sensible man, an excellent man, one who will make any amiable woman he marries happy. I am convinced of it, or I should not, as I do, wish to see him married to my niece—yet I never thought him suited to you. Yours is a character without pretension, yet one which, in love and marriage, would not, I believe, be easily satisfied, would require great qualities, a high tone of thought and action, a character superior and lofty as your own."

Mrs. Hungerford paused, and seemed lost in thought. Caroline felt that this lady had seen deeply into her mind. This conviction, beyond all praise, and all demonstrations of fondness, increases affection, confidence, and gratitude, in strong and generous minds. Caroline endeavoured, but could not well express in words what she felt at this instant.

"My dear," said Mrs. Hungerford, "we know that we are speaking plain truth to each other—we need no flowers of speech—I understand you, and you understand me. We are suited to each other—yes, notwithstanding the difference of age, and a thousand other differences, we are suited to each other. This possibility of a friendship between youth and age is one of the rewards Heaven grants to the early and late cultivation of the understanding and of the affections. Late as it is with me in life, I have not, thank God, survived my affections. How can I ever, whilst I have such children, such friends!" After a pause of a few moments of seemingly pleasurable reflections, Mrs. Hungerford continued, "I have never considered friendship as but a name—as a mere worldly commerce of interest: I believe in disinterested affection, taking the word disinterested in its proper sense; and I have still, believe me, the power of sympathizing with a young friend—such a young friend as Caroline Percy. Early as it is with her in life, she has so cultivated her understanding, so regulated her mind, that she cannot consider friendship merely as a companionship in frivolous amusement, or a mixture of gossiping confidences and idle sentiment; therefore, I am proud enough to hope that she can and will be the friend of such an old woman as I am."

"It would be the pride of my life to have—to deserve such a friend," cried Caroline: "I feel all the condescension of this kindness. I know you are much too good to me. I am afraid you think too highly of me. But Mrs. Hungerford's praise does not operate like flattery: though it exalts me in my own opinion, it shall not make me vain; it excites my ambition to be—all she thinks me."

"You are all I think you," said Mrs. Hungerford; "and that you may hereafter be something yet nearer than a friend to me is the warmest wish of my heart—But, no, I will not indulge myself in expressing that wish; Such wishes are never wise where we have no power, no right to act—such wishes often counteract their own object—anticipations are always imprudent. But—about my niece, Lady Mary Pembroke. I particularly admire the discretion, still more than the kindness, with which you have acted with respect to her and Mr. Barclay—you have left things to their natural course. You have not by any imprudent zeal or generosity hazarded a word that could hurt the delicacy of either party. You seem to have been fully aware that wherever the affections are concerned, the human mind is most tenacious of what one half of the philosophers in the world will not allow to exist, and the other half cannot define. Influenced as we all are every moment in our preferences and aversions, sometimes imperceptibly, sometimes avowedly, by the most trifling and often the silliest causes, yet the wisest of us start, and back, and think it incumbent on our pride in love affairs, to resist the slightest interference, or the best advice, from the best friends. What! love upon compulsion! No—Jupiter is not more tenacious of his thunderbolt than Cupid is of his arrows. Blind as he is, none may presume to direct the hand of that little urchin."

Here the conversation was interrupted by the entrance of a servant, who brought the post-bag, with many letters for Mrs. Hungerford.

CHAPTER XVIII

The arrival of the post was at this time an anxious moment to Mrs. Hungerford, as she had so many near relations and friends in the army and navy. This day brought letters, with news that lighted up her countenance with dignified joy, one from Captain Hungerford, her second son, ten minutes after an action at sea with the French.

"Dear mother—English victorious, of course; for particulars, see Gazette. In the cockle shell I have, could do nothing worth mentioning, but am promised a ship soon, and hope for opportunity to show myself worthy to be your son.

"F. HUNGERFORD."

"I hope I am grateful to Providence for such children!" cried Mrs. Hungerford.

Mrs. Mortimer darted upon Captain Hungerford's name in the Gazette—"And I cannot refrain from mentioning to your lordships the gallant manner in which I was seconded by Captain Hungerford."

"Happy mother that I am! And more happiness still—a letter also from my colonel! Thanks of commanding officer—gallant conduct abroad—leave of absence for three weeks—and will be here to-morrow!"

This news spread through the castle in a few minutes, and the whole house was in motion and in joy.

"What is the matter?" said Rosamond, who had been out of the room when the colonel's letter was read. "As I came down stairs, I met I can't tell how many servants running different ways, with faces of delight. I do believe Colonel Hungerford is come."

"Not come, but coming," said Mrs. Hungerford; "and I am proud that you, my friends, should see what a sensation the first sound of his return makes in his own home. There it is, after all, that you may best judge what a man really is."

Every thing conspired to give Caroline a favourable idea of Colonel Hungerford. He arrived—and his own appearance and manners, far from contradicting, fully justified all that his friends had said. His appearance was that of a soldier and a gentleman, with a fine person and striking countenance, with the air of command, yet without presumption; not without a consciousness of his own merit, but apparently with only a consciousness sufficient to give value and grace to his deference for others. To those he respected or loved, his manner was particularly engaging; and the appropriate attentions he paid to each of his friends proved that their peculiar tastes, their characteristic merits, and their past kindnesses, were ever full in his remembrance. To his mother his grateful affection, and the tender reverence he showed, were quite touching; and the high opinion he had of her character, and the strong influence she held over his mind, he seemed proud to avow in words and actions. To his sister Mortimer, in a different but not less pleasing manner, his affection appeared in a thousand little instances, which the most polite courtiers, with the most officious desire to please, could not without the happy inspiration of truth have invented. There were innumerable slight strokes in his conversation with his sister which marked the pleasure he felt in the recollection of their early friendship, allusions to trivial passages in the history of their childhood, which none of the important scenes in which he had since been engaged had effaced from his mind; and at other times a playful carelessness, that showed the lightness, the expanding freedom of heart, which can be felt only in the perfect confidence and intimacy of domestic affection. In his manner towards his cousins, the Lady Pembrokes, who, since he had last seen them, had grown up from children into fine young women, there were nice differences; with all the privileged familiarity of relationship he met the sprightly frankness of Lady Mary, and by a degree of delicate tender respect put the retiring sensitive timidity of Lady Elizabeth at ease. None of these shades of manner were lost upon Caroline's discriminating observation. For some time after his arrival, the whole attention of every individual at Hungerford Castle was occupied by Colonel Hungerford. All were alternately talking of him or listening to him. The eagerness which every body felt to hear from him accounts of public and private affairs, and the multitude and variety of questions by which he was assailed, drew him out continually; so that he talked a great deal, yet evidently more to gratify others than himself. He was always unwilling to engross the conversation, and sometimes anxious to hear from his mother and sister of domestic occurrences; but he postponed his own gratification, and never failed to satisfy general curiosity, even by the repetition of narratives and anecdotes, till he was exhausted. Conscious that he did not wish to make himself the hero of his tale, he threw himself upon the mercy of his friends, or their justice; and without any of the provoking reserve of affected or cowardly humility, he talked naturally of the events in which he had taken a share, and of what concerned himself as well as others. With polite kindness, which gratified them peculiarly, he seemed to take the Percy family, as his mother's friends, directly upon trust as his own: he spoke before them, freely, of all his confidential opinions of men and things. He did them justice in considering them as safe auditors, and they enjoyed and fully appreciated the value of his various conversation. In his anecdotes of persons, there was always something decidedly characteristic of the individual, or illustrative of some general principle. In his narratives there were strong marks of the Froissart accuracy of detail, which interests by giving the impression of reality, and the proof of having been an eye-witness of the scene; and sometimes, scorning detail, he displayed the power of keeping an infinite number of particulars in subordination, and of seizing those large features which gave a rapid and masterly view of the whole. For his profession he felt that enthusiasm which commands sympathy. Whilst he spoke of the British army, those who heard him seemed to see every thing, as he did, in a military point of view. Yet his love of military glory had not hardened his heart so as to render him insensible of the evils and sufferings which, alas! it necessarily produces. The natural expression of great feeling and humanity burst from him; but he turned hastily and firmly from the contemplation of evils, which he could not prevent, and would not uselessly deplore. In conversing one day privately with Mr. Percy, he showed that bitter and deep philosophic reflections on the horrors and folly of war had passed through his mind, but that he had systematically and resolutely shut them out.

"We are now," said he, "less likely than ever to see the time when all the princes of Europe will sign the good Abbé de St. Pierre's project for a perpetual peace; and, in the mean time, while kingdoms can maintain their independence, their existence, only by superiority in war, it is not for the defenders of their country to fix their thoughts upon 'the price of victory.'"

After explaining the plan of a battle, or the intrigues of a court, Colonel Hungerford would turn with delight to plans of cottages, which his sister Mortimer was drawing for him; and from a map of the seat of war he would go to a map of his own estate, eagerly asking his mother where she would recommend that houses should be built, and consulting her about the characters and merits of those tenants with whom his absence on the continent had prevented him from becoming acquainted. These and a thousand other little traits showed that his military habits had not destroyed his domestic tastes.

Caroline had taken an interest in the military profession ever since her eldest brother had gone into the army. Colonel Hungerford was seven or eight years older than Godfrey Percy, and had a more formed, steady, and exalted character, with more knowledge, and a far more cultivated understanding; but many expressions, and some points of character, were similar. Caroline observed this, and wished and hoped that, when her brother should have had as many opportunities of improvement as Colonel Hungerford's experience had given him, he might be just such a man. This idea increased the interest she took in observing and listening to Colonel Hungerford. After he had been some time at home, and that every day more and more of his amiable character had been developed, Rosamond said to herself, "This is certainly the man for Caroline, and I suspect she begins to think so. If she does not, I never will forgive her."

One day, when the sisters were by themselves, Rosamond tried to sound Caroline on this subject. She began, as she thought, at a safe distance from her main object. "How very much esteemed and beloved Colonel Hungerford is in his own family!"

"Very much and very deservedly," answered Caroline. She spoke without any hesitation or embarrassment.

Rosamond, rather dissatisfied even with the fulness of the assent to her first proposition, added, "And not only by his own family, but by all who know him."

Caroline was silent.

"It is surprising," continued Rosamond, "that a man who has led a soldier's wandering life should have acquired so much literature, such accurate knowledge, and should have retained such simple and domestic tastes."

Full assent again from Caroline, both of look and voice—but still not the exact look and voice Rosamond desired.

"Do you know, Caroline," continued she, "I think that in several things Colonel Hungerford is very like my brother Godfrey."

"Yes, and in some points, I think Colonel Hungerford is superior to Godfrey," said Caroline.

"Well, I really think so too," cried Rosamond, "and I am sure Godfrey would think and say so himself. How he would admire Colonel Hungerford, and how desirous, how ambitious he would be to make such a man his friend, his—in short, I know if Godfrey was here this minute, he would think just as I do about Colonel Hungerford, and about—all other things."

"All other things," repeated Caroline, smiling: "that includes a great deal."

"Yes, it does, that is certain," said Rosamond, significantly. "And," continued she, "I know another person of excellent judgment too, who, if I mistake not, is of my way of thinking, of wishing at least, in some things, that is a comfort. How Mrs. Hungerford does adore her son! And I think she loves you almost as much." Caroline expressed strong gratitude for Mrs. Hungerford's kindness to her, and the warmest return of affection.

"Then, in one word," continued Rosamond, "for out it must come, sooner or later—I think she not only loves you as if you were her daughter, but that—Now confess, Caroline, did not the idea ever occur to you? And don't you see that Mrs. Hungerford wishes it?—Oh! that blush is answer enough—I'll say no more—I do not mean to torment or distress—good bye, I am satisfied."

"Stay, my dear Rosamond, stay one moment, and I will tell you exactly all I think and feel."

"I will stay as long as you please," said Rosamond, "and I thank you for this confidence."

"You have a right to it," said Caroline: "I see, my dear sister, and feel all your kindness towards me, and all Mrs. Hungerford's—I see what you both wish."

"There's my own sister Caroline, above all artifice and affectation."

"But," said Caroline.

"But—Oh! Caroline, don't go back—don't palter with us—abide by your own words, and your own character, and don't condescend to any pitiful buts."

"You do not yet know the nature of my but."

"Nor do I wish to know it, nor will I hear it," cried Rosamond, stopping her ears, "because I know, whatever it is, it will lower you in my opinion. You have fairly acknowledged that Colonel Hungerford possesses every virtue, public and private, that can make him worthy of you—not a single fault on which to ground one possible, imaginable, rational but. Temper, manners, talents, character, fortune, family, fame, every thing the heart of woman can desire."

"Every thing against which the heart of woman should guard itself," said Caroline.

"Guard!—Why guard?—What is it you suspect? What crime can you invent to lay to his charge?"

"I suspect him of nothing. It is no crime—except, perhaps, in your eyes, dear Rosamond," said Caroline, smiling—"no crime not to love me."

"Oh! is that all? Now I understand and forgive you," said Rosamond, "if it is only that you fear."

"I do not recollect that I said I feared it," said Caroline.

"Well, well—I beg pardon for using that unguarded word—of course your pride must neither hope nor fear upon the occasion; you must quite forget yourself to stone. As you please, or rather as you think proper; but you will allow me to hope and fear for you. Since I have not, thank Heaven! made proud and vain professions of stoicism—have not vowed to throw away the rose, lest I should be pricked by the thorn."

"Laugh, but hear me," said Caroline. "I make no professions of stoicism; it is because I am conscious that I am no stoic that I have endeavoured to guard well my heart.—I have seen and admired all Colonel Hungerford's good and amiable qualities; I have seen and been grateful for all that you and Mrs. Hungerford hoped and wished for my happiness—have not been insensible to any of the delightful, any of the romantic circumstances of the vision; but I saw it was only a vision—and one that might lead me into waking, lasting misery."

"Misery! lasting! How?" said Rosamond.

"Neither your wishes nor Mrs. Hungerford's, you know, can or ought to decide, or even to influence the event, that is to be determined by Colonel Hungerford's own judgment and feelings, and by mine. In the mean time, I cannot forget that the delicacy, honour, pride, prudence of our sex, forbid a woman to think of any man, as a lover, till he gives her reason to believe that he feels love for her."

"Certainly," said Rosamond; "but I take it for granted that Colonel Hungerford does love you."

"But why should we take it for granted?" said Caroline: "he has not shown me any preference."

"Why—I don't know, I am not skilled in these matters," said Rosamond—"I am not sure—but I think— and yet I should be sorry to mislead you—at any rate there is no harm in hoping—"

"If there be no harm, there might be much danger," said Caroline: "better not to think of the subject at all, since we can do no good by thinking of it, and may do harm."

After a pause of surprise, disappointment, and reflection, Rosamond resumed: "So I am to understand it to be your opinion, that a woman of sense, delicacy, proper pride, honour, and prudence, must, can, and ought to shut her eyes, ears, understanding, and heart, against all the merit and all the powers of pleasing a man may possess, till said man shall and do make a matrimonial proposal for her in due form—hey! Caroline?"

"I never thought any such thing," answered Caroline, "and I expressed myself very ill if I said any such thing. A woman need not shut her eyes, ears, or understanding to a man's merit—only her heart."

"Then the irresistible charm, the supreme merit, the only merit that can or ought to touch her heart in any man, is the simple or glorious circumstance of his loving her?"

"I never heard that it was a man's supreme merit to love," said Caroline; "but we are not at present inquiring what is a man's but what is a woman's characteristic excellence. And I have heard it said to be a woman's supreme merit, and grace, and dignity, that her love should not unsought be won."

"That is true," said Rosamond, "perfectly true—in general; but surely you will allow that there may be cases in which it would be difficult to adhere to the letter as well as to the spirit of this excellent rule. Have you never felt—can't you imagine this?"

"I can well imagine it," said Caroline; "fortunately, I have never felt it. If I had not early perceived that Colonel Hungerford was not thinking of me, I might have deceived myself with false hopes: believe me, I never was insensible to his merit."

"But where is the merit or the glory, if there was no struggle, no difficulty?" said Rosamond, in a melancholy tone.

"Glory there is none," said Caroline; "nor do I claim any merit: but is not it something to prevent struggle and difficulty? Is it nothing to preserve my own happiness?"

"Something, to be sure," said Rosamond. "But, on the other hand, you know there is the old proverb, 'Nothing hazard, nothing have.'"

"That is a masculine, not a feminine proverb," said Caroline.

"All I meant to say was, that there is no rule without an exception, as all your philosophers, even the most rigid, allow; and if an exception be ever permitted, surely in such a case as this it might, in favour of such a man as Colonel Hungerford."

"Dangerous exceptions!" said Caroline. "Every body is too apt to make an exception in such cases in their own favour: that, you know, is the common error of the weak. Oh! my dear sister, instead of weakening, strengthen my mind—instead of trying to raise my enthusiasm, or reproaching me for want of sensibility, tell me that you approve of my exerting all my power over myself to do that which I think right. Consider what evil I should bring upon myself, if I became attached to a man who is not attached to me; if you saw me sinking, an object of pity and contempt, the victim, the slave of an unhappy passion."

"Oh! my dear, dear Caroline, that could never be—God forbid; oh! God forbid!" cried Rosamond, with a look of terror: but recovering herself, she added, "This is a vain fear. With your strength of mind, you could never be reduced to such a condition."

"Who can answer for their strength of mind in the second trial, if it fail in the first?" said Caroline. "If a woman once lets her affections go out of her power, how can she afterwards answer for her own happiness?"

"All very right and very true," said Rosamond: "but for a young person, Caroline, I could spare some of this premature reason. If there be some folly, at least there is some generosity, some sensibility often joined with a romantic temper: take care lest you 'mistake reverse of wrong for right,' and in your great zeal to avoid romance, run into selfishness."

"Selfishness!"

"Why, yes—after all, what are these cold calculations about loving or not loving such a character as Colonel Hungerford—what is all this wonderfully long-sighted care of your own individual happiness, but selfishness?—moral, very moral selfishness, I grant."

Caroline coloured, paused, and when she answered, she spoke in a lower and graver tone and manner than usual.

"If it be selfish to pursue, by the best means in my power, and by means which cannot hurt any human being, my own happiness, must I deserve to be called selfish?—Unless a woman be quite unconnected with others in society, without a family, and without friends—which, I thank God, is not my situation—it is impossible to hazard or to destroy our own happiness by any kind of imprudence, without destroying the happiness of others. Therefore imprudence, call it romance, or what you please, is often want of generosity—want of thought for the happiness of our friends, as well as for our own."

"Well come off!" said Rosamond, laughing: "you have proved, with admirable logic, that prudence is the height of generosity. But, my dear Caroline, do not speak so very seriously, and do not look with such 'sweet austere composure.'—I don't in earnest accuse you of selfishness—I was wrong to use that ugly word; but I was vexed with you for being more prudent than even good old Mrs. Hungerford."

At these words tears filled Caroline's eyes. "Dear, kind Mrs. Hungerford," she exclaimed, "in the warmth of her heart, in the fulness of her kindness for me, once in her life Mrs. Hungerford said perhaps an imprudent word, expressed a wish of which her better judgment may have repented."

"No, no!" cried Rosamond—"her better, her best judgment must have confirmed her opinion of you. She never will repent of that wish. Why should you think she has repented of it, Caroline?"

"Because she must by this time see that there is no probability of that wish being accomplished: she must, therefore, desire that it should be forgotten. And I trust I have acted, and shall always act, as if it were forgotten by me, except as to its kindness—that I shall remember while I have life and feeling. But if I had built a romance upon that slight word, consider how much that excellent friend would blame herself, when she found that she had misled me, that she had been the cause of anguish to my heart, that she had lowered in the opinion of all, even in her own opinion, one she had once so exalted by her approbation and friendship. And, oh! consider, Rosamond, what a return should I make for that friendship, if I were to be the occasion of any misunderstanding, any disagreement between her and her darling son. If I were to become the rival of her beloved niece!"

"Rival!—Niece!—How?—Which?" cried Rosamond, "Which?" repeated she, eagerly; "I cannot think of any thing else, till you say which."

"Suppose Lady Elizabeth."

"The thought never occurred to me—Is it possible?—My dear Caroline, you have opened my eyes—But are you sure? Then you have acted wisely, rightly, Caroline; and I have as usual been very, very imprudent. Forgive what I said about selfishness—I was unjust. You selfish! you, who thought of all your friends, I thought only of you. But tell me, did you think of Lady Elizabeth from the first? Did you see how it would be from the very first?"

"No; I never thought of it till lately, and I am not sure of it yet."

"So you never thought of it till lately, and you are not sure of it yet?—Then I dare say you are mistaken, and wrong, with all your superfluous prudence. I will observe with my own eyes, and trust only my own judgment."

With this laudable resolution Rosamond departed.

The next morning she had an opportunity of observing, and deciding by her own judgment. Lady Elizabeth Pembroke and Caroline had both been copying a picture of Prince Rupert when a boy. They had finished their copies. Mrs. Hungerford showed them to her son. Lady Elizabeth's was rather the superior painting. Colonel Hungerford instantly distinguished it, and, in strong terms, expressed his admiration; but, by some mistake, he fancied that both copies were done by Caroline: she explained to him that that which he preferred was Lady Elizabeth's.

"Yours!" exclaimed Colonel Hungerford, turning to Lady Elizabeth with a look and tone of delighted surprise. Lady Elizabeth coloured, Lady Mary smiled: he forbore adding one word either of praise or observation. Caroline gently relieved Mrs. Hungerford's hand from her copy of the picture which she still held.

Rosamond, breathless, looked and looked and waited for something more decisive.

"My mother wished for a copy of this picture," said Lady Elizabeth, in a tremulous voice, and without raising her eyes, "for we have none but a vile daub of him at Pembroke."

"Perhaps my aunt Pembroke would be so good to accept of the original?" said Colonel Hungerford; "and my mother would beg of Lady Elizabeth to give her copy to—our gallery."

"Do, my dear Elizabeth," said Mrs. Hungerford. Lady Elizabeth shook her head, yet smiled.

"Do, my dear; you cannot refuse your cousin."

"Cousin! there's hope still," thought Rosamond.

"If it were but worthy of his acceptance," said Lady Elizabeth.—Colonel Hungerford, lost in the enjoyment of her self-timidity and retiring grace, quite forgot to say how much he thought the picture worthy of his acceptance.

His mother spoke for him.

"Since Hungerford asks you for it, my dear, you may be certain that he thinks highly of it, for my son never flatters."

"Who? I!—flatter!" cried Colonel Hungerford; "flatter!" added he, in a low voice, with a tenderness of accent and look, which could scarcely be misunderstood. Nor was it misunderstood by Lady Elizabeth, as her quick varying colour showed. It was well that, at this moment, no eye turned upon Rosamond, for all her thoughts and feeling would have been read in her face.

"Come," cried Lady Mary, "let us have the picture in its place directly—come all of you to the gallery, fix where it shall be hung." Colonel Hungerford seized upon it, and following Lady Elizabeth, accompanied Lady Mary to the gallery. Mrs. Hungerford rose deliberately—Caroline offered her arm.

"Yes, my dear child, let me lean upon you."

They walked slowly after the young party—Rosamond followed.

"I am afraid," said Mrs. Hungerford, as she leaned more upon Caroline, "I am afraid I shall tire you, my dear."

"Oh! no, no!" said Caroline, "not in the least."

"I am growing so infirm, that I require a stronger arm, a kinder I can never have."

The door of the antechamber, which opened into the gallery, closed after the young people.

"I am not one of those exigeante mothers who expect always to have possession of a son's arm," resumed Mrs. Hungerford: "the time, I knew, would come, when I must give up my colonel."

"And with pleasure, I am sure, you now give him up, secure of his happiness," said Caroline.

Mrs. Hungerford stopped short, and looked full on Caroline, upon whom she had previously avoided to turn her eyes. From what anxiety did Caroline's serene, open countenance, and sweet ingenuous smile, at this instant, relieve her friend! Old as she was, Mrs. Hungerford had quick and strong feelings. For a moment she could not speak—she held out her arms to Caroline, and folded her to her heart.

"Excellent creature!" said she—"Child of my affections—that you must ever be!"

"Oh! Mrs. Hungerford! my dear madam," cried Rosamond, "you have no idea how unjust and imprudent I have been about Caroline."

"My love," said Mrs. Hungerford, smiling, and wiping tears from her eyes, "I fancy I can form a competent idea of your imprudence from my own. We must all learn discretion from this dear girl—you, early—I, late in life."

"Dear Rosamond, do not reproach yourself for your excessive kindness to me," said Caroline; "in candour and generous feeling, who is equal to you?"

"Kissing one another, I protest," cried Lady Mary Pembroke, opening the door from the gallery, "whilst we were wondering you did not come after us. Aunt Hungerford, you know how we looked for the bow and arrows, and the peaked shoes, with the knee-chains of the time of Edward the Fourth. Well, they are all behind the great armoury press, which Gustavus has been moving to make room for Elizabeth's copy of Prince Rupert. Do come and look at them—but stay, first I have a favour to beg of you, Caroline. I know Gustavus will ask my sister to ride with him this morning, and the flies torment her horse so, and she is such a coward, that she will not be able to listen to a word that is said to her—could you lend her your pretty gentle White Surrey?"

"With pleasure," said Caroline, "and my net."

"I will go and bring it to your ladyship," said Rosamond.

"My ladyship is in no hurry," cried Lady Mary—"don't run away, don't go: it is not wanted yet."

But Rosamond, glad to escape, ran away, saying, "There is some of the fringe off—I must sew it on."

Rosamond, as she sewed on the fringe, sighed—and worked—and wished it was for Caroline, and said to herself, "So it is all over—and all in vain!"

The horses for the happy riding party came to the door. Rosamond ran down stairs with the net; Caroline had it put on her horse, and Lady Elizabeth Pembroke thanked her with such a look of kindness, of secure faith in her friend's sympathy, that even Rosamond forgave her for being happy. But Rosamond could not wish to stay to witness her happiness just at this time; and she was not sorry when her father announced the next day that business required his immediate return home. Lamentations, loud and sincere, were heard from every individual in the castle, especially from Mrs. Hungerford, and from her daughter. They were, however, too well bred to persist in their solicitations to have the visit prolonged.

They said they were grateful for the time which had been given to them, and appeared kindly satisfied with their friends' promise to repeat their visit, whenever they could with convenience.

Caroline, tenderly and gratefully attached to Mrs. Hungerford, found it very difficult and painful to part from her; the more painful because she feared to express all the affection, admiration, and gratitude she felt for this excellent friend, lest her emotion might be misinterpreted. Mrs. Hungerford understood her thoroughly. When she took leave of her, she kissed her at first in silence, and then, by a few strong words, and more by her manner than by her words, expressed her high esteem and affection for her young friend.

CHAPTER XIX

LETTER FROM DR. PERCY TO HIS SISTER ROSAMOND.

"I never told you, my dear Rosamond, that the beautiful Constance was Mr. Gresham's daughter; I told you only that I saw her at his house. To the best of my belief she is no relation to him. She is daughter to Mr. Gresham's sick partner; and this partner—now, Rosamond, here is coincidence, if not romance, enough to please you—this partner is Mr. Panton, the London correspondent of the shipwrecked Dutch merchants, the very Panton and Co. to whom my father lately wrote to recommend Godfrey's friend, young Captain Henry—captain no more. I have not seen him yet; he is invisible, in the counting-house, in the remote city, in ultimate Broad-street, far as pole from pole from me at Mrs. Panton's fine house in Grosvenor-square.

"But now to have done with an old story, before I begin with a new—I will tell you at once all I know, or probably shall ever know, about Constance. She is sole heiress to her father's fortune, which, on his repeated word, I believe, amounts to hundreds of thousands. She is accomplished and amiable, and, as I told you before, beautiful: but luckily her style of beauty, which is that of one of Rubens' wives, does not particularly strike my fancy. Besides, I would really and truly rather have a profession than be an idle gentleman: I love my profession, and feel ambitious to distinguish myself in it, and to make you all proud of your brother, Dr. Percy. These general principles are strengthened beyond the possibility of doubt, by the particular circumstances of the present case. A young unknown physician, I have been introduced by a friend to this family, and have, in my medical capacity, been admitted to a degree of familiarity in the house which none shall ever have cause to repent. Physicians, I think, are called upon for scrupulous good faith, because in some respects, they are more trusted in families, and have more opportunities of intimacy, than those of any other profession. I know, my dear Rosamond, you will not suspect me of assuming fine sentiments that are foreign to my real feelings; but I must now inform you, that if I could make myself agreeable and acceptable to Miss Panton, and if it were equally in my will and in my power, yet I should never be, in the language of the market, one shilling the better for her. Her father, a man of low birth, and having, perhaps, in spite of his wealth, suffered from the proud man's contumely, has determined to ennoble his family by means of his only child, and she is not to enjoy his fortune unless she marry one who has a title. If she unites herself with any man, below the rank of a baron's son, he swears she shall never see the colour of sixpence of his money. I understand that a certain Lord Roadster, eldest son of Lord Runnymede, is the present candidate for her favour—or rather for her wealth; and that his lordship is patronized by her father. Every thing that could be done by the vulgar selfishness and moneyed pride of her father and mother-in-law to spoil this young lady, and to make her consider herself as the first and only object of consequence in this world, has been done—and yet she is not in the least spoiled. Shame to all systems of education! there are some natures so good, that they will go right, where all about them go wrong. My father will not admit this, and will exclaim, Nonsense!—I will try to say something that he will allow to be sense. Miss Panton's own mother was of a good family, and, I am told, was an amiable woman, of agreeable manners, and a cultivated mind, who had been sacrificed for fortune to this rich city husband. Her daughter's first principles and ideas of manners and morals were, I suppose, formed by her precepts and example. After her mother's death, I know she had the advantage of an excellent and enlightened friend in her father's partner, Mr. Gresham, who, having no children of his own, took pleasure, at all his leisure moments, in improving little Constance. Then the contrast between her father and him, between their ignorance and his enlightened liberality, must have early struck her mind, and thus, I suppose, by observing their faults and follies, she learned to form for herself an opposite character and manners. The present Mrs. Panton is only her step-mother. Mrs. Panton is a huge, protuberant woman, with a full-blown face, a bay wig, and artificial flowers; talking in an affected little voice, when she is in company, and when she has on her company clothes and manners; but bawling loud, in a vulgarly broad cockney dialect, when she is at her ease in her own house. She has an inordinate passion for dress, and a rage for fine people. I have a chance of becoming a favourite, because I am 'of a good fammully," and Mrs. Panton says she knows very well I have been egg and bird in the best company.

"My patient—observe, my patient is the last person of whom I speak or think—is nervous and hypochondriac; but as I do not believe that you have much taste for medical detail, I shall not trouble you with the particulars of this old gentleman's case, but pray for his recovery—for if I succeed in setting him up again, it will set me up.... For the first time I have, this day, after many calls, seen Godfrey's friend, young Mr. Henry. He is handsome, and, as you ladies say, interesting. He is particularly gentlemanlike in his manners; but he looks unhappy, and I thought he was reserved towards me; but I have no right yet to expect that he should be otherwise. He spoke of Godfrey with strong affection.

"Yours, truly,

"ERASMUS PERCY."

In the care of Mr. Panton's health, Dr. Percy was now the immediate successor to a certain apothecary of the name of Coxeater, who, by right of flattery, had reigned for many years over the family with arbitrary sway, till he offended the lady of the house by agreeing with her husband upon some disputed point about a julep. The apothecary had a terrible loss of old Panton, for he swallowed more drugs in the course of a week than any man in the city swallows in a year. At the same time, he was so economical of these very drugs, that when Dr. Percy ordered the removal from his bedchamber of a range of half full phials, he was actually near crying at the thoughts of the waste of such a quantity of good physic: he finished by turning away a footman for laughing at his ridiculous distress. Panton was obstinate by fits, but touch his fears about his health, and he would be as docile as the bon vivant seigneur in Zadig, whose physician had no credit with him when he digested well, but who governed him despotically whenever he had an indigestion; so that he was ready to take any thing that could be prescribed, even a basilisk stewed in rose-water. This merchant, retired from business, was now as much engrossed with his health as ever he had been with his wealth.

When Dr. Percy was first called in, he found his patient in a lamentable state, in an arm-chair, dying with the apprehension of having swallowed in a peach a live earwig, which he was persuaded had bred, was breeding, or would breed in his stomach. However ridiculous this fancy may appear, it had taken such hold of the man, that he was really wasting away—his appetite failing as well as his spirits. He would not take the least exercise, or stir from his chair, scarcely move or permit himself to be moved, hand, foot, or head, lest he should disturb or waken this nest of earwigs. Whilst these "reptiles" slept, he said, he had rest; but when they wakened, he felt them crawling about and pinching his intestines. The wife had laughed, and the apothecary had flattered in vain: Panton angrily persisted in the assertion that he should die—and then they'd "see who was right." Dr. Percy recollected a case, which he had heard from a celebrated physician, of a hypochondriac, who fancied that his intestines were sealed up by a piece of wax which he had swallowed, and who, in this belief, refused to eat or drink any thing. Instead of fighting against the fancy, the judicious physician humoured it—showed the patient sealing-wax dissolving in spirit of wine, and then persuaded him to take some of that spirit to produce the same effect. The patient acceded to the reasoning, took the remedy, said that he felt that his intestines were unsealing—were unsealed: but, alas! they had been sealed so long, that they had lost their natural powers and actions, and he died lamenting that his excellent physician had not been called in soon enough.

Dr. Percy was more fortunate, for he came in time to kill the earwigs for his patient before they had pinched him to death. Erasmus showed Mr. Panton the experiment of killing one of these insects, by placing it within a magic circle of oil, and prevailed upon him to destroy his diminutive enemies with castor oil. When this hallucination, to speak in words of learned length, when this hallucination was removed, there was a still more difficult task, to cure our hypochondriac of the three remote causes of his disease—idleness of mind—indolence of body—and the habit of drinking every day a bottle of London particular: to prevail upon him to diminish the quantity per diem was deemed impossible by his wife; especially as Mr. Coxeater, the apothecary, had flattered him with the notion, that to live high was necessary for a gouty constitution, and that he was gouty.—N.B. He never had the gout in his life.

Mrs. Panton augured ill of Dr. Percy's success, and Constance grew pale when he touched upon this dangerous subject—the madeira. Yet he had hopes. He recollected the ingenious manner in which Dr. Brown [Footnote: Vide Life of Dr. Brown.] worked upon a Highland chieftain, to induce him to diminish his diurnal quantity of spirituous potation. But there was no family pride to work upon, at least no family arms were to be had. Erasmus found a succedaneum, however, in the love of titles and of what are called fine people. Lord Runnymede had given Mr. Panton a gold beaker, of curious workmanship, on which his lordship's arms were engraved; of this present the citizen was very fond and vain: observing this, Dr. Percy was determined to render it subservient to his purposes. He knew they would be right glad of any opportunity of producing and talking of this beaker to all their acquaintance. He therefore advised—no, not advised; for with some minds if you advise you are not listened to, if you command you are obeyed—he commanded that his patient should have his madeira always decanted into the curious beaker, for certain galvanic advantages that every knowing porter-drinker is aware of: Erasmus emptied a decanter of madeira into the beaker to show that it held more than a quart. This last circumstance decided Mr. Panton to give a solemn promise to abide by the advice of his physician, who seized this auspicious moment to act upon the imagination of his patient, by various medical anecdotes. Mr. Panton seemed to be much struck with the account of bottles made of antimonial glass, which continue, for years, to impregnate successive quantities of liquor with the same antimonial virtues. Dr. Percy then produced a piece of coloured crystal about the size of a large nut, which he directed his patient to put into the beaker, and to add another of these medicated crystals every day, till the vessel should be half full, to increase the power of the drug by successive additions; and by this arrangement, Panton was gradually reduced to half his usual quantity of wine.

Dr. Percy's next difficulty was how to supply the purse-full and purse-proud citizen with motive and occupation. Mr. Panton had an utter aversion and contempt for all science and literature; he could not conceive that any man "could sit down to read for amusement," but he enjoyed a party of pleasure in a good boat on the water, to one of the aits or islets in the Thames at the right season, to be regaled with eel-pie. One book he had read, and one play he liked—no, not a play, but a pantomime. The book was Robinson Crusoe—the pantomime, Harlequin Friday. He had been heard to say, that if ever he had a villa, there should be in it an island like Robinson Crusoe's; and why not a fortress, a castle, and a grotto? this would be something new; and why should he not have his fancy, and why should not there be Panton's Folly as well as any of the thousand Follies in England? Surely he was rich enough to have a Folly. His physician cherished this bright idea. Mrs. Panton was all this time dying to have a villa on the Thames. Dr. Percy proposed that one should be made on Mr. Panton's plan. The villa was bought, and every day the hypochondriac—hypochondriac now no more—went to his villa-Crusoe, where he fussed, and furbished, and toiled at his desert island in the Thames, as hard as ever he laboured to make his plum in the counting-house. In due course he recovered his health, and, to use his own expression, "became as alert as any man in all England of his inches in the girth, thanks be to Dr. Percy!"

We find the following letter from Dr. Percy, written, as it appears, some months after his first attendance upon Mr. Panton.

"Yes, my dear friends at home, Alfred tells you truth, and does not flatter much. The having set up again this old citizen, who was thought bankrupt in constitution, has done me honour in the city; and, as Alfred assures you, has spread my name through Broad-street, and Fleet-street, and Milk-street, embracing the wide extremes between High-Holborn and St. Mary Axe,

'And even Islington has heard my fame.'

"In earnest, I am getting fast into practice in the city—and Rosamond must not turn up her aristocratic lip at the city—very good men, in every sense of the word, some of the best men I know, inhabit what she is pleased to call the wrong end of the town.

"Mr. Gresham is unceasing and indefatigable in his kindness to me. I consider it as an instance of this kindness that he has found employment for my poor friend, O'Brien; has made him his porter—a pleasanter place than he had with the painter that pleased nobody: O'Brien sees me almost every day, and rejoices in what he calls my prosperity.

"'Heaven for ever prosper your honour' is the beginning and end of all he says, and, I believe, of all he thinks. Is not it singular, that my first step towards getting into practice should have been prepared by that which seemed to threaten my ruin—the quarrel with Frumpton about O'Brien and the hospital?

"A delicacy strikes me, and begins at this moment, in the midst of my prosperity, to make my pride uneasy.

"I am afraid that my father should say Erasmus gets on by patronage, after all—by the patronage of a poor Irish porter and a rich English merchant.

"Adieu, my dear friends; you must not expect such long letters from me now that I am becoming a busy man. Alfred and I see but little of one another, we live at such a distance, and we are both so gloriously industrious. But we have holiday minutes, when we meet and talk more in the same space of time than any two wise men—I did not say, women—that you ever saw.

"Yours, affectionately,

"ERASMUS PERCY.

"P.S. I have just recollected that I forgot to answer your question about Mr. Henry. I do see him whenever I have time to go, and whenever he will come to Mr. Gresham's, which is very seldom. Mr. Gresham has begged him repeatedly to come to his house every Sunday, when Henry must undoubtedly be at leisure; yet Mr. Henry has been there but seldom since the first six weeks after he came to London. I cannot yet understand whether this arises from pride, or from some better motive. Mr. Gresham says he likes what he has seen of him, and well observes, that a young officer, who has lived a gay life in the army, must have great power over his own habits, and something uncommon in his character, to be both willing and able thus suddenly and completely to change his mode of life, and to conform to all the restraints and disagreeable circumstances of his new situation."

EXTRACT OF A LETTER FROM MR. PERCY TO ERASMUS PERCY.

"... Let me take the opportunity of your playful allusion to your present patrons, a porter and a hypochondriac, seriously to explain to you my principles about patronage—I never had any idea that you ought not to be assisted by friends: friends which have been made for you by your parents I consider as part of your patrimony. I inherited many from my father, for which I respect and bless his name. During the course of my life, I have had the happiness of gaining the regard of some persons of talents and virtue, some of them in high station; this regard will extend to my children while I live, and descend to them when I am no more. I never cultivated them with a view to advancing my family, but I make no doubt that their friendship will assist my sons in their progress through their several professions. I hold it to be just and right that friends should give, and that young men should gratefully accept, all the means and opportunities of bringing professional acquirements and abilities into notice. Afterwards, the merit of the candidate, and his fitness for any given situation, ought, and probably will, ultimately decide whether the assistance has been properly or improperly given. If family friends procure for any young man a reward of any kind which he has not merited, I should object to that as much as if the place or the reward had been bestowed by a professed patron from political or other interested motives. If my friends were to assist you merely because you were my sons, bore my name, or represented the Percy estate, I should not think this just or honourable; but they know the principles which have been instilled into you, and the education you have received: from these they can form a judgment of what you are likely to be, and for what situations you are qualified; therefore it is but reasonable that they should recommend you preferably to strangers, even of equal ability. Every young man has friends, and they will do all they can to assist him: if they do so according to his merits, they do well; if in spite of his demerits, they do ill; but whilst nothing is practised to prevent the course of free competition, there can be no evil to the community, and there is no injurious patronage. So much for family friends. Now as to friends of your own making, they are as much your own earning, and all the advantage they can be of to you is as honourably yours, as your fees. Whatever assistance you may receive from Mr. Gresham I consider in this light. As to gratitude—I acknowledge that in some cases gratitude might be guilty of partial patronage.

"If you had saved a minister of state from breaking his neck, and he in return had made you surgeon-general to our armies, without knowing whether you were qualified for that situation, I should call that partial and pernicious patronage; but if you had cured a great man of a dangerous disease, and he afterwards exerted himself to recommend you as a physician to his friends and acquaintance, this I should consider as part of your fit reward.

"So now, my dear son, I hope you fully understand me, and that you will not attribute to me false delicacies, and a prudery, a puritanism of independence, which I utterly disclaim.—Go on, and prosper, and depend upon the warm sympathy and entire approbation of your affectionate father,

"L. PERCY."

LETTER FROM ALFRED PERCY TO ROSAMOND.

"MY DEAR ROSAMOND,

"Thank you for your letters from Hungerford Castle. If Mr. Barclay had been but ten years younger, and if he had been ten degrees more a laughing philosopher, and if Caroline could but have loved him, I should have had no objection to him for a brother-in-law; but as my three ifs could not be, I regret the Leicestershire estate as little as possible, and I will console myself for not having the marriage settlements to draw.

"Your letters were great delights to me. I kept them to read when the business of the day was done, and I read them by my single candle in my lone chamber. I would rather live in my lone chamber all my days, and never see a wax-light all my nights, than be married to your Lady Angelica Headingham. I give Mr. Barclay joy of having escaped from her charms. I prefer an indenture tripartite, however musty or tiresome, to a triple tyrant, however fair or entertaining.

"So you expect me to be very entertaining next vacation, and you expect to hear all I have seen, heard, felt, and understood since I came to London. Alas! Rosamond, I have no wonders to relate; and lest you should be disappointed when we meet, I had best tell you now and at once all I have to say about myself. My history is much like that of the first years at the bar of every young lawyer—short and bitter—much law and few fees. Some, however, I have received.

"A few of my father's friends, who are so unfortunate as to be at law, have been so good as to direct their attorneys to give me briefs. But most of his friends, to my loss—I am too generous, observe, to say to my sorrow—are wise enough to keep clear of lawsuits. I heard his friend, the late chancellor, say the other day to some one who wanted to plunge into a suit in Chancery, 'If any body were to take a fancy to a corner of my estate, I would rather—provided always that nobody knew it—let him have it than go to law for it.'

"But to go on with my own affairs.

"A little while after my interview with Lord Oldborough, his lordship, to my surprise—for I thought his offer to assist me in my profession, if ever it should lie in his line, was a mere courtier's promise—sent his attorney to me, with a brief in a cause of Colonel Hauton's. The colonel has gone to law (most ungrateful as he is) with his uncle, who was his guardian, and who managed all his affairs for years. I need not explain to you the merits of the suit, or the demerits of the plaintiff. It is enough to tell you that I was all-glorious, with the hope of making a good point which had escaped the other counsel employed on our side; but the senior counsel never acknowledged the assistance he had received from me—obtained a nonsuit against the colonel, and had all the honour and triumph of the day. Some few gentlemen of the bar knew the truth, and they were indignant. I hear that my senior, whose name I will never tell you lest you should hate it, has got into great practice by the gaining of this suit. Be that as it may, I would not change places and feelings with him at this moment.

'Grant me an honest fame, or grant me none!'

"Mr. Grose, Lord Oldborough's solicitor, a rich rogue and very saucy, was obliged to employ me, because his client ordered it, and Lord Oldborough is not a man to be disobeyed, either in private or public affairs: but the attorney was obviously vexed and scandalized by his lordship's employing me, a young barrister, of whom nobody had ever heard, and who was not recommended by him, or under the protection even of any solicitor of eminence. Mr. Grose knew well how the suit was gained, but he never mentioned it to Lord Oldborough; on the contrary, he gave all the credit to my senior. This dry story of a point law is the most interesting thing I have to tell you about myself. I have seen nothing, heard nothing, know nothing, but of law, and I begin to feel it difficult to write, speak, or think, in any but professional language. Tell my father, that I shall soon come to talking law Latin and law French.

"I know no more of what is going on in this great metropolis than if I were at Tobolski. Buckhurst Falconer used to be my newspaper, but since he has given up all hopes of Caroline, he seldom comes near me. I have lost in him my fashionable Daily Advertiser, my Belle Assemblée, and tête-à-tête magazine.

"Last Sunday, I went to his fashionable chapel to hear him preach: he is much admired, but I don't like his manner or his sermons—too theatrical and affected—too rhetorical and antithetical, evidently more suited to display the talents of the preacher than to do honour to God or good to man. He told me, that if he could preach himself into a deanery, he should think he had preached to some purpose; and could die with a safe conscience, as he should think he had not laboured in vain in his vocation. Of all men, I think a dissipated clergyman is the most contemptible. How much Commissioner Falconer has to answer for, who forced him, or who lured him, knowing how unfit he was for it, into the church! The commissioner frets because the price of iniquity has not yet been received—the living of Chipping Friars is not yet Buckhurst's. The poor paralytic incumbent, for whose death he is praying daily, is still living; and, as Buckhurst says, may shake on many a long year. How Buckhurst lives in the mean time at the rate he does I cannot tell you—that art of living in style upon nothing is an art which I see practised by numbers, but which is still a mystery to me. However, the Falconers seem in great favour at present; the commissioner hopes Lord Oldborough may do something for Buckhurst. Last Sunday, when I went to hear him preach, I saw the whole family of the Falconers, in grandeur, in the Duke of Greenwich's seat.

The Marchioness of Twickenham was there, and looked beautiful, but, as I thought, unhappy. After the sermon, I heard Lady Somebody, who was in the next seat to me, whisper to a Lady Otherbody, just as she was rising after the blessing, 'My dear madam, did you hear the shocking report about the Marchioness of Twickenham?' then a very close and confidential whisper; then, loud enough for me to hear, 'But I do suppose, as there are hopes of an heir, all will be hushed—for the present.'

"Just then the Duke of Greenwich and the marquis and marchioness came down the aisle, and as they passed, my scandal-mongers smiled, and curtsied, and were so delighted to see their dear marchioness! The Miss Falconers, following in the wake of nobility, seemed too much charmed with themselves, to see or know me—till Lord Oldborough, though listening to the duke, espied me, and did me the honour to bow; then the misses put up their glasses to see who I could be, and they also smiled, and curtsied, and were delighted to see me.

"It is well for us that we don't live on their smiles and curtsies. They went off in the Marchioness of Twickenham's superb equipage. I had a full view of her as she drew up the glass, and a more melancholy countenance than hers I have seldom seen. Lord Oldborough hoped my father was well—but never mentioned Godfrey. The marchioness does not know me, but she turned at the name of Percy, and I thought sighed. Now, Rosamond, I put that sigh in for you—make what you can of it, and of the half-heard mysterious whisper. I expect that you will have a romance in great forwardness, before Monday, the 3rd of next month, when I hope to see you all.

"No letters from Godfrey.—Erasmus has been so busy of late, he tells me, he has not had time to record for you all his doings. In one word, he is doing exceedingly well. His practice increases every day in the city in spite of Dr. Frumpton. Adieu till Monday, the 3rd—Happy Monday!—'Restraint that sweetens liberty.' My dear Rosamond, which do you think loves vacation-time most, a lawyer or a school-boy?

"I was interrupted just now by a letter from a certain farmer of the name of Grimwood, who has written to me, 'because I am a friend to justice, and my father's son,' &c., and has given me a long account of a quarrel he has with Dr. Leicester about the tithe of peaches—said Grimwood is so angry, that he can neither spell nor write intelligibly, and he swears that if it cost him a thousand guineas in gold, he will have the law of the doctor. I wish my father would be so kind as to send to Mr. Grimwood (he lives at Pegginton), and advise him to keep clear of Attorney Sharpe, and to keep cool, if possible, till Monday, the 3rd, and then I will make up the quarrel if I can. Observe, more is to be done on Monday, the 3rd, than ever was done on any other Monday.

"Your affectionate brother,

"ALFRED PERCY.

"P.S.—I open my letter to tell you a delightful piece of news—that Lord Oldborough has taken Temple for his private secretary, and will bring him in for the borough of —. How his lordship found him out to be the author of that famous pamphlet, which bore Cunningham's name, I do not know. I know that I kept the secret, as in honour bound; but Lord Oldborough has the best ways and means of obtaining intelligence of any man in England. It is singular that he never said one word about the pamphlet to Temple, nor ever appeared to him to know that it was his writing. I cannot understand this."

To comprehend why Lord Oldborough had never mentioned the pamphlet to Mr. Temple, it was necessary to know more than Alfred had opportunities of discovering of this minister's character. His lordship did not choose to acknowledge to the world that he had been duped by Cunningham Falconer. Lord Oldborough would sooner repair an error than acknowledge it. Not that he was uncandid; but he considered candour as dangerous and impolitic in a public character.

Upon some occasion, soon after Mr. Temple came to be his lordship's secretary, Mr. Temple acknowledged to a gentleman, in Lord Oldborough's presence, some trifling official mistake he had made: Lord Oldborough, as soon as the gentleman was gone, said to his secretary, "Sir, if you make a mistake, repair it—that is sufficient. Sir, you are young in political life—you don't know, I see, that candour hurts a political character in the opinion of fools—that is, of the greater part of mankind. Candour may be advantageous to a moral writer, or to a private gentleman, but not to a minister of state. A statesman, if he would govern public opinion, must establish a belief in his infallibility."

Upon this principle Lord Oldborough abided, not only by his own measures, but by his own instruments—right or wrong, he was known to support those whom he had once employed or patronised. Lucky this for the Falconer family!

LETTER FROM ALFRED TO ERASMUS.

"MY DEAR DOCTOR,

"How I pity you who have no vacations! Please, when next you sum up the advantages and disadvantages of the professions of law and medicine, to set down vacations to the credit side of the law. You who work for life and death can have no pause, no respite; whilst I from time to time may, happily, leave all the property, real and personal, of my fellow-creatures, to its lawful or unlawful owners. Now, for six good weeks to come, I may hang sorrow and cast away care, and forget the sound and smell of parchments, and the din of the courts.

"Here I am, a happy prisoner at large, in this nutshell of a house at the Hills, which you have never seen since it has become the family mansion. I am now in the actual tenure and occupation of the little room, commonly called Rosamond's room, bounded on the N. E. W. and S. by blank—[N.B. a very dangerous practice of leaving blanks for your boundaries in your leases, as an eminent attorney told me last week.] Said room containing in the whole 14 square feet 4-1/2 square inches, superficial measure, be the same more or less. I don't know how my father and mother, and sisters, who all their lives were used to range in spacious apartments, can live so happily, cooped up as they now are; but their bodies, as well as minds, seem to have a contractile power, which adapts them to their present confined circumstances. Procrustes, though he was a mighty tyrant, could fit only the body to the bed. I found all at home as cheerful and contented as in the days when we lived magnificently at Percy-hall. I have not seen the Hungerfords yet; Colonel H. is, I hear, attached to Lady Elizabeth Pembroke. I know very little of her, but Caroline assures me she is an amiable, sensible woman, well suited to him, and to all his family. I need not, however, expatiate on this subject, for Caroline says that she wrote you a long letter, the day after she returned from Hungerford Castle.

"I must tell you what has happened to me since I came to the country. Do you remember my receiving a very angry, very ill-spelled letter, from a certain Farmer Grimwood of Pegginton, who swore, that if it cost him a thousand guineas in gold he would have the law of the doctor—viz. Dr. Leicester—about a tithe of peaches? My father, at my request, was so good as to send for said Grimwood, and to prevent him from having recourse in his ire to Attorney Sharpe. With prodigious difficulty, the angry farmer was restrained till my arrival; when I came home, I found him waiting for me, and literally foaming at the mouth with the furious desire for law. I flatter myself, I did listen to his story with a patience for which Job might have been admired. I was well aware that till he had exhausted himself, and was practically convinced that he had nothing more to say, he would be incapable of listening to me, or to the voice of the angel of peace. When at last absolute fatigue of reiteration had reduced him to silence, when he had held me by the button till he was persuaded he had made me fully master of his case, I prevailed upon him to let me hear what could be said on the opposite side of the question; and after some hours' cross-examination of six witnesses, repeaters, and reporters, and after an infinite confusion of said I's, and said he's, it was made clearly to appear that the whole quarrel originated in the mistake of a few words in a message which Dr. Leicester's agent had given to his son, a boy of seven years old, who had left it with a deaf gate-keeper of seventy-six, who repeated it to Farmer Grimwood, at a moment when the farmer was over-heated and overtired, and consequently prone to misunderstanding and to anger. The most curious circumstance in the whole business is, that the word peaches had never been mentioned by Dr. Leicester's agent in the original message; and Dr. Leicester really did not know that Mr. Grimwood of Pegginton was possessed of a single peach. Grimwood, though uncommonly obstinate and slow, is a just man; and when I at last brought the facts with indisputable evidence home to his understanding, he acknowledged that he had been too hasty, rejoiced that he had not gone to law, begged the doctor and the doctor's agent's pardon, thanked me with his whole honest heart, and went home in perfect charity with all mankind. Mr. Sharpe, who soon heard of the amicable conclusion of this affair, laughs at me, and pronounces that I shall never make a lawyer, and that my friends need never flatter themselves with the notion of my rising at the bar.

"Yours truly,

"A. PERCY.

"My letter was forgotten yesterday, and I am glad of it. Blessings on Farmer Grimwood of Pegginton! Little did I think that he and his quarrel about tithe peaches would have such happy influence on my destiny. Blessings on Farmer Grimwood of Pegginton! I repeat: he has been the cause of my seeing such a—of my receiving such a look of approbation—such a smile! She is niece to our good rector—come to spend a few days with him. Grimwood went to the vicarage to make up his quarrel with Dr. Leicester—I do not know what he said of me, but I find it has left a very favourable impression in the good doctor's mind. He came here yesterday, and brought with him his charming niece. My dear Erasmus, you know that I have often prayed that I might never fall in love seriously, till I had some reasonable prospect of being able to marry; but I begin to retract my prayer for indifference, and to be of opinion that the most prudent thing a professional man can do is to fall in love—to fall in love with such a woman as Sophia Leicester. What a new motive for exertion! Animated by delightful hope, perseverance, even in the most stupid drudgery, will be pleasure. Hope!—but I am far from hope—far at this instant from knowing distinctly what I hope—or wish—or mean. I will write again soon and explain."

CHAPTER XX

In several successive letters of Alfred to his brother, the progress of his attachment to Miss Leicester is described. Instead of paying a visit of a few days to her uncle, it appears that she stayed at the vicarage during the whole of Alfred's vacation. Her mother died, and, contrary to the expectation of some of her admirers, Miss Leicester was left in possession of only a moderate fortune. She showed much dignity under these adverse circumstances, with a charming mixture of spirit and gentleness of disposition. The change in her expectations, which deprived her of some of her fashionable admirers, showed her the superior sincerity and steadiness of Alfred's sentiments. No promises were given on either side; but it appears, that Alfred was permitted to live and labour upon hope. He returned to London more eager than ever to pursue his profession.

We trust that our readers will be fully satisfied with this abridgment of the affair, and will be more inclined to sympathize with Alfred, and to wish well to his attachment, than if they had been fatigued with a volume of his love-letters, and with those endless repetitions of the same sentiments with which most lovers' letters abound.

Let us now go on to the affairs of Erasmus Percy.

Mr. Panton, provoked by his daughter's coldness towards Lord Roadster, had begun shrewdly to suspect that the lady must be in love with some other person. His young physician was the only man on whom he could fix his suspicions. Constance seemed to be on a more confidential footing with him than with any of the visitors who frequented his house; she had spoken of him in terms of high approbation, and had not contradicted her father when he had, purposely to try her, pronounced Dr. Percy to be the handsomest young fellow he knew. While these suspicions were secretly gaining strength in the father's mind, a circumstance occurred which confirmed them at once, and caused them to burst forth with uncontrolled violence of expression.

Dr. Percy was called in to prescribe for a sick lawyer, and from this lawyer's conversation he learnt that Lord Runnymede was a ruined man, and that his son Lord Roadster's extravagance had been the cause of his ruin. Erasmus determined to put Mr. Panton upon his guard, and thus, if possible, to prevent the amiable Constance from becoming a victim to her father's absurd ambition. With this view he went to Mr. Panton's. The old gentleman was gone to dine with his club. Mrs. Panton, in her elegant language, desired he would leave his business with her. When he had explained the purport of his visit, after a variety of vulgar exclamations denoting surprise and horror, and after paying many compliments to her own sagacity, all which appeared incompatible with her astonishment, Mrs. Panton expressed much gratitude to Erasmus, mixed with suppressed satisfaction, and significant nods which he could not quite comprehend. Her gratitude was interrupted, and the whole train of her ideas changed, by the entrance of a milliner with new caps and artificial flowers. She, however, retained sufficient recollection of what had passed, to call after Erasmus when he had taken his leave, and to insist upon his coming to her party that evening. This he declined. Then she said he must dine with her next day, for let him be never so busy, he must dine somewhere, and as good dine with somebody as with nobody—in short, she would take no denial. The next day Erasmus was received with ungracious oddity of manner by old Panton— the only person in the drawing-room when he arrived. Erasmus was so much struck with the gloom of his countenance, that he asked whether Mr. Panton felt himself ill. Panton bared his wrist, and held out his hand to Erasmus to feel his pulse—then withdrawing his hand, he exclaimed, "Nonsense! I'm as well as any man in England. Pray, now, Doctor Percy, why don't you get a wig?"—"Why should I, sir, when I have hair?" said Erasmus, laughing.—"Pshaw! doctor, what signifies laughing when I am serious!—Why, sir, in my youth every decent physician wore a wig, and I have no notion of a good physician without a wig—particularly a young one. Sir, many people have a great objection to a young physician for many reasons. And take my advice in time, Doctor Percy—a wig, a proper wig, not one of your modern natural scratches, but a decent powdered doctor's bob, would make you look ten years older at one slap, and trust me you'd get into practice fast enough then, and be sent for by many a sober family, that would never think of letting you within their doors without the wig; for, sir, you are too young and too handsome for a physician—Hey! what say you to the wig?" concluded Panton, in a tone of such serious, yet comical impatience, that Erasmus found it difficult to restrain a smile, whilst he answered that he really did not think his charms were so dangerous that it was necessary to disguise them by a wig; that as to his youth, it was an objection which every day would tend to lessen; and that he trusted he might obtain the credit of being a good physician if he could cure people of their diseases; and they would feel it to be a matter of indifference whether they were restored to health by a doctor in a wig or without one.

"Indifference!" cried Panton, starting upright in his chair with passion. "I don't know what you call a matter of indifference, sir; I can tell you its no matter of indifference to me—If you mean me; for say that with God's mercy you carried me through, what then, if you are doing your best to break my heart after all—"

Mr. Panton stopped short, for at this instant Constance came into the room, and her father's look of angry suspicion, and her blush, immediately explained to Erasmus what had the moment before appeared to him unintelligible. He felt provoked with himself for colouring in his turn, and being embarrassed without any reason, but he recovered his presence of mind directly, when Constance, with a dignified ingenuous modesty of manner, advanced towards him, notwithstanding her father's forbidding look, and with a sweet, yet firm voice, thanked him for his yesterday's friendly visit to her mother.

"I wonder you a'n't ashamed of yourself, girl!" cried old Panton, choking with passion.

"And I'm sure I wonder you a'n't ashamed of yourself, Mr. Panton, if you come to that," cried Mrs. Panton, "exposing of your family affairs this way by your unseasonable passions, when one has asked people to dinner too."

"Dinner or no dinner," cried old Panton, and he must have been strangely transported beyond himself when he made that exclamation, "dinner or no dinner, Mrs. Panton, I will speak my mind, and be master in my own house! So, Doctor Percy, if you please, we'll leave the ladies, and talk over our matters our own way, in my own room here within."

Dr. Percy willingly acceded to this proposal. Old Panton waddled as fast as he could to show the way through the antechamber, whilst Mrs. Panton called after him, "Don't expose yourself no more than you can help, my dear!" And as Erasmus passed her, she whispered, "Never mind him, doctor—stand by yourself—I'll stand by you, and we'll stand by you—won't we, Constance?—see her colour!"—"We have reason to be grateful to Dr. Percy," said Constance, gravely, with an air of offended modesty; "and I hope," added she, with softened sweetness of tone, as she looked at him, and saw his feelings in his countenance, "I hope Doctor Percy is assured of my gratitude, and of my perfect esteem."

"Come! what the devil?" cried old Panton, "I thought you were close behind me."

"Now, doctor," cried he, as soon as he had fairly got Erasmus into his closet, and shut the door, "now, doctor, I suppose you see I am not a man to be imposed upon?"

"Nor, if you were, am I a man to impose upon you, sir," said Erasmus. "If I understand you rightly, Mr. Panton, you suspect me of some designs upon your daughter? I have none."

"And you won't have the assurance to deny that you are in love with her?"

"I am not in love with Miss Panton, sir: she has charms and virtues which might create the strongest attachment in the heart of any man of feeling and discernment who could permit himself to think of her; but I am not in a situation in which I could, with honour, seek to win her affections, and, fortunately for me, this reflection has probably preserved my heart from danger. If I felt any thing like love for your daughter, sir, you may be assured that I should not, at this instant, be in your house."

"A mighty fine speech, sir! and well delivered, for aught I know. You are a scholar, and can speak sentences; but that won't impose on me, a plain man that has eyes. Why—tell me!—didn't I see you within these two minutes blushing up to the eyes, both of you, at one another? Don't I know when I see men and women in love—tell me! Mrs. Panton—fudge!—And did not I see behind my back, just now, the women conjuring with you?—And aren't you colouring over head and ears with conscience this very instant?—Tell me!"

Erasmus in vain asserted his own and the young lady's innocence, and maintained that blushing was no proof of guilt—he even adverted to the possibility of a man's blushing for others instead of himself.

"Blush for me as much as you please, if it's me you allude to," cried the coarse father; "but when my daughter's at stake, I make no bones of speaking plain, and cutting the matter short in the beginning—for we all know what love is when it comes to a head. Marrow-bones! don't I know that there must be some reason why that headstrong girl won't think of my Lord Runnymede's son and heir, and such a looking youth, title and all, as my Lord Roadster! And you are the cause, sir; and I thank you for opening my eyes to it, as you did by your information to Mrs. Panton yesterday, in my absence."

Erasmus protested with such an air of truth as would have convinced any person capable of being convinced, that, in giving that information, he had been actuated solely by a desire to save Miss Panton from a ruinous match, by honest regard for her and all her family.

"Ruinous!—You are wrong, sir—I know better—I know best—I saw my Lord Runnymede himself this very morning—a little temporary want of cash only from the estate's being tied up, as they sometimes tie estates, which all noble families is subject to—Tell me! don't I know the bottom of these things? for though I haven't been used to land, I know all about it. And at worst, my Lord Roadster, my son-in-law that is to be, is not chargeable with a penny of his father's debts. So your informer is wrong, sir, every way, and no lawyer, sir, for I have an attorney at my back—and your information's all wrong, and you had no need to interfere."

Erasmus felt and acknowledged the imprudence of his interference, but hoped it might be forgiven in favour of the motive—and he looked so honestly glad to hear that his information was all wrong, that old Panton at the moment believed in his integrity, and said, stretching out his hand towards him, "Well, well, no harm done—then it's all as it should be, and we may ring for dinner—But," recurring again to his favourite idea, "you'll get the wig, doctor?"

"Excuse me," said Erasmus, laughing, "your confidence in me cannot depend upon a wig."

"It can, sir, and it does," cried Panton, turning again with all his anger revived. "Excuse you! No, sir, I won't; for the wig's my test, and I told Mrs. Panton so last night—the wig's my test of your uprightness in this matter, sir; and I fairly tell you, that if you refuse this, all the words you can string don't signify a button with me."

"And by what right, sir, do you speak to me in this manner?" cried Erasmus, proudly, for he lost all sense of the ludicrous in indignation at the insolent doubt of his integrity, which, after all the assurances he had given, these last words from Mr. Panton implied: "By what right, sir, do you speak to me in this manner?—And what reason can you have to expect that I should submit to any tests to convince you of the truth of my assertions?"

"Right! Reason!" cried Panton. "Why, doctor, don't you know that I'm your patron?"

"My patron!" repeated Erasmus, in a tone which would have expressed much to the mind of any man of sense or feeling, but which conveyed no idea to the gross apprehension of old Panton except that Dr. Percy was ignorant of the fact.

"Your patron—yes, doctor—why, don't you know, that ever since you set me upon my legs I have been going up and down the city puffing—that is, I mean, recommending you to all my friends? and you see you're of consequence—getting into fine practice for so young a man. And it stands to reason that when one takes a young man by the hand, one has a right to expect one's advice should be followed; and as to the wig, I don't make it a test—you've an objection to a test—but, as I've mentioned it to Mrs. Panton, I must make it a point, and you know I am not a man to go back. And you'll consider that if you disoblige me, you can't expect that I should continue my friendship, and protection, and patronage, and all that."

"Be assured, sir, I expect nothing from you," said Erasmus, "and desire nothing: I have the happiness and honour to belong to a profession, in which, if a man merits confidence, he will succeed, without requiring any man's patronage."—Much less the patronage of such a one as you! Erasmus would have said, but that he commanded his indignation, or, perhaps, it was extinguished by contempt.

A servant now came to announce that the company was arrived, and dinner was waiting. In very bad humour, Mr. Panton, nevertheless, ate an excellent dinner, growling over every thing as he devoured it. Constance seemed much grieved by her father's unseasonable fit of rudeness and obstinacy; with sweetness of temper and filial duty she bore with his humour, and concealed it as far as she could from observation. Mrs. Panton was displeased with this, and once went so far as to whisper to Erasmus that her step-daughter wanted spirit sadly, but that he ought never to mind that, but to take a broad hint, and keep his ground. Erasmus, who, with great simplicity and an upright character, had quick observation and tact, perceived pretty nearly what was going on in the family. He saw that the step-mother, under an air of frank and coarse good-nature, was cunning and interested; that she wished to encourage the daughter to open war with the father, knowing that nothing could incense him so much as Constance's thinking of a poor physician instead of accepting of an earl's son; Mrs. Panton wished then to fan to a flame the spark which she was confident existed in his daughter's heart. Erasmus, who was not apt to fancy that ladies liked him, endeavoured to relieve Constance from the agonizing apprehension which he saw she felt of his being misled by her mother's hints: he appeared sometimes not to hear, and at other times not to understand, what Mrs. Panton whispered; and at last talked so loud across the table to Mr. Henry, about letters from Godfrey, and the officers of all the regiments in or out of England, that no other subject could be introduced, and no other voice could be heard. As soon as he decently could, after dinner, Dr. Percy took his leave, heartily glad to escape from his awkward situation, and from the patronage of Mr. Panton. Erasmus was mistaken, however, in supposing that Mr. Panton could do him no harm. It is true that he could not deny that Dr. Percy had restored him to health, and the opinion, which had spread in the city, of Dr. Percy's skill, was not, and could not, be diminished by Mr. Panton's railing against him; but when he hinted that the young physician had practised upon his daughter's heart, all the rich citizens who had daughters to watch began to consider him as a dangerous person, and resolved never to call him in, except in some desperate case. Mrs. Panton's gossiping confidences did more harm than her husband's loud complaints; and the very eagerness which poor Constance showed to vindicate Dr. Percy, and to declare the truth, served only to confirm the sagaciously-nodding mothers and overwise fathers in their own opinions. Mr. Henry said and did what he could for Erasmus; but what could be done by a young man shut up all day in a counting-house? or who would listen to any thing that was said by a youth without station or name? Mr. Gresham unluckily was at this time at his country-seat. Poor Erasmus found his practice in the city decline as rapidly as it had risen, and he began a little to doubt the truth of that noble sentiment which he had so proudly expressed. He was comforted, however, by letters from his father, who strongly approved his conduct, and who maintained that truth would at last prevail, and that the prejudice which had been raised against him would, in time, be turned to his advantage.

It happened that, while old Panton, in his present ludicrous fit of obstinacy, was caballing against our young physician with all his might in the city, the remote consequences of his absurdities were operating in Dr. Percy's favour at the west end of the town. Our readers may recollect having heard of a footman, whom Mr. Panton turned away for laughing at his perversity. Erasmus had at the time pleaded in the poor fellow's favour, and had, afterwards, when the servant was out of place, in distress, and ill, humanely attended him, and cured a child of his, who had inflamed eyes. This man was now in the service of a rich and very fine lady, who lived in Grosvenor-square—Lady Spilsbury. Her ladyship had several sickly children—children rendered sickly by their mother's overweening and injudicious care. Alarmed successively by every fashionable medical terror of the day, she dosed her children with every specific which was publicly advertised or privately recommended. No creatures of their age had taken such quantities of Ching's lozenges, Godbold's elixir, or Dixon's antibilious pills. The consequence was, that the dangers, which had at first been imaginary, became real: these little victims of domestic medicine never had a day's health: they looked, and were, more dead than alive. Still the mother, in the midst of hourly alarms, was in admiration of her own medical skill, which she said had actually preserved, in spite of nature, children of such sickly constitutions. In consequence of this conviction, she redoubled her vigilance, and the most trivial accident was magnified into a symptom of the greatest importance.

It happened on the day when the eldest Miss Spilsbury had miraculously attained her seventh year, a slight inflammation was discerned in her right eye, which was attributed by her mother to her having neglected the preceding day to bathe it in elder-flower water; by her governess, to her having sat up the preceding night to supper; by her maid, to her having been found peeping through a windy key-hole; and by the young lady herself, to her having been kept poring for two hours over her French lesson.

Whatever might have been the original cause, the inflammation evidently increased, either in consequence or in spite of the innumerable remedies applied internally and externally—the eye grew redder and redder, and as red as blood, the nose inflamed, and the mother, in great alarm for the beauty as well as health of her child, sent for Sir Amyas Courtney. He had already won Lady Spilsbury's heart by recommending to her the honan tcha, or Tartar tea, which enables the Tartars to digest raw flesh, and tinges water of a red colour.

Sir Amyas pronounced that the young lady had hereditary nerves, besought Lady Spilsbury to compose herself, assured her the inflammation was purely symptomatic, and as soon as he could subdue the continual nervous inclination to shrivel up the nose, which he trusted he could in time master, all would go well. But Sir Amyas attended every day for a month, yet never got the mastery of this nervous inclination. Lady Spilsbury then was persuaded it could not be nerves, it must be scrofula; and she called in Dr. Frumpton, the man for scrofula. He of course confirmed her ladyship in her opinion; for a week d—d nerves and Sir Amyas; threw in desperate doses of calomel for another month, reduced the poor child to what the maid called an attomy, and still the inflammation increased. Lady Spilsbury desired a consultation of physicians, but Dr. Frumpton would not consult with Sir Amyas, nor would Sir Amyas consult with Dr. Frumpton. Lady Spilsbury began to dread that the sight of the eye would be injured, and this idea terrified the mother almost out of her senses. In the suspension of authority which terror produces in a family, the lady's-maid usually usurps considerable power.

Now her ladyship's maid had been offended by Dr. Frumpton's calling her my good girl, and by Sir Amyas Courtney's having objected to a green silk bandage which she had recommended; so that she could not abide either of the gentlemen, and she was confident the young lady would never get well while they had the management of affairs: she had heard—but she did not mention from whom, she was too diplomatic to give up her authority—she had heard of a young physician, a Dr. Percy, who had performed wonderful great cures in the city, and had in particular cured a young lady who had an inflamed eye, just for all the world like Miss Spilsbury's. In this last assertion, there was, perhaps, some little exaggeration; but it produced a salutary effect upon Lady Spilsbury's imagination: the footman was immediately despatched for Dr. Percy, and ordered to make all possible haste. Thus by one of those petty underplots of life, which, often unknown to us, are continually going on, our young physician was brought into a situation where he had an opportunity of showing his abilities. These favourable accidents happen to many men who are not able to make use of them, and thus the general complaint is preferred of want of good fortune, or of opportunity for talents to distinguish themselves.

Upon Dr. Percy's arrival at Lady Spilsbury's, he immediately perceived that parties ran high, and that the partisans were all eager to know whether he would pronounce the young lady's case to be nervous or scrofulous. He was assailed by a multitude of female voices, and requested particularly to attend to innumerable contradictory symptoms, before he was permitted even to see his patient. He attended carefully to whatever facts he could obtain, pure from opinion and misrepresentation. The young lady was in a darkened room—he begged to have a little more light admitted, though she was in such pain that she could scarcely endure it. Our young physician had the great advantage of possessing the use of his senses and understanding, unbiassed by medical theories, or by the authority of great names: he was not always trying to force symptoms to agree with previous descriptions, but he was actually able to see, hear, and judge of them as they really appeared. There was a small protuberance on the left side of the nose, which, on his pressing it, gave great pain to the child.

"Dear me! miss, you know," said the maid, "it is not in your nose you feel the great pain—you know you told Sir Amyas Courtney t'other day—that is, Sir Amyas Courtney told you—"

Dr. Percy insisted that the child should be permitted to speak for herself; and, relieved from the apprehension of not saying the thing that she was expected to say, she described her present and past feelings. She said, "that the pain seemed lately to have changed from where it was before—that it had changed ever since Dr. Frumpton's opening his snuff-box near her had made her sneeze." This sneeze was thought by all but Dr. Percy to be a circumstance too trivial to be worth mentioning; but on this hint he determined to repeat the experiment. He had often thought that many of the pains which are supposed to be symptoms of certain diseases, many disorders which baffle the skill of medicine, originate in accidents, by which extraneous substances are taken or forced into different parts of the body. He ordered some cephalic snuff to be administered to the patient. All present looked with contempt at the physician who proposed such a simple remedy. But soon after the child had sneezed violently and repeatedly, Dr. Percy saw a little bit of green silk appear, which was drawn from the nostril, to the patient's great and immediate relief. Her brothers and sisters then recollected having seen her, two months before, stuffing up her nose a bit of green riband, which she said she liked because it smelt of some perfume. The cause of the inflammation removed, it soon subsided; the eye and nose recovered their natural size and colour, and every body said, "Who would have thought it?" all but Dr. Frumpton and Sir Amyas Courtney, who, in the face of demonstration, maintained each his own opinion; declaring that the green riband had nothing to do with the business. The sudden recovery of the child, Sir Amyas said, proved to him, in the most satisfactory manner, that the disease was, as he at first pronounced—nervous. Dr. Frumpton swore that scrofula would soon break out again in another shape; and, denouncing vengeance against generations yet unborn, he left Lady Spilsbury's children to take the consequences of trusting to a youngster, whose impertinent interference he could never forget or forgive. In spite of all that the two angry and unsuccessful physicians could say, the recovery of the child's eye redounded much to Dr. Percy's honour, and introduced him to the notice of several men of science and celebrity, who frequented Lady Spilsbury's excellent dinners. Even the intemperance of Dr. Frumpton's anger was of service; for in consequence of his furious assertions, inquiry was made into the circumstances, and the friends of Erasmus had then an opportunity of producing in his defence the Irish porter. His cause could not be in better hands.

With that warmth and eloquence of gratitude characteristic of his country, the poor fellow told his story so as to touch every heart. Among others it particularly affected an officer just returned from our armies on the continent: and by him it was the next day repeated at the table of a celebrated general, when the conversation turned upon the conduct of certain army surgeons. Lord Oldborough happened to be one of the company; the name of Percy struck his ear; the moment Erasmus was thus brought to his recollection, he attended particularly to what the officer was saying; and, after hearing two circumstances, which were so marked with humanity and good sense, his lordship determined to give what assistance he could to the rising credit of the son of his old friend, by calling him in for Lady Oldborough, who was in a declining state of health. But Sir Amyas Courtney, who had long attended her ladyship, endeavoured, with all the address of hatred, to prejudice her against his young rival, and to prevent her complying with her lord's request. Depending on her habitual belief that he was essential to her existence, Sir Amyas went so far as to declare that if Dr. Percy should be sent for, he must discontinue his visits. Lord Oldborough, however, whom the appearance of opposition to his will always confirmed in his purpose, cut short the matter by a few peremptory words.

Sir Amyas, the soft silken Sir Amyas, could not for an instant stand before the terror of Lord Oldborough's eye: the moment he was told that he was at perfect liberty to discontinue his visits, his regard—his attachment—his devotion for Lady Oldborough, prevented the possibility of abandoning her ladyship; he was willing to sacrifice his private feelings, perhaps his private prejudices, his judgment, in short any thing, every thing, sooner than disoblige Lord Oldborough, or any of his family. Lord Oldborough, satisfied with the submission, scarcely stayed to hear the end of the speech, but rang the bell, ordered that Dr. Percy should be sent for, and went to attend a cabinet council.

Lady Oldborough received him as it might be supposed that a very sickly, very much prejudiced, very proud lady of quality would receive a physician without a name, who was forced upon her in opposition to her long habits of reliance on her courtly favourite. Her present disease, as Dr. Percy believed, was water upon her chest, and there was some chance of saving her, by the remedies which have been found successful in a first attack of that complaint; but Sir Amyas had pronounced that her ladyship's disorder was merely nervous spasms, consequent upon a bilious attack, and he could not, or would not, recede from his opinion: his prescriptions, to which her ladyship devoutly adhered to the last, were all directed against bile and nerves. She would not hear of water on the chest, or take any of the remedies proposed by Dr. Percy. Lady Oldborough died ten days after he was called in. Those who knew nothing of the matter, that is, above nine-tenths of all who talked about it, affirmed that poor Lady Oldborough's death was occasioned by her following the rash prescriptions of a young physician, who had been forced upon her by Lord Oldborough; and who, unacquainted with her ladyship's constitution, had mistaken the nature of her complaint. All her ladyship's female relations joined in this clamour, for they were most of them friends or partizans of Sir Amyas Courtney. The rank and conspicuous situation of Lord Oldborough interested vast numbers in the discussion, which was carried on in every fashionable circle the day after her ladyship's decease.

Dr. Percy took a decided step in this emergency. He went to the minister, to whom no one, friend or enemy, had ventured to give the slightest hint of the reports in circulation. Dr. Percy plainly stated the facts, represented that his character and the fate of his whole life were at stake, and besought his lordship to have the truth examined into by eminent and impartial physicians. Erasmus was aware of all he hazarded in making this request—aware that he must hurt Lord Oldborough's feelings—that he must irritate him by bringing to his view at once, and in this critical moment, a number of family cabals, of which he was ignorant—aware that Lord Oldborough was oppressed with business, public and private; and that, above all things, he was impatient of any intrusion upon his hours of privacy. But all these subordinate considerations vanished before Lord Oldborough's magnanimity. Without saying one word, he sat down and wrote an order, that proper means should be taken to ascertain the disease of which Lady Oldborough died.

The report made, in consequence of this order, by the surgeons, confirmed Dr. Percy's opinion that her ladyship's disease was water on the chest—and Lord Oldborough took effectual means to give the truth publicity.

"You need not thank me, Dr. Percy—you have a right to expect justice, more you will never want. My assistance might, it seems, have been injurious, but can never be necessary to your reputation."

These few words—much from Lord Oldborough—and which he took care to say when they could be heard by numbers, were quickly circulated. The physicians and surgeons who had given in their report were zealous in maintaining the truth; medical and political parties were interested in the affair; the name of Dr. Percy was joined with the first names in the medical world, and repeated by the first people in the great world, so that with surprising celerity he became known and fashionable. And thus the very circumstance that threatened his ruin was, by his civil courage and decided judgment, converted into the means of his rising into eminence.

Late one night, after a busy and fatiguing day, just as Erasmus had got into bed, and was settling himself comfortably to sleep, he heard a loud knock at the door.

"Mr. Henry, sir, from Mr. Panton's in the city, wishes to speak with you."

"Show him in.—So, old Panton, I suppose—some indigestion has brought him to reason?"

"Oh! no such thing," interrupted Mr. Henry—"I would not have disturbed you at this time of night for any such trifle; but our excellent friend, Mr. Gresham—"

"What of him?" cried Erasmus, starting up in bed.

"Is ill,—but whether dangerously or not, I cannot tell you. An express from his house in the country has just arrived; I heard the letter read, but could not get it to bring to you. It was written to old Panton from Mr. Gresham's housekeeper, without her master's knowledge, as he has no opinion of physicians, she said, except of a young Dr. Percy, and did not like to send for him for such a trifle as a sore throat, lest it should hurt his practice to leave town at this season."

Erasmus stayed to hear no more, but ordered horses instantly, set out, and travelled with all possible expedition. He had reason to rejoice that he had not made a moment's delay. He found Mr. Gresham actually suffocating from a quinsy. A surgeon had been sent for from the next town, but was not at home. Erasmus, the instant he saw Mr. Gresham, perceiving the danger, without saying one syllable, sprang to the bed, lanced the throat, and saved the life of his valuable friend. The surgeon, who came the next day, said that Dr. Percy ought to have waited for his arrival, and that a physician might be severely blamed for performing a surgical operation—that it was a very indelicate thing.

But Mr. Gresham, who had fallen into a comfortable sleep, did not hear him; nor did Dr. Percy, who was writing the following letter to his father:

"... You will sympathize with me, my dear father, and all my friends at home will sympathize in the joy I feel at seeing this excellent man, this kind friend, recovering under my care. These are some of the happy moments which, in my profession, repay us for years of toil, disappointment, and sufferings—yes, sufferings—for we must suffer with those that suffer: we must daily and hourly behold every form of pain, acute or lingering; numbers, every year of our lives, we must see perish, the victims of incurable disease. We are doomed to hear the groans of the dying, and the lamentations, sometimes the reproaches, of surviving friends; often and often must the candid and humane physician deplore the insufficiency of his art. But there are successful, gloriously successful moments, which reward us for all the painful duties, all the unavailing regrets of our profession.

"This day I shall recall to my mind whenever my spirits sink, or whenever my fortitude begins to fail. I wish you could see the gratitude and joy in the looks of all Mr. Gresham's servants. His death would have been a public loss, for the beneficent use he makes of his princely fortune has rendered numbers dependent on him for the comforts of life. He lives here in a palace, and every thing he has done, whether in building or planting, in encouraging the useful or the fine arts, has been done with a judicious and magnificent spirit. Surely this man ought to be happy in his own reflections, and yet he does not seem to me as happy as he deserves to be. I shall stay here till I see him out of all danger of relapse.—He has just awakened—Adieu for the present."

In continuation of this letter the following was written the next day:

"All danger is over—my friend is convalescent, and I shall return to town to-morrow. But would you think, my dear father, that the real cause of Mr. Gresham's being unhappy is patronage? By accident I made use of that word in speaking of old Panton's quarrel with me, and he cursed the word the moment I pronounced it: 'Yes,' he exclaimed, 'it is twice accursed—once in the giving, and once in the receiving.' Then he began, in a most feeling manner, to describe the evils attendant upon being a patron. He has done his utmost to relieve and encourage genius in distress; but among all the poets, painters, artists, and men of letters, whom in various ways he has obliged, he has scarcely been able to satisfy the vanity or the expectations of any. Some have passed from excessive adulation to gross abuse of him—many more torment him continually with their complaints and invectives against each other; and, instead of having done good by his generosity, he finds that, in a variety of instances, of which he detailed the circumstances, he has done much mischief, and, as he says, infinite injury to his own peace of mind—for he has burdened himself with the care of a number of people, who cannot be made happy. He has to deal with men but partially cultivated; with talents, unaccompanied by reason, justice, or liberality of sentiment. With great feeling himself, he suffers acutely from all their jealousies and quarrels, and from the near and perpetual view of the littleness by which artists too often degrade themselves. Another man in Mr. Gresham's situation would become a misanthropist, and would comfort himself by railing against the ingratitude of mankind; but this would not comfort Mr. Gresham. He loves his fellow-creatures, and sees their faults in sorrow rather than in anger. I have known him, and intimately, for a considerable time, and yet I never heard him speak on this subject but once before, when the painter, whom I used to call the irritable genius, had caricatured him in return for all his kindness.

"Though it is not easy to change the habits or to alter the views and objects of a man, like Mr. Gresham, past the meridian of life, yet I cannot help flattering myself that this might be effected. If he would, by one bold effort, shake off these dependents, the evening of his days might yet be serene and happy. He wants friends, not protégées. I have advised him, as soon as his strength will permit, to take a little tour, which will bring him into your part of the country. He wishes much to become acquainted with all our family, and I have given him a note of introduction. You, my dear father, can say to him more than I could with propriety.

"Mr. Gresham knows how to accept as well as to give. He allows me to have the pleasure of proving to him, that where my friends are concerned, I am above pecuniary considerations. My love to my dear mother, Rosamond, and Caroline.

"Your affectionate son,

"E. PERCY."

Though Mr. Gresham would not hurt the feelings of his young friend and physician, by pressing upon him at the moment any remuneration, or by entering into any calculation of the loss he would sustain by his absence from London at this critical season, he took his own methods of justly recompensing Dr. Percy. Erasmus found at his door, some time after his return to town, a plain but excellent chariot and horses, with a note from Mr. Gresham, written in such terms as precluded the possibility of refusing the offer.

The celebrated London physician, who said that he was not paid for three weeks' attendance in the country, by a draft of two thousand pounds; and who, when the pen was put into his own hands, wrote four in the place of two, would smile in scorn at the generosity of Mr. Gresham and the disinterestedness of Dr. Percy.

CHAPTER XXI

LETTER FROM CAROLINE TO ERASMUS.

"MY DEAR ERASMUS,

"Your friend and patient, Mr. Gresham, was so eager to take your advice, and so quick in his movements, that your letter, announcing his intended visit, reached us but a few days before his arrival at the Hills. And—mark how great and little events, which seem to have no possible link of connexion, depend upon one another—Alfred or Mr. Gresham must have sat up all night, or slept on the floor, had not Alfred, that morning, received a letter from Mrs. Hungerford, summoning him to town to draw her son's marriage settlements. It is thought that Colonel Hungerford, whose leave of absence from his regiment has, by special favour, been repeatedly protracted, will be very soon sent abroad. Lady Elizabeth Pembroke has, therefore, consented to his urgent desire for their immediate union; and Alfred will, I am sure, give them as little reason as possible to complain of the law's delay. Lady Elizabeth, who has all that decision of mind and true courage which you know is so completely compatible with the most perfect gentleness of disposition and softness, even timidity of manners, resolves to leave all her relations and friends, and to go abroad. She says she knew what sacrifices she must make in marrying a soldier, and she is prepared to make them without hesitation or repining.

"And now to return to your friend, Mr. Gresham. The more we see of him the more we like him. Perhaps he bribed our judgment a little at first by the kind, affectionate manner in which he spoke of you; but, independently of this prepossession, we should, I hope, soon have discovered his merit. He is a good English merchant. Not a 'M. Friport, qui sçait donner, mais qui ne sçait pas vivre,' but a well-bred, well-informed gentleman, upright, liberal, and benevolent, without singularity or oddities of any sort. His quiet, plain manners, free from ostentation, express so well the kind feelings of his mind, that I prefer them infinitely to what are called polished manners. Last night Rosamond and I were amusing ourselves by contrasting him with our recollection of the polished M. de Tourville—but as you were not at home at the memorable time of the shipwreck, and of M. de Tourville's visit, you cannot feel the force of our parallel between these two beings, the most dissimilar I have ever seen—an English merchant and a diplomatic Frenchman. You will ask, what put it into our heads to make the comparison? A slight circumstance which happened yesterday evening. Rosamond was showing Mr. Gresham some of my drawings, and among them the copy of that beautiful miniature in M. de Tourville's snuff-box. My father told him the history of Euphrosyne, of her German prince, and Count Albert. Mr. Gresham's way of listening struck us, by its contrast to the manner of M. de Tourville—and this led us on to draw a parallel between their characters. Mr. Gresham, instead of shrugging his shoulders, and smiling disdainfully, like the Frenchman, at the Quixotism of the young nobleman, who lost his favour at court by opposing the passion of his prince, was touched with Count Albert's disinterested character; and quite forgetting, as Rosamond observed, to compliment me upon my picture of Euphrosyne, he laid down the miniature with a negligence of which M. de Tourville never would have been guilty, and went on eagerly to tell some excellent traits of the count. For instance, when he was a very young man in the Prussian or Austrian service, I forget which, in the heat of an engagement he had his sabre lifted over the head of one of the enemy's officers, when, looking down, he saw that the officer's right arm was broken. The count immediately stopped, took hold of the disabled officer's bridle, and led him off to a place of safety. This and many other anecdotes Mr. Gresham heard, when he spent some time on the continent a few years ago, whilst he was transacting some commercial business. He had full opportunities of learning the opinions of different parties; and he says, that it was the prayer of all the good and wise in Germany, whenever the hereditary prince should succeed to the throne, that Count Albert Altenberg might be his minister.

"By-the-bye, Mr. Gresham, though he is rather an elderly man, and looks remarkably cool and composed, shows all the warmth of youth whenever any of his feelings are touched.

"I wish you could see how much my father is pleased with your friend. He has frequently repeated that Mr. Gresham, long as he has been trained in the habits of mercantile life, is quite free from the spirit of monopoly in small or great affairs. My father rejoices that his son has made such a friend. Rosamond charged me to leave her room to write to you at the end of my letter; but she is listening so intently to something Mr. Gresham is telling her, that I do not believe she will write one line. I hear a few words, which so much excite my curiosity, that I must go and listen too. Adieu.

"Affectionately yours,

"CAROLINE PERCY."

Another letter from Caroline to Erasmus, dated some weeks after the preceding.

"Tuesday, 14th.

"Yes, my dear Erasmus, your friend, Mr. Gresham, is still with us; and he declares that he has not, for many years, been so happy as since he came here. He is now sufficiently intimate in this family to speak of himself, and of his own feelings and plans. You, who know what a horror he has of egotism, will consider this as a strong proof of his liking us, and of his confidence in our regard. He has related many of the instances, which, I suppose, he told you, of the ingratitude and disappointments he has met with from persons whom he attempted to serve. He has kept us all, for hours, Rosamond especially, in a state of alternate pity and indignation. For all that has happened, he blames himself more than he blames any one else; and with a mildness and candour which make us at once admire and love him, he adverts to the causes of his own disappointment.

"My father has spoken to him as freely as you could desire. He has urged, that as far as the public good is concerned, free competition is more advantageous to the arts and to artists than any private patronage can be.

"If the productions have real merit, they will make their own way; if they have not merit, they ought not to make their way. And the same argument he has applied to literary merit, and to the merit, generally speaking, of persons as well as of things. He has also plainly told Mr. Gresham that he considers the trade of a patron as one of the most thankless, as it is the least useful, of all trades.

"All this has made such an impression upon your candid friend, that he has declared it to be his determination to have no more protégées, and to let the competition of talents work fairly without the interference, or, as he expressed it, any of the bounties and drawbacks of patronage. 'But then,' he added, with a sigh, 'I am a solitary being: am I to pass the remainder of my days without objects of interest or affection? While Constance Panton was a child, she was an object to me; but now she must live with her parents, or she will marry: at all events, she is rich—and is my wealth to be only for my selfish gratification? How happy you are, Mr. Percy, who have such an amiable wife, such a large family, and so many charming domestic objects of affection!'

"Mr. Gresham then walked away with my father to the end of the room, and continued his conversation in a low voice, to which I did not think I ought to listen, so I came up stairs to write to you. I think you told me that Mr. Gresham had suffered some disappointment early in life, which prevented his marrying; but if I am not mistaken, his mind now turns again to the hopes of domestic happiness. If I am not mistaken, Rosamond has made an impression on his heart. I have been as conveniently and meritoriously deaf, blind, and stupid, for some time past as possible; but though I shut my eyes, and stop my ears, yet my imagination will act, and I can only say to myself, as we used to do when we were children—I will not think of it till it comes, that I may have the pleasure of the surprise....

"Affectionately yours,

"CAROLINE PERCY."

Caroline was right—Rosamond had made a great impression upon Mr. Gresham's heart. His recollection of the difference between his age and Rosamond's, and his consciousness of the want of the gaiety and attractions of youth, rendered him extremely diffident, and for some time suppressed his passion, at least delayed the declaration of his attachment. But Rosamond seemed evidently to like his company and conversation, and she showed that degree of esteem and interest for him which, he flattered himself, might be improved into a more tender affection. He ventured to make his proposal—he applied first to Mrs. Percy, and entreated that she would make known his sentiments to her daughter.

When Mrs. Percy spoke to Rosamond, she was surprised at the very decided refusal which Rosamond immediately gave. Both Mrs. Percy and Caroline were inclined to think that Rosamond had not only a high opinion of Mr. Gresham, but that she had felt a preference for him which she had never before shown for any other person; and they thought that, perhaps, some refinement of delicacy about accepting his large fortune, or some fear that his want of high birth, and what are called good connexions, would be objected to by her father and mother, might be the cause of this refusal. Mrs. Percy felt extremely anxious to explain her own sentiments, and fully to understand Rosamond's feelings. In this anxiety Caroline joined most earnestly; all the kindness, sympathy, and ardent affection, which Rosamond had ever shown for her, when the interests of her heart were in question, were strong in Caroline's recollection, and these were now fully returned. Caroline thought Mr. Gresham was too old for her sister; but she considered that this objection, and all others, should yield to Rosamond's own opinion and taste. She agreed with her mother in imagining that Rosamond was not quite indifferent to his merit and to his attachment.

Mrs. Percy began by assuring Rosamond that she should be left entirely at liberty to decide according to her own judgment and feelings. "You have seen, my dear, how your father and I have acted towards your sister; and you may be sure that we shall show you equal justice. Though parents are accused of always rating 'a good estate above a faithful lover,' yet you will recollect that Mr. Barclay's good estate did not induce us to press his suit with Caroline. Mr. Gresham has a large fortune; and, to speak in Lady Jane Granville's style, it must be acknowledged, my dear Rosamond, that this would be a most advantageous match; but for this very reason we are particularly desirous that you should determine for yourself: at the same time, let me tell you, that I am a little surprised by the promptness of your decision. Let me be sure that this negative is serious—let me be sure that I rightly understand you, my love: now, when only your own Caroline is present, tell me what are your objections to Mr. Gresham?"

Thanks for her mother's kindness; thanks repeated, with tears in her eyes, were, for a considerable time, all the answer that could be obtained from Rosamond. At length she said, "Without having any particular objection to a person, surely, if I cannot love him, that is sufficient reason for my not wishing to marry him."

Rosamond spoke these words in so feeble a tone, and with so much hesitation, colouring at the same time so much, that her mother and sister were still uncertain how they were to understand her if—and

Mrs. Percy replied, "Undoubtedly, my dear, if you cannot love him; but that is the question. Is it quite certain that you cannot?"

"Oh! quite certain—I believe."

"This certainty seems to have come very suddenly," said her mother, smiling.

"What can you mean, mother?"

"I mean that you did not show any decided dislike to him, till within these few hours, my dear."

"Dislike! I don't feel—I hope I don't show any dislike—I am sure I should be very ungrateful. On the contrary, it would be impossible for any body, who is good for any thing, to dislike Mr. Gresham."

"Then you can neither like him nor dislike him?—You are in a state of absolute indifference."

"That is, except gratitude—gratitude for all his kindness to Erasmus, and for his partiality to me—gratitude I certainly feel."

"And esteem?"

"Yes; to be sure, esteem."

"And I think," continued her mother, "that before he committed this crime of proposing for you, Rosamond, you used to show some of the indignation of a good friend against those ungrateful people who used him so ill.

"Indignation! Yes," interrupted Rosamond, "who could avoid feeling indignation?"

"And pity?—I think I have heard you express pity for poor Mr. Gresham."

"Well, ma'am, because he really was very much to be pitied—don't you think so?"

"I do—and pity—" said Mrs. Percy, smiling.

"No, indeed, mother, you need not smile—nor you, Caroline; for the sort of pity which I feel is not—it was merely pity by itself, plain pity: why should people imagine and insist upon it, that more is felt than expressed?"

"My dear," said Mrs. Percy, "I do not insist upon your feeling more than you really do; but let us see— you are in a state of absolute indifference, and yet you feel esteem, indignation, pity—how is this, Rosamond? How can this be?"

"Very easily, ma'am, because by absolute indifference, I mean—Oh! you know very well what I mean— absolute indifference as to—"

"Love, perhaps, is the word which you cannot pronounce this morning."

"Now, mother! Now, Caroline! You fancy that I love him. But, supposing there were any if in the case on my side, tell me only why I should refuse him?"

"Nay, my dear, that is what we wait to hear from you," said Mrs. Percy.

"Then I will tell you why," said Rosamond: "in the first place, Mr. Gresham has a large fortune, and I have none. And I have the greatest horror of the idea of marrying for money, or of the possibility of its being suspected that I might do so."

"I thought that was the fear!" cried Caroline: "but, my dear Rosamond, with your generous mind, you know it is quite impossible that you should marry from interested motives."

"Absolutely impossible," said her mother. "And when you are sure of your own mind, it would be weakness, my dear, to dread the suspicions of others, even if such were likely to be formed."

"Oh! do not, my dearest Rosamond," said Caroline, taking her sister's hand, pressing it between hers, and speaking in the most urgent, almost supplicating tone, "do not, generous as you are, sacrifice your happiness to mistaken delicacy!"

"But," said Rosamond, after a moment's silence, "but you attribute more than I deserve to my delicacy and generosity: I ought not to let you think me so much better than I really am. I had some other motives: you will think them very foolish—very ridiculous—perhaps wrong; but you are so kind and indulgent to me, mother, that I will tell you all my follies. I do not like to marry a man who is not a hero—you are very good not to laugh, Caroline."

"Indeed, I am too seriously interested at present to laugh," said Caroline.

"And you must be sensible," continued Rosamond, "that I could not, by any effort of imagination, or by any illusion of love, convert a man of Mr. Gresham's time of life and appearance, with his wig, and sober kind of understanding, into a hero."

"As to the wig," replied Mrs. Percy, "you will recollect that both Sir Charles Grandison and Lovelace wore wigs; but, my dear, granting that a man cannot, in these days, be a hero in a wig, and granting that a hero cannot or should not have a sober understanding, will you give me leave to ask, whether you have positively determined that none but heroes and heroines should live, or love, or marry, or be happy in this mortal world?"

"Heaven forbid!" said Rosamond, "particularly as I am not a heroine."

"And as only a few hundred millions of people in the world are in the same condition," added Mrs. Percy.

"And those perhaps, not the least happy of human beings," said Caroline. "Be that as it may, I think it cannot be denied that Mr. Gresham has, in a high degree, one of the qualities which ought to distinguish a hero."

"What?" said Rosamond, eagerly.

"Generosity," replied Caroline; "and his large fortune puts it in his power to show that quality upon a scale more extended than is usually allowed even to the heroes of romance."

"True—very true," said Rosamond, smiling: "generosity might make a hero of him if he were not a merchant—a merchant!—a Percy ought not to marry a merchant."

"Perhaps, my dear," said Mrs. Percy, "you don't know that half, at least, of all the nobility in England have married into the families of merchants; therefore, in the opinion of half the nobility of England, there can be nothing discreditable or derogatory in such an alliance."

"I know, ma'am, such things are; but then you will allow they are usually done for money, and that makes the matter worse. If the sons of noble families marry the daughters of mercantile houses, it is merely to repair the family fortune. But a nobleman has great privileges. If he marry beneath himself, his low wife is immediately raised by her wedding-ring to an equality with the high and mighty husband— her name is forgotten in her title—her vulgar relations are left in convenient obscurity: the husband never thinks of taking notice of them; and the wife, of course, may let it alone if she pleases. But a woman, in our rank of life, must bear her husband's name, and must also bear all his relations, be they ever so vulgar. Now, Caroline, honestly—how should you like this?"

"Honestly, not at all," said Caroline; "but as we cannot have every thing we like, or avoid every thing we dislike, in life, we must balance the good against the evil, when we are to make our choice: and if I found certain amiable, estimable qualities in a character, I think that I might esteem, love, and marry him, even though he had a vulgar name and vulgar connexions. I fairly acknowledge, however, that it must be something superior in the man's character which could balance the objection to vulgarity in my mind."

"Very well, my dear," said Rosamond, "do you be a martyr to vulgarity and philosophy, if you like it—but excuse me, if you please. Since you, who have so much strength of mind, fairly acknowledge that this objection is barely to be overcome by your utmost efforts, do me the favour, do me the justice, not to expect from me a degree of civil courage quite above my powers."

Caroline, still believing that Rosamond was only bringing forward all the objections that might be raised against her wishes, replied, "Fortunately, my dear Rosamond, you are not called upon for any such effort of philosophy, for Mr. Gresham is not vulgar, nor is even his name vulgar, and he cannot have any vulgar relations, because he has no relations of any description—I heard him say, the other day, that he was a solitary being."

"That is a comfort," said Rosamond, laughing; "that is a great thing in his favour; but if he has not relations, he has connexions. What do you think of those horrible Pantons? This instant I think I see old Panton cooling himself—wig pushed back—waistcoat unbuttoned—and protuberant Mrs. Panton with her bay wig and artificial flowers. And not the Pantons only, but you may be sure there are hordes of St. Mary Axe cockneys, that would pour forth upon Mrs. Gresham, with overwhelming force, and with partnership and old-acquaintance-sake claims upon her public notice and private intimacy. Come, come, my dear Caroline, don't speak against your conscience—you know you never could withstand the hordes of vulgarians."

"These vulgarians in buckram," said Caroline, "have grown from two to two hundred in a trice, in your imagination, Rosamond: but consider that old Panton, against whom you have such an invincible horror, will, now that he has quarrelled with Erasmus, probably very soon eat himself out of the world; and I don't see that you are bound to Mr. Gresham's dead partner's widow—is this your only objection to Mr. Gresham?"

"My only objection! Oh, no! don't flatter yourself that in killing old Panton you have struck off all my objections. Independently of vulgar relations or connexions, and the disparity of age, my grand objection remains. But I will address myself to my mother, for you are not a good person for judging of prejudices—you really don't understand them, my dear Caroline; one might as well talk to Socrates. You go to work with logic, and get one between the horns of a wicked dilemma directly—I will talk to my mother; she understands prejudices."

"Your mother thanks you," said Mrs. Percy, smiling, "for your opinion of her understanding."

"My mother is the most indulgent of mothers, and, besides, the most candid, and therefore I know she will confess to me that she herself cherishes a little darling prejudice in favour of birth and family, a leetle prejudice—well covered by good-nature and politeness—but still a secret, invincible antipathy to low-born people."

"To low-bred people, I grant."

"Oh, mother! you are upon your candour—my dear mother, not only low-bred but low-born: confess you have a—what shall I call it?—an indisposition towards low-born people."

"Since you put me upon my candour," said Mrs. Percy, "I am afraid I must confess that I am conscious of a little of the aristocratic weakness you impute to me."

"Impute!—No imputation, in my opinion," cried Rosamond. "I do not think it any weakness."

"But I do," said Mrs. Percy—"I consider it as a weakness; and bitterly should I reproach myself, if I saw any weakness, any prejudice of mine, influence my children injuriously in the most material circumstance of their lives, and where their happiness is at stake. So, my dear Rosamond, let me intreat—"

"Oh! mother, don't let the tears come into your eyes; and, without any intreaties, I will do just as you please."

"My love," said Mrs. Percy, "I have no pleasure but that you should please yourself and judge for yourself, without referring to any prepossession of mine. And lest your imagination should deceive you as to the extent of my aristocratic prejudices, let me explain. The indisposition, which I have acknowledged I feel towards low-born people, arises, I believe, chiefly from my taking it for granted that they cannot be thoroughly well-bred. I have accidentally seen examples of people of inferior birth, who, though they had risen to high station, and though they had acquired, in a certain degree, polite manners, and had been metamorphosed by fashion, to all outward appearance, into perfect gentry, yet betrayed some marks of their origin, or of their early education, whenever their passions or their interests were touched: then some awkward gesture, some vulgar expression, some mean or mercenary sentiment, some habitual contraction of mind, recurred."

"True, true, most true!" said Rosamond. "It requires two generations, at least, to wash out the stain of vulgarity: neither a gentleman nor a gentlewoman can be made in less than two generations; therefore I never will marry a low-born man, if he had every perfection under the sun."

"Nay, my dear, that is too strong," said Mrs. Percy. "Hear me, my dearest Rosamond. I was going to tell you, that my experience has been so limited, that I am not justified in drawing from it any general conclusion. And even to the most positive and rational general rules you know there are exceptions."

"That is a fine general softening clause," said Rosamond; "but now positively, mother, would you have ever consented to marry a merchant?"

"Certainly, my dear, if your father had been a merchant, I should have married him," replied Mrs. Percy.

"Well, I except my father. To put the question more fairly, may I ask, do you wish that your daughter should marry a merchant?"

"As I endeavoured to explain to you before, that depends entirely upon what the merchant is, and upon what my daughter feels for him."

Rosamond sighed.

"I ought to observe, that merchants are now quite in a different class from what they were at the first rise of commerce in these countries," continued her mother. "Their education, their habits of thinking, knowledge, and manners, are improved, and, consequently, their consideration, their rank in society is raised. In our days, some of the best informed, most liberal, and most respectable men in the British dominions are merchants. I could not therefore object to my daughter's marrying a merchant; but I should certainly inquire anxiously what sort of a merchant he was. I do not mean that I should inquire whether he was concerned in this or that branch of commerce, but whether his mind were free from every thing mercenary and illiberal. I have done so with respect to Mr. Gresham, and I can assure you solemnly, that Mr. Gresham's want of the advantage of high birth is completely counterbalanced in my opinion by his superior qualities. I see in him a cultivated, enlarged, generous mind. I have seen him tried, where his passions and his interests have been nearly concerned, and I never saw in him the slightest tincture of vulgarity in manner or sentiment: therefore, my dear daughter, if he has made an impression on your heart, do not, on my account, conceal or struggle against it; because, far from objecting to Mr. Gresham for a son-in-law, I should prefer him to any gentleman or nobleman who had not his exalted character."

"There!" cried Caroline, with a look of joyful triumph, "there! my dear Rosamond, now your heart must be quite at ease!"

But looking at Rosamond at this moment, she saw no expression of joy or pleasure in her countenance; and Caroline was now convinced that she had been mistaken about Rosamond's feelings.

"Really and truly, mother, you think all this?"

"Really and truly, my dear, no motive upon earth would make me disguise my opinions, or palliate even my prejudices, when you thus consult me, and depend upon my truth. And now that I have said this much, I will say no more, lest I should bias you on the other side: I will leave you to your own feelings and excellent understanding."

Rosamond's affectionate heart was touched so by her mother's kindness, that she could not for some minutes repress her tears. When she recovered her voice, she assured her mother and Caroline, with a seriousness and an earnest frankness which at once convinced them of her truth, that she had not the slightest partiality for Mr. Gresham; that, on the contrary, his age was to her a serious objection. She had feared that her friends might wish for the match, and that being conscious she had no other objection to make to Mr. Gresham except that she could not love him, she had hesitated for want of a better reason, when her mother first began this cross-examination.

Relieved by this thorough explanation, and by the conviction that her father, mother, and sister, were perfectly satisfied with her decision, Rosamond was at ease as far as she herself was concerned. But she still dreaded to see Mr. Gresham again. She was excessively sorry to have given him pain, and she feared not a little that in rejecting the lover she should lose the friend.

Mr. Gresham, however, was of too generous a character to cease to be the friend of the woman he loved, merely because she could not return his passion: it is wounded pride, not disappointed affection, that turns immediately from love to hatred.

Rosamond was spared the pain of seeing Mr. Gresham again at this time, for he left the Hills, and set out immediately for London, where he was recalled by news of the sudden death of his partner. Old Mr. Panton had been found dead in his bed, after having supped inordinately the preceding night upon eel-pie. It was indispensably necessary that Mr. Gresham should attend at the opening of Panton's will, and Mrs. Panton wrote to represent this in urgent terms. Mr. Henry was gone to Amsterdam; he had, for some time previously to the death of Mr. Panton, obtained the partnership's permission to go over to the Dutch merchants, their correspondents in Amsterdam, to fill a situation in their house, for which his knowledge of the Dutch, French, and Spanish languages eminently qualified him.

When Mr. Henry had solicited this employment, Mr. Gresham had been unwilling to part with him, but had yielded to the young man's earnest entreaties, and to the idea that this change would, in a lucrative point of view, be materially for Mr. Henry's advantage.

Some apology to the lovers of romance may be expected for this abrupt transition from the affairs of the heart to the affairs of the counting-house—but so it is in real life. We are sorry, but we cannot help it— we have neither sentiments nor sonnets, ready for every occasion.

CHAPTER XXII

LETTER FROM ALFRED.

This appears to have been written some months after the vacation spent at the Hills.

'Oh! thoughtless mortals, ever blind to fate,
Too soon dejected, and too soon elate.'

"You remember, I am sure, my dear father, how angry we were some time ago with that man, whose name I never would tell you, the man whom Rosamond called Counsellor Nameless, who snatched a good point from me in arguing Mr. Hauton's cause. This very circumstance has been the means of introducing me to the notice of three men, all eminent in their profession, and each with the same inclination to serve me, according to their respective powers—a solicitor, a barrister, and a judge. Solicitor Babington (by-the-by, pray tell Rosamond in answer to her question whether there is an honest attorney, that there are no such things as attorneys now in England—they are all turned into solicitors and agents, just as every shop is become a warehouse, and every service a situation), Babington the solicitor employed against us in that suit a man who knows, without practising them, all the tricks of the trade, and who is a thoroughly honest man. He saw the trick that was played by Nameless, and took occasion afterwards to recommend me to several of his own clients. Upon the strength of this point briefs appeared on my table day after day—two guineas, three guineas, five guineas! comfortable sight! But far more comfortable, more gratifying, the kindness of Counsellor Friend: a more benevolent man never existed. I am sure the profession of the law has not contracted his heart, and yet you never saw or can conceive a man more intent upon his business. I believe he eats, drinks, and sleeps upon law: he has the reputation, in consequence, of being one of the soundest of our lawyers—the best opinion in England. He seems to make the cause of every client his own, and is as anxious as if his private property depended on the fate of each suit. He sets me a fine example of labour, perseverance, professional enthusiasm and rectitude. He is one of the very best friends a young lawyer like me could have; he puts me in the way I should go, and keeps me in it by showing that it is not a matter of chance, but of certainty, that this is the right road to fortune and to fame.

"Mr. Friend has sometimes a way of paying a compliment as if he were making a reproach, and of doing a favour as a matter of course. Just now I met him, and apropos to some observations I happened to make on a cause in which he is engaged, he said to me, as if he were half angry, though I knew he was thoroughly pleased, 'Quick parts! Yes, so I see you have: but take care—in your profession 'tis often "Most haste, worst speed;" not but what there are happy exceptions, examples of lawyers, who have combined judgment with wit, industry with genius, and law with eloquence. But these instances are rare, very rare; for the rarity of the case, worth studying. Therefore dine with me to-morrow, and I will introduce you to one of these exceptions.'

"The person in question, I opine, is the lord chief justice—and Friend could not do me a greater favour than to introduce me to one whom, as you know, I have long admired in public, and with whom, independently of any professional advantage, I have ardently wished to be acquainted.

"I have been told—I cannot tell you what—for here's the bell-man. I don't wonder 'the choleric man' knocked down the postman for blowing his horn in his ear.

"Abruptly yours,

"ALFRED PERCY."

Alfred had good reason to desire to be acquainted with this lord chief justice. Some French writer says, "Qu'il faut plier les grandes ailes de l'éloquence pour entrer dans un salon." The chief justice did so with peculiar ease. He possessed perfect conversational tact, with great powers of wit, humour, and all that felicity of allusion, which an uncommonly recollective memory, acting on stores of varied knowledge, can alone command. He really conversed; he did not merely tell stories, or make bonmots, or confine himself to the single combat of close argument, or the flourish of declamation; but he alternately followed and led, threw out and received ideas, knowing how to listen full as well as how to talk, remembering always Lord Chesterfield's experienced maxim, "That it is easier to hear than to talk yourself into the good opinion of your auditors." It was not, however, from policy, but from benevolence, that the chief justice made so good a hearer. It has been said, and with truth, that with him a good point never passed unnoticed in a public court, nor was a good thing ever lost upon him in private company. Of the number of his own good things fewer are in circulation than might be expected. The best conversation, that which rises from the occasion, and which suits the moment, suffers most from repetition. Fitted precisely to the peculiar time and place, the best things cannot bear transplanting.

The day Alfred Percy was introduced to the chief justice, the conversation began, from some slight remarks made by one of the company, on the acting of Mrs. Siddons. A lady who had just been reading the memoirs of the celebrated French actress, Mademoiselle Clairon, spoke of the astonishing pains which she took to study her parts, and to acquire what the French call l'air noble, continually endeavouring, on the most common occasions, when she was off the stage, to avoid all awkward motions, and in her habitual manner to preserve an air of grace and dignity. This led the chief justice to mention the care which Lord Chatham, Mr. Pitt, and other great orators, have taken to form their habits of speaking, by unremitting attention to their language in private as well as in public. He maintained that no man can speak with ease and security in public till custom has brought him to feel it as a moral impossibility that he could be guilty of any petty vulgarism, or that he could be convicted of any capital sin against grammar.

Alfred felt anxious to hear the chief justice farther on this subject, but the conversation was dragged back to Mademoiselle Clairon. The lady by whom she was first mentioned declared she thought that all Mademoiselle Clairon's studying must have made her a very unnatural actress. The chief justice quoted the answer which Mademoiselle Clairon gave, when she was reproached with having too much art.— "De l'art! et que voudroit-on done que j'eusse? Etois-je Andromaque? Etois-je Phédre?"

Alfred observed that those who complained of an actress's having too much art should rather complain of her having too little—of her not having art enough to conceal her art.

The chief justice honoured Alfred by a nod and a smile.

The lady, however, protested against this doctrine, and concluded by confessing that she always did and always should prefer nature to art.

From this commonplace confession, the chief justice, by a playful cross-examination, presently made it apparent that we do not always know what we mean by art and what by nature; that the ideas are so mixed in civilized society, and the words so inaccurately used, both in common conversation, and in the writings of philosophers, that no metaphysical prism can separate or reduce them to their primary meaning. Next he touched upon the distinction between art and artifice. The conversation branched out into remarks on grace and affectation, and thence to the different theories of beauty and taste, with all which he played with a master's hand.

A man accustomed to speak to numbers perceives immediately when his auditors seize his ideas, and knows instantly, by the assent and expression of the eye, to whom they are new or to whom they are familiar. The chief justice discovered that Alfred Percy had superior knowledge, literature, and talents, even before he spoke, by his manner of listening. The conversation presently passed from l'air noble to le style noble, and to the French laws of criticism, which prohibit the descending to allusions to arts and manufactures. This subject he discussed deeply, yet rapidly observed how taste is influenced by different governments and manners—remarked how the strong line of demarcation formerly kept in France between the nobility and the citizens had influenced taste in writing and in eloquence, and how our more popular government not only admitted allusions to the occupations of the lower classes, but required them. Our orators at elections, and in parliament, must speak so as to come home to the feelings and vocabulary of constituents. Examples from Burke and others, the chief justice said, might be brought in support of this opinion.

Alfred was so fortunate as to recollect some apposite illustrations from Burke, and from several of our great orators, Wyndham, Erskine, Mackintosh, and Romilly. As Alfred spoke, the chief justice's eye brightened with approbation, and it was observed that he afterwards addressed to him particularly his conversation; and, more flattering still, that he went deeper into the subject which he had been discussing. From one of the passages which had been mentioned, he took occasion to answer the argument of the French critics, who justify their taste by asserting that it is the taste of the ancients. Skilled in classical as in modern literature, he showed that the ancients had made allusions to arts and manufactures, as far as their knowledge went; but, as he observed, in modern times new arts and sciences afford fresh subjects of allusion unknown to the ancients; consequently we ought not to restrict our taste by exclusive reverence for classical precedents. On these points it is requisite to reform the pandects of criticism.

Another passage from Burke, to which Alfred had alluded, the chief justice thought too rich in ornament. "Ornaments," he said, "if not kept subordinate, however intrinsically beautiful, injure the general effect—therefore a judicious orator will sacrifice all such as draw the attention from his principal design."

Alfred Percy, in support of this opinion, cited the example of the Spanish painter, who obliterated certain beautiful silver vases, which he had introduced in a picture of the Lord's Supper, because he found, that at first view, every spectator's eye was caught by these splendid ornaments, and every one extolled their exquisite finish, instead of attending to the great subject of the piece.

The chief justice was so well pleased with the conversation of our young barrister, that, at parting, he gave Alfred an invitation to his house. The conversation had been very different from what might have been expected: metaphysics, belles-lettres, poetry, plays, criticism—what a range of ideas, far from Coke and Selden, was gone over this evening in the course of a few hours! Alfred had reason to be more and more convinced of the truth of his father's favourite doctrine, that the general cultivation of the understanding, and the acquirement of general knowledge, are essential to the attainment of excellence in any profession, useful to a young man particularly in introducing him to the notice of valuable friends and acquaintance.

An author well skilled in the worst parts of human nature has asserted, that "nothing is more tiresome than praises in which we have no manner of share." Yet we, who have a better opinion of our kind, trust that there are some who can sympathize in the enthusiasm of a good and young mind, struck with splendid talents, and with a superior character; therefore we venture to insert some of the warm eulogiums, with which we find our young lawyer's letters filled.

"My DEAR FATHER,

"I have only a few moments to write, but cannot delay to answer your question about the chief justice. Disappointed—no danger of that—he far surpasses my expectations. It has been said that he never opened a book, that he never heard a common ballad, or saw a workman at his trade, without learning something, which he afterwards turned to good account. This you may see in his public speeches, but I am more completely convinced of it since I have heard him converse. His illustrations are drawn from the workshop, the manufactory, the mine, the mechanic, the poet—from every art and science, from every thing in nature, animate or inanimate.

'From gems, from flames, from orient rays of light,
The richest lustre makes his purple bright.'

"Perhaps I am writing his panegyric because he is my lord chief justice, and because I dined with him yesterday, and am to dine with him again to-morrow.

"Yours affectionately,

"ALFRED PERCY."

In a subsequent letter he shows that his admiration increased instead of diminishing, upon a more intimate acquaintance with its object.

"High station," says Alfred, "appears to me much more desirable, since I have known this great man. He makes rank so gracious, and shows that it is a pleasurable, not a 'painful pre-eminence,' when it gives the power of raising others, and of continually doing kind and generous actions. Mr. Friend tells me, that, before the chief justice was so high as he is now, without a rival in his profession, he was ever the most generous man to his competitors. I am sure he is now the most kind and condescending to his inferiors. In company he is never intent upon himself, seems never anxious about his own dignity or his own fame. He is sufficiently sure of both to be quite at ease. He excites my ambition, and exalts its nature and value.

"He has raised my esteem for my profession, by showing the noble use that can be made of it, in defending right and virtue. He has done my mind good in another way: he has shown me that professional labour is not incompatible with domestic pleasures. I wish you could see him as I do, in the midst of his family, with his fine children playing about him, with his wife, a charming cultivated woman, who adores him, and who is his best companion and friend. Before I knew the chief justice, I had seen other great lawyers and judges, some of them crabbed old bachelors, others uneasily yoked to vulgar helpmates—having married early in life women whom they had dragged up as they rose, but who were always pulling them down—had seen some of these learned men sink into mere epicures, and become dead to intellectual enjoyment—others, with higher minds, and originally fine talents, I had seen in premature old age, with understandings contracted and palsied by partial or overstrained exertion, worn out, mind and body, and only late, very late in life, just attaining wealth and honours, when they were incapable of enjoying them. This had struck me as a deplorable and discouraging spectacle—a sad termination of a life of labour. But now I see a man in the prime of life, in the full vigour of all his intellectual faculties and moral sensibility, with a high character, fortune, and professional honours, all obtained by his own merit and exertions, with the prospect of health and length of days to enjoy and communicate happiness. Exulting in the sight of this resplendent luminary, and conscious that it will guide and cheer me forwards, I 'bless the useful light.'"

Our young lawyer was so honestly enthusiastic in his admiration of this great man, and was so full of the impression that had been made on his mind, that he forgot in this letter to advert to the advantage which, in a professional point of view, he might derive from the good opinion formed of him by the chief justice. In consequence of Solicitor Babington's telling his clients the share which Alfred had in winning Colonel Hauton's cause, he was employed in a suit of considerable importance, in which a great landed property was at stake. It was one of those standing suits which last from year to year, and which seem likely to linger on from generation to generation. Instead of considering his brief in this cause merely as a means of obtaining a fee, instead of contenting himself to make some motion of course, which fell to his share, Alfred set himself seriously to study the case, and searched indefatigably for all the precedents that could bear upon it. He was fortunate enough, or rather he was persevering enough, to find an old case in point, which had escaped the attention of the other lawyers. Mr. Friend was one of the senior counsel in this cause, and he took generous care that Alfred's merit should not now, as upon a former occasion, he concealed. Mr. Friend prevailed upon his brother barristers to agree in calling upon Alfred to speak to his own case in point; and the chief justice, who presided, said, "This case is new to me. This had escaped me, Mr. Percy; I must take another day to reconsider the matter, before I can pronounce judgment."

This from the chief justice, with the sense which Alfred's brother barristers felt of his deserving such notice, was of immediate and material advantage to our young lawyer. Attorneys and solicitors turned their eyes upon him, briefs began to flow in, and his diligence increased with his business. As junior counsel, he still had little opportunity in the common course of things of distinguishing himself, as it frequently fell to his share only to say a few words; but he never failed to make himself master of every case in which he was employed. And it happened one day, when the senior counsel was ill, the judge called upon the next barrister.—"Mr. Trevors, are you prepared?"

"My lord—I can't say—no, my lord."

"Mr. Percy, are you prepared?"

"Yes, my lord."

"So I thought—always prepared: go on, sir—go on, Mr. Percy."

He went on, and spoke so ably, and with such comprehensive knowledge of the case and of the law, that he obtained a decision in favour of his client, and established his own reputation as a man of business and of talents, who was always prepared. For the manner in which he was brought forward and distinguished by the chief justice he was truly grateful. This was a species of patronage honourable both to the giver and the receiver. Here was no favour shown disproportionate to deserts, but here was just distinction paid to merit, and generous discernment giving talents opportunity of developing themselves. These opportunities would only have been the ruin of a man who could not show himself equal to the occasion; but this was not the case with Alfred. His capacity, like the fairy tent, seemed to enlarge so as to contain all that it was necessary to comprehend: and new powers appeared in him in new situations.

Alfred had been introduced by his brother Erasmus to some of those men of literature with whom he had become acquainted at Lady Spilsbury's good dinners. Among these was a Mr. Dunbar, a gentleman who had resided for many years in India, from whom Alfred, who constantly sought for information from all with whom he conversed, had learned much of Indian affairs. Mr. Dunbar had collected some curious tracts on Mohammedan law, and glad to find an intelligent auditor on his favourite subject, a subject not generally interesting, he willingly communicated all he knew to Alfred, and lent him his manuscripts and scarce tracts, which Alfred, in the many leisure hours that a young lawyer can command before he gets into practice, had studied, and of which he had made himself master. It happened a considerable time afterwards that the East India Company had a cause—one of the greatest causes ever brought before our courts of law—relative to the demand of some native bankers in Hindostan against the company for upwards of four millions of rupees. This Mr. Dunbar, who had a considerable interest in the cause, and who was intimate with several of the directors, recommended it to them to employ Mr. Alfred Percy, who, as he knew, had had ample means of information, and who had studied a subject of which few of his brother barristers had any knowledge. The very circumstance of his being employed in a cause of such importance was of great advantage to him; and the credit he gained by accurate and uncommon knowledge in the course of the suit at once raised his reputation among the best judges, and established him in the courts.

On another occasion, Alfred's moral character was as serviceable as his literary taste had been in recommending him to his clients. Buckhurst Falconer had introduced him to a certain Mr. Clay, known by the name of French Clay. In a conversation after dinner, when the ladies had retired, Mr. Clay had boasted of his successes with the fair sex, and had expressed many sentiments that marked him for a profligate coxcomb.

Alfred felt disgust and indignation for this parade of vice. There was one officer in company who strongly sympathized in his feelings; this led to farther acquaintance and mutual esteem. This officer soon afterwards married Lady Harriet —, a beautiful young woman, with whom he lived happily for some time, till, unfortunately, while her husband was abroad with his regiment, chance brought the wife, at a watering-place, into the company of French Clay, and imprudence, the love of flattery, coquetry, and self-confidence, made her a victim to his vanity. Love he had none—nor she either—but her disgrace was soon discovered, or revealed; and her unhappy and almost distracted husband immediately commenced a suit against Clay. He chose Alfred Percy for his counsel. In this cause, where strong feelings of indignation were justly roused, and where there was room for oratory, Alfred spoke with such force and pathos that every honest heart was touched. The verdict of the jury showed the impression which he had made upon them: his speech was universally admired; and those who had till now known him only as a man of business, and a sound lawyer, were surprised to find him suddenly display such powers of eloquence. Counsellor Friend's plain advice to him had always been, "Never harangue about nothing: if your client require it, he is a fool, and never mind him; never speak till you've something to say, and then only say what you have to say.

'Words are like leaves, and where they most abound,
Much fruit of solid sense is seldom found.'"

Friend now congratulated Alfred with all his honest affectionate heart, and said, with a frown that struggled hard with a smile, "Well, I believe I must allow you to be an orator. But, take care—don't let the lawyer merge in the advocate. Bear it always in mind, that a mere man of words at the bar—or indeed any where else—is a mere man of straw."

The chief justice, who knew how to say the kindest things in the most polite manner, was heard to observe, that "Mr. Percy had done wisely, to begin by showing that he had laid a solid foundation of law, on which the ornaments of oratory could be raised high, and supported securely."

French Clay's affair with Lady Harriot had been much talked of in the fashionable world; from a love of scandal or a love of justice, from zeal in the cause of morality or from natural curiosity, her trial had been a matter of general interest to the ladies, young and old. In consequence Mr. Alfred Percy's speech was prodigiously read, and, from various motives, highly applauded. When a man begins to rise, all hands—all hands but the hands of his rivals—are ready to push him up, and all tongues exclaim, "'Twas I helped!" or, "'Twas what I always foretold!"

The Lady Angelica Headingham now bethought herself that she had a little poem, written by Mr. Alfred Percy, which had been given to her long ago by Miss Percy, and of which, at the time she received it, her ladyship had thought so little, that hardly deigning to bestow the customary tribute of a compliment, she had thrown it, scarcely perused, into her writing-box. It was now worth while to rummage for it, and now, when the author had a name, her ladyship discovered that the poem was charming—absolutely charming! Such an early indication of talents! Such a happy promise of genius!—Oh! she had always foreseen that Mr. Alfred Percy would make an uncommon figure in the world!

"Bless me! does your ladyship know him?"

"Oh! intimately!—That is, I never saw him exactly—but all his family I've known intimately—ages ago in the country."

"I should so like to meet him! And do pray give me a copy of the verses—and me!—and me!"

To work went the pens of all the female amateurs, in scribbling copies of "The Lawyer's May-day."—And away went the fair patroness in search of the author—introduced herself with unabashed grace, invited him for Monday, Tuesday, Wednesday, Thursday—Engaged? how unfortunate!—Well, for next week? a fortnight hence? three weeks? positively she must have him at her conversazione—she must give him— No, he must give her a day, he must consent to lose a day—so many of her friends and real judges were dying to see him.

To save the lives of so many judges, he consented to lose an evening—the day was fixed—Alfred found her conversazione very brilliant—was admired—and admired others in his turn as much as was expected. It was an agreeable variety of company and of thought to him, and he promised to go sometimes to her ladyship's parties—a promise which delighted her much, particularly as he had not yet given a copy of the verses to Lady Spilsbury. Lady Spilsbury, to whom the verses quickly worked round, was quite angry that her friend Erasmus had not given her an early copy; and now invitations the most pressing came from Lady Spilsbury to her excellent literary dinners. If Alfred had been so disposed, he might, among these fetchers and carriers of bays, have been extolled to the skies; but he had too much sense and prudence to lose the substance for the shadow, to sink a solid character into a drawing-room reputation. Of this he had seen the folly in Buckhurst Falconer's case, and now, if any farther warning on this subject had been wanting, he would have taken it from the example of poor Seebright, the poet, whom he met the second time he went to Lady Angelica Headingham's. Poor Seebright, as the world already began to call him, from being an object of admiration, was beginning to sink into an object of pity. Instead of making himself independent by steady exertions in any respectable profession, instead of making his way in the republic of letters by some solid work of merit, he frittered away his time among fashionable amateurs, feeding upon their flattery, and living on in the vain hope of patronage. Already the flight of his genius had been restrained, the force of his wing impaired; instead of soaring superior, he kept hovering near the earth; his "kestrel courage fell," he appeared to be almost tamed to the domestic state to which he was reduced—yet now and then a rebel sense of his former freedom, and of his present degradation, would appear. "Ah! if I were but independent as you are! If I had but followed a profession as you have done!" said he to Alfred, when, apart from the crowd, they had an opportunity of conversing confidentially.

Alfred replied that it was not yet too late, that it was never too late for a man of spirit and talents to make himself independent; he then suggested to Mr. Seebright various ways of employing his powers, and pointed out some useful and creditable literary undertakings, by which he might acquire reputation. Seebright listened, his eye eagerly catching at each new idea the first moment, the next turning off to something else, raising objections futile or fastidious, seeing nothing impossible in any dream of his imagination, where no effort of exertion was requisite, but finding every thing impracticable when he came to sober reality, where he was called upon to labour. In fact, he was one of the sort of people who do not know what they want, or what they would be, who complain and complain; disappointed and discontented, at having sunk below their powers and their hopes, and are yet without capability of persevering exertion to emerge from their obscurity. Seebright was now become an inefficient being, whom no one could assist to any good purpose. Alfred, after a long, mazy, fruitless conversation, was convinced that the case was hopeless, and, sincerely pitying him, gave it up as irremediable. Just as he had come to this conclusion, and had sunk into silence, a relation of his, whom he had not seen for a considerable time, entered the room, and passed by without noticing him. She was so much altered in her appearance, that he could scarcely believe he saw Lady Jane Granville; she looked out of spirits, and care-worn. He immediately observed that less attention was paid to her than she used to command; she had obviously sunk considerably in importance, and appeared to feel this keenly. Upon inquiry, Alfred learnt that she had lost a large portion of her fortune by a lawsuit, which she had managed, that is to say, mismanaged, for herself; and she was still at law for the remainder of her estate, which, notwithstanding her right was undoubted, it was generally supposed that she would lose, for the same reason that occasioned her former failure, her pertinacity in following her own advice only. Alfred knew that there had been some misunderstanding between Lady Jane and his family, that she had been offended by his sister Caroline having declined accepting her invitation to town, and from Mr. and Mrs. Percy having differed with her in opinion as to the value of the patronage of fashion: she had also been displeased with Erasmus about Sir Amyas Courtney. Notwithstanding all this, he was convinced that Lady Jane, whatever her opinions might be, and whether mistaken or not, had been actuated by sincere regard for his family, for which he and they were grateful; and now was the time to show it, now when he was coming into notice in the world, and she declining in importance. Therefore, though she had passed by him without recognizing him, he went immediately and spoke to her in so respectful and kind a manner, paid her the whole evening such marked attention, that she was quite pleased and touched. In reality, she had been vexed with herself for having persisted so long in her resentment; she wished for a fair opportunity for a reconciliation, and she rejoiced that Alfred thus opened the way for it. She invited him to come to see her the next day, observing, as she put her card into his hand, that she no longer lived in her fine house in St. James's place. Now that his motives could not be mistaken, he was assiduous in his visits; and when he had sufficiently obtained her confidence, he ventured to touch upon her affairs. She, proud to convince him of her abilities as a woman of business, explained her whole case, and descanted upon the blunders and folly of her solicitors and counsellors, especially upon the absurdity of the opinions which she had not followed. Her cause depended upon the replication she was to put in to a plea in special pleading: she thought she saw the way straight before her, and exclaimed vehemently against that love of the crooked path by which her lawyers seemed possessed.

Without disputing the legal soundness of her ladyship's opinion in her own peculiar case, Alfred, beginning at a great distance from her passions, quietly undertook, by relating to her cases which had fallen under his own knowledge, to convince her that plain common sense and reason could never lead her to the knowledge of the rules of special pleading, or to the proper wording of those answers, on the letter of which the fate of a cause frequently depends. He confessed to her that his own understanding had been so shocked at first by the apparent absurdity of the system, that he had almost abandoned the study, and that it had been only in consequence of actual experience that he had at last discovered the utility of those rules. She insisted upon being also convinced before she could submit; but as it is not quite so easy as ladies sometimes think it is to teach any art or science in two words, or to convey, in a moment, to the ignorant, the combined result of study and experience, Alfred declined this task, and could undertake only to show her ladyship, by asking her opinion on various cases which had been decided in the courts, that it was possible she might be mistaken; and that, however superior her understanding, a court of law would infallibly decide according to its own rules.

"But, good Heavens! my dear sir," exclaimed Lady Jane, "when, after I have paid the amount of my bond, and every farthing that I owe a creditor, yet this rogue says I have not, is not it a proper answer that I owe him nothing?"

"Pardon me, this would be considered as an evasive plea by the court, or as a negative pregnant."

"Oh! if you come to your negative pregnants," cried Lady Jane, "it is impossible to understand you—I give up the point."

To this conclusion it had been Alfred's object to bring her ladyship; and when she was fully convinced of the insufficient limits of the human—he never said the female—understanding to comprehend these things without the aid of men learned in the law, he humbly offered his assistance to guide her out of that labyrinth, into which, unwittingly and without any clue, she had ventured farther and farther, till she was just in the very jaws of nonsuit and ruin. She put her affairs completely into his hands, and promised that she would no farther interfere, even with her advice; for it was upon this condition that Alfred engaged to undertake the management of her cause. Nothing indeed is more tormenting to men of business, than to be pestered with the incessant advice, hopes and fears, cautions and explanations, cunning suggestions, superficial knowledge, and profound ignorance, of lady or gentlemen lawyers. Alfred now begged and obtained permission from the court to amend the Lady Jane Granville's last plea—he thenceforward conducted the business, and played the game of special pleading with such strict and acute attention to the rules, that there were good hopes the remaining portion of her ladyship's fortune, which was now at stake, might be saved. He endeavoured to keep up her spirits and her patience, for of a speedy termination to the business there was no chance. They had to deal with adversaries who knew how, on their side, to protract the pleadings, and to avoid what is called coming to the point.

It was a great pleasure to Alfred thus to have it in his power to assist his friends, and the hope of serving them redoubled his diligence. About this time he was engaged in a cause for his brother's friend and Rosamond's admirer, Mr. Gresham. A picture-dealer had cheated this gentleman, in the sale of a picture of considerable value. Mr. Gresham had bargained for, and bought, an original Guido, wrote his name on the back of it, and directed that it should be sent to him. The painting which was taken to his house had his name written on the back, but was not the original Guido for which he had bargained—it was a copy. The picture-dealer, however, and two respectable witnesses, were ready to swear positively that this was the identical picture on which Mr. Gresham wrote his name—that they saw him write his name, and heard him order that it should be sent to him. Mr. Gresham himself acknowledged that the writing was so like his own that he could not venture to deny that it was his, and yet he could swear that this was not the picture for which he had bargained, and on which he had written his name. He suspected it to be a forgery; and was certain that, by some means, one picture had been substituted for another. Yet the defendant had witnesses to prove that the picture never was out of Mr. Gresham's sight, from the time he bargained for it, till the moment when he wrote his name on the back, in the presence of the same witnesses.

This chain of evidence they thought was complete, and that it could not be broken. Alfred Percy, however, discovered the nature of the fraud, and, regardless of the boasts and taunts of the opposite party, kept his mind carefully secret, till the moment when he came to cross-examine the witnesses; for, as Mr. Friend had observed to him, many a cause had been lost by the impatience of counsel, in showing, beforehand, how it might certainly be won [Footnote: See Deinology.]. By thus revealing the intended mode of attack, opportunity is given to prepare a defence by which it may be ultimately counteracted. In the present case, the defendant, however, came into court secure of victory, and utterly unprepared to meet the truth, which was brought out full upon him when least expected. The fact was, that he had put two pictures into the same frame—the original in front, the copy behind it: on the back of the canvass of the copy Mr. Gresham had written his name, never suspecting that it was not the original for which he bargained, and which he thought he actually held in his hand. The witnesses, therefore, swore literally the truth, that they saw him write upon that picture; and they believed the picture, on which he wrote, was the identical picture that was sent home to him. One of the witnesses was an honest man, who really believed what he swore, and knew nothing of the fraud, to which the other, a rogue in confederacy with the picture-dealer, was privy. The cross-examination of both was so ably managed, that the honest man was soon made to perceive and the rogue forced to reveal the truth. Alfred had reason to be proud of the credit he obtained for the ability displayed in this cross-examination, but he was infinitely more gratified by having it in his power to gain a cause for his friend, and to restore to Mr. Gresham his favourite Guido.

A welcome sight—a letter from Godfrey! the first his family had received from him since he left England. Two of his letters, it appears, had been lost. Alluding to one he had written immediately on hearing of the change in his father's fortune, he observes, that he has kept his resolution of living within his pay; and, after entering into some other family details, he continues as follows: "Now, my dear mother, prepare to hear me recant what I have said against Lord Oldborough. I forgive his lordship all his sins, and I begin to believe, that though he is a statesman, his heart is not yet quite ossified. He has recalled our regiment from this unhealthy place, and he has promoted Gascoigne to be our lieutenant-colonel. I say that Lord Oldborough has done all this, because I am sure, from a hint in Alfred's last letter, that his lordship has been the prime mover in the business. But not to keep you in suspense about the facts.

"In my first letter to my father, I told you, that from the moment our late lethargic lieutenant-colonel came to the island, he took to drinking rum, pure rum, to waken himself—claret, port, and madeira, had lost their power over him. Then came brandy, which he fancied was an excellent preservative against the yellow fever, and the fever of the country. So he died 'boldly by brandy.' Poor fellow! he was boasting to me, the last week of his existence, when he was literally on his deathbed, that his father taught him to drink before he was six years old, by practising him every day, after dinner, in the sublime art of carrying a bumper steadily to his lips. He, moreover, boasted to me, that when a boy of thirteen, at an academy, he often drank two bottles of claret at a sitting; and that, when he went into the army, getting among a jolly set, he brought himself never to feel the worse for any quantity of wine. I don't know what he meant by the worse for it—at forty-five, when I first saw him, he had neither head nor hand left for himself or his country. His hand shook so, that if he had been perishing with thirst, he could not have carried a glass to his lips, till after various attempts in all manner of curves and zigzags, spilling half of it by the way. It was really pitiable to see him—when he was to sign his name I always went out of the room, and left Gascoigne to guide his hand. More helpless still his mind than his body. If his own or England's salvation had depended upon it, he could not, when in the least hurried, have uttered a distinct order, have dictated an intelligible letter; or, in time of need, have recollected the name of any one of his officers, or even his own name—quite imbecile and embruted. But, peace to his ashes—or rather to his dregs—and may there never be such another British colonel!

"Early habits of temperance have not only saved my life, but made my life worth saving. Neither Colonel Gascoigne nor I have ever had a day's serious illness since we came to the island—but we are the only two that have escaped. Partly from the colonel's example, and partly from their own inclination, all the other officers have drunk hard. Lieutenant R— is now ill of the fever; Captain H— (I beg his pardon), now Major H—, will soon follow the colonel to the grave, unless he takes my very disinterested advice, and drinks less. I am laughed at by D— and V—and others for this; they ask why the deuce I can't let the major kill himself his own way, and as fast as he pleases, when I should get on a step by it, and that step such a great one. They say none but a fool would do as I do, and I think none but a brute could do otherwise—I can't stand by with any satisfaction, and see a fellow-creature killing himself by inches, even though I have the chance of slipping into his shoes: I am sure the shoes would pinch me confoundedly. If it is my brother-officer's lot to fall in battle—it's very well—I run the same hazard—he dies, as he ought to do, a brave fellow; but to stand by, and see a man die as he ought not to do, and die what is called an honest fellow!—I can't do it. H— at first had a great mind to run me through the body; but, poor man, he is now very fond of me, and if any one can keep him from destroying himself, I flatter myself I shall.

"A thousand thanks to dear Caroline for her letter, and to Rosamond for her journal. They, who have never been an inch from home, cannot conceive how delightful it is, at such a distance, to receive letters from our friends. You remember, in Cook's voyage, his joy at meeting in some distant island with the spoon marked London.

"I hope you received my letters, Nos. 1 and 2. Not that there was any thing particular in them. You know I never do more than tell the bare facts—not like Rosamond's journal—with which, by-the-bye, Gascoigne has fallen in love. He sighs, and wishes that Heaven had blessed him with such a sister—for sister, read wife. I hope this will encourage Rosamond to write again immediately. No; do not tell what I have just said about Gascoigne, for—who knows the perverse ways of women?—perhaps it might prevent her from writing to me at all. You may tell her, in general, that it is my opinion ladies always write better and do every thing better than men—except fight, which Heaven forbid they should ever do in public or private!

"I am glad that Caroline did not marry Mr. Barclay, since she did not like him; but by all accounts he is a sensible, worthy man, and I give my consent to his marriage with Lady Mary Pembroke, though, from Caroline's description, I became half in love with her myself. N.B. I have not been in love above six times since I left England, and but once any thing to signify. How does the Marchioness of Twickenham go on?

"Affectionate duty to my father, and love to all the happy people at home.

"Dear mother,

"Your affectionate son,

"G. PERCY."

CHAPTER XXIII

LETTER FROM ALFRED TO CAROLINE.

"MY DEAR CAROLINE,

"I am going to surprise you—I know it is the most imprudent thing a story-teller can do to give notice or promise of a surprise; but you see, I have such confidence at this moment in my fact, that I hazard this imprudence—Whom do you think I have seen? Guess—guess all round the breakfast-table—father, mother, Caroline, Rosamond—I defy you all—ay, Rosamond, even you, with all your capacity for romance; the romance of real life is beyond all other romances—its coincidences beyond the combinations of the most inventive fancy—even of yours, Rosamond—Granted—go on—Patience, ladies, if you please, and don't turn over the page, or glance to the end of my letter to satisfy your curiosity, but read fairly on, says my father.

"You remember, I hope, the Irishman, O'Brien, to whom Erasmus was so good, and whom Mr. Gresham, kind as he always is, took for his porter: when Mr. Gresham set off last week for Amsterdam, he gave this fellow leave to go home to his wife, who lives at Greenwich. This morning, the wife came to see my honour to speak to me, and when she did see me she could not speak, she was crying so bitterly; she was in the greatest distress about her husband: he had, she said, in going to see her, been seized by a press-gang, and put on board a tender now on the Thames. Moved by the poor Irishwoman's agony of grief, and helpless state, I went to Greenwich, where the tender was lying, to speak to the captain, to try to obtain O'Brien's release. But upon my arrival there, I found that the woman had been mistaken in every point of her story. In short, her husband was not on board the tender, had never been pressed, and had only stayed away from home the preceding night, in consequence of having met with the captain's servant, one of his countrymen, from the county of Leitrim dear, who had taken him home to treat him, and had kept him all night to sing 'St. Patrick's day in the morning,' and to drink a good journey, and a quick passage, across the salt water to his master, which he could not refuse. Whilst I was looking at my watch, and regretting my lost morning, a gentleman, whose servant had really been pressed, came up to speak to the captain, who was standing beside me. The gentleman had something striking and noble in his whole appearance; but his address and accent, which were those of a foreigner, did not suit the fancy of my English captain, who, putting on the surly air, with which he thought it for his honour and for the honour of his country to receive a Frenchman, as he took this gentleman to be, replied in the least satisfactory manner possible, and in the short language of some seamen, 'Your footman's an Englishman, sir; has been pressed for an able-bodied seaman, which I trust he'll prove; he's aboard the tender, and there he will remain.' The foreigner, who, notwithstanding the politeness of his address, seemed to have a high spirit, and to be fully sensible of what was due from others to him as well as from him to them, replied with temper and firmness. The captain, without giving any reasons, or attending to what was said, reiterated, 'I am under orders, sir; I am acting according to my orders—I can do neither more nor less. The law is as I tell you, sir.'

"The foreigner bowed submission to the law, but expressed his surprise that such should be law in a land of liberty. With admiration he had heard, that, by the English law and British constitution, the property and personal liberty of the lowest, the meanest subject, could not be injured or oppressed by the highest nobleman in the realm, by the most powerful minister, even by the king himself. He had always been assured that the king could not put his hand into the purse of the subject, or take from him to the value of a single penny; that the sovereign could not deprive the meanest of the people unheard, untried, uncondemned, of a single hour of his liberty, or touch a hair of his head; he had always, on the continent, heard it the boast of Englishmen, that when even a slave touched English ground he became free: 'Yet now, to my astonishment,' pursued the foreigner, 'what do I see?—a freeborn British subject returning to his native land, after an absence of some years, unoffending against any law, innocent, unsuspected of all crime, a faithful domestic, an excellent man, prevented from returning to his family and his home, put on board a king's ship, unused to hard labour, condemned to work like a galley slave, doomed to banishment, perhaps to death!—Good Heavens! In all this where is your English liberty? Where is English justice, and the spirit of your English law?'

"'And who the devil are you, sir?' cried the captain, 'who seem to know so much and so little of English law?'

"'My name, if that be of any consequence, is Count Albert Altenberg.'

"'Well, Caroline, you are surprised.—'No,' says Rosamond; 'I guessed it was he, from the first moment I heard he was a foreigner, and had a noble air.''

"'Altenberg,' repeated the captain; 'that's not a French name:—Why, you are not a Frenchman!'

"'No, sir—a German.'

"'Ah ha!' cried the captain, suddenly changing his tone, 'I thought you were not a Frenchman, or you could not talk so well of English law, and feel so much for English liberty; and now, since that's the case, I'll own to you frankly, that in the main I'm much of your mind—and for my own particular share, I'd as lieve the Admiralty had sent me to hell as have ordered me to press on the Thames. But my business is to obey orders—which I will do, by the blessing of God—so good morning to you. As to law, and justice, and all that, talk to him,' said the captain, pointing with his thumb over his left shoulder to me as he walked off hastily.

"'Poor fellow!' said I; 'this is the hardest part of a British captain's duty, and so he feels it.'

"'Duty!' exclaimed the count—'Duty! pardon me for repeating your word—but can it be his duty? I hope I did not pass proper bounds in speaking to him; but now he is gone, I may say to you, sir—to you, who, if I may presume to judge from your countenance, sympathize in my feelings—this is a fitter employment for an African slave-merchant than for a British officer. The whole scene which I have just beheld there on the river, on the banks, the violence, the struggles I have witnessed there, the screams of the women and children,—it is not only horrible, but in England incredible! Is it not like what we have heard of on the coast of Africa with detestation—what your humanity has there forbidden—abolished? And is it possible that the cries of those negroes across the Atlantic can so affect your philanthropists' imaginations, whilst you are deaf or unmoved by these cries of your countrymen, close to your metropolis, at your very gates? I think I hear them still,' said the count, with a look of horror. 'Such a scene I never before beheld! I have seen it—and yet I cannot believe that I have seen it in England.'

"I acknowledged that the sight was terrible; I could not be surprised that the operation of pressing men for the sea service should strike a foreigner as inconsistent with the notion of English justice and liberty, and I admired the energy and strength of feeling which the count showed; but I defended the measure as well as I could, on the plea of necessity.

"'Necessity!' said the count: 'Pardon me if I remind you that necessity is the tyrant's plea.'

"I mended my plea, and changed necessity into utility—general utility. It was essential to England's defence—to her existence—she could not exist without her navy, and her navy could not be maintained without a press-gang—as I was assured by those who were skilled in naval affairs.

"The count smiled at my evident consciousness of the weakness of my concluding corollary, and observed that, by my own statement, the whole argument depended on the assertions of those who maintained that a navy could not exist without a press-gang. He urged this no further, and I was glad of it; his horses and mine were at this moment brought up, and we both rode together to town.

"I know that Rosamond, at this instant, is gasping with impatience to hear whether in the course of this ride I spoke of M. de Tourville—and the shipwreck. I did—but not of Euphrosyne: upon that subject I could not well touch. He had heard of the shipwreck, and of the hospitality with which the sufferers had been treated by an English gentleman, and he was surprised and pleased, when I told him that I was the son of that gentleman. Of M. de Tourville, the count, I fancy, thinks much the same as you do. He spoke of him as an intriguing diplomatist, of quick talents, but of a mind incapable of any thing great or generous. The count went on from speaking of M. de Tourville to some of the celebrated public characters abroad, and to the politics and manners of the different courts and countries of Europe. For so young a man, he has seen and reflected much. He is indeed a very superior person, as he convinced me even in this short ride. You know that Dr. Johnson says, 'that you cannot stand for five minutes with a great man under a shed, waiting till a shower is over, without hearing him say something that another man could not say.' But though the count conversed with me so well and so agreeably, I could see that his mind was, from time to time, absent and anxious; and as we came into town, he again spoke of the press-gang, and of his poor servant—a faithful attached servant, he called him, and I am sure the count is a good master, and a man of feeling. He had offered money to obtain the man's release in vain. A substitute it was at this time difficult to find—the count was but just arrived in London, had not yet presented any of his numerous letters of introduction; he mentioned the names of some of the people to whom these were addressed, and he asked me whether application to any of them could be of service. But none of his letters were to any of the men now in power. Lord Oldborough was the only person I knew whose word would be law in this case, and I offered to go with him to his lordship. This I ventured, my dear father, because I wisely—yes, wisely, as you shall see, calculated that the introduction of a foreigner, fresh from the continent, and from that court where Cunningham Falconer is now resident envoy, would be agreeable, and might be useful to the minister.

"My friend, Mr. Temple, who is as obliging and as much my friend now he is secretary to the great man as he was when he was a scrivening nobody in his garret, obtained audience for us directly. I need not detail—indeed I have not time—graciously received—count's business done by a line—Temple ordered to write to Admiralty: Lord Oldborough seemed obliged to me for introducing the count—I saw he wished to have some private conversation with him—rose, and took my leave. Lord Oldborough paid me for my discretion on the spot by a kind look—a great deal from him—and following me to the door of the antechamber, 'Mr. Percy, I cannot regret that you have followed your own independent professional course—I congratulate you upon your success—I have heard of it from many quarters, and always, believe me, with pleasure, on your father's account, and on your own.'

"Next day I found on my table when I came from the courts, the count's card—when I returned his visit, Commissioner Falconer was with him in close converse—confirmed by this in opinion that Lord Oldborough is sucking information—I mean, political secrets—out of the count. The commissioner could not, in common decency, help being 'exceedingly sorry that he and Mrs. Falconer had seen so little of me of late,' nor could he well avoid asking me to a concert, to which he invited the count, for the ensuing evening. As the count promised to go, so did I, on purpose to meet him. Adieu, dearest Caroline.

"Most affectionately yours,

"ALFRED PERCY."

To give an account of Mrs. Falconer's concert in fashionable style, we should inform the public that Dr. Mudge for ever established his fame in "Buds of Roses;" and Miss La Grande was astonishing, absolutely astonishing, in "Frenar vorrei le lagrime"—quite in Catalani's best manner; but Miss Georgiana Falconer was divine in "O Giove omnipotente," and quite surpassed herself in "Quanto O quanto è amor possente," in which Dr. Mudge was also capital: indeed it would be doing injustice to this gentleman's powers not to acknowledge the universality of his genius.

Perhaps our readers may not feel quite satisfied with this general eulogium, and may observe, that all this might have been learnt from the newspapers of the day. Then we must tell things plainly and simply, but this will not sound nearly so grand, and letting the public behind the scenes will destroy all the stage effect and illusion. Alfred Percy went to Mrs. Falconer's unfashionably early, in hopes that, as Count Altenberg dined there, he might have a quarter of an hour's conversation with him before the musical party should assemble. In this hope Alfred was mistaken. He found in the great drawing-room only Mrs. Falconer and two other ladies, whose names he never heard, standing round the fire; the unknown ladies were in close and eager converse about Count Altenberg. "He is so handsome—so polite—so charming!"—"He is very rich—has immense possessions abroad, has not he?"—"Certainly, he has a fine estate in Yorkshire."—"But when did he come to England?"—"How long does he stay?"—"15,000l., no, 20,000l. per annum."—"Indeed!"—"Mrs. Falconer, has not Count Altenberg 20,000l. a year?"

Mrs. Falconer, seemingly uninterested, stood silent, looking through her glass at the man who was lighting the argand lamps. "Really, my dear," answered she, "I can't say—I know nothing of Count Altenberg—Take care! that argand!—He's quite a stranger to us—the commissioner met him at Lord Oldborough's, and on Lord Oldborough's account, of course—Vigor, we must have more light, Vigor—wishes to pay him attention—But here's Mr. Percy," continued she, turning to Alfred, "can, I dare say, tell you all about these things. I think the commissioner mentioned that it was you, Mr. Percy, who introduced the Count to Lord Oldborough."

The ladies immediately fixed their surprised and inquiring eyes upon Mr. Alfred Percy—he seemed to grow in an instant several feet in their estimation: but he shrunk again when he acknowledged that he had merely met Count Altenberg accidentally at Greenwich—that he knew nothing of the count's estate in Yorkshire, or of his foreign possessions, and was utterly incompetent to decide whether he had 10,000l. or 20,000l. per annum.

"That's very odd!" said one of the ladies. "But this much I know, that he is passionately fond of music, for he told me so at dinner."

"Then I am sure he will be charmed to-night with Miss Georgiana," said the confidants.

"But what signifies that," replied the other lady, "if he has not—"

"Mr. Percy," interrupted Mrs. Falconer, "I have never seen you since that sad affair of Lady Harriot H— and Lewis Clay;" and putting her arm within Alfred's, she walked him away, talking over the affair, and throwing in a proper proportion of compliment. As she reached the folding doors, at the farthest end of the room, she opened them.

"I have a notion the young people are here." She introduced him into the music-room. Miss Georgiana Falconer, at the piano-forte, with performers, composers, masters, and young ladies, all with music-books round her, sat high in consultation, which Alfred's appearance interrupted—a faint struggle to be civil—an insipid question or two was addressed to him. "Fond of music, Mr. Percy? Captain Percy, I think, likes music? You expect Captain Percy home soon?"

Scarcely listening to his answers, the young ladies soon resumed their own conversation, forgot his existence, and went on eagerly with their own affairs.

As they turned over their music-books, Alfred, for some minutes, heard only the names of La Tour, Winter, Von Esch, Lanza, Portogallo, Mortellari, Guglielmi, Sacchini, Sarti, Paisiello, pronounced by male and female voices in various tones of ecstasy and of execration. Then there was an eager search for certain favourite duets, trios, and sets of cavatinas. Next he heard, in rapid succession, the names of Tenducci, Pachierotti, Marchesi, Viganoni, Braham, Gabrielli, Mara, Banti, Grassini, Billington, Catalani. Imagine our young barrister's sense of his profound ignorance, whilst he heard the merits of all dead and living composers, singers, and masters, decided upon by the Miss Falconers. By degrees he began to see a little through the palpable obscure, by which he had at first felt himself surrounded: he discerned that he was in a committee of the particular friends of the Miss Falconers, who were settling what they should sing and play. All, of course, were flattering the Miss Falconers, and abusing their absent friends, those especially who were expected to bear a part in this concert; for instance—"Those two eternal Miss Byngs, with voices, like cracked bells, and with their old-fashioned music, Handel, Corelli, and Pergolese, horrid!—And odious little Miss Crotch, who has science but no taste, execution but no expression!" Here they talked a vast deal about expression. Alfred did not understand them, and doubted whether they understood themselves. "Then her voice! how people can call it fine!—powerful, if you will—but overpowering! For my part, I can't stand it, can you?—Every body knows an artificial shake, when good, is far superior to a natural shake. As to the Miss Barhams, the eldest has no more ear than the table, and the youngest such a thread of a voice!"

"But, mamma," interrupted Miss Georgiana Falconer, "are the Miss La Grandes to be here to-night?"

"Certainly, my dear—you know I could not avoid asking the Miss La Grandes."

"Then, positively," cried Miss Georgiana, her whole face changing, and ill-humour swelling in every feature, "then, positively, ma'am, I can't and won't sing a note!"

"Why, my dear love," said Mrs. Falconer, "surely you don't pretend to be afraid of the Miss La Grandes?"

"You!" cried one of the chorus of flatterers—"You! to whom the La Grandes are no more to be compared—"

"Not but that they certainly sing finely, I am told," said Mrs. Falconer; "yet I can't say I like their style of singing—and knowledge of music, you know, they don't pretend to."

"Why, that's true," said Miss Georgiana; "but still, somehow, I can never bring out my voice before those girls. If I have any voice at all, it is in the lower part, and Miss La Grande always chooses the lower part—besides, ma'am, you know she regularly takes 'O Giove omnipotente' from me. But I should not mind that even, if she would not attempt poor 'Quanto O quanto è amor possente'—there's no standing that! Now, really, to hear that so spoiled by Miss La Grande—"

"Hush! my dear," said Mrs. Falconer, just as Mrs. La Grande appeared—"Oh! my good Mrs. La Grande, how kind is this of you to come to me with your poor head! And Miss La Grande and Miss Eliza! We are so much obliged to you, for you know that we could not have done without you."

The Miss La Grandes were soon followed by the Miss Barhams and Miss Crotch, and they were all "so good, and so kind, and such dear creatures." But after the first forced compliments, silence and reserve spread among the young ladies of the Miss Falconers' party. It was evident that the fair professors were mutually afraid and envious of each other, and there was little prospect of harmony of temper. At length the gentlemen arrived. Count Altenberg appeared, and came up to pay his compliments to the Miss Falconers: as he had not been behind the scenes, all was charming illusion to his eyes. No one could appear more good-humoured, agreeable, and amiable than Miss Georgiana; she was in delightful spirits, well dressed, and admirably supported by her mother. The concert began. But who can describe the anxiety of the rival mothers, each in agonies to have their daughters brought forward and exhibited to the best advantage! Some grew pale, some red—all, according to their different powers of self-command and address, endeavoured to conceal their feelings. Mrs. Falconer now shone superior in ease inimitable. She appeared absolutely unconcerned for her own daughter, quite intent upon bringing into notice the talents of the Miss Barhams, Miss Crotch, the Miss La Grandes, &c.

These young ladies in their turn knew and practised the various arts by which at a musical party the unfortunate mistress of the house may be tormented. Some, who were sensible that the company were anxious for their performance, chose to be "quite out of voice," till they had been pressed and flattered into acquiescence; one sweet bashful creature must absolutely be forced to the instrument, as a new speaker of the House of Commons was formerly dragged to the chair. Then the instrument was not what one young lady was used to; the lights were so placed that another who was near-sighted could not see a note—another could not endure such a glare. One could not sing unless the windows were all open—another could not play unless they were all shut. With perfect complaisance Mrs. Falconer ordered the windows to be opened and shut, and again shut and opened; with admirable patience she was, or seemed to be, the martyr to the caprices of the fair musicians. While all the time she so manoeuvred as to divide, and govern, and finally to have every thing arranged as she pleased. None but a perfectly cool stander-by, and one previously acquainted with Mrs. Falconer's character, could have seen all that Alfred saw. Perhaps the interest he began to take about Count Altenberg, who was the grand object of all her operations, increased his penetration. While the count was engaged in earnest political conversation in one of the inner rooms with the commissioner, Mrs. Falconer besought the Miss La Grandes to favour the company. It was impossible for them to resist her polite entreaties. Next she called upon Miss Crotch, and the Miss Barhams; and she contrived that they should sing and play, and play and sing, till they had exhausted the admiration and complaisance of the auditors. Then she relieved attention with some slight things from Miss Arabella Falconer, such as could excite no sensation or envy. Presently, after walking about the room, carelessly joining different conversation parties, and saying something obliging to each, she approached the count and the commissioner. Finding that the commissioner had finished all he had to say, she began to reproach him for keeping the count so long from the ladies, and leading him, as she spoke, to the piano-forte, she declared that he had missed such charming things. She could not ask Miss Crotch to play any more till she had rested—"Georgiana! for want of something better, do try what you can give us—She will appear to great disadvantage, of course—My dear, I think we have not had O Giove omnipotente."

"I am not equal to that, ma'am," said Georgiana, drawing back: "you should call upon Miss La Grande."

"True, my love; but Miss La Grande has been so very obliging, I could not ask—Try it, my love—I am not surprised you should be diffident after what we have heard; but the count, I am sure, will make allowances."

With amiable and becoming diffidence Miss Georgiana was compelled to comply—the count was surprised and charmed by her voice: then she was prevailed upon to try "Quanta O quanto è amor possente"—the count, who was enthusiastically fond of music, seemed quite enchanted; and Mrs. Falconer took care that he should have this impression left full and strong upon his mind—supper was announced. The count was placed at the table between Mrs. Falconer and Lady Trant—but just as they were sitting down, Mrs. Falconer called to Georgiana, who was going, much against her will, to another table, "Take my place, my dear Georgiana, for you know I never eat supper."

Georgiana's countenance, which had been black as night, became all radiant instantly. She took her mamma's place beside the count. Mrs. Falconer walked about all supper-time smiling, and saying obliging things with self-satisfied grace. She had reason indeed to be satisfied with the success of this night's operations. Never once did she appear to look towards the count, or her daughter; but assuredly she saw that things were going on as she wished.

In the mean time Alfred Percy was as heartily tired by the exhibitions of this evening as were many fashionable young men who had been loud in their praises of the performers. Perhaps Alfred was not however a perfectly fair judge, as he was disappointed in his own manoeuvres, not having been able to obtain two minutes' conversation with the count during the whole evening. In a letter to Rosamond, the next day, he said that Mrs. Falconer's concert had been very dull, and he observed that "People can see more of one another in a single day in the country than they can in a year in town." He was further very eloquent "on the folly of meeting in crowds to say commonplace nothings to people you do not care for, and to see only the outsides of those with whom you desire to converse."

"Just as I was writing this sentence," continues Alfred, "Count Altenberg called—how fortunate!—how obliging of him to come so early, before I went to the courts. He has put me into good humour again with the whole world—even with the Miss Falconers. He came to take leave of me—he is going down to the country—with whom do you think?—With Lord Oldborough, during the recess. Did I not tell you that Lord Oldborough would like him—that is, would find that he has information, and can be useful? I hope you will all see the count; indeed I am sure you will. He politely spoke of paying his respects to my father, by whom the shipwrecked foreigners had been so hospitably succoured in their distress. I told him that our family no longer lived in the same place; that we had been obliged to retire to a small estate, in a distant part of the county. I did not trouble him with the history of our family misfortunes;

nor did I even mention how the shipwreck, and the carelessness of the Dutch sailors, had occasioned the fire at Percy Hall—though I was tempted to tell him this when I was speaking of M. de Tourville.

"I forgot to tell my father, that the morning when I went with the count to Lord Oldborough's, among a heap of books of heraldry, with which his table was covered, I spied an old book of my father's on the arte of deciphering, which he had lent Commissioner Falconer years ago. Lord Oldborough, whose eye is quick as a hawk's, saw my eye turn towards it, and he asked me if I knew any thing of that book, or of the art of deciphering? Nothing of the art, but something of the book, which I recollected to be my father's. His lordship put it into my hands, and I showed some pencil notes of my father's writing. Lord Oldborough seemed surprised, and said he did not know this had been among the number of your studies. I told him that you had once been much intent upon Wilkins and Leibnitz's scheme of a universal language, and that I believed this had led you to the art of deciphering. He repeated the words 'Universal language—Ha!—then I suppose it was from Mr. Percy that Commissioner Falconer learnt all he knew on this subject?'

"'I believe so, my lord.'

"'Ha!' He seemed lost for a moment in thought, and then added, 'I wish I had known this sooner—Ha!'

"What these Haes meant, I was unable to decipher; but I am sure they related to some matter very interesting to him. He explained himself no farther, but immediately turned away from me to the count, and began to talk of the affairs of his court, and of M. de Tourville, of whom he seems to have some knowledge, I suppose through the means of his envoy, Cunningham Falconer.

"I understand that a prodigious party is invited to Falconer-court. The count asked me if I was to be one of them, and seemed to wish it—I like him much. They are to have balls, and plays, and great doings. If I have time, I will write to-morrow, and tell you who goes, and give you a sketch of their characters. Mrs. Falconer cannot well avoid asking you to some of her entertainments, and it will be pleasant to you to know who's who beforehand."

CHAPTER XXIV

Notwithstanding all the patronage of fashion, which the Miss Falconers had for some time enjoyed, notwithstanding all their own accomplishments, and their mother's address and knowledge of the world, the grand object had not been obtained—for they were not married. Though every where seen, and every where admired, no proposals had yet been made adequate to their expectations. In vain had one young nobleman after another, heir apparent after heir apparent, been invited, cherished, and flattered by Mrs. Falconer, had been constantly at her balls and concerts, had stood beside the harp and the piano-forte, had danced or flirted with the Miss Falconers, had been hung out at all public places as a pendant to one or other of the sisters.

The mother, seeing project after project fail for the establishment of her daughters, forced to bear and to conceal these disappointments, still continued to form new schemes with indefatigable perseverance. Yet every season the difficulty increased; and Mrs. Falconer, in the midst of the life of pleasure which she seemed to lead, was a prey to perpetual anxiety. She knew that if any thing should happen to the commissioner, whose health was declining; if he should lose Lord Oldborough's favour, which seemed not impossible; if Lord Oldborough should not be able to maintain himself in power, or if he should die; she and her daughters would lose every thing. From a small estate, overwhelmed with debt, there would be no fortune for her daughters; they would be left utterly destitute, and absolutely unable to do any thing for themselves—unlikely to suit plain country gentlemen, after the high style of company in which they had lived, and still more incapable than she would be of bearing a reverse of fortune. The young ladies, confident of their charms, unaccustomed to reflect, and full of the present, thought little of these probabilities of future evil, though they were quite as impatient to be married as their mother could wish. Indeed, this impatience becoming visible, she was rather anxious to suppress it, because it counteracted her views. Mrs. Falconer had still two schemes for their establishment. Sir Robert Percy had luckily lost his wife within the last twelvemonth, had no children, and had been heard to declare that he would marry again as soon as he decently could, because, if he were to die without heirs, the Percy estate might revert to the relations, whom he detested. Mrs. Falconer had persuaded the commissioner to cultivate Sir Robert Percy's acquaintance; had this winter watched for the time when law business called him to town; had prevailed upon him to go to her house, instead of staying, as he usually did, at an hotel, or spending his day at his solicitor's chambers. She had in short made things so agreeable to him, and he seemed so well pleased with her, she had hopes he would in time be brought to propose for her daughter Arabella. To conciliate Sir Robert Percy, it was necessary to avoid all connexion with the other Percys; and it was for this reason that the commissioner had of late avoided Alfred and Erasmus. Mrs. Falconer's schemes for Georgiana, her beautiful daughter, were far more brilliant. Several great establishments she had in view. The appearance of Count Altenberg put many old visions to flight—her whole fancy fixed upon him. If she could marry her Georgiana to Count Altenberg!—There would be a match high as her most exalted ambition could desire; and this project did not seem impossible. The count had been heard to say that he thought Miss Georgiana Falconer the handsomest woman he had seen since he had been in London. He had admired her dancing, and had listened with enthusiastic attention to her music, and to her charming voice; the young lady herself was confident that he was, would be, or ought to be, her slave. The count was going into the country for some weeks with Lord Oldborough. Mrs. Falconer, though she had not seen Falconer-court for fifteen years, decided to go there immediately. Then she should have the count fairly away from all the designing mothers and rival daughters of her acquaintance, and besides—she might, by this seasonable visit to the country, secure Sir Robert Percy for her daughter Arabella. The commissioner rejoiced in his lady's determination, because he knew that it would afford him an opportunity of obliging Lord Oldborough. His lordship had always been averse from the trouble of entertaining company. He disliked it still more since the death of Lady Oldborough; but he knew that it was necessary to keep up his interest and his popularity in the country, and he would, therefore, be obliged by Mrs. Falconer's giving dinners and entertainments for him. This game had succeeded, when it had been played—at the time of the Marchioness of Twickenham's marriage. Mr. Falconer was particularly anxious now to please Lord Oldborough, for he was fully aware that he had lost ground with his patron, and that his sons had all in different ways given his lordship cause of dissatisfaction. With Buckhurst Falconer Lord Oldborough was displeased for being the companion and encourager of his nephew, Colonel Hauton, in extravagance and gaming. In paying his court to the nephew, Buckhurst lost the uncle. Lord Oldborough had hoped that a man of literature and talents, as Buckhurst had been represented to him, would have drawn his nephew from the turf to the senate, and would have raised in Colonel Hauton's mind some noble ambition.

"A clergyman! sir," said Lord Oldborough to Commissioner Falconer, with a look of austere indignation.—"What could induce such a man as Mr. Buckhurst Falconer to become a clergyman?" The commissioner, affecting to sympathize in this indignation, declared that he was so angry with his son that he would not see him. All the time, however, he comforted himself with the hope that his son would, in a few months, be in possession of the long-expected living of Chipping-Friars, as the old incumbent was now speechless. Lord Oldborough had never, after this disowning of Buckhurst, mentioned his name to the father, and the commissioner thought this management had succeeded.

Of John Falconer, too, there had been complaints. Officers returned from abroad had spoken of his stupidity, his neglect of duty, and, above all, of his boasting that, let him do what he pleased, he was sure of Lord Oldborough's favour—certain of being a major in one year, a lieutenant-colonel in two. At first his boasts had been laughed at by his brother officers, but when, at the year's end, he actually was made a major, their surprise and discontent were great. Lord Oldborough was blamed for patronizing such a fellow. All this, in course of time, came to his lordship's knowledge. He heard these complaints in silence. It was not his habit suddenly to express his displeasure. He heard, and saw, without speaking or acting, till facts and proofs had accumulated in his mind. He seemed to pass over many things unobserved, but they were all registered in his memory, and he would judge and decide at last in an instant, and irrevocably. Of this Commissioner Falconer, a cunning man, who watched parts of a character narrowly, but could not take in the whole, was not aware. He often blessed his good fortune for having escaped Lord Oldborough's displeasure or detection, upon occasions when his lordship had marked all that the commissioner imagined he had overlooked; his lordship was often most awake to what was passing, and most displeased, when he appeared most absent or unmoved.

For instance, many mistakes, and much ignorance, had frequently appeared in his envoy Cunningham Falconer's despatches; but except when, in the first moment of surprise at the difference between the ineptitude of the envoy, and the talents of the author of the pamphlet, his lordship had exclaimed, "A slovenly despatch," these mistakes, and this ignorance, had passed without animadversion. Some symptoms of duplicity, some evasion of the minister's questions, had likewise appeared, and the commissioner had trembled lest the suspicions of his patron should be awakened.

Count Altenberg, without design to injure Cunningham, had accidentally mentioned in the presence of the commissioner and of Lord Oldborough something of a transaction which was to be kept a profound secret from the minister, a private intrigue which Cunningham had been carrying on to get himself appointed envoy to the court of Denmark, by the interest of the opposite party, in case of a change of ministry. At the moment when this was alluded to by Count Altenberg, the commissioner was so dreadfully alarmed that he perspired at every pore; but perceiving that Lord Oldborough expressed no surprise, asked no explanation, never looked towards him with suspicion, nor even raised his eyes, Mr. Falconer flattered himself that his lordship was so completely engrossed in the operation of replacing a loose glass in his spectacles, that he had not heard or noticed one word the count had said. In this hope the commissioner was confirmed by Lord Oldborough's speaking an instant afterwards precisely in his usual tone, and pursuing his previous subject of conversation, without any apparent interruption in the train of his ideas. Yet, notwithstanding that the commissioner fancied that he and his son had escaped, and were secure in each particular instance, he had a general feeling that Lord Oldborough was more reserved towards him; and he was haunted by a constant fear of losing, not his patron's esteem or confidence, but his favour. Against this danger he constantly guarded. To flatter, to keep Lord Oldborough in good humour, to make himself agreeable and necessary by continual petty submissions and services, was the sum of his policy.

It was with this view that he determined to go into the country; and with this view he had consented to various expenses, which were necessary, as Mrs. Falconer declared, to make it practicable for her and her daughters to accompany him. Orders were sent to have a theatre at Falconer-court, which had been long disused, fitted up in the most elegant manner. The Miss Falconers had been in the habit of acting at Sir Thomas and Lady Flowerton's private theatre at Richmond, and they were accomplished actresses.

Count Altenberg had declared that he was particularly fond of theatrical amusements. That hint was sufficient. Besides, what a sensation the opening of a theatre at Falconer-court would create in the country! Mrs. Falconer observed that the only possible way to make the country supportable was to have a large party of town friends in your house—and this was the more necessary for her, as she was almost a stranger in her own county.

Alfred kept his promise, and sent Rosamond a list of the persons of whom the party was to consist. Opposite to several names he wrote—commonplace young—or, commonplace old ladies:—of the latter number were Lady Trant and Lady Kew: of the former were the Miss G—s, and others not worth mentioning. Then came the two Lady Arlingtons, nieces of the Duke of Greenwich.

"The Lady Arlingtons," continues Alfred, "are glad to get to Mrs. Falconer, and Mrs. Falconer is glad to have them, because they are related to my lord duke. I have met them at Mrs. Falconer's, at Lady Angelica Headingham's, and often at Lady Jane Granville's. The style and tone of the Lady Anne is languishing—of Lady Frances, lively: both seem mere spoilt selfish ladies of quality. Lady Anne's selfishness is of the cold, chronic, inveterate nature; Lady Frances' of the hot, acute, and tormenting species. She 'loves everything by fits, and nothing long.' Every body is an angel and a dear creature, while they minister to her fancies—and no longer. About these fancies she is restless and impatient to a degree which makes her sister look sick and scornful beyond description. Lady Anne neither fancies nor loves any thing or any body. She seems to have no object upon earth but to drink barley-water, and save herself from all manner of trouble or exertion, bodily or mental. So much for the Lady Arlingtons.

"Buckhurst Falconer cannot be of this party—Colonel Hauton has him at his regiment. But Buckhurst's two friends, the Clays, are earnestly pressed into the service. Notwithstanding the fine sanctified speech Mrs. Falconer made me, about that sad affair of Lewis Clay with Lady Harriot H—, she invites him; and I have a notion, if Count Altenberg had not appeared, that she would have liked to have had him, or his brother, for her son-in-law. That you may judge how much my mother would like them for her sons-in-law, I will take the trouble to draw you portraits of both gentlemen.

"French Clay and English Clay, as they have been named, are brothers, both men of large fortune, which their father acquired respectably by commerce, and which they are spending in all kinds of extravagance and profligacy, not from inclination, but merely to purchase admission into fine company. French Clay is a travelled coxcomb, who, à propos de bottes, begins with, 'When I was abroad with the Princess Orbitella—' But I am afraid I cannot speak of this man with impartiality, for I cannot bear to see an Englishman apeing a Frenchman. The imitation is always so awkward, so ridiculous, so contemptible. French Clay talks of tact, but without possessing any; he delights in what he calls persiflage, but in his persiflage, instead of the wit and elegance of Parisian raillery, there appears only the vulgar love and habit of derision. He is continually railing at our English want of savoir vivre, yet is himself an example of the ill-breeding which he reprobates. His manners have neither the cordiality of an Englishman nor the polish of a foreigner. To improve us in l'esprit de société, he would introduce the whole system of French gallantry—the vice without the refinement. I heard him acknowledge it to be 'his principle' to intrigue with every married woman who would listen to him, provided she has any one of his four requisites, wit, fashion, beauty, or a good table. He says his late suit in Doctors'-commons cost him nothing; for 10,000l. are nothing to him.

"Public virtue, as well as private, he thinks it a fine air to disdain, and patriotism and love of our country, he calls prejudices of which a philosopher ought to divest himself. Some charitable people say that he is not so unfeeling as he seems to be, and that above half his vices arise from affectation, and from a mistaken ambition to be what he thinks perfectly French.

"His brother, English Clay, is a cold, reserved, proud, dull-looking man, whom art, in despite of nature, strove, and strove in vain, to quicken into a 'gay deceiver.' He is a grave man of pleasure—his first care being to provide for his exclusively personal gratifications. His dinner is a serious, solemn business, whether it be at his own table or at a tavern, which last he prefers—he orders it so that his repast shall be the very best of its kind that money can procure. His next care is, that he be not cheated in what he is to pay. Not that he values money, but he cannot bear to be taken in. Then his dress, his horses his whole appointment and establishment, are complete, and accurately in the fashion of the day—no expense spared. All that belongs to Mr. Clay, of Clay-hall, is the best of its kind, or, at least, had from the best hand in England. Every thing about him is English; but I don't know whether this arises from love of his country or contempt of his brother. English Clay is not ostentatious of that which is his own, but he is disdainful of all that belongs to another. The slightest deficiency in the appointments of his companions he sees, and marks by a wink to some bystander, or with a dry joke laughs the wretch to scorn. In company he delights to sit by silent and snug, sneering inwardly at those who are entertaining the company, and committing themselves. He never entertains, and is seldom entertained. His joys are neither convivial nor intellectual; he is gregarious, but not companionable; a hard drinker, but not social. Wine sometimes makes him noisy, but never makes him gay; and, whatever be his excesses, he commits them seemingly without temptation from taste or passion. He keeps a furiously expensive mistress, whom he curses, and who curses him, as Buckhurst informs me, ten times a day; yet he prides himself on being free and unmarried! Scorning and dreading women in general, he swears he would not marry Venus herself unless she had 100,000l. in each pocket; and now that no mortal Venus wears pockets, he thanks Heaven he is safe. Buckhurst, I remember, assured me that beneath this crust of pride there is some good-nature. Deep hid under a large mass of selfishness there may be some glimmerings of affection. He shows symptoms of feeling for his horses, and his mother, and his coachman, and his country. I do believe he would fight for old England, for it is his country, and he is English Clay. Affection for his coachman, did I say?—He shows admiration, if not affection, for every whip of note in town. He is their companion—no, their pupil, and, as Antoninus Pius gratefully prided himself in recording the names of those relations and friends from whom he learnt his several virtues, this man may boast to after-ages of having learnt from one coachman how to cut a fly off his near leader's ear, how to tuck up a duck from another, and the true spit from a third—by-the-bye, it is said, but I don't vouch for the truth of the story, that this last accomplishment cost him a tooth, which he had had drawn to attain it in perfection. Pure slang he could not learn from any one coachman, but from constantly frequenting the society of all. I recollect Buckhurst Falconer telling me that he dined once with English Clay, in company with a baronet, a viscount, an earl, a duke, and the driver of a mail-coach, to whom was given, by acclamation, the seat of honour. I am told there is a house, at which these gentlemen and noblemen meet regularly every week, where there are two dining-rooms divided by glass doors. In one room the real coachmen dined, in the other the amateur gentlemen, who, when they are tired of their own conversation, throw open the glass doors, that they may be entertained and edified by the coachmen's wit and slang; in which dialect English Clay's rapid proficiency has, it is said, recommended him to the best society, even more than his being the master of the best of cooks, and of Clay-hall.

"I have said so much more than I intended of both these brothers, that I have no room for more portraits; indeed, the other gentlemen are zeros.

"Yours affectionately,

"ALFRED PERCY."

Notwithstanding the pains which Mrs. Falconer took to engage these Mr. Clays to accompany her, she could obtain only a promise that they would wait upon her, if possible, some time during the recess.

Count Altenberg also, much to Mrs. Falconer's disappointment, was detained in town a few days longer than he had foreseen, but he promised to follow Lord Oldborough early in the ensuing week. All the rest of the prodigious party arrived at Falconer-court, which was within a few miles of Lord Oldborough's seat at Clermont-park.

The day after Lord Oldborough's arrival in the country, his lordship was seized with a fit of the gout, which fixed in his right hand. Commissioner Falconer, when he came in the morning to pay his respects, and to inquire after his patron's health, found him in his study, writing a letter with his left hand. "My lord, shall not I call Mr. Temple—or—could I offer my services as secretary?"

"I thank you, sir—no. This letter must be written with my own hand."

Whom can this letter be to, that is of so much consequence? thought the commissioner; and glancing his eye at the direction, he saw, as the letter was given to a servant, "To L. Percy, Esq."—his surprise arrested the pinch of snuff which he was just going to take. "What could be the business—the secret—only a few lines, what could they contain?"

Simply these words

"MY DEAR SIR,

"I write to you with my left hand, the gout having, within these few hours, incapacitated my right. Since this gout keeps me a prisoner, and I cannot, as I had intended, go to you, may I beg that you will do me the favour to come to me, if it could suit your convenience, to-morrow morning, when I shall be alone from twelve till four.

"With true esteem,

"Yours,

"OLDBOROUGH."

In the course of the day the commissioner found out, by something Lord Oldborough let fall, what his lordship had no intention to conceal, that he had requested Mr. Percy to come to Clermont-park the next morning; and the commissioner promised himself that he would be in the way to see his good cousin Percy, and to satisfy his curiosity. But his manoeuvres and windings were, whenever it was necessary, counteracted and cut short by the unexpected directness and peremptory plain dealing of his patron. In the morning, towards the hour of twelve, the commissioner thought he had well begun a conversation that would draw out into length upon a topic which he knew must be interesting to his lordship, and he held in his hand private letters of great consequence from his son Cunningham; but Lord Oldborough, taking the letters, locked them up in his desk, saying, "To-night I will read them—this morning I have set apart for a conversation with Mr. Percy, whom I wish to see alone. In the mean time, my interest in the borough has been left too much to the care of that attorney Sharpe, of whom I have no great opinion. Will you be so good to ride over, as you promised me that you would, to the borough, and see what is doing there?"

The commissioner endeavoured not to look disconcerted or discomfited, rang the bell for his horses, and took his leave, as Lord Oldborough had determined that he should, before the arrival of Mr. Percy, who came exactly at twelve.

"I thank you for this punctuality, Mr. Percy," said Lord Oldborough, advancing in his most gracious manner; and no two things could be more strikingly different than his gracious and ungracious manner. "I thank you for this kind punctuality. No one knows better than I do the difference between the visit of a friend and all other visits."

Without preface, Lord Oldborough always went directly to the point. "I have requested you to come to me, Mr. Percy, because I want from you two things, which I cannot have so much to my satisfaction from any other person as from you—assistance and sympathy. But, before I go to my own affairs, let me—and not by way of compliment, but plainly and truly—let me congratulate you, my dear sir, on the success of your sons, on the distinction and independence they have already acquired in their professions. I know the value of independence—of that which I shall never have," added his lordship, with a forced smile and a deep sigh. "But let that be. It was not of that I meant to speak. You pursue your course; I, mine. Firmness of purpose I take to be the great difference between man and man. I am not one of those who habitually covet sympathy. It is a sign of a mind insufficient to its own support, to look for sympathy on every trivial occurrence; and on great occasions it has not been my good fortune to meet many persons who could sympathize with me."

"True," said Mr. Percy, "people must think with you, before they can feel with you."

"It is extraordinary, Mr. Percy," continued Lord Oldborough, "that, knowing how widely you differ from me in political principles, I should choose, of all men living, to open my mind to you. But the fact is, that I am convinced, however we may differ about the means, the end we both have in view is one and the same—the good and glory of the British empire."

"My lord, I believe it," cried Mr. Percy—with energy and warmth he repeated, "My lord, I believe it."

"I thank you, sir," said Lord Oldborough; "you do me justice. I have reason to be satisfied when such men as you do me justice; I have reason also to be satisfied that I have not to make the common complaint of those who serve princes. From him whom I have served I have not met with any ingratitude, with any neglect: on the contrary, I am well assured, that so firm is his conviction of my intending the good of his throne and of his people, that to preserve me his minister is the first wish of his heart. I am confident that without hesitation he would dismiss from his councils any who should obstruct my views, or be inimical to my interests."

"Then, my lord, you are happy; if man can be happy at the summit of ambition."

"Pardon me. It is a dizzy height at best; but, were it attained, I trust my head would be strong enough to bear it."

"Lord Verulam, you know, my lord," said Mr. Percy, smiling, "tells us, that people, by looking down precipices, do put their spirits in the act of falling."

"True, true," said Lord Oldborough, rather impatient at Mr. Percy's going to Lord Verulam and philosophy. "But you have not yet heard the facts. I am encompassed with enemies, open and secret. Open enemies I meet and defy—their strength I can calculate and oppose; but the strength of my secret enemies I cannot calculate, for that strength depends on their combination, and that combination I cannot break till I know of what it consists. I have the power and the will to strike, but know not where to aim. In the dark I will not strike, lest I injure the innocent or destroy a friend. Light I cannot obtain, though I have been in search of it for a considerable time. Perhaps by your assistance it may be obtained."

"By my assistance!" exclaimed Mr. Percy: "ignorant, as I am, of all parties, and of all their secret transactions, how, my dear lord, can I possibly afford you any assistance?"

"Precisely by your being unconnected with all parties—a cool stander-by, you can judge of the play— you can assist me with your general knowledge of human nature, and with a particular species of knowledge, of which I should never have guessed that you were possessed, but for an accidental discovery of it made to me the other day by your son Alfred—your knowledge of the art of deciphering."

Lord Oldborough then produced the Tourville papers, related how they had been put into his hands by Commissioner Falconer, showed him what the commissioner and his son had deciphered, pointed out where the remaining difficulty occurred, and explained how they were completely at a stand from their inability to decipher the word Gassoc, or to decide who or what it could mean. All the conjectures of the commissioner, the cassock, and the bishop, and the gosshawk, and the heraldic researches, and the French misnomers, and the puns upon the coats of arms, and the notes from Wilkins on universal language, and an old book on deciphering, which had been lent to the commissioner, and the private and public letters which Cunningham had written since he went abroad, were all laid before Mr. Percy.

"As to my envoy, Mr. Cunningham Falconer," said Lord Oldborough, as he took up the bundle of Cunningham's letters, "I do not choose to interrupt the main business before us, by adverting to him or to his character, farther than to point out to you this mark," showing a peculiar pencil mark, made on certain papers. "This is my note of distrust, observe, and this my note for mere circumlocution, or nonsense. And here," continued his lordship, "is a list of all those in, or connected with the ministry, whom it is possible may be my enemies." The list was the same as that on which the commissioner formerly went to work, except that the name of the Duke of Greenwich had been struck out, and two others added in his place, so that it stood thus: "Dukes of Doncaster and Stratford; Lords Coleman, Naresby, Skreene, Twisselton, Waltham, Wrexfield, Chelsea, and Lancaster; Sir Thomas Cope, Sir James Skipworth; Secretaries Arnold and Oldfield." This list was marked with figures, in different coloured inks, prefixed to each name, denoting the degrees of their supposed enmity to Lord Oldborough, and these had been calculated from a paper, containing notes of the probable causes and motives of their disaffection, drawn up by Commissioner Falconer, but corrected, and in many places contradicted, by notes in Lord Oldborough's hand-writing. His lordship marked which was his calculation of probabilities, and made some observations on the character of each, as he read over the list of names rapidly.

Doncaster, a dunce—Stratford, a miser—Coleman, a knave—Naresby, non compos—Skreene, the most corrupt of the corrupt—Twisselton, puzzle headed—Waltham, a mere theorist—Wrexfield, a speechifier—Chelsea, a trimmer—Lancaster, deep and dark—Sir Thomas Cope, a wit, a poet, and a fool—Sir James Skipworth, finance and finesse—Arnold, able and active—and Oldfield, a diplomatist in grain.

"And is this the summary of the history of the men with whom your lordship is obliged to act and live?" said Mr. Percy.

"It is—I am: but, my dear sir, do not let us fly off at a tangent to morality or philosophy; these have nothing to do with the present purpose. You have before you all the papers relative to this transaction. Now, will you do me the favour, the service, to look them over, and try whether you can make out le mot d'énigme? I shall not disturb you."

Lord Oldborough sat down at a small table by the fire, with a packet of letters and memorials beside him, and in a few minutes was completely absorbed in these, for he had acquired the power of turning his attention suddenly and entirely from one subject to another.

Without reading the mass of Commissioner Falconer's explanations and conjectures, or encumbering his understanding with all that Cunningham had collected, as if purposely to puzzle the cause, Mr. Percy examined first very carefully the original documents—then Lord Oldborough's notes on the views and characters of the suspected persons, and the reasons of their several enmities or dissatisfaction. From the scale of probabilities, which he found had been with great skill calculated on these notes, he selected the principal names, and then tried with these, whether he could make out an idea that had struck him the moment he had heard of the Gassoc. He recollected the famous word Cabal, in the reign of Charles the Second, and he thought it possible that the cabalistical word Gassoc might be formed by a similar combination. But Gassoc was no English word, was no word of any language. Upon close examination of the Tourville papers, he perceived that the commissioner had been right in one of his suggestions, that the G had been written instead of a C: in some places it had been a c turned into a g, and the writer seemed to be in doubt whether the word should be Gassoc or Cassoc. Assuming, therefore, that it was Cassock, Mr. Percy found the initials of six persons, who stood high in Lord Oldborough's scale of probabilities: Chelsea—Arnold—Skreene—Skipworth—Oldfield—Coleman; and the last k, for which he hunted in vain a considerable time, was supplied by Kensington (one of the Duke of Greenwich's titles), whose name had been scratched out of the list, since his reconciliation and connexion by marriage with Lord Oldborough, but who had certainly at one time been of the league of his lordship's enemies. Every circumstance and date in the Tourville papers exactly agree with this explanation: the Cassock thus composed cleared up all difficulties; and passages, that were before dark and mysterious, were rendered by this reading perfectly intelligible. The interpretation, when once given, appeared so simple, that Lord Oldborough wondered how it was possible that it had not before occurred to his mind. His satisfaction was great—he was at this moment relieved from all danger of mistaking friend for foe; he felt that his enemies were in his power, and his triumph secure.

"My dear sir," cried he, "you do not know, you cannot estimate, the extent of the service you have done me: far from wishing to lessen it in your eyes, I wish you to know at this moment its full importance. By Lady Oldborough's death, and by circumstances with which I need not trouble you, I lost the support of her connexions. The Duke of Greenwich, though my relation, is a weak man, and a weak man can never be a good friend. I was encompassed, undermined, the ground hollow under me—I knew it, but I could not put my finger upon one of the traitors. Now I have them all at one blow, and I thank you for it. I have the character, I believe, of being what is called proud, but you see that I am not too proud to be assisted and obliged by one who will never allow me to oblige or assist him or any of his family. But why should this be? Look over the list of these men. In some one of these places of trust, give me a person in whom I can confide, a friend to me, and to your country. Look over that list, now in your hand, and put your finger upon any thing that will suit you."

"I thank you, my lord," said Mr. Percy; "I feel the full value of your good opinion, and true gratitude for the warmth of your friendship, but I cannot accept of any office under your administration. Our political principles differ as much as our private sentiments of honour agree; and these sentiments will, I trust, make you approve of what I now say—and do."

"But there are places, there are situations which you might accept, where your political opinions and mine could never clash. It is an extraordinary thing for a minister to press a gentleman to accept of a place, unless he expects more in return than what he gives. But come—I must have Mr. Percy one of us. You have never tried ambition yet," added Lord Oldborough, with a smile: "trust me, you will find ambition has its pleasures, its proud moments, when a man feels that he has his foot on the neck of his enemies."

Lord Oldborough stood, as if he felt this pride at the instant. "You do not know the charms of ambition, Mr. Percy."

"It may be delightful to feel one's foot on the neck of one's enemies, but, for my part, I rather prefer having no enemies."

"No enemies!" said Lord Oldborough: "every man that has character enough to make friends has character enough to make enemies—and must have enemies, if not of his power or place, of his talents and property—the sphere lower, the passion's the same. No enemies!—What is he, who has been at law with you, and has robbed you of your estate?"

"I forgot him—upon my word, I forgot him," said Mr. Percy. "You see, my lord, if he robbed me of my estate, he did not rob me of my peace of mind. Does your lordship think," said Mr. Percy, smiling, "that any ambitious man, deprived of his place, could say as much?"

"When I can tell you that from my own experience, you shall know," said Lord Oldborough, replying in the same tone; "but, thanks to your discovery, there seems to be little chance, at present, of my being competent to answer that question. But to business—we are wasting life."

Every word or action that did not tend to a political purpose appeared to Lord Oldborough to be a waste of life.

"Your ultimatum? Can you be one of us?"

"Impossible, my lord. Pardon me if I say, that the nearer the view your confidence permits me to take of the workings of your powerful mind, and of the pains and penalties of your exalted situation, the more clearly I feel that ambition is not for me, that my happiness lies in another line."

"Enough—I have done—the subject is at rest between us for ever." A cloud, followed instantaneously by a strong radiance of pleasure, passed across Lord Oldborough's countenance, while he pronounced, as if speaking to himself, the words, "Singular obstinacy! Admirable consistency! And I too am consistent, my dear sir," said he, sitting down at the table. "Now for business; but I am deprived of my right hand." He rang, and desired his secretary, Mr. Temple, to be sent to him. Mr. Percy rose to take leave, but Lord Oldborough would not permit him to go. "I can have no secrets for you, Mr. Percy—stay and see the end of the Cassock."

Mr. Temple came in; and Lord Oldborough, with that promptitude and decision by which he was characterised, dictated a letter to the king, laying before his majesty the whole intrigue, as discovered by the Tourville papers, adding a list of the members of the Cassock—concluding by begging his majesty's permission to resign, unless the cabal, which had rendered his efforts for the good of the country and for his majesty's service in some points abortive, should be dismissed from his majesty's councils. In another letter to a private friend, who had access to the royal ear, Lord Oldborough named the persons, whom, if his majesty should do him the favour of consulting him, he should wish to recommend in the places of those who might be dismissed. His lordship farther remarked, that the marriage which had taken place between his niece and the eldest son of the Duke of Greenwich, and the late proofs of his grace's friendship, dissipated all fears and resentment arising from his former connexion with the Cassock. Lord Oldborough therefore entreated his majesty to continue his grace in his ministry. All this was stated in the shortest and plainest terms.

"No rounded periods, no phrases, no fine writing, Mr. Temple, upon this occasion, if you please; it must be felt that these letters are straight from my mind, and that if they are not written by my own hand, it is because that hand is disabled. As soon as the gout will let me stir, I shall pay my duty to my sovereign in person. These arrangements will be completed, I trust, by the meeting of parliament. In the mean time I am better here than in London; the blow will be struck, and none will know by whom—not but what I am ready to avow it, if called upon. But—let the coffee-house politicians decide, and the country gentlemen prose upon it," said Lord Oldborough, smiling—"some will say the ministry split on India affairs, some on Spanish, some on French affairs. How little they, any of them, know what passes or what governs behind the curtain! Let them talk—whilst I act."

The joy of this discovery so raised Lord Oldborough's spirits, and dilated his heart, that he threw himself open with a freedom and hilarity, and with a degree of humour unusual to him, and unknown except to the few in his most intimate confidence. The letters finished, Mr. Temple was immediately despatched with them to town.

"There," said Lord Oldborough, as soon as Mr. Temple had left him, "there's a secretary I can depend upon; and there is another obligation I owe to your family—to your son Alfred."

Now this business of the Tourville papers was off his mind, Lord Oldborough, though not much accustomed to turn his attention to the lesser details of domestic life, spoke of every individual of the Percy family with whom he was acquainted; and, in particular, of Godfrey, to whom he was conscious that he had been unjust. Mr. Percy, to relieve him from this regret, talked of the pleasure his son had had in his friend Gascoigne's late promotion to the lieutenant-colonelcy. Whilst Mr. Percy spoke, Lord Oldborough searched among a packet of letters for one which made honourable mention of Captain Percy, and put it into the hands of the happy father.

"Ah! these are pleasurable feelings denied to me," said Lord Oldborough.

After a pause he added, "That nephew of mine, Colonel Hauton, is irretrievably profligate, selfish, insignificant. I look to my niece, the Marchioness of Twickenham's child, that is to say, if the mother—"

Another long pause, during which his lordship rubbed the glasses of his spectacles, and looked through them, as if intent that no speck should remain; while he did this very slowly, his mind ran rapidly from the idea of the Marchioness of Twickenham to John Falconer, and thence to all the causes of distrust and discontent which he felt towards all the different individuals of the Falconer family. He considered, that now the Tourville papers had been completely deciphered, the necessity for engaging the secrecy of the commissioner, and of his son Cunningham, would soon cease.

Lord Oldborough's reverie was interrupted by seeing, at this instant, the commissioner returning from his ride.

"Not a word, Mr. Percy, of what has passed between us, to Commissioner Falconer—not a word of the Gassoc. I put you on your guard, because you live with those in whom you have entire confidence," said Lord Oldborough; "but that is what a public man, a minister, cannot do."

Another reason why I should not like to be a minister, thought Mr. Percy. "I took it for granted that the commissioner was entirely in your lordship's confidence."

"I thought you were too good a philosopher to take any thing for granted, Mr. Percy. Consider, if you please, that I am in a situation where I must have tools, and use them, as long as I can make them serviceable to my purposes. Sir, I am not a missionary, but a minister. I must work with men, and upon men, such as I find them. I am not a chemist, to analyze and purify the gold. I make no objection to that alloy, which I am told is necessary, and fits it for being moulded to my purposes. But here comes the ductile commissioner."

Lord Oldborough began to talk to him of the borough, without any mercy for his curiosity, and without any attempt to evade the various dexterous pushes he made to discover the business which had this morning occupied his lordship. Mr. Percy was surprised, in the course of this day, to see the manner in which the commissioner, a gentleman well-born, of originally independent fortune and station, humbled and abased himself to a patron. Mr. Falconer had contracted a certain cringing servility of manner, which completely altered his whole appearance, and which quite prevented him even from looking like a gentleman. It was his principle never to contradict a great man, never to give him any sort of pain; and his idea of the deference due to rank, and of the danger of losing favour by giving offence, was carried so far, that not only his attitude and language, but his whole mind, seemed to be new modified. He had not the free use of his faculties. He seemed really so to subdue and submit his powers, that his understanding was annihilated. Mr. Percy was astonished at the change in his cousin; the commissioner was equally surprised, nay, actually terrified, by Mr. Percy's freedom and boldness. "Good Heavens! how can you speak in this manner?" said Mr. Falconer, as they were going down stairs together, after parting with Lord Oldborough.

"And why not?—I have nothing to fear or to hope, nothing to gain or to lose. Lord Oldborough can give me nothing that I would accept, but his esteem, and that I am sure of never losing."

Heigho! if I had your favour with my lord, what I would make of it! thought the commissioner, as he stepped into his chariot. Mr. Percy mounted his horse, and rode back to his humble home, glad to have done his friend Lord Oldborough a service, still more glad that he was not bound to the minister by any of the chains of political dependence. Rejoiced to quit Tourville papers—state intrigues—lists of enemies,—and all the necessity for reserve and management, and all the turmoil of ambition.

CHAPTER XXV

Count Altenberg arrived at Clermont-park, and as Lord Oldborough was still confined by the gout, Commissioner Falconer, to his lady's infinite satisfaction, was deputed to show him every thing that was worth seeing in this part of the country. Every morning some party was formed by Mrs. Falconer, and so happily arranged that her Georgiana and the count were necessarily thrown together. The count rode extremely well; Miss Falconers had been taught to ride in a celebrated riding-house, and were delighted to display their equestrian graces. When they were not disposed to ride, the count had a phaeton; and Mrs. Falconer a barouche; and either in the phaeton, or the barouche seat, Miss Georgiana Falconer was seated with the count, who, as she discovered, drove uncommonly well.

The count had expressed a desire to see the place where M. de Tourville had been shipwrecked, and he really wished to be introduced to the Percy family, of whom, from the specimen he had seen in Alfred, and from all the hospitality they had shown the distressed mariners (some of whom were his countrymen), he had formed a favourable opinion. Half his wish was granted, the rest dispersed in empty air. Mrs. Falconer with alacrity arranged a party for Percy-hall, to show the count the scene of the shipwreck. She should be so glad to see it herself, for she was absent from the country at the time of the sad disaster; but the commissioner, who knew the spot, and all the circumstances, better than any other person, would show them every thing—and Sir Robert Percy, she was sure, would think himself much honoured by Count Altenberg's visiting his place.

Count Altenberg had some confused recollection of Mr. Alfred Percy's having told him that his father no longer lived at Percy hall; but this speech of Mrs. Falconer's led the count to believe that he had misunderstood what Alfred had said.

The party arranged for Percy-hall consisted of the Miss Falconers, the two Lady Arlingtons, and some other young people, who were at Falconer-court. It was a fine morning, Mrs. Falconer was all suavity and smiles, both the Miss Falconers in charming hopes, and consequently in charming spirits.

Percy-hall was really a beautiful place, and Miss Arabella Falconer now looked at it with the pleasure of anticipated possession. Sir Robert Percy was not at home, he had been obliged that morning to be absent on some special business; but he had left orders with his steward and housekeeper to show the party of visitors the house and grounds. In going through the apartments they came to the gallery leading to the library, where they were stopped by some workmen's trestles, on which were lying two painted glass windows, one that had been taken down, and another which was to be put in its stead. Whilst the workmen were moving the obstacles out of the way, the company had leisure to admire the painted windows. One of them was covered with coats of arms: the other represented the fire at Percy-hall, and the portrait of Caroline assisting the old nurse down the staircase. This painting immediately fixed Count Altenberg's eye, and Miss Georgiana Falconer, not knowing whose portrait it was, exclaimed, as she looked at the figure of Caroline, "Beautiful! Exquisite! What a lovely creature that is assisting the old woman!"

"Yes," said Count Altenberg, "it is one of the finest countenances I ever beheld."

All the ladies eagerly pressed forward to look at it.

"Beautiful! Don't you think it is something like Lady Anne Cope?" said Miss Falconer.

"Oh! dear, no!" cried Miss Georgiana Falconer: "it is a great deal handsomer than any of the Copes ever were, or ever will be!"

"It has a look of Lady Mary Nesbitt," said one of the Lady Arlingtons.

"The eyes are so like Lady Coningsby, who is my delight," said Georgiana.

"And it has quite the Arlington nose," said Mrs. Falconer, glancing her eye upon the Lady Arlingtons. Count Altenberg, without moving his eye, repeated, "It is the most beautiful face I ever beheld."

"Not nearly so beautiful as the original, sir," said the painter.

"The original?—Is it a copy?"

"A portrait, sir."

"Oh! a family portrait of one of our great, great grandmother Percys, I suppose," said Miss Georgiana, "done in her youth—in a fancy piece, you know, according to the taste of those times—she must have been superlatively lovely."

"Ma'am," said the painter, "the young lady, of whom this is a portrait, is, I hope and believe, now living."

"Where?—and who can she be?—for I am sure I don't recollect ever having seen her in all my life—never met her in town any where—Pray, sir, who may it be?" added she, turning to the artist, with a mixture of affected negligence and real pride.

"Miss Caroline Percy, ma'am."

"A daughter of Sir Robert Percy—of the gentleman of this house?" said Count Altenberg eagerly.

Mrs. Falconer, and her daughter Georgiana, answered rapidly, with looks of alarm, as they stood a little behind the count.

"Oh! no, no, Count Altenberg," cried Mrs. Falconer, advancing, "not a daughter of the gentleman of this house—another family, relations, but distant relations of the commissioner's: he formerly knew something of them, but we know nothing of them."

The painter however knew a great deal, and seemed anxious to tell all he knew: but Mrs. Falconer walked on immediately, saying, "This is our way, is not it? This leads to the library, where, I dare say, we shall find the book which the count wanted." The count heard her not, for with his eyes fixed on the picture he was listening to the account which the painter was giving of the circumstance it recorded of the fire at Percy-hall—of the presence of mind and humanity of Miss Caroline Percy, who had saved the life of the poor decrepit woman, who in the picture was represented as leaning upon her arm. The painter paused when he came to this part of his story—"That woman was my mother, sir."—He went on, and with all the eloquence of filial affection and of gratitude, pronounced in a few words a panegyric on the family who had been his first and his best benefactors: all who heard him were touched with his honest warmth, except the Miss Falconers.

"I dare say those Percys were very good people in their day," said Miss Falconer; "but their day is over, and no doubt you'll find, in the present possessor of the estate, sir, as good a patron at least."

The artist took up his pencil without making any reply, and went on with some heraldic devices he was painting.

"I am amazed how you could see any likeness in that face or figure to Lady Anne Cope, or Lady Mary Nesbitt, or any of the Arlingtons," said Miss Georgiana Falconer, looking through her hand at the portrait of Caroline: "it's the most beautiful thing I ever saw, certainly; but there's nothing of an air of fashion, and without that—"

"Count Altenberg, I have found for you the very book I heard you tell the commissioner last night you wished so much to see," said Mrs. Falconer. The count went forward to receive the book, and to thank the lady for her polite attention; she turned over the leaves, and showed him some uncommonly fine prints, which he was bound to admire—and whilst he was admiring, Mrs. Falconer found a moment to whisper to her daughter Georgiana, "Not a word more about the picture: let it alone, and it is only a picture—dwell upon it, and you make it a reality."

Miss Georgiana had quickness and ability sufficient to feel the value of her mother's knowledge of the world and of human nature, but she had seldom sufficient command of temper to imitate or to benefit by Mrs. Falconer's address. On this occasion she contented herself with venting her spleen on the poor painter, whose colouring and drapery she began to criticize unmercifully. Mrs. Falconer, however, carried off the count with her into the library, and kept him there, till the commissioner, who had been detained in the neighbouring village by some electioneering business, arrived; and then they pursued their walk together through the park. Miss Falconer was particularly delighted with the beauties of the grounds. Miss Georgiana, recovering her good-humour, was again charming—and all went on well; till they came near the sea-shore, and the count asked Commissioner Falconer to show him the place where the shipwreck had happened. She was provoked that his attention should be withdrawn from her, and again by these Percys. The commissioner called to one of the boatmen who had been ordered to be in readiness, and asked him to point out the place where the Dutch vessel had been wrecked. The man, who seemed rather surly, replied that they could not see the right place where they stood, and if they had a mind to see it, they must come into the boat, and row a piece up farther.

Now some of these town-bred ladies were alarmed at the idea of going to sea, and though Miss Georgiana was very unwilling to be separated from the count, and though her mother encouraged the young lady to vanquish her fears as much by precept and as little by example as possible, yet when she was to be handed into the boat, she drew back in pretty terror, put her hands before her face, and protested she could not venture even with Count Altenberg. After as much waste of words as the discussion of such arrangements on a party of pleasure usually involves, it was at length settled that only the commissioner should accompany the count, that the rest of the gentlemen and ladies should pursue their walk, and that they should all meet again at the park-gate. The surly boatman rowed off, but he soon ceased to be surly when the count spoke of the humanity and hospitality which had been shown to some of his countrymen by Mr. Percy. Immediately the boatman's tongue was loosed.

"Why, ay, sir, if you bees curious about that there gentleman, I can tell you a deal about him. But them as comes to see the new man does not covet to hear talk of the old master; but, nevertheless, there's none like him—he gave me and wife that there white cottage yonder, half ways up the bank, where you see the smoke rising between the trees—as snug a cottage it is!—But that is no matter to you, sir. But I wish you had but seed him the night of the shipwreck, he and his son, God above bless him, and them—wherever they are, if they're above ground. I'd row out the worse night ever we had, to set my eyes on them again before I die, but for a minute. Ay, that night of the shipwreck, not a man was willing to go out with them, or could be got out the first turn, but myself."

Upon this text he spoke at large, entering into a most circumstantial and diffuse history of the shipwreck, mingling his own praises with those which he heartily bestowed upon the Percys of the right good old branch. Commissioner Falconer meantime was not in a condition to throw in any thing in favour of his new friend Sir Robert Percy; he was taking pinch after pinch of snuff, looking alternately at the water and the boat, sitting stiffly upright in anxious silence. Although in the incessant practice of suppressing his own feelings, corporeal and mental, from respect or complaisance to his superiors in rank and station, yet he presently found it beyond the utmost efforts of his courtly philosophy to endure his qualms of mind and body. Interrupting the talkative boatman, he first conjured the orator to mind what he was about; at last, Mr. Falconer complaining of growing very sick, the count gave up all thoughts of proceeding farther, and begged the boatman to put them ashore as soon as he could. They landed near the village, which it was necessary that they should pass through, before they could reach the appointed place of meeting. The poor commissioner, whose stomach was still disordered, and whose head was giddy, observed that they had yet a long walk to take, and proposed sending for one of the carriages—accordingly they waited for it at the village inn. The commissioner, after having made a multitude of apologies to the count, retired to rest himself—during his absence, the count, who, wherever he was, endeavoured to see as much as possible of the manners of the people, began talking to the landlord and landlady. Again the conversation turned upon the characters of the late and the present possessors of Percy-hall; and the good people, by all the anecdotes they told, and still more by the warm attachment they expressed for the old banished family, increased every moment his desire to be personally acquainted with those who in adversity were preferred to persons in present power and prosperity. Count Altenberg, young as he was, had seen enough of the world to feel the full value of eulogiums bestowed on those who are poor, and who have no means of serving in any way the interests of their panegyrists.

When the carriage came, and the commissioner was sufficiently refitted for conversation, the count repeatedly expressed his earnest wish to become acquainted with that Mr. Percy and his family, to whom his countrymen had been so much obliged, and of whom he said he had this morning heard so many interesting anecdotes. The commissioner had not been present when the count saw the picture of Caroline, nor indeed did he enter into Mrs. Falconer's matrimonial designs for her daughter Georgiana. The commissioner generally saw the folly, and despaired of the success, of all castle-building but his own, and his castles in the air were always on a political plan. So without difficulty he immediately replied that nothing would give him more pleasure than to introduce the count to his relations, the Percys. The moment this was mentioned, however, to Mrs. Falconer, the commissioner saw through the complacent countenance, with which she forced herself to listen to him, that he had made some terrible blunder, for which he should have to answer in private.

Accordingly the first moment they were alone, Mrs. Falconer reproached him with the rash promise he had made. "I shall have all the difficulty in the world to put this out of the count's head. I thought, Mr. Falconer, that you had agreed to let those Percys drop."

"So I would if I could, my dear; but how can I, when Lord Oldborough persists in holding them up?—You must go and see them, my dear."

"I!" cried Mrs. Falconer, with a look of horror; "I!—not I, indeed! Lord Oldborough holds up only the gentlemen of the family—his lordship has nothing to do with the ladies, I suppose. Now, you know visiting can go on vastly well, to all eternity, between the gentlemen of a family without the ladies having any sort of intimacy or acquaintance even. You and Mr. Percy—if it is necessary for appearance sake with Lord Oldborough—may continue upon the old footing; but I charge you, commissioner, do not involve me—and whatever happens, don't take Count Altenberg with you to the Hills."

"Why not, my dear?"

"My dear, I have my reasons. You were not in the gallery at Percy-hall this morning, when the count saw that painted glass window?"

The commissioner begged an explanation; but when he had heard all Mrs. Falconer's reasons, they did not seem to strike him with the force she desired and expected.

"I will do as you please, my dear," said he, "and, if I can, I will make the count forget my promised introduction to the Percys; but all the time, depend upon it, your fears and your hopes are both equally vain. You ladies are apt to take it for granted that men's heads are always running on love."

"Young men's heads sometimes are," said Mrs. Falconer.

"Very seldom in these days," said the commissioner. "And love altogether, as one should think you might know by this time, Mrs. Falconer—a sensible woman of the world, as you are; but no woman, even the most sensible, can ever believe it—love altogether has surprisingly little to do in the real management and business of the world."

"Surprisingly little," replied Mrs. Falconer, placidly. "But seriously, my dear, here is an opportunity of making an excellent match for Georgiana, if you will be so obliging as not to counteract me."

"I am the last man in the world to counteract you, my dear; but it will never do," said Mr. Falconer; "and you will only make Georgiana ridiculous, as she has been several times already, from the failure of these love-matches. I tell you, Mrs. Falconer, Count Altenberg is no more thinking of love than I am—nor is he a man in the least likely to fall in love."

"He is more than half in love with my Georgiana already," said the mother, "if I have any eyes."

"You have eyes, and very fine eyes, my dear, as every body knows, and no one better than myself—they have but one defect."

"Defect!"

"They sometimes see more than exists."

"You would not be so incredulous, Mr. Falconer, if you had seen the rapture with which the count listens to Georgiana when she plays on the harp. He is prodigiously fond of music."

"And of painting too," said the commissioner; "for, by your account of the matter, he seemed to have been more than half in love also with a picture this morning."

"A picture is no very dangerous rival, except in a modern novel," replied Mrs. Falconer. "But beware, commissioner—and remember, I understand these things—I warn you in time—beware of the original of that picture, and never again talk to me of going to see those Percys; for though the girl may be only an unfashioned country beauty, and Georgiana has so many polished advantages, yet there is no knowing what whim a young man might take into his head."

The commissioner, though he remained completely of his own opinion, that Mrs. Falconer's scheme for Georgiana would never do, disputed the point no farther, but left the room, promising all she required, for promises cost him nothing. To do him justice, he recollected and endeavoured to the best of his power to keep his word; for the next morning he took his time so well to propose a ride to the Hills, just at the moment when Lord Oldborough and the count were deep in a conversation on the state of continental politics, that his lordship would not part with him. The commissioner paid his visit alone, and Mrs. Falconer gave him credit for his address; but scarcely had she congratulated herself, when she was thrown again into terror—the commissioner had suggested to Lord Oldborough the propriety and policy of giving, whilst he was in the country, a popularity ball! His lordship assented, and Mrs. Falconer, as usual, was to take the trouble off his hands, and to give an entertainment, to his lordship's friends. Lord Oldborough had not yet recovered from the gout, and he was glad to accept of her offer: his lordship not being able to appear, or to do the honours of the fête, was a sufficient apology for his not giving it at Clermont-park.

The obsequious commissioner begged to have a list of any friends whom Lord Oldborough particularly wished to have invited; but his lordship, with a look of absence, replied, that he left all that entirely to Mrs. Falconer; however, the very evening of the day on which the commissioner paid his visit alone at the Hills, Lord Oldborough put into his hands a list of the friends whom he wished should be invited to the ball, and at the head of his list were the Percys.

"The Percys! the very people I first thought of!" said Mr. Falconer, commanding his countenance carefully: "but I fear we cannot hope to have them, they are at such a distance, and they have no carriage."

"Any of my carriages, all of them, shall be at their command," said Lord Oldborough.

The commissioner reported this to Mrs. Falconer, observing that he had gone to the very brink of offending Lord Oldborough to oblige her, as he knew by his lordship's look and tone of voice; and that nothing now could be done, but to visit the Percys, and as soon as possible, and to send them a card of invitation for the ball.

"And, my dear, whatever you do, I am sure will be done with a good grace," added the commissioner, observing that his lady looked excessively discomfited.

"Very well, commissioner; you will have your daughter upon your hands, that's all."

"I should be as sorry for that, my love, as you could be; but what can be done? we must not lose the substance in running after the shadow. Lord Oldborough might turn short round upon us."

"Not the least likely upon such a trifling occasion as this, where no politics are in question. What can Mrs. or Miss Percy's being or not being at this ball signify to Lord Oldborough?—a man who never in his life thought of balls or cared any thing about women, and these are women whom he has never seen. What interest can it possibly be of Lord Oldborough's?"

"I cannot tell you, my dear—I don't see any immediate interest. But there's an old private friendship in the case. Some way or other, I declare I cannot tell you how, that old cousin Percy of mine has contrived to get nearer to Lord Oldborough than any one living ever could do—nearer to his heart."

"Heart!—Private friendship!" repeated Mrs. Falconer, with a tone of ineffable contempt. "Well, I only wish you had said nothing about the matter to Lord Oldborough; I could have managed it myself. Was there ever such want of address! When you saw the Percys at the head of the list, was that a time to say any thing about your fears of their not coming? Do you think Lord Oldborough could not translate fears into hopes? Then to mention their having no carriages!—when, if you had kept your own counsel, that would have been our sufficient excuse at last. They must have refused: nothing need have been said about it till the night of the ball; and I would lay my life, Lord Oldborough would never, in the mean time, have thought of it, or of them. But so silly! to object in that way, when you know that the slightest contradiction wakens Lord Oldborough's will, and then indeed you might as well talk to his own Jupiter Tonans. If his lordship had set a beggar-woman's name at the head of his list, and you had objected that she had no carriage, he would directly have answered 'She shall have mine.' Bless me! It's wonderful that people can pique themselves on address, and have so little knowledge of character."

"My dear," said the commissioner, "if you reproach me from this time till to-morrow, the end of the matter will be, that you must go and see the Percys. I say, Mrs. Falconer," added he, assuming a peremptory tone, for which he had acquired a taste from Lord Oldborough, but had seldom courage or opportunity to indulge in it, "I say, Mrs. Falconer, the thing must be done." He rang the bell in a gloriously authoritative manner, and ordered the carriage.

A visit paid thus upon compulsion was not likely to be very agreeable; but the complaints against the roads, the dreadful distance, and the horrid necessity of being civil, need not be recorded. Miss Falconers exclaimed when they at last came to the Hills, "La! I did not think it was so tolerable a place!" Miss Georgiana hoped that they should, at least, see Miss Caroline—she owned she was curious to see that beautiful original, of whom the painter at Percy Hall, and her brother Buckhurst, had said so much.

Mrs. Percy and Rosamond only were at home. Caroline had taken a walk with her father to a considerable distance.

Mrs. Falconer, who had, by this time, completely recovered her self-command, presented herself with such smiling grace, and expressed, in such a tone of cordiality, her earnest desire, now that she had been so happy as to get into the country, to enjoy the society of her friends and relations, that Rosamond was quite charmed into a belief of at least half of what she said. Rosamond was willing to attribute all that had appeared, particularly of late, in contradiction of this lady's present professions, to some political motives of Commissioner Falconer, whom she disliked for his conduct to Buckhurst, and whom she was completely willing to give up as a worldly-minded courtier. But whilst the manners of the mother operated thus with Rosamond in favour of her moral character, even Rosamond's easy faith and sanguine benevolence could not see or hear any thing from the daughters that confirmed Mrs. Falconer's flattering speeches; they sat in languid silence, looking upon the animate and inanimate objects in the room with the same air of supercilious listlessness. They could not speak so as to be heard, they could not really understand any thing that Rosamond said to them; they seemed as if their bodies had been brought into the room by mistake, and their souls left behind them: not that they were in the least timid or abashed; no, they seemed fully satisfied with their own inanity, and proud to show that they had absolutely no ideas in common with those into whose company they had been thus unfortunately compelled. Once or twice they turned their heads with some signs of vivacity, when the door opened, and when they expected to see Miss Caroline Percy enter: but though the visit was protracted, in hopes of her return, yet at last they were obliged to depart without having their curiosity satisfied.

Mrs. Falconer's fears of rivalship for her Georgiana were not diminished by this visit. By those of the family whom she saw this day, she judged of Caroline, whom she had not seen; and she had tact sufficient to apprehend, that the conversation and manners of Mrs. Percy and of Rosamond were such as might, perhaps, please a well-bred and well-informed foreigner better, even, than the fashionable tone and air of the day, of which he had not been long enough in England to appreciate the conventional value. Still Mrs. Falconer had a lingering hope that some difficulties about dress, or some happy cold, might prevent these dangerous Percys from accepting the invitation to the ball. When their answers to her card came, she gave one hasty glance at it.

"Will do themselves the honour."

"My dear, you are alarming yourself unnecessarily," cried the commissioner, who pitied the distress visible, at least to his eyes, in her countenance; or who feared, perhaps, a renewal of reproaches for his own want of address, "quite unnecessarily, believe me. I have had a great deal of conversation with Count Altenberg since I spoke of him to you last, and I am confirmed in my opinion that he merely feels the curiosity natural to an enlightened traveller to become acquainted with Mr. Percy, a man who has been described to him as a person of abilities. And he wants to thank him in the name of his countrymen, who were assisted, you know I told you, by the Percys, at the time of the shipwreck. You will see, my dear, that the ladies of the family will be nothing to him."

Mrs. Falconer sighed, and bit her lips.

"In half an hour's conversation, I would engage to find out the ruling passion of any man, young or old. Now, remember I tell you, Mrs. Falconer, Count Altenberg's ruling passion is ambition."

"Ruling passion!" repeated Mrs. Falconer; "one of your book-words, and book-notions, that are always misleading you in practice. Ruling passion!—Metaphysical nonsense! As if men were such consistent creatures as to be ruled regularly by one passion—when often ten different passions pull a man, even before your face, ten different ways, and one cannot tell one hour what will be the ruling passion of the next. Tell me the reigning fashion, and I will tell you the ruling passion!—Luckily," continued Mrs. Falconer, after a pause of deep consideration, "Georgiana is very fashionable—one of the most fashionable young women in England, as the count might have seen when he was in London. But then, on the other hand, whether he is judge enough of English manners—Georgiana must be well dressed—and I know the Count's taste in dress; I have made myself mistress of that—commissioner, I must trouble you for some money."

"Mrs. Falconer, I have no money; and if I had," said the commissioner, who always lost his temper when that subject was touched upon, "if I had, I would not give it to you to throw away upon such a losing game—a nonsensical speculation! Georgiana has not the least chance, nor has any other English woman, were she as handsome as Venus and dressed in bank notes—why, Mrs. Falconer, since you put me in a passion, I must tell you a secret."

But checking himself, Mr. Falconer stood for a moment silent, and went on with "Count Altenberg has made up his quarrel with the hereditary prince, and I have it from undoubted authority, that he is to be the prince's prime minister when he comes to the throne; and the present prince, you know, as Cunningham says, is so infirm and asthmatic, that he may be carried off at any moment."

"Very well—very likely—I am glad of it," said Mrs. Falconer: "but where's the secret?"

"I've thought better of that, and I cannot tell it to you. But this much I tell you positively, Mrs. Falconer, that you will lose your labour, if you speculate upon the Count for Georgiana."

"Is he married? Answer me that question, and I will ask no more—and that I have a right to ask."

"No—not married; but I can tell no more. Only let me beg that you will just put all love notions out of Georgiana's head and your own, or you'll make the girl ridiculous, and expose yourself, my dear. But, on the other hand, let there be no deficiency of attention to the count, for all our civilities to him will pay a hundred fold, and, perhaps, sooner than you expect—for he may be prime minister and prime favourite at Cunningham's court in a month, and of course will have it in his power to forward Cunningham's interests. That is what I look to, Mrs. Falconer; for I am long-sighted in my views, as you will find."

"Well, time will show. I am glad you tell me he positively is not married," concluded Mrs. Falconer: "as to the rest, we shall see."

CHAPTER XXVI

The evening appointed for Mrs. Falconer's ball at length arrived; and all the neighbouring gentry assembled at Falconer-court. They were received by Mrs. Falconer in a splendid saloon, newly furnished for this occasion, which displayed in its decorations the utmost perfection of modern taste and magnificence.

Mrs. Falconer was fitted, both by art and nature, to adorn a ball-room, and conduct a ball. With that ease of manner which a perfect knowledge of the world and long practice alone can give, she floated round the circle, conscious that she was in her element. Her eye, with one glance, seemed to pervade the whole assembly; her ear divided itself amongst a multitude of voices; and her attention diffused itself over all with equal grace. Yet that attention, universal as it seemed, was nicely discriminative. Mistress of the art of pleasing, and perfectly acquainted with all the shades of politeness, she knew how to dispose them so as to conceal their boundaries, and even their gradation, from all but the most skilful observers. They might, indeed, have formed, from Mrs. Falconer's reception of each of her guests, an exact estimate of their rank, fashion, and consequence in the world; for by these standards she regulated her opinion, and measured her regard. Every one present knew this to be her theory, and observed it to be her practice towards others; but each flattered themselves by turns that they discovered in her manner a personal exception in their own favour. In the turn of her countenance, the tone of her voice, her smile or her anxiety, in her distant respect or her affectionate familiarity, some distinction was discerned peculiar to each individual.

The Miss Falconers, stationary at one end of the room, seemed to have adopted manners diametrically opposite to those of their mother: attraction being the principle of the mother, repulsion of the daughters. Encircled amongst a party of young female friends, Miss Falconers, with high-bred airs, confined to their own coterie their exclusive attention.

They left to their mother the responsibility and all the labour of doing the honours of her own house, whilst they enjoyed the glory of being remarked and wondered at by half the company; a circumstance which, far from embarrassing, seemed obviously to increase their gaiety.

The ball could not begin till the band of a regiment, quartered in the neighbourhood, arrived. Whilst they were waiting for the music, the Miss Falconers and their party stationed themselves directly opposite to the entrance of the saloon, so as to have a full view of the antechamber through which the company were to pass—no one passed uncensured by this confederacy. The first coup-d'oeil decided the fate of all who appeared, and each of the fair judges vied with the others in the severity of the sentence pronounced on the unfortunate persons who thus came before their merciless tribunal.

"But I am astonished the Percys do not make their appearance," cried Miss Georgiana Falconer.

"Has Sir Robert Percy any one with him?" asked one of the young ladies.

"I am not speaking of Sir Robert Percy," replied Miss Georgiana, "but of the other branch, the fallen branch of the Percys—our relations too—but we know nothing of them—only mamma was obliged to ask them for to-night—And, Bell, only conceive how horribly provoking! because they come, we sha'n't have Sir Robert Percy—just sent to excuse himself."

"Abominable! Now, really!—And for people quite out of the world, that nobody ever heard of, except Lord Oldborough, who, ages ago, had some political connexion, I think they say, with the father," said Miss Arabella.

"No, they met abroad, or something of that sort," replied Miss Georgiana.

"Was that it? Very likely—I know nothing about them: I only wish they had stayed at home, where they are so fond of staying, I hear. You know, Georgiana, Buckhurst told us, that when they had something to live upon they never lived like other people, but always were buried alive in the country; and Lady Jane Granville, with her own lips, told me, that, even since they lost their fortune, she had asked one of these girls to town with her and to Tunbridge—Now only conceive how kind! and what an advantage that would have been—And, can you believe it? Mr. Percy was so unaccountable, and they all so odd, that they refused—Lady Jane, of course, will never ask them again. But now, must not they be the silliest creatures in the universe?"

"Silly! Oh! dear, no: there you are wrong, Bell; for you know they are all so wise, and so learned, so blue, such a deep blue, and all that sort of thing, that, for my part, I shall never dare to open my lips before them."

"Fortunately," said one of the young ladies, "you have not much to fear from their learning at a ball; and as dancers I don't apprehend you have much to dread from any of them, even from the beauty."

"Why, scarcely," said Miss Georgiana; "I own I shall be curious to see how they will get on—'comment ces savantes se tireront d'affaire.' I wonder they are not here. Keep your eye on the door, dear Lady Frances—I would not miss their entrée for millions."

In vain eyes and glasses were fixed in expectation of the arrival of these devoted objects of ridicule—another, and another, and another came, but not the Percys.

The band was now ready, and began to play—Count Altenberg entered the room. Quick as grace can venture to move, Mrs. Falconer glided to receive him. Miss Georgiana Falconer, at the same moment, composed her features into their most becoming position, and gave herself a fine air of the head. The Count bowed to her—she fanned herself, and her eye involuntarily glanced, first at a brilliant star he wore, and then at her mother, whilst, with no small degree of anxiety, she prepared to play off, on this decisive evening, all her artillery, to complete her conquest—to complete her victory, for she flattered herself that only the finishing blow was wanting. In this belief her female companions contributed to confirm her, though probably they were all the time laughing at her vanity.

Mrs. Falconer requested Count Altenberg to open the ball with Lady Frances Arlington. After having obeyed her orders, he next led out Miss Georgiana Falconer, evidently to her satisfaction; the more so, as she was conscious of being, at that moment, the envy of at least half the company.

Count Altenberg, quite unconscious of being himself the object of any attention, seemed to think only of showing his partner to advantage; if he danced well, it appeared to be only because he habitually moved with ease and dignity, and that whatever he did he looked like a gentleman. His fair partner danced admirably, and now surpassed herself.

It was repeated to Mrs. Falconer, that Colonel Bremen, the Count's friend, had told some one that the Count had declared he had never seen any thing equal to Miss Georgiana Falconer, except at the opera at Paris. At this triumphant moment Miss Georgiana could have seen, with security and complacency, the arrival of Miss Caroline Percy. The more prudent mother, however, was well satisfied with her absence. Every thing conspired to Mrs. Falconer's satisfaction. The ball was far advanced, and no Percys appeared. Mrs. Falconer wondered, and deplored, and at length it came near the hour when supper was ordered—the commissioner inquired whether Mrs. Falconer was certain that she had named the right day on the card?

"Oh! certain—But it is now so late, I am clear they will not be here to-night."

"Very extraordinary, to keep Lord Oldborough's carriage and servants!" said the commissioner: "they went in time, I am sure, for I saw them set out."

"All I know is, that we have done every thing that is proper," said Mrs. Falconer, "and Lord Oldborough cannot blame us—as to the Count, he seems quite content."

Mrs. Falconer's accent seemed to imply something more than content; but this was not a proper time or place to contest the point. The husband passed on, saying to himself "Absurd!" The wife went on, saying "Obstinate!"

Count Altenberg had led his partner to a seat, and as soon as he quitted her, the young ladies of her party all flattered her, in congratulatory whispers: one observed that there was certainly something very particular in Count Altenberg's manner, when he first spoke to Miss Georgiana Falconer; another remarked that he always spoke to Miss Georgiana Falconer with emotion and embarrassment; a third declared that her eye was fixed upon the Count, and she saw him several times change colour—all, in short, agreed that the Count's heart was Miss Georgiana Falconer's devoted prize. She the while, with well-affected incredulity and secret complacency, half repressed and half encouraged these remarks by frequent exclamations of "La! how can you think so!—Why will you say such things!—Dear! how can you be so tormenting—so silly, now, to have such fancies!—But did he really change colour?"—In love with her! She wondered how such an idea could ever come into their heads—she should, for her part, never have dreamed of such a thing—indeed, she was positive they were mistaken. Count Altenberg in love with her!—Oh, no, there could be nothing in it.

Whilst she spoke, her eyes followed the Count, who, quite unconscious of his danger, undisturbed by any idea of Miss Georgiana Falconer and love, two ideas which probably never had entered his mind together, was carelessly walking down the room, his thoughts apparently occupied with the passing scene. He had so much the habit of observing men and manners, without appearing to observe them, that, under an air of gaiety, he carried his understanding, as it were, incognito. His observation glanced on all the company as he passed. Miss Georgiana Falconer lost sight of him as he reached the end of the saloon; he disappeared in the antechamber.

Soon afterwards a report reached her that the Percy family were arrived; that Count Altenberg had been particularly struck by the sight of one of the Miss Percys, and had been overheard to whisper to his friend Colonel Bremen, "Very like the picture! but still more mind in the countenance!"

At hearing this, Miss Georgiana Falconer grew first red and then turned pale; Mrs. Falconer, though scarcely less confounded, never changed a muscle of her face, but leaving every body to choose their various comments upon the Count's words, and simply saying, "Are the Percys come at last?" she won her easy way through the crowd, whispering to young Petcalf as she passed, "Now is your time, Petcalf, my good creature—Georgiana is disengaged."

Before Mrs. Falconer got to the antechamber, another report met her, "that the Percys had been overturned, and had been terribly hurt."

"Overturned!—terribly hurt!—Good Heavens!" cried Mrs. Falconer, as she entered the antechamber. But the next person told her they were not in the least hurt—still pressing forward, she exclaimed, "Mrs. Percy! Where is Mrs. Percy? My dear madam! what has happened? Come the wrong road, did you?—broken bridge—And were you really overturned?"

"No, no, only obliged to get out and walk a little way."

"Oh! I am sorry—But I am so glad to see you all safe!—When it grew late, I grew so uneasy!" Then turning towards Caroline, "Miss Caroline Percy, I am sure, though I had never, till now, the pleasure of seeing her."

An introduction of Caroline by Mrs. Percy, in due form, took place. Mrs. Falconer next recognized Mr. Percy, declared he did not look a day older than when she had seen him fifteen years before—then recurring to the ladies, "But, my dear Mrs. Percy, are you sure that your shoes are not wet through?—Oh! my dear madam, Miss Percy's are terribly wet! and Miss Caroline's!—Positively, the young ladies must go to my dressing-room—the shoes must be dried." Mrs. Falconer said that perhaps her daughters could accommodate the Miss Percys with others.

It was in vain that Rosamond protested her shoes were not wet, and that her sister's were perfectly dry; a few specks on their white justified Mrs. Falconer's apprehensions.

"Where is my Arabella? If there was any body I could venture to trouble—"

Count Altenberg instantly offered his services. "Impossible to trouble you, Count! But since you are so very good, perhaps you could find one of my daughters for me—Miss Falconer—if you are so kind, sir— Georgiana I am afraid is dancing."

Miss Falconer was found, and despatched with the Miss Percys, in spite of all they could say to the contrary, to Mrs. Falconer's dressing-room. Rosamond was permitted, without much difficulty, to do as she pleased; but Mrs. Falconer's infinite fears lest Caroline should catch her death of cold could not be appeased, till she had submitted to change her shoes.

"Caroline!" said Rosamond, in a low voice, "Caroline! do not put on those shoes—they are too large— you will never be able to dance in them."

"I know that—but I am content. It is better to yield than to debate the point any longer," said Caroline.

When they returned to the ball-room, Count Altenberg was in earnest conversation with Mr. Percy; but Mrs. Falconer observed that the Count saw Miss Caroline Percy the moment she re-appeared.

"Now is not it extraordinary," thought she, "when Georgiana dances so well! is infinitely more fashionable, and so charmingly dressed!—What can strike him so much in this girl's appearance?"

It was not her appearance that struck him. He was too well accustomed to see beauty and fashion in public places to be caught at first sight by a handsome face, or by a young lady's exhibition of her personal graces at a ball; but a favourable impression had been made on his mind by what he had previously heard of Miss Caroline Percy's conduct and character: her appearance confirmed this impression precisely, because she had not the practised air of a professed beauty, because she did not seem in the least to be thinking of herself, or to expect admiration. This was really uncommon, and, therefore, it fixed the attention of a man like Count Altenberg. He asked Caroline to dance; she declined dancing. Mr. Temple engaged Rosamond, and the moment he led her away, the Count availed himself of her place, and a conversation commenced, which soon made Mrs. Falconer regret that Caroline had declined dancing. Though the Count was a stranger to the Percy family, yet there were many subjects of common interest of which he knew how to avail himself. He began by speaking of Mr. Alfred Percy, of the pleasure he had had in becoming acquainted with him, of the circumstance which led to this acquaintance: then he passed, to Lord Oldborough—to M. de Tourville—to the shipwreck. He paused at Percy-hall, for he felt for those to whom he was speaking. They understood him, but they did not avoid the subject; he then indulged himself in the pleasure of repeating some of the expressions of attachment to their old landlord, and of honest affection and gratitude, which he had heard from the peasants in the village.

Mrs. Falconer moved away the moment she foresaw this part of the conversation, but she was only so far removed as to prevent the necessity of her taking any part in it, or of appearing to hear what it might be awkward for her to hear, considering her intimacy with Sir Robert Percy. She began talking to an old lady about her late illness, of which she longed to hear from her own lips all the particulars; and whilst the old lady told her case, Mrs. Falconer, with eyes fixed upon her, and making, at proper intervals, all the appropriate changes of countenance requisite to express tender sympathy, alarm, horror, astonishment, and joyful congratulation, contrived, at the same time, through the whole progress of fever, and the administration of half the medicines in the London Pharmacopoeia, to hear every thing that was said by Count Altenberg, and not to lose a word that was uttered by Caroline. Mrs. Falconer was particularly anxious to know what would be said about the picture in the gallery at Percy-hall, with which the Count had been so much charmed. When he got into the gallery, Mrs. Falconer listened with breathless eagerness, yet still smiling on the old lady's never-ending history of her convalescence, and of a shawl undoubtedly Turkish, with the true, inestimable, inimitable, little border.

Not a word was said of the picture—but a pause implied more to alarm Mrs. Falconer than could have been expressed by the most flattering compliment.

Mrs. Falconer wondered why supper was so late. She sent to order that it might be served as soon as possible; but her man, or her gentleman cook, was not a person to be hurried. Three successive messengers were sent in vain. He knew his importance, and preserved his dignity. The caramel was not ready, and nothing could make him dispense with its proper appearance.

How much depended on this caramel! How much, of which the cook never dreamed! How much Mrs. Falconer suffered during this half hour, and suffered with a smiling countenance! How much, with a scowling brow, Miss Georgiana Falconer made poor Petcalf endure!

Every thing conspired to discomfit Mrs. Falconer. She saw the manner in which all the principal gentry in the country, one after another, expressed satisfaction at meeting the Percy family. She saw the regard and respect with which they were addressed, notwithstanding their loss of fortune and station. It was quite astonishing to Mrs. Falconer. Every body in the rooms, except her own set of town friends, seemed so strangely interested about this family. "How provoking that I was obliged to ask them here!—And Count Altenberg sees and hears all this!"

Yes—all this confirmed, by the testimony of their equals in rank, the favourable ideas he had first received of the Percys from their inferiors and dependants. Every person who spoke to or of Caroline— and he heard many speak of her who had known her from childhood—showed affection in their countenance and manner.

At length, supper was announced, and Mrs. Falconer requested Count Altenberg would take Lady Frances Arlington into the supper-room. Miss Georgiana Falconer was anxious to sit as near as possible to her dear Lady Frances, and this was happily accomplished.

The Count was more than usually agreeable; but whether this arose from his desire to please the ladies who sat beside him, or those who sat opposite to him, those to whom he was in politeness bound to address his conversation, or those whose attention he might hope it would attract, were questions of difficult solution.

As they were returning into the ball-room, Rosamond watched her opportunity, made her way along a passage which led to Mrs. Falconer's dressing-room, seized her sister's shoes, returned with the prize before Caroline reached the antechamber, and, unseen by all, made her put them on—"Now promise me not to refuse to dance, if you are asked again."

Count Altenberg engaged Miss Georgiana Falconer the first two dances—when these were finished, he asked Caroline to dance, and Mrs. Falconer, who dreaded the renewal of conversation between them, and who knew nothing of Rosamond's counter-manoeuvre about the shoes, was surprised and rejoiced when she saw Caroline comply, and suffer herself to be led out by Count Altenberg. But Miss Georgiana, who had observed that Rosamond danced well, had fears—the mother's hopes were disappointed, the daughter's fears were justified. Caroline showed all the capability of dancing without being a dancer, and it certainly did not escape the Count's observation that she possessed what is most desirable in female accomplishments, the power to excel without the wish to display. Immediately after she had finished these dances, the favour of her hand was solicited by a certain Colonel Spandrill. Colonel Spandrill, celebrated for his fashionable address and personal accomplishments, had been the hoped-for partner of many rival ladies, and his choice excited no small degree of emotion. However, it was settled that he only danced with Miss Percy because Mrs. Falconer had made it her particular request. One of these ladies declared she had overheard that request; Colonel Spandrill then was safe from all blame, but the full fire of their resentment was directed against poor Caroline. Every feature of her face was criticised, and even the minutiæ of her dress. They all allowed that she was handsome, but each found some different fault with her style of beauty. It was curious to observe how this secondary class of young ladies, who had without discomfiture or emotion seen Caroline the object of Count Altenberg's attention, were struck with indignation the moment they suspected her of pleasing Colonel Spandrill. Envy seldom takes two steps at once: it is always excited by the fear of losing the proximate object of ambition; it never exists without some mixture of hope as well as of fear. These ladies having no hope of captivating Count Altenberg, Caroline did not then appear to be their rival; but now that they dreaded her competition with a man whom they had hopes of winning, they pulled her to pieces without mercy.

The Miss Falconers and their quadrille-set were resting themselves, whilst this country dance was going on. Miss Georgiana was all the time endeavouring to engage Count Altenberg in conversation. By all the modern arts of coquetry, so insipid to a man of the world, so contemptible to a man of sense, she tried to recall the attention of the Count. Politeness obliged him to seem to listen, and he endeavoured to keep up that kind of conversation which is suited to a ball-room; but he relapsed continually into reverie, till at last, provoked by his absence of mind, Miss Georgiana, unable to conceal her vexation, unjustly threw the blame upon her health. She complained of the headache, of heat, of cold, of country dances—such barbarous things!—How could any one bear any thing but quadrilles? Then the music—the band was horrid!—they played vastly too fast—shocking! there was no such thing as keeping time—did not Count Altenberg think so?

Count Altenberg was at that moment beating time with his foot, in exact cadence to Miss Caroline Percy's dancing: Miss Falconer saw this, but not till she had uttered her question, not till it had been observed by all her companions. Lady Frances Arlington half smiled, and half a smile instantly appeared along a whole line of young ladies. Miss Georgiana suddenly became sensible that she was exposed to the ridicule or sarcastic pity of those who but an hour before had flattered her in the grossest manner: she had expected to produce a great effect at this ball—she saw another preferred. Her spirits sunk, and even the powers of affectation failed. The struggle between the fine lady and the woman ceased. Passion always conquers art at a coup de main. When any strong emotion of the soul is excited, the natural character, temper, and manners seldom fail to break through all that is factitious—those who had seen Miss Georgiana Falconer only through the veil of affectation were absolutely astonished at the change that appeared when it was thrown aside. By the Count the metamorphosis was unnoticed, for he was intent on another object; but by many of the spectators it was beheld with open surprise, or secret contempt. She exhibited at this moment the picture of a disappointed coquette—the spasm of jealousy had seized her heart; and, unable to conceal or endure the pain in this convulsion of mind, she forgot all grace and decorum. Her mother from afar saw the danger at this crisis, and came to her relief. The danger in Mrs. Falconer's opinion was, that the young lady's want of temper should be seen by Count Altenberg; she therefore carried him off to a distant part of the room, to show him, as she said, "a bassoon player, who was the exact image of Hogarth's enraged musician."

In the mean time Colonel Spandrill and Caroline had finished their dance: and the colonel, who made it a principle to engross the attention of the prettiest woman in the room, was now, after his manner, paying his adorations to his fair partner. Promising himself that he should be able to recede or advance as he thought proper, he used a certain happy ambiguity of phrase, which, according to the manner in which it is understood, or rather according to the tone and look with which it is accompanied, says every thing—or nothing. With prudent caution, he began with darts, flames, wounds, and anguish; words which every military man holds himself privileged to use towards every fine woman he meets. Darts, flames, wounds, and anguish, were of no avail. The colonel went on, as far as bright eyes—bewitching smiles—and heavenly grace. Still without effect. With astonishment he perceived that the girl, who looked as if she had never heard that she was handsome, received the full fire of his flattery with the composure of a veteran inured to public admiration.

Mrs. Falconer was almost as much surprised and disappointed by this as the colonel could be. She had purposely introduced the gallant Colonel Spandrill to the Miss Percys, in hopes that Caroline's head might be affected by flattery; and that she might not then retain all that dignity of manner which, as Mrs. Falconer had sense enough to see, was her distinguishing charm in the eyes of the Count. Frustrated, and dreading every instant that with all her address she should not be able to manage her Georgiana's temper, Mrs. Falconer became excessively impatient for the departure of the Percy family.

"Mr. Falconer!" cried she; "Commissioner! Mrs. Percy ordered her carriage a considerable time ago. They have a great way to return, and a dreadful road—I am uneasy about them—do pray be so good to see what detains her carriage."

The commissioner went out of the room, and a few minutes afterwards returned, and taking Mrs. Falconer aside, said, "I have something to tell you, my dear, that will surprise you—indeed I can scarcely believe it. Long as I have known Lord Oldborough, I never knew him do, or think of doing such a thing— and he ill—at least ill enough with the gout, for an excuse—an excuse he thought sufficient for the whole county—and there are people of so much more consequence—I protest I cannot understand it."

"Understand what, commissioner?—Will you tell me what has happened, and you may be as much surprised as you please afterwards? Lord Oldborough has the gout," added she, in an accent which expressed "Well, all the world knows that."

"Lord Oldborough's own confidential man Rodney, you know—"

"Well, well, Rodney I do know—what of him?"

"He is here—I have seen him this instant—from his lord, with a message to Mr. Percy, to let him know that there are apartments prepared for him and all his family at Clermont-park; and that he insists upon their not returning this night to the Hills, lest the ladies should be tired."

"Lord Oldborough!" repeated Mrs. Falconer; "Lord Oldborough!—the ladies!—Clermont-park! where none but persons of the first distinction are invited!"

"Ay, now you are surprised," cried the commissioner.

"Surprised! beyond all power of expression," said Mrs. Falconer.

"Beyond all power of dissimulation," she should have said.

"Count Altenberg, too, going to hand them to their carriage—going to Clermont-park with them!—I wish to Heaven," said Mrs. Falconer to herself, "I had never given this unfortunate ball!"

Mrs. Falconer was mistaken in this idea. It was not the circumstance of meeting Caroline at a ball that made this impression on Count Altenberg; wherever he had seen her, if he had had opportunity of conversing, and of observing the dignity and simplicity of her manner, the same effect would have been produced—but in fact Mrs. Falconer's fears, and her daughter's jealousy, had much magnified the truth. Count Altenberg had not, as they fancied, fallen desperately in love at first sight with Caroline—he had only been pleased and interested sufficiently to make him desirous to see more of her. Caroline, though so much the object of jealousy, had not the slightest idea that she had made a conquest—she simply thought the count's conversation agreeable, and she was glad that she should see him again at breakfast the next morning.

CHAPTER XXVII

Mr. and Mrs. Percy accepted of Lord Oldborough's invitation. They found apartments prepared for them at Clermont-park, and servants ready to attend, with the officious promptitude with which a great man's domestics usually wait upon those who are supposed to stand high in their master's favour.

During his illness Lord Oldborough had always breakfasted in his own room; but his lordship appeared at the breakfast-table the morning after the ball, ready to receive his guests. Nothing could be more gracious, more polite, more kind, than his reception of Mr. Percy and his family. From the moment he was introduced to the wife and daughters of his friend, he seemed to throw aside the reserve and coldness of his manner—to forget at once the statesman and the minister, the affairs of Europe and the intrigues of the cabinet—to live entirely for the present moment and the present company. The company consisted of the Percy family, Count Altenberg, and Mr. Temple. It was a common practice with Lord Oldborough to set conversation a-going, then to become silent, and to retire to his own thoughts—he would just throw the ball, and leave others to run for it. But now he condescended at least to join in the pursuit, though apparently without ambition to obtain distinction in the race. After breakfast he showed the ladies into his library; and, as he was himself disabled, requested Mr. Temple to take down such books or prints as he thought most worthy of their attention. Literature had been neglected, perhaps undervalued, by Lord Oldborough, since he had devoted himself to politics; but he could at will recall the classical stores of his youth; and on modern books his quick eye and ear, joined to his strong and rapid judgment, enabled him to decide better than many who make it the only business of their lives to read. Even Mr. Percy, who knew him best, was surprised; and still more surprised was Mr. Temple, who had seen him in varieties of company, some of the highest rank and fashion both in wit and literature, where his lordship had appeared either absent of mind or a silent listener; but he now exerted those powers of conversation which he usually suffered to lie dormant. Instead of waiting in proud expectation that those who were in his company should prove their claims to his attention, he now produced his own intellectual treasures; evidently not for the vanity of display, but to encourage his guests to produce those talents which he seemed to take it for granted that they possessed. It appeared to be his sole object, his pride and pleasure, to pay attention to the wife and daughters of his friend; and to show them and him to advantage to an illustrious foreigner.

"Yes," said he, apart to Count Altenberg, "I am proud to show you a specimen of a cultivated independent country gentleman and his family."

With his usual penetration, Lord Oldborough soon discerned the characteristics of each of the ladies of this family—the good sense and good breeding of Mrs. Percy, the wit and generous simplicity of Rosamond, the magnanimity and the superior understanding of Caroline. As instances of these different qualities appeared, his quick and brightening eye marked his approbation, sometimes by a glance at Count Altenberg, by a nod to Mr. Temple, or by a congratulatory smile as he turned to Mr. Percy.

"I now comprehend," said his lordship, "why Mr. Percy could never be induced to take a part in public business. Ladies, you have done a great injury to your country—you have made this gentleman too happy in domestic life."

Lord Oldborough spoke this in a tone of raillery, and with a smile—but the smile was succeeded by a deep sigh, and a dark gloom of countenance. At this moment one of his secretaries, Mr. Shaw, came in with papers to be signed. The minister reappeared. Lord Oldborough's mind turned instantly to business; he withdrew to a table apart, sat down, and began to look over the first paper that was laid before him. Mr. Percy rang the bell, and something was said about not intruding on his lordship's time— he looked up: "Mr. Temple, you are free. Mr. Shaw shall finish whatever letters it is necessary should be written this morning. You shall have the pleasure of being with your friends. It is a pleasure you deserve, sir, and can appreciate. Mrs. Percy expressed a wish to see the grounds—you will show them to these ladies. I am a prisoner still," said his lordship, looking down at his gouty hand, "and always shall be a prisoner," added he, turning his eye upon the papers which Mr. Shaw held.

The ladies, accompanied by Mr. Temple, and by Count Altenberg, went out to walk. Mr. Percy stayed one moment to express his sense of the extraordinary politeness and kindness with which Lord Oldborough had honoured him and his family.

"You owe me no thanks, my dear sir. Kindness can be repaid only by kindness. It is a species of debt, which in the course of my life I have seldom been called upon to pay."

This was said not in a voice either of sentiment or of compliment, but rather in an austere tone, and with a stern countenance of conquered emotion. Without looking at Mr. Percy, he received and answered the farewell shake of the hand; his lips were instantly after strongly compressed; and, taking up his pen, the man was again absorbed in the minister.

Mr. Percy joined the party who were going to walk in the park. Count Altenberg had been unusually silent in Lord Oldborough's company: with the becoming deference of a young man, in the presence of one superior in age, and in high station, he had listened, eager to learn, instead of impatient to talk. Attention of course now turned upon him, as the stranger and the foreigner.

With the same perfect taste and good-breeding with which he knew how to pay honour due, he received it, and appeared as much at his ease, whether he was in the shade or the light, whether he was unnoticed or the object of general attention. He had that air of self-possession, which characterizes a person secure of his own resources, and not afraid to produce his abilities.

The conversation turned at first upon the beauties of nature—Clermont-park was one of the really magnificent places in England which an Englishman may feel proud to show to a foreigner.

Count Altenberg politely and justly observed how different the country seats of our nobility are from the ruinous and comfortless chateaux of most of the French nobility.

Clermont-park, however, was not new to the count. Commissioner Falconer had the day after his arrival shown him every thing that was to be seen: his attention, therefore, as they pursued their walk, was not so much distracted by external objects as to prevent him from wishing to converse. Finding that Mr. Percy had travelled, he spoke of Switzerland and Italy; and, without any of the jargon of a connoisseur, showed that he felt with sensibility and enthusiasm the beautiful and sublime. It soon appeared that he had seen various countries, not merely with the eye of a painter and a poet, but of a philosophical traveller, who can allow for the differences of national taste, and discern how its variations are influenced by climate, education, government, and local circumstances. In his rapid panorama of foreign countries, he showed variety of knowledge, and without illiberal prejudice against any nation, an amiable predilection for his native country. Next to his own country he preferred England, which, as he said, by the mother's side, he might call his own. She had early instilled into him an admiration for our free constitution, and a love of our domestic habits; but he had never before visited this country, and he was particularly desirous to obtain an accurate knowledge of England, and of the manners and modes of life of its inhabitants. He seemed thus eager to obtain information, not merely to gratify a cursory or selfish curiosity, but with a view to the future, and with a hope of doing permanent good. It was clear that he was not only a philosophical but a benevolent traveller, to whom nothing that concerns his fellow-creatures is foreign or indifferent. His treasuring up all he had seen abroad, that could be useful at home, reminded Caroline of Colonel Hungerford; but she observed that Count Altenberg's views were more enlarged; he was unbiassed by professional habits; his sphere of action was higher; heir to extensive property, with all the foreign rights of territorial dominion hereditarily his; and with a probability of obtaining the political power of ministerial station; plans, which in other circumstances might have been romantic, with Count Altenberg's prospects and abilities, were within the bounds of sound judgment and actual practicability. But whatever these intentions might be, they were only to be inferred from his conversation; he scarcely spoke of himself, or of his own designs; whatever he was led to say on such subjects, he seemed, immediately after he had said it, to feel as an impropriety, not justified by the slight interest which the acquaintance of a few hours could inspire.

He changed the conversation by asking some questions about a celebrated English writer. In return for the information Mr. Percy gave him, he spoke of some recent foreign publications—related several anecdotes of literary foreigners. His anecdotes were interesting, because, in each, there was something characteristic of the individual, or illustrative of some general principle of human nature. To gratify Mr. Percy, the Count spoke of some public events of which he had had means of obtaining information. He had not neglected any of the opportunities he enjoyed, and whether he talked of civil or military affairs, he showed the same efficient knowledge, and the same superior ability.

Caroline, leaning on her father's arm, listened with a countenance full of intelligence, animation, and sympathy; she looked alternately at the Count and at her father, whose satisfaction she saw and enjoyed. Feeling that he was appreciated by the father, inspired by the charms of the daughter, and excited by the idea he had formed of her character, Count Altenberg had indeed been uncommonly agreeable, entertaining, and eloquent. During this walk, though Caroline said but little, yet that little, to a man of the Count's discernment, was sufficient to show good judgment and great capacity. This increased the admiration and interest which her beauty and manners, and all he had heard of her conduct, created.

It is said to be one of the characteristics of genius, that it is able quickly to discover and elicit genius, wherever it exists. It is certain that with the celerity of intuition, of sympathy, or of practised penetration, Count Altenberg perceived Caroline's intellectual superiority. He had been, at first, curious to discover whether her mental qualifications were equal to her extraordinary personal beauty; but he had soon forgotten his intention of trying her abilities, in anxiety to convince her of his own. The whole turn and style of his conversation now proved, more than any compliment could possibly have shown, the high opinion he had of her understanding, and of the elevation of her mind. A woman may always judge of the real estimation in which she is held, by the conversation which is addressed to her.

All this time, where were Rosamond, Mrs. Percy, and Mr. Temple? Mr. Temple had taken them to see a fine view; Mr. Percy proposed to sit down and quietly wait their return; Caroline and the Count seemed to have no objection to oblige him, and they placed themselves under a spreading beech. They had not been seated many minutes, before they were interrupted by the appearance of Commissioner Falconer, who came, by a cross path, from the house.

"At last I have found you. What a prodigious walk you have taken!" cried the commissioner, wiping his forehead. "But where's Mrs. Percy and the rest of your party? I have so walked to catch you—rode over on purpose to pay my compliments to the ladies before they return home—and I come chargé d'affaires from Mrs. Falconer to Mrs. Percy. I must see Mrs. Percy—Oh! here she is, coming down the hill—ay, from the point of view—Mercy! how you have walked: I am not equal to the grand tour—it kills me. But I am so sorry I was not here time enough to do the honours of Clermont-park, as Lord Oldborough is confined. Who has Mrs. Percy for her cicerone? Ha! Mr. Temple—I thought he was always so busy—deputed by Lord Oldborough—really!—Hum—I hope Lord Oldborough did not conceive that there was any want of empressement on my part—I should have been here a full hour sooner, but that my ladies were so late at breakfast after sitting up—and I thought your ladies might have been fatigued too—but Miss Caroline Percy, I see, fresh as a rose—"

The commissioner then, as if half in jest, half in earnest, paid Caroline a profusion of compliments upon her appearance the preceding night—numbered on his fingers the conquests she had made, and the hearts she had broken. Mrs. Percy, Rosamond, and Mr. Temple came up; and as soon as they had expressed their raptures on the beauty of this view, the commissioner presented his note from Mrs. Falconer to Mrs. Percy, to which, he said, he was most anxious to be the bearer of a favourable answer, as he knew that he should otherwise be ill-received at home, and the disappointment would be great. The note contained a pressing invitation to a play, which the young people at Falconer-court had it in contemplation to represent. Whether it was to be Zara or Cato, they had not yet positively decided—for Cato they were in terrible distress for a Marcia—could Miss Caroline Percy be prevailed upon to try Marcia? She would look the part so well, and, no doubt, act it so well. Or if she preferred Zara, Miss Georgiana Falconer would, with pleasure, take the part of the confidante. Dresses in great forwardness, Turkish or Roman, convertible, in a few hours' notice—should wait Miss Percy's decision.

"Well, my dear Caroline, what say you?" cried Mrs. Percy.

Caroline was going to answer.

"No, no, don't answer yet," interrupted the commissioner: "let me add, what I find Mrs. Falconer took it for granted I would say, that there can be no possible difficulty or inconvenience about the goings and comings, and horses and carriages, and beds, and all that sort of thing—for our horses and carriages can have nothing to do whilst the ladies are rehearsing—shall attend you any day—any hour—and beds we can contrive: so, I beseech you, let none of these vulgar sublunary considerations deprive us of a Zara or a Marcia—But say, which shall it be?—Which character, my charming cousin, will you do us the honour and pleasure to take?"

Count Altenberg advanced a step, full of eager expectation. When he heard Caroline pronounce, with great politeness, a refusal, for the first moment he looked disappointed, but the next seemed satisfied and pleased. It would have highly gratified and interested him to have seen Caroline act either the sublime or the tender heroine, but he preferred seeing her support her own character with modest dignity.

Commissioner Falconer pleaded and pressed in vain; Caroline was steady in her refusal, though the manner of it was so gentle, that every instant he thought he should vanquish her reluctance. At length he turned from the ladies to the gentlemen for assistance.

"Mr. Temple, I am sure you will join my entreaties—Count Altenberg—"

Count Altenberg "would not presume to ask a favour, which had been refused to the commissioner and to Mrs. Falconer." Caroline understood, and gave him credit for his politeness.

"Then, if I must give up this point," said the commissioner, "at least do not let me return disappointed in every respect—let me hope that you will all favour us with your company at our play."

This invitation was accepted with many thanks.

"And, remember, you must not run away from us that night," added the commissioner. "Mrs. Falconer will have reason to be jealous of Clermont-park, if she finds that it draws our friends and relations away from Falconer-court."

The carriage, which had been ordered to the great gate of the park, was now waiting there, and the commissioner took leave of his relations, with many shakes of the hand and many expressions of regret. Count Altenberg continued talking to Caroline till the last moment; and after he had handed her into the carriage, as he took leave of Mr. Percy, he said that he had to thank him and his family for some of the most agreeable among the many agreeable hours he had passed since he came to England.

On their way home, this happy family-party eagerly talked over every thing and every body that had interested them—first and chiefly they spoke of Count Altenberg. Caroline said how often, during their walk, she had regretted her mother's and sister's absence. She recollected and reminded her father of some of the striking circumstances they had heard, and Mr. Percy and she repeated so many curious and interesting anecdotes, so many just observations and noble sentiments, that Mrs. Percy and Rosamond were quite charmed with the Count. Rosamond, however, was surprised by the openness and ease with which Caroline praised and talked of this gentleman.

"I will say nothing," thought she; "for I am determined to be prudent this time. But certainly here is no danger that her love should unsought be won. Only this I may and must think, that Caroline cannot, without affectation, avoid seeing that she has made a conquest."

Mistaken again, Rosamond—Caroline had neither seen nor suspected it. Count Altenberg's gratitude for the hospitality shown to his countrymen at the time of the shipwreck, his recent acquaintance with her brother Alfred, and all he had heard of her father from the grateful tenants at Percy-hall, accounted, as Caroline justly thought, for the eagerness he had shown to be introduced to her family. His conversing so much with her, she thought, was natural, as he was a stranger to most of the company, and had some subjects of conversation in common with her and her family. Caroline was not apt to imagine admiration in every word or look; she was not expert in construing every compliment into a declaration or an innuendo of love.

His conversation, during their walk, had been perfectly free from all compliment. It had been on subjects so interesting, that she had been carried on without having had time to think of love. A good and great character had opened to her view, and she had been so absorbed in sympathy, that though she had thought of nothing but Count Altenberg, she had never thought of him with any reference to herself.

The morning after their return home, Count Altenberg came to the Hills, accompanied by Mr. Temple. They stayed till it was late; for the Count seemed to forget the hour of the day, till reminded of it by Mr. Temple. Caroline, in her own family, at her home, pleased Count Altenberg particularly. The interest he felt about her increased, and he afterwards took or made frequent opportunities of calling at the Hills: his conversation was generally addressed to Mr. Percy, but he observed Caroline with peculiar attention—and Rosamond was confirmed in her opinion. A few weeks passed in this manner, while the play was preparing at Falconer-court. But before we go to the play, let us take a peep behind the scenes, and inquire what is and has been doing by the Falconer family. Even they who are used to the ennui subsequent to dissipation, even they who have experienced the vicissitudes of coquetry, the mortifications of rivalship, and the despair of disappointed vanity, can scarcely conceive the complication of disagreeable ideas and emotions with which Miss Georgiana Falconer awoke the morning after the magnificent ball.

The image of her beautiful rival disturbed her morning dreams, and stood before her fancy the moment she opened her eyes. Wakening, she endeavoured to recollect and compare all that had passed the preceding night; but there had been such tumult in her mind, that she had only a vague remembrance of the transactions: she had a confused idea that the Count was in love, and that he was not in love with her: she had fears that, during the heat of competition, she had betrayed unbecoming emotion; but gradually, habitual vanity predominated; her hopes brightened; she began to fancy that the impression made by her rival might be easily effaced, and that they should see no more of the fair phantom. That branch of the Percy family, she recollected, were to be considered only as decayed gentry; and she flattered herself that they would necessarily and immediately sink again into that obscurity from which her mother's ill-fated civility had raised them. Her mother, she knew, had invited these Percys against her will, and would be particularly careful on account of Sir Robert Percy (and Arabella) not to show them any further attention. Thus things would, in a day or two, fall again into their proper train. "No doubt the Count will call this morning, to know how we do after the ball."

So she rose, and resolved to dress herself with the most becoming negligence.

Very different was the result of her experienced mother's reflections. Mrs. Falconer saw that her daughter's chance of the Count was now scarcely worth considering; that it must be given up at once, to avoid the danger of utter ruin to other speculations of a more promising kind. The mother knew the unmanageable violence of her daughter's temper: she had seen her Georgiana expose herself the preceding night at the ball to her particular friends, and Mrs. Falconer knew enough of the world to dread reports originating from particular friends; she dreaded, also, that on some future similar occasion, the young lady's want of command over her jealousy should produce some terribly ridiculous scene, confirm the report that she had an unhappy passion for Count Altenberg, stigmatize her as a forlorn maiden, and ruin her chance of any other establishment. In this instance she had been misled by her own and her daughter's vanity. It was mortifying, to be sure, to find that she had been wrong; and still more provoking to be obliged to acknowledge that Mr. Falconer was right; but in the existing circumstances it was absolutely necessary, and Mrs. Falconer, with a species of satisfaction, returned to her former habits of thinking, and resumed certain old schemes, from which the arrival of the Count had diverted her imagination. She expected the two Mr. Clays at Falconer-court the next day. Either of them, she thought, might be a good match for Georgiana. To be sure, it was said that French Clay had gaming debts to a large amount upon his hands—this was against him; but, in his favour, there was the chance of his elder brother's dying unmarried, and leaving him Clay-hall. Or, take it the other way, and suppose English Clay to be made the object—he was one of the men who professedly have a horror of being taken in to marry; yet no men are more likely "to run into the danger to avoid the apprehension." Suppose the worst, and that neither of the Clays could be worked to any good purpose, Mrs. Falconer had still in reserve that pis aller Petcalf, whose father, the good general, was at Bath, with the gout in his stomach; and if he should die, young Petcalf would pop into possession of the general's lodge in Asia Minor [Footnote: A district in England so called.]: not so fine a place, to be sure, nor an establishment so well appointed as Clay-hall; but still with a nabob's fortune a great deal might be done—and Georgiana might make Petcalf throw down the lodge and build. So at the worst she might settle very comfortably with young Petcalf, whom she could manage as she pleased, provided she never let him see her penchant for Count Altenberg. Mrs. Falconer determined to turn the tables dexterously, and to make it appear that the Count admired Georgiana, but saw she could not be induced to leave England. "We must," said she to herself, "persuade English Clay that I would not for any consideration give my daughter to a foreigner."

In consequence of these plans and reflections, Mrs. Falconer began her new system of operations, by writing that note full of superfluous civility to Mrs. Percy, with which Commissioner Falconer had been charged: the pressing Caroline to play Zara or Marcia, the leaving to her the choice of dresses and characters, the assurance that Miss Georgiana Falconer would take the confidante's part with pleasure, were all strokes of Mrs. Falconer's policy. By these means she thought she could most effectually do away all suspicion of her own or her daughter's jealousy of Miss Caroline Percy. Mrs. Falconer foresaw that, in all probability, Caroline would decline acting; but if she had accepted, Mrs. Falconer would have been sincerely pleased, confident, as she was, that Caroline's inferiority to her Georgiana, who was an accomplished actress, would be conspicuously manifest.

As soon as Mrs. Percy's answer, and Caroline's refusal, arrived, Mrs. Falconer went to her daughter Georgiana's apartment, who was giving directions to her maid, Lydia Sharpe, about some part of Zara's dress.

"My dear," said Mrs. Falconer, looking carelessly at the dress, "you won't want a very expensive dress for Zara."

"Indeed, ma'am, I shall," cried Georgiana: "Zara will be nothing, unless she is well dressed."

"Well, my dear, you must manage as well as you can with Lydia Sharpe. Your last court-dress surely she can make do vastly well, with a little alteration to give it a Turkish air."

"Oh! dear me, ma'am!—a little alteration!" cried Lydia: "no alteration upon the face of Heaven's earth, that I could devise from this till Christmas, would give it a Turkish air. You don't consider, nor conceive, ma'am, how skimping these here court-trains are now—for say the length might answer, its length without any manner of breadth, you know, ma'am—look, ma'am, a mere strip!—only two breadths of three quarters bare each—which gives no folds in nature, nor drapery, nor majesty, which, for a Turkish queen, is indispensably requisite, I presume."

"Another breadth or two would make it full enough, and cotton velvet will do, and come cheap," said Mrs. Falconer.

"Cotton velvet!" cried Miss Georgiana. "I would not wear cotton velvet—like the odious, shabby Miss Chattertons, who are infamous for it."

"But on the stage, what eye could detect it, child?" said Mrs. Falconer.

"Eye, ma'am! no, to be sure, at that distance: but the first touch to any body that understands velvets would betray it—and them that is on the stage along with Miss Georgiana, or behind the scenes, will detect it. And I understood the ladies was to sup in their dresses, and on such an occasion I presumed you would like Miss Georgiana to have an entire cap a pie new dress, as the Lady Arlingtons and every body has seen her appear in this, and has it by heart, I may say—and the Count too, who, of course, will expect, to see Zara spick and span—But I leave it all to your own better judgment, ma'am—I am only just mentioning—"

"All I know is, that the play will be nothing unless it is well dressed," cried Miss Georgiana; "and I never will play Zara in old trumpery."

"Well, my dear, there's your amber satin, or your pink, or your green, or your white, or—I am sure you have dresses enough. Lydia, produce them, and let me see."

Lydia covered the bed with various finery; but to every dress that was produced some insuperable objection was started by the young lady or by her maid.

"I remember you had a lavender satin, that I do not see here, Georgiana," said Mrs. Falconer.

"The colour did not become me, ma'am, and I sold it to Lydia."

Sold! gave, perhaps some innocent reader may suspect that the young lady meant to say.—No: this buying and selling of finery now goes on frequently between a certain class of fashionable maids and mistresses; and some young ladies are now not ashamed to become old clothes-women.

"Vastly well," said Mrs. Falconer, smiling; "you have your own ways and means, and I am glad of it, for I can tell you there is no chance of my getting you any money from your father; I dare not speak to him on that subject—for he was extremely displeased with me about Mrs. Sparkes' last bill: so if you want a new dress for Zara, you and Lydia Sharpe must settle it as well as you can between you. I will, in the mean time, go and write a note, while you make your bargain."

"Bargain! Me, ma'am!" cried Lydia Sharpe, as Mrs. Falconer left the room; "I am the worst creature extant at bargaining, especially with ladies. But any thing I can do certainly to accommodate, I shall, I'm sure, be happy."

"Well, then," said Miss Georgiana, "if you take this white satin off my hands, Lydia, I am sure I shall be happy."

"I have no objection, ma'am—that is, I'm in duty bound to make no manner of objections," said Lydia, with a very sentimental air, hanging her head aside, and with one finger rubbing her under-lip slowly, as she contemplated the white satin, which her young mistress held up for sale. "I am really scrupulous—but you're sensible, Miss Georgiana, that your white satin is so all frayed with the crape sleeves. Lady Trant recommended—"

"Only a very little frayed."

"But in the front breadth, ma'am; you know that makes a world of difference, because there's no hiding, and with satin no turning—and not a bit neither to new body."

"The body is perfectly good."

"I beg pardon for observing, but you know, ma'am, you noticed yourself how it was blacked and soiled by wearing under your black lace last time, and that you could not wear it again on that account."

"I!—but you—"

"To be sure, ma'am, there's a great deal of difference between I and you: only when one comes to bargaining—"

She paused, seeing wrath gathering black and dire in her young lady's countenance; before it burst, she changed her tone, and continued, "All I mean to say, ma'am, is, that white satin being a style of thing I could not pretend to think of wearing in any shape myself, I could only take it to part with again, and in the existing circumstances, I'm confident I should lose by it. But rather than disoblige, I'll take it at whatever you please."

"Nay, I don't please about the matter, Lydia; but I am sure you had an excellent bargain of my lavender satin, which I had only worn but twice."

"Dear heart!—La, ma'am! if you knew what trouble I had with Mrs. Sparkes, the dress-maker, about it, because of the coffee-stain—And I vow to my stars I am ashamed to mention it; but Mrs. Scrags, Lady Trant's woman, and both the Lady Arlingtons' maids, can vouch for the truth of it. I did not make a penny, but lost, ma'am, last year, by you and Miss Bell; that is, not by you nor Miss Bell, but by all I bought, and sold to disadvantage; which, I am morally certain, you would not have permitted, had you known of it, as I told Mrs. Scrags, who was wondering and pitying of me: my young ladies, Mrs. Scrags, says I—"

"No matter," interrupted Georgiana; "no matter what you said to Mrs. Scrags, or Mrs. Scrags to you—but tell me at once, Lydia, what you can afford to give me for these three gowns."

"I afford to give!" said Lydia Sharpe. "Well, the times is past, to be sure, and greatly changed, since ladies used to give, but now it's their maids must give—then, suppose—let's see, ma'am—for the three, the old white satin, and the amber satin, and the black lace—why, ma'am, if you'd throw me the pink crape into the bargain, I don't doubt but I could afford to give you nine guineas, ma'am," said the maid.

"Then, Lydia Sharpe, you will never have them, I promise you," cried the mistress: "Nine guineas! how can you have the assurance to offer me such a sum? As if I had never bought a gown in my life, and did not know the value or price of any thing! Do you take me for a fool?"

"Oh! dear no, miss—I'm confident that you know the value and price to the uttermost penny—but only you forget that there's a difference betwixt the buying and selling price for ladies; but if you please, ma'am—I would do any thing to oblige and accommodate you—I will consult the Lady Arlingtons' women, Miss Flora, and Miss Prichard, who is judges in this line—most honourable appraisers; and if they praise the articles, on inspection, a shilling higher, I am sure I shall submit to their jurisdiction—if they say ten guineas, ma'am, you shall have it, for I love to be at a word and a blow—and to do every thing genteel: so I'll step and consult my friends, ma'am, and give you my ultimatum in half an hour."

So saying, whilst her young mistress stood flushed and swelling with pride and anger, which, however, the sense of her own convenience and interest controlled, the maid swept up the many coloured robes in her arms, and carried them up the back stairs, to hold her consultation with her friends, the most honourable of appraisers.

"Well, my dear," said Mrs. Falconer, returning as she heard the maid quit the room, "have you driven your bargain for the loan? Have you raised the supplies?"

"No, indeed, ma'am—for Lydia is grown a perfect Jew. She may well say she is related to Sharpe, the attorney—she is the keenest, most interested creature in the world—and grown very saucy too."

"Like all those people, my dear; but one can't do without them."

"But one can change them."

"But, to use their own language, one is not sure of bettering oneself—and then their wages are to be paid—and all one's little family secrets are at their mercy."

"It's very provoking—it is very provoking!" repeated Miss Georgiana, walking up and down the room. "Such an extortioner!—for my amber satin, and my white satin, and my black lace, and my pink crape, only nine guineas! What do you think of that, ma'am?"

"I think, my dear, you pay a prodigious premium for ready money; but nine guineas will dress Zara decently, I dare say, if that's your object."

"Nine guineas! ma'am," cried Miss Georgiana, "impossible! I can't act at all—so there's an end of the matter."

"Not an end of the matter quite," said Mrs. Falconer, coolly; "for in that case I must look out for another Zara."

"And where will you find one, ma'am?"

"The Lady Arlingtons have both fine figures—and, I dare say, would either of them oblige me."

"Not they. Lady Anne, with her indolence and her languor—a lady who looks as if she was saying, 'Quasha, tell Quaco to tell Fibba to pick up this pin that lies at my foot;' do you think she'd get a part by heart, ma'am, to oblige you—or that she could, if she would, act Zara?—No more than she could fly!"

"But her sister, Lady Frances, would and could," said Mrs. Falconer. "She is quick enough, and I know she longs to try Zara."

"Longs!—Lord, ma'am, she longs for fifty things in a minute!—Quick!—Yes, but don't depend on her, I advise you; for she does not know, for two seconds together, what she would have or what she would do."

"Then I have resource in one who, I am persuaded, will not disappoint me or any body else," said Mrs. Falconer.

"Whom can you mean, ma'am?"

"Miss Caroline Percy. Count Altenberg put it into my head: he observed that she would look the character remarkably well—and I will write to her directly."

Without power of articulating, Miss Georgiana Falconer fixed her eyes upon her mother for some moments.

"You think I have lost my senses this morning—I thought, and I am afraid so did many other people, that you had lost yours last night. Another such scene, your friends the Lady Arlingtons for spectators, you are ridiculous, and, of course, undone for life in the fashionable world—establishment, and every thing else that is desirable, irrevocably out of the question. I am surprised that a girl of your understanding and really polished manners, Georgiana, should, the moment any thing crosses or vexes you, show no more command of temper, grace, or dignity, than the veriest country girl. When things go wrong, do you see me lose all presence of mind; or rather, do you ever see me change a muscle of my countenance?"

"The muscles of some people's countenance, ma'am, I suppose, are differently made from others—mine will change with my feelings, and there is no remedy, for my feelings unfortunately are uncommonly acute."

"That is a misfortune, indeed, Georgiana; but not without remedy, I trust. If you will take my advice—"

"Were you ever in love, ma'am?"

"Properly—when every thing was settled for my marriage; but not improperly, or it might never have come to my wedding-day. Headstrong child! listen to me, or you will never see that day with Count Altenberg."

"Do you mean, ma'am, to ask Miss Caroline Percy to play Zara?"

"I will answer no question, Georgiana, till you have heard me patiently."

"I only hope, ma'am, you'll put it in the play-bill—or, if you don't, I will—Zara, Miss Caroline Percy—by particular desire of Count Altenberg."

"Whatever I do, you may hope and be assured, Georgiana, shall be properly done," cried Mrs. Falconer, rising with dignity; "and, since you are not disposed to listen to me, I shall leave you to your own inventions, and go and write my notes."

"La, mamma! dear mamma! dear'st mamma!" cried the young lady, throwing her arms round her mother, and stopping her. "You that never change a muscle of your countenance, how hasty you are with your own Georgiana!—sit down, and I'll listen patiently!"

Mrs. Falconer seated herself, and Miss Georgiana prepared to listen patiently, armed with a piece of gold fringe, which she rolled and unrolled, and held in different lights and varied festoons whilst her mother spoke, or, as the young lady would say, lectured. Mrs. Falconer was too well aware of the impracticableness of her daughter's temper to tell her upon this occasion the whole truth, even if her own habits would have permitted her to be sincere. She never mentioned to Georgiana that she had totally given up the scheme of marrying her to Count Altenberg, and that she was thoroughly convinced there was no chance of her winning him; but, on the contrary, she represented to the young lady that the Count had only a transient fancy for Miss Caroline Percy, which would never come to any serious proposal, unless it was opposed; that in a short time they should go to town, and the Count, of course, would return with Lord Oldborough: then the game would be in her own hands, provided, in the mean time, Georgiana should conduct herself with prudence and temper, and let no creature see or suspect any sort of anxiety; for that would give such an advantage against her, and such a triumph to Caroline and her friends, who, as Mrs. Falconer said, were, no doubt, all on the watch to "interpret," or misinterpret, "motions, looks, and eyes." "My dear," concluded the mother, "your play is to show yourself always easy and happy, whatever occurs; occupied with other things, surrounded by other admirers, and encouraging them properly—properly of course to pique the jealousy of your Count."

"My Count!" said Georgiana, with half a smile; "but Miss—You say this fancy of his will pass away—but when? When?"

"You young people always say, 'but when?' you have no idea of looking forward: a few months, a year, more or less, what does it signify? Georgiana, are you in such imminent danger of growing old or ugly?"

Georgiana turned her eyes involuntarily towards the glass, and smiled.

"But, ma'am, you were not in earnest then about getting another Zara."

"The offer I made—the compliments I paid in the note I wrote this morning, were all necessary to cover your mistakes of the night."

"Made! Wrote!" cried the young lady, with terror in her voice and eyes: "Good Heavens! mother, what have you done?"

"I had no doubt at the time I wrote," continued Mrs. Falconer, coolly, "I had no other idea, but that Miss Caroline Percy would decline."

"Oh! ma'am," cried Georgiana, half crying, then stamping with passion, "Oh! ma'am, how could you imagine, or affect to imagine, that that girl, that odious girl, who was born to be my plague, with all her affected humility, would decline?—Decline!—no, she will be transported to come sweeping in, in gorgeous tragedy—Zara! Marcia! If the whole family can beg or borrow a dress for her, we are undone—that's our only chance. Oh! mother, what possessed you to do this?"

"Gently, pretty Passionate, and trust to my judgment in future," putting into her daughter's hands Mrs. Percy's note.

"Miss Caroline Percy—sorry—out of her power!—Oh! charming!—a fine escape!" cried Georgiana, delighted. "You may be sure it was for want of the dress, though, mamma."

"No matter—but about yours, my dear?"

"Oh! yes, ma'am—my dress; that's the only difficulty now."

"I certainly wish you, my darling, to appear well, especially as all the world will be here: the two Clays— by-the-bye, here's their letter—they come to-morrow—and in short the whole world; but, as to money, there's but one way of putting your father into good-humour enough with you to touch upon that string."

"One way—well, if there be one way—any way."

"Petcalf!"

"Oh! Petcalf is my abhorrence—"

"There is the thing! He was speaking to your father seriously about you, and your father sounded me: I said you would never agree, and he was quite displeased—that and Mrs. Sparkes' bill completely overset him. Now, if you had your wish, Georgiana—what would be your taste, child?"

"My wish! My taste!—Oh! that would be for a delicate, delicate, soft, sentimental blue satin, with silver fringe, looped with pearl, for my first act; and in my last—"

"Two dresses! Oh! you extravagant! out of all possibility."

"I am only wishing, telling you my taste, dear mamma. You know there must be a change of dress, in the last act, for Zara's nuptials—now for my wedding dress, mamma, my taste would be—

'Shine out, appear, be found, my lovely Zara,'

—in bridal white and silver. You know, ma'am, I am only supposing."

"Well then, supposition for supposition," replied Mrs. Falconer: "supposing I let your father hope that you are not so decided to abhor poor Petcalf—"

"Oh! dear mamma, I am so persecuted about that Petcalf! and compared with Count Altenberg, my father must be blind, or think me an idiot."

"Oh! between him and the Count there is no comparison, to be sure; but I forgot to mention, that what your father builds upon is our poor old friend the general's death—Clay here, in a postscript, you see, mentions the gout in his stomach—so I am afraid he is as good as gone, as your father says, and then The Lodge in Asia Minor is certainly a pretty place to sit down upon if one could do no better."

"But, ma'am, the Count's vast possessions and rank!"

"I grant you all that, my dear; but our present object is the play—Zara's royal robes cannot be had for nothing, you know—you never listened to my infallible means of obtaining your wish: I think I can engage that the commissioner will not refuse us, if you will empower me to say to him, that by this time twelvemonth, if nothing better offers—mind my if—Petcalf shall be rewarded for his constancy."

"If—Oh! dear me! But before this time twelvemonth the Count—"

"Or one of the Clays might offer, and in that case, my if brings you off safe with your father."

"Well, then, mamma, upon condition that you will promise me, upon your word, you will lay a marked emphasis upon your if—I believe, for Zara's sake, I must—"

"I knew you would behave at last like a sensible girl," said Mrs. Falconer: "I'll go and speak to your father directly."

Mrs. Falconer thus fairly gained her point, by setting Georgiana's passion for dress against her passion for Count Altenberg; and having, moreover, under false pretences, extorted from the young lady many promises to keep her temper prudently, and to be upon the best terms possible with her rival, the mother went away perfectly satisfied with her own address.

The father was brought to perform his part, not without difficulty—Carte blanche for Zara's sentimental blue and bridal white robes was obtained, silver fringe and pearls inclusive: the triumphant Zara rang for the base confidante of her late distresses—Lydia Sharpe re-entered, with the four dresses upon sale; but she and her guineas, and the most honourable appraisers, all were treated with becoming scorn—and as Lydia obeyed her young lady's orders to replace her clothes in her wardrobe, and never to think of them more, they suddenly rose in value in her estimation, and she repented that she had been quite so much of an extortioner. She knew the difference of her mistress's tone when disappointed or successful, and guessed that supplies had been obtained by some means or other: "New dresses, I smell, are the order of the day," said Lydia Sharpe to herself; "but I'll engage she will want me presently to make them up: so I warrant I won't come down off my high horse till I see why—Miss Georgiana Falconer, ma'am, I beg pardon—you are the mistress—I meant only to oblige and accommodate when called upon—but if I'm not wanted, I'm not wanted—and I hope ladies will find them that will be more abler and willinger to serve them."

So saying, half flouncing, half pouting, she retired. Her young mistress, aware that Lydia's talents and expeditious performance, as a mantua-maker and a milliner, were essential to the appearance of Zara, suppressed her own resentment, submitted to her maid's insolence, and brought her into humour again that night, by a present of the famous white satin.

In due time, consequently, the Turkish dresses were in great forwardness. Lest we should never get to the play, we forbear to relate all the various frettings, jealousies, clashing vanities, and petty quarrels, which occurred between the actresses and their friends, during the getting up of this piece and its rehearsals. We need mention, only that the seeds of irreconcileable dislike were sown at this time, between the Miss Falconers and their dear friends, the Lady Arlingtons: there was some difficulty made by Lady Anne about lending her diamond crescent for Zara's turban—Miss Georgiana could never forgive this; and Lady Frances, on her part, was provoked, beyond measure, by an order from the duke, her uncle, forbidding her to appear on the stage. She had some reason to suspect that this order came in consequence of a treacherous hint in a letter of Georgiana's to Lady Trant, which went round, through Lady Jane Granville to the duke, who otherwise, as Lady Frances observed, "in the midst of his politics, might never have heard a word of the matter."

Mrs. Falconer had need of all her power over the muscles of her face, and all her address, in these delicate and difficult circumstances. Her daughter Arabella, too, was sullen—the young lady was subject to her brother John's fits of obstinacy. For some time she could not be brought to undertake the part of Selima; and no other Selima was to be had. She did not see why she should condescend to play the confidante for Georgiana's Zara—why she was to be sacrificed to her sister; and Sir Robert Percy, her admirer, not even to be invited, because the other Percys were to come.

Mrs. Falconer plied her well with flattery, through Colonel Spandrill; and at last Arabella was pacified by a promise that the following week "Love in a Village," or "The Lord of the Manor," should be acted, in which she should choose her part, and in which her voice and musical talents would be brought forward—and Sir Robert Percy and his friends should be the principal auditors.

Recovered, or partly recovered, from her fit of the sullens, she was prevailed upon to say she would try what she could do in Selima.

The parts were learnt by heart; the dresses, after innumerable alterations, finished to the satisfaction of the heroes and heroines of the drama.

Their quarrels, and the quarrels of their friends and of their servants, male and female, were at last hushed to temporary repose, and—the great, the important day arrived.

The preceding evening, Mrs. Falconer, as she sat quite exhausted in the green-room, was heard to declare, she was so tired, that she would not go through the same thing again, for one month, to be Queen of England.

CHAPTER XXVIII

The theatre at Falconer-court was not very spacious, but it was elegantly fitted up, extremely well lighted, and had a good effect. There was a brilliant audience, an excellent band of music, and the whole had a gay and festive appearance.

The Percy family, as they came from a great distance, were late. The house was crowded. Mrs. Falconer was obliged to seat Mrs. Percy and her daughters with the Lady Arlingtons on a bench upon the stage: a conspicuous situation, which had been reserved for their ladyships.

Every eye instantly turned upon the beautiful Caroline. She bore the gaze of public admiration with a blushing dignity, which interested every body in her favour. Count Altenberg, who had anxiously expected the moment of her arrival, was, however, upon his guard. Knowing that he was watched by Mrs. Falconer's friends, he was determined that his secret thoughts should not be seen. One involuntary glance he gave, but immediately withdrew his eye, and continued his conversation with the gentleman next to him. After a few moments had elapsed, he could indulge himself in looking at Caroline unobserved, for the gaze of public admiration is as transient as it is eager. It is surprising how short a time any face, however beautiful, engages numbers who meet together to be seen.

The audience were now happily full of themselves, arranging their seats, and doing civilities to those of their friends who were worthy of notice.

"Lady Trant! won't your ladyship sit in the front row?"

"I'm vastly well, thank you."

"Lady Kew, I am afraid you won't see over my head."

"Oh! I assure you—perfectly—perfectly."

"Colonel Spandrill, I'll trouble you—my shawl."

"Clay, lend me your opera-glass.—How did you leave all at Bath?"

"I'm so glad that General Petcalf's gout in his stomach did not carry him off—for young Petcalf could not have acted, you know, to-night.—Mrs. Harcourt is trying to catch your eye, Lady Kew."

All those who were new to the theatre at Falconer-court, or who were not intimate with the family, were in great anxiety to inform themselves on one important point, before the prologue should begin. Stretching to those who were, or had the reputation of being, good authorities, they asked in whispers, "Do you know if there is to be any clapping of hands?—Can you tell me whether it is allowable to say any thing?"

It seems that at some private theatres loud demonstrations of applause were forbidden. It was thought more genteel to approve and admire in silence,—thus to draw the line between professional actors and actresses, and gentlemen and lady performers. Upon trial, however, in some instances, it had been found that the difference was sufficiently obvious, without marking it by any invidious distinction. Young and old amateurs have acknowledged, that the silence, however genteel, was so dreadfully awful, that they preferred even the noise of vulgar acclamations.

The cup of flattery was found so sweet, that objections were no longer made to swallowing it in public.

The overture finished, the prologue, which was written by Mr. Seebright, was received with merited applause. And, after a buzz of requests and promises for copies, the house was silent—the curtain drew up, and the first appearance of Zara, in the delicate sentimental blue satin, was hailed with plaudits, long and loud—plaudits which were reiterated at the end of her first speech, which was, indeed, extremely well recited. Count Altenberg leaned forward, and seemed to listen with delight; then stood up, and several times renewed his plaudits; at first, with an appearance of timidity, afterwards, with decision and energy. Miss Georgiana Falconer really acted uncommonly well, so that he could without flattery applaud; and if he did exaggerate a little in the expression of his admiration, he deemed it allowable. He had another object: he was absolutely determined to see whether or not Caroline was capable of the mean passions which had disgusted him in her rival. He reflected that he had seen her only when she was triumphant; and he was anxious to know how she would appear in different circumstances. Of her high intellectual endowments he could not doubt; but temper is not always a blessing given to the fair, or even to the wise. It may seem strange that a gallant man should think of a beauty's temper; and, probably, if Count Altenberg had considered Caroline only as a beauty, he would not have troubled himself to make, on this point, any severe and dangerous scrutiny.

The play went on—Zara sustaining the interest of the scene. She was but feebly supported by the sulky Selima, and the other parts were but ill performed. The faults common to unpractised actors occurred: one of Osman's arms never moved, and the other sawed the air perpetually, as if in pure despite of Hamlet's prohibition. Then, in crossing over, Osman was continually entangled in Zara's robe; or, when standing still, she was obliged to twitch her train thrice before she could get it from beneath his leaden feet. When confident that he could repeat a speech fluently, he was apt to turn his back upon his mistress; or, when he felt himself called upon to listen to his mistress, he would regularly turn his back upon the audience. But all these are defects permitted by the licence of a private theatre, allowable by courtesy to gentlemen-actors; and things went on as well as could be expected. Osman had not his part by heart, but still Zara covered all deficiencies: and Osman did no worse than other Osmans had done before him, till he came to the long speech, beginning with,

"The sultans, my great ancestors, bequeath'd
Their empire to me, but their tastes they gave not."

Powerful prompting got him through the first six lines decently enough, till he came to

—"wasting tenderness in wild profusion,
I might look down to my surrounded feet,
And bless contending beauties,"

At this he bungled sadly—his hearing suddenly failing as well as his memory, there was a dead stop. In vain the prompter, the scene-shifter, the candle-snuffer, as loud as they could, and much louder than they ought, reiterated the next sentence,

"I might speak,
Serenely slothful."

It was plain that Osman could not speak, nor was he "serene." He had begun, as in dangers great he was wont, to kick his left ankle-bone rapidly with his right heel; and through the pomp of Osman's oriental robes and turban young Petcalf stood confessed. He threw back an angry look at the prompter—Zara terrified, gave up all for lost—the two Lady Arlingtons retreated behind the scenes to laugh—the polite audience struggled not to smile. Count Altenberg at this moment looked at Caroline, who, instead of joining in the laugh, showed by her countenance and manner the most good-natured sympathy.

Zara, recovering her presence of mind, swept across the stage in such a manner as to hide from view her kicking sultan; and as she passed, she whispered the line to him so distinctly, that he caught the sound, left off kicking, went on with his speech, and all was well again. Count Altenberg forgot to join in the cheering plaudits, he was so much charmed at that instant by Caroline's smile.

Fortunately for Zara, and for the audience, in the next scenes the part of Lusignan was performed by a gentleman who had been well used to acting—though he was not a man of any extraordinary capacity, yet, from his habit of the boards, and his being perfect in his part, he now seemed quite a superior person. It was found unaccountably easier to act with this son of labour than with any other of the gentlemen-performers, though they were all natural geniuses.

The moment Zara appeared with Lusignan, her powers shone forth—nothing spoiled the illusion, the attention of the audience was fixed, their interest was sustained, their feelings touched. The exercise of the fan ceased in the front rows, glasses of lemonade were held untasted, and nobody consulted the play-bill. Excited by success, sympathy, and applause the most flattering, Zara went on with increasing éclat.

Meanwhile the Percy family, who were quite intent upon the play, began to find their situation disagreeable from some noise behind the scenes. A party of ladies, among whom was Lady Frances Arlington, stood whispering so loud close to Caroline that their voices were heard by her more distinctly than those of the actors. Lady Frances stood half hid between the side scenes, holding a little white dog in her arms.

"Hush!" cried her ladyship, putting her fingers on her lips—her companions became silent instantly. The house was now in profound attention. Zara was in the midst of her favourite speech,

"Would you learn more, and open all my heart?
Know then that, spite of this renew'd injustice,
I do not—cannot—wish to love you less;
—That long before you look'd so low as Zara,
She gave her heart to Osman."

At the name of Osman, the dog started and struggled—Lady Frances appeared to restrain him, but he ran on the stage—leaped up on Zara—and at the repetition of the name of Osman sat down on his hind legs, begged with his fore-paws, and began to whine in such a piteous manner that the whole audience were on the brink of laughter—Zara, and all her attendants and friends, lost their presence of mind.

Caroline sprang forward quite across the stage, caught the dog in her arms, and carried him off. Count Altenberg, no longer master of himself, clapped his hands, and the whole house resounded with applause.

Miss Georgiana Falconer misunderstood the cause of the plaudits, imagined that she was encored, cast down her eyes, and, as soon as there was silence, advanced and recommenced her speech, of which Count Altenberg did not hear one word.

This malicious trick had been contrived by Lady Frances Arlington, to revenge herself on Miss Georgiana Falconer for having prevented her from taking a part in the play. Her ladyship had, in the course of the rehearsals, privately drilled her dog to answer to the name of Osman, when that name was pronounced in Zara's tragic tone. The dog had been kept out of the way till Zara was in the midst of that speech in which she calls repeatedly on the name of Osman. This trick had been so well contrived, that all but those who were in the secret imagined that the appearance of the dog at this unlucky moment had been accidental. The truth began indeed to be soon whispered in confidence.

But to return to Count Altenberg. At the commencement of the play, when the idea of trying Caroline's temper had occurred to him, he had felt some anxiety lest all the high expectations he had formed, all the bright enchantment, should vanish. In the first act, he had begun by joining timidly in the general applause of Zara, dreading lest Caroline should not be blessed with that temper which could bear the praises of a rival "with unwounded ear." But the count applauded with more confidence in the second act; during the third was quite at his ease; and in the fifth could not forgive himself for having supposed it possible that Caroline could be liable to any of the foibles of her sex.

In the mean time Miss Georgiana Falconer, in high spirits, intoxicated with vanity, was persuaded that the Count had returned to his senses; and so little did she know of his character, or of the human heart, as to expect that a declaration of love would soon follow this public profession of admiration. Such was the confusion of her ideas, that she was confident Zara was on the point of becoming Countess of Altenberg.

After the play was over, and a thousand compliments had been paid and received, most of the company called for their carriages. The house emptied fast: there remained only a select party, who were to stay supper. They soon adjourned to the green-room to repeat their tribute of applause to the actors. High in the midst stood Miss Georgiana Falconer, receiving incense from a crowd of adorers. As Count Altenberg approached, she assumed a languishing air of softness and sensibility. The Count said all that could reasonably be expected, but his compliments did not seem quite to satisfy the lady. She was in hopes that he was going to say something more to her taste, when French Clay pressed forward, which he did with an air neither French nor English. He protested that he could not have conceived it possible for the powers of any actress upon earth to interest him for the English Zara; "but you, madam," said he, "have done the impossible; and now I should die content, if I could see your genius do justice to Zaïre. How you would shine in the divine original, when you could do such wonders for a miserable translation!"

Several gentlemen, and among others Mr. Percy, would not allow that the English translation deserved to be called miserable. "The wrong side of the tapestry we cannot expect should be quite equal to the right side." said he: "Voltaire pointed out a few odds and ends here and there, which disfigured the work, and required to be cut off; but upon the whole, if I recollect, he was satisfied with the piece, and complimented Mr. Hill upon having preserved the general design, spirit, and simplicity of the original."

"Mere politeness in M. de Voltaire!" replied French Clay; "but, in effect, Zaïre is absolutely incapable of any thing more than being done into English. For example, will any body have the goodness to tell me," said he, looking round, and fixing his look of appeal on Miss Caroline Percy, "how would you translate the famous 'Zaïre!—vous pleurez!'"

"Is not it translated," said Caroline, "by 'Zara! you weep?'"

"Ah! pardonnez moi!" cried French Clay, with a shrug meant to be French, but which English shoulders could not cleverly execute—"Ah! pardonnez! to my ears now that says nothing."

"To our feelings it said a great deal just now," said Caroline, looking at Zara in a manner which was lost upon her feelings, but not upon Count Altenberg's.

"Ah! indubitably I admit," cried Mr. Clay, "la beauté est toujours dans son pays, and tears fortunately need no translation; but when we come to words, you will allow me, ma'am, that the language of fine feeling is absolutely untranslateable, untransfusible."

Caroline seemed to wish to avoid being drawn forward to farther discussion, but Mr. Clay repeated, in a tone of soft condescension, "Your silence flatters me with the hope, ma'am, that we agree?"

Caroline could not submit to this interpretation of her silence, and blushing, but without being disconcerted, she answered, that she had always heard, and believed, it was the test of true feeling, as of true wit, that it can be easily understood, and that its language is universal.

"If I had ever doubted that truth," said Count Altenberg, "I should have been convinced of it by what I have seen and heard this night."

Miss Georgiana Falconer bowed her head graciously to the Count, and smiled, and sighed. Lady Frances Arlington and Rosamond smiled at the same moment, for they perceived by the universal language of the eye, that what Count Altenberg said was not intended for the lady who took it so decidedly to herself. This was the second time this night that Miss Georgiana Falconer's vanity had appropriated to herself a compliment in which she had no share. Yet, even at this moment, which, as she conceived, was a moment of triumph, while she was encircled by adorers, while the voice of praise yet vibrated in her ears, she felt anguish at perceiving the serenity of her rival's countenance; and, however strange it may appear, actually envied Caroline for not being envious.

Mrs. Falconer, skilled in every turn of her daughter's temper, which she was now obliged to follow and humour, or dexterously to counteract, lest it should ruin all schemes for her establishment, saw the cloud gathering on Zara's brow, and immediately fixed the attention of the company upon the beauty of her dress and the fine folds of her velvet train. She commenced lamentations on the difference between English and French velvets. French Clay, as she had foreseen, took up the word, and talked of velvets till supper was announced.

When Mrs. Falconer attended Lady Trant and Lady Kew to their rooms, a nocturnal conference was held in Lady Trant's apartment, where, of course, in the most confidential manner, their ladyships sat talking over the events of the day, and of some matters too interesting to be spoken of in general society. They began to congratulate Mrs. Falconer upon the impression which Zara had made on Count Altenberg; but the wily mother repressed their premature felicitations. She protested she was positively certain that the person in question had now no thoughts of Georgiana, such as their ladyships' partiality to her might lead them to suppose; and now, when the business was over, she might venture to declare that nothing could have persuaded her to let a daughter of hers marry a foreigner. She should have been sorry to give offence to such an amiable and well-informed young nobleman; and she really rejoiced that, if her sentiments had been, as no doubt by a person of his penetration they must have been, discovered, Count Altenberg had taken the hint without being offended: indeed, she had felt it a point of conscience to let the truth be seen time enough, to prevent his coming to a downright proposal, and having the mortification of an absolute refusal. Other mothers, she knew, might feel differently about giving a daughter to a foreigner, and other young ladies might feel differently from her Georgiana. Where there was so great an establishment in prospect, and rank, and fashion, and figure, to say nothing of talents, it could hardly be expected that such temptations should be resisted in a certain family, where it was so very desirable, and indeed necessary, to get a daughter married without a portion. Mrs. Falconer declared that on every account she should rejoice, if things should happen to turn out so. The present object was every way worthy, and charming. She was a young lady for whom, even from the little she had seen of her, she confessed she felt uncommonly interested—putting relationship out of the question.

Thus having with able generalship secured a retreat for herself and for her daughter, Mrs. Falconer retired to rest.

Early the next morning one of Lord Oldborough's grooms brought a note for Mr. Percy. Commissioner Falconer's confidential servant took the note immediately up to his master's bedchamber, to inquire whether it would be proper to waken Mr. Percy to give it to him, or to make the groom wait till Mr. Percy should come down to breakfast.

The commissioner sat up in his bed, rubbed his eyes, read the direction of the note, many times turned and returned it, and desired to see the man who brought it. The groom was shown in.

"How is my lord's gout?"

"Quite well, sir: my lord was out yesterday in the park—both a horseback and afoot."

"I am very happy to hear it. And pray, did any despatches come last night from town, can you tell, sir?"

"I really can't particularly say, sir—I was out with the horses."

"But about this note?" said the commissioner.

The result of the cross-examination that followed gave reason to believe that the note contained an invitation to breakfast, because he had heard Mr. Rodney, my lord's own gentleman, tell the man whose business it was to attend at breakfast, that my lord would breakfast in his own room, and expected a friend to breakfast with him.

"A friend—Hum! Was there no note to me?—no message?"

"None, sir—as I know."

"Very extraordinary." Mr. Falconer inclined to keep the man till breakfast-time, but he would not be kept—he had orders to return with an answer immediately; and he had been on the fidgets all the time the commissioner had been detaining him; for Lord Oldborough's messengers could not venture to delay. The note was consequently delivered to Mr. Percy immediately, and Mr. Percy went to breakfast at Clermont-park. The commissioner's breakfast was spoiled by the curiosity this invitation excited, and he was obliged to chew green tea for the heartburn with great diligence. Meantime the company were all talking the play over and over again, till at last, when even Zara appeared satiated with the subject, the conversation diverged a little to other topics. Unluckily French Clay usurped so large a portion of attention, that Count Altenberg's voice was for some time scarcely heard—the contrast was striking between a really well-bred polished foreigner, and a man who, having kept bad company abroad, and having formed himself on a few bad models, presented an exaggerated imitation of those who were ridiculous, detested, or unknown, in good society at Paris; and whom the nation would utterly disclaim as representatives of their morals or manners. At this period of their acquaintance with Count Altenberg, every circumstance which drew out his character, tastes, and opinions, was interesting to the Percy family in general, and in particular to Caroline. The most commonplace and disagreeable characters often promoted this purpose, and thus afforded means of amusement, and materials for reflection. Towards the end of breakfast, the newspapers were brought in—the commissioner, who had wondered frequently what could make them so late, seized upon the government-paper directly, which he pocketed, and retired, after handing other newspapers to Count Altenberg and to the Mr. Clays. English Clay, setting down his well-sugared cup of tea, leaving a happily-prepared morsel of ham and bread and butter on his plate, turned his back upon the ladies; and comfortably settling himself with his arm over his chair, and the light full upon London news, began to read to himself. Count Altenberg glanced at Continental News, as he unfolded his paper, but instantly turned to Gazette Extraordinary, which he laid before Mrs. Falconer. She requested him, if it was not too much trouble, to read it aloud. "I hope my foreign accent will not make it unintelligible," said he; and without farther preface, or considering how he was to appear himself, he obeyed. Though he had not a perfectly English accent, he showed that he had a thoroughly English heart, by the joy and pride he took in reading an account of a great victory.

English Clay turned round upon his chair, and setting his arms a-kimbo, with the newspaper still fast in his hand, and his elbow sticking out across Lady Anne Arlington, sat facing the count, and listening to him With a look of surprise. "Why, d—m'me, but you're a good fellow, after all!" exclaimed he, "though you are not an Englishman!"

"By the mother's side I am, sir," replied Count Altenberg. "I may boast that I am at least half an Englishman."

"Half is better than the whole," said French Clay, scornfully.

"By the Lord, I could have sworn his mother, or some of his blood, was English!" cried English Clay. "I beg your pardon, ma'am—'fraid I annoy your ladyship?" added he, perceiving that the Lady Anne haughtily retreated from his offending elbow.

Then sensible of having committed himself by his sudden burst of feeling, he coloured all over, took up his tea, drank as if he wished to hide his face for ever in the cup, recovered his head with mighty effort, turned round again to his newspaper, and was cold and silent as before. His brother meanwhile was, or affected to be, more intent upon some eau sucrée, that he was preparing for himself, than upon the fate of the army and navy of Spain or England. Rising from the breakfast table, he went into the adjoining room, and threw himself at full length upon a sofa; Lady Frances Arlington, who detested politics, immediately followed, and led the way to a work-table, round which the ladies gathered, and formed themselves in a few minutes into a committee of dress, all speaking at once; Count Altenberg went with the ladies out of the breakfast-room, where English Clay would have been happy to have remained alone; but being interrupted by the entrance of the servants, he could not enjoy peaceable possession, and he was compelled also to follow:—getting as far as he could from the female committee, he took Petcalf into a window to talk of horses, and commenced a history of the colts of Regulus, and of the plates they had won.

French Clay, rising from the sofa, and adjusting his cravat at a looking-glass, carelessly said, addressing himself to Count Altenberg, "I think, M. le Comte, I heard you say something about public feelings. Now, I do not comprehend precisely what is meant by public feelings; for my part, I am free to confess that I have none."

"I certainly must have expressed myself ill," replied Count Altenberg; "I should have said, love of our country."

Mrs. Percy, Rosamond, and Caroline, escaped from the committee of dress, were now eagerly listening to this conversation.

"And if you had, M. le Comte, I might, en philosophe, have been permitted to ask," replied French Clay, "what is love of our country, but a mere prejudice? and to a person of an emancipated mind, that word prejudice says volumes. Assuredly M. le Comte will allow, and must feel well, that no prejudice ever was or can be useful to mankind."

The Count fully admitted that utility is the best human test by which all sentiment, as well as every thing else, can be tried: but he observed that Mr. Clay had not yet proved love of our country to be a useless or pernicious principle of action: and by his own argument, if it can be proved to be useful, it should not be called, in the invidious sense of the word, a prejudice.

"True—but the labour of the proof fortunately rests with you, M. le Comte."

Count Altenberg answered in French, speaking very rapidly. "It is a labour saved me fortunately, by the recorded experience of all history, by the testimony of the wisest and the best in all countries, ancient and modern—all agree in proclaiming love of our country to be one of the most powerful, most permanent motives to good and great actions; the most expansive, elevating principle—elevating without danger—expansive without waste; the principle to which the legislator looks for the preservative against corruption in states—to which the moralist turns for the antidote against selfishness in individuals. Recollect, name any great character, ancient or modern—is not love of his country one of his virtues? Can you draw—can you conceive a great character—a great or a good character, or even a safe member of society without it? A man hangs loose upon society, as your own Burke says—"

"Ah! M. le Comte!" cried Clay, shrinking with affected horror, "I repent—I see what I have brought upon myself; after Burke will come Cicero; and after Cicero all Rome, Carthage, Athens, Lacedemon. Oh! spare me! since I was a schoolboy, I could never suffer those names. Ah! M. le Comte, de grâce!—I know I have put myself in the case to be buried alive under a load of quotations."

The Count, with that good humour which disappoints ridicule, smiled, and checked his enthusiasm.

"Is there not a kind of enthusiasm," said Mrs. Percy, "which is as necessary to virtue as to genius?"

French Clay shook his head. He was sorry to differ from a lady; as a gallant man, he knew he was wrong, but as a philosopher he could not patronize enthusiasm. It was the business, he apprehended, of philosophy to correct and extinguish it.

"I have heard it said," interposed Rosamond, "that it is a favourite maxim of law, that the extreme of justice is the extreme of injustice—perhaps this maxim may be applied to philosophy as well as to law."

"Why extinguish enthusiasm?" cried Caroline. "It is not surely the business of philosophy to extinguish, but to direct it. Does not enthusiasm, well directed, give life and energy to all that is good and great?"

There was so much life and energy in Caroline's beautiful countenance, that French Clay was for a moment silenced by admiration.

"After all," resumed he, "there is one slight circumstance, which persons of feeling should consider, that the evils and horrors of war are produced by this very principle, which some people think so useful to mankind, this famous love of our country."

Count Altenberg asked, whether wars had not more frequently arisen from the unlawful fancies which princes and conquerors are apt to take for the territories of their neighbours, than from the legitimate love of their own country?

French Clay, hurried by a smile he saw on Rosamond's lips, changed his ground again for the worse, and said he was not speaking of wars, of foreign conquests, but of defensive wars, where foolish people, from an absurd love of their own country, that is, of certain barren mountains, of a few acres of snow, or of collections of old houses and churches, called capital cities, will expose themselves to fire, flame, and famine, and will stand to be cut to pieces inchmeal, rather than to submit to a conqueror, who might, ten to one, be a more civilized or cleverer sort of a person than their own rulers; and under whom they might enjoy all the luxuries of life—changing only the name of their country for some other equally well-sounding name; and perhaps adopting a few new laws, instead of what they might have been in the habit from their childhood of worshipping, as a wittenagemote, or a diet, or a constitution. "For my part," continued French Clay, "I have accustomed myself to go to the bottom of things. I have approfondied. I have not suffered my understanding to be paralysed—I have made my own analysis of happiness, and find that your legislators, and moralists, and patriots, would juggle me out of many solid physical comforts, by engaging me to fight for enthusiasms which do me no manner of good."

Count Altenberg's countenance had flushed with indignation, and cooled with contempt, several times during Mr. Clay's speech. Beginning in a low composed voice, he first answered, whatever pretence to reason it contained, in the analysis of human happiness, he observed, Mr. Clay had bounded his to physical comforts—this was reducing civilized man below even the savage, and nearly to the state of brutes. Did Mr. Clay choose to leave out all intellectual pleasures—all the pleasures of self-complacency, self-approbation, and sympathy? But, supposing that he was content to bound his happiness, inelegant and low, to such narrow limits, Count Altenberg observed, he did not provide for the security even of that poor portion. If he were ready to give up the liberty or the free constitution of the country in which he resided, ready to live under tyrants and tyranny, how could he be secure for a year, a day, even an hour, of his epicurean paradise?

Mr. Clay acknowledged, that, "in this point of view, it might be awkward to live in a conquered country; but if a man has talents to make himself agreeable to the powers that be, and money in his purse, that can never touch him, chacun pour soi—et honi soit qui mal y pense."

"Is it in England!—Oh! can it be in England, and from an Englishman, that I hear such sentiments!" exclaimed Count Altenberg. "Such I have heard on the continent—such we have heard the precursors of the ruin, disgrace, destruction of the princes and nations of Europe!"

Some painful reflections or recollections seemed to absorb the Count for a few moments.

"Foi d'honnête homme et de philosophe," French Clay declared, that, for his own part, he cared not who ruled or how, who was conqueror, or what was conquered, provided champagne and burgundy were left to him by the conqueror.

Rosamond thought it was a pity Mr. Clay was not married to the lady who said she did not care what revolutions happened, as long as she had her roast chicken, and her little game at cards.

"Happen what will," continued French Clay, "I have two hundred thousand pounds, well counted—as to the rest, it is quite indifferent to me, whether England be called England or France; for," concluded he, walking off to the committee of dress, "after all I have heard, I recur to my first question, what is country—or, as people term it, their native land?"

The following lines came full into Caroline's recollection as French Clay spoke:

"Breathes there the man with soul so dead,
Who never to himself has said,
This is my own, my native land?
Whose heart has ne'er within him burn'd,
As home his footsteps he hath turn'd,
From wandering on a foreign strand?
If such there he, go, mark him well;
High though his titles, proud his fame,
Boundless his wealth, as wish can claim,
Despite these titles, power and pelf,
The wretch, concentred all in self,
Living shall forfeit fair renown,
And doubly dying shall go down
To the vile dust from whence he sprung.
Unwept, unhonour'd, and unsung."

Caroline asked Count Altenberg, who seemed well acquainted with English literature, if he had ever read Scott's Lay of the Last Minstrel?

The Count smiled, and replied,

"'Breathes there the man with soul so dead,
Who never to himself has said'
any of those beautiful lines?"

Caroline, surprised that the Count knew so well what had passed in her mind, blushed.

At this moment Mrs. Falconer returned, and throwing a reconnoitring glance round the room to see how the company had disposed of themselves, was well pleased to observe French Clay leaning on the back of Georgiana's chair, and giving her his opinion about some artificial flowers. The ladies had been consulting upon the manner in which the characters in "Love in a Village,"—or, "The Lord of the Manor," should be dressed, and Miss Arabella Falconer had not yet completely determined which piece or which dress she preferred. She was glad that the Percys had been kept from this committee, because, as they were not to be asked to the entertainment, it was a subject she could not discuss before them. Whenever they had approached the table, the young ladies had talked only of fashions in general; and now, as Mrs. Percy and Caroline, followed by Count Altenberg, joined them, Mrs. Falconer put aside a volume of plays, containing "The Lord of the Manor," &c.; and, taking up another book, said something about the immortal bard to English Clay, who happened to be near her. He replied, "I have every edition of Shakspeare that ever was printed or published, and every thing that ever was written about him, good, bad, or indifferent, at Clay-hall. I made this a principle, and I think every Englishman should do the same. Your Mr. Voltaire," added this polite Englishman, turning to Count Altenberg, "made a fine example of himself by dashing at our Shakspeare?"

"Undoubtedly, Voltaire showed he did not understand Shakspeare, and therefore did not do him justice," replied Count Altenberg. "Even Voltaire had some tinge of national prejudice, as well as other men. It was reserved for women to set us, in this instance, as in many others, an example at once of superior candour and superior talent."

English Clay pulled up his boots, and, with a look of cool contempt, said, "I see you are a lady's man, monsieur."

Count Altenberg replied, that if a lady's man means an admirer of the fair sex, he was proud to feel that he deserved that compliment; and with much warmth he pronounced such a panegyric upon that sex, without whom "le commencement de la vie est sans secours, le milieu sans plaisir, et la fin sans consolation," that even Lady Anne Arlington raised her head from the hand on which it reclined, and every female eye turned upon him with approbation.

"Oh! what a lover he will make, if ever he is in love," cried Lady Frances Arlington, who never scrupled saying any thing that came into her head. "I beg pardon, I believe I have said something very shocking. Georgiana, my dear, I protest I was not thinking of—But what a disturbance I have made amongst all your faces, ladies—and gentlemen," repeated her ladyship, looking archly at the Count, whose face at this moment glowed manifestly; "and all because gentlemen and ladies don't mind their grammar and their tenses. Now don't you recollect—I call upon Mrs. Falconer, who really has some presence of—countenance—I call upon Mrs. Falconer to witness that I said 'if;' and, pray comprehend me, M. le Comte, else I must appear excessively rude, I did not mean to say any thing of the present or the past, but only of the future."

The Count, recovering his presence of mind, and presence of countenance, turned to a little Cupid on the mantel-piece; and, playfully doing homage before it, repeated,

"Qui que tu sois voici ton maître,
Il l'est, le fut—ou le doit être."

"Oh! charming—oh! for a translation!" cried Mrs. Falconer, glad to turn the attention from Georgiana:—"Lady Frances—ladies some of you, Miss Percy, here's my pencil."

Here they were interrupted by Mr. Percy's return from Lord Oldborough's.

The commissioner followed Mr. Percy into the room, and asked, and was answered, a variety of questions about despatches from town; trying, but, in vain, to find out what had been going forward. At last he ended with a look of absence, and a declaration that he was quite happy to hear that Lord Oldborough had so completely got rid of his gout.

"Completely," said Mr. Percy; "and he desires me to tell you, that it will be necessary for him to return to town in a few days."

"In a few days!" cried the commissioner.

"In a few days!" repeated several voices, in different tones.

"In a few days!—Gracious Heaven! and what will become of 'the Lord of the Manor!'" cried Miss Falconer.

"Gently, my Arabella! never raise your voice so high—you, who are a musician," said Mrs. Falconer, "and so sweet a voice as you have—in general. Besides," added she, drawing her apart, "you forget that you should not speak of 'the Lord of the Manor' before the Percys, as they are not to be asked."

"To be sure. Pray keep your temper, Bell, if you can, for a minute," whispered Miss Georgiana; "you see they have rung for the carriage."

Mrs. Falconer began to entreat Mrs. Percy would not be in a hurry to run away; but to her great joy the carriage came to the door.

At parting with Count Altenberg, Mr. Percy said that he regretted that they were so soon to lose his company in this part of the world. "We, who live so much retired, shall feel the loss particularly."

The Count, evidently agitated, only said, in a low voice, "We are not parting yet—we shall meet again—I hope—do you ever go to London?"

"Never."

"At all events, we must meet again," said the Count.

The ladies had all collected at the open windows, to see the departure of the Percys; but Miss Georgiana Falconer could learn nothing from the manner in which the Count handed Caroline into the carriage. It did not appear even that he spoke to her.

On his return, the Miss Falconers, and the Lady Arlingtons, were of course talking of those who had just left the house. There was at first but one voice in praise of Caroline's beauty and talents, elegance, and simplicity of manner. Mrs. Falconer set the example; Lady Frances Arlington and Miss Georgiana Falconer extolled her in the highest terms—one to provoke, the other not to appear provoked.

"La!" said Lady Frances, "how we may mistake even the people we know best—Georgiana, can you conceive it? I never should have guessed, if you had not told me, that Miss Caroline Percy was such a favourite of yours. Do you know now, so little penetration have I, I should have thought that you rather disliked her?"

"You are quite right, my dear Lady Frances," cried Mrs. Falconer; "I give you credit for your penetration: entre nous, Miss Caroline Percy is no favourite of Georgiana."

Georgiana actually opened her eyes with astonishment, and thought her mother did not know what she was saying, and that she certainly did not perceive that Count Altenberg was in the room.

"Count Altenberg, is this the book you are looking for?" said the young lady, pronouncing Count Altenberg's name very distinctly, to put her mother on her guard.

Mrs. Falconer continued precisely in the same tone. "Georgiana does justice, I am sure, to Miss Percy's merit and charms; but the truth is, she does not like her, and Georgiana has too much frankness to conceal it; and now come here, and I will tell you the reason." In a half whisper, but perfectly intelligible to every one in the room, Mrs. Falconer went on—"Georgiana's favourite brother, Buckhurst—did you never hear it? In days of yore, there was an attachment—Buckhurst, you know, is very ardent in his attachments—desperately in love he was—and no wonder. But at that time he was nobody—he was unprovided for, and the young lady had a good fortune then—her father would have him go to the bar— against the commissioner's wishes. You know a young man will do any thing if he is in love, and is encouraged—I don't know how the thing went on, or off, but Buckhurst found himself disappointed at last, and was so miserable about it! ready to break his heart! you would have pitied him! Georgiana was so sorry for him, that she never could forgive the young lady—though I really don't imagine, after all, she was to blame. But sisters will feel for their brothers."

Georgiana, charmed to find this amiable mode of accounting for her dislike to Caroline, instantly pursued her mother's hint, and frankly declared that she never could conceal either her likings or dislikings—that Miss Caroline Percy might have all the merit upon earth, and she did not doubt but she had; yet she never could forgive her for jilting Buckhurst—no, never! never! It might be unjust, but she owned that it was a prepossession she could not conquer.

"Why, indeed, my dear young lady, I hardly know how to blame you," cried Lady Trant; "for certainly a jilt is not a very amiable character."

"Oh! my dear Lady Trant, don't use such a word—Georgiana!—Why will you be so warm, so very unguarded, where that darling brother is concerned? You really—Oh! my dear Lady Trant, this must not go farther—and positively the word jilt must never be used again; for I'm confident it is quite inapplicable."

"I'd not swear for that," cried Lady Trant; "for, now I recollect, at Lady Angelica Headingham's, what was it we heard, my dear Lady Kew, about her coquetting with that Mr. Barclay, who is now going to be married to Lady Mary Pembroke, you know?"

"Oh! yes, I did hear something, I recollect—but, at the time, I never minded, because I did not know, then, who that Miss Caroline Percy was—true, true, I recollect it now. And all, you know, we heard about her and Sir James Harcourt—was there not something there? By all accounts, it is plain she is not the simple country beauty she looks—practised!—practised! you see."

Miss Georgiana Falconer's only fear was, that Count Altenberg might not hear Lady Kew, who had lowered her voice to the note of mystery. Mrs. Falconer, who had accomplished her own judicious purpose, of accounting for Georgiana's dislike of Miss Caroline Percy, was now afraid that her dear friends would overdo the business; she made many efforts to stop them, but once upon the scent of scandal, it was no easy matter to change the pursuit.

"You seem to have found something that has caught your attention delightfully, Count Altenberg," said Mrs. Falconer; "how I envy any one who is completely in a book—what is it?"

"Johnson's preface to Shakspeare."

Miss Georgiana Falconer was vexed, for she recollected that Miss Caroline Percy had just been speaking of it with admiration.

Mrs. Falconer wondered how it could have happened that she had never read it.

Lady Kew persevered in her story. "Sir James Harcourt, I know, who is the most polite creature in the whole world, and who never speaks an ill word of any body, I assure you, said of Miss Caroline Percy in my hearing—what I shall not repeat. Only this much I must tell you, Mrs. Falconer—Mrs. Falconer!—She won't listen because the young lady is a relation of her own—and we are very rude; but truth is truth, notwithstanding, you know. Well, well, she may talk of Miss Percy's beauty and abilities—very clever she is, I don't dispute; but this I may say, that Mrs. Falconer must never praise her to me for simplicity of character."

"Why, no," said Miss Georgiana; "one is apt to suppose that a person who has lived all her life in the country must, of course, have great simplicity. But there is a simplicity of character, and a simplicity of manner, and they don't always go together. Caroline Percy's manner is fascinating, because, you know, it is what one does not meet with every day in town—that was what struck my poor brother—that and her great talents, which can make her whatever she pleases to be: but I am greatly afraid she is not quite the ingenuous person she looks."

Count Altenberg changed colour, and was putting down his book suddenly, when Mrs. Falconer caught it, and stopping him, asked how far he had read.

Whilst he was turning over the leaves, Lady Trant went on, in her turn—"With all her practice, or her simplicity, whichever it may be—far be it from me to decide which—I fancy she has met with her match, and has been disappointed in her turn."

"Really!" cried Georgiana, eagerly: "How! What! When!—Are you certain?"

"Last summer—Oh! I have it from those who know the gentleman well. Only an affair of the heart that did not end happily: but I am told she was very much in love. The family would not hear of it—the mother, especially, was averse: so the young gentleman ended by marrying—exceedingly well—and the young lady by wearing the willow, you know, a decent time."

"Oh! why did you never tell me this before?" said Miss Georgiana.

"I protest I never thought of it, till Lady Kew brought it to my recollection, by talking of Lady Angelica Headingham, and Sir James Harcourt, and all that."

"But who was the gentleman?"

"That's a secret," replied Lady Trant.

"A secret!—A secret!—What is it? What is it?" cried Lady Frances Arlington, pressing into the midst of the party; for she was the most curious person imaginable.

Then heads joined, and Lady Trant whispered, and Lady Frances exclaimed aloud, "Hungerford?—Colonel Hungerford!"

"Fie! fie! Lady Frances," cried Georgiana—and "Fie! fie! you are a pretty person to keep a secret," cried Lady Trant: "I vow I'll never trust your ladyship with a secret again—when you publish it in this way."

"I vow you will," said Lady Frances. "Why, you all know, in your hearts, you wish to publish it—else why tell it—especially to me? But all this time I am not thinking in the least about the matter, nor was I when I said Hungerford—I was and am thinking of my own affairs. What did I do with the letter I received this morning? I had it here—no, I hadn't it—yes, I had—Anne!—Anne!—Lady Anne! the duchess's letter: I gave it to you; what did you do with it?"

"La! it is somewhere, I suppose," said Lady Anne, raising her head, and giving a vague look round the room.

Lady Frances made every one search their work-boxes, writing-boxes, and reticules; then went from table to table, opening and shutting all the drawers.

"Frances!—If you would not fly about so! What can it signify?" expostulated Lady Anne. But in vain; her sister went on, moving every thing and every body in the room, displacing all the cushions of all the chairs in her progress, and, at last, approached Lady Anne's sofa, with intent to invade her repose.

"Ah! Frances!" cried Lady Anne, in a deprecating tone, with a gesture of supplication and anguish in her eyes, "do let me rest!"

"Never, till I have the letter."

With the energy of anger and despair Lady Anne made an effort to reach the bell-cord—but it missed—the cord swung—Petcalf ran to catch it, and stumbled over a stool—English Clay stood still and laughed—French Clay exclaimed, "Ah! mon Dieu! Cupidon!"

Count Altenberg saved Cupid from falling, and rang the bell.

"Sir," said Lady Anne to the footman, "I had a letter—some time this morning, in my hand."

"Yes, my lady."

"I want it."

"Yes, my lady."

"Pray, sir, tell somebody to tell Pritchard, to tell Flora, to go up stairs to my dressing-room, sir, to look every where for't; and let it be brought to my sister, Lady Frances, if you please, sir."

"No, no, sir, don't do any thing about the matter, if you please—I will go myself," said Lady Frances.

Away the lady ran up stairs, and down again, with the letter in her hand.

"Yes! exactly as I thought," cried she; "my aunt does say, that Mrs. Hungerford is to be down to-day—I thought so."

"Very likely," said Lady Anne; "I never thought about it."

"But, Anne, you must think about it, for my aunt desires we should go and see her directly."

"I can't go," said Lady Anne—"I've a cold—your going will do."

"Mrs. Falconer, my dear Mrs. Falconer, will you go with me to-morrow to Hungerford Castle?" cried Lady Frances, eagerly.

"Impossible! my dear Lady Frances, unfortunately quite impossible. The Hungerfords and we have no connexion—there was an old family quarrel—"

"Oh! never mind family quarrels and connexions—you can go, and I am sure it will be taken very well—and you know you only go with me. Oh! positively you must—now there's my good dear Mrs. Falconer—yes, and order the carriage this minute for to-morrow early," said Lady Frances, in a coaxing yet impatient tone.

Mrs. Falconer adhered to its being absolutely impossible.

"Then, Anne, you must go."

No—Anne was impenetrable.

"Then I'll go by myself," cried Lady Frances, pettishly—"I'll take Pritchard with me, in our own carriage, and I'll speak about it directly—for go I must and will."

"Now, Frances, what new fancy is this for Mrs. Hungerford? I am sure you used not to care about her," said Lady Anne.

"And I dare say I should not care about her now," replied Lady Frances, "but that I am dying to see an old pair of shoes she has."

"An old pair of shoes!" repeated Lady Anne, with a look of unutterable disdain.

"An old pair of shoes!" cried Mrs. Falconer, laughing.

"Yes, a pair of blue damask shoes as old as Edward the Fourth's time—with chains from the toe to the knee, you know—or do you know, Count Altenberg? Miss Percy was describing them—she saw Colonel Hungerford put them on—Oh! he must put them on for me—I'll make him put them on, chains and all, to-morrow."

"Colonel Hungerford is on his way to India by this time," said Georgiana Falconer, drily.

"May I ask," said Count Altenberg, taking advantage of the first pause in the conversation—"may I ask if I understood rightly, that Mrs. Hungerford, mother of Colonel Hungerford, lives in this neighbourhood, and is coming into the country to-morrow?"

"Yes—just so," said Lady Frances.

What concern can it be of his? thought Miss Georgiana Falconer, fixing her eyes upon the Count with alarmed curiosity.

"I knew Colonel Hungerford abroad," continued the Count, "and have a great regard for him."

Lady Kew, Lady Trant, and Miss Georgiana Falconer, exchanged looks.

"I am sorry that he is gone to India," said Mrs. Falconer, in a sentimental tone; "it would have been so pleasant to you to have renewed an acquaintance with him in England."

Count Altenberg regretted the absence of his friend, the colonel; but, turning to Lady Frances, he congratulated himself upon having an opportunity of presenting his letters of introduction, and paying his respects to Mrs. Hungerford, of whom he had heard much from foreigners who had visited England, and who had been charmed with her, and with her daughter, Mrs. Mortimer—his letters of introduction had been addressed to her town residence, but she was not in London when he was there.

"No, she was at Pembroke," said Lady Kew.

I'm sure I wish she were there still, thought Miss Georgiana.

"But, after all, Lady Frances, is the duchess sure that Mrs. Hungerford is actually come to the country?—May be, she is still in town."

"I shall have the honour of letting your ladyship know; for, if Lord Oldborough will permit, I shall certainly go, very soon, to pay my respects at Hungerford Castle," said Count Altenberg.

The prescient jealousy of Miss Georgiana Falconer boded ill of this visit to Hungerford Castle. A few days afterwards a note was received from Count Altenberg, returning many thanks to Mr. and Mrs. Falconer for the civilities he had received from them, paying all proper compliments to Zara, announcing his intention of accepting an invitation to stay some time at Mrs. Hungerford's, and taking a polite leave of the Falconer family.

Here was a death-blow to all Georgiana's hopes! But we shall not stay to describe her disappointment, or the art of her mother in concealing it; nor shall we accompany Mrs. Falconer to town, to see how her designs upon the Clays or Petcalf prospered. We must follow Count Altenberg to Hungerford Castle.

CHAPTER XXIX

"Who would prize the tainted posies,
  Which on ev'ry breast are worn?
Who could pluck the spotless roses
  From their never touched thorn?"

The feeling expressed in these lines will be acknowledged by every man of sense and delicacy. "No such man ever prized a heart much hackneyed in the ways of love." It was with exquisite pain that Count Altenberg had heard all that had been said of Caroline—he did not give credit to half the insinuations—he despised those who made them: he knew that some of the ladies spoke from envy, others from the mere love of scandal; but still, altogether, an impression unfavourable to Caroline, or rather unfavourable to his passion for Caroline, was left on his mind. The idea that she had been suspected, the certainty that she had been talked of, that she had even been named as one who had coquetted with many admirers—the notion that she had been in love—passionately in love—all this took from the freshness, the virgin modesty, the dignity, the charm, with which she had appeared to his imagination, and without which she could not have touched his heart—a heart not to be easily won.

In his own country, at the court where he resided, in the different parts of the continent which he had visited, Germany, Poland, Switzerland, France, he had seen women celebrated for beauty and for wit, many of the most polished manners, many of the highest accomplishments, some of exquisite sensibility, a few with genuine simplicity of character, but in all there had been something which had prevented his wishing to make any one of them the companion of his life. In some there was a want of good temper—in others of good sense; there was some false taste for admiration or for notoriety—some love of pleasure, or some love of sway, inconsistent with his idea of the perfection of the female character, incompatible with his plans of life, and with his notions of love and happiness.

In England, where education, institutions, opinion, manners, the habits of society, and of domestic life, happily combine to give the just proportion of all that is attractive, useful, ornamental, and amiable to the female character—in England, Count Altenberg had hopes of finding a woman who, to the noble simplicity of character that was once the charm of Switzerland, joined the polish, the elegance, that was once the pride of France; a woman possessing an enlarged, cultivated, embellished understanding, capable of comprehending all his views as a politician and a statesman; yet without any wish for power, or love of political intrigue. Graced with knowledge and taste for literature and science, capable of being extended to the highest point of excellence, yet free from all pedantry, or pretension—with wit, conversational talents, and love of good society, without that desire of exhibition, that devouring diseased appetite for admiration, which preys upon the mind insatiably, to its torture—to its destruction; without that undefineable, untranslateable French love of succès de société, which substitutes a precarious; factitious, intoxicated existence in public, for the safe self-approbation, the sober, the permanent happiness of domestic life. In England Count Altenberg hoped to find a woman raised by "divine philosophy" [Footnote: Milton.] far above all illiberal prejudice, but preserving a just and becoming sense of religion; unobtrusive, mild, and yet firm. Every thing that he had seen of Caroline had confirmed his first hope, and exalted his future expectation; but, by what he had just heard, his imagination was checked in full career, suddenly, and painfully. His heavenly dream was disturbed by earthly voices—voices of malignant spirits—mysterious—indistinct—yet alarming. He had not conceived it possible that the breath of blame could approach such a character as Caroline's—he was struck with surprise, and shocked, on hearing her name profaned by common scandal, and spoken of as the victim of a disappointed passion, the scorn of one of the most distinguished families in England. Such were the first painful thoughts and feelings of Count Altenberg. At the time he heard the whispers which gave rise to them, he had been actually penning a letter to his father, declaring his attachment—he now resolved not to write. But he determined to satisfy himself as to the truth or falsehood of these reports. He was not a man to give ear lightly to calumny—he detested its baseness; he would not suffer himself for a moment to brood over suspicion, nor yet would he allow himself for present ease and pleasure to gloss over, without examination, that which might afterwards recur to his mind, and might create future unjust or unhappy jealousy. Either the object of his hopes was worthy of him, or not—if not worthy, better tear her from his heart for ever. This determined him to go immediately to Mrs. Hungerford's. Count Altenberg trusted to his own address and penetration for discovering all he wished to know, without betraying any peculiar interest in the subject.

The first sight of Mrs. Hungerford, the gracious dignity of her appearance and manners, the first five minutes' conversation he had with her, decided him in the opinion, that common report had done her justice; and raised in his mind extreme anxiety to know her opinion of Caroline. But, though he began the history of Zara, and of the play at Falconer-court, for the express purpose of introducing the Percys, in speaking of the company who had been present, yet, conscious of some unusual emotion when he was going to pronounce that name, and fancying some meaning in Mrs. Hungerford's great attention as he spoke, he mentioned almost every other guest, even the most insignificant, without speaking of Caroline, or of any of her family. He went back to his friend Colonel Hungerford. Mrs. Hungerford opened a letter-case, and took from it the last letter she had received from her son since he left England, containing some interesting particulars.—Towards the conclusion of the letter, the writing changed to a small feminine hand, and all India vanished from the view of Count Altenberg, for, as he turned the page, he saw the name of Caroline Percy: "I suppose I ought to stop here," said he, offering the letter to Mrs. Hungerford. "No," she replied, the whole letter was at his service—they were only a few lines from her daughter Lady Elizabeth.

These few lines mentioned Caroline Percy among the dear and intimate friends whom she regretted most in Europe, and to whom she sent a message expressive of the warmest affection and esteem. A glow of joy instantly diffused itself over his whole frame. As far as related to Colonel Hungerford, he was sure that all he had heard was false. There was little probability that his wife should, if those circumstances were true, be Caroline's most intimate friend. Before these thoughts had well arranged themselves in his head, a pleasing, sprightly young lady came into the room, who he at first thought was Mrs. Hungerford's daughter; but she was too young to answer exactly the description of Mrs. Mortimer.

"Lady Mary Pembroke, my niece," said Mrs. Hungerford.

Her ladyship was followed by Mr. Barclay—Count Altenberg seemed in a fair way to have all his doubts satisfied; but, in the hurry of his mind, he had almost forgotten to ask for Mrs. Mortimer.

"You will not see her to-day," said Mrs. Hungerford; "she is gone to see some friends, who live at distance too great for a morning visit. But I hope," continued Mrs. Hungerford, turning to Lady Mary, "that my daughter will make me amends for losing a day of her company, by bringing me our dear Caroline to-morrow."

"Is there a chance of Caroline's coming to us?" cried Lady Mary with affectionate eagerness.

"Is there any hope of our seeing Miss Caroline Percy?" said Mr. Barclay, with an air of respectful regard, very different from what must have been the feelings of a man who had trifled with a woman, or who had thought that she had trifled with him.

Count Altenberg rejoiced that he had come without a moment's delay to Hungerford Castle.

"You are really a good creature, my dear," continued Mrs. Hungerford to Lady Mary, "for being so anxious to have Caroline here—many a niece might be jealous of my affection, for certainly I love her as well as if she were my own child. To-morrow, sir," said she, turning to Count Altenberg, "I hope I shall have the pleasure to introduce you to this young friend of ours: I shall feel proud to show her to a foreigner, whom I wish to prepossess in favour of my countrywomen."

The Count said that he had already had the honour of being presented to Miss Caroline Percy—that he had seen her frequently at Falconer-court, and at her own home—and that he was not surprised at the interest which she excited at Hungerford Castle. Count Altenberg showed the interest she had excited in his own mind, whilst he pronounced, in the most sober manner in his power, those few words.

Mrs. Hungerford perceived it, nor had it escaped her observation, that he had forborne to mention the name of Percy when enumerating the persons he had met at Falconer-court. She was both too well bred in general, and too discreet on Caroline's account, to take any notice of this circumstance. She passed immediately and easily to a different subject of conversation.

The next day Mrs. Mortimer returned with Caroline. The Count saw the affection with which she was embraced by Mrs. Hungerford. The family had crowded to the door of the antechamber to receive her, so that Caroline, encompassed with friends, could not immediately see the Count, and he enjoyed these moments so exquisitely, that the idea which had previously engrossed all his soul, anxiety to see how she would look on meeting him thus unexpectedly, was absolutely forgotten. When the crowd opened, and Mrs. Hungerford led her forward, a smile of frank surprise and pleasure appeared on her countenance upon seeing Count Altenberg; but her colour had been previously so much raised, and so much pleasure had sparkled in her eyes, that there was no judging what share of emotion was to be attributed to this surprise. He was, and he had reason to be, satisfied with perceiving, that in the midst of the first pleasure of meeting intimate friends, and when she did not expect to meet any but friends, she was not chilled by the sight of one who was, to her, as yet but a new acquaintance.

After introducing Count Altenberg to Mrs. Mortimer, Mrs. Hungerford said, "Till I had my daughter and all my friends in full force about me, I prudently did not make any attempt, Count Altenberg, upon your liberty; but now that you see my resources, I trust you will surrender yourself, without difficulty, my prisoner, as long as we can possibly detain you in this castle."

Never was man less disposed to refuse an invitation than Count Altenberg at this moment. He wrote to Mrs. Falconer immediately that farewell note which had shocked Miss Georgiana so much.

As Lord Oldborough was preparing to return to town, and likely to be engrossed by ministerial business, his lordship, with less reluctance, relinquished his company; and the Count, with infinite satisfaction, found himself established at once upon a footing of intimacy at Hungerford Castle. The letter he had intended to write to his father was now written and sent; but it was expressed in yet stronger terms than he had originally designed—he concluded by conjuring his father, as he valued the happiness of his son, not to take a step in any of the treaties of marriage that had been planned for him, and besought him to write as soon as it was possible, to relieve his mind from suspense, and to set him at liberty to declare his attachment, if, upon further acquaintance with the English lady who had touched his heart, he should feel any hope of making such an impression on her affections as could induce her to make for him the great sacrifice of country, family, and friends. In the mean time, the hours and days passed on most happily at Hungerford Castle. Every succeeding day discovered to him some new excellence in the object of his affection. Mrs. Hungerford, with judicious, delicate kindness, forbore all attempts to display even those qualities and talents in Caroline which she most valued, certain that she might safely leave them to the discernment of her lover. That Count Altenberg loved, Mrs. Hungerford had too much penetration to doubt; and it rejoiced her heart, and satisfied all her hopes, to see a prospect of her young friend being united to such a man. Mrs. Mortimer felt as much joy and as much delicacy upon the subject as her mother showed.

In that near examination in domestic life, so dangerous to many women of the highest pretensions, Caroline shone superior. His love, approved by the whole strength of his reason, and exalted by the natural enthusiasm of his temper, was now at the highest. His impatience was extreme for the arrival of that answer to his letter, which he hoped would set him at liberty to declare his passion.

The letter at last arrived; very different were its contents from what he had hoped. A previous letter from his father to him, sent in a packet with government despatches by Mr. Cunningham Falconer, had not reached him. That letter, of which his father now sent him a copy, contained an account of the steps which had been taken, relative to a treaty of marriage between his son and the Countess Christina, a lady of high birth, beauty, and talents, who had lately appeared for the first time at that court. Count Altenberg's father described the countess as one who, he was sure, must charm his son; and as the alliance was eagerly desired by the lady's friends, and in every respect honourable for his whole family, the old Count was impatient to have the affair concluded. Receiving no answer to this letter, and pressed by circumstances, he had gone forward in his son's name with the treaty, and had pledged him so far, that there was now, he declared, no possibility of retracting with honour. He lamented that his son should, in the mean time, have taken a fancy to an English lady; but, as Count Albert's letter gave the assurance to his family that he would not take any decisive step till he should receive an answer, nothing could have been done in England that would commit his honour—absence would soon efface a transient impression—the advantages of the alliance proposed in his own country would appear stronger the more they should be examined—the charms of the Countess Christina, with her superior understanding, would have an irresistible effect; "and," concluded the old count, "I beseech you, my dear Albert, as your friend—I will say more—I command you as your father, return to your own country as soon as you can obtain passports after receiving this letter."

Count Altenberg would have left Hungerford Castle immediately, but he had still a lingering hope that his last letter to his father would produce a change in his mind, and for an answer to this he determined to wait; but a sudden change appeared in his manner: he was grave and absent; instead of seeking

Caroline's company and conversation as usual, he studiously avoided her; and when he did speak to her, his behaviour was so cold and reserved—so unlike his natural or his former manner, that the difference struck not only Caroline herself, but Rosamond and Mrs. Percy, who were, at this time, at Hungerford Castle. It happened that, on the very day, and nearly at the very hour, when Count Altenberg received this letter from his father, of which no one knew any thing but himself, there arrived at Hungerford Castle another of Mrs. Hungerford's nieces, a young lady of uncommon beauty, and of the most attractive and elegant manners, Lady Florence Pembroke. She was just returned from Italy with an uncle, who had resided there for some time. Count Altenberg, from the moment he was introduced to Lady Florence, devoted to her his whole attention—he sat beside her—whenever he conversed, his conversation was addressed to her; and the evident absence of mind he occasionally betrayed, and all the change in his manner, seemed to have been caused by her ladyship's appearance. Some sage philosophers know little more of cause and effect than that the one precedes the other; no wonder then that Rosamond, not famous for the accuracy of her reasoning, should, in this instance, be misled by appearances. To support her character for prudence, she determined not to seem to observe what passed, and not to mention her suspicions to her sister; who, as she remarked, was sensible of the count's altered manner; and who, as she rightly conjectured, did not perceive it with indifference. The accomplishments, good sense, and exalted sentiments of Count Altenberg, and the marked attentions he had paid her, had made an unusual impression on the mind of Caroline. He had never declared his love, but involuntarily it had betrayed itself on several occasions. Insensibly Caroline was thus led to feel for him more than she dared to avow even to herself, when the sudden change in his manner awakened her from this delightful forgetfulness of every object that was unconnected with her new feelings, and suddenly arrested her steps as she seemed entering the paradise of love and hope.

At night, when they were retiring to rest, and Caroline and Rosamond were in their mother's room, Rosamond, unable longer to keep her prudent silence, gave vent to her indignation against Count Altenberg in general reflections upon the fickleness of man. Even men of the best understanding were, she said, but children of a larger growth—pleased with change—preferring always the newest to the fairest, or the best. Caroline did not accede to these accusations.

Rosamond, astonished and provoked, exclaimed, "Is it possible that you are so blind as not to see that Count Altenberg—" Rosamond stopped short, for she saw Caroline's colour change. She stood beside her mother motionless, and with her eyes fixed on the ground. Rosamond moved a chair towards her.

"Sit down, my dear love," said her mother, tenderly taking Caroline's hand—"sit down and compose yourself."

"My dear mother, you required one, and but one promise from me—I gave it you, firmly intending to keep it; and yet I fear that you will think I have broken it. I promised to tell you whenever I felt the first symptom of preference for any person. I did not know my own mind till this day. Indeed I thought I felt nothing but what every body else expressed, esteem and admiration."

"In common minds," replied Mrs. Percy, "esteem and admiration may be very safely distant from love; but in such a mind as yours, Caroline, the step from perfect esteem to love is dangerously near—scarcely perceptible."

"Why dangerously?" cried Rosamond: "why should not perfect love follow perfect esteem? that is the very thing I desire for Caroline. I am sure he is attached to her, and he is all we could wish for her, and—"

"Stop!" cried Caroline. "Oh! my dear sister! as you wish me to be good and happy, name him to me no more—for it cannot be."

"Why?" exclaimed Rosamond, with a look of dismay: "Why cannot it be? It can, it must—it shall be."

Caroline sighed, and turning from her sister, as if she dreaded to listen to her, she repeated, "No;—I will not flatter myself—I see that it cannot be—I have observed the change in his manner. The pain it gave me first awakened me to the state of my own affections. I have given you some proof of sincerity by speaking thus immediately of the impression made on my mind. You will acknowledge the effort was difficult.—Mother, will you answer me one question—which I am afraid to ask—did you, or do you think that any body else perceived my sentiments by my manner?" Caroline paused, and her mother and sister set her heart at ease on that point.

"After all," said Rosamond, addressing herself to her mother, "I may be mistaken in what I hinted about Count Altenberg. I own I thought the change in his manner arose from Lady Florence Pembroke—I am sorry I said any thing of it—I dare say when he sees more of her—she is very pretty, very pleasing, very elegant, and amiable, no doubt; but surely, in comparison with Caroline—but I am not certain that there is any rivalship in the case."

"I am certain that there shall be none," said Caroline. "How extraordinary it is that the best, the noblest, the most delightful feelings of the heart, may lead to the meanest, the most odious! I have, within a few hours, felt enough to be aware of this. I will leave nothing to chance. A woman should never expose herself to any hazard. I will preserve my peace of mind, my own esteem. I will preserve my dear and excellent friends; and that I may preserve some of them, I am sensible that I must now quit them."

Mrs. Percy was going to speak, but Rosamond interposed.

"Oh! what have I done!" exclaimed she: "imprudent creature that I was, why did I speak? why did I open your eyes, Caroline? I had resolved not to say a single word of the change I perceived in the Count."

"And did you think I should not perceive it?" said Caroline. "Oh, you little know how quickly—the first look—the first tone of his voice—But of that I will think no more. Only let me assure you, that you, my dear Rosamond, did no harm—it was not what any body said that alarmed me: before you pointed it out, I had felt that change in his manner, for which I cannot account."

"You cannot account?—Can you doubt that Lady Florence is the cause?" said Rosamond.

"Yes, I have great doubts," said Caroline.

"So have I," said Mrs. Percy.

"I cannot believe," said Caroline, "that a man of his sense and character would be so suddenly captivated: I do not mean to detract from Lady Florence's merits, but before they could make the impression you suspect on Count Altenberg, there must have been time for them to be known and appreciated. Shall I go on, and tell you all that has passed in my mind? Yes, my mother and sister should see me as I am—perhaps under the delusion of vanity—or self-love—or—But if I am wrong, you will set me right—you will help me to set myself right: it has never been declared in words, therefore perhaps I am vain and presumptuous to believe or to imagine—yet I do feel persuaded that I am preferred—that I am—"

"Loved! Oh, yes!" said Rosamond, "a thousand times I have thought so, I have felt certain, that Count Altenberg loved you; but now I am convinced, alas! of my mistake—convinced at least that his love is of that light, changeable sort, which is not worth having—not worth your having."

"That last," cried Caroline, "I can never believe." She stopped, and blushed deeply. "What does my mother say?" added she, in a timid voice.

"My mother, I am sure, thought once that he loved Caroline—did not you, mother?" said Rosamond.

"Yes, my dear," answered Mrs. Percy, "I have thought so, and I am not yet convinced that we were mistaken; but I entirely agree with Caroline that this is a subject upon which we ought not to let our thoughts dwell."

"Oh! so I have thought, so I have said on former occasions, how often, how sincerely!" said Caroline. "But this is the first time I ever felt it difficult to practise what I know to be wise and right. Mother, I beg it as a favour that you will take me away from this place—this place, where but yesterday I thought myself so happy!"

"But why, Caroline—why, mother, should she do this?" expostulated Rosamond. "If she thinks, if you think that he loves her, if you do not believe that he has changed, if you do not believe that he is struck with a new face, why should Caroline go? For Heaven's sake do not take her away till you are sure that it is necessary."

"I will be guided by her opinion," said Mrs. Percy; "I can depend entirely on her own prudence."

"Indeed, I think it will be most prudent that I should not indulge myself in staying longer," said Caroline. "From what I have seen of Count Altenberg, we have reason to think that he acts in general from wise and good motives. We should therefore believe that in the present instance his motives are good and adequate—I cannot suspect that he acts from caprice: what the nature of the obstacle may be, I can only guess; but I am inclined to think that some opposing duty—"

"His duty," said Rosamond, "I suppose he must have known before to-day. What new duty can he have discovered? No, no; men are not so very apt in love matters to think of opposing duties as women do: much more likely that he has heard something to your disadvantage, Caroline, from the Falconers. I can tell you that Lady Frances Arlington gave me a hint that strange things had been said, and great pains taken to misrepresent you to the count."

"If injurious representations have been made of me to him," replied Caroline, "he will in time discover the falsehood of such report; or, if he believe them without examination, he is not what I imagine him to be. No; I am convinced he has too noble a mind, too just an understanding, to be misled by calumny."

Mrs. Percy declared she was decidedly of this opinion. "The obstacle, whatever it may be, my dear mother," continued Caroline, with the earnest tone and expression of countenance of a person of strong mind, at once feeling and thinking deeply, "the difficulty, whatever it is, must be either such as time will obviate or increase; the obstacle must be either conquerable or unconquerable: if he love me, as I thought he did, if he have the energy of character I think he possesses, he will conquer it, if it can be conquered; if it be unconquerable, what misery, what madness, to suffer my affections to be irrevocably engaged! or what base vanity to wish, if it were in my power, to inspire him with an unhappy passion! Then, in every point of view, mother, surely it is best that I should leave this—dangerous place," said Caroline, smiling. "Yet you are both so happy here, I am sorry to be the cause."

"My love," said her mother, "to us all things are trifles, compared with what it is right and becoming that you should do. I entirely approve and applaud your prudence and resolution: what you desire shall be done as soon as possible. We will go home to-morrow morning."

"But, my dear ma'am! so suddenly! consider," cried Rosamond, "how very strange this will appear to Mrs. Hungerford, and to every body!"

"My dear Rosamond, these are some of the small difficulties, the false delicacies, which so often prevent people from doing what is right, or what is essentially necessary for the security of the peace and happiness of their whole lives," said Mrs. Percy.

"That is true," replied Rosamond; "and I do not object to doing the thing, but I only wish we had some good, decent excuse for running away: you don't expect that Mrs. Hungerford will part with you without remonstrance, without struggle, without even inquiring, why you must run away? I am sure I hope she will not ask me, for I am not prepared with an answer, and my face would never do, and would give way at the first glance of her penetrating eye—what will you say to Mrs. Hungerford?"

"The truth," replied Caroline. "Mrs. Hungerford has ever treated me with so much kindness, has shown me so much affection and esteem, feels such a warm interest in all that concerns me, and is herself of so noble a character, that she commands my entire confidence—and she shall have it without reserve. Since my mother agrees with me in thinking that Lady Florence has not been in any degree the cause of the change of manner we have observed, there can be no impropriety on that account in our speaking of the subject to Mrs. Hungerford. It may be painful, humiliating—but what is meant by confidence, by openness towards our friends?—We are all of us ready enough to confess our virtues," said she, smiling; "but our weaknesses, what humbles our pride to acknowledge, we are apt to find some delicate reason for keeping secret. Mother, if you do not disapprove of it, I wish you to tell Mrs. Hungerford the whole truth."

Mrs. Percy entirely approved of Caroline's placing confidence in this excellent friend. She observed, that this was very different from the girlish gossiping sort of confidences, which are made often from one young lady to another, merely from the want of something to say, or the pleasure of prattling about love, or the hope of being encouraged by some weak young friend, to indulge some foolish passion.

The next morning, before Mrs. Hungerford had left her apartment, Mrs. Percy went to her, and explained the reasons which induced Caroline to refuse herself the pleasure of prolonging her visit at Hungerford Castle.

Mrs. Hungerford was touched by the confidence which Caroline placed in her. "Believe me," said she, "it is not misplaced—I feel all its value. And must I lose her? I never parted with her without regret, and that regret increases the more I see of her. I almost forget that she is not my own, till I am called upon to relinquish her: but much as I value her, much as I enjoy her society, I cannot be so selfish as to wish to detain her when her peace of mind is at stake. How few, how very few are there, of all the various young women I know, who would have the good sense and resolution, I will say it, the integrity of mind, to act as she does! There is usually some sentimental casuistry, some cowardly fear, or lingering hope, that prevents young people in these circumstances from doing the plain right thing—any thing but the plain right thing they are ready to do—and there is always some delicate reason for not telling the truth, especially to their friends; but our daughters, Mrs. Percy, are above these things." With respect to Count Altenberg, Mrs. Hungerford said, that, from many observations she had made, she felt no doubt of his being strongly attached to Caroline. "Their characters, their understandings, are suited to each other; they have the same high views, the same magnanimity. With one exception—you must allow a mother's partiality to make an exception in favour of her own son—with one exception Count Altenberg is the man of all others to whom I could wish to see Caroline united. I never till yesterday doubted that it would be; but I was as much struck with the change in his manner as you have been. I agree with Caroline, that some obstacle, probably of duty, has arisen, and I hope—but no, I will imitate her example, and as you tell me she forbids herself to hope, so will I—if possible. At all events she raises herself, high as she was in my esteem, still higher by her present conduct. Tell her so, my dear Mrs. Percy—you, her mother, may give this praise, without hurting her delicacy; and tell her that, old as I am, I have not forgotten so completely the feelings of my youth, as not to be aware that suspense in some situations is the worst of evils. She may be assured that my attention shall be as much awake as even her mother's could be—and when any thing that I think important or decisive occurs, she shall hear from me immediately, or see me, unless I should lose the use of my limbs, or my faculties."

A messenger came to summon Mrs. Hungerford to breakfast—soon afterwards a ride was proposed by Mrs. Mortimer. Count Altenberg was to be one of this party, and he looked for a moment surprised and disappointed, when he found that Caroline was not going with them; but he forebore to ask why she did not ride, and endeavoured to occupy himself solely in helping Mrs. Mortimer to mount her horse—Rosamond was glad to perceive that he did not well know what he was doing.

Before they returned from their ride, the Percys were on their way to the Hills. Till this moment the sight of home, even after a short absence, had, on returning to it, always been delightful to Caroline; but now, for the first time in her life, every object seemed to have lost its brightness. In the stillness of retirement, which she used to love, she felt something sad and lifeless. The favourite glade, which formerly she thought the very spot so beautifully described by Dryden, as the scene of his "Flower and the Leaf," even this she found had lost its charm. New to love, Caroline was not till now aware, that it throws a radiance upon every object, which, when passed away, seems to leave all nature changed.

To banish recollections which she knew that she ought not to indulge, she employed herself unremittingly. But her mind did not turn with its wonted energy to her occupations, nor was it acted upon by those small motives of ordinary life, by which it had formerly been excited. When reading, her thoughts would wander even from her favourite authors: every subject they discussed would remind her of some conversation that had passed at Hungerford Castle; some coincidence or difference of opinion would lead her to digress; some observation more just or more striking; some better expression, or some expression which pleased her better than the author's, would occur, and the book was laid down. These digressions of fancy were yet more frequent when she was endeavouring to fix her attention to drawing, needle-work, or to any other sedentary employment. Exercise she found useful. She spent more time than usual in planting and in gardening—a simple remedy; but practical philosophy frequently finds those simple remedies the best which Providence has put within the reach of all.

One morning, soon after her return home, when she was alone and busy in her garden, she heard voices at a distance; as they approached nearer, she thought she distinguished Mrs. Hungerford's. She listened, and looked towards the path whence the voices had come. All was silent—but a minute afterwards, she saw Mrs. Hungerford coming through the narrow path in the thicket: Caroline at first sprang forward to meet her, then stopped short, her heart beating violently—she thought that, perhaps, Mrs. Hungerford was accompanied by Count Altenberg; but she was alone. Ashamed of the hope which had glanced across her mind, and of the sudden stop which had betrayed her thoughts, Caroline now went forward, blushing.

Mrs. Hungerford embraced her with tenderness, and then assuming a cheerful tone, "Your mother and sister wanted to persuade me," said she, "that I should never find my way to you—but I insisted upon it that I could. Had I not the instinct of a true friend to guide me?—So now let me sit down and rest myself on this pretty seat—a very comfortable throne!—and that is saying much for a throne. So these are your territories?" continued she, looking round, and talking with an air of playfulness, to give Caroline time to recover herself.

"Why did you never invite me to your garden?—Perhaps, you think me a mere fire-side, arm-chair old woman, dead to all the beauties of nature; but I can assure you that I have, all my life, from principle, cultivated this taste, which I think peculiarly suited to women, salutary not only to their health, but to their happiness and their virtues—their domestic virtues, increasing the interest they take in their homes, heightening those feelings of associated pleasure which extend from persons to places, and which are at once a proof of the strength of early attachments and a security for their continuance to the latest period of life. Our friend, Count Altenberg, was observing to me the other day that we Englishwomen, among our other advantages, from our modes of life, from our spending so many months of the year in the country, have more opportunity of forming and indulging these tastes than is usual among foreign ladies in the same rank of life. Fortunately for us, we are not like Mr. Clay's French countess, or duchess, who declared that she hated innocent pleasures."

After mentioning French Clay, Mrs. Hungerford passed to a comparison between him and Count Altenberg. She had met Mr. Clay in town, and disliked him. "He is an Englishman only by birth, and a Frenchman only by affectation; Count Altenberg, on the contrary, a foreigner by birth, has all the tastes and principles that make him worthy to be an Englishman. I am convinced that, if he had liberty of choice, he would prefer residing in England to living in any country in the world. Indeed, he expressed that sentiment at parting from us yesterday."

"He is gone then," said Caroline.

"He is, my love."

Caroline wished to ask where? and whether he was gone for ever? Yet she continued silent—and became extremely pale.

Mrs. Hungerford, without appearing to take any notice of her emotion, continued, and answered all the questions which she wished to ask.

"He is gone back to Germany to his own court—recalled, as he told me, by some imperious duty."

Caroline revived.

"So far you see, my dear, we were right, as those usually are who judge from general principles. It was not, indeed, to be credited," continued Mrs. Hungerford, "that a man of his character and understanding should act merely from caprice. What the nature of the duty may be, whether relating to his duty as a public or a private man, he did not explain—the latter, I fear: I apprehend some engagement, that will prevent his return to England. In this case he has done most honourably, at whatever risk or pain to himself, to avoid any attempt to engage your affections, my dear; and you have, in these trying circumstances, acted as becomes your sex and yourself."

"I hope so," said Caroline, timidly: "my mother and Rosamond endeavoured to re-assure me on one point—you have seen more since, and must therefore be better able to judge—Count Altenberg has none of that presumption of manner which puts a woman upon her guard against his inferences. But, in secret, do you think he ever suspected—"

"I cannot, my love, tell what passes in the secret recesses of man's heart—much more difficult to penetrate than woman's," replied Mrs. Hungerford, smiling. "But let this satisfy you—by no word, hint, or look, could I ever guess that he had formed such a hope. Of your whole family he spoke in terms of the highest regard. Of you he dared not trust himself to say much; but the little he did venture to say was expressive of the highest respect and esteem: more he did not, and ought not, I am convinced, to have allowed himself."

"I am satisfied—quite satisfied," said Caroline, relieving her heart by a deep sigh; "and I thank you, my kind Mrs. Hungerford. You have put this subject at rest for ever in my mind. If Count Altenberg can love me with honour, he will; if he cannot, Heaven forbid I should wish it!"

From this time forward Caroline never spoke more upon the subject, never mentioned the name of Count Altenberg. She exerted all the strong command she possessed over herself to conquer the languor and indolence to which she had found herself disposed.

It is a difficult task to restore what may be called the tone of the mind, to recover the power of being acted upon by common and every day motives, after sensibility has been unusually excited. Where the affections have been deeply and long engaged, this is a task which the most severe philosophy cannot accomplish without the aid of time—and of that superior power which it would be irreverent here to name.

By using no concealment with her friends, by permitting no self-delusion, by having the courage to confess the first symptom of partiality of which she was conscious, Caroline put it out of her own power to nourish a preference into a passion which must ultimately have made herself and her friends unhappy. Besides the advantages which she derived from her literary tastes, and her habits of varying her occupations, she at this time found great resources in her warm and affectionate attachment to her own family.

She had never yet arrived at that state of egoisme, which marks the height of passion, when all interests and affections sink and vanish before one exclusive and tyrant sentiment.

CHAPTER XXX

When Count Altenberg went to London to obtain his passports, he went to pay his parting respects to Lord Oldborough, whose talents and uncommon character had made an indelible impression on his mind.

When he asked whether his lordship had any commands that he could execute at his own court, he was surprised by receiving at once a commission of a difficult and delicate nature. Lord Oldborough, whose penetration had seen into Count Altenberg's character, and who knew how and when to trust, though he was supposed to be the most reserved of men, confided to the Count his dissatisfaction with the proceedings of Cunningham Falconer; his suspicions that the envoy was playing double, and endeavouring to ingratiate himself abroad and at home with a party inimical to his lordship's interests.

"Diplomatists are all, more or less, insincere," said Lord Oldborough. "But to have chosen an envoy who joins ingratitude to duplicity would reflect no credit upon the minister by whom he was appointed. Were I speaking to a common person, I should not admit the possibility of my having committed such an error. But Count Altenberg will judge by the whole and not by a part. He knows that every man in power is sometimes the slave of circumstances. This Cunningham Falconer—all these Falconers were forced upon me—how, it is of little consequence to you to hear. It is sufficient for me to assure you, Count, that it was not my judgment that erred. Now the necessity has ceased. By other means my purpose has been accomplished. The Falconers are useless to me. But I will not abandon those whom I have undertaken to protect, till I have proof of their perfidy."

Lord Oldborough then explained the points on which he desired to inform himself before he should decide with regard to Cunningham. Count Altenberg undertook to procure for his lordship the means of ascertaining the fidelity of his envoy; and Lord Oldborough then turned the conversation on general politics. He soon perceived that the Count was not as much interested in these subjects as formerly. At parting, Lord Oldborough smiled, and said, "You have been, since I saw you last, Count Altenberg, too much in the company of a philosopher, who prefers the happiness of a country gentleman's life to the glory of a statesman's career. But height will soon recall high thoughts. Ambition is not dead, only dormant within you. It will, I hope and trust, make you in time the minister and pride of your country. In this hope I bid you farewell."

Commissioner Falconer having been told, by one of the people in the antechamber, that Count Altenberg had arrived, and was now with the minister, waited anxiously to see him, caught him in his way out, and eagerly pressed an invitation from Mrs. Falconer to dine or spend the evening with them—but the Count had now his passports, and pleaded the absolute necessity for his immediately setting out on his return to his own country. The commissioner, from a word or two that he hazarded upon the subject, had the vexation to perceive that his hopes of engaging Count Altenberg to assist the views of his son Cunningham were vain, and he regretted that he had wasted so much civility upon a foreigner who would make him no return.

Miss Georgiana Falconer's mortification at the Count's leaving England was much alleviated by finding that he had not been detained by the charms of Miss Caroline Percy, and she was almost consoled for losing the prize herself, by seeing that it had not been won by her rival. Mrs. Falconer, too, though she had long abandoned all hopes of the Count as a son-in-law, yet rejoiced to be spared the humiliation of writing to congratulate Mr. and Mrs. Percy upon the marriage and splendid establishment of their daughter.

"After all, how ill they have managed!" said Mrs. Falconer; "the game was in their own hands. Certainly Mrs. Percy must be the worst mother in the world, and the daughter, with all her sense, a perfect simpleton, or they might have made up the match when they had the Count to themselves at Hungerford Castle."

"I told you long ago, but you would never believe, Mrs. Falconer," cried the commissioner, "that Count Altenberg's ruling passion was ambition, and that he was not the least likely to fall in love, as you ladies call it. The old Prince of — is going fast, and Count Altenberg's father has sent for him, that he may be on the spot to secure his favour with the hereditary prince—I am sure I hope Count Altenberg will not be minister; for from the few words he said to me just now when I met him, he will not enter into my views with regard to Cunningham."

"No, those political visions of yours, commissioner, seldom end in any thing but disappointment," said Mrs. Falconer. "I always said it would be so."

Then followed a scene of recrimination, such as was the usual consequence of the failure of any of the plans of this intriguing pair.

"And, Mrs. Falconer," concluded the commissioner, "I augur as ill of your present scheme for Georgiana as I did of the last. You will find that all your dinners and concerts will be just as much thrown away upon the two Clays as your balls and plays were upon Count Altenberg. And this is the way, ma'am, you go on plunging me deeper and deeper in debt," said the commissioner, walking about the room much disturbed, "If any thing was to go wrong with Lord Oldborough, what would become of us!"

"My dear, that is a very unseasonable apprehension; for Lord Oldborough, as I hear on all sides, is firmer in power now than he ever was—of that, you know, you were but yesterday giving me assurance and proof. His favour, you know, is so high, that all who were leagued against him in that combination he detected, were, in consequence of his lordship's letter, instantly dismissed from office: his colleagues are now of his choosing—the cabinet, I understand, completely his own friends. What more security can you desire?"

"You don't understand me, Mrs. Falconer: I am not thinking of the security of Lord Oldborough's power—of that, after all I have seen, I can have no doubt; but I am not so sure of—"

"The continuance of my own favour," he was going to say, but it was painful to him to utter the words, and he had a superstitious dread, common to courtiers, of speaking of their decline of favour, Besides, he knew that reproaches for want of address in managing Lord Oldborough's humour would immediately follow from Mrs. Falconer, if he gave any hint of this kind; and on his address the commissioner piqued himself, not without reason. Abruptly changing his tone, and taking that air of authority which every now and then he thought fit to assume, he said, "Mrs. Falconer, there's one thing I won't allow—I won't allow Georgiana and you to make a fool of young Petcalf."

"By no means, my love; but if he makes a fool of himself, you know?"

"Mrs. Falconer, you recollect the transaction about the draught."

"For Zara's dress?"

"Yes, ma'am. The condition you made then in my name with Georgiana I hold her to, and I expect that she be prepared to be Mrs. Petcalf within the year."

"I told her so, my dear, and she acquiesces—she submits—she is ready to obey—if nothing better offers."

"If—Ay, there it is!—All the time I know you are looking to the Clays; and if they fail, somebody else will start up, whom you will think a better match than Petcalf, and all these people are to be fêted, and so you will go on, wasting my money and your own time. Petcalf will run restive at last, you will lose him, and I shall have Georgiana left upon my hands after all."

"No danger, my dear. My principle is the most satisfactory and secure imaginable. To have a number of tickets in the wheel—then, if one comes up a blank, still you have a chance of a prize in the next. Only have patience, Mr. Falconer."

"Patience! my dear: how can a man have patience, when he has seen the same thing going on for years? And I have said the same thing to you over and over a hundred times, Mrs. Falconer."

"A hundred times at least, I grant, and that, perhaps, is enough to try my patience you'll allow, and yet, you see how reasonable I am. I have only to repeat what is incontrovertible, that when a girl has been brought up, and has lived in a certain line, you must push her in that line, for she will not do in any other. You must be sensible that no mere country gentleman would ever think of Georgiana—we must push her in the line for which she is fit—the fashionable line."

"Push! Bless my soul, ma'am! you have been pushing one or other of those girls ever since they were in their teens, but your pushing signifies nothing. The men, don't you see, back as fast as the women advance?"

"Coarse!—Too coarse an observation for you, commissioner!" said Mrs. Falconer, with admirable temper; "but when men are angry they will say more than they think."

"Ma'am, I don't say half as much as I think—ever."

"Indeed!—That is a candid confession, for which I owe you credit, at all events."

"It's a foolish game—it's a foolish game—it's a losing game," continued the commissioner; "and you will play it till we are ruined."

"Not a losing game if it be played with temper and spirit. Many throw up the game like cowards, when, if they had but had courage to double the bet, they would have made their fortune."

"Pshaw! Pshaw!" said the commissioner: "Can you double your girls' beauty? can you double their fortune?"

"Fashion stands in the place both of beauty and fortune, Mr. Falconer; and fashion, my girls, I hope you will allow, enjoy."

"Enjoy! What signifies that? Fashion, you told me, was to win Count Altenberg—has it won him? Are we one bit the better for the expense we were at in all those entertainments?"

"All that, or most of it—at least the popularity-ball—must be set down to Lord Oldborough's account; and that is your affair, commissioner."

"And the play, and the play-house, and the dresses! Was Zara's dress my affair? Did I not tell you, you were wasting your time upon that man?"

"No waste, nothing has been wasted, my dear commissioner; believe me, even in point of economy we could not have laid out money better; for at a trifling expense we have obtained for Georgiana the credit of having refused Count Altenberg. Lady Kew and Lady Trant have spread the report. You know it is not my business to speak—and now the Count is gone, who can contradict it with any propriety?—The thing is universally believed. Every body is talking of it, and the consequence is, Georgiana is more in fashion now than ever she was. There's a proposal I had for her this morning," said Mrs. Falconer, throwing a letter carelessly before the commissioner.

"A proposal! That is something worth attending to," said the commissioner, putting on his spectacles.

"No, nothing worth our attention," said Mrs. Falconer, "only eighteen hundred a year, which, you know, Georgiana could not possibly live upon."

"Better than nothing, surely," said the commissioner; "let me see."

"Not better than Petcalf, not within a thousand a year so good, putting Asia Minor out of the question. So, you know, I could not hesitate an instant."

"But I hope your answer was very civil. People are not aware what dangerous enemies they make on these occasions," said Mr. Falconer: "I hope your answer was very polite."

"Oh! the pink of courtesy," said Mrs. Falconer. "I lamented that my daughter's fortune was so small as to put it out of her power, &c., and I added a great deal about merit, and the honour done our family, and so on. But I wonder the man had the assurance to propose for Georgiana, when he had nothing better to say for himself."

"Petcalf, to be sure, if the general dies, is a thousand a year better. I believe you are right there," said Mr. Falconer; and with an air of calculating consideration, he took up a pen.

"But what are you about, commissioner? going to write on that letter, as if it were waste paper!" said Mrs. Falconer, starting up, and taking it hastily from him: "I must have it for Lady Trant, Lady Kew, and some more of our intimate friends, that they may be able to say they have seen the proposal; for mothers and daughters too, in these days, are so apt to boast, that it is quite necessary to have some written document to produce, and there's no going beyond that."

"Certainly—quite necessary. And what written document," said the commissioner, smiling, "have you to produce in the case of Count Altenberg?"

"Oh! that is another affair," said Mrs. Falconer, smiling in her turn. "One must not in all cases have recourse to the same expedients. Besides, if we produce our proofs on one occasion, we shall depend upon having our word taken on trust another time; and it would be too much to make a practice of showing gentlemen's letters: it is not what I should always do—certainly not with regard to a man of Count Altenberg's rank and pretensions, who merits to be treated with somewhat more consideration, surely, than a man who hazards such a proposal as this. I merely produced it to show you that Georgiana is in no absolute distress for admirers. And now, my dear, I must trouble you—those public singers are terribly expensive; yet at a concert we must have them, and one cannot have them without coming up to their price—I must trouble you to sign this draft, for our concert last week."

"Now, Mrs. Falconer, I have signed it," cried the commissioner, "and it is the last, for a similar purpose, I ever will sign—upon my honour."

"I have invited every body to a concert here next week," said Mrs. Falconer: "What can I do?"

"Do as others do," said the commissioner; "let these musical professors give a concert at your house: then, instead of paying them, you share their profits, and you have the best company at your house into the bargain."

"Such things are done, I know," said Mrs. Falconer, "and by people of rank; but Lady Jane Granville would not do it, when she was more distressed for money than we are, and I know many say it is what they would not do."

"It must be done by you, Mrs. Falconer, or you must give up having concerts altogether," said the commissioner, leaving the room.

To give up concerts was quite impossible, especially as French Clay was, or pretended to be, passionately fond of music, and it was at her musical parties that he never failed to attend assiduously. The next concert was given by a celebrated performer at Mrs. Falconer's house, and she and the singers shared the profit. To such meanness can the slaves of fashion condescend!

At this concert it happened that there was a new and remarkably handsome, graceful, female Italian singer, who was much admired by all the gentlemen present, and particularly by French Clay, who had set up, with little ear, and less taste, for a great judge of music. He was ambitious of appearing as the patron of this young performer. He went about every where talking of her in raptures, and making interest for her with all the great people of his acquaintance. Her own voice and her own charms needed not the protection of Mr. Clay; from the night she was first produced at Mrs. Falconer's, she became at once the height of the fashion. Every body was eager to have her at their parties, especially as she had never yet been upon the stage. Admirers crowded round her, and among them were many of rank and fortune: an old earl and a young baronet were of the number. The ardour of competition so much increased the zeal of French Clay, that what was at first only affectation, became real enthusiasm. He was resolved to win the lady from all his rivals. He had frequent opportunities of seeing her at Mrs. Falconer's, where he appeared always in glory as her patron.

Seraphina, the fair Italian, considering Mrs. Falconer as her first patroness, made it a point of gratitude to hold her concerts frequently at her house. Mrs. Falconer was proud of the distinction. Fresh éclat was thrown upon her and upon her daughters.

French Clay was always near Miss Georgiana Falconer, or near Seraphina; and he applauded each by turns with all the raptures of an amateur. Mrs. Falconer saw that rivalship with the old earl and the young baronet had worked Mr. Clay into a passion for Seraphina; but she thought she knew how a passion for a singer must end, and as this did not interfere with her matrimonial designs, it gave her little uneasiness. Bets ran high in the fashionable world upon the three candidates. Mrs. Falconer had no doubt that the old earl would carry off the prize, as he was extremely rich, and was ready to make any settlement and any establishment. Her prophecy would, probably, have been accomplished, but that French Clay, strongly urged by the immediate danger of losing the lady, and flattered by Seraphina's mother, who, in another style of life, was equal to Mrs. Falconer in address and knowledge of the world, was drawn in to offer what alone could balance the charms of the baronet's youth and of the earl's wealth—a week after the offer was made, Seraphina became Mrs. French Clay. Upon this marriage Commissioner Falconer hastened immediately to reproach his wife.

"There! Mrs. Falconer, I told you it would never do—There is another son-in-law who has escaped you!"

Never did Mrs. Falconer's genius appear so great as in circumstances which would have confounded one of inferior resource. It is true, she had been thrown into surprise and consternation by the first news of this marriage; but by an able stroke she had turned defeat into victory. With a calm air of triumph she replied to her husband, "I beg your pardon, Mr. Falconer,—French Clay was only my ostensible object: I should have been very sorry to have had him for my son-in-law; for, though it is a secret, I know that he is overwhelmed with debt. The son-in-law I really wished for has not escaped me, sir—the elder brother, English Clay—Clay, of Clay-hall, I apprehend, you will allow, is rather a better match for your daughter; and his proposal for Georgiana, his relation, Lady Trant, was last night authorized to make to me in form. And now, commissioner, there is an end of your fears that your daughter should be left, at last, upon your hands; and now, I flatter myself, you will acknowledge that I always knew what I was about— mistress of Clay-hall, and of seven thousand a year—I think that is doing pretty well for a girl who has nothing."

The commissioner was so much delighted, that he willingly permitted his lady to enjoy her triumph over him.

"Now only consider, commissioner," she pursued, "if I had huddled up that match with Petcalf!—Petcalf, I'll answer for it, in case of necessity, that is, in case of any difficulty on the part of Sir Robert Percy, I can turn over to Bell. Poor Petcalf!" added she, with a smile: "I really have a regard for that ever-lasting partner, and wish to leave him a chance of being partner for life to one of my daughters. I am sure he has reason to be excessively obliged to me for thinking of him at this moment—I must go to Georgiana and talk about wedding-clothes, laces, jewels, equipages—Mr. Clay, of Clay-hall, piques himself upon having every thing the best of its kind, and in the highest style—Happy—happy girl!"

"Happy—happy father, who has got her off his hands!" cried the commissioner.

"'Twas my doing—'twas all my doing!" said Mrs. Falconer.

"It was, my dear; and how was it brought about?" said Mr. Falconer: "stay one minute from the wedding-clothes, and tell me."

Mrs. Falconer returned, and in the pride of successful intrigue explained all—that is, all she chose her husband to know.

Lady Trant was Mr. Clay's near relation, and Mrs. Falconer's intimate friend—how she had engaged her ladyship so zealously in her cause was the point which Mrs. Falconer did not choose to explain, and into which the commissioner never thought of inquiring. There are moments in which the most selfish may be betrayed into a belief that others act from generous motives; and the very principles which they hold infallible applied to all other cases, they think admit in their own of an exception: so Commissioner Falconer, notwithstanding his knowledge of the world, and his knowledge of himself, took it for granted, that, in this instance, Lady Trant acted from the impulse of disinterested friendship. This point happily admitted without question, all the rest Mrs. Falconer could satisfactorily explain. Lady Trant being a friend she could trust entirely, Mrs. Falconer had opened her mind to her ladyship, and, by her suggestion, Lady Trant had seized the happy moment when English Clay was enraged against his brother for his strange marriage, and had deplored that Clay-hall, and the fine estate belonging to it, should go to the children of an Italian singer: English Clay took fresh fire at this idea, and swore that, much as he hated the notion of a wife and children, he had a great mind to marry on purpose to punish his brother, and to cut him off, as he deserved, for ever from Clay-hall. Lady Trant commended his spirit, and urged him to put his resolution into execution—English Clay, however, balked a little at this: women now-a-days, he said, were so cursed expensive, that scarce any fortune could suffice for a wife, and horses, and all in style; and as to taking a wife, who would not be of a piece with the rest of his establishment, that was what he was not the man to do. Lady Trant answered, that of course he would wish to have a fashionable wife; that was the only thing that was wanting to make Clay-hall complete.

"But then an establishment that was quite correct, and in the first style for a bachelor, would be quite incorrect for a married man, and every thing to do over again."

"True; but then to grow into an old bachelor, and to hear every body saying, or to know that every body is saying, behind your back, 'He will never marry, you know; and all his estate will go to his brother, or the children of Seraphina, the singer.'"

There are some men who might feel tired of having the same idea repeated, and the self-same words reiterated; but English Clay was not of the number: on the contrary, repetition was necessary, in the first place, to give his mind time to take in an idea; and afterwards, reiteration was agreeable, as it impressed him with a sense of conviction without the trouble of thought. After Lady Trant had reiterated a sufficient time, he assented, and declared what her ladyship observed was d—d true; but after a silence of several minutes, he added, "There's such a cursed deal of danger of being taken in by a woman, especially by one of those fashionable girls, who are all in the catch-match line." Lady Trant, who had been well tutored and prepared with replies by Mrs. Falconer, answered that as Mr. Clay, of Clay-hall, had a fortune that entitled him to ask any woman, so he was, for the same reason, at full liberty to please himself; and though family connexion and fashion would of course be indispensable to him, yet money could be no object to a man of his fortune—he was not like many needy young men, obliged to sell themselves for a wife's fortune, to pay old debts: no, Lady Trant said, she was sure her relation and friend, Mr. Clay, of Clay-hall, would never bargain for a wife, and, of course, where there was no bargaining there could be no fear of being taken in.

English Clay had never considered the matter in this view before; but now it was pointed out, he confessed it struck him as very fair—very fair: and his pride, of which he had a comfortable portion, being now touched, he asserted both his disinterestedness and his right to judge and choose in this business entirely for himself. Who had a right to blame him? his fortune was his own, and he would marry a girl without sixpence, if she struck his fancy. Lady Trant supported him in his humour, and he began to name some of the young ladies of his acquaintance: one would look well in a curricle; another would do the honours of his house handsomely; another danced charmingly, and would be a credit to him in a ball-room; another would make a sweet-tempered nurse when he should have the gout: but Lady Trant found some objection to every one he mentioned, till, at last, when he had named all he could think of in remainder to his heart, Lady Trant proposed Miss Georgiana.

But she was intended for his brother.

"Oh! no." Lady Trant had very particular reasons for being positive that neither Mrs. nor Miss Falconer had ever such an idea, however they might have let it go abroad, perhaps, to conceal their real wishes— Miss Georgiana Falconer had refused so many gentlemen—Count Altenberg, report said, among others; and it was plain to Lady Trant that the young lady could not be easily pleased—that her affections were not to be engaged very readily: yet she had a notion, she owned, that if—But she was not at liberty to say more. She was only convinced that no girl was more admired than Miss Georgiana Falconer, and no woman would do greater credit to the taste of a man of fashion: she had all the requisites Mr. Clay had named: she would look well in a curricle; she would do the honours of his house charmingly; she sung and danced divinely: and Lady Trant summed up all by reiterating, that Miss Georgiana Falconer never would have married his brother.

This persuasive flattery, combining with English Clay's anger against his brother, had such effect, that he protested, if it was not for the trouble of the thing, he did not care if he married next week. But the making the proposal, and all that, was an awkward, troublesome business, to which he could not bring himself. Lady Trant kindly offered to take all trouble of this sort off his hands—undertook to speak to Mrs. Falconer, if she had his authority for so doing, and engaged that he should be married without any kind of awkwardness or difficulty. In consequence of this assurance, Lady Trant was empowered by Mr. Clay to make the proposal, which was received with so much joy and triumph by Mrs. Falconer and by her Georgiana.

But their joy and triumph were not of long duration. In this family, where none of the members of it acted in concert, or well knew what the others were doing,—where each had some separate interest, vanity, or vice, to be pursued or indulged, it often happened that one individual counteracted the other, and none were willing to abandon their selfish purpose, whether of interest or pleasure. On the present occasion, by a curious concatenation of circumstances, it happened that Buckhurst Falconer, who had formerly been the spoiled darling of his mother, was the person whose interest immediately crossed hers; and if he pursued his object, it must be at the risk of breaking off his sister Georgiana's marriage with English Clay. It is necessary to go back a few steps to trace the progress of Buckhurst Falconer's history. It is a painful task to recapitulate and follow the gradual deterioration of a disposition such as his; to mark the ruin and degradation of a character which, notwithstanding its faults, had a degree of generosity and openness, with a sense of honour and quick feeling, which early in life promised well; and which, but for parental weakness and mistaken system, might have been matured into every thing good and great. After his mother had, by introducing him early to fashionable company, and to a life of idleness and dissipation, disgusted him with the profession of the law, in which, with talents such as his, he might, with application and perseverance, have risen to wealth and eminence—after his father had, by duplicity and tyranny, forced him into that sacred profession for which the young man felt himself unfit, and which his conscience long refused to consider merely as the means of worldly provision—the next step was to send him with a profligate patron, as chaplain to a regiment, notorious for gambling. The first sacrifice of principle made, his sense of honour, duty, and virtue, once abandoned, his natural sensibility only hastened his perversion. He had a high idea of the clerical character; but his past habits and his present duties were in direct opposition. Indeed, in the situation in which he was placed, and with the society into which he was thrown, it would have required more than a common share of civil courage, and all the steadiness of a veteran in virtue, to have withstood the temptations by which he was surrounded. Even if he had possessed sufficient resolution to change his former habits, and to become a good clergyman, his companions and his patron, instead of respecting, would have shunned him as a censor. Unwilling to give up the pleasures of conviviality, and incapable of sustaining the martyrdom of ridicule, Buckhurst Falconer soon abjured all the principles to which he could not adhere—he soon gloried in the open defiance of every thing that he had once held right. Upon all occasions, afraid of being supposed to be subject to any restraint as a clergyman, or to be influenced by any of the prejudices of his profession, he strove continually to show his liberality and spirit by daring, both in words and actions, beyond what others dared. He might have been checked and stopped in his career of extravagance by the actual want of money and of credit, had he not unluckily obtained, at this early period, a living, as a reward for saving Bishop Clay from being choked: this preferment, obtained in circumstances so ludicrous, afforded him matter of much temporary amusement and triumph; and confirmed him in the idea his father had long laboured to inculcate, that merit was unnecessary to rising in the world or in the church. But however he might endeavour to blind himself to the truth, and however general opinion was shut out from him for a time by those profligate persons with whom he lived, yet he could not help now and then seeing and feeling that he had lost respectability; and in the midst of noisy merriment he was often to himself an object of secret and sad contempt. Soon after he was separated for a time from Colonel Hauton and his companions, by going to take possession of his living, he made an effort to regain his self-complacency—he endeavoured to distinguish himself as an eloquent preacher.—Ashamed of avowing to his associates better motives, by which he was partly actuated, he protested that he preached only for fame and a deanery. His talents were such as soon accomplished half his wish, and ensured him celebrity—he obtained opportunities of preaching in a fashionable chapel in London—he was prodigiously followed—his theatrical manner, perhaps, increased the effect of his eloquence upon a certain class of his auditors; but the more sober and nice-judging part of his congregation objected to this dramatic art and declamatory style, as tending to draw the attention from the doctrine to the preacher, and to obtain admiration from man more than to do honour to God. This, however, might have passed, as a matter of speculative opinion or difference of taste; provided the preacher is believed to be in earnest, the style of his preaching is of little comparative consequence. But the moment he is suspected of being insincere, the moment it is found that he does not practise what he preaches, his power over the rational mind ceases; and to moral feeling such a clergyman becomes an object, not only of contempt, but of disgust and abhorrence. Murmurs were soon heard against the private conduct of the celebrated preacher—perhaps envy for his talents and success mingled her voice with the honest expressions of virtuous indignation. The murmurs grew louder and louder; and Buckhurst Falconer, to avoid having inquiries made and irregularities brought to light, was obliged to yield to a rival preacher of far inferior talents, but of more correct conduct.

Commissioner Falconer was glad that his son was disappointed in this manner, as he thought it would make him more attentive than he had been of late to Colonel Hauton; and the living of Chipping-Friars was better worth looking after than the fleeting fame of a popular preacher. Buckhurst, however, still held fame in higher estimation than it had ever been held by his father, who never valued it but as subordinate to interest. But the love of fame, however superior to mercenary habits, affords no security for the stability of conduct; on the contrary, without good sense and resolution, it infallibly accelerates the degeneracy of character. Buckhurst's hopes of obtaining literary celebrity being lost, he sunk another step, and now contented himself with the kind of notoriety which can be gained by a man of talents, who condescends to be the wit of private circles and of public dinners. Still he met with many competitors in this line. In the metropolis, the mendicants for fame, like the professional beggars, portion out the town among them, and whoever ventures to ply beyond his allotted walk is immediately jostled and abused; and the false pretensions of the wit, and all the tricks to obtain admiration, are as sure to be exposed by some rivals of the trade, as the false legs, arms, and various impostures of the beggar are denounced by the brother-beggar, on whose monopoly he has infringed. Our wit was soon compelled to confine himself to his own set, and gradually he degenerated from being the wit to being the good story-teller of the company. A man who lives by pleasing must become whatever the society in which he lives desire. Colonel Hauton and his associates had but little taste for pure wit—low humour and facetious stories were more suited to their capacities—slang and buffoonery were their delight. Buckhurst had early become a proficient in all these: the respect due to the clerical character had not restrained him from the exercise of arts for his own amusement, which now he found indispensably requisite for the entertainment of others, and to preserve favour with his patron. Contrary to all calculation, and, as the commissioner said, to all reasonable expectation, the old paralytic incumbent had continued to exist, and so many years had passed since the promise had been made to Buckhurst of this living, the transaction in consequence of which it was promised was now so completely forgotten, that the commissioner feared that Colonel Hauton, no longer under the influence of shame, might consider the promise as merely gratuitous, not binding: therefore the cautious father was solicitous that his son should incessantly stick close to the colonel, who, as it was observed, never recollected his absent friends. Buckhurst, though he knew him to be selfish and silly, yet had no suspicion of his breaking his promise, because he piqued himself on being a man of honour; and little as he cared, in general, for any one but himself, Colonel Hauton had often declared that he could not live without Buckhurst Falconer. He was always driving with the colonel, riding, betting with him, or relieving him from the sense of his own inability by making a jest of some person. Buckhurst's talents for mimicry were an infallible resource. In particular, he could mimick the two Clays to perfection, could take off the affected tone, foreign airs, and quick talkative vanity of French Clay; and represent the slow, surly reserve, supercilious silence, and solemn self-importance of English Clay. He used to imitate not only their manners, gesture, and voice, but could hold conversations in their characters, fall naturally into their train of thinking, and their modes of expression. Once a week, at least, the two Clays were introduced for the amusement of their friend Colonel Hauton, who, at the hundredth representation, was as well pleased as at the first, and never failed to "witness his wonder with an idiot laugh," quite unconscious that, the moment afterwards, when he had left the room, this laugh was mimicked for the entertainment of the remainder of the band of friends. It happened one night that Buckhurst Falconer, immediately after Colonel Hauton had quitted the party, began to set the table in a roar, by mimicking his laugh, snuffling voice, and silly observations; when, to his utter confusion, his patron, who he thought had left the room, returned from behind a screen, and resumed his place opposite to Buckhurst. Not Banquo's ghost could have struck more terror into the heart of the guilty. Buckhurst grew pale as death, and sudden silence ensued. Recovering his presence of mind, he thought that it was possible the colonel might be such a fool as not to have recognized himself; so by a wink to one of the company, and a kick under the table to another, he endeavoured to make them join in his attempt to pass off the whole as mimicry of a Colonel Hallerton. His companions supported him as he continued the farce, and the laughter recommenced. Colonel Hauton filled his glass, and said nothing; by degrees, however, he joined or pretended to join in the laugh, and left the company without Buckhurst's being able exactly to determine whether he had duped him or not. After the colonel was fairly gone,—for this time Buckhurst took care not only to look behind the screen, but even to shut the doors of the antechamber, and to wait till he heard the parting wheels,—they held a conference upon the question— duped or not duped? All agreed in flattering Buckhurst that he had completely succeeded in giving the colonel the change, and he was particularly complimented on his address by a Mr. Sloak, chaplain to a nobleman, who was one of the company. There was something of a hypocritical tone in Sloak's voice— something of a doubtful cast in his eyes, which, for a moment, raised in Buckhurst's mind a suspicion of him. But, the next day, Colonel Hauton appeared as usual. Buckhurst rode, drove, and jested with him as before; and the whole transaction was, on his part, forgotten. A month afterwards the rector of Chipping-Friars actually died—Commissioner Falconer despatched an express to Buckhurst, who stood beside his bed, with the news, the instant he opened his eyes in the morning. Buckhurst sent the messenger on to Colonel Hauton's at the barracks, and before Buckhurst was dressed, the colonel's groom brought him an invitation to meet a large party at dinner: "the colonel would be unavoidably engaged, by regimental business, all morning."

Buckhurst's friends and acquaintance now flocked to congratulate him, and, by dinner-time, he had, in imagination, disposed of the second year's tithes, and looked out for a curate to do the duty of Chipping-Friars. The company assembled at dinner, and the colonel seemed in uncommonly good spirits, Buckhurst jovial and triumphant—nothing was said of the living, but every thing was taken for granted. In the middle of dinner the colonel cried, "Come, gentlemen, fill your glasses, and drink with me to the health of the new rector of Chipping-Friars." The glasses were filled instantly, all but Buckhurst Falconer's, who, of course, thought he should not drink his own health.

"Mr. Sloak, I have the pleasure to drink your health; Mr. Sloak, rector of Chipping-Friars," cried the patron, raising his voice. "Buckhurst," added he, with a malicious smile, "you do not fill your glass."

Buckhurst sat aghast. "Colonel, is this a jest?"

"A jest?—by G—! no," said the colonel; "I have had enough of jests and jesters."

"What can this mean?"

"It means," said the colonel, coolly, "that, idiot as you take me, or make me to be, I'm not fool enough to patronize a mimick to mimick myself; and, moreover, I have the good of the church too much at heart, to make a rector of one who has no rectitude—I can have my pun, too."

The laugh was instantly turned against Buckhurst. Starting from table, he looked alternately at Colonel Hauton and at Mr. Sloak, and could scarcely find words to express his rage. "Hypocrisy! Treachery! Ingratitude! Cowardice! If my cloth did not protect you, you would not dare—Oh! that I were not a clergyman!" cried Buckhurst.

"It's a good time to wish it, faith!" said the colonel; "but you should have thought better before you put on the cloth."

Cursing himself, his patron, and his father, Buckhurst struck his forehead, and rushed out of the room: an insulting laugh followed from Colonel Hauton, in which Mr. Sloak and all the company joined— Buckhurst heard it with feelings of powerless desperation. He walked as fast as possible—he almost ran through the barrack-yard and through the streets of the town, to get as far as he could from this scene—from these people. He found himself in the open fields, and leaning against a tree—his heart almost bursting—for still he had a heart: "Oh! Mr. Percy!" he exclaimed aloud, "once I had a friend—a good, generous friend—and I left him for such a wretch as this! Oh! if I had followed his advice! He knew me—knew my better self! And if he could see me at this moment, he would pity me. Oh! Caroline! you would pity—no, you would despise me, as I despise myself—I a clergyman!—Oh! father! father! what have you to answer for!"

To this sudden pang of conscience and feeling succeeded the idea of the reproaches which his father would pour upon him—the recollection of his debts, and the impossibility of paying them—his destitute, hopeless condition—anger against the new rector of Chipping-Friars, and against his cold, malicious patron, returned with increased force upon his mind. The remainder of that day, and the whole of the night, were passed in these fluctuations of passion. Whenever he closed his eyes and began to doze, he heard the voice of Colonel Hauton drinking the health of Mr. Sloak; and twice he started from his sleep, after having collared both the rector and his patron. The day brought him no relief: the moment his creditors heard the facts, he knew he should be in immediate danger of arrest. He hurried to town to his father—his father must know his situation sooner or later, and something must be done.

We spare the reader a shocking scene of filial and parental reproaches.

They were both, at last, compelled to return to the question, What is to be done? The father declared his utter inability to pay his son's debts, and told him, that now there remained but one way of extricating himself from his difficulties—to turn to a better patron.

"Oh! sir, I have done with patrons," cried Buckhurst.

"What, then, will you do, sir? Live in a jail the remainder of your life?"

Buckhurst gave a deep sigh, and, after a pause, said, "Well, sir, go on—Who is to be my new patron?"

"Your old friend, Bishop Clay."

"I have no claim upon him. He has done much for me already."

"Therefore he will do more."

"Not pay my debts—and that is the pressing difficulty. He cannot extricate me, unless he could give me a good living immediately, and he has none better than the one I have already, except Dr. Leicester's—his deanery, you know, is in the gift of the crown. Besides, the good dean is likely to live as long as I shall."

"Stay; you do not yet, quick sir, see my scheme—a scheme which would pay your debts and put you at ease at once—Miss Tammy Clay, the bishop's sister."

"An old, ugly, cross, avaricious devil!" cried Buckhurst.

"Rich! passing rich! and well inclined toward you, Buckhurst, as you know."

Buckhurst said that she was his abhorrence—that the idea of a man's selling himself in marriage was so repugnant to his feelings, that he would rather die in a jail.

His father let him exhaust himself in declamation, certain that he would be brought to think of it at last, by the necessity to which he was reduced. The result was what the commissioner saw it must be. Creditors pressed—a jail in immediate view—no resource but Miss Tammy Clay. He went down to the country to the bishop's, to get out of the way of his creditors, and—to consider about it. He found no difficulty likely to arise on the part of the lady. The bishop, old, and almost doting, governed by his sister

Tammy, who was an admirable housekeeper, and kept his table exquisitely, was brought, though very reluctantly, to consent to their marriage.

Not so acquiescent, however, were Miss Tammy's two nephews, French and English Clay. They had looked upon her wealth as their indefeasible right and property. The possibility of her marrying had for years been, as they thought, out of the question; and of all the young men of their acquaintance, Buckhurst Falconer was the very last whom they would have suspected to have any design upon aunt Tammy—she had long and often been the subject of his ridicule. French Clay, though he had just made an imprudent match with a singer, was the more loud and violent against the aunt; and English Clay, though he was not in want of her money, was roused by the idea of being duped by the Falconers. This was just at the time he had commissioned Lady Trant to propose for Miss Georgiana. Aunt Tammy had promised to give him six thousand pounds whenever he should marry: he did not value her money a single sixpence, but he would not be tricked out of his rights by any man or woman breathing. Aunt Tammy, resenting certain words that had escaped him derogatory to her youth and beauty, and being naturally unwilling to give—any thing but herself—refused to part with the six thousand pounds. In these hard times, and when she was going to marry an expensive husband, she laughing said, that all she had would be little enough for her own establishment. Buckhurst would willingly have given up the sum in question, but English Clay would not receive it as a consequence of his intercession. His pride offended Buckhurst: they came to high words, and high silence. English Clay went to his relation, Lady Trant, and first reproaching her with having been too precipitate in executing his first commission, gave her a second, in which he begged she would make no delay: he requested her ladyship would inform Mrs. Falconer that a double alliance with her family was more than he had looked for—and in one word, that either her son Buckhurst's marriage with his aunt Tammy, or his own marriage with Miss Georgiana, must be given up. He would not have his aunt at her age make herself ridiculous, and he would not connect himself with a family who could uphold a young man in duping an old woman: Lady Trant might shape his message as she pleased, but this was to be its substance.

In consequence of Lady Trant's intimation, which of course was made with all possible delicacy, Georgiana and Mrs. Falconer wrote to Buckhurst in the strongest terms, urging him to give up his intended marriage. There were, as they forcibly represented, so many other old women with large fortunes who could in the course of a short time be found, who would be quite as good matches for him, that it would argue a total insensibility to the interests and entreaties of his beloved mother and sister, if he persisted in his present preposterous design. Buckhurst answered,

"MY DEAR MOTHER AND GEORGY,

"I was married yesterday, and am as sorry for it to-day as you can be.

"Yours truly,

"B.F.

"P.S.—There are other young men, with as good fortunes as English Clay, in the world."

The letter and the postscript disappointed and enraged Mrs. Falconer and Georgiana beyond description.

English Clay left his D.I.O. at Mrs. Falconer's door, and banged down to Clay-hall.

Georgiana, violent in the expression of her disappointment, would have exposed herself to Lady Trant, and to half her acquaintance; but Mrs. Falconer, in the midst of her mortification, retained command of temper sufficient to take thought for the future. She warned Lady Trant to be silent, and took precautions to prevent the affair from being known; providently determining, that, as soon as her daughter should recover from the disappointment of losing Clay-hall, she would marry her to Petcalf, and settle her at once at the lodge in Asia Minor.

"Till Georgiana is married," said she to herself, "the commissioner will never let me have peace: if English Clay's breaking off the match gets wind, we are undone; for who will think of a rejected girl, beautiful or fashionable though she be? So the best thing that can be done is to marry her immediately to Petcalf. I will have it so—and the wedding-clothes will not have been bought in vain."

The bringing down the young lady's imagination, however, from Clay-hall to a lodge was a task of much difficulty; and Mrs. Falconer often in the bitterness of her heart exclaimed, that she had the most ungrateful children in the world. It seems that it is a tacit compact between mothers and daughters of a certain class, that if the young ladies are dressed, amused, advertised, and exhibited at every fashionable public place and private party, their hearts, or hands at least, are to be absolutely at the disposal of their parents.

It was just when Mrs. Falconer was exasperated by Georgiana's ingratitude, that her son Buckhurst was obliged to come to London after his marriage, to settle with his creditors. His bride insisted upon accompanying him, and chose this unpropitious time for being introduced to his family. And such a bride! Mrs. Buckhurst Falconer! Such an introduction! Such a reception! His mother cold and civil, merely from policy to prevent their family-quarrels from becoming public; his sisters—

But enough. Here let us turn from the painful scene, and leave this house divided against itself.

CHAPTER XXXI

LETTER FROM ALFRED TO HIS FATHER.

"MY DEAR FATHER,

"I send you two pamphlets on the causes of the late changes in the ministry, one by a friend, the other by an enemy, of Lord Oldborough. Temple, I should have thought the author of the first, but that I know he has not time to write, and that there does not appear any of that behind the scene knowledge which his situation affords. All the pamphleteers and newspaper politicians write as if they knew the whole— some confident that the ministry split on one question—some on another; long declamations and abuse follow as usual on each side, but WISE people, and of course myself among that number, suspect 'that all that we know is, that we know nothing.' That there was some private intrigue in the cabinet, which has not yet transpired, I opine from Temple's reserve whenever I have mentioned the subject. This morning, when I asked him to frank these pamphlets, he laughed, and said that I was sending coals to Newcastle: what this meant he refused to explain, or rather he attempted to explain it away, by observing, that people of good understanding often could judge better at a distance of what was passing in the political world, than those who were close to the scene of action, and subject to hear the contradictory reports of the day; therefore, he conceived that I might be sending materials for thinking, to one who could judge better than I can. I tormented Temple for a quarter of an hour with a cross-examination so able, that it was really a pity to waste it out of the courts; but I could get nothing more from him. Is it possible, my dear father, that you are at the bottom of all this?

"Lord Oldborough certainly told me the other day, and in a very significant manner, and, as I now recollect, fixing his inquiring eye upon me as he said the words, that he not only felt esteem and regard for Mr. Percy, but gratitude—gratitude for tried friendship. I took it at the time as a general expression of kindness; now I recollect the look, and the pause after the word gratitude, I put this with Temple's coals to Newcastle. But, if it be a secret, I must not inquire, and if it be not, you will tell it to me. So I shall go on to my own affairs.

"The other day I was surprised by a visit at my chambers from an East-India director. Lord Oldborough, I find, recommended it to him to employ me in a very important cause, long pending, for a vast sum of money: the whole, with all its accumulated and accumulating interest, depending on a point of law. Heaven send me special sense, or special nonsense, sufficient to avoid a nonsuit, of which there have been already no less than three in this cause.

"What do you think of Lord Oldborough's kindness? This is only one of many instances in which I have traced his desire to serve me. It is not common with politicians, thus to recollect those who have no means of serving them, and who have never reminded them even of their existence by paying court in any way actively or passively.

"The Falconers are all discontented with his lordship at this moment, because he has disposed of a sinecure place on which the commissioner had long had his eye. His lordship has given it to an old disabled sea-captain, whom he knew only by reputation.

"The accounts you have heard of Buckhurst's marriage are, alas! too true; and what you have been told of the lady's age and ugliness is not exaggerated. As to her temper and her avarice, I am afraid that what you have heard of them is also true; for a brother lawyer of mine, who was employed to draw the settlements, says she has taken care to keep every penny she could in her own power; and that, in the whole course of his practice, he never saw so hard a battle between love and parsimony. Poor Buckhurst! who could have foreseen that this would be his fate! I met him in the street yesterday with his bride, and he looked as if he would rather be hanged than receive my congratulations: I passed without seeming to have seen them.

"I have just received Mr. Barclay's letter, and am going to work upon his settlements. So Caroline's wishes for Lady Mary Pembroke will be accomplished. I asked Temple whether Lord Oldborough had heard any thing of Count Altenberg since his return to his own country. Yes—one private letter to Lord Oldborough, from which nothing had transpired but one line of general thanks for civilities received in England. Temple, who seems to have formed the same notion and the same wishes that we had, told me yesterday, without my questioning him, that Lord Oldborough had written with his own hand an answer to the Count, which none of the secretaries have seen. Temple, in sealing up the packet, ventured to ask whether there was any chance of seeing Count Altenberg again in England. 'None that he knew,' Lord Oldborough answered. Temple, who of all men is least like Commissioner Falconer in circumlocutory address, at once blurted out, 'Is Count Altenberg going to be married?' Lord Oldborough turned and looked upon him with surprise—whether surprise at his curiosity, or at the improbability of the Count's making his lordship the confidant of his love-affairs, Temple declares he was in too much confusion to be able to decide. Lord Oldborough made no reply, but took up an answer to a memorial, which he had ordered Temple to draw, pointed out some unlucky mistakes in it, and finished by saying to him, 'Mr. Temple, your thoughts are not in your business. Sir, I do believe you are in love;' which sentence Temple declares his lordship pronounced with a look and accent that would have suited, Sir, I do believe you have the plague.' And if so, do me the justice to let me employ Mr. Shaw to do your business, till you are married.'

"Temple says that Lord Oldborough is proud of showing himself a foe to love, which he considers as the bane of ambition, and as one of the weaknesses of human nature, to which a great man ought to be superior.

"Whether the secretary be right or wrong in this opinion of his lordship, I have not seen enough to be able to determine; and I suspect that Temple is not at present a perfectly calm observer. Ever since his visit to the country he seems not to be entirely master of himself: his heart is still hovering round about some absent object—what object, I do not know; for though he does not deny my charge, he will not tell me the name of his fair one. I suspect Lady Frances Arlington of having stolen his heart. I am very sorry for it—for I am clear she is only coquetting with him. Temple says that he is too poor to marry. He is so amiable, that I am sure he will make any woman he marries happy, if it be not her own fault, and if they have but enough to live upon. It grieves me to hear his unavailing daily regrets for having quitted the bar. Had he continued in his original profession, he might, and in all probability would have been, at this moment (as his competitor, a man much his inferior in talent, actually is), in the receipt of four thousand good pounds per annum, independent of all men; and might have married any woman in any rank. Besides, even with such a patron as Lord Oldborough, Temple feels dependence grievous to his spirit. He is of a very good family, and was not early used to a subservient situation. His health too will be hurt by his close confinement to the business of office—and he has no time for indulging his literary taste—no play for his genius: that was his original grievance at the bar, but his present occupations are less congenial to his taste than law ever was. His brother-secretary, Mr. Shaw, is a mere matter-of-fact man, who is particularly unsuited to him—an objector to every thing new, a curtailer and contemner of all eloquence: poor Temple is uneasy and discontented; he would give up his situation to-morrow but that he cannot quit Lord Oldborough. He says that he has a hundred times resolved to resign—that he has had his letter written, and the words on his lips; but he never could, when it came to the point, present the letter, or pronounce the farewell to Lord Oldborough. Wonderful the ascendancy this man has over the mind!—Extraordinary his power of attaching, with manners so little conciliatory! Adieu, my dear father; I have indulged myself too long in writing to you. I have to read over the late Mr. Panton's will, and to give our friend Mr. Gresham an opinion upon it—notwithstanding Rosamond's cruelty to him, he is as much our friend, and her friend, as ever. Panton's will is on ten skins of parchment: and then I have a plea in rejoinder to draw for Lady Jane Granville; and, worse than all, to read and answer four of her ladyship's notes now on my table. By-the-bye, I would rather carry on a suit for any four men, than for one such woman of business as poor Lady Jane. She is never at rest one moment; never can believe that either lawyer or solicitor knows what he is about—always thinks her letters and notes can do more than bills in chancery, or than the lord chancellor himself. She frets incessantly. I must request Erasmus to medicine her to repose; she has absolutely a law fever. Erasmus is at Richmond—sent for by some grandee: he is in high practice. He told me he began last week to write to Rosamond, from the bedside of some sleeping patient, a full and true answer to all her questions about Miss Panton; but the sleeper awakened, and the doctor had never time to finish his story.

"Adieu a second time. Love to all.

"Dear father, yours affectionately,

"ALFRED PERCY.

"Just as I began the second skin of Panton's will, a note was brought to me from—whom do you think? Lord Oldborough, requesting to see me at four o'clock. What can his lordship want with me?—I must send this frank before I can satisfy my own curiosity on this point—or yours, Rosamond."

After finishing the perusal of Mr. Panton's long-winded will, writing an opinion upon it for Mr. Gresham, and penning a quieting note for poor Lady Jane Granville, Alfred, eager to be punctual to the appointed hour, went to the minister. He need not have looked at his watch so often, or have walked so fast, for when he arrived it wanted five minutes of the time appointed, and his lordship had not returned from a visit to the Duke of Greenwich. He was told, however, that orders had been given for his admittance; and he was shown into an apartment where he had leisure, during a full quarter of an hour, to admire his own punctuality. At last he heard a noise of loud huzzas in the street, and looking out of the window, he saw a crowd at the farthest end of the street; and as it moved nearer, perceived that the populace had taken the horses from Lord Oldborough's carriage, and were drawing him to his own door with loud acclamations. His lordship bowed to the multitude as he got out of his carriage rather proudly and coldly, yet still the crowd threw up their hats and huzzaed. He apologized to Alfred, as he entered the room, for having been later than his appointment. Commissioner Falconer and Mr. Temple were with him, and the commissioner immediately began to tell how they had been delayed by the zeal of the people. Lord Oldborough took a paper from his pocket, and walked to the window to read it, without seeming to hear one word that the commissioner was saying, and without paying any attention to the acclamations of the multitude below, which were again repeated on their seeing him at the window. When his lordship had finished looking over the paper, he called upon Alfred to witness it, and then presenting it to Mr. Falconer, he said, in his haughtiest manner, "An equivalent, sir, for that sinecure place which you asked for, and which it was out of my power to obtain for you. That was given as the just reward of merit, and of public services. My private debts—" [Alfred Percy observed that his lordship did not use the word obligation]. "My private debts to your family, Mr. Falconer, could not be paid from the public fund with which I am entrusted, but you will not, I hope, find me the less desirous that they should be properly acknowledged. The annuity," continued he, putting his finger on the amount, which the commissioner longed to see, but at which he had not dared yet to look, "the annuity is to the full amount of that place which, I think you assured me, would satisfy your and Mrs. Falconer's expectations."

"Oh! my lord, more than satisfy: but from your lordship's private fortune—from your lordship's own emoluments of office, I cannot possibly think—Mrs. Falconer would, I am sure, be excessively distressed—"

"Do me the favour, sir, to let no more be said upon this subject," interrupted Lord Oldborough. "As you return home, will you speak to those poor people whom I still hear in the street, and advise them now to return peaceably to their homes. My man Rodney, I am afraid, has thought it for my honour to be too liberal to these good people—but you will speak to them, commissioner."

The commissioner, who never completely felt Lord Oldborough's character, imagined that at this moment his lordship secretly enjoyed the clamour of popular applause, and that this cold indifference was affected; Mr. Falconer therefore protested, with a smile, that he would do his best to calm the enthusiasm of the people, but that it was a hard, if not impossible task, to stem the tide of Lord

Oldborough's popularity. "Enjoy it, my lord!" concluded Mr. Falconer; "Enjoy it!—No minister in my memory ever was so popular!"

As soon as the commissioner, after saying these words, had left the room, Lord Oldborough, in a tone of sovereign contempt, repeated the word, "Popularity! There goes a man, now, who thinks me fit to be a fool to fame!"

"Popularity," said Mr. Temple, "is a bad master, but a good servant. A great man will," as Burke says, "disdain to veer like the weathercock on the temple of fashion with every breath of wind. But may he not, my lord—say, for you know—may he not wisely take advantage of the gale, and direct this great power, so as to work the state-machinery to good purpose?"

"A dangerous power," replied Lord Oldborough, turning from his secretary to Alfred, as if he were impatient to speak of business. Temple, who had more of the habits of a man of letters than of a man of business or of a courtier, was apt unseasonably to pursue a discussion, and to pique himself upon showing sincerity by declaring a difference of opinion from his patron. Utterly repugnant as this was to the minister's habits and temper, yet in admiration of the boldness of the man, and in consideration for his true attachment, Lord Oldborough bore it with magnanimous patience—when he had time—and when he had not, would cut it short at once.

"In a mixed government, popularity, philosophically speaking, if I may differ from your lordship—" Temple began.

"Permit me, sir, first," interrupted Lord Oldborough, "to settle my business with Mr. Alfred Percy, who, being a professional man, and in high practice, probably sets a just value upon his time."

Mr. Temple, who was a man of quick feelings, felt a word or glance of reproof from Lord Oldborough with keen sensibility. Alfred could not fix his own attention upon what his lordship was now beginning to say. Lord Oldborough saw reflected in Alfred's countenance the disturbance in his friend's: and immediately returning, and putting a key into Mr. Temple's hand—"You will do me a service, sir," said he, "by looking over my father's papers marked private in red letters. They may be necessary in this business—they are papers which I could trust only to one who has my interests at heart."

Mr. Temple's face brightened instantly, and bowing much lower than usual, he received the key with great respect, and hurried away to search for the papers.

"For a similar reason, Mr. Alfred Percy," said Lord Oldborough, "they shall, if you please, be put into your hands." His lordship moved a chair towards Alfred, and seated himself. "My law-agent has not satisfied me of late. A suit, into which I have been plunged by those who had the direction of my business, has not been carried on with ability or vigour. I had not leisure to look into any affairs that merely concerned myself. Circumstances have just wakened me to the subject, and to the perception that my private fortune has suffered, and will suffer yet more materially, unless I am fortunate enough to find united in the same person a lawyer and a friend. I have looked round and see many older barristers than Mr. Alfred Percy, but none so likely to be interested in my affairs as the son of my earliest friend, and few more capable of conducting them with diligence and ability. May I hope, sir, for hereditary kindness from you, as well as for professional services?"

No one knew better than Lord Oldborough how to seem receiving whilst he conferred a favour; and if ever he appeared harsh, it was only where he knew that the people to whom he spoke had not feelings worthy of his consideration. His lordship was as much pleased by the manner in which this trust was accepted, as our young lawyer could be by the manner in which it was offered.

"My papers then shall be sent to you directly," said Lord Oldborough. "Look over them, and if you are of opinion that my case is a bad one, I will stop where I am. If, on the contrary, you find that justice and law are on my side, proceed, persist. I shall trust the whole to you, sir, without a farther question."

Lord Oldborough next spoke of a steward of his at Clermont-park, who, as he had reason to suspect, was leagued with a certain Attorney Sharpe in fraudulent designs: his lordship hoped that Mr. Alfred Percy, during his vacations, when spent in that neighbourhood, might, consistently with his professional duties, find time to see into these affairs; and, in his lordship's absence, might supply the want of the master's eye.

Alfred assured his lordship that no effort or care should be wanting on his part to justify the high confidence with which he was honoured.

"Since you are going to take charge of my business, sir," pursued Lord Oldborough, "it is fit you should know my views relative to my affairs. In my present situation, with the favour I enjoy, and the opportunities I command, it would be easy to make my fortune whatever I pleased. Avarice is not my passion. It is my pride not to increase the burdens of my country. Mine is a generous country, ever ready to reward her public servants, living or dying. But, whilst I live, never will I speculate upon her generosity, and, when I die, never shall my heirs appeal to her compassion. My power at its zenith, and my character being known, I can afford to lay aside much of that adventitious splendour which adds nothing to true dignity. Economy and dignity are compatible—essential to each other. To preserve independence, and, consequently, integrity, economy is necessary in all stations. Therefore, sir, I determine—for I am not stringing sentences together that are to end in nothing—I determine, at this moment, to begin to make retrenchments in my expenditure. The establishment at Clermont-park, whither I have no thoughts of returning, may be reduced. I commit that, sir, to your discretion."

Mr. Temple returned with the papers, on which Lord Oldborough put his seal, and said his solicitor should deliver them, with all others that were necessary, the next morning to Mr. Percy. Alfred, careful never to intrude a moment on the time of the minister, rose, and, without repeating his thanks, made his bow.

"I consider this lawsuit as a fortunate circumstance," said Lord Oldborough, "since it affords me means at last of engaging Mr. Alfred Percy in my service, in a mode which cannot," added his lordship, smiling, "interfere with his family horror of ministerial patronage."

Alfred said something respectfully expressive of his sense of the professional advantage he must derive from being employed by Lord Oldborough—a species of patronage, by which he felt himself most highly honoured, and for which he was sure his whole family would feel properly grateful.

"Sir," said Lord Oldborough, following him to the door, "if I had ever doubted it, you would convince me that perfect propriety of manner is consistent with independence of mind. As to the rest, we all know the difference between a client and a patron."

The management of Lord Oldborough's business necessarily led to an increase of intercourse between his lordship and Alfred, which was peculiarly agreeable to our young barrister, not only as it gave him opportunities of seeing more of the character of this minister, but as it put it into his power to be of service occasionally to his friend Mr. Temple. Chained to a desk, his genius confined to the forms of office, and with a master too high, and an associate too low, to afford him any of the pleasures of society, he had languished for want of a companion. Alfred encouraged him by example to submit to the drudgery of business, showed him that a man of letters may become a man of business, and that the habits of both may be rendered compatible. Temple now performed the duties of his office with all that regularity which is supposed to be peculiar to dulness. About this time he had been brought into parliament by Lord Oldborough, and in the intervals of business, in that leisure which order afforded him, he employed and concentrated his powers on a political question of considerable importance; and when he was completely master of the subject, he rose in the House of Commons, and made a speech, which from all parties obtained deserved applause. The speech was published. A few days afterwards, Mr. Temple happened to enter Lord Oldborough's cabinet earlier than usual: he found his lordship reading; and reading with so much attention, that he did not observe him—he heard his lordship's quick and decided pencil mark page after page. At length, rising and turning to throw the book on the table, Lord Oldborough saw his secretary copying a letter.

"An excellent speech—to the purpose, sir," said Lord Oldborough. "It had its effect on the house, I understand; and I thank your friend, Mr. Alfred Percy, for putting it into my hands when I had leisure to peruse it with attention."

Lord Oldborough thought for some moments, then looked over some official papers which he had ordered Mr. Temple to draw up.

"Very well, sir—very well. A man of genius, I see, can become a man of business."

His lordship signed the papers, and, when that was finished, turned again to Mr. Temple.

"Sir, some time ago a place was vacant, which, I know, you had reason to expect. It was given to Mr. Shaw, because it was better suited to him than to you. The manner in which you took your disappointment showed a confidence in my justice. Have you any objection, Mr. Temple, to the diplomatic line?"

"I fear—or I should say, I hope—my lord, that I have not the habits of dissimulation, which, as I have always understood, are necessary to success in the diplomatic line."

"You have understood wrongly, sir," replied Lord Oldborough. "I, who have seen something of courts, and know something of diplomacy, am of opinion that a man of sense, who knows what he is about, who says the thing that is, who will tell at once what he can do, and what he cannot, would succeed better as a negotiator in the present state of Europe, than could any diplomatist with all the simulation and dissimulation of Chesterfield, or with the tact of Mazarin."

"Indeed, my lord!" said Mr. Temple, looking up with an air of surprise that almost expressed, Then why did you choose Cunningham Falconer for an envoy?

"Pray," said Lord Oldborough, taking a long inspiration with a pinch of snuff, "pray with that despatch this morning from Mr. Cunningham Falconer were there any private letters?"

"One for Commissioner Falconer, my lord."

"None from Count Altenberg to me?"

"None, my lord."

The minister took a walk up and down the room, and then returning to Mr. Temple, said, "His majesty thinks proper, sir, to appoint you envoy in the place of Mr. Cunningham Falconer, who is recalled."

"I thank you, my lord—his majesty does me great honour," cried Mr. Temple, with sudden gratitude: then, his countenance and tone instantly changing from joy to sorrow, he added, "His majesty does me great honour, my lord, but—"

"But not great pleasure, it seems, sir," said Lord Oldborough. "I thought, Mr. Temple, you had trusted to me the advancement of your fortune."

"My fortune! My lord, I am struck with surprise and gratitude by your lordship's goodness in taking thought for the advancement of my fortune. But I have other feelings."

"And may I ask what is the nature of your other feelings, sir?"

"My lord—excuse me—I cannot tell them to you."

"One word more, sir. Do you hesitate, from any motives of delicacy with respect to the present envoy?"

"No, my lord, you look too high for my motive; and the higher I am sensible that I stand in your lordship's opinion, the greater is my fear of falling. I beg you will excuse me: the offer that your lordship has had the goodness to make would be the height of my ambition; but when opposing motives draw the will in contrary directions—"

"Sir, if you are going into the bottomless pit of metaphysics, excuse me," said Lord Oldborough—"there I must leave you. I protest, sir, you are past my comprehension."

"And past my own," cried Mr. Temple, "for," with effort he uttered the words, "unfortunately I have formed an—I have become attached to—"

"In short, sir, you are in love, I think," said Lord Oldborough, coolly. "I think I told you so, sir, more than a month ago."

"I have said it! and said it to Lord Oldborough!" exclaimed Mr. Temple, looking as one uncertain whether he were dreaming or awake.

"It is undoubtedly uncommon to select a minister of state for the confidant of a love affair," said Lord Oldborough, with an air of some repressed humour.

"I knew I should expose myself to your lordship's derision," exclaimed Mr. Temple.

He was too much engrossed by his own feelings, as he pronounced these words, to observe in his lordship's countenance an extraordinary emotion. It was visible but for one instant.

With a look more placid, and a tone somewhat below his usual voice, Lord Oldborough said, "You have misjudged me much, Mr. Temple, if you have conceived that your feelings, that such feelings would be matter of derision to me. But since you have touched upon this subject, let me give you one hint—Ambition wears better than Love."

Lord Oldborough sat down to write, and added, "For one fortnight I can spare you, Mr. Temple—Mr. Shaw will undertake your part of the business of office. At the end of the ensuing fortnight, I trust you will let me have your answer."

Full of gratitude, Mr. Temple could express it only by a bow—and retired. The antechamber was now filling fast for the levee. One person after another stopped him; all had some pressing business, or some business which they thought of consequence, either to the nation or themselves.

"Mr. Temple, I must trouble you to look over these heads of a bill."

"Mr. Temple!—My memorial—just give me your advice."

"Sir—I wrote a letter, three weeks ago, to Lord Oldborough, on the herring-fishery, to which I have not had the honour of an answer."

"Mr. Temple—the address from Nottingham—Where's the reply?"

"Mr. Temple, may I know whether his lordship means to see us gentlemen from the city about the loan?"

"Sir—Pray, sir!—My new invention for rifling cannon—Ordnance department!—Sir, I did apply—War-office, too, sir!—It's very hard I can't get an answer—bandied about!—Sir, I can't think myself well used—Government shall hear more."

"One word, Mr. Temple, if you please, about tithes. I've an idea—"

"Temple, don't forget the Littleford turnpike bill."

"Mr. Temple, who is to second the motion on Indian affairs?"

"Temple, my good friend, did you speak to Lord Oldborough about my little affair for Tom?"

"Mr. Temple, a word in your ear—the member for the borough, you know, is dead; letters must be written directly to the corporation."

"Temple, my dear friend, before you go, give me a frank."

At last Mr. Temple got away from memorialists, petitioners, grievances, men of business, idle men, newsmen, and dear friends, then hastened to Alfred to unburden his mind—and to rest his exhausted spirits.

CHAPTER XXXII

The moment that Mr. Temple reached his friend's chambers, he threw himself into a chair.

"What repose—what leisure—what retirement is here!" cried he. "A man can think and feel a moment for himself."

"Not well, I fear, in the midst of the crackling of these parchments," said Alfred, folding up the deeds at which he had been at work. "However, I have now done my business for this day, and I am your man for what you please—if you are not engaged by some of your great people, we cannot do better than dine together."

"With all my heart," said Mr. Temple.

"And where shall we dine?" said Alfred.

"Any where you please. But I have a great deal to say to you, Alfred—don't think of dining yet."

"At the old work!" cried Alfred.

"'You think of convincing, while I think of dining.'"

But, as he spoke, Alfred observed his friend's agitated countenance, and immediately becoming serious, he drew a chair beside Mr. Temple, and said, "I believe, Temple, you have something to say that you are anxious about. You know that if there is any thing I can do, head, hand, and heart are at your service."

"Of that I am quite sure, else I should not come here to open my heart to you," replied Mr. Temple. Then he related all that had just passed between Lord Oldborough and himself, and ended by asking Alfred, whether he thought there was any chance of success for his love?

"You have not told me who the lady is," said Alfred.

"Have not I?—but, surely, you can guess."

"I have guessed—but I wish to be mistaken—Lady Frances Arlington?"

"Quite mistaken. Guess again—and nearer home."

"Nearer home!—One of my sisters!—Not Caroline, I hope?"

"No."

"Then it must be as I once hoped. But why did you never mention it to me before?"

Mr. Temple declared that he had thought there was so little chance of his ever being in circumstances in which he could marry, especially a woman who had not some fortune of her own, that he had scarcely ventured to avow, even to himself, his attachment.

"I thought my love would wear itself out," added he. "Indeed I did not know how serious a business it was, till this sudden proposal was made to me of leaving England: then I felt that I should drag, at every step, a lengthening chain. In plain prose, I cannot leave England without knowing my fate. But don't let me make a fool of myself, Alfred. No man of sense will do more than hazard a refusal: that every man ought to do, or he sacrifices the dignity of the woman he loves to his own false pride. I know that in these days gentlemen-suitors are usually expert in sounding the relations of the lady they wish to address. To inquire whether the lady is engaged or not is, I think, prudent and honourable: but beyond this, I consider it to be treacherous and base to endeavour, by any indirect means, to engage relations to say what a lover should learn only from the lady herself. Therefore, my dear friend, all I ask is whether you have reason to believe that your sister Rosamond's heart is pre-engaged; or if you think that there is such a certainty of my being rejected, as ought, in common prudence, to prevent my hazarding the mortification of a refusal?"

Alfred assured his friend, that, to the best of his belief, Rosamond's heart was disengaged. "And," continued he, "as a witness is or ought to be prepared to tell his cause of belief, I will give you mine. Some time since I was commissioned by a gentleman, who wished to address her, to make the previous inquiry, and the answer was, quite disengaged. Now as she did not accept of this gentleman, there is reason to conclude that he did not engage her affections—"

"Was he rich or poor, may I ask?" interrupted Mr. Temple.

"That is a leading question," said Alfred.

"I do not want you to tell me who the gentleman was—I know that would not be a fair question, and I trust I should be as far from asking, as you from answering it. But there are so many rich as well as so many poor men in the world, that in answering to the inquiry rich or poor, what city or court man do you name? I want only to draw a general inference as to your sister's taste for wealth."

"Her taste is assuredly not exclusively for wealth; for her last admirer was a gentleman of very large fortune."

"I am happy, at least, in that respect, in not resembling him," said Mr. Temple. "Now for my other question—what chance for myself?"

"Of that, my good friend, you must judge for yourself. By your own rule all you have a right to hear is, that I, Rosamond's brother, have no reason for believing that she has such a repugnance to you as would make a refusal certain. And that you may not too much admire my discretion, I must add, that if I had a mind to tell you more, I could not. All I know is, that Rosamond, as well as the rest of my family, in their letters spoke of you with general approbation, but I do not believe the idea of considering you as her lover ever entered into her head or theirs."

"But now the sooner it enters the better," cried Mr. Temple. "Will you—can you—Have not you business to do for Lord Oldborough at Clermont-park?"

"Yes—and I am glad of it, as it gives me an opportunity of indulging myself in going with you, my dear Temple. I am ready to set out at any moment."

"God bless you! The sooner the better, then. This night in the mail, if you please. I'll run and take our places," said he, snatching up his hat.

"Better send," cried Alfred stopping him: "my man can run and take places in a coach as well as you. Do you stay with me. We will go to the coffee-house, dine, and be ready to set off."

Mr. Temple acceded.

"In the mean time," said Alfred, "you have relations and connexions of your own who should be consulted."

Mr. Temple said he was sure that all his relations and connexions would highly approve of an alliance with the Percy family. "But, in fact," added he, "that is all they will care about the matter. My relations, though high and mighty people, have never been of any service to me: they are too grand, and too happy, to mind whether a younger son of a younger son sinks or swims; whether I live in single wretchedness or double blessedness. Not one relation has nature given, who cares for me half as much as the friend I have made for myself."

Sincerely as Alfred was interested for his success, yet he did not let this friendship interfere with the justice due to his sister, of leaving her sole arbitress of a question which most concerned her happiness.

During the last stage of their journey, they were lucky enough to have the coach to themselves, and Mr. Temple made himself amends for the restraint under which he had laboured during the preceding part of the journey, whilst he had been oppressed by the presence of men, whose talk was of the lower concerns of life. After he had descanted for some time on the perfections of his mistress, he ended with expressing his surprise that his friend, who had often of late rallied him upon his being in love, had not guessed sooner who was the object of his passion.

Alfred said that the idea of Rosamond had occurred to him, because his friend's absence of mind might be dated from the time of his last visit to Clermont-park; "but," said Alfred, "as Lady Frances Arlington was there, and as I had formerly fancied that her ladyship's wish to captivate or dazzle you, had not been quite without effect, I was still in doubt, and thought even your praises of Rosamond's disposition and temper, compared with her ladyship's, might only be ruse de guerre, or ruse d'amour."

"There was no ruse in the case," said Mr. Temple; "I confess that when I first emerged from my obscurity into all the light and life of the world of fashion, my eyes were dazzled, and before I recovered the use of them sufficiently to compare the splendid objects by which I found myself surrounded, I was wonderfully struck with the appearance of Lady Frances Arlington, and did not measure, as I ought, the immense difference between Lord Oldborough's secretary, and the niece of the Duke of Greenwich. Lady Frances, from mere gaieté de coeur likes to break hearts; and she continually wishes to add one, however insignificant, to the number of her conquests. I, a simple man of literature, unskilled in the wicked ways of the fair, was charmed by her ladyship's innocent naïveté and frank gaiety, and all that was

'Strangely wild, or madly gay,

I call'd it only pretty Fanny's way.'

"Fortunately, just as I was in imminent danger of exchanging true sighs for false smiles, I became acquainted with your sister Rosamond. In the country, and under circumstances more favourable for the development of character than any which might occur for months or years in a town-life, where all the men and women are merely actors, I had leisure to see and mark the difference and the resemblance between Lady Frances Arlington's character, and that of your sister. They resembled each other in natural quickness of intellect and of feeling; in wit, sprightliness, and enthusiasm, they were also to a certain degree alike. I was amused by Lady Frances Arlington's lively nonsense, till I heard your sister's lively sense. Her ladyship hazards saying every thing that occurs to her, and often makes happy hits; but your sister's style of wit is far superior, and far more agreeable, because it has the grace, elegance, and, above all, the infinite variety which literary allusion supplies. I found myself pleased, not only with what she said, but with the trains of ideas, that, by a single word, she often suggested. Conversing with her, my mind was kept always active, without ever being over-exerted or fatigued. I can look back, and trace the whole progress of my attachment. I began in this way, by finding her conversation most delightful— but soon discovered that she was not only more entertaining and more cultivated, but far more amiable than my idol, Lady Frances, because she had never been an idol, and did not expect to be adored. Then she was more interesting, because more capable of being interested. Lady Frances requires much sympathy, but gives little; and for that enthusiasm of temper which had, at first, charmed me in her ladyship, I began to lose my taste, when I observed that it was always excited by trifles, and by trifles that concerned herself more than any one else. I used to think her—what every body calls her, a perfectly natural character; and so, perhaps, she is: but not the better for that—since she is what, I am afraid, we all are naturally—selfish. Her ladyship, if I may use the expression, is enthusiastically selfish. Your sister—enthusiastically generous. Lady Frances's manners are caressing, yet I doubt whether she feels affection for any one living, except just at the moment when they are ministering to her fancies. It was Miss Percy's warm affection for her sister Caroline which first touched my heart. I saw each in her own family. The contrast was striking—in short, by the joint effect of contrast and resemblance, my love for one lady decreased as fast as it increased for the other; and I had just wit and judgment enough to escape from snares that could not have held me long, to chains that have power to hold me for ever."

To this history of the birth and progress of his love, Mr. Temple added many expressions of his hopes, fears, and regrets, that he had not five thousand a year, instead of five hundred, to offer his mistress; he at length became absolutely silent. They were within view of the Hills, and too many feelings crowded upon his mind to be expressed in words.

And now we might reasonably contrive to fill—

"Twelve vast French romances neatly gilt,"

with the history of the following eventful fortnight, including the first surprise at the arrival of the travellers—the declaration of Mr. Temple's love—the astonishment of Rosamond on discovering that she was the object of this passion—of a passion so generous and ardent—the consequent and rapid discovery of a hundred perfections in the gentleman which had before escaped her penetration—the strong peculiar temptation to marry him, because he had not enough to live upon—the reaction of generosity on the other side of the question, which forbade to ruin her lover's fortune—the fluctuations of sentiment and imagination, the delicacies of generosity, gratitude, love, and finally the decision of common sense.

It was fortunate for Rosamond, not only that she had prudent friends, but that they had not made her in the least afraid of their superior wisdom, so that she had, from the time she was a child, told them every idea, as it rose in her vivid imagination, and every feeling of her susceptible heart; imprudent as she might appear in her confidential conversation, this never passed from words to actions. And now, when she was called upon in an important event of life to decide for herself, she acted with consummate discretion.

Mr. Temple's character and manners peculiarly pleased her, and his being a man of birth and family certainly operated much in his favour. Her parents now, as in Mr. Gresham's case, did not suffer their own tastes or prepossessions to interfere with her happiness.

Caroline, grateful for the sympathy which Rosamond had always shown her, took the warmest interest in this affair. Caroline was the most excellent, indulgent, yet safe confidante; and as a hearer, she was absolutely indefatigable. Rosamond never found her too busy, too lazy, or too sleepy to listen to her: late at night, early in the morning, or in the most hurried moment, of the day, it was all the same— Caroline seemed to have nothing to do but to hear, think, and feel for Rosamond.

The fortnight allowed by Lord Oldborough having now nearly elapsed, it was absolutely necessary Rosamond should come to some decision. Mr. Temple's understanding, temper, disposition, and manners, she allowed to be excellent—his conversation was particularly agreeable. In short, after searching in vain for an objection, she was obliged to confess that she liked him. Indeed, before she had allowed this in words her mother and sister had made the discovery, and had seen the struggle in her mind between love and prudence. Mr. Temple's fortune was not sufficient for them to live upon, and she knew that a wife in his present circumstances must be a burden to him; therefore, notwithstanding all that his passion and all that her own partiality could urge, she decidedly refused his proposal of an immediate union, nor would she enter into any engagement, or suffer him to bind himself by any promise for the future; but he obtained permission to correspond with her during his absence from England, and with the hope that she was not quite indifferent to him, he took leave of her—returned to town—waited upon Lord Oldborough—accepted of the embassy, and prepared for his departure to the continent.

Now that there was an approaching possibility and probability of hearing of Count Altenberg, Caroline felt it extremely difficult to adhere to her resolution of never thinking of him, especially as her mind, which had been actively occupied and deeply interested in her sister's concerns, was now left to return upon itself in all the leisure of retirement. Fortunately for her, about this time she was again called upon for that sympathy which she was ever ready to give to her friends. She received the following letter from Mrs. Hungerford.

LETTER FROM MRS. HUNGERFORD TO MISS CAROLINE PERCY.

"Come, my beloved Caroline, my dear young friend, friend of my family, and of all who are most near and dear to me—come, and enjoy with me and them that happiness, which your judicious kindness long since foresaw, and your prudence promoted.

"My niece, Lady Mary Pembroke, is at last persuaded that she has it in her power to make Mr. Barclay permanently happy. He has been obliged to take a considerable length of time to convince her of the steadiness of his attachment. Indeed, her objection—that he had been charmed by such a coquette as the lady by whom we first saw him captivated, appeared to me strong; and I thought my niece right for adhering to it, more especially as I believed that at the time her affections pleaded against her reason in his favour, and that, if she had been convinced long ago, it would not have been against her will.

"Mr. Barclay has behaved like a man of sense and honour. Without disguise he told her of his former attachment to you. She instantly made an answer, which raised her high in my estimation. She replied, that Mr. Barclay's being detached from Lady Angelica Headingham by your superior merit was to her the strongest argument in his favour. She must, she said, have felt insecure in the possession of a heart, which had been transferred directly from Lady Angelica to herself, because she was conscious that her own disposition was so different from her ladyship's; but in succeeding to the affection which he had felt for a woman of your character, she should feel perfect security, or at least reasonable hope, that by similar, though certainly inferior qualities, she might ensure his happiness and her own. They are to be married next week. Lady Mary particularly wishes that you should be one of her bride-maids—come then, my love, and bring all my Percys. I shall not perfectly enjoy my own and my niece's happiness till you share it with me. My daughter Mortimer insists upon signing this as well as myself.

"MARY-ELIZABETH HUNGERFORD.

"KATE MORTIMER."

Caroline and all Mrs. Hungerford's Percys obeyed her summons with alacrity. Lady Mary Pembroke's marriage with Mr. Barclay was solemnized under the happiest auspices, and in the midst of approving and sympathizing friends. As soon as the ceremony was over, and she had embraced and congratulated her niece, Mrs. Hungerford turned to Mrs. Percy, and in a low voice said, "If it were not too much for one so happy as I am, so rich in blessings, to ask one blessing more, I should ask to be permitted to live to see the day when our dear Caroline—" Mrs. Hungerford pressed Mrs. Percy's hand, but could say no more; the tears rolled down her cheeks as she looked up to heaven. Some minutes afterwards, following Caroline with her eyes, "Look at her, Mrs. Percy!" said Mrs. Hungerford. "Did ever selfish coquette, in the height of triumph over lover or rival, enjoy such pleasure as you see sparkling at this moment in that dear girl's countenance?"

The bride and bridegroom set off immediately for Mr. Barclay's seat in Berkshire. Lady Florence accompanied her sister; and Mrs. Hungerford, after parting from both her nieces, entreated that Caroline might be left with her. "It is a selfish request, I know, my dear; but at my age I cannot afford to be generous of the society of those I love. Allow me to plead my age, and my—Well, I will not say more since I see it gives you pain, and since I see you will grant the prayer of my petition, rather than hear my claims to your compassion."

Caroline liked particularly to stay with Mrs. Hungerford at this time, when there was not any company at the castle, no one but Mrs. Hungerford and her daughter, so that she had the full and quiet enjoyment of their society. At this time of her life, and in the state of her mind at this period, no society could have been more agreeable, soothing, and useful to Caroline, than that of such a friend. One, who had not forgotten the passions of youth; who could give at once sympathy and counsel; who was willing to allow to love its full and exquisite power to exalt the happiness of human life, yet appeared herself, in advanced and serene old age, a constant example of the falsehood of the notion, that the enthusiasm of passion is essential to felicity. An elegant and just distinction has been made by a philosophical writer between delicacy of passion and delicacy of taste. One leading to that ill-governed susceptibility, which transports the soul to ecstasy, or reduces it to despair, on every adverse or prosperous change of fortune; the other enlarging our sphere of happiness, by directing and increasing our sensibility to objects of which we may command the enjoyment, instead of wasting it upon those over which we have no control. Mrs. Hungerford was a striking example of the advantage of cultivating delicacy of taste.

At an advanced age, she showed exquisite perception of pleasure in every work of genius; in conversation, no stroke of wit or humour escaped her quick intelligence, no shade of sentiment or politeness was lost upon her; and on hearing of any trait of generosity or greatness of soul, her whole countenance beamed with delight; yet with all this quickness of feeling she was quite free from fastidiousness, and from that irritability about trifles, into which those who indulge the delicacy of passion in youth are apt to degenerate in age. Caroline felt, every day, increasing affection as well as admiration for Mrs. Hungerford, and found time pass delightfully in her company. Besides that general and well-chosen acquaintance with literature which supplied her with perpetual resources, she had that knowledge of life and of the world which mixes so well, in conversation, with the knowledge of books. She had known, intimately, most of the celebrated people of the last century, and had store of curious and interesting anecdotes, which she produced with so much taste and judgment, and told so well, as never to fatigue attention. Caroline found that her mind was never passive or dormant in Mrs. Hungerford's company; she was always excited to follow some train of thought, to discuss some interesting question, or to reflect upon some new idea. There was, besides, in the whole tenor of her conversation and remarks such an indulgence for human nature, with all its faults and follies, as left the most pleasing and encouraging impression on the mind, and inspired hope and confidence. Her anecdotes and her philosophy all tended to prove that there is more virtue than vice, more happiness than misery, in life; and, above all, that there is a greater probability that the world should improve than that it should degenerate. Caroline felt pleased continually to find her own favourite opinions and hopes supported and confirmed by the experience and judgment of such a woman; and there was something gratifying to her, in being thus distinguished and preferred by one who had read so much and thought so deeply.

As Mrs. Hungerford had heard nothing more of Count Altenberg, she wisely forbore to touch upon the subject, or even to mention his name to Caroline; and she saw, with satisfaction, the care with which her young friend turned her mind from every dangerous recollection. Sometimes, however, the remembrance of the Count was unavoidably recalled; once, in particular, in turning over the life of Sir Philip Sidney, there was a passage copied in his hand, on a slip of paper, which had accidentally been left in the book.

"Algernon Sidney, in a letter to his son, says, that in the whole of his life he never knew one man, of what condition soever, arrive at any degree of reputation in the world, who made choice of, or delighted in the company or conversation of those, who in their qualities were inferior, or in their parts not much superior to himself."

"What have you there, my love? Something that pleases and interests you particularly, I see," said Mrs. Hungerford, not knowing what it was that Caroline was reading: "show it me, my dear—I am sure I shall like it."

Caroline, deeply blushing, gave her the paper. She recollected the hand-writing, and folding up the paper, put it in her pocket-book.

"It is an observation," said she, "that I wish I could write in letters of gold for the advantage of all the young men in the world in whom I take any interest."

The energetic warmth with which Mrs. Hungerford spoke relieved Caroline, as it seemed to justify the delight she had involuntarily expressed—the sentiments for the individual seemed now enveloped in general approbation and benevolence. She never loved Mrs. Hungerford better than at this instant.

Mrs. Hungerford observed that none of the common sentimental passages, either in poetry or novels, ever seemed to affect Caroline; and to the romantic descriptions of love she was so indifferent that it might have appeared to a common observer as if she was, and ever would be, a stranger to the passion. By the help of the active and plastic powers of the imagination, any and every hero of a novel could be made, at pleasure, to appear the exact resemblance of each lady's different lover. Some, indeed, professed a peculiar and absolute exclusive attachment, founded on unintelligible or indescribable merits or graces; but these ladies, of all others, she had found were most liable to change, and on farther acquaintance with the world to discover, on generalizing their notions, similar or superior attractions in new models of perfection. In Caroline, Mrs. Hungerford saw none of these capricious fancies, and that it was not her imagination, but her reason which gave Count Altenberg the exalted place he held in her esteem. It was therefore with pleasure, that this kind lady perceived, that her young friend's residence with her soothed her mind and restored it to its former tone.

But Caroline was soon obliged to leave Hungerford Castle, A letter from Erasmus informed her that poor Lady Jane Granville was ill of a nervous fever, that she had no companion, no one to attend her but a maid-servant, and that she was much in want of some judicious friend who could raise her spirits and tranquillize her mind, which was in a state of continual agitation about her lawsuit. Caroline, remembering Lady Jane's former kindness, thought this a fit opportunity to show her gratitude; and, happy as she was with her friends at Hungerford Castle, she hesitated not a moment to sacrifice her own pleasure.—Her father and mother approved of her determination, and her brother Alfred carried her to London.

CHAPTER XXXIII

In these days, people travel with so much safety, ease, and celerity, that heroines have little chance of adventures on the road; and a journey is now so common a thing, that, as Rosamond observed, the most brilliant imagination has no hope of having wonders to relate. To Rosamond's mortification, Caroline and her brother reached London without any event having occurred better worth recording than the loss of an umbrella. They drove into town when it was nearly dark, just before the lamps were lighted; Caroline, therefore, had little satisfaction from the first view of the metropolis. She found Lady Jane Granville in a small lodging in Clarges-street—the room dark—a smell of smoke—the tea-equipage prepared—Lady Jane lying on a shabby-looking sofa—drops and a smelling-bottle on a little table beside her. She raised herself as Caroline entered, looked half pleased, half ashamed to see her; and, stretching out her hand, said, in a complaining voice, "Ah! my dear Caroline, are you really come? This is too good! Sadly changed, you find—and every thing about me—Sit down, my dear—Keppel, do let us have tea as soon as you can," said Lady Jane.

"As soon as ever Eustace comes in, my lady," answered Keppel, peevishly.

"In the mean time, for Heaven's sake, allow us a little more light—I cannot live without light. Come nearer to me, my dear Caroline, and tell me how did you leave all our friends at the Hills?"

Whilst Caroline was answering her ladyship, more candles were brought, and Lady Jane moved them on the table till she threw the light full on Caroline's face.

"Handsomer than ever! And altogether so formed. One would not think, Alfred, she had been buried all this time in the country. Ah! perverse child; why would not you come when I could have been of some use to you—when, at least, I could, have received you as I ought? This is not a fit place, you see; nor am I now in circumstances, or in a style of life—Heigho!"

"Dr. Percy is not come yet," resumed she. "This is his usual hour—and I wrote a note to tell him that he would meet his sister Caroline to-night."

In all her ladyship said, in every look and motion, there was the same nervous hurry and uneasiness. Dr. Percy arrived, and for a moment Lady Jane forgot herself in sympathy with the pleasure the brother and sister showed at meeting. Soon, however, she would have relapsed into melancholy comparisons, but, that Dr. Percy checked the course of her thoughts; and with the happy art, by which a physician of conversational powers can amuse a nervous patient, he, without the aid of poppy or mandragora, medicined her to rest, though not to sleep.

When Erasmus was alone with his sister, he observed that no permanent amendment could be expected in Lady Jane's health till her mind should be at ease about her lawsuit. While this was undecided, her imagination vacillated between the horror of neglected poverty, and the hopes of recovering her former splendour and consideration. The lawsuit was not to be decided for some weeks, and Caroline saw that all that could be done in the mean time was as much as possible to soothe and amuse her patient: however tiresome and difficult the task, she went through it with the utmost cheerfulness and sweetness of temper. Day after day she passed alone with Lady Jane, hearing her complaints, bodily and mental, and listening to the eternally repeated history of her lawsuit. But Caroline's patience was ensured by a sense of gratitude, which, in her, was not a sentimental phrase, but a motive for long endurance, still more difficult than active exertion.

One half hour in the day, however, she was sure of being happy—the half hour when her brother Erasmus paid his visit. Of Alfred she saw little, for he was so much engaged with business, that a few minutes now and then were all he could possibly spare from his professional duties. Mr. Temple called. She was surprised to see him, for she thought he had been on his way to the continent; but he told her that difficulties had occurred, chiefly through the manoeuvres of Cunningham Falconer, and that he did not know when there would be an end of these—that Lord Oldborough was glad of the delay at present, because he wanted Mr. Temple's assistance, as the other secretary had been taken ill, and his lordship had not yet fixed upon a confidential person to supply his place. Of course, in these circumstances, Mr. Temple was so much occupied, that Caroline saw very little of him; and she experienced what thousands have observed, that, however people may wish to meet in great towns, it is frequently impracticable, from small difficulties as to time, distance, and connexions. Of Mr. Gresham, Caroline had hoped that she should see a great deal—her brother Erasmus had long since introduced him to Lady Jane Granville; and, notwithstanding his being a merchant, her ladyship liked him. He was as much disposed as ever to be friendly to the whole Percy family; and the moment he heard of Caroline's being in town, he hastened to see her, and showed all his former affectionate regard in his countenance and manner. But his time and his thoughts were now engrossed by an affair very near his heart, which he was impatient to bring to a termination. As soon as this should be accomplished, he was to set out for Amsterdam, where the concerns of his late partner, old Mr. Panton, as his correspondents wrote, imperiously demanded his presence.

This affair, which was so near Mr. Gresham's heart, related to his dear Constance. Alfred had alluded to it in one of his letters, and Erasmus had begun to write the particulars to Rosamond; but he had not at the time leisure to finish the letter, and afterwards burnt it, being uncertain how the romance, as Alfred called it, might end. He therefore thought it prudent to say nothing about it. The whole story was now told to Caroline, and, briefly, was this.

After old Panton's rage against Dr. Percy, in consequence of the suspicion that his daughter was in love with him; after the strange wig-scene, and the high words that followed, had driven Erasmus from the house, Constance went to her father, and, intent upon doing justice to Erasmus, at whatever hazard to herself, protested that he had not been the cause of her refusal of Lord Roadster. To convince her father of this, she confessed that her heart was not entirely disengaged—no threats, no persuasion, could, however, draw from her the name of the person whom she preferred: she knew that to name him would be only to ruin his fortune—that her father never would consent to her marrying him; nor had the object of her preference ever given her reason to think that he felt any thing more for her than regard and respect. Old Panton, the last man in the world to understand any delicacies, thought her whole confession "nonsense:" the agitation and hesitation with which it was made, and her eagerness to clear Dr. Percy's credit, and to reinstate him in her father's favour, conspired to convince the old man that his "own first original opinion was right." Of this, indeed, he seldom needed any additional circumstances to complete the conviction on any occasion. During the remainder of his life he continued obstinate in his error: "If she likes any body else, why can't the girl name him? Nonsense—that cursed Dr. Percy is the man, and he never shall be the man." In this belief old Panton died, and what is of much more consequence, in this belief he made his will. On purpose to exclude Dr. Percy, and in the hope of accomplishing his favourite purpose of ennobling his descendants, he, in due legal form, inserted a clause in his will, stating, "that he bequeathed his whole fortune (save his wife's dower) to his beloved daughter, upon condition, that within the twelve calendar months next ensuing, after his decease, she, the said Constance, should marry a man not below the rank of the son of a baron. But in case she, the said Constance, should not marry within the said twelve calendar months, or should marry any man below the rank of a baron, then and after the expiration of said twelve calendar months, the said fortune to go to his beloved wife, except an annuity of two hundred pounds a year, to be paid thereout to his daughter Constance." Mr. Gresham was appointed sole executor to his will. As soon as it was decently possible, after old Panton's decease, Lord Roadster renewed his suit to Constance, and was civilly but very steadily refused. Many other suitors, coming within the description of persons favoured by the will, presented themselves, but without success. Some making their application to Constance herself, some endeavouring to win her favour through the intercession of her guardian, Mr. Gresham— all in vain. Month after month had passed away, and Mr. Gresham began to be much in dread, and Mrs. Panton, the step-mother, somewhat in hopes, that the twelve calendar months would elapse without the young lady's having fulfilled the terms prescribed by the will. Mr. Gresham, one morning, took his fair ward apart, and began to talk to her seriously upon the subject. He told her that he thought it impossible she should act from mere perverseness or caprice, especially as, from her childhood upwards, he had never seen in her any symptoms of an obstinate or capricious disposition; therefore he was well convinced that she had some good reason for refusing so many offers seemingly unexceptionable: he was grieved to find that he had not sufficiently won or deserved her confidence, to be trusted with the secret of her heart. Constance, who revered and loved him with the most grateful tenderness, knelt before him; and clasping his hand in hers, while tears rolled over her blushing cheeks, endeavoured to speak, but could not for some moments. At last, she assured him that delicacy, and the uncertainty in which she was whether she was beloved, were the only causes which had hitherto prevented her from speaking on this subject, even to him, who now stood in the place of her father, and who had ever treated her with more than a father's kindness.

Mr. Gresham named Erasmus Percy.

"No."

"Mr. Henry!"

"How was it possible that Mr. Gresham had never thought of him?"

Mr. Gresham had thought of him—had suspected that Mr. Henry's love for Constance had been the cause of his quitting England—had admired the young man's honourable silence and resolution—had recalled him from Amsterdam, and he was now in London.

But young Henry, who knew nothing of Mr. Gresham's favourable disposition towards him, who had only commercial correspondence with him, and knew little of his character, considered him merely as the executor of Mr. Panton, and, with this idea, obeyed his summons home to settle accounts. When they met, he was much surprised by Mr. Gresham's speaking, not of accounts, but of Constance. When Mr. Gresham told him the terms of Mr. Panton's will, far from appearing disappointed or dejected, Mr. Henry's face flushed with hope and joy. He instantly confessed to her guardian that he loved Constance passionately; and that now, when it could not be supposed he had mercenary views; now, when no duty, no honour forbad him, he would try his fate. He spoke with a spirit given by strong passion long repressed, and with a decision of character which his modesty and reserve of manner had, till now, prevented from appearing.

"Did he consider," Mr. Gresham asked, "what he expected Miss Panton to sacrifice for him?"

"Yes, fortune, not duty—duty he could never have asked her to sacrifice; he could not have esteemed her if she had sacrificed duty. As to the rest," added he, proudly, "Miss Panton is now to decide between love and fortune."

"This from the modest Mr. Henry! from whom, till this moment, I never heard a syllable that savoured of presumption!" said Mr. Gresham.

Mr. Henry was silent—and stood with an air of proud determination. Regardless of the surprise and attention with which Mr. Gresham considered him during this silence, he thought for a few moments, and asked, "Sir, when may I see Miss Panton?"

"And would you," said Mr. Gresham, "if it were in your power, sir, reduce the woman you love from opulence to poverty—to distress?"

"I have four hundred a year, Miss Panton has two—six hundred a year is not poverty, sir. Distress—the woman I marry shall never know whilst I have life and health. No, sir, this is not romance. Of my perseverance in whatever I undertake, even when least congenial to my habits, you have had proofs. Mr. Gresham, if Miss Panton approves of me, and if love can make her happy, I fear not to assert to you, her guardian, that I will make her happy. If she love me not, or," added he, his whole countenance changing from the expression of ardent love to that of cold disdain, "or, if love be not in her mind superior to fortune, then I have little to regret. Wealth and honours wait her command. But," resumed he, "the trial I will make—the hazard I will run. If I am mistaken—if I am presumptuous—the humiliation be mine—the agony all my own: my heart will bear it—or—break!"

"Heroics!" said Mr. Gresham. "Now let me ask—"

"Let me ask, sir—pardon me," interrupted Mr. Henry—"Let me beg to see Miss Panton."

"Stay, listen to me, young man—"

"Young gentleman, sir, if you please."

"Young gentleman, sir, if you please," repeated Mr. Gresham, mildly; "I can make allowance for all this—you were bred a soldier, jealous of honour—but listen to me: there is one thing I must tell you before you see Miss Panton—though I apprehend it may somewhat mortify you, as it will interfere with your boast of disinterestedness and your vow of poverty—Miss Panton I have from her cradle been in the habit of considering partly as my own—my own child—and, as such, I have left her in my will ten thousand pounds. As she will want this money before my death, if she marries you, I must convert my legacy into a marriage-portion, and you shall not, sir, have love without fortune, whatever your heroics may think of it. Now go to your mistress, and keep my secret."

Young Henry was evidently more touched by this generosity than by this bounty; and with a gentleness and humility the most feeling he said, "How shall I thank you, sir, for bearing with me as you did?"

"Oh!" said Mr. Gresham, "old as I am, I know what it is to be in love, and can conceive too what it is to fear that a guardian might be cross, and that the executor and the partner of Mr. Panton might act like Mr. Panton himself. Say no more—I understand it all, you see—Go to your Constance."

Even in the haughtiness and spirit this young man had shown, Mr. Gresham saw the sincerity, strength, and disinterestedness of his affection; and in Mr. Gresham's estimation these were no trifling merits. We pass over—shall we be forgiven?—the love scenes between Mr. Henry and Constance. In these cases it is well when there is some sober friend to look to the common sense of the thing, and in the midst of the exaltation to do the necessary business of life. Mr. Gresham laid Mr. Panton's will before counsel learned in the law, took opinions from two different counsel; from Alfred Percy, whose friendship was likely to quicken his attention, and from another barrister of long standing, who, being totally unconnected with the parties might probably give a perfectly unbiassed and dispassionate advice. Both agreed that there was no avoiding the clause in the will; that Miss Panton, if she married a man below the rank of a baron's son, must give up her fortune to her step-mother at the end of twelve calendar months from the time of her father's decease; but both barristers gave it as their opinion, that the income during those twelve months belonged to Constance: this was a considerable sum, which, by Mr. Gresham's advice, was to be vested with the rest of Mr. Henry's capital in the firm of the house of Panton and Co. In consequence of Mr. Gresham's earnest recommendation, and of his own excellent conduct and ability, Mr. Henry was from this time joined in the firm, and as one of the partners had a secure income proportioned to his part of the capital, besides a share in the very advantageous speculations in which the house was engaged. Mr. Gresham undertook to supply Mr. Henry's place at Amsterdam, whither he was under the necessity of going. His house he would leave to Constance during his absence. She had best begin by taking possession of it, and establish herself there, he observed, that she might not have the inconvenience and mortification of being turned out of her own at the end of the year. "And if," said he, "I should be able, when I return, to make Mr. Henry's residence with me agreeable to him, I shall hope he will not, while I live, take my Constance quite away from me—I look to her as my chief happiness in life."

If Rosamond had heard the sigh which closed this speech, and if she had seen the simplicity and delicacy of Mr. Gresham's generosity on this occasion, she would have reproached herself for refusing him, and would almost have reasoned herself into the belief that she had done very wrong not to marry him; but this belief would only, could only, have lasted till she should see Mr. Temple again: so that, upon the whole, it was best for poor Mr. Gresham that she knew nothing of the matter.

All things being arranged thus in the kindest and most convenient manner by this excellent man, and the day being fixed for the marriage of Constance and Mr. Henry, Caroline was asked to be bride's-maid, and the honour of Lady Jane Granville's company was requested. It is inconceivable how much importance Lady Jane attached to the idea of her accepting or refusing this request, and the quantity she talked about it was wonderful! Notwithstanding the habitual theme of her being of no consequence now to any one, of her being utterly forgotten and out of the world, yet she had still a secret, very secret belief, that all she did would be known and commented upon; and she worked herself up to think, also, that the honour to be conferred, or the offence that would be taken in consequence of her decision, would be immortal. Every five minutes for two hours after the first reading of Mr. Gresham's note, she took it up, laid it down, and argued the matter pro and con to Caroline.

A long and loud knocking at the door came to Caroline's relief: it was repeated with imperious impatience. "Who is it, my dear? look out of the window, but don't let yourself be seen."

Caroline did not know any of the fashionable equipages, which to Lady Jane appeared a great defect in her education: upon this occasion, however, she thought she recollected the livery to be Mrs. Falconer's.

"Oh! no, my dear, quite impossible—the Falconers have not been near me this age. I will tell you whose livery it is—there is a resemblance, but it is astonishing to me a girl of your sense cannot learn the difference—it is old Lady Brangle's livery."

"It might very possibly be so," Caroline allowed.

The servant however brought in cards and a note from Mrs. Falconer—the note was to announce to Lady Jane Granville the approaching marriage of Miss Falconer with Sir Robert Percy—the day was named, and the honour of Lady Jane Granville's company was requested at the wedding. Lady Jane knew that this communication was made, not in the least in the kindness, but in the pride of Mrs. Falconer's heart; and precisely in the same spirit in which it was written Lady Jane thought it incumbent upon her to receive and answer it. Her ladyship was really warm and honest in her friendships, and very grateful to her branch of the Percy family, for the kindness they had shown her in adversity.

"I think it extremely ill-judged and ill-bred of Mrs. Falconer to invite me to this wedding. Does she think I have no feeling? My own near relations and best friends deprived of their birth-right by this Sir Robert Percy—does she conceive it possible that I could go to such a wedding?—No; nor did she wish or expect it; she only wrote from vanity, and I shall answer her with pride, which, at least, is somewhat superior to that mean passion; and I shall go, I am now determined, to Mr. Gresham's—I do nothing by halves."

Her ladyship immediately wrote answers to both the invitations. Nothing for months had done her so much good as the exertion, interest, and imaginary self-importance these two notes created. At Mr. Gresham's on the day of the wedding her ladyship appeared with great dignity, and was satisfied that she had conferred honour and serious obligation. Could she have seen into the minds of all the company, she would have been astonished to find how little she occupied their thoughts. It would be difficult to determine whether it is more for the happiness or misery of man and womankind that politeness should cherish, or truth destroy, these little delusions of self-love.

Presently there appeared in the newspapers a splendid account of the marriage at St. George's church, Hanover-square, of Sir Robert Percy, of Percy-hall, with Arabella, the eldest daughter of J. Falconer, Esquire: present at the ceremony was a long list of fashionable friends, who, as Lady Jane Granville observed, "would not have cared if the bride had been hanged the next minute." The happy pair, after partaking of an elegant collation, set out in a barouche and four for Percy-hall, the seat of Sir Robert Percy.

"So!" cried Lady Jane, throwing down the paper, "Mrs. Falconer has accomplished that match at last, and has got one of her daughters well off her hands—the ugly one too. Upon my word, she is amazingly clever. But, after all, the man has a horrid temper, and a very bad character. Now it is over, my dear Caroline, I must tell you, that long ago, before I was so well aware of what sort of a man he was, I had formed the plan of marrying him to you, and so uniting the two branches, and bringing the estate into your family; but we have often reason to rejoice that our best-concerted schemes don't succeed. I give Mrs. Falconer joy. For worlds I would not have such a man married to any relation or friend of mine—Oh! if I recover my fortune, Caroline, I have hopes for you!"

Her ladyship was interrupted by the arrival of Mr. Gresham, who came to take leave, as he was just setting out for Holland. He was a man who said less and did more for his friends, as Caroline observed, than almost any person she knew. On seeing his gallery of paintings, she had noticed some beautiful miniatures; he now brought all those which she had admired, and begged to leave them with her during his absence, that she might at her leisure copy any of them she liked. He knew she painted in miniature, for he had long ago, when at the Hills, seen her copy of M. de Tourville's picture of Euphrosyne.

"If," said Mr. Gresham, observing that Caroline scrupled to take charge of so many precious pictures, "if you are too proud to receive from me the slightest kindness without a return, I am willing to put myself under an obligation to you. While I am away, at your leisure, make me a copy of that Euphrosyne—I shall love it for your sake, and as reminding me of the time when I first saw it—the happiest time perhaps of my life," added he, in a low voice.

"Oh, Rosamond!" thought Caroline, "if you had heard that!—and if you knew how generously kind he has been to your brothers!"

At parting from Alfred and Erasmus, he said to them, "My good young friends, why don't either of you marry? To be sure, you are young enough; but think of it in time, and don't put off, put off, till you grow into old bachelors. I know young men generally in these days say, they find it too expensive to marry—some truth in that, but more selfishness: here's young Mr. Henry has set you a good example. Your practice in your professions, I suppose, puts you as much at ease in the world by this time as he is. Malthus, you know, whom I saw you studying the other day, objects only to people marrying before they can maintain a family. Alfred, when I was at the Hills, I heard of a certain Miss Leicester. If you shall think of marrying before I come back again, you'll want a house, and I've lent mine already—but money, you know, can place one in any part of the town you might like better—I have a sum lying idle at my bankers, which I have just had transferred to the account of Alfred and Erasmus Percy—whichever of you marry before I come back, must do me the favour to purchase a good house—I must have it at the polite end of the town, or I shall be worse than an old bachelor—let me find it well furnished and aired—nothing airs a house so well as a warm friend: then, you know, if I should not fancy your purchase, I leave it on your hands, and you pay me the purchase-money year by year, at your leisure—if you can trust that I will not throw you into jail for it."

The warmth of Alfred's thanks in particular showed Mr. Gresham that he had not been mistaken about Miss Leicester.

"I wish I had thought, or rather I wish I had spoken of this sooner," added Mr. Gresham: "perhaps I might have had the pleasure of seeing you married before my leaving England; but—no—it is best as it is—I might have hurried things—and in these matters every body likes to go their own pace, and their own way. So fare ye well—God bless you both, and give you good wives—I can ask nothing better for you from Heaven."

No man could he more disposed than Alfred felt himself at this instant to agree with Mr. Gresham, and to marry immediately—visions of beauty and happiness floated before his imagination; but a solicitor knocking at the door of his chambers recalled him to the sense of the sad necessity of finishing some law-papers instead of going into the country to see his fair mistress. His professional duty absolutely required his remaining in town the whole of this term—Lady Jane Granville's business, in particular, depended upon him—he gave his mind to it. She little knew how difficult it was to him at this time to fix his attention, or how much temper it required in these circumstances to bear with her impatience. The week before her cause was expected to come to trial, her ladyship's law-fever was at its height—Alfred avoided her presence, and did her business.

The day arrived—her cause came on—Alfred's exertions proved successful—and hot from the courts he brought the first joyful news—a decree in her favour!

Lady Jane started up, clasped her hands, embraced Alfred, embraced Caroline, returned thanks to Heaven—again and again, in broken sentences, tried to express her gratitude. A flood of tears came to her relief. "Oh! Alfred, what pleasure your generous heart must feel!"

From this day—from this hour, Lady Jane's health rapidly recovered; and, as Erasmus observed, her lawyer had at last proved her best physician.

When Caroline saw Lady Jane restored to her strength, and in excellent spirits, preparing to take possession of a handsome house in Spring-Gardens, she thought she might be spared to return to her own family. But Lady Jane would not part with her; she insisted upon keeping her the remainder of the winter, promising to carry her back to the Hills in a few weeks. It was plain that refusing this request would renew the ire of Lady Jane, and render irreconcilable the quarrel between her ladyship and the Percy family. Caroline felt extremely unwilling to offend one whom she had obliged, and one who really showed such anxiety for her happiness.

"I know, my dear Lady Jane," said she, smiling, "that if I stay with you, you will form a hundred kind schemes for my establishment; but forgive me when I tell you, that it is upon the strength of my belief in the probability that they will none of them be accomplished, that I consent to accept your ladyship's invitation."

"Perverse! provoking and incomprehensible!—But since you consent to stay, my dear, I will not quarrel with your motives: I will let them rest as philosophically unintelligible as you please. Be satisfied, I will never more accuse you of perversity in refusing me formerly; nor will I convict you of inconsistency for obliging me now. The being convicted of inconsistency I know is what you people, who pique yourselves upon being rational, are so afraid of. Now we every-day people, who make no pretensions to be reasonable, have no character for consistency to support—you cannot conceive what delightful liberty we enjoy. In lieu of whole tomes of casuistry, the simple phrase, 'I've changed my mind,' does our business. Do let me hear if you could prevail upon yourself to say so."

"I've changed my mind," said Caroline, playfully.

"That's candid—now I love as well as admire you."

"To be entirely candid, then," said Caroline, "I must, my dear Lady Jane, if you will give me leave, tell you more."

"As much as you please," said Lady Jane, "for I am naturally curious, particularly when young ladies blush."

Caroline thought, that however Lady Jane and she might differ on some points, her ladyship's anxiety to promote her happiness, in the way she thought most advantageous, deserved not only her gratitude but her confidence. Besides, it would be the most effectual way, she hoped, of preventing Lady Jane from forming any schemes for her establishment, to confess at once that she really believed it was not likely she should meet with any person, whose character and merits were equal to those of Count Altenberg, and any one inferior to him she was determined never to marry. She added a few words, as delicately as she could, upon the dread she felt of being presented in society as a young lady wishing for an establishment.

Lady Jane heard all she said upon this subject with much attention; but when she had finished, her ladyship said to herself, "Nonsense!—Every young lady thinks one lover perfect till she has seen another. Before Caroline has passed a month in fashionable society, provided she has a fashionable admirer, we shall hear no more of this Count Altenberg."

"Well, my dear," said she, holding out her hand to Caroline, "I will give you my word I will, to the best of my ability, comply with all your conditions. You shall not be advertised as a young lady in search of a husband—but just as if you were a married woman, you will give me leave to introduce my acquaintance to you; and if they should find out, or if in time you should find out, that you are not married, you know, I shall not be to blame."

CHAPTER XXXIV

Behold Lady Jane Granville reinstated in her fortune, occupying a fine house in a fashionable situation, with suitable equipage and establishment! carriages rolling to her door; tickets crowding her servants' hands; an influx, an affluence of friends, and congratulations such as quite astonished Caroline.

"Where were these people all the time she lived in Clarges-street?" thought she.

Lady Jane, though she knew from experience the emptiness and insincerity of such demonstrations of regard, was, nevertheless, habitually pleased by them, and proud to be in a situation where numbers found it worth while to pay her attentions. But notwithstanding her foibles, she was not a mere fashionable friend. She was warm in her affection for Caroline. The producing her young friend in the great London world was her prime object.

The pretensions of individuals are often cruelly mortified when they come to encounter the vast competition of a capital city. As King James said to the country-gentleman at court, "The little vessels, that made a figure on the lake, appear insignificant on the ocean!"

Happily for Caroline, she had not formed high expectations of pleasure, any hope of producing effect, or even sensation, upon her first appearance in the fashionable world. As she said in her letters to her friends at home, nothing could be more dull or tiresome than her first experience of a young lady's introduction into life; nothing, as she assured Rosamond, could be less like the reality than the delightful representations in novels, where every day produces new scenes, new adventures, and new characters. She was ashamed to write such stupid letters from London; but unless she were to have recourse to invention, she literally had not any thing entertaining to tell. She would, if Rosamond was in despair, invent a few conquests; and like great historians, put in some fine speeches supposed to have been spoken by celebrated characters.

In reality, Caroline's beauty had not passed so completely unobserved as her modesty and inexperience imagined. She did not know the signs of the times. On her first entrance into a public room eyes turned upon her—the eyes of mothers with apprehension, of daughters with envy. Some gentlemen looked with admiration, others with curiosity.

"A new face! Who is she?"

"A relation of Lady Jane Granville."

"What has she?"

"I don't know—nothing, I believe."

"Nothing, certainly—a daughter of the Percy who lost his fortune."

All apprehensions ceased on the part of the ladies, and generally all admiration on the part of the gentlemen. Opera-glasses turned another way. Pity succeeding to envy, a few charitably disposed added, "Ah! poor thing! unprovided for—What a pity!"

"Do you dance to-night?"

"Does our quadrille come next?"

Some gentleman, an abstract admirer of beauty, perhaps, asked the honour of her hand—to dance; but there the abstraction generally ended. A few, indeed, went farther, and swore that she was a fine girl, prophesied that she would take, and declared they would be d—d if they would not think of her, if they could afford it.

From their prophecies or their oaths nothing ensued, and even the civilities and compliments she received from Lady Jane's particular friends and acquaintance, though in a more polite style, were equally unmeaning and unproductive. Days passed without leaving a trace behind.

Unluckily for Caroline, her brother Alfred was about this time obliged to leave town. He was summoned to the country by Dr. Leicester. Dr. Percy was so continually employed, that she could scarcely have a few minutes in a week of his company, now that Lady Jane's health no longer required his professional attendance. Caroline, who had always been used to domestic society and conversation, was thus compelled to live completely in public, without the pleasures of home, and without the amusement young people generally enjoy in company, when they are with those of their own age to whom they can communicate their thoughts. Lady Jane Granville was so much afraid of Caroline's not appearing fashionable, that she continually cautioned her against expressing her natural feelings at the sight of any thing new and surprising, or at the perception of the tiresome or ridiculous. Her ladyship would never permit her protégée to ask the name of any person in public places or at private parties—because not to know certain people "argues yourself unknown."

"I'll tell you who every body is when we go home;" but when she was at home, Lady Jane was generally too much tired to explain or to comprehend the description of these nameless bodies; and even when her ladyship was able to satisfy her curiosity, Caroline was apt to mistake afterwards the titles and histories of the personages, and by the misnomers of which she was guilty, provoked Lady Jane past endurance. Whether it was from want of natural genius in the scholar, or interest in the study, or from the teacher's thus unphilosophically separating the name and the idea, it is certain that Caroline made but slow progress in acquiring her fashionable nomenclature. She was nearly in despair at her own want of memory, when fortunately a new instructress fell in her way, who was delighted with her ignorance, and desired nothing better than to tell her who was who; in every private party and public place to point out the ridiculous or notorious, and at the moment the figures were passing, whether they heard or not, to relate anecdotes characteristic and illustrative: this new, entertaining preceptress was Lady Frances Arlington. Her ladyship having quarrelled with Miss Georgiana Falconer, hated to go out with Mrs. Falconer, hated still more to stay at home with the old tapestry-working duchess her aunt, and was delighted to have Lady Jane Granville to take her every where. She cared little what any person thought of herself, much less what they thought of Caroline: therefore, free from all the delicacies and anxieties of Lady Jane's friendship and systems, Lady Frances, though from different premises coming to the same conclusion, agreed that thinking of Caroline's advantage was stuff! and that all she had to do was to amuse herself in town. Caroline was the most convenient companion to go out with, for she never crossed her ladyship about partners, or admirers, never vied with her for admiration, or seemed to mind her flirtations; but quietly suffering her to draw off all the fashionable beaux, whom Lady Jane stationed upon duty, she let Lady Frances Arlington talk, or dance, to her heart's content, and was satisfied often to sit still and be silent. The variety of words and ideas, facts and remarks, which her lively and practised companion poured into her mind, Caroline was left to class for herself, to generalize, and to make her own conclusions. Now she had means of amusement, she took pleasure in observing all that was going on, and she knew something of the characters and motives of the actors in such different scenes. As a spectator, she was particularly struck by the eagerness of all the players, at their different games of love, interest, or ambition; and in various sets of company, she was diverted by observing how each thought themselves the whole world: here a party of young ladies and gentlemen, practising, morning, noon, and night, steps for their quadrille; and while they are dancing the quadrille, jockey gentlemen ranged against the wall in the ball-room, talking of their horses; grave heads and snuff-boxes in a corner settling the fate of Europe, proving that, they were, are, or ought to be, behind the scenes; at the card-tables, sharpened faces seeing nothing in the universe but their cards; and at the piano-forte a set of signers and signoras, and ladies of quality, mingled together, full of duets, solos, overtures, cavatinas, expression, execution, and thorough bass—mothers in agonies, daughters pressed or pressing forward—some young and trembling with shame—more, though young, yet confident of applause—others, and these the saddest among the gay, veteran female exhibitors, tired to death, yet forced to continue the unfruitful glories. In one grand party, silence and state; in another group, rival matrons chasing round the room the heir presumptive to a dukedom, or wedging their daughters closer and closer to that door-way through which Lord William must pass. Here a poet acting enthusiasm with a chapeau bras—there another dying of ennui to admiration; here a wit cutting and slashing right or wrong; there a man of judgment standing by, silent as the grave—all for notoriety. Whilst others of high rank, birth, or wealth, without effort or merit, secure of distinction, looked down with sober contempt upon the poor stragglers and wranglers for fame.

Caroline had as yet seen but few of the literary candidates for celebrity; only those privileged few, who, combining the pretensions of rank and talent, had a natural right to be in certain circles; or those who, uniting superior address to superior abilities, had risen or forced their way into fine company. Added to these were two or three, who were invited to parties as being the wonder and show of the season—persons whom the pride of rank found it gratifying to have at command, and who afforded to them a most happy relief from the dulness of their habitual existence. Caroline, though pitying the exhibitors, whenever she met any of this description, had great curiosity, to see more of literary society; but Lady Jane systematically hung back on this point, and evaded her promises.

"Yes, my dear, I did promise to take you to Lady Angelica Headingham's, and Lady Spilsbury's, but there's time enough—not yet—not till I have established you in a higher society: not for your advantage to get among the blue-stockings—the blue rubs off—and the least shade might ruin you with some people. If you were married, I should introduce you to that set with pleasure, for they entertain me vastly, and it is a great privation to me this winter—a long fast; but even this abstinence from wit I can endure for your sake, my dear Caroline—you are my first object. If you would take the bel esprit line decidedly—Talents you have, but not courage sufficient; and even if you had, you are scarce old enough: with your beauty and grace, you have a better chance in the circle you are in, my dear."

But Lady Frances Arlington, who thought only of her own chance of amusement, seconded Caroline's wish to see the literary set. Nothing could be more stupid, her ladyship said, than running round always in the same circle; for her part, she loved to see clever odd people, and though her aunt-duchess would not let her go to Lady Spilsbury's, yet Lady Frances was sure that, with Lady Jane Granville for her chaperon, she could get a passport for Lady Angelica Headingham's, "because Lady Angelica is a sort of cousin, I can't tell you how many times removed, but just as many as will serve my present purpose—a connexion quite near enough to prove her fashionable, and respectable, and all that: so, my dear Lady Jane—I'll ask leave," concluded Lady Frances, "and we will go next conversazione day."

No—Lady Jane was firm to what she believed to be for Caroline's interest, and she refused to take her into that set, and therefore declined the honour of chaperoning her ladyship to Lady Angelica Headingham's.

"Oh! my dear Lady Jane, you couldn't, you wouldn't be so cruel! When I am dying with impatience to see my cousin make herself ridiculous, as I hear she does more and more every day with that Baron Wilhelmberg—Wilhelmberg, I said, not Altenberg—Miss Caroline Percy need not have turned her head so quickly. Lady Angelica's man is a German, and yours was a Pole, or Prussian, was not he?—Do you know, the ugliest man I ever saw in my life, and the handsomest, were both Poles—but they are all well-bred."

"But about Lady Angelica's German baron?" interrupted Lady Jane.

"Yes, what sort of a person is he?" said Caroline.

"As unlike your Count Altenberg as possible—an oddish looking genius—oldish, too—like one's idea of an alchymist, or a professor, or a conjuror—like any thing rather than a man of fashion; but, nevertheless, since he has got into fashion, the ladies have all found out that he is very like a Roman emperor—and so he is—like any head on an old coin."

"But how comes there to be such a value set on this head?—How came he into fashion?" said Lady Jane.

"Is it possible you don't know? Oh! it was when you were out of the world he first made the great noise—by dreaming—yes, dreaming—dreaming himself, and making every body else dream as he pleases; he sported last season a new theory of dreaming—joins practice to theory, too—very extraordinary—interprets all your dreams to your satisfaction, they say—and, quite on philosophical principles, can make you dream whatever he pleases. True, upon my veracity."

"Did your ladyship ever try his skill?" said Lady Jane.

"Not I; for the duchess would not hear of him—but I long the more to know what he could make me dream. He certainly is very clever, for he was asked last winter everywhere. All the world ran mad—Lady Spilsbury, and my wise cousin, I understand, came to pulling wigs for him. Angelica conquered at last; you know Angelica was always a little bit of a coquette—not a little bit neither. At first, to be sure, she thought no more of love for the German emperor than I do this minute; but he knew how to coquet also—Who would have thought it?—So there were notes, and verses, and dreams, and interpretations, and I can't tell you what. But, so far, the man is no charlatan—he has made Lady Angelica dream the very dream he chose—the strangest, too, imaginable—that she is in love with him. And the interpretation is, that she will take him 'for better for worse.'"

"That is your own interpretation, is not it, Lady Frances?" said Caroline.

"Is it possible there is any truth in it?" said Lady Jane.

"All true, positively, I hear. And of all things, I should like to see Lady Angelica and the baron face to face—tête-à-tête—or profile by profile, in the true Roman emperor and empress medal style."

"So should I, I confess," said Lady Jane, smiling.

"The best or the worst of it is," continued Lady Frances, "that, after all, this baron bold is, I've a notion, no better than an adventurer: for I heard a little bird sing, that a certain ambassador hinted confidentially, that the Baron de Wilhelmberg would find it difficult to prove his sixteen quarterings. But now, upon both your honours, promise me you'll never mention this—never give the least confidential hint of it to man, woman, or child; because it might get round, spoil our sport, and never might I have the dear delight of drawing the caricature."

"Now your ladyship is not serious, I am sure," said Caroline.

"Never more serious—never so serious in my life; and, I assure you," cried Lady Frances, speaking very earnestly and anxiously, "if you give the least hint, I will never forgive you while I live; for I have set my heart on doing the caricature."

"Impossible that, for the mere pleasure of drawing a caricature, you would let your own cousin expose herself with an adventurer!" said Caroline.

"La! Lady Angelica is only my cousin a hundred removes. I can't help her being ridiculous: every body, I dare say, has ridiculous cousins—and laugh one must. If one were forbidden to laugh at one's relatives, it would be sad indeed for those who have extensive connexions. Well, Lady Jane, I am glad to see that you don't pique yourself on being too good to laugh: so I may depend on you. Our party for Lady Angelica's is fixed for Monday."

No—Lady Jane had, it is certain, some curiosity and some desire to laugh at her neighbour's expense. So far, Lady Frances had, with address, touched her foible for her purpose; but Lady Jane's affection for Caroline strengthened her against the temptation. She was persuaded that it would be a disadvantage to her to go to this conversazione. She would not upon any account have Miss Percy be seen in the blue-stocking set at present—she had her reasons. To this resolution her ladyship adhered, though Lady Frances Arlington, pertinacious to accomplish any purpose she took into her fancy, returned morning after morning to the charge. Sometimes she would come with intelligence from her fetcher and carrier of news, as she called him, Captain Nuttall.

One day, with a very dejected countenance, her ladyship came in saying, "It's off—it's all off! Nuttall thinks it will never be a match."

The next day, in high spirits, she brought word, "It's on—it's on again! Nuttall thinks it will certainly be a match—and Angelica is more delightfully ridiculous than ever! Now, my dear Lady Jane, Tuesday?—next week?—the week afterwards? In short, my dearest Lady Jane, once for all, will you ever take me to her conversazione?"

"Never, my dear Lady Frances, till Miss Caroline Percy is married," said Lady Jane: "I have my own reasons."

"Then I wish Miss Caroline Percy were to be married to-morrow—I have my own reasons. But, after all, tell me, is there any, the least chance of Miss Percy's being married?"

"Not the least chance," said Caroline.

"That is her own fault," said Lady Jane, looking mortified and displeased.

"That cannot be said of me, there's one comfort," cried Lady Frances. "If I'm not married, 'tis not my fault; but my papa's, who, to make an eldest son, left me only a poor 5000l. portion. What a shame to rob daughters for sons, as the grandees do! I wish it had pleased Heaven to have made me the daughter of an honest merchant, who never thinks of this impertinence: then with my plum or plums, I might have chosen the first spend-thrift lord in the land, or, may be, I might have been blessed with an offer from that paragon of perfection, Lord William —. Do you know what made him such a paragon of perfection? His elder brother's falling sick, and being like to die. Now, if the brother should recover, adieu to my Lord William's perfections."

"Not in the opinion of all," said Lady Jane. "Lord William was a favourite of mine, and I saw his merit long ago, and shall see it, whether his elder brother die or recover."

"At all events," continued Lady Frances, "he will be a paragon, you will see, only till he is married, and then—

'How shall I your true love know
From any other man?'

"By-the-bye, the other day, Lord William, in flying from the chase of matrons, in his fright (he always looks like a frightened hare, poor creature!) took refuge between you two ladies. Seriously, Lady Jane, do you know I think you manage vastly well for your protégée—you are not so broad as Mrs. Falconer."

"Broad! I beg your ladyship's pardon for repeating your word," cried Lady Jane, looking quite angry, and feeling too angry to parry, as she usually did, with wit: "I really don't understand your ladyship."

"Then I must wish your ladyship a good morning, for I've no time or talents for explanation," said Lady Frances, running off, delighted to have produced a sensation.

Lady Jane rang for her carriage, and made no observations on what had passed. But in the evening she declared that she would not take Lady Frances Arlington out with her any more, that her ladyship's spirits were too much for her. "Besides, my dear Caroline, when she is with you, I never hear you speak a word—you leave it entirely to her ladyship. After all, she is, if you observe, a perfectly selfish creature."

Lady Jane recollected various instances of this.

"She merely makes a tool of me—my carriage, my servants, my time, myself, always to be at her service, whenever the aunt-duchess cannot, or will not, do her ladyship's behests. For the slightest errand she could devise, she would send me to the antipodes; bid me fetch her a toothpick from the farthest inch of the city. Well! I could pardon all the trouble she gives for her fancies, if she would take any trouble for others in return. No—ask her to do the least thing for you, and she tells you, she'd be very glad, but she does not know how; or, she would do it this minute, but that she has not time; or, she would have remembered it certainly, but that she forgot it."

Caroline admitted that Lady Frances was thoughtless and giddy, but she hoped not incurably selfish, as Lady Jane now seemed to suppose.

"Pardon me, she is incurably selfish. Her childishness made me excuse her for a great while: I fancied she was so giddy that she could not remember any thing; but I find she never forgets any thing on which she has set her own foolish head. Giddy! I can't bear people who are too giddy to think of any body but themselves."

Caroline endeavoured to excuse her ladyship, by saying that, by all accounts, she had been educated in a way that must make her selfish. "Idolized, and spoiled, I think you told me she was?"

"True, very likely; let her mother, or her grandmother, settle that account—I am not to blame, and I will not suffer for it. You know, if we entered like your father into the question of education, we might go back to Adam and Eve, and find nobody to blame but them. In the mean time, I will not take Lady Frances Arlington out with me any more—on this point I am determined; for, suppose I forgave her selfishness and childishness, and all that, why should I be subject to her impertinence? She has been suffered to say whatever comes into her head, and to think it wit. Now, as far as I am concerned, I will teach her better."

Caroline, who always saw the best side of characters, pleaded her freedom from art and dissimulation.

"My dear Caroline, she is not half so free from dissimulation as you are from envy and jealousy. She is always in your way, and you never see it. I can't bear to hear you defend her, when I know she would and does sacrifice you at any time and at all times to her own amusement. But she shall not stand in your light—for you are a generous, unsuspicious creature. Lady Frances shall never go out with me again—and I have just thought of an excellent way of settling that matter. I'll change my coach for a vis-à-vis, which will carry only two."

This Lady Jane, quick and decided, immediately accomplished; she adhered to her resolution, and never did take Lady Frances Arlington out with her more.

Returning from a party this evening—a party where they met Lord William, who had sat beside Caroline at supper—Lady Jane began to reproach her with having been unusually reserved and silent.

Caroline said she was not conscious of this.

"I hope and trust I am not too broad," continued Lady Jane, with a very proud and proper look; "but I own, I think there is as much indelicacy in a young lady's hanging back too much as in her coming too forward. And gentlemen are apt to over-rate their consequence as much, if they find you are afraid to speak to them, as if you were to talk—like Miss Falconer herself."

Caroline assented fully to the truth of this remark; assured Lady Jane that she had not intentionally hung back or been reserved; that she had no affectation of this sort. In a word, she promised to exert herself more in conversation, since Lady Jane desired it.

"I do wish it, my dear: you don't get on—there's no getting you on. You certainly do not talk enough to gentlemen when they sit beside you. It will be observed."

"Then, ma'am, I hope it will be observed too," said Caroline, smiling, "that the gentlemen do not talk to me."

"No matter—you should find something to say to them—you have plenty of gold, but no ready change about you. Now, as Lord Chesterfield tells us, you know, that will never do."

Caroline was perfectly sensible of this—she knew she was deficient in the sort of conversation of the moment, requisite for fine company and public places.

"But when I have nothing to say, is not it better for me to say nothing, ma'am?"

"No, my dear—half the world are in that predicament; but would it mend our condition to reduce our parties to quakers' silent meetings? My dear, you must condescend to talk, without saying any thing—and you must bear to hear and say the same words a hundred times over; and another thing, my dear Caroline—I wish you could cure yourself of looking fatigued. You will never be thought agreeable, unless you can endure, without showing that you are tired, the most stupid people extant—"

Caroline smiled, and said she recollected her father's telling her that "the Prince de Ligne, the most agreeable man of his day, declared that his secret depended, not on his wit or talents for conversation, but on his power of concealing the ennui he felt in stupid company."

"Well, my dear, I tell you so, as well as the Prince de Ligne, and let me see that you benefit by it to-morrow."

The next night they went to a large party at a very fine lady's. It was dull, but Caroline did her best to look happy, and exerted herself to talk to please Lady Jane, who, from her card-table, from time to time, looked at her, nodded and smiled. When they got into their carriage, Lady Jane, before she had well drawn up the glass, began to praise her for her performance this evening. "Really, my dear, you got on very well to-night; and I hear Miss Caroline Percy is very agreeable. And, shall I tell you who told me so?—No; that would make you too vain. But I'll leave you to sleep upon what has been said—to-morrow you shall hear more."

The next morning, Caroline had stolen away from visitors, and quietly in her own room was endeavouring to proceed in her copy of the miniature for Mr. Gresham, when Lady Jane came into her apartment, with a letter and its cover in her hand. "A letter in which you, Caroline, are deeply concerned."

A sudden hope darted across Caroline's imagination and illuminated her countenance. As suddenly it vanished, when she saw on the cover of the letter, no foreign post-mark, no foreign hand—but a hand unknown to her.

"Deeply concerned! How can I—how—how am I concerned in this, ma'am?" she asked—with difficulty commanding her voice to articulate the words.

"Only a proposal for you, my dear," said Lady Jane, smiling: "not a proposal for which you need blush, as you'll see if you'll read."

But observing that Caroline was not at this moment capable of reading, without seeming to notice the tremor of her hand, and that she was holding the letter upside down before her eyes, Lady Jane, with kind politeness, passed on to the picture at which her young friend had been at work, and stooping to examine the miniature with her glass, made some observations on the painting, and gave Caroline time to recover. Nor did her ladyship look up till Caroline exclaimed, "John Clay!—English Clay!"

"Yes—Clay, of Clay-hall, as Mrs. Falconer would say. You see, my love, I told you truly, it was no blushing matter. I am sorry I startled you by my abruptness. Surprises are generally ill-judged—and always ill-bred. Acquit me, I beseech you, of all but thoughtlessness," said Lady Jane, sitting down by Caroline, and kindly taking her hand: "I hope you know I am not Mrs. Falconer."

"I do, indeed," said Caroline, pressing her hand: "I feel all your kindness, all your politeness."

"Of course, I knew that a proposal from Clay, of Clay-hall, would be to you—just what it is to me," said Lady Jane. "I hope you cannot apprehend that, for the sake of his seven or ten thousand, whatever he has per annum, I should press such a match upon you, Caroline? No, no, you are worth something much better."

"Thank you, my dear Lady Jane," cried Caroline, embracing her with warm gratitude.

"Why, child, you could not think me so—merely mercenary. No; touch me upon family, or fashion—any of my aristocratic prejudices as your father calls them—and I might, perhaps, be a little peremptory. But John Clay is a man just risen from the ranks, lately promoted from being a manufacturer's son, to be a subaltern in good company, looking to rise another step by purchase: no, no—a Percy could not accept such an offer—no loss of fortune could justify such a mésalliance. Such was my first feeling, and I am sure yours, when you read at the bottom of this awkwardly folded epistle, 'Your ladyship's most devoted, &c. John Clay'—"

"I believe I had no feeling, but pure surprise," said Caroline. "I scarcely think Mr. Clay can be in earnest—for, to the best of my recollection, he never spoke five words to me in his life!"

"English Clay, my dear. Has not he said every thing in one word?—I should have been a little surprised, but that I have been seeing this good while the dessous des cartes. Don't flatter yourself that love for you offers Clay-hall—no; but hatred to Mrs. and Miss Falconer. There have been quarrels upon quarrels, and poor Lady Trant in the middle of them, unable to get out—and John Clay swearing he is not to be taken in—and Miss Falconer buffeting Lady Trant with the willow he left on her brows—and Mrs. Falconer smiling through the whole, and keeping the secret, which every body knows: in short, my dear, 'tis not worth explaining to you—but John Clay certainly hopes to complete the mortification of the Falconers by giving himself to you. Besides, you are in fashion. Too much has been said about him—I'm tired of him. Write your answer, my dear—or I'm to write, am I? Well, give me some gilt paper—let us do the thing properly." Properly the thing was done—the letter folded, not awkwardly, was sealed and sent, Caroline delighted with Lady Jane, and Lady Jane delighted with herself.

"So there's an end of that matter," said Lady Jane. "I saw how it would be long ago; but I was glad you saw nothing of it, lest you should not have let it come to a declaration. A refusal is always creditable; therefore, I own, I should have been mortified, if the season had passed without your having one proposal. But now you have nothing to be ashamed of—you've killed your man—and I hope and trust I shall live to see you kill another."

Caroline laughed, but said she was glad Lady Jane was not one of those who count refusals as so many proofs of a young lady's merit; for her own part, she acknowledged she was inclined to think that they were sometimes proofs rather of coquetry and duplicity.

Lady Jane hesitated, and said she did not see this—she could not agree to this.

The conversation went on till her ladyship and Caroline came to a complete opposition of opinion on a principle, which, though it was only stated in general, and in the abstract, her ladyship defended with an urgency, and Caroline resisted with a steadiness, which are seldom shown about any merely speculative point, unless there is some secret apprehension of their being soon reduced to practice.

Lady Jane asserted that "a woman should always let an attachment come to a declaration, before she permits a man to see her mind, even though determined upon a refusal."

Caroline thought this would be using the man ill.

Lady Jane maintained that it would be using him much worse to refuse him before he asked.

"But without refusing," Caroline said that "a gentleman might be led to perceive when he was not likely to be accepted, and thus would be saved the pain and humiliation of a rejected proposal."

"It was not a young lady's first business to think of that—her first duty was to do what was right and proper for herself," Lady Jane said.

"Certainly; but the very question is, what is right and proper?"

"To give a distinct answer when a distinct question is asked, neither more nor less," said Lady Jane. "Caroline, on these subjects you must trust to one who knows the world, to tell you the opinion of the world. A woman is safe, and cannot be blamed by friend or foe, if she adhere to the plain rule, 'Stay till you are asked.' Till a gentleman thinks proper, in form, to declare his attachment, nothing can be more indelicate than for a lady to see it."

"Or, in some cases, more disingenuous, more cruel, than to pretend to be blind to it."

"Cruel!—Cruel is a word of the last century, or the century before the last. Cruelty is never heard of now, my dear—gentlemen's hearts don't break in these our days; or suppose an odd heart should break, if the lady is treating it according to rule, she is not to blame. Why did not the proud tongue speak? Whatever happens, she is acquitted by the world."

"And by her own conscience? Surely not, if she deceive, and injure by deception."

Lady Jane warmly repeated that she knew the world—that at her time of life she ought to know the world—and that she was certain any line of conduct but that which she had pointed out would expose a woman to the charge of indelicacy, and perhaps of impertinence.

These were heavy charges, Caroline felt; but she thought that, when not deserved, they could be borne better than self-reproaches for the want of candour and truth.

Lady Jane observed, that, in the catalogue of female virtues, delicacy must have the foremost place.

Caroline made a distinction between real delicacy and punctilio.

Lady Jane was inclined to call it a distinction without a difference. She, however, more prudently said, that punctilio was necessary as the guard of female delicacy.

Undoubtedly; but the greater virtue should not be sacrificed to the less. Truth and sincerity, Caroline thought, must be classed among the highest virtues of woman, as well as of man, and she hoped they were perfectly consistent with the utmost feminine modesty. She asked whether, after all, the plea of delicacy and punctilio was not sometimes used to conceal the real motives? Perhaps ladies, in pretending to be too delicate to see a gentleman's sentiments, were often, in fact, gratifying their own vanity, and urging him to that declaration which was to complete the female triumph.

Lady Jane grew angry: but, fearing lest Caroline should perceive that she had some particular object in view—doubtful whether Caroline knew, or did not know, her aim—and farther, having a secret hope, that, like other young ladies who support fine sentiments about love and generosity, in conversation, she might, when it came to the test, forget them, her ladyship urged her opinion no farther.

Indeed, she candidly acknowledged, that much might be said on Caroline's side of the question—and there the matter ended.

CHAPTER XXXV

The object that Lady Jane had in view was to prevent Caroline from discouraging, by premature candour, a passion which she saw rising in the heart of a young nobleman.

Lord William —,

"Well pleased to 'scape from flattery to wit,"

had always preferred Lady Jane Granville's company to the society of those who courted him more, or with less delicacy. Since Miss Caroline Percy's arrival and appearance in town Lady Jane had, to do her justice, preserved with his lordship exactly the same even tenor of conduct; whatever her wishes might be, she had too much proper pride to compromise her own or her young friend's dignity. Moreover, her ladyship had sense and knowledge of character sufficient to perceive that such a sacrifice, or the least appearance of a disposition to make it, would be not only degrading, but vain: it would, she knew, for ever disgust and ruin them in the opinion of a man, who had infinitely more penetration and feeling than those who flattered him were aware that he possessed.

Lord William had excellent abilities, knowledge, and superior qualities of every sort, all depressed by excessive timidity, to such a degree as to be almost useless to himself and to others. Whenever he was, either for the business or pleasure of life, to meet or mix with numbers, the whole man was, as it were, snatched from himself. He was subject to that nightmare of the soul, who seats herself upon the human breast, oppresses the heart, palsies the will, and raises spectres of dismay, which the sufferer combats in vain—that cruel enchantress, who hurls her spell even upon childhood; and when she makes the youth her victim, pronounces, "Henceforward you shall never appear in your natural character: innocent, you shall look guilty; wise, you shall look silly; never shall you have the use of your natural faculties. That which you wish to say, you shall not say—that which you wish to do, you shall not do: you shall appear reserved when you are enthusiastic, insensible when your heart sinks into melting tenderness. In the presence of those you most wish to please, you shall be most awkward; and when approached by her you love, you shall become lifeless as a statue, under the irresistible spell of mauvaise honte."

Strange that France should give a name to that malady of the mind which she never knew, or of which she knows less than any other nation upon the surface of the civilized globe! Under the spell of mauvaise honte poor Lord William—laboured—fast bound—and bound the faster by all the efforts made for his relief by the matrons and young damsels who crowded round him continually. They were astonished that all their charms, and all the encouragement they held out, failed to free this young nobleman from his excessive timidity.

"What a pity! it was his only fault, they were sure."—"Ten thousand pities he could not be made to speak—they were certain he had a vast deal to say."—"And he could be so agreeable, they were confident, if he would."—"Most extraordinary that a man of his rank and fortune, whom every creature admired, should be so timid."

True; but the timid Lord William all the time esteemed himself more highly than these ladies who affected to admire him. Mixed with his apparent timidity there was a secret pride. Conscious of the difference between what he was, and what he appeared to be, he was at once mortified and provoked, and felt disdain and disgust for those who pretended to admire his outward man, or who paid to his fortune that tribute which he thought due to his merit. With some few, some very few, by whom he was appreciated, his pride and his timidity were equally at ease, his reserve vanished in an astonishing manner, and the man came out of the marble. Of this small number in his confidence Lady Jane Granville was one. Even from his boyish years she had discerned his worth and value, and he now distinguished her by his grateful and constant regard. But Lady Jane Granville, though a woman of considerable talents, could not be a judge of the whole of his mind, or the extent of his powers: her talent was chiefly wit—her knowledge, knowledge of the world—her mind cultivated but slightly, and for embellishment—his deeply, extensively, and with large views. When he became acquainted with Miss Caroline Percy, he soon found that to her all this appeared, and by her was justly valued. His assiduity in cultivating his friend Lady Jane's acquaintance increased; and his taste for the conversation at her house became so great, that he was always the first, and usually the last, at her parties. His morning visits were frequent and long; he knew, by instinct, the hours when the two ladies were disengaged, but not always so exactly the time when he ought to take leave. His ear never informed him when Lady Jane's carriage came to the door, nor did he always hear the servant announce its being in readiness. Her ladyship might fidget as much as her politeness would permit without danger of its being observed. His lordship never was wakened to the sense of its being necessary to stir, till Miss Caroline Percy, by some strong indication, such as putting away her drawing, and the books, or by plainly saying, "We must go out now," made it manifest to him that he must depart. For this Caroline was regularly reproved afterwards by Lady Jane—but she never found that it gave Lord William any offence; nor did she for some time observe that it caused him much uneasiness. He seemed to her to stay from mere habitual absence of mind, and unwillingness to remove from a retreat where he was safe and comfortable, to some place where he was liable to be annoyed by his fair persecutors. That he liked her company and conversation she did not affect to deny, nor could she doubt that he felt for her esteem and regard—he expressed both, and he was not a man to express more than he felt, or the truth of whose professions could be suspected; but she thought that his regard for her, and for Lady Jane, were both of the same nature. She thought him a friend, not a lover. This was not with Caroline a mere commonplace phrase. She believed this to be true; and at the time she believed it, she was right. But constantly in the society of an amiable, sensible, and beautiful young woman, with a man of feeling, taste, and understanding, whose heart is disengaged, the passage from friendship to love is found so easy and rapid, as to be scarcely perceptible. And to this, which generally happens in similar circumstances, Lord William was peculiarly liable. For though, from the crowds who courted his attention, it might seem that his liberty of choice was unlimited, yet, in fact, his power of choosing was contracted and reduced to the few "whom choice and passion both approve." Among these few his fastidious judgment, and his apprehensions of domestic unhappiness, saw frequently, and sometimes too justly, objection to the family connexion of the young lady: some want of union in it—want of principle, or train of dissipation, which he dreaded, or some folly he disliked; so that among the numbers of his own rank who sought his alliance, it was not easy for him to satisfy himself, even as to connexion—still more difficult to satisfy him as to love, "the modern fair one's jest," or, what is worse, her affectation. His lordship was well aware that among the numbers of young ladies who were ready at a moment's warning to marry him, not one of these would love him for his own sake. Now in common with Marmontel's Alcibiades, and with most men of rank who have any superiority of character, Lord William had an anxious desire to be loved for his own sake; for though, in the opinion of most people of the world, and of some philosophers, the circumstances of rank and fortune form a part of personal merit; yet as these are not indissolubly associated with the individual, he rather preferred affection and esteem arising from merit, of which he could not be deprived by any revolution of fate or turn of fancy. If he were ever loved by Caroline Percy, it would be for his own sake; and of the constancy of her affection, if once obtained, the whole tenor of her character and conduct gave him the most secure pledge. Her education, manners, talents, and beauty, were all such as would honour and grace the highest rank of life. She had no fortune—but that was of no consequence to him—he was likely to have a princely income: he had no debts, he had at present all that satisfied his wishes, and that could enable him to live married, as well as single, in a manner that suited his station. His friends, eager to have him marry, and almost despairing of his complying, in this point, with their wishes, left him entirely at liberty in his choice. Reason and passion both determined on that choice, just about the time when English Clay proposed for Caroline, and when the conversation about declarations and refusals had passed between her and Lady Jane. That conversation, instead of changing or weakening the opinions Caroline then expressed, had confirmed her in her own sentiments, by drawing out more fully the strength of the reasons, and the honourable nature of the feelings, on which they were founded. Some slight circumstances, such as she could scarcely state in words, occurred about this time, which first gave her the idea, that Lord William — felt for her more than esteem. The tender interest he showed one day when she had a slight indisposition—the extreme alarm he expressed one night when there occurred an embarrassment between their carriages at the door of the opera-house, by which Lady Jane's vis-à-vis was nearly overturned—an alarm much greater than Caroline thought the occasion required—was succeeded by anger against his coachman, so much more violent and vehement than the error or offence justified, or than his lordship had ever before been seen to show; these things, which in a man of gallantry might mean nothing but to show his politeness, from Lord William seemed indicative of something more. Caroline began to see that the friend might become a lover, and now, for the first time, questioned her own heart. She thought highly of Lord William's abilities and character—she saw, as she had once said to Lady Jane, "signs which convinced her that this volcano, covered with snow, and often enveloped in clouds, would at some time burst forth in torrents of fire." Little indication as Lord William now showed to common observers of being or of becoming an orator, she perceived in him the soul of eloquence; and she foresaw, that on some great occasion, from some great motive, he would at once vanquish his timidity, and burst forth upon the senate. She felt convinced that whether eloquent or silent, speaking or acting, in public or private life, Lord William would in every circumstance of trial fill and sustain the character of an upright, honourable, enlightened English nobleman. Notwithstanding that she thought thus highly of him, Count Altenberg, in her opinion, far surpassed him in the qualities they both possessed, and excelled in many, in which Lord William was deficient—in manner especially; and manner goes a great way in love, even with people of the best understanding. Besides all the advantages of manner, Count Altenberg had far superior talents, or at least far superior habits of conversation—he was altogether as estimable and more agreeable than his rival. He also had had the advantage of finding Caroline's mind disengaged—he had cultivated her society in the country, where he had had time and opportunity to develope his own character and hers—in one word, he had made the first impression on her heart; and such an impression, once made on a heart like hers, cannot be easily effaced. Though there seemed little chance of his returning to claim his place in her affections— though she had made the most laudable efforts to banish him from her recollection, yet

"En songeant qu'il faut qu'on l'oublie
On s'en souvient;"

and now she found, that not only all others compared with him were indifferent to her, but that any, whom she was forced to put in comparison and competition with Count Altenberg, immediately sunk in her opinion.

Thus distinctly knowing her own mind, Caroline was however still in doubt as to Lord William's, and afraid of mistaking the nature of his sentiments. She well remembered Lady Jane's cautions; and though she was fully resolved to spare by her candour the suspense and pain which coquetry might create and prolong, yet it was necessary to be certain that she read aright, and therefore to wait for something more decisive, by which to interpret his meaning. Lady Jane wisely forbore all observations on the subject, and never said or looked a word that could recall the memory of her former debate. With the most scrupulous, almost haughty delicacy, and the most consummate prudence, she left things to take their course, secure of what the end would be.

One night Lady Jane and Caroline were at a party. When they arrived, they descried Lord William, in the midst of a group of the fair and fashionable, looking as if he was suffering martyrdom. His eye caught Caroline as she passed, and his colour changed. The lady next him put up her glass, to look for the cause of that change—but the glass was put down again, and no apprehensions excited. By degrees, Lord William worked his way towards Caroline—no, not towards Caroline, but to Lady Jane Granville. The company near her were talking of a proposal, which a gentleman had lately made for a celebrated beauty—his suit had been rejected. Some said that the lady must have seen that he was attached to her, and that she had been to blame in allowing him so long to pay her attentions, if she were determined to refuse him at last; others defended the lady, saying that the gentleman had never made a distinct declaration, and that therefore the lady was quite correct in not appearing to know that his intentions meant any thing more than was avowed. Lord William listened, perfectly silent, and with an appearance of some anxiety. Lady Jane Granville supported warmly the same side of the question which she had taken in a similar conversation with Caroline.

Miss Percy was appealed to for her opinion, "Would it not be strange, indeed, if a lady were to reject a gentleman before she was asked?"

Lord William with increasing anxiety listened, but dared not look at Caroline, who with becoming modesty, but with firmness in what she believed to be right, answered, "that if a woman saw that a gentleman loved her, and felt that she could not return his attachment, she might, without any rude or premature rejecting, simply by a certain ease of manner, which every man of sense knows how to interpret, mark the difference between esteem and tenderer sentiments; and might, by convincing him that there was no chance of his obtaining any farther interest in her heart, prevent his ever having the pain of a decided refusal."

The discussion ended here. Fresh company joined them; other subjects were started. Lord William continued silent: he did not take any share in any conversation, but was so absent and absorbed in his own thoughts, that several times he was spoken to, without his being able to give a plausible answer—then he stood covered with confusion—confusion increasing from the sense that it was observed, and could not be conquered. The company moved different ways, but his lordship continued fixed near Caroline. At last the attention of all near him was happily diverted and drawn away from him by the appearance of some new and distinguished person. He seized the moment, and summoned courage sufficient to address some slight question to Caroline: she answered him with an ease of manner which he felt to be unfavourable to his wishes. The spell was upon him, and he could not articulate—a dead silence might have ensued, but that Lady Jane happily went on saying something about pine-apple ice. Lord William assented implicitly, without knowing to what, and replied, "Just so—exactly so—" to contradictory assertions; and if he had been asked at this instant whether what he was eating was hot or cold, he could not have been able to decide. Lady Jane composedly took a biscuit, and enjoyed the passing scene, observing that this was the pleasantest party she had been at this season.

Mrs. Crabstock came up, and Lady Jane, with wit at will, kept the pattern-lady in play by an opportunely-recollected tale of scandal; with ears delighted, eyes riveted, stood Mrs. Crabstock, while Lord William, again relieved from the fear of observation, breathed once more; and, partly recovering his senses, through the mist that hung over him, looked at Caroline, in hopes of drawing some encouraging omen from her countenance. He had come to this party determined to say something that should explain to her his sentiments. He thought he could speak to her better in a crowd than alone. Now or never! said he to himself. With desperate effort, and with an oppressed voice, he said—the very thing he did not mean to say.

"Miss Percy, I never was so inclined in all my life to quarrel with ease of manner in any body as in you." Then, correcting himself, and blushing deeply, he added, "I don't mean that I don't admire your ease of manner in general—but—in short, it is impossible, I think, that with your penetration, you can be in any doubt as to my sentiments. If I thought—"

He stopped short: he felt as if his life hung upon a thread—as if the first look, the first sound of her voice, the next word spoken, must decide his fate. He longed, yet feared to see that look, and to hear that word. "And I think it is impossible that, with your lordship's penetration, you should mistake mine," said Caroline.

There was an ingenuous sweetness in her look and voice, a fear of giving pain, yet a resolution to be sincere. Lord William felt and understood it all. He saw there was no hope. Caroline heard from him a deep sigh. With great and painful emotion, in the most calm voice she could command, but in the kindest tone, she added, "For the sentiments of regard and esteem your lordship has expressed for me, believe me, I am truly grateful."

Mrs. Crabstock moved towards them, and Caroline paused.

"Are you to be at Lady Arrowsmith's concert to-morrow, my lord?" said Mrs. Crabstock, who was now at liberty to ask questions; for even scandal will not hold curiosity in check for ever.

"Are you to be at Lady Arrowsmith's, my lord, to-morrow night?" repeated she, for her first attack was unheard.

"I do not know, indeed," said he, starting from his fit of absence.

Mrs. Crabstock persisted. "Were you at the opera last night, my lord?"

"I really, ma'am, do not recollect."

"Bless me!" cried Mrs. Crabstock.

And "Bless me!" cried Lady Jane Granville. "We are to be at the Duchess of Greenwich's ball: Caroline, my dear—time for us to move. My lord, might I trouble your lordship to ask if our carriage is to be had?"

Lord William, before she had completed the request, obeyed. As they went down the staircase, Lady Jane laughing said, "I am afraid I shall be as impertinently curious as Mrs. Crabstock—I was going to ask your lordship whether you are engaged to-morrow, or whether you can come to us—to me?"

"Unhappily," the accent on the word showed it was no expression of course. "Unhappily I cannot—I am engaged—I thank your ladyship."

Lady Jane looked back at Caroline, who was a little behind her.

"Though I could not recollect in time to tell Mrs. Crabstock where I was last night, or where I am to be to-morrow," continued his lordship, making an effort to smile, "yet I can satisfy your ladyship—I shall be at Tunbridge."

"Tunbridge!" cried Lady Jane, stopping short, and turning to Lord William, as the light shone full on his face: "Tunbridge, at this season?"

"All seasons are alike to me—all seasons and their change," replied Lord William, scarcely knowing what he answered—the powers of mind and body engrossed in suppressing emotion.

They had now reached the bottom of the stairs—a shawl of Lady Jane's was not to be found; and while the servants were searching for it, she and Caroline, followed by Lord William, went into one of the supper-rooms, which was open.

"To Tunbridge!" repeated Lady Jane. "No, my lord, you must not leave us."

"What is there to prevent me?" said Lord William, hastily, almost harshly; for though at the time he felt her kindness, yet, irresistibly under the power of his demon, he said the thing he did not mean: his voice and look expressed the reverse of what his heart felt.

"Nay, if there is nothing to prevent your lordship," said Lady Jane, walking away with dignity, "I have only to wish your lordship a good journey."

"I would stay, if I could see any thing to keep me," said Lord William, impelled, contrary to his better judgment, to appeal once more to Caroline's countenance. Then cursed himself for his weakness.

Lady Jane, turning back, saw his lordship's look; and now, convinced that Caroline was to blame for all, reproached herself for misinterpreting his words and manner.

"Well, my lord," cried she, "you will not be in such haste to set out for Tunbridge, I am sure, as to go before you hear from me in the morning. Perhaps I may trouble your lordship with some commands."

He bowed, and said he should do himself the honour of waiting her ladyship's commands. She passed on quickly towards the hall. Lord William offered his arm to Caroline.

"I must speak to you, Miss Percy—and have but a moment—"

Caroline walked more slowly.

"Thank you, madam—yes, I do thank you. Much pain you have given; but as little as you could. Better now than later. Like yourself—and I thank you for preserving the idea of excellence in my mind in all its integrity—in all—I shall detain you but a moment—you are not impatient?"

"No," said Caroline, in a tremulous voice; yet for his sake, as well as for the sake of her own consistency, trying to suppress emotion which she thought he might misinterpret.

"Fear not—I shall not misinterpret—I know too well what love is. Speak freely of my sentiments to Lady Jane, when I am gone—her friendship deserves it from me."

He stopped speaking. "Stay," said Caroline. "It may give your noble mind some ease to know that my heart was engaged before we ever met."

He was silent. It was the silence of deep feeling. They came within view of the servants—he walked quietly to the carriage—assisted her into it, pressed her hand—and said in a low voice, "Farewell—for ever."

The carriage-door was shut.

"Where to, my lady?" said the footman.

"The Duchess of Greenwich's, or home, Caroline?"

"Oh! home, if I may choose," said Caroline.

"Home!" said Lady Jane.

And the moment the glass was up, "Caroline, my dear, tell me this instant, what is all this between you and Lord William?—Is it as I hope?—or, is it as I fear?—speak."

Caroline could not—she was in tears.

"What have you done?—If you have said any thing irrevocable, and without consulting me, I never, never will forgive you, Caroline. Speak, at all events."

Caroline tried to obey her ladyship.

"What have you done?—What have you said?"

"I have said the truth—I have done, I hope, what I ought," said Caroline; "but I have given great pain—"

Lady Jane now perceiving by her voice that she was in sorrow, spoke no more in anger; but, checking herself, and changing her tone, said, "It is not irremediable, my dear. Whatever pain you may have given, you know the power to give pleasure is still in your own hands."

Caroline sighed—"Alas! no, madam, it is not."

"Why so, my love? He will not leave town in the morning without my commands; and I am at your command. A note, a line, a word, will set all to rights."

"But that word I cannot say."

"Then let me say it for you. Trust your delicacy to me—I will be dignity itself. Can you doubt it? Believe me, much as I wish to see you what and where you ought to be in society, I would not—there it is, begging Lady Frances Arlington's pardon, that Mrs. Falconer and I differ in character essentially, and de fond en comble. I would never yield a point of real delicacy; I would not descend the thousandth part of a degree from proper dignity, to make you—any more than to make myself—a princess. And now, without reserve, open your heart, and tell me what you wish to have done or said."

"Nothing, my dear Lady Jane."

"Nothing? my dear Caroline."

"I have no more to say—I have said all I can say."

The carriage stopped at their own door.

"We are all in the dark," said Lady Jane: "when I have more light I shall be able better to tell what we are about."

"Now, I can see as well as hear," continued she, as her woman met her with lights. "Keppel, you may go to bed; we shall not want you to-night."

"Now, Caroline, take care: remember your countenance is open to me, if not your heart."

"Both, both are open to you, my dear friend!" cried Caroline. "And Lord William, who said you deserved it from him, desired me to speak as freely for him as for myself."

"He's a noble creature! There's the difference between reserve of character and reserve of manner—I always said so. Go on, my dear."

Caroline related every thing that had passed; and Lady Jane, when she had finished, said, "A couple of children!—But a couple of charming children. Now I, that have common sense, must set it all to rights, and turn no prettily into yes."

"It cannot be done," said Caroline.

"Pardon me, solemn fair one, it can."

"Pardon me, my dear Lady Jane, it must not be done."

"Children should not say must," cried Lady Jane, in a playful tone; for never did she feel in more delightful spirits than at this moment, when all her hopes for Caroline, as she thought, were realized; "and to complete 'the pleasing history,' no obstacle remained," she said, "but the Chinese mother-of-pearl curtain of etiquette to be withdrawn, by a dexterous, delicate hand, from between Shuey-Ping-Sin and her lover." Lady Jane, late as it was at night, took up a pen, to write a note to Lord William.

"What are you going to do, may I ask, my dear madam?" cried Caroline.

"My dear madam, I am going my own way—let me alone."

"But if you mean to write for me—"

"For you!—not at all—for myself. I beg to see Lord William in the morning, to trouble him with my commands."

"But seriously, my dear Lady Jane, do not give him unnecessary pain—for my mind is decided."

"So every young lady says—it is a ruled case—for the first three days." Lady Jane wrote on as fast as she could.

"My dear Lady Jane," cried Caroline, stopping her ladyship's hand, "I am in earnest."

"So, then," cried Lady Jane, impatiently, "you will not trust me—you will not open your heart to me, Caroline?"

"I do—I have trusted you entirely, my dear friend. My heart I opened to you long ago."

A dead pause—and blank consternation in Lady Jane's countenance.

"But surely since then it must have changed?"

"Not in the least."

"But it will change: let Lord William try to change it."

Caroline shook her head. "It will not—I cannot."

"And you won't do this, when I ask it as a favour for my friend, my particular friend?"

"Excuse me, dear, kind Lady Jane; I know you wish only my happiness, but this would make me unhappy. It is the only thing you could ask with which I would not comply."

"Then I'll never ask any thing else while I live from you, Miss Percy," cried Lady Jane, rising and throwing her pen from her. "You are resolved to throw your happiness from you—do so. Wish your happiness!— yes, I have wished it anxiously—ardently! but now I have done: you are determined to be perverse and philosophical. Good night to you."

Lady Jane snatched up her candle, and in haste retired. Caroline, sensible that all her ladyship's anger at this moment arose from warm affection, was the more sorry to have occasioned it, and to feel that she could not, by yielding, allay it instantly.—A sleepless night.

Early in the morning, Keppel, half-dressed and not half awake, came, with her ladyship's love, and begged to speak a word to Miss Percy.

"Love!" repeated Caroline, as she went to Lady Jane's apartment: "how kind she is!"

"My dear, you have not slept, I see—nor I neither; but I am sure you have forgiven my hastiness;" said Lady Jane, raising herself on her pillow.

Caroline kissed her affectionately.

"And let these tears, my dearest Caroline," continued Lady Jane, "be converted into tears of joy: for my sake—for your whole family—for your own sake, my sweet girl, be advised, and don't throw away your happiness for life. Here's a note from Lord William—he waits my commands—that's all. Let me only desire to see him."

"On my account? I cannot," said Caroline—the tears streaming down her face, though she spoke calmly.

"Then it is your pride to refuse the man for whom every other young woman is sighing."

"No, believe me that I do not act from pride: I feel none—I have no reason to feel any."

"No reason to feel pride! Don't you know—yes, you know as well as I do, that this is the man of men— the man on whom every mother's—every daughter's eye is fixed—the first unmarried nobleman now in England—the prize of prizes. The most excellent man, you allow, and universally allowed to be the most agreeable."

"But if he be not so to me?" said Caroline.

"That can only be because—you are conscious of the cause, Caroline—it is your own fault."

"And therefore I said, that I felt I had no reason to be proud," said Caroline.

"Then have reason to be proud; conquer this weakness, and then you may have cause to be proud. You pique yourself on being reasonable: is it reasonable to leave your affections in the possession of a man, of whom, in all human probability, you will never hear more?"

"Too probable," said Caroline.

"And will you, Caroline Percy, like Lady Angelica Headingham, leave your heart at the mercy of a foreign adventurer?"

"Oh! stop, ma'am," cried Caroline, putting her hand before Lady Jane's mouth: "don't say that word—any thing else I could bear. But if you knew him—education, character, manners—no, you would not be so unjust."

"You know you told me you were sensible you ought not to indulge such a weakness, Caroline?"

"I did—I am sensible of it—oh! you see I am; and my best—my very best have I done to drive him from my memory; and never, till I was forced to make this comparison, did I recollect—did I feel—Weak, I may be," said Caroline, changing from great agitation to perfect decision; "but wicked will not be: I will never marry one man, and love another. My own happiness if I sacrifice, mine be the consequence; but will never injure the happiness of another. Do not, madam, keep that noble heart, this excellent Lord William, in suspense—What are your commands?"

"My commands!" cried Lady Jane, raising her voice, trembling with anger. "Then this is your gratitude—this your generosity!"

"I cannot be generous—I must be just. I have concealed nothing from Lord William—he knows that my heart was engaged before we met."

"And this your affection for all your friends—all who wish for your happiness? You would sacrifice nothing—nothing—no, not the slightest fancy, disgraceful fancy of your own, to please them, when you know how ardently too they wish to see you happily married."

"To marry to please others, against my own inclination, against my own conscience, must be weakness indeed—self-deception; for if my friends wish my happiness, and I make myself miserable, how can that please them? Any sacrifice I could make, except that of principle, I would; but that I never will make, nor will my friends, nor do they, desire it—Forgive me, dear Lady Jane."

"I never will forgive you," interrupted Lady Jane. "Ring!—yes, ring the bell—and when rung, never expect my forgiveness."

It must be done, thought Caroline, sooner or later.

"My compliments, Keppel, to Lord William," said Lady Jane; "I have no commands to trouble him with. Stay, I must find something—that parcel for Mrs. Baggot, Tunbridge—I must write—I cannot write."

"With great difficulty, in the agitation of her mind and hand, Lady Jane wrote a few lines, and holding the note up, looked at Caroline—a last appeal—in vain.

"Take it, Keppel—I'm sorry Lord William's servant has been kept waiting," cried her ladyship, and suddenly closed the curtain. Caroline retired softly, hoping that Lady Jane might sleep, and sleep off her anger; but no—the morning passed—the day passed—and the sun went down upon her wrath. At night she would not, she could not, go out any where. Caroline, alone with her, endured a terrible tête-à-tête. Lady Jane never spoke. Caroline tried all she could, by affectionate kindness of look and voice, and by contrite gentleness, to soothe her perturbed spirit. Lady Jane's anger admitted of no alleviation: her disappointment increased the more she reflected, and the more she thought of what others would think, if they could know it. And that they did not know, might never know it, (for Lady Jane was too honourable to betray Lord William's secret,) was an additional mortification. It was not till after ninety-six hours that Caroline perceived in her ladyship any change for the better. The first favourable symptom was her giving vent to her natural feelings in the following broken sentences: "After all my pains! When I was just thinking of writing to your father—when I might have carried you home in triumph, Lady William! A duke in all human probability—a duchess—absolutely a duchess you might have been! And such a well-informed—such an amiable man!—every thing your own family could have wished—And Rosamond!—Ah! poor Rosamond—Rosamond, you little know!—And nobody will ever know—no creature will ever be a bit the wiser. If you would have let him even come to a declaration—properly, decently to a declaration—let him attend you in public once or twice, your declared admirer—what harm could it possibly have done him, you, or any body? Then there would have been some credit, at least—and some comfort to me. But now, at the end of the campaign, just where we were before! The season over, under Lady Jane Granville's chaperonage, the beautiful Miss Caroline Percy has received one proposal and a quarter!—No, while I live, I will never forgive it."

CHAPTER XXXVI

No less an event than Alfred's marriage, no event calling less imperatively upon her feelings, could have recovered Lady Jane's sympathy for Caroline. But Alfred Percy, who had been the restorer of her fortune, her friend in adversity, what pain it would give him to find her, at the moment when he might expect her congratulations, quarrelling with his sister—that sister, too, who had left her home, where she was so happy, and Hungerford Castle, where she was adored, on purpose to tend Lady Jane in sickness and obscurity!

Without being put exactly into these words, or, perhaps, into any words, thoughts such as these, with feelings of gratitude and affection, revived for Caroline in Lady Jane's mind the moment she heard of Alfred's intended marriage.

"Good young man!—Excellent friend!—Well, tell me all about it, my dear."

It was the first time that her ladyship had said my dear to Caroline since the day of the fatal refusal.

Caroline was touched by this word of reconciliation—and the tears it brought into her eyes completely overcame Lady Jane, who hastily wiped her own.

"So, my dear Caroline—where were we? Tell me about your brother's marriage—when is it to be?— How has it been brought about?—The last I heard of the Leicesters was the good dean's death—I remember pitying them very much—Were they not left in straitened circumstances, too? Will Alfred have any fortune with Miss Leicester?—Tell me every thing—read me his letters."

To go back to Dr. Leicester's death. For some months his preferments were kept in abeyance. Many were named, or thought of, as likely to succeed him. The deanery was in the gift of the crown, and as it was imagined that the vicarage was also at the disposal of government, applications had poured in, on all sides, for friends, and friends' friends, to the remotest link of the supporters of ministry—But—to use their own elegant, phrase—the hands of government were tied.

It seems that in consequence of some parliamentary interest, formerly given opportunely, and in consideration of certain arrangements in his diocese, to serve persons whom ministers were obliged to oblige, a promise had long ago been given to Bishop Clay that his recommendation to the deanery should be accepted on the next vacancy. The bishop, who had promised the living to his sister's husband, now presented it to Mr. Buckhurst Falconer, with the important addition of Dr. Leicester's deanery.

To become a dean was once the height of Buckhurst's ambition, that for which in a moment of elation he prayed, scarcely hoping that his wishes would ever be fulfilled: yet now that his wish was accomplished, and that he had attained this height of his ambition, was he happy? No!—far from it; farther than ever. How could he be happy—dissatisfied with his conduct, and detesting his wife? In the very act of selling himself to this beldam, he abhorred his own meanness; but he did not know how much reason he should have to repent, till the deed was done. It was done in a hurry, with all the precipitation of a man who hates himself for what he feels forced to do. Unused to bargain and sale in any way, in marriage never having thought of it before, Buckhurst did not take all precautions necessary to make his sacrifice answer his own purpose. He could not conceive the avaricious temper and habits of his lady, till he was hers past redemption. Whatever accession of income he obtained from his marriage, he lived up to; immediately, his establishment, his expenses, surpassed his revenue. His wife would not pay or advance a shilling beyond her stipulated quota to their domestic expenses. He could not hear the parsimonious manner in which she would have had him live, or the shabby style in which she received his friends. He was more profuse in proportion as she was more niggardly; and whilst she scolded and grudged every penny she paid, he ran in debt magnanimously for hundreds. When the living and deanery came into his possession, the second year's fruits had been eaten beforehand. Money he must have, and money his wife would not give—but a litigious agent suggested to him a plan for raising it, by demanding a considerable sum from the executors of the late Dr. Leicester, for what is called dilapidation. The parsonage-house seemed to be in good repair; but to make out charges of dilapidation was not difficult to those who understood the business—and fifteen hundred pounds was the charge presently made out against the executors of the late incumbent. It was invidious, it was odious for the new vicar, in the face of his parishioners, of all those who loved and respected his predecessor, to begin by making such a demand—especially as it was well known that the late dean had not saved any of the income of his preferment, but had disposed of it amongst his parishioners as a steward for the poor. He had left his family in narrow circumstances. They were proud of his virtues, and not ashamed of the consequences. With dignity and ease they retrenched their expenses; and after having lived as became the family of a dignitary of the church, on quitting the parsonage, the widow and her niece retired to a small habitation, suited to their altered circumstances, and lived with respectable and respected economy. The charge brought against them by the new dean was an unexpected blow. It was an extortion, to which Mrs. Leicester would not submit—could not without injury to her niece, from whose fortune the sum claimed, if yielded, must be deducted.

Alfred Percy, from the first moment of their distress, from the time of good Dr. Leicester's death, had been assiduous in his attentions to Mrs. Leicester; and by the most affectionate letters, and, whenever he could get away from London, by his visits to her and to his Sophia, had proved the warmth and constancy of his attachment. Some months had now passed—he urged his suit, and besought Sophia no longer to delay his happiness. Mrs. Leicester wished that her niece should now give herself a protector and friend, who might console her for the uncle she had lost. It was at this period the dilapidation charge was made. Mrs. Leicester laid the whole statement before Alfred, declaring that for his sake, as well as for her niece's, she was resolute to defend herself against injustice. Alfred could scarcely bring himself to believe that Buckhurst Falconer had acted in the manner represented, with a rapacity, harshness, and cruelty, so opposite to his natural disposition. Faults, Alfred well knew that Buckhurst had; but they were all, he thought, of quite a different sort from those of which he now stood accused. What was to be done? Alfred was extremely averse from going to law with a man who was his relation, for whom he had early felt, and still retained, a considerable regard: yet he could not stand by, and see the woman he loved, defrauded of nearly half the small fortune she possessed. On the other hand, he was employed as a professional man, and called upon to act. He determined, however, before he should, as a last resource, expose the truth and maintain the right in a court of justice, previously to try every means of conciliation in his power. To all his letters the new dean answered evasively and unsatisfactorily, by referring him to his attorney, into whose hands he said he had put the business, and he knew and wished to hear nothing more about it. The attorney, Solicitor Sharpe, was impracticable— Alfred resolved to see the dean himself; and this, after much difficulty, he at length effected. He found the dean and his lady tête-à-tête. Their raised voices suddenly stopped short as he entered. The dean gave an angry look at his servant as Alfred came into the room.

"Your servants," said Alfred, "told me that you were not at home, but I told them that I knew the dean would be at home to an old friend."

"You are very good,—(said Buckhurst)—you do me a great deal of honour," said the dean.

Two different manners appeared in the same person: one natural—belonging to his former, the other assumed, proper, as he thought, for his present self, or rather for his present situation.

"Won't you be seated? I hope all our friends—" Mrs. Buckhurst, or, as she was called, Mrs. Dean Falconer, made divers motions, with a very ugly chin, and stood as if she thought there ought to be an introduction. The dean knew it, but being ashamed to introduce her, determined against it. Alfred stood in suspension, waiting their mutual pleasure.

"Won't you sit down, sir?" repeated the dean.

Down plumped Mrs. Falconer directly, and taking out her spectacles, as if to shame her husband, by heightening the contrast of youth and age, deliberately put them on; then drawing her table nearer, settled herself to her work.

Alfred, who saw it to be necessary, determined to use his best address to conciliate the lady.

"Mr. Dean, you have never yet done me the honour to introduce me to Mrs. Falconer."

"I thought—I thought we had met before—since—Mrs. Falconer, Mr. Alfred Percy."

The lady took off her spectacles, smiled, and adjusted herself, evidently with an intention to be more agreeable. Alfred sat down by her work-table, directed his conversation to her, and soon talked, or rather induced her to talk herself into fine humour. Presently she retired to dress for dinner, and "hoped Mr. Alfred Percy had no intention of running away—she had a well-aired bed to offer him."

The dean, though he cordially hated his lady, was glad, for his own sake, to be relieved from her fits of crossness; and was pleased by Alfred's paying attention to her, as this was a sort of respect to himself, and what he seldom met with from those young men who had been his companions before his marriage—they usually treated his lady with a neglect or ridicule which reflected certainly upon her husband.

Alfred never yet had touched upon his business, and Buckhurst began to think this was merely a friendly visit. Upon Alfred's observing some alteration which had been lately made in the room in which they were sitting, the dean took him to see other improvements in the house; in pointing out these, and all the conveniences and elegancies about the parsonage, Buckhurst totally forgot the dilapidation suit; and every thing he showed and said tended unawares to prove that the house was in the most perfect repair and best condition possible. Gradually, whatever solemnity and beneficed pomp there had at first appeared in the dean's manner, wore off, or was laid aside; and, except his being somewhat more corpulent and rubicund than in early years, he appeared like the original Buckhurst. His gaiety of heart, indeed, was gone, but some sparkles of his former spirits remained.

"Here," said he, showing Alfred into his study, "here, as our good friend Mr. Blank said, when he showed us his study, 'Here is where I read all day long—quite snug—and nobody's a bit the wiser for it.'"

The dean seated himself in his comfortable arm-chair. "Try that chair, Alfred, excellent for sleeping in at one's ease."

"To rest the cushion and soft dean invite."

"Ah!" said Alfred, "often have I sat in this room with my excellent friend, Dr. Leicester!"

The new dean's countenance suddenly changed: but endeavouring to pass it off with a jest, he said, "Ay, poor good old Leicester, he sleeps for ever,—that's one comfort—to me—if not to you." But perceiving that Alfred continued to look serious, the dean added some more proper reflections in a tone of ecclesiastical sentiment, and with a sigh of decorum—then rose, for he smelt that the dilapidation suit was coming.

"Would not you like, Mr. Percy, to wash your hands before dinner?"

"I thank you, Mr. Dean, I must detain you a moment to speak to you on business."

Black as Erebus grew the face of the dean—he had no resource but to listen, for he knew it would come after dinner, if it did not come now; and it was as well to have it alone in the study, where nobody might be a bit the wiser.

When Alfred had stated the whole of what he had to say, which he did in as few and strong words as possible, appealing to the justice and feelings of Buckhurst—to the fears which the dean must have of being exposed, and ultimately defeated, in a court of justice—"Mrs. Leicester," concluded he, "is determined to maintain the suit, and has employed me to carry it on for her."

"I should very little have expected," said the dean, "that Mr. Alfred Percy would have been employed in such a way against me."

"Still less should I have expected that I could be called upon in such a way against you," replied Alfred. "No one can feel it more than I do. The object of my present visit is to try whether some accommodation may not be made, which will relieve us both from the necessity of going to law, and may prevent me from being driven to the performance of this most painful professional duty."

"Duty! professional duty!" repeated Buckhurst: "as if I did not understand all those cloak-words, and know how easy it is to put them on and off at pleasure!"

"To some it may be, but not to me," said Alfred, calmly.

Anger started into Buckhurst's countenance: but conscious how inefficacious it would be, and how completely he had laid himself open, the dean answered, "You are the best judge, sir. But I trust— though I don't pretend to understand the honour of lawyers—I trust, as a gentleman, you will not take advantage against me in this suit, of any thing my openness has shown you about the parsonage."

"You trust rightly, Mr. Dean," replied Alfred, in his turn, with a look not of anger, but of proud indignation; "you trust rightly, Mr. Dean, and as I should have expected that one who has had opportunities of knowing me so well ought to trust."

"That's a clear answer," said Buckhurst. "But how could I tell?—so much jockeying goes on in every profession—how could I tell that a lawyer would be more conscientious than another man? But now you assure me of it—I take it upon your word, and believe it in your case. About the accommodation— accommodation means money, does not it?—frankly, I have not a shilling. But Mrs. Falconer is all accommodation. Try what you can do with her—and by the way you began, I should hope you would do a great deal," added he, laughing.

Alfred would not undertake to speak to his lady, unless the dean would, in the first instance, make some sacrifice. He represented that he was not asking for money, but for a relinquishment of a claim, which he apprehended not to be justly due: "And the only use I shall ever make of what you have shown me here, is to press upon your feelings, as I do at this moment, the conviction of the injustice of that claim, which I am persuaded your lawyers only instigated, and that you will abandon."

Buckhurst begged him not to be persuaded of any such thing. The instigation of an attorney, he laughing said, was not in law counted the instigation of the devil—at law no man talked of feelings. In matters of property judges did not understand them, whatever figure they might make with a jury in criminal cases—with an eloquent advocate's hand on his breast.

Alfred let Buckhurst go on with his vain wit and gay rhetoric till he had nothing more to say, knowing that he was hiding consciousness of unhandsome conduct. Sticking firmly to his point, Alfred showed that his client, though gentle, was resolved, and that, unless Buckhurst yielded, law must take its course—that though he should never give any hint, the premises must be inspected, and disgrace and defeat must follow.

Forced to be serious, fretted and hurried, for the half-hour bell before dinner had now rung, and the dean's stomach began to know canonical hours, he exclaimed, "The upshot of the whole business is, that Mr. Alfred Percy is in love, I understand, with Miss Sophia Leicester, and this fifteen hundred pounds, which he pushes me to the bare wall to relinquish, is eventually, as part of her fortune, to become his. Would it not have been as fair to have stated this at once?"

"No—because it would not have been the truth."

"No!—You won't deny that you are in love with Miss Leicester?"

"I am as much in love as man can be with Miss Leicester; but her fortune is nothing to me, for I shall never touch it."

"Never touch it! Does the aunt—the widow—the cunning widow, refuse consent?"

"Far from it: the aunt is all the aunt of Miss Leicester should be—all the widow of Dr. Leicester ought to be. But her circumstances are not what they ought to be; and by the liberality of a friend, who lends me a house, rent free, and by the resources of my profession, I am better able than Mrs. Leicester is to spare fifteen hundred pounds: therefore, in the recovery of this money I have no personal interest at present. I shall never receive it from her."

"Noble! Noble!—just what I could have done myself—once! What a contrast!"

Buckhurst laid his head down upon his arms flat on the table, and remained for some moments silent— then, starting upright, "I'll never claim a penny from her—I'll give it all up to you! I will, if I sell my band for it, by Jove!"

"Oh! what has your father to answer for, who forced you into the church!" thought Alfred.

"My dear Buckhurst," said he, "my dear dean—"

"Call me Buckhurst, if you love me."

"I do love you, it is impossible to help it, in spite of—"

"All my faults—say it out—say it out—in spite of your conscience," added Buckhurst, trying to laugh.

"Not in spite of my conscience, but in favour of yours," said Alfred, "against whose better dictates you have been compelled all your life to act."

"I have so, but that's over. What remains to be done at present? I am in real distress for five hundred pounds. Apropos to your being engaged in this dilapidation suit, you can speak to Mrs. Falconer about it. Tell her I have given up the thing; and see what she will do."

Alfred promised he would speak to Mrs. Falconer. "And, Alfred, when you see your sister Caroline, tell her that I am not in one sense such a wretch—quite, as she thinks me. But tell her that I am yet a greater wretch—infinitely more miserable than she, I hope, can conceive—beyond redemption—beyond endurance miserable." He turned away hastily in an agony of mind. Alfred shut the door and escaped, scarcely able to bear his own emotion.

When they met at dinner, Mrs. Dean Falconer was an altered person—her unseemly morning costume and well-worn shawl being cast aside, she appeared in bloom-coloured gossamer gauze, and primrose ribbons, a would-be young lady. Nothing of that curmudgeon look, or old fairy cast of face and figure, to which he had that morning been introduced, but in their place smiles, and all the false brilliancy which rouge can give to the eyes, proclaimed a determination to be charming.

The dean was silent, and scarcely ate any thing, though the dinner was excellent, for his lady was skilled in the culinary department, and in favour of Alfred had made a more hospitable display than she usually condescended to make for her husband's friends. There were no other guests, except a young lady, companion to Mrs. Falconer. Alfred was as agreeable and entertaining as circumstances permitted; and Mrs. Buckhurst Falconer, as soon as she got out of the dining-room, even before she reached the drawing-room, pronounced him to be a most polite and accomplished young man, very different indeed from the common run, or the usual style, of Mr. Dean Falconer's dashing bachelor beaux, who in her opinion were little better than brute bears.

At coffee, when the gentlemen joined the ladies in the drawing-room, as Alfred was standing beside Mrs. Falconer, meditating how and when to speak of the object of his visit, she cleared the ground by choosing the topic of conversation, which, at last fairly drove her husband out of the room. She judiciously, maliciously, or accidentally, began to talk of the proposal which she had heard a near relation of hers had not long since made to a near relation of Mr. Alfred Percy's—Mr. Clay, of Clay-hall, her nephew, had proposed for Mr. Alfred's sister, Miss Caroline Percy. She was really sorry the match was not to take place, for she had heard a very high character of the young lady in every way, and her nephew was rich enough to do without fortune—not but what that would be very acceptable to all men—especially young men, who are now mostly all for money instead of all for love—except in the case of very first rate extraordinary beauty, which therefore making a woman a prey, just as much one as the other, might be deemed a misfortune as great, though hardly quite, Mrs. Buckhurst said, as she had found a great fortune in her own particular case. The involution of meaning in these sentences rendering it not easy to be comprehended, the dean stood it pretty well, only stirring his coffee, and observing that it was cold; but when his lady went on to a string of interrogatories about Miss Caroline Percy—on the colour of her eyes and hair—size of her mouth and nose—requiring in short a complete full-length portrait of the young lady, poor Buckhurst set down his cup, and pleading business in his study, left the field open to Alfred.

"Near-sighted glasses! Do you never use them, Mr. Percy?" said Mrs. Dean Falconer, as she thought Alfred's eyes fixed upon her spectacles, which lay on the table.

No—he never used them, he thanked her: he was rather far-sighted than short-sighted. She internally commended his politeness in not taking them up to verify her assertion, and put them into her pocket to avoid all future danger.

He saw it was a favourable moment, and entered at once into his business—beginning by observing that the dean was much out of spirits. The moment money was touched upon, the curmudgeon look returned upon the lady; and for some time Alfred had great difficulty in making himself heard: she poured forth such complaints against the extravagance of the dean, with lists of the debts she had paid, the sums she had given, and the vow she had made, never to go beyond the weekly allowance she had, at the last settlement, agreed to give her husband.

Alfred pleaded strongly the expense of law, and the certainty, in his opinion, of ultimate defeat, with the being obliged to pay all the costs, which would fall upon the dean. The dean was willing to withdraw his claim—he had promised to do so, in the most handsome manner; and therefore, Alfred said, he felt particularly anxious that he should not be distressed for five hundred pounds, a sum for which he knew Mr. Falconer was immediately pressed. He appealed to Mrs. Falconer's generosity. He had been desired by the dean to speak to her on the subject, otherwise he should not have presumed—and it was as a professional man, and a near relation, that he now took the liberty: this was the first transaction he had ever had with her, and he hoped he should leave the vicarage impressed with a sense of her generosity, and enabled to do her justice in the opinion of those who did not know her.

That was very little to her, she bluntly said—she acted only up to her own notions—she lived only for herself.

"And for her husband." Love, Alfred Percy said, he was assured, was superior to money in her opinion. "And after all, my dear madam, you set me the example of frankness, and permit me to speak to you without reserve. What can you, who have no reason, you say, to be pleased with either of your nephews, do better with your money, than spend it while you live and for yourself, in securing happiness in the gratitude and affection of a husband, who, generous himself, will be peculiarly touched and attached by generosity?"

The words, love, generosity, generous, sounded upon the lady's ear, and she was unwilling to lose that high opinion which she imagined Alfred entertained of her sentiments and character. Besides, she was conscious that he was in fact nearer the truth than all the world would have believed. Avaricious in trifles, and parsimonious in those every-day habits which brand the reputation immediately with the fault of avarice, this woman was one of those misers who can be generous by fits and starts, and who have been known to give hundreds of pounds, but never without reluctance would part with a shilling.

She presented the dean, her husband, with an order on her banker for the money he wanted, and Alfred had the pleasure of leaving his unhappy friend better, at least, than he found him. He rejoiced in having compromised this business so successfully, and in thus having prevented the litigation, ill-will, and disgraceful circumstances, which, without his interference, must have ensued.

The gratitude of Mrs. Leicester and her niece was delightful. The aunt urged him to accept what he had been the means of saving, as part of her niece's fortune; but this he absolutely refused, and satisfied Mrs. Leicester's delicacy, by explaining, that he could not, if he would, now yield to her entreaties, as he had actually obtained the money from poor Buckhurst's generous repentance, upon the express faith that he had no private interest in the accommodation.

"You would not," said Alfred, "bring me under the act against raising money upon false pretences?"

What Alfred lost in money he gained in love. His Sophia's eyes beamed upon him with delight. The day was fixed for their marriage, and at Alfred's suggestion, Mrs. Leicester consented, painful as it was, in some respects, to her feelings, that they should be married by the dean in the parish church.

Alfred brought his bride to town, and as soon as they were established in their own house, or rather in that house which Mr. Gresham insisted upon their calling their own, Lady Jane Granville was the first person to offer her congratulations.—Alfred begged his sister Caroline from Lady Jane, as he had already obtained his father's and mother's consent. Lady Jane was really fond of Caroline's company, and had forgiven her, as well as she could; yet her ladyship had no longer a hope of being of use to her, and felt that even if any other offer were to occur—and none such as had been made could ever more be expected—it would lead only to fresh disappointment and altercation; therefore she, with the less reluctance, relinquished Caroline altogether.

Caroline's new sister had been, from the time they were first acquainted, her friend, and she rejoiced in seeing all her hopes for her brother's happiness accomplished by this marriage. His Sophia had those habits of independent occupation which are essential to the wife of a professional man, and which enable her to spend cheerfully many hours alone, or at least without the company of her husband. On his return home every evening, he was sure to find a smiling wife, a sympathizing friend, a cheerful fireside.—She had musical talents—her husband was fond of music; and she did not lay aside the accomplishments which had charmed the lover, but made use of them to please him whom she had chosen as her companion for life. Her voice, her harp, her utmost skill, were ready at any moment, and she found far more delight in devoting her talents to him than she had ever felt in exhibiting them to admiring auditors. This was the domestic use of accomplishments to which Caroline had always been accustomed; so that joining in her new sister's occupations and endeavours to make Alfred's evenings pass pleasantly, she felt at once as much at home as if she had been in the country; for the mind is its own place, and domestic happiness may be naturalized in a capital city.

At her brother's house, Caroline had an opportunity of seeing a society that was new to her, that of the professional men of the first eminence both in law and medicine, the men of science and of literature, with whom Alfred and Erasmus had been for years assiduously cultivating acquaintance. They were now happy to meet at Alfred's house, for they liked and esteemed him, and they found his wife and sister sensible, well-informed women, to whom their conversation was of real amusement and instruction; and who, in return, knew how to enliven their leisure hours by female sprightliness and elegance. Caroline now saw the literary and scientific world to the best advantage: not the amateurs, or the mere show people, but those who, really excelling and feeling their own superiority, had too much pride and too little time to waste upon idle flattery, or what to them were stupid, uninteresting parties. Those who refused to go to Lady Spilsbury's, or to Lady Angelica Headingham's, or who were seen there, perhaps, once or twice in a season as a great favour and honour, would call three or four evenings every week at Alfred's.

The first news, the first hints of discoveries, inventions, and literary projects, she heard from time to time discussed. Those men of talent, whom she had heard were to be seen at conversaziones, or of whom she had had a glimpse in fine society, now appeared in a new point of view, and to the best advantage; without those pretensions and rivalships with which they sometimes are afflicted in public, or those affectations and singularities, which they often are supposed to assume, to obtain notoriety among persons inferior to them in intellect and superior in fashion. Instead of playing, as they sometimes did, a false game to amuse the multitude, they were obliged now to exert their real skill, and play fair with one another.

Sir James Harrington tells us, that in his days the courtiers who played at divers games in public, had a way of exciting the admiration and amazement of the commoner sort of spectators, by producing heaps of golden counters, and seeming to stake immense sums, when all the time they had previously agreed among one another, that each guinea should stand for a shilling, or each hundred guineas for one: so that in fact two modes of calculation were used for the initiated and uninitiated; and this exoteric practice goes on continually to this hour, among literary performers in the intellectual, as well as among courtiers in the fashionable world.

Besides the pleasure of studying celebrated characters, and persons of eminent merit, at their ease and at her own, Caroline had now opportunities of seeing most of those objects of rational curiosity, which with Lady Jane Granville had been prohibited as mauvais ton. With men of sense she found it was not mauvais ton to use her eyes for the purposes of instruction or entertainment.

With Mrs. Alfred Percy she saw every thing in the best manner; in the company of well-informed guides, who were able to point out what was essential to be observed; ready to explain and to illustrate; to procure for them all those privileges and advantages as spectators, which common gazers are denied, but which liberal and enlightened men are ever not only ready to allow, but eager to procure for intelligent, unassuming females.

Among the gentlemen of learning, talents, and eminence in Alfred's own profession, whom Caroline had the honour of seeing at her brother's, were Mr. Friend, the friend of his early years at the bar; and that great luminary, who in a higher orbit had cheered and guided him in his ascent. The chief justice was in a station, and of an age, where praise can be conferred without impropriety, and without hurting the feelings of delicacy or pride. He knew how to praise—a difficult art, but he excelled in it. As Caroline once, in speaking of him, said, "Common compliments compared to praise from him, are as common coin compared to a medal struck and appropriated for the occasion."

About this time Mr. Temple came to tell Alfred, that a ship had been actually ordered to be in readiness to carry him on his intended embassy; that Mr. Shaw had recovered; that Cunningham Falconer had no more excuses or pretences for delay; despatches, the last Lord Oldborough said he should ever receive from him as envoy, had now arrived, and Temple was to have set out immediately; but that the whole embassy had been delayed, because Lord Oldborough had received a letter from Count Altenberg, giving an account of alarming revolutionary symptoms, which had appeared in the capital, and in the provinces, in the dominions of his sovereign, Lord Oldborough had shown Mr. Temple what related to public affairs, but had not put the whole letter into his hands. All that he could judge from what he read was, that the Count's mind was most seriously occupied with the dangerous state of public affairs in his country. "I should have thought," added Mr. Temple, "that the whole of this communication was entirely of a political nature, but that in the last page which Lord Oldborough put into my hand, the catch-words at the bottom were Countess Christina."

Alfred observed, "that, without the aid of Rosamond's imagination to supply something more, nothing could be made of this. However, it was a satisfaction to have had direct news of Count Altenberg."

The next day Mr. Temple came for Alfred. Lord Oldborough desired to see him.

"Whatever his business may be, I am sure it is important and interesting," said Mr. Temple; "by this time I ought to be well acquainted with Lord Oldborough—I know the signs of his suppressed emotion, and I have seldom seen him put such force upon himself to appear calm, and to do the business of the day, before he should yield his mind to what pressed on his secret thoughts."

CHAPTER XXXVII

When Alfred arrived, Lord Oldborough was engaged with some gentlemen from the city about a loan. By the length of time which the negotiators stayed, they tried Alfred's patience; but the minister sat with immoveable composure, till they knew their own minds, and till they departed. Then, the loan at once dismissed from his thoughts, he was ready for Alfred.

"You have married, I think, Mr. Alfred Percy, since I saw you last—I congratulate you."

His lordship was not in the habit of noticing such common events; Alfred was surprised and obliged by the interest in his private affairs which this congratulation denoted.

"I congratulate you, sir, because I understand you have married a woman of sense. To marry a fool—to form or to have any connexion with a fool," continued his lordship, his countenance changing remarkably as he spoke, "I conceive to be the greatest evil, the greatest curse, that can be inflicted on a man of sense."

He walked across the room with long, firm, indignant strides—then stopping short, he exclaimed, "Lettres de cachet!—Dangerous instruments in bad hands!—As what are not?—But one good purpose they answered—they put it in the power of the head of every noble house to disown, and to deprive of the liberty to disgrace his family, any member who should manifest the will to commit desperate crime or desperate folly."

Alfred was by no means disposed to join in praise even of this use of a lettre de cachet, but he did not think it a proper time to argue the point, as he saw Lord Oldborough was under the influence of some strong passion. He waited in silence till his lordship should explain himself farther.

His lordship unlocked a desk, and produced a letter.

"Pray, Mr. Percy—Mr. Alfred Percy—have you heard any thing lately of the Marchioness of Twickenham?"

"No, my lord."

Alfred, at this instant, recollected the whisper which he had once heard at chapel, and he added, "Not of late, my lord."

"There," said Lord Oldborough, putting a letter into Alfred's hands—"there is the sum of what I have heard."

The letter was from the Duke of Greenwich, informing Lord Oldborough that an unfortunate discovery had been made of an affair between the Marchioness of Twickenham and a certain Captain Bellamy, which rendered an immediate separation necessary.

"So!" thought Alfred, "my brother Godfrey had a fine escape of this fair lady!"

"I have seen her once since I received that letter, and I never will see her again," said Lord Oldborough: "that's past—all that concerns her is past and irremediable. Now as to the future, and to what concerns myself. I have been informed—how truly, I cannot say—that some time ago a rumour, a suspicion of this intrigue was whispered in what they call the fashionable world."

"I believe that your lordship has been truly informed," said Alfred; and he then mentioned the whisper he had heard at the chapel.

"Ha!—Farther, it has been asserted to me, that a hint was given to the Marquis of Twickenham of the danger of suffering that—what is the man's name?—Bellamy, to be so near his wife; and that the hint was disregarded."

"The marquis did very weakly or very wickedly," said Alfred.

"All wickedness is weakness, sir, you know: but to our point. I have been assured that the actual discovery of the intrigue was made to the marquis some months previously to the birth of his child—and that he forbore to take any notice of this, lest it might affect the legitimacy of that child. After the birth of the infant—a boy—subsequent indiscretions on the part of the marchioness, the marquis would make it appear, gave rise to his first suspicions. Now, sir, these are the points, of which, as my friend, and as a professional man, I desire you to ascertain the truth. If the facts are as I have thus heard, I presume no divorce can be legally obtained."

"Certainly not, my lord."

"Then I will direct you instantly to the proper channels for information."

Whilst Lord Oldborough wrote directions, Alfred assured him he would fulfil his commission with all the discretion and celerity in his power.

"The next step," continued Lord Oldborough—"for, on such a subject, I wish to say all that is necessary at once, that it may be banished from my mind—your next step, supposing the facts to be ascertained, is to go with this letter—my answer to the Duke of Greenwich. See him—and see the marquis. In matters of consequence have nothing to do with secondary people—deal with the principals. Show in the first place, as a lawyer, that their divorce is unattainable—next, show the marquis that he destroys his son and heir by attempting it. The duke, I believe, would be glad of a pretext for dissolving the political connexion between me and the Greenwich family. He fears me, and he fears the world: he dares not abandon me without a pretence for the dissolution of friendship. He is a weak man, and never dares to act without a pretext; but show him that a divorce is not necessary for his purpose—a separation will do as well—Or without it, I am ready to break with him at council, in the House of Lords, on a hundred political points; and let him shield himself as he may from the reproach of desertion, by leaving the blame of quarrel on my impracticability, or on what he will, I care not—so that my family be saved from the ignominy of divorce."

As he sealed his letter, Lord Oldborough went on in abrupt sentences.

"I never counted on a weak man's friendship—I can do without his grace—Woman! Woman! The same—ever since the beginning of the world!"

Then turning to Alfred to deliver the letter into his hand, "Your brother, Major Percy, sir—I think I recollect—He was better in the West Indies."

"I was just thinking so, my lord," said Alfred.

"Yes—better encounter the plague than a fool."

Lord Oldborough had never before distinctly adverted to his knowledge of his niece's partiality for Godfrey, but his lordship now added, "Major Percy's honourable conduct is not unknown: I trust honourable conduct never was, and never will be, lost upon me.—This to the Duke of Greenwich—and this to the marquis.—Since it was to be, I rejoice that this Captain Bellamy is the gallant.—Had it been your brother, sir—could there have been any love in the case—not, observe, that I believe in love, much less am I subject to the weakness of remorse—but a twinge might have seized my mind—I might possibly have been told that the marchioness was married against her inclination.—But I am at ease on that point—my judgment of her was right.—You will let me know, in one word, the result of your negotiation without entering into particulars—divorce, or no divorce, is all I wish to hear."

Alfred did not know all the circumstances of the Marchioness of Twickenham's marriage, nor the peremptory manner in which it had been insisted upon by her uncle, otherwise he would have felt still greater surprise than that which he now felt, at the stern, unbending character of the man. Possessed as Lord Oldborough was by the opinion, that he had at the time judged and acted in the best manner possible, no after-events could make him doubt the justice of his own decision, or could at all shake him in his own estimation.

Alfred soon brought his report. "In one word—no divorce, my lord."

"That's well—I thank you, sir."

His lordship made no farther inquiries—not even whether there was to be a separation.

Alfred was commissioned by the Duke of Greenwich to deliver a message, which, like the messages of the gods in Homer, he delivered verbatim, and without comment: "His grace of Greenwich trusts Lord Oldborough will believe, that, notwithstanding the unfortunate circumstances, which dissolved in some degree the family connexion, it was the farthest possible from his grace's wish or thoughts to break with Lord Oldborough, as long as private feelings, and public principles, could be rendered by any means compatible."

Lord Oldborough smiled in scorn—and Alfred could scarcely command his countenance.

Lord Oldborough prepared to give his grace the opportunity, which he knew he desired, of differing with him on principle: his lordship thought his favour and power were now sufficiently established to be able to do without the Duke of Greenwich, and his pride prompted him to show this to his grace and to the world. He carried it with a high hand for a short time; but even whilst he felt most secure, and when all seemed to bend and bow before his genius and his sway, many circumstances and many persons were combining to work the downfall of his power.

One of the first slight circumstances which shook his favour, was a speech he had made to some gentleman, about the presentation of the deanery to Buckhurst Falconer. It had been supposed by many, who knew the court which Commissioner Falconer paid to Lord Oldborough, that it was through his lordship's interest, that this preferment was given to the son; but when some person, taking this for granted, spoke of it to his lordship, he indignantly disclaimed all part in the transaction, and it is said that he added, "Sir, I know what is due to private regard as a man—and as a minister what must be yielded to parliamentary influence; but I never could have advised the bestowing ecclesiastical benefice and dignity upon any one whose conduct was not his first recommendation."

This speech, made in a moment of proud and perhaps unguarded indignation, was repeated with additions, suppressions, variations, and comments. Any thing will at court serve the purpose of those who wish to injure, and it is inconceivable what mischief was done to the minister by this slight circumstance. In the first place, the nobleman high in office, and the family connexions of the nobleman who had made the exchange of livings, and given the promise of the deanery to Bishop Clay, were offended beyond redemption—because they were in the wrong. Then, all who had done, or wished to do wrong, in similar instances, were displeased by reflection or by anticipation. But Lord Oldborough chiefly was injured by misrepresentation in the quarter where it was of most consequence to him to preserve his influence. It was construed by the highest authority into disrespect, and an imperious desire to encroach on favour, to control prerogative, and to subdue the mind of his sovereign. Insidious arts had long been secretly employed to infuse these ideas; and when once the jealousy of power was excited, every trifle confirmed the suspicion which Lord Oldborough's uncourtier-like character was little calculated to dispel. His popularity now gave umbrage, and it was hinted that he wished to make himself the independent minister of the people.

The affairs of the country prospered, however, under his administration; there was trouble, there was hazard in change. It was argued, that it was best to wait at least for some reverse of fortune in war, or some symptom of domestic discontent, before an attempt should be made to displace this minister, formidable by his talents, and by the awe his commanding character inspired.

The habit of confidence and deference for his genius and integrity remained, and to him no difference for some time appeared, in consequence of the secret decay of favour.

Commissioner Falconer, timid, anxious, restless, was disposed by circumstances and by nature, or by second nature, to the vigilance of a dependent's life; accustomed to watch and consult daily the barometer of court favour, he soon felt the coming storm; and the moment he saw prognostics of the change, he trembled, and considered how he should best provide for his own safety before the hour of danger arrived. Numerous libels against the minister appeared, which Lord Oldborough never read, but the commissioner, with his best spectacles, read them all; for he well knew and believed what the sage Selden saith, that "though some make slight of libels, yet you may see by them how the wind sets."

After determining by the throwing up of these straws which way the wind set, the commissioner began with all possible skill and dexterity to trim his boat. But dexterous trimmer though he was, and "prescient of change," he did yet not foresee from what quarter the storm would come.

Count Altenberg's letters had unveiled completely the envoy Cunningham Falconer's treachery, as far as it related to his intrigues abroad, and other friends detected some of his manoeuvres with politicians at home, to whom he had endeavoured to pay court, by betraying confidence reposed in him respecting the Tourville papers. Much of the mischief Cunningham had done this great minister still operated, unknown to his unsuspicious mind: but sufficient was revealed to determine Lord Oldborough to dismiss him from all future hopes of his favour.

"Mr. Commissioner Falconer," he began one morning, the moment the commissioner entered his cabinet, "Mr. Commissioner Falconer," in a tone which instantly dispelled the smile at entrance from the commissioner's countenance, and in the same moment changed his whole configurature. "My confidence is withdrawn from your son, Mr. Cunningham Falconer—for ever—and not without good reason—as you may—if you are not aware of it already—see, by those papers."

Lord Oldborough turned away, and asked his secretaries for his red box, as he was going to council.

Just as he left his cabinet, he looked back, and said, "Mr. Falconer, you should know, if you be not already apprised of it, that your son Cunningham is on his road to Denmark. You should be aware that the journey is not made by my desire, or by his majesty's order, or by any official authority; consequently he is travelling to the court of Denmark at his own expense or yours—unless he can prevail upon his Grace of Greenwich to defray his ambassadorial travelling charges, or can afford to wait for them till a total change of administration—of which, sir, if I see any symptoms to-day in council," added his lordship, in the tone of bitter irony; "I will give you fair notice—for fair dealing is what I practise."

This said, the minister left the commissioner to digest his speech as he might, and repaired to council, where he found every thing apparently as smooth as usual, and where he was received by all, especially by the highest, with perfect consideration.

Meantime Commissioner Falconer was wretched beyond expression—wretched in the certainty that his son, that he himself, had probably lost, irrecoverably, one excellent patron, before they had secured, even in case of change, another. This premature discovery of Cunningham's intrigues totally disconcerted and overwhelmed him; and, in the bitterness of his heart, he cursed the duplicity which he had taught and encouraged, still more by example, than by precept. But Cunningham's duplicity had more and closer folds than his own. Cunningham, conceited of his diplomatic genius, and fearful of the cautious timidity of his father, did not trust that father with the knowledge of all he did, or half of what he intended; so that the commissioner, who had thought himself at the bottom of every thing, now found that he, too, had been cheated by his son with false confidences; and was involved by him in the consequences of a scheme, of which he had never been the adviser. Commissioner Falconer knew too well, by the experience of Cumberland and others, the fate of those who suffer themselves to be lured on by second-hand promises; and who venture, without being publicly acknowledged by their employers, to undertake any diplomatic mission. Nor would Cunningham, whose natural disposition to distrust was greater than his father's, have sold himself to any political tempter, without first signing and sealing the compact, had he been in possession of his cool judgment, and had he been in any other than the desperate circumstances in which he was placed. His secret conscience whispered that his recall was in consequence of the detection of some of his intrigues, and he dreaded to appear before the haughty, irritated minister. Deceived also by news from England that Lord Oldborough's dismission or resignation could not be distant, Cunningham had ventured upon this bold stroke for an embassy.

On Lord Oldborough's return from council, the commissioner, finding, from his secret informants, that every thing had gone on smoothly, and being over-awed by the confident security of the minister, began to doubt his former belief; and, in spite of all the symptoms of change, was now inclined to think that none would take place. The sorrow and contrition with which he next appeared before Lord Oldborough were, therefore, truly sincere; and when he found himself alone once more with his lordship, earnest was the vehemence with which he disclaimed his unworthy son, and disavowed all knowledge of the transaction.

"If I had seen cause to believe that you had any part in this transaction, sir, you would not be here at this moment: therefore your protestations are superfluous—none would be accepted if any were necessary."

The very circumstance of the son's not having trusted the father completely, saved the commissioner, for this time, from utter ruin: he took breath; and presently—oh, weak man! doomed never to know how to deal with a strong character—fancying that his intercession might avail for his son, and that the pride of Lord Oldborough might be appeased, and might be suddenly wrought to forgiveness, by that tone and posture of submission and supplication used only by the subject to offended majesty, he actually threw himself at the feet of the minister.

"My gracious lord—a pardon for my son!"

"I beseech you, sir!" cried Lord Oldborough, endeavouring to stop him from kneeling—the commissioner sunk instantly on his knee.

"Never will the unhappy father rise till his son be restored to your favour, my lord."

"Sir," said Lord Oldborough, "I have no favour for those who have no sense of honour: rise, Mr. Falconer, and let not the father degrade himself for the son—unavailingly."

The accent and look were decisive—the commissioner rose. Instead of being gratified, his patron seemed shocked, if not disgusted: far from being propitiated by this sacrifice of dignity, it rendered him still more averse; and no consolatory omen appearing, the commissioner withdrew in silence, repenting that he had abased himself. After this, some days and nights passed with him in all the horrors of indecision—Could the minister weather the storm or not?—should Mr. Falconer endeavour to reinstate himself with Lord Oldborough, or secure in time favour with the Duke of Greenwich?—Mrs. Falconer, to whom her husband's groans in the middle of the night at last betrayed the sufferings of his mind, drew from him the secret of his fears and meditations. She advised strongly the going over, decidedly, and in time, but secretly, to the Greenwich faction.

The commissioner knew that this could not be done secretly. The attention of the minister was now awake to all his motions, and the smallest movement towards his grace of Greenwich must be observed and understood. On the other hand, to abide by a falling minister was folly, especially when he had positively withdrawn his favour from Cunningham, who had the most to expect from his patronage. Between these opposite difficulties, notwithstanding the urgent excitations of Mrs. Falconer, the poor commissioner could not bring himself to decide, till the time for action was past.

Another blow came upon him for which he was wholly unprepared—there arrived from abroad accounts of the failure of a secret expedition; and the general in his despatches named Colonel John Falconer as the officer to whose neglect of orders he principally attributed the disappointment. It appeared that orders had been sent to have his regiment at a certain place at a given hour. At the moment these orders came, Colonel John Falconer was out on a shooting party without leave. The troops, of course, on which the general had relied, did not arrive in time, and all his other combinations failed from this neglect of discipline and disobedience of orders. Colonel Falconer was sent home to be tried by a court-martial.

"I pity you, sir," said Lord Oldborough, as Commissioner Falconer, white as ashes, read in his presence these despatches—"I pity you, sir, from my soul: here is no fault of yours—the fault is mine."

It was one of the few faults of this nature which Lord Oldborough had ever committed. Except in the instance of the Falconer family, none could name any whom his lordship had placed in situations, for which they were inadequate or unfit. Of this single error he had not foreseen the consequences; they were more important, more injurious to him and to the public, than he could have calculated or conceived. It appeared now as if the Falconer family were doomed to be his ruin. That the public knew, in general, that John Falconer had been promoted by ministerial favour, Lord Oldborough was aware; but he imagined that the peculiar circumstances of that affair were known only to himself and to Commissioner Falconer's family. To his astonishment he found, at this critical moment, that the whole transaction had reached the ear of majesty, and that it was soon publicly known. The commissioner, with protestations and oaths, declared that the secret had never, by his means, transpired—it had been divulged by the baseness of his son Cunningham, who betrayed it to the Greenwich faction. They, skilled in all the arts of undermining a rival, employed the means that were thus put into their power with great diligence and effect.

It was observed at the levee, that the sovereign looked coldly upon the minister. Every courtier whispered that Lord Oldborough had been certainly much to blame. Disdainful of their opinions, Lord Oldborough was sensibly affected by the altered eye of his sovereign.

"What! After all my services!—At the first change of fortune!"

This sentiment swelled in his breast; but his countenance was rigidly calm, his demeanour towards the courtiers and towards his colleagues more than usually firm, if not haughty.

After the levee, he demanded a private audience.

Alone with the king, the habitual influence of this great minister's superior genius operated. The cold manner was changed, or rather, it was changed involuntarily. From one "not used to the language of apology," the frank avowal of a fault has a striking effect. Lord Oldborough took upon himself the whole blame of the disaster that had ensued, in consequence of his error, an error frequent in other ministers, in him, almost unprecedented.

He was answered with a smile of royal raillery, that the peculiar family circumstances which had determined his lordship so rapidly to promote that officer, must, to all fathers of families and heads of houses, if not to statesmen and generals, be a sufficient and home apology.

Considering the peculiar talent which his sovereign possessed, and in which he gloried, that of knowing the connexions and domestic affairs, not only of the nobility near his person, but of private individuals remote from his court, Lord Oldborough had little cause to be surprised that this secret transaction should be known to his majesty. Something of this his lordship, with all due respect, hinted in reply. At the termination of this audience, he was soothed by the condescending assurance, that whilst the circumstances of the late unfortunate reverse naturally created regret and mortification, no dissatisfaction with his ministerial conduct mixed with these feelings; on the contrary, he was assured that fear of the effect a disappointment might have on the mind of the public, in diminishing confidence in his lordship's efforts for the good of the country, was the sentiment which had lowered the spirits and clouded the brow of majesty.

His lordship returned thanks for the gracious demonstration of these sentiments—and, bowing respectfully, withdrew. In the faces and behaviour of the courtiers, as in a glass, he saw reflected the truth. They all pretended to be in the utmost consternation; and he heard of nothing but "apprehensions for the effect on the public mind," and "fears for his lordship's popularity." His secretary, Mr. Temple, heard, indeed, more of this than could reach his lordship's ear directly; for, even now, when they thought they foresaw his fall, few had sufficient courage to hazard the tone of condolence with Lord Oldborough, or to expose the face of hypocrisy to the severity of his penetrating eye. In secret, every means had been taken to propagate in the city, the knowledge of all the circumstances that were unfavourable to the minister, and to increase the dissatisfaction which any check in the success of our armies naturally produces. The tide of popularity, which had hitherto supported the minister, suddenly ebbed; and he fell, in public opinion, with astonishing rapidity. For the moment all was forgotten, but that he was the person who had promoted John Falconer to be a colonel, against whom the cry of the populace was raised with all the clamour of national indignation. The Greenwich faction knew how to take advantage of this disposition. It happened to be some festival, some holiday, when the common people, having nothing to do, are more disposed than at any other time to intoxication and disorder. The emissaries of designing partisans mixed with the populace, and a mob gathered round the minister's carriage, as he was returning home late one day—the same carriage, and the same man, whom, but a few short weeks before, this populace had drawn with loud huzzas, and almost with tears of affection. Unmoved of mind, as he had been when he heard their huzzas, Lord Oldborough now listened to their execrations, till from abuse they began to proceed to outrage. Stones were thrown at his carriage. One of his servants narrowly escaped being struck. Lord Oldborough was alone—he threw open his carriage-door, and sprang out on the step.

"Whose life is it you seek?" cried he, in a voice which obtained instant silence. "Lord Oldborough's? Lord Oldborough stands before you. Take his life who dares—a life spent in your service. Strike! but strike openly. You are Englishmen, not assassins."

Then, turning to his servants, he added, in a calm voice, "Home—slowly. Not a man here will touch you. Keep your master in sight. If I fall, mark by what hand."

Then stepping down into the midst of the people, he crossed the street to the flagged pathway, the crowd opening to make way for him. He walked on with a deliberate firm step; the mob moving along with him, sometimes huzzaing, sometimes uttering horrid execrations in horrid tones. Lord Oldborough, preserving absolute silence, still walked on, never turned his head, or quickened his pace, till he reached his own house. Then, facing the mob, as he stood waiting till the door should be opened, the people, struck with his intrepidity, with one accord joined in a shout of applause.

The next instant, and before the door was opened, they cried, "Hat off!—Hat off!"

Lord Oldborough's hat never stirred. A man took up a stone.

"Mark that man!" cried Lord Oldborough.

The door opened. "Return to your homes, my countrymen, and bless God that you have not any of you to answer this night for murder!"

Then entering his house, he took off his hat, and gave it to one of his attendants. His secretary, Temple, had run down stairs to meet him, inquiring what was the cause of the disturbance.

"Only," said Lord Oldborough, "that I have served the people, but never bent to them."

"Curse them! they are not worth serving. Oh! I thought they'd have taken my lord's life that minute," cried his faithful servant Rodney. "The sight left my eyes. I thought he was gone for ever. Thank God! he's safe. Take off my lord's coat—I can't—for the soul of me. Curse those ungrateful people!"

"Do not curse them, my good Rodney," said Lord Oldborough, smiling. "Poor people, they are not ungrateful, only mistaken. Those who mislead them are to blame. The English are a fine people. Even an English mob, you see, is generous, and just, as far as it knows."

Lord Oldborough was sound asleep this night, before any other individual in the house had finished talking of the dangers he had escaped.

The civil and military courage shown by the minister in the sudden attack upon his character and person were such as to raise him again at once to his former height in public esteem. His enemies were obliged to affect admiration. The Greenwich party, foiled in this attempt, now disavowed it. News of a victory effaced the memory of the late disappointment. Stocks rose—addresses for a change of ministry were quashed—addresses of thanks and congratulation poured in—Lord Oldborough gave them to Mr. Temple to answer, and kept the strength of his attention fixed upon the great objects which were essential to the nation and the sovereign he served.

Mr. Falconer saw that the storm had blown over, the darkness was past—Lord Oldborough, firm and superior, stood bright in power, and before him the commissioner bent more obsequious, more anxious than ever. Anxious he might well be—unhappy father! the life, perhaps, of one of his sons, his honour, certainly, at stake—the fortune of another—his existence ruined! And what hopes of propitiating him, who had so suffered by the favour he had already shown, who had been betrayed by one of the family and disgraced by another. The commissioner's only hope was in the recollection of the words, "I pity you from my soul, sir," which burst from Lord Oldborough even at the moment when he had most reason to be enraged against Colonel Falconer. Following up this idea, and working on the generous compassion, of which, but for this indication, he should not have supposed the stern Lord Oldborough to be susceptible, the commissioner appeared before him every day the image of a broken-hearted father. In silence Lord Oldborough from time to time looked at him; and by these looks, more than by all the promises of all the great men who had ever spoken to him, Mr. Falconer was reassured; and, as he told Mrs. Falconer, who at this time was in dreadful anxiety, he felt certain that Lord Oldborough would not punish him for the faults of his sons—he was satisfied that his place and his pension would not be taken from him—and that, at least in fortune, they should not be utterly ruined. In this security the commissioner showed rather more than his customary degree of strength of mind, and more knowledge of Lord Oldborough's character than he had upon most other occasions evinced.

Things were in this state, when, one morning, after the minister had given orders that no one should be admitted, as he was dictating some public papers of consequence to Mr. Temple, the Duke of Greenwich was announced. His grace sent in a note to signify that he waited upon Lord Oldborough by order of his majesty; and that, if this hour were not convenient, he begged to have the hour named at which his grace could be admitted. His grace was admitted instantly. Mr. Temple retired—for it was evident this was to be a secret conference. His grace of Greenwich entered with the most important solemnity—

infinitely more ceremonious than usual; he was at last seated, and, after heavy and audible sighs, still hesitated to open his business. Through the affected gloom and dejection of his countenance Lord Oldborough saw a malicious pleasure lurking, whilst, in a studied exordium, he spoke of the infinite reluctance with which he had been compelled, by his majesty's express orders, to wait upon his lordship on a business the most painful to his feelings. As being a public colleague—as a near and dear connexion—as a friend in long habits of intimacy with his lordship, he had prayed his majesty to be excused; but it was his majesty's pleasure: he had only now to beg his lordship to believe that it was with infinite concern, &c. Lord Oldborough, though suffering under this circumlocution, never condescended to show any symptom of impatience; but allowing his grace to run the changes on the words and forms of apology, when these were exhausted, his lordship simply said, that "his majesty's pleasure of course precluded all necessity for apology."

His grace was vexed to find Lord Oldborough still unmoved—he was sure this tranquillity could not long endure: he continued, "A sad business, my lord—a terrible discovery—I really can hardly bring myself to speak—"

Lord Oldborough gave his grace no assistance.

"My private regard," he repeated.

A smile of contempt on Lord Oldborough's countenance.

"Your lordship's hitherto invulnerable public integrity—"

A glance of indignation from Lord Oldborough.

"Hitherto invulnerable!—your grace will explain."

"Let these—these fatal notes—letters—unfortunately got into the hands of a leading, impracticable member of opposition, and by him laid—Would that I had been apprised, or could have conceived it possible, time enough to prevent that step; but it was done before I had the slightest intimation—laid before his majesty—"

Lord Oldborough calmly received the letters from his grace.

"My own handwriting, and private seal, I perceive."

The duke sighed—and whilst Lord Oldborough drew out, opened, and read the first letter in the parcel, his grace went on—"This affair has thrown us all into the greatest consternation. It is to be brought before parliament immediately—unless a resignation should take place—which we should all deplore. The impudence, the inveteracy of that fellow, is astonishing—no silencing him. We might hush up the affair if his majesty had not been apprised; but where the interest of the service is concerned, his majesty is warm."

"His majesty!" cried Lord Oldborough: "His majesty could not, I trust, for a moment imagine these letters to be I mine?"

"But for the hand and seal which I understood your lordship to acknowledge, I am persuaded his majesty could not have believed it."

"Believed! My king! did he believe it?" cried Lord Oldborough. His agitation was for a moment excessive, uncontrollable. "No! that I will never credit, till I have it from his own lips." Then commanding himself, "Your grace will have the goodness to leave these letters with me till to-morrow."

His grace, with infinite politeness and regret, was under the necessity of refusing this request. His orders were only to show the letters to his lordship, and then to restore them to the hands of the member of opposition who had laid them before his majesty.

Lord Oldborough took off the cover of one of the letters, on which was merely the address and seal. The address was written also at the bottom of the letter enclosed, therefore the cover could not be of the least importance. The duke could not, Lord Oldborough said, refuse to leave this with him.

To this his grace agreed—protesting that he was far from wishing to make difficulties. If there were any thing else he could do—any thing his lordship would wish to have privately insinuated or publicly said—

His lordship, with proud thanks, assured the duke he did not wish to have any thing privately insinuated; and whatever it was necessary to say or do publicly, he should do himself, or give orders to have done. His lordship entered into no farther explanation. The duke at last was obliged to take his leave, earnestly hoping and trusting that this business would terminate to his lordship's entire satisfaction.

No sooner was the duke gone than Lord Oldborough rang for his carriage.

"Immediately—and Mr. Temple, instantly."

Whilst his carriage was coming to the door, in the shortest manner possible Lord Oldborough stated the facts to his secretary, that letters had been forged in his lordship's name, promising to certain persons promotion in the army—and navy—gratification—and pensions. Some were addressed to persons who had actually obtained promotion, shortly after the time of these letters; others contained reproaches for having been ill-used. Even from the rapid glance Lord Oldborough had taken of these papers, he had retained the names of several of the persons to whom they were addressed—and the nature of the promotion obtained. They were persons who could have had no claim upon an honest minister. His lordship left a list of them with Mr. Temple—also the cover of the letter, on which was a specimen of the forged writing and the private seal.

"I am going to the king. In my absence, Mr. Temple, think for me—I know you feel for me. The object is to discover the authors of this forgery."

"My lord, may I consult with Mr. Alfred Percy?"

"Yes—with no other person."

It was not Lord Oldborough's day for doing business with the king. He was late—the king was going out to ride. His majesty received the minister as usual; but notwithstanding the condescension of his majesty's words and manner, it was evident to Lord Oldborough's penetration, that there was a coldness and formality in the king's countenance.

"I beg I may not detain your majesty—I see I am late," said Lord Oldborough.

"Is the business urgent, my lord?"

"No, sir; for it concerns principally myself: it can, therefore, wait your majesty's leisure at any hour your majesty may appoint."

The king dismounted instantly.

"This moment, my lord, I am at leisure for any business that concerns your lordship."

The king returned to the palace—Lord Oldborough followed, and all the spectators on foot and horseback were left full of curiosity.

Notwithstanding the condescension of his majesty's words and manner, and the polite promptitude to attend to any business that concerned his lordship, it was evident to Lord Oldborough's penetration that there was an unusual coldness and formality in the king's countenance and deportment, unlike the graciousness of his reception when satisfied and pleased. As soon as the business of the day had been gone through, Lord Oldborough said he must now beg his majesty's attention on a subject which principally concerned himself. The king looked as one prepared to hear, but determined to say as little as possible.

Lord Oldborough placed himself so as to give the king the advantage of the light, which he did not fear to have full on his own countenance.

"Sir, certain letters, signed with my name, and sealed with my seal, have, I am informed, been laid before your majesty."

"Your lordship has been rightly informed."

"I trust—I hope that your majesty—"

At the firm assertion, in the tone with which Lord Oldborough pronounced, I trust—his majesty's eye changed—and moved away from Lord Oldborough's, when he, with respectful interrogation of tone, added, "I hope your majesty could not believe those letters to be mine."

"Frankly, my lord," said the king, "the assertions, the insinuations of no man, or set of men, of any rank or weight in my dominions, could by any imaginable means have induced me to conceive it possible that such letters had been written by your lordship. Not for one moment could my belief have been compelled by any evidence less strong than your lordship's handwriting and seal. I own, I thought I knew your lordship's seal and writing; but I now see that I have been deceived, and I rejoice to see it."

"I thank your majesty. I cannot feel surprise that a forgery and a counterfeit which, at first view, compelled my own belief of their being genuine, should, for a moment, have deceived you, sir; but, I own, I had flattered myself that my sovereign knew my heart and character, yet better than my seal and signature."

"Undoubtedly, my lord."

"And I should have hoped that, if your majesty had perused those letters, no assertions could have been necessary, on my part, to convince you, sir, that they could not be mine. I have now only to rejoice that your majesty is undeceived; and that I have not intruded unnecessarily with this explanation. I am fully sensible, sir, of your goodness, in having thus permitted me to make, as early as possible, this assertion of my innocence. For the proofs of it, and for the detection of the guilty, I am preparing; and I hope to make these as clear to you, sir, as your majesty's assurance of the pleasure you feel in being undeceived is satisfactory—consolatory to me," concluded Lord Oldborough, with a bow of profound yet proud respect.

"My lord," said the king, "I have no doubt that this affair will redound to your honour, and terminate to your lordship's entire satisfaction."

The very phrase used by the Duke of Greenwich.

"As to myself, your lordship can have no farther anxiety; but I wish your lordship's endeavours to detect and bring proofs home to the guilty may be promptly successful—for the gratification of your own feelings, and the satisfaction of the public mind, before the matter should be brought forward in parliament."

His majesty bowed, and as Lord Oldborough retired, he added some gracious phrases, expressive of the high esteem he felt for the minister, and the interest he had always, and should always take, in whatever could contribute to his public and private—satisfaction—(again).

To an eye and ear less practised in courts than this minister's, all that had been said would have been really satisfactory: but Lord Oldborough discerned a secret embarrassment in the smile, a constraint in the manner, a care, an effort to be gracious in the language, a caution, a rounding of the periods, a recurrence to technical phrases of compliment and amity, a want of the free fluent language of the heart; language which, as it flows, whether from sovereign or subject, leaves a trace that the art of courtier or of monarch cannot imitate. In all attempts at such imitation, there is a want, of which vanity and even interest is not always sensible, but which feeling perceives instantly. Lord Oldborough felt it— and twice, during this audience, he was on the point of offering his resignation, and twice, exerting strong power over himself, he refrained.

He saw plainly that he was not where he had been in the king's confidence; that his enemies had been at work, and, in some measure, had succeeded; that suspicions had been infused into the king's mind. That his king had doubted him, his majesty had confessed—and Lord Oldborough discerned that there was no genuine joy at the moment his majesty was undeceived, no real anxiety for his honour, only the ostensible manifestation suitable to the occasion—repeatable—or recordable.

Still there was nothing of which he could complain; every expression, if written down or repeated, must have appeared proper and gracious from the sovereign to his minister; and for that minister to resign at such a moment, from pride or pique, would have been fatal to the dignity, perhaps to the integrity, of his character.

Lord Oldborough reasoned thus as he stood in the presence of the king, and compelled himself, during the whole audience, and to the last parting moment, to preserve an air and tone of calm, respectful self-possession.

CHAPTER XXXVIII

During Lord Oldborough's absence, his faithful secretary had been active in his service. Mr. Temple went immediately to his friend Alfred Percy. Alfred had just returned fatigued from the courts, and was resting himself, in conversation with his wife and Caroline.

"I am sorry to disturb you, Alfred," said Mr. Temple, "but I must take you away from these ladies to consult you on particular business."

"Oh! let the particular business wait till he has rested himself," said Mrs. Percy, "unless it be a matter of life and death."

"Life and death!" cried Lady Frances Arlington, running in at the open door—"Yes, it is a matter of life and death!—Stay, Mr. Temple! Mr. Percy! going the moment I come into the room—Impossible!"

"Impossible it would be," said Mr. Temple, "in any other case; but—"

"'When a lady's in the case,
You know all other things give place,'"

cried Lady Frances. "So, positively, gentlemen, I stop the way. But, Mr. Temple, to comfort you—for I never saw a man, gallant or ungallant, look so impatient—I shall not be able to stay above a moment— Thank you, Mrs. Percy, I can't sit down—Mrs. Crabstock, the crossest of Crabstocks and stiffest of pattern-women, is in the carriage waiting for me. Give me joy—I have accomplished my purpose, and without Lady Jane Granville's assistance—obtained a permit to go with Lady Trant, and made her take me to Lady Angelica's last night. Grand conversazione!—Saw the German baron! Caught both the profiles—have 'em here—defy you not to smile. Look," cried her ladyship, drawing out of her reticule a caricature, which she put into Caroline's hand; and, whilst she was looking at it, Lady Frances went on speaking rapidly. "Only a sketch, a scrawl in pencil, while they thought I was copying a Sonnet to Wisdom—on the worst bit of paper, too, in the world—old cover of a letter I stole from Lady Trant's reticule while she was at cards. Mr. Temple, you shall see my chef-d'oeuvre by and by; don't look at the reverse of the medal, pray. Did not I tell you, you were the most impatient man in the world?"

It was true that Mr. Temple was at this instant most impatient to get possession of the paper, for on the back of that cover of the letter, on which the caricature was drawn, the hand-writing of the direction appeared to him—He dared scarcely believe his eyes—his hopes.

"Mrs. Crabstock, my lady," said the footman, "is waiting."

"I know, sir," said Lady Frances: "so, Caroline, you won't see the likeness. Very well; if I can't get a compliment, I must be off. When you draw a caricature, I won't praise it. Here! Mr. Temple, one look, since you are dying for it."

"One look will not satisfy me," cried Mr. Temple, seizing the paper: "your ladyship must leave the drawing with us till to-morrow."

"Us—must. Given at our court of St. James's. Lord Oldborough's own imperative style."

"Imperative! no; humbly I beseech your ladyship, thus humbly," cried Mr. Temple, kneeling in jest, but keeping in earnest fast hold of the paper.

"But why—why? Are you acquainted with Lady Angelica? I did not know you knew her."

"It is excellent!—It is admirable!—I cannot let it go. This hand that seized it long shall hold the prize."

"The man's mad! But don't think I'll give it to you—I would not give it to my mother: but I'll lend it to you, if you'll tell me honestly why you want it."

"Honestly—I want to show it to a particular friend, who will be delighted with it."

"Tell me who, this minute, or you shall not have it."

"Mrs. Crabstock, my lady, bids me say, the duchess—"

"The duchess—the deuce!—if she's come to the duchess, I must go. I hope your man, Mrs. Percy, won't tell Mrs. Crabstock he saw this gentleman kneeling."

"Mrs. Crabstock's getting out, my lady," said the footman, returning.

"Mr. Temple, for mercy's sake, get up."

"Never, till your ladyship gives the drawing."

"There! there! let me go—audacious!"

"Good morning to you, Mrs. Percy—Good bye, Caroline—Be at Lady Jane's to-night, for I'm to be there."

Her ladyship ran off, and met Mrs. Crabstock on the stairs, with whom we leave her to make her peace as she pleases.

"My dear Temple, I believe you are out of your senses," said Alfred: "I never saw any man so importunate about a drawing that is not worth a straw—trembling with eagerness, and kneeling!—Caroline, what do you think Rosamond would have thought of all this?"

"If she knew the whole, she would have thought I acted admirably," said Mr. Temple. "But come, I have business."

Alfred took him into his study, and there the whole affair was explained. Mr. Temple had brought with him the specimen of the forgery to show to Alfred, and, upon comparing it with the handwriting on the cover of the letter on which the caricature was drawn, the similarity appeared to be strikingly exact. The cover, which had been stolen, as Lady Frances Arlington said, from Lady Trant's reticule, was directed to Captain Nuttall. He was one of the persons to whom forged letters had been written, as appeared by the list which Lord Oldborough had left with Mr. Temple. The secretary was almost certain that his lordship had never written with his own hand to any Captain Nuttall; but this he could ask the moment he should see Lord Oldborough again. It seemed as if this paper had never been actually used as the cover of a letter, for it had no post-mark, seal, or wafer. Upon farther inspection, it was perceived that a t had been left out in the name of Nuttall; and it appeared probable that the cover had been thrown aside, and a new one written, in consequence of this omission. But Alfred did not think it possible that Lady Trant could be the forger of these letters, because he had seen some of her ladyship's notes of invitation to Caroline, and they were written in a wretched cramped hand.

"But that cramped hand might be feigned to conceal the powers of penmanship," said Mr. Temple.

"Well! granting her ladyship's talents were equal to the mere execution," Alfred persisted in thinking she had not abilities sufficient to invent or combine all the parts of such a scheme. "She might be an accomplice, but she must have had a principal—and who could that principal be?"

The same suspicion, the same person, came at the same moment into the heads of both gentlemen, as they sat looking at each other.

"There is an intimacy between them," said Alfred. "Recollect all the pains Lady Trant took for Mrs. Falconer about English Clay—they—"

"Mrs. Falconer! But how could she possibly get at Lord Oldborough's private seal—a seal that is always locked up—a seal never used to any common letter, never to any but those written by his own hand to some private friend, and on some very particular occasion? Since I have been with him I have not seen him use that seal three times."

"When and to whom, can you recollect?" said Alfred.

"I recollect!—I have it all!" exclaimed Mr. Temple, striking the table—"I have it! But, Lady Frances Arlington—I am sorry she is gone."

"Why! what of her?—Lady Frances can have nothing more to do with the business."

"She has a great deal more, I can assure you—but without knowing it."

"Of that I am certain, or all the world would have known it long ago: but tell me how."

"I recollect, at the time when I was dangling after Lady Frances—there's good in every thing—just before we went down to Falconer-court, her ladyship, who, you know, has always some reigning fancy, was distracted about what she called bread-seals. She took off the impression of seals with bread—no matter how, but she did—and used to torment me—no, I thought it a great pleasure at the time—to procure for her all the pretty seals I could."

"But, surely, you did not give her Lord Oldborough's?"

"I!—not I!—how could you imagine such a thing?"

"You were in love, and might have forgotten consequences."

"A man in love may forget every thing, I grant—except his fidelity. No, I never gave the seal; but I perfectly recollect Lady Frances showing it to me in her collection, and my asking her how she came by it."

"And how did she?"

"From the cover of a note which the duke, her uncle, had received from Lord Oldborough; and I, at the time, remembered his lordship's having written it to the Duke of Greenwich on the birth of his grandson. Lord Oldborough had, upon a former occasion, affronted his grace by sending him a note sealed with a wafer—this time his lordship took special care, and sealed it with his private seal of honour."

"Well! But how does this bring the matter home to Mrs. Falconer?" said Alfred.

"Stay—I am bringing it as near home to her as possible. We all went down to Falconer-court together; and there I remember Lady Frances had her collection of bread-seals, and was daubing and colouring them with vermilion—and Mrs. Falconer was so anxious about them—and Lady Frances gave her several—I must see Lady Frances again directly, to inquire whether she gave her, among the rest, Lord Oldborough's—I'll go to Lady Jane Granville's this evening on purpose. But had I not better go this moment to Lady Trant?"

Alfred advised, that having traced the matter thus far, they should not hazard giving any alarm to Lady Trant or to Mrs. Falconer, but should report to Lord Oldborough what progress had been made.

Mr. Temple accordingly went home, to be in readiness for his lordship's return. In the mean time the first exaltation of indignant pride having subsided, and his cool judgment reflecting upon what had passed, Lord Oldborough considered that, however satisfactory to his own mind might be the feeling of his innocence, the proofs of it were necessary to satisfy the public; he saw that his character would be left doubtful, and at the mercy of his enemies, if he were in pique and resentment hastily to resign, before he had vindicated his integrity. "If your proofs be produced, my lord!"—these words recurred to him, and his anxiety to obtain these proofs rose high; and high was his satisfaction the moment he saw his secretary, for by the first glance at Mr. Temple's countenance he perceived that some discovery had been made.

Alfred, that night, received through Mr. Temple his lordship's request, that he would obtain what farther information he could relative to the private seal, in whatever way he thought most prudent. His lordship trusted entirely to his discretion—Mr. Temple was engaged with other business.

Alfred went with Caroline to Lady Jane Granville's, to meet Lady Frances Arlington; he entered into conversation, and by degrees brought her to his point, playing all the time with her curiosity, and humouring her childishness, while he carried on his cross-examination.

At first she could not recollect any thing about making the seals he talked of. "It was a fancy that had passed—and a past fancy," she said, "was like a past love, or a past beauty, good for nothing but to be forgotten." However, by proper leading of the witness, and suggesting time, place, and circumstance, he did bring to the fair lady's mind all that he wanted her to remember. She could not conceive what interest Mr. Percy could take in the matter—it was some jest about Mr. Temple, she was sure. Yes, she did recollect a seal with a Cupid riding a lion, that Mr. Temple gave her just before they went to Falconer-court—was that what he meant?

"No—but a curious seal—" (Alfred described the device.)

"Lord Oldborough's! Yes, there was some such odd seal." But it was not given to her by Mr. Temple—she took that from a note to her uncle, the Duke of Greenwich.

Yes—that, Alfred said, he knew; but what did her ladyship do with it?

"You know how I got it! Bless me! you seem to know every thing I do and say. You know my affairs vastly well—you act the conjuror admirably—pray, can you tell me whom I am to marry?"

"That I will—when your ladyship has told me to whom you gave that seal."

"That I would, and welcome, if I could recollect—but I really can't. If you think I gave it to Mr. Temple, I assure you, you are mistaken—you may ask him."

"I know your ladyship did not give it to Mr. Temple—but to whom did you give it?"

"I remember now—not to any gentleman, after all—you are positively out. I gave it to Mrs. Falconer."

"You are certain of that, Lady Frances Arlington?"

"I am certain, Mr. Alfred Percy."

"And how can you prove it to me, Lady Frances?"

"The easiest way in the world—by asking Mrs. Falconer. Only I don't go there now much, since Georgiana and I have quarrelled—but what can make you so curious about it?"

"That's a secret."—At the word secret, her attention was fixed.—"May I ask if your ladyship would know the seal again if you saw it?—Is this any thing like the impression?" (showing her the seal on the forged cover.)

"The very same that I gave Mrs. Falconer, I'll swear to it—I'll tell you how I know it particularly. There's a little outer rim here, with points to it, which there is not to the other. I fastened my bread-seal into an old setting of my own, from which I had lost the stone. Mrs. Falconer took a fancy to it, among a number of others, so I let her have it. Now I have answered all your questions—answer mine—Whom am I to marry?"

"Your ladyship will marry whomsoever—your ladyship pleases."

"That was an ambiguous answer," she observed; "for that she pleased every body." Her ladyship was going to run on with some further questions, but Alfred pretending that the oracle was not permitted to answer more explicitly, left her completely in the dark as to what his meaning had been in this whole conversation.

He reported progress to Lord Oldborough—and his lordship slept as soundly this night as he did the night after he had been attacked by the mob.

The next morning the first person he desired to see was Mr. Falconer—his lordship sent for him into his cabinet.

"Mr. Commissioner Falconer, I promised to give you notice, whenever I should see any probability of my going out of power."

"Good Heaven! my lord," exclaimed the commissioner, starting back. The surprise, the consternation were real—Lord Oldborough had his eye upon him to determine that point.

"Impossible, surely!—I hope—"

His hope flitted at the moment to the Duke of Greenwich—but returned instantly: he had made no terms—had missed his time. If Lord Oldborough should go out of office—his place, his pension, gone—utter ruin.

Lord Oldborough marked the vacillation and confusion of his countenance, and saw that he was quite unprepared.

"I hope—Merciful Powers! I trust—I thought your lordship had triumphed over all your enemies, and was firmer in favour and power than ever. What can have occurred?"

Without making any answer, Lord Oldborough beckoned to the commissioner to approach nearer the window where his lordship was standing, and then suddenly put into his hand the cover with the forged handwriting and seal.

"What am I to understand by this, my lord?" said the bewildered commissioner, turning it backwards and forwards. "Captain Nuttall!—I never saw the man in my life. May I ask, my lord, what I am to comprehend from this?"

"I see, sir, that you know nothing of the business."

The whole was explained by Lord Oldborough succinctly. The astonishment and horror in the poor commissioner's countenance and gestures, and still more, the eagerness with which he begged to be permitted to try to discover the authors of this forgery, were sufficient proofs that he had not the slightest suspicion that the guilt could be traced to any of his own family.

Lord Oldborough's look, fixed on the commissioner, expressed what it had once before expressed—"Sir, from my soul, I pity you!"

The commissioner saw this look, and wondered why Lord Oldborough should pity him at a time when all his lordship's feelings should naturally be for himself.

"My lord, I would engage we shall discover—we shall trace it."

"I believe that I have discovered—that I have traced it," said Lord Oldborough; and he sighed.

Now that sigh was more incomprehensible to the commissioner than all the rest, and he stood with his lips open for a moment before he could utter, "Why then resign, my lord?"

"That is my affair," said Lord Oldborough. "Let us, if you please, sir, think of yours; for, probably, this is the only time I shall ever more have it in my power to be of the least service to you."

"Oh! my lord—my lord, don't say so!" said the commissioner quite forgetting all his artificial manner, and speaking naturally: "the last time you shall have it in your power!—Oh! my dear lord, don't say so!"

"My dear sir, I must—it gives me pain—you see it does."

"At such a time as this to think of me instead of yourself! My lord, I never knew you till this moment—so well."

"Nor I you, sir," said Lord Oldborough. "It is the more unfortunate for us both, that our connexion and intercourse must now for ever cease."

"Never, never, my lord, if you were to go out of power to-morrow—which Heaven, in its mercy and justice, forbid! I could never forget the goodness—I would never desert—in spite of all interest—I should continue—I hope your lordship would permit me to pay my duty—all intercourse could never cease."

Lord Oldborough saw, and almost smiled at the struggle between the courtier and the man—the confusion in the commissioner's mind between his feelings and his interest. Partly his lordship relieved, and partly he pained Mr. Falconer, by saying, in his firm tone, "I thank you, Mr. Falconer; but all intercourse must cease. After this hour, we meet no more. I beg you, sir, to collect your spirits, and to listen to me calmly. Before this day is at an end, you will understand why all farther intercourse between us would be useless to your interest, and incompatible with my honour. Before many hours are past, a blow will be struck which will go to your heart—for I see you have one—and deprive you of the power of thought. It is my wish to make that blow fall as lightly upon you as possible."

"Oh! my lord, your resignation would indeed be a blow I could never recover. The bare apprehension deprives me at this moment of all power of thought; but still I hope—"

"Hear me, sir, I beg, without interruption: it is my business to think for you. Go immediately to the Duke of Greenwich, make what terms with him you can—make what advantage you can of the secret of my approaching resignation—a secret I now put in your power to communicate to his grace, and which no one yet suspects—I having told it to no one living but to yourself. Go quickly to the duke—time presses—I wish you success—and a better patron than I have been, than my principles would permit me to be. Farewell, Mr. Falconer."

The commissioner moved towards the door when Lord Oldborough said "Time presses;" but the commissioner stopped—turned back—could not go: the tears—real tears—rolled down his cheeks— Lord Oldborough went forward, and held out his hand to him—the commissioner kissed it, with the reverence with which he would have kissed his sovereign's hand; and bowing, he involuntarily backed to the door, as if quitting the presence of majesty.

"It is a pity that man was bred a mere courtier, and that he is cursed with a family on none of whom there is any dependence," thought Lord Oldborough, as the door closed upon the commissioner for ever.

Lord Oldborough delayed an hour purposely, to give Mr. Falconer advantage of the day with the Duke of Greenwich: then ordered his carriage, and drove to—Mrs. Falconer's.

Great was her surprise at the minister's entrance.—"Concerned the commissioner was not at home."

"My business is with Mrs. Falconer."

"My lord—your lordship—the honour and the pleasure of a visit—Georgiana, my dear."

Mrs. Falconer nodded to her daughter, who most unwillingly, and as if dying with curiosity, retired.

The smile died away upon Mrs. Falconer's lips as she observed the stern gravity of Lord Oldborough's countenance. She moved a chair towards his lordship—he stood, and leaning on the back of the chair, paused, as he looked at her.

"What is to come?—Cunningham, perhaps," thought Mrs. Falconer; "or perhaps something about John. When will he speak?—I can't—I must—I am happy to see your lordship looking so well."

"Is Mrs. Falconer acquainted with Lady Trant?"

"Lady Trant—yes, my lord."

"Mercy! Is it possible?—No, for her own sake she would not betray me," thought Mrs. Falconer.

"Intimately?" said Lord Oldborough.

"Intimately—that is, as one's intimate with every body of a certain sort—one visits—but no farther—I can't say I have the honour—"

Mrs. Falconer was so distracted by seeing Lord Oldborough searching in his pocket-book for a letter, that in spite of all her presence of mind, she knew not what she said; and all her presence of countenance failed, when Lord Oldborough placed before her eyes the cover directed to Captain Nuttall.

Can you guess how this came into Lady Trant's possession, madam?"

"I protest, my lord," her voice trembling, in spite of her utmost efforts to command it, "I don't know—nor can I conceive—"

"Nor can you conceive by whom it was written, madam?"

"It appears—it bears a resemblance—some likeness—as far as I recollect—but it is so long since I have seen your lordship's own hand—and hands are so like—sometimes—and I am so bad a judge—every hand, all fashionable hands, are so like."

"And every seal like every seal?" said Lord Oldborough, placing the counterfeit seal before Mrs. Falconer. "I recommend it to you, madam, to waste no farther time in evasion; but to deliver to me the counterpart of this seal, the impression of my private seal, which you had from Lady Frances Arlington."

"A mere bread-seal! Her ladyship surely has not said—I really have lost it—if I ever had it—I declare your lordship terrifies me so, by this strange mode—"

"I recommend it to you once more, madam, and for the last time I earnestly recommend it to you, to deliver up to me that seal, for I have sworn to my belief that it is in your possession; a warrant will in consequence be issued, to seize and search your papers. The purport of my present visit, of which I should gladly have been spared the pain, is to save you, madam, from the public disgrace of having a warrant executed. Do not faint, madam, if you can avoid it, nor go into hysterics; for if you do, I must retire, and the warrant must be executed. Your best course is to open that desk, to give me up the seal, to make to me at this instant a full confession of all you know of this transaction. If you do thus, for your husband's sake, madam, I will, as far as I can consistently with what is due to myself, spare you the shame of an arrest."

Mrs. Falconer, with trembling hands, unlocked the desk, and delivered the seal.

"And a letter which I see in the same hand-writing, madam, if you please."

She gave it; and then, unable to support herself longer, sunk upon a sofa: but she neither fainted nor screamed—she was aware of the consequences. Lord Oldborough opened the window to give her air. She was relieved by a burst of tears, and was silent—and nothing was heard but her sobs, which she endeavoured to suppress in vain. She was more relieved on looking up by one glance at Lord Oldborough's countenance, where she saw compassion working strongly.

But before she could take any advantage of it, the expression was changed, the feeling was controlled: he was conscious of its weakness—he recollected what public justice, and justice to his own character, required—he recollected all the treachery, the criminality, of which she had been guilty.

"Madam, you are not now in a condition, I see, to explain yourself farther—I will relieve you from my presence: my reproaches you will never hear; but I shall expect from you, before one hour, such an avowal in writing of this whole transaction, as may, with the written confession of Lady Trant, afford the proofs which are due to my sovereign, and to the public, of my integrity."

Mrs. Falconer bowed her head, covered her face, clasped her hands in agony: as Lord Oldborough retired, she sprang up, followed to throw herself at his feet, yet without knowing what she could say.

"The commissioner is innocent!—If you forsake him, he is undone—all, all of us, utterly ruined! Oh! Georgiana! Georgiana! where are you? speak for me!"

Georgiana was in an inner apartment, trying on a new robe à la Georgienne.

"Whatever you may wish farther to say to me, madam," said Lord Oldborough, disengaging himself from her, and passing decidedly on, before Georgiana appeared, "you will put in writing, and let me have within this hour—or never."

Within that hour, Commissioner Falconer brought, for Lord Oldborough, the paper his wife had drawn up, but which he was obliged to deliver to Mr. Temple; for Lord Oldborough had so ordered, and his lordship persevered in refusing to see him more. Mrs. Falconer's paper was worded with all the art and address of which she was mistress, and all the pathos she could command—Lord Oldborough looked only for facts—these he marked with his pencil, and observed where they corroborated and where they differed from Lady Trant's confession, which Mr. Temple had been charged to obtain during his lordship's visit to Mrs. Falconer. The greater part of the night Lord Oldborough and Mr. Alfred Percy were employed arranging these documents, so as to put the proofs in the clearest and shortest form, to be laid before his majesty the succeeding day.

It appeared that Mrs. Falconer had been first tempted to these practices by the distress for money into which extravagant entertainments, or, as she stated, the expenses incident to her situation—expenses which far exceeded her income—had led her. It was supposed, from her having kept open house at times for the minister, that she and the commissioner had great influence; she had been applied to—presents had been offered, and she had long withstood. But at length, Lady Trant acting in concert with her, they had been supplied with information by a clerk in one of the offices, a relation of Lady Trant, who was a vain, incautious youth, and, it seems, did not know the use made of his indiscretion: he told what promotions he heard spoken of—what commissions were making out. The ladies prophesied, and their prophecies being accomplished, they gained credit. For some time they kept themselves behind the scenes—and many, applying to A.B., and dealing with they did not know whom, paid for promotions which would have come unpaid for; others paid, and were never promoted, and wrote letters of reproach—Captain Nuttall was among these, and he it was, who, finding himself duped, first stirred in the business; and by means of an active member of opposition, to whom he made known his secret grievance, brought the whole to light.

The proofs arranged (and Lord Oldborough never slept till they were perfected), he reposed tranquilly. The next day, asking an audience of his majesty, he simply laid the papers on his majesty's table, observing that he had been so fortunate as to succeed in tracing the forgery, and that he trusted these papers contained all the necessary proofs.

His lordship bowed and retired instantly, leaving his majesty to examine the papers alone.

The resolution to resign his ministerial station had long been forming in Lord Oldborough's mind. It was not a resolution taken suddenly in pride or pique, but after reflection, and upon strong reasons. It was a measure which he had long been revolving in his secret thoughts. During the enthusiasm of political life, the proverbial warnings against the vanity of ambition, and the danger of dependence on the favour of princes, had passed on his ear but as a schoolboy's lesson: a phrase "to point a moral, or adorn a tale." He was not a reading man, and the maxims of books he disregarded or disbelieved; but in the observations he made for himself he trusted: the lessons he drew from life were never lost upon him, and he acted in consequence of that which he believed, with a decision, vigour, and invariability, seldom found even among philosophers. Of late years he had, in real life, seen striking instances of the treachery of courtiers, and had felt some symptoms of insecurity in the smile of princes. Fortune had been favourable to him—she was fickle—he determined to quit her before she should change. Ambition, it is true, had tempted him—he had risen to her highest pinnacle: he would not be hurled from high—he would descend voluntarily, and with dignity. Lord Oldborough's habits of thought were as different as possible from those of a metaphysician: he had reflected less upon the course of his own mind than upon almost any other subject; but he knew human nature practically; disquisitions on habit, passion, or the sovereign good, were unread by him, nor, in the course of his life, had he ever formed a system, moral or prudential; but the same penetration, the same longanimity, which enabled him to govern the affairs of a great nation, gave him, when his attention turned towards himself, a foresight for his own happiness. In the meridian of life, he had cherished ambition, as the only passion that could supply him with motive strong enough to call great powers into great action. But of late years he had felt something, not only of the waywardness of fortune, but of the approaches of age—not in his mind, but in his health, which had suffered by his exertions. The attacks of hereditary gout had become more violent and more frequent. If he lived, these would, probably, at seasons, often incapacitate him from his arduous ministerial duties: much, that he did well, must be ill done by deputy. He had ever reprobated the practice of leaving the business of the nation to be done by clerks and underlings in office. Yet to this the minister, however able, however honest, must come at last, if he persist in engrossing business and power beyond what an individual can wield. Love for his country, a sense of his own honour, integrity, and consistency, here combined to determine this great minister to retire while it was yet time—to secure, at once, the dignity and happiness of the evening of life. The day had been devoted to good and high purposes—that was enough—he could now, self-satisfied and full of honour, bid adieu to ambition. This resolution, once formed, was fixed. In vain even his sovereign endeavoured to dissuade him from carrying it into execution.

When the king had examined the papers which Lord Oldborough had laid before him, his majesty sent for his lordship again, and the moment the minister entered the cabinet, his majesty expressed his perfect satisfaction in seeing that his lordship had, with so little trouble, and with his usual ability, got to the bottom of this affair.

What was to be done next? The Duke of Greenwich was to be summoned. His grace was in astonishment when he saw the papers which contained Lord Oldborough's complete vindication, and the crimination of Mrs. Falconer. Through the whole, as he read on, his grace had but one idea, viz. "Commissioner Falconer has deceived me with false intelligence of the intended resignation." Not one word was said by Lord Oldborough to give his grace hope of that event—till the member of opposition by whom the forged letters had been produced—till all those who knew or had heard any thing of the transaction were clearly and fully apprised of the truth. After this was established, and that all saw Lord Oldborough clear and bright in honour, and, at least apparently, as firm in power as he had ever been, to the astonishment of his sovereign his lordship begged permission to resign.

Whatever might have been the effect of misrepresentation, to lower Lord Oldborough's favour, at the moment when he spoke of retiring, his king recollected all his past services—all that must, in future, be hazarded and lost in parting with such a minister—so eminent in abilities, of such tried integrity, of such fidelity, such attachment to his person, such a zealous supporter of royalty, such a favourite with his people, so successful as well as so able a minister! Never was he so much valued as at this moment. All his sovereign's early attachment returned in full strength and warmth.

"No, my lord, you must not—you will not leave me."

These simple words, spoken with the warmth of the heart, touched Lord Oldborough more than can be told. It was difficult to resist them, especially when he saw tears in the eyes of the monarch whom he loved.

But his resolution was taken. He thanked his majesty, not with the common-place thanks of courtiers, but with his whole heart and soul he thanked his majesty for this gracious condescension—this testimony of approbation—these proofs of sensibility to his attachment, which paid—overpaid him, in a moment, for the labours of a life. The recollection of them would be the glory, the solace of his age—could never leave his memory while life lasted—would, he thought, be present to him, if he should retain his senses, in his dying moment. But he was, in the midst of this strong feeling, firm to the resolution his reason had taken. He humbly represented, that he had waited for a favourable time when the affairs of the country were in a prosperous train, when there were few difficulties to embarrass those whom his majesty might name to succeed to his place at the head of administration: there were many who were ambitious of that station—zeal, talents, and the activity of youth were at his majesty's command. For himself, he found it necessary for his health and happiness to retire from public business; and to resign the arduous trust with which he had been honoured.

"My lord, if I must accept of your resignation, I must—but I do it with regret. Is there any thing your lordship wishes—any thing you will name for yourself or your friends, that I can do, to show my sense of your services and merit?"

"For myself, your majesty's bounty has left me nothing to wish."

"For your friends, then, my lord?—Let me have the satisfaction of obliging you through them."

Nothing could be more gracious or more gratifying than the whole of this parting audience. It was Lord Oldborough's last audience.

The news of his resignation, quickly whispered at court, was not that day publicly known or announced. The next morning his lordship's door was crowded beyond example in the memory of ministers. Mr. Temple, by his lordship's order, announced as soon as possible the minister's having resigned. All were in astonishment—many in sorrow: some few—a very few of the most insignificant of the crowd, persons incapable of generous sympathy, who thought they could follow their own paltry interests unnoticed—left the room, without paying their farewell respects to this great minister—minister now no more.

The moment he appeared, there was sudden silence. All eyes were fixed upon him, every one pressing to get into the circle.

"Gentlemen, thank you for these marks of attention—of regard. Mr. Temple has told you—you know, my friends, that I am a man without power."

"We know," answered a distinguished gentleman, "that you are Lord Oldborough. With or without power, the same in the eyes of your friends, and of the British nation."

Lord Oldborough bowed low, and looked gratified. His lordship then went round the circle with an air more cheerful, more free from reserve, than usual; with something in his manner more of sensibility, but nothing less of dignity. All who merited distinction he distinguished by some few appropriate words, which each remembered afterwards, and repeated to their families and friends. He spoke or listened to each individual with the attention of one who is courting, not quitting, popularity. Free from that restraint and responsibility which his public and ministerial duties had imposed upon him, he now entered into the private concerns of all, and gave his parting assistance or counsel. He noted all grievances—registered all promises that ought to be recommended to the care of his successor in office. The wishes of many, to whom he had forborne to give any encouragement, he now unexpectedly fulfilled and surpassed. When all were satisfied, and had nothing more to ask or to hope from him, they yet delayed, and parted from Lord Oldborough with difficulty and regret.

A proof that justice commands more than any other quality the respect and gratitude of mankind. Take time and numbers into the calculation, and all discover, in their turn, the advantage of this virtue. This minister, a few regretted instances excepted, had shown no favour, but strict justice, in his patronage.

All Lord Oldborough's requests for his friends were granted—all his recommendations attended to: it was grateful to him to feel that his influence lasted after his power had ceased. Though the sun had apparently set, its parting rays continued to brighten and cheer the prospect.

Under a new minister, Mr. Temple declined accepting of the embassy which had been offered to him. Remuneration suitable to his services, and to the high terms in which Lord Oldborough had spoken of his merit, was promised; and without waiting to see in what form, or manner, this promise would be accomplished, the secretary asked and obtained permission to accompany his revered master to his retirement. Alfred Percy, zealous and ardent in Lord Oldborough's service, the more this great man's character had risen upon his admiration, had already hastened to the country to prepare every thing at Clermont-park for his reception. By his orders, that establishment had been retrenched; by Alfred Percy's activity it was restored. Services, which the richest nobleman in the land could not have purchased, or the highest have commanded, Alfred was proud to pay as a voluntary tribute to a noble character.

Lord Oldborough set out for the country at a very early hour in the morning, and no one previously knew his intentions, except Mr. Temple. He was desirous to avoid what it had been whispered was the design of the people, to attend him in crowds through the streets of the metropolis.

As they drove out of town, Lord Oldborough recollected that in some account, either of the Duke of Marlborough, or the Duke of Ormond's leaving London, after his dismission from court, it is said, that of all those whom the duke had served, all those who had courted and flattered him in the time of his prosperity and power, none showed any gratitude or attachment, excepting one page, who appeared at the coach-door as his master was departing, and gave some signs of genuine sorrow and respect.

"I am fortunate," said Lord Oldborough, "in having few complaints to make of ingratitude. I make none. The few I might make," continued his lordship, who now rewarded Mr. Temple's approved fidelity, by speaking to him with the openness and confidence of friendship, "the few I might make have been chiefly caused by errors of my own in the choice of the persons I have obliged. I thank Heaven, however, that upon the whole I leave public life not only with a good conscience, but with a good opinion of human nature. I speak not of courtiers—there is nothing of nature about them—they are what circumstances make them. Were I to live my life over again, the hours spent with courtiers are those which I should most wish to be spared; but by a statesman, or a minister, these cannot be avoided. For myself, in resigning my ministerial office, I might say, as Charles the Fifth, when he abdicated, said to his successor, 'I leave you a heavy burthen; for since my shoulders have borne it, I have not passed one day exempt from anxiety.'

"But from the first moment I started in the course of ambition, I was aware that tranquillity must be sacrificed; and to the last moment I abided by the sacrifice. The good I had in view, I have reached—the prize at which I aimed, I have won. The glory of England was my object—her approbation my reward. Generous people!—If ever I bore toil or peril in your cause, I am rewarded, and never shall you hear me say that 'the unfruitful glories please no more.' The esteem of my sovereign!—I possess it. It is indefeasibly mine. His favour, his smiles, are his to give, or take away. Never shall he hear from me the wailings of disappointed ambition."

CHAPTER XXXIX

Caroline took advantage of the opportunity of returning home with her brother Alfred, when he went to the country, to prepare Clermont-park for the reception of Lord Oldborough. And now she saw her home again with more than wonted delight. Every thing animate and inanimate seemed to smile upon her, every heart rejoiced at her return; and she enjoyed equally the pleasure of loving, and of being beloved by, such friends. She had been amused and admired during her residence in London; but a life of dissipation she had always thought, and now she was convinced from experience, could never suit her taste or character. She would immediately have resumed her former occupations, if Rosamond would have permitted; but Rosamond took entire possession of her at every moment when her father or mother had not claimed their prior right to hear and to be heard.

"Caroline, my dear, don't natter yourself that you shall be left in peace—See!—she is sitting down to write a letter, as if she had not been away from us these six months—You must write to Lady Jane Granville!—Well, finish your gratitude quickly—and no more writing, reading, or drawing, this day; you must think of nothing but talking, or listening to me."

Much as she loved talking in general, Rosamond now so far preferred the pleasure of hearing, that, with her eyes fixed on Caroline, her countenance varying with every variety of Caroline's expression, she sat perfectly silent all the time her sister spoke. And scarcely was her voice heard, even in exclamation. But, during the pauses of narrative, when the pause lasted more than a minute, she would say, "Go on, my dear Caroline, go on. Tell us something more."

The conversation was interrupted by the sudden entrance of Mr. Temple—and Rosamond did not immediately find her fluency of speech increase. Mr. Temple had seized the first moment that duty and gratitude to his master and friend permitted to hasten to the Hills, nor had Lord Oldborough been unmindful of his feelings. Little as his lordship was disposed to think of love affairs, it seems he recollected those of his secretary; for, the morning after their arrival at Clermont-park, when he proffered his services, Lord Oldborough said, that he had only to trouble Mr. Temple to pay a visit for him, if it would not be disagreeable, to his old friend Mr. Percy.

"Tell him that I know his first wish will be to come to show me that it is the man, not the minister, for whom he had a regard: tell him this proof of his esteem is unnecessary. He will wish to see me for another reason: he is a philosopher—and will have a philosophical curiosity to discover how I exist without ambition. But of that he cannot yet form a judgment—nor can I: therefore, if he pleases, let his visit be delayed till next week. I have some papers to arrange, which I should wish to show him, and I cannot have them sooner in readiness. If you, Mr. Temple, can contrive to pass this week at Mr. Percy's, let me not detain you. There is no fear," added he, smiling, that "in solitude I should be troubled by the spectre which haunted the minister in Gil Blas in his retirement."

Never was man happier than Mr. Temple, when he found himself in the midst of the family circle at the Hills, and seated beside Rosamond, free from all cares, all business, all intrigues of courtiers, and restraints of office; no longer in the horrors of, attendance and dependence, but with the promise of a competent provision for life—with the consciousness of its having been, honourably obtained; and to brighten all, the hope, the delightful hope, of soon prevailing on the woman he loved, to become his for ever.

Alfred Percy had been obliged to return directly to London, and for once in his life Mr. Temple benefited by the absence of his friend. In the small house at the Hills, Alfred's was the only room that could have been spared for him; and in this room, scarcely fourteen feet square, the ex-secretary found himself lodged more entirely to his satisfaction than he had ever been in the sumptuous apartments of the great. The happy are not fastidious as to their accommodations; they never miss the painted ceiling, or the long arcade, and their slumbers require no bed of down. The lover's only fear was, that this happy week would pass too swiftly; and, indeed, time flew unperceived by him, and by Rosamond. One fine day, after dinner, Mrs. Percy proposed, that instead of sitting longer in the house, they should have their dessert of strawberries in some pleasant place in the lawn or wood. Rosamond eagerly seconded this proposal, and whispered, "Caroline's bower."

Thither they went. This bower of Caroline, this favourite spot, Rosamond, during her sister's absence, had taken delight in ornamenting, and it did credit as much to her taste as to her kindness. She had opened a view on one side to a waterfall among the rocks; on the other, to a winding path descending through the glen. Honey-suckle, rose, and eglantine, near the bower, were in rich and wild profusion; all these, the song of birds, and even the smell of the new-mown grass, seemed peculiarly delightful to Mr. Temple. Of late years he had been doomed to close confinement in a capital city; but all his tastes were rural, and, as he said, he feared he should expose himself to the ridicule Dr. Johnson throws on those "who talk of sheep and goats, and who babble of green fields."

Mr. Percy thought Dr. Johnson was rather too intolerant of rural description, and of the praises of a country life, but acknowledged that he quite agreed with him in disliking, pastorals—excepting always that beautiful drama, "The Gentle Shepherd." Mr. Percy said, that, in his opinion, a life purely pastoral must, if it could be realized, prove as insufferably tiresome in reality, as it usually is found to be in fiction. He hated Delias and shepherdesses, and declared that he should soon grow tired of any companion with whom he had no other occupation in common but "tending a few sheep." There was a vast difference, he thought, between pastoral and domestic life. His idea of domestic life comprised all the varieties of literature, exercise, and amusement for the faculties, with the delights of cultivated society.

The conversation turned from pastoral life and pastorals to Scotch and English ballads and songs. Their various merits of simplicity, pathos, or elegance, were compared and discussed. After the Reliques of Ancient Poetry had been sufficiently admired, Rosamond and Caroline mentioned two modern compositions, both by the same author, each exquisite in its different style of poetry—one beautiful, the other sublime. Rosamond's favourite was the Exile of Erin; Caroline's, the Mariners of England. To justify their tastes, they repeated the poems. Caroline fixed the attention of the company on the flag, which has

"Braved a thousand years the battle and the breeze,"

when suddenly her own attention seemed to be distracted by some object in the glen below. She endeavoured to go on, but her voice faltered—her colour changed. Rosamond, whose quick eye followed her sister's, instantly caught a glimpse of a gentleman coming up the path from the glen. Rosamond started from her seat, and clasping her hands, exclaimed, "It is! It is he!—It is Count Altenberg!"

They had not recovered from their astonishment when Count Altenberg stood before them. To Mr. Percy, to Mrs. Percy, to Rosamond, to each he spoke, before he said one word to Caroline. But one look had said all, had spoken, and had been understood.

That he was not married she was certain—for that look said he loved her—and her confidence in his honour was secure: Whatever had delayed his return, or had been mysterious in his conduct, she felt convinced that he had never been to blame.

And on his part did he read as distinctly the truth in her countenance?—Was the high colour, the radiant pleasure in that countenance unmarked? The joy was so veiled by feminine modesty, that he doubted, trembled, and if at last the rapid feelings ended in hope, it was respectful hope. With deference the most marked, mingled with dignity, tenderness, and passion, he approached Caroline. He was too delicate, too well-bred, to distress her by distinguishing her more particularly; but as he took the seat, which she left for him beside her mother, the open and serene expression of her eye, with the soft sound of her voice, in the few words she answered to what he said, were enough to set his heart at ease. The sight of Mr. Temple had at first alarmed the Count, but the alarm was only momentary. One glance at Rosamond re-assured him.

Ideas, which it requires many words to tell, passed instantaneously with the rapidity of light. After they were seated, some minutes were spent in common-place questions and answers, such as those which Benjamin Franklin would wisely put all together, into one formula, to satisfy curiosity. Count Altenberg landed the preceding day—had not stopped to see any one in England—had not even heard of Lord Oldborough's resignation—had proceeded directly to the Hills—had left his equipage at a town a few miles distant—thought he had been fully master of the well-known road, but the approach having been lately changed, he had missed his way.

This settled, to make room for a more interesting explanation, Mr. Temple had the politeness to withdraw. Rosamond had the humanity, and Caroline the discretion, to accompany him in his walk.

Count Altenberg then said, addressing himself to Mr. Percy, on whose regard he seemed to have reliance, and to Mrs. Percy, whom he appeared most anxious to interest in his favour, "You certainly, sir, as a man of penetration, and a father; you, madam, as a mother, and as a lady who must have been accustomed to the admiration of our sex, could not avoid seeing, when I was in this country before, that I felt the highest admiration, that I had formed the strongest attachment for your daughter—Miss Caroline Percy."

Mr. and Mrs. Percy both acknowledged that they thought Count Altenberg had shown some preference for Caroline; but as he had never declared his attachment, they had not felt themselves justified in inferring more from his attentions than his general good opinion. A change in his manner, which they observed shortly before they quitted Hungerford Castle, had impressed them with the idea that he had no such views as they had once been led to imagine, and their never having heard any thing from him since, had confirmed them in this belief.

"Painful—exquisitely painful, as it was to me," said Count Altenberg, "I felt myself bound in honour to leave you in that error; and, at all hazards to myself, to suffer you to continue under that persuasion, as I was then, and have been till within these few days, in dread of being obliged to fulfil an engagement, made without my concurrence or knowledge, and which must for ever have precluded me from indulging the first wish of my heart. The moment, literally the moment I was at liberty, I hastened hither, to declare my real sentiments, and to solicit your permission to address your daughter. But before I can expect that permission, before I can hope for your approbation of my suit—an approbation which, I am well aware, must depend entirely upon your opinion of my character—I must, to explain whatever may have appeared unintelligible in my conduct, be permitted to make you fully acquainted with the circumstances in which I have been placed."

Beginning with the history of his father's letters and his own, respecting the projected marriage with the Countess Christina, he related, nearly as follows, all that passed, after his having, in obedience to his father's summons, returned home. He found contracts drawn up and ready for his signature—the friends of both families apprized of the proposed alliance, and every thing actually prepared for his marriage. Remonstrances with his father were vain. The old Count said that it was impossible to break off the match, that his honour and the honour of his house was pledged. But independently of all promises, he considered the accomplishment of this marriage as most desirable and advantageous: with all the vehemence of affection, and all the force of parental authority, he charged his son to fulfil his engagements. The old Count was a fond but an imperious father; a good but an ambitious man. It was his belief that love is such a transient passion, that it is folly to sacrifice to its indulgence any of the solid and permanent interests of life. His experience at courts, and his observation on the gallantries of young princes and nobles, had taught him to believe that love is not only a transient, but a variable and capricious feeling, easily changing its object, and subsisting only by novelty. All that his son said of his attachment to Caroline, of the certainty of its permanence, and of its being essential to the happiness of his life, the father heard but as the common language of every enamoured youth. He let his son speak without interruption, but smiled incredulous, and listened only as to the voice of one in the paroxysm of a passion, which, however violent, would necessarily subside. Between the fits, he endeavoured to control the fever of his mind, and as a spell repeated these words, "Albert! see the young Countess Christina—but once—I ask no more."

Albert, with the respect due to a father, but with the firmness due to himself, and with all the courage which love only could have given to oppose the authority and affection of a parent, refused to ratify the contract that had been prepared, and declined the proposed interview. He doubted not, he said, that the lady was all his father described—beautiful, amiable, and of transcendant talents; he doubted not her power to win any but a heart already won. He would enter into no invidious comparisons, nor bid defiance to her charms—his own choice was made, he was sure of his constancy, and he thought it not only the most honourable course, but the most respectful to the Lady Christina, ingenuously at once, and without having any interview with her, or her friends, to state the truth—that the treaty had been commenced by his father without his knowledge, and carried on under total ignorance of an attachment he had formed in England. The father, after some expressions of anger and disappointment, was silent, and appeared to acquiesce. He no longer openly urged the proposed interview, but he secretly contrived that it should take place. At a masked ball at court, Count Albert entered into conversation with a Minerva, whose majestic air and figure distinguished her above her companions, whose language, thoughts, and sentiments, perfectly sustained the character which she assumed. He was struck with admiration by her talents, and by a certain elevation of thought and sentiment, which, in all she said, seemed the habitual expression of a real character, not the strained language of a feigned personage.

She took off her mask—he was dazzled by her beauty. They were at this moment surrounded by numbers of her friends and of his, who were watching the effect produced by this interview. His father, satisfied by the admiration he saw in Count Albert's countenance, when they both took off their masks, approached and whispered, "the Countess Christina." Count Altenberg grew pale, and for a moment stood in silent consternation. The lady smiled with an air of haughty superiority, which in some degree relieved him, by calling his own pride to his aid, and by convincing him that tenderness, or feminine timidity, which he would have most dreaded to wound, were not the characteristics of her mind. He instantly asked permission to pay his respects to her at her father's palace the ensuing day. She changed colour—darted a penetrating glance at the Count; and after an incomprehensible and quick alternation of pleasure and pain in her countenance, she replied, that "she consented to grant Count Albert Altenberg that interview which he and their mutual friends desired." She then retired with friends from the assembly.

In spite of the haughtiness of her demeanour, it had been obvious that she had desired to make an impression upon Count Albert; and all who knew her agreed that she had never on any occasion been seen to exert herself so much to shine and please. She shone, but had not pleased. The father, however, was content; an interview was promised—he trusted to the charms and talents of the Countess—he trusted to her flattering desire to captivate, and with impatience and confidence, he waited for the event of the succeeding day. Some intervening hours, a night of feverish and agonizing suspense, would have been spared to Count Albert, had he at this time known any thing of an intrigue—an intrigue which an artful enemy had been carrying on, with design to mortify, disgrace, and ruin his house. The plan was worthy of him by whom it was formed—M. de Tourville—a person, between whom and Count Albert there seemed an incompatibility of character, and even of manner; an aversion openly, indiscreetly shown by the Count, even from his boyish years, but cautiously concealed on the part of M. de Tourville, masked in courtly smiles and a diplomatic air of perfect consideration. Fear mixed with M. de Tourville's dislike. He was aware that if Count Albert continued in confidence with the hereditary prince, he would, when the prince should assume the reins of government, become, in all probability, his prime minister, and then adieu to all M. de Tourville's hopes of rising to favour and fortune. Fertile in the resources of intrigue, gallant and political, he combined them, upon this occasion, with exquisite address. When the Countess Christina was first presented at court, he had observed that the Prince was struck by her beauty. M. de Tourville took every means that a courtier well knows how to employ, to flatter the taste by which he hoped to benefit. In secret he insinuated into the lady's ear that she was admired by the prince. M. de Tourville knew her to be of an aspiring character, and rightly judged that ambition was her strongest passion. When once the hope of captivating the prince had been suggested to her, she began to disdain the proposed alliance with the house of Altenberg; but she concealed this disdain, till she could show it with security: she played her part with all the ability, foresight, and consummate prudence, of which ambition, undisturbed by love, is capable. Many obstacles opposed her views: the projected marriage with Count Albert Altenberg—the certainty that the reigning prince would never consent to his son's forming an alliance with the daughter of a subject. But the old Prince was dying, and the Lady Christina calculated, that till his decease, she could protract the time appointed for her marriage with Count Albert. The young Prince might then break off the projected match, prevail upon the Emperor to create her a Princess of the empire, and then, without derogating from his rank, or giving offence to German ideas of propriety, he might gratify his passion, and accomplish the fulness of her ambition. Determined to take no counsel but her own, she never opened her scheme to any of her friends, but pursued her plan secretly, in concert with M. de Tourville, whom she considered but as a humble instrument devoted to her service. He all the while considering her merely as a puppet, played by his art, to secure at once the purposes of his interest and of his hatred. He thought he foresaw that Count Albert would never yield his intended bride peaceably to his prince—he knew nothing of the

Count's attachment in England—the Lady Christina was charming—the alliance highly advantageous to the house of Altenberg—the breaking off such a marriage, and the disappointment of a passion which he thought the young Countess could not fail to inspire, would, as M. de Tourville hoped, produce an irreparable breach between the Prince and his favourite. On Count Albert's return from England, symptoms of alarm and jealousy had appeared in the Prince, unmarked by all but by the Countess Christina, and by the confidant, who was in the secret of his passion.

So far M. de Tourville's scheme had prospered, and from the character of the hereditary Prince, it was likely to succeed in its ultimate view. He was a Prince of good dispositions, but wanting in resolution and civil courage: capable of resisting the allurements of pleasure for a certain time, but soon weary of painful endurance in any cause; with a taste for virtue, but destitute of that power to bear and forbear, without which there is no virtue: a hero, when supported by a stronger mind, such as that of his friend, Count Albert; but relaxing and sinking at once, when exposed to the influence of a flatterer such as M. de Tourville: subject to exquisite shame and self-reproach, when he had acted contrary to his own idea of right; yet, from the very same weakness that made him err, disposed to be obstinate in error. M. de Tourville argued well from his knowledge of his character, that the Prince, enamoured as he was of the charms of the fair Christina, would not long be able to resist his passion; and that if once he broke through his sense of honour, and declared that passion to the destined bride of his friend, he would ever afterwards shun and detest the man whom he had injured. All this M. de Tourville had admirably well combined: no man understood and managed better the weaknesses of human nature, but its strength he could not so well estimate; and as for generosity, as he could not believe in its sincerity, he was never prepared for its effects. The struggles which the Prince made against his passion were greater, and of longer duration, than M. de Tourville had expected. If Count Albert had continued absent, the Prince might have been brought more easily to betray him; but his return recalled, in the midst of love and jealousy, the sense of respect he had for the superior character of this friend of his early days: he knew the value of a friend—even at the moment he yielded his faith to a flatterer. He could not at once forfeit the esteem of the being who esteemed him most—he could not sacrifice the interest, and as he thought, the happiness, of the man who loved him best. The attachment his favourite had shown him, his truth, his confiding openness of temper, the pleasure in his countenance when he saw him first upon his return from England, all these operated on the heart of the Prince, and no declaration of his passion had been made at the time when the appointed interview took place between Count Albert and the Countess Christina at her father's palace. Her friends not doubting that her marriage was on the eve of its accomplishment, had no scruple, even in that court of etiquette, in permitting the affianced lovers to have as private a conference as each seemed to desire. The lady's manner was this morning most alarmingly gracious. Count Albert was, however, struck by a difference in her air the moment she was alone with him, from what it had been whilst in the presence of her friends. All that he might without vanity have interpreted as marking a desire to please, to show him favour, and to evince her approbation, at least, of the choice her friends had made for her, vanished the moment they withdrew. What her motives might be, Count Altenberg could not guess; but the hope he now felt, that she was not really inclined to consider him with partiality, rendered it more easy to enter into that explanation, upon which he was, at all events, resolved. With all the delicacy due to her sex, with all the deference due to her character, and all the softenings by which politeness can soothe and conciliate pride, he revealed to the Countess Christina the real state of his affections: he told her the whole truth, concluding, by repeating the assurance of his belief, that her charms and merit would be irresistible to any heart that was disengaged.

The lady heard him in astonishment: for this turn of fate she had been wholly unprepared—the idea of his being attached to another had never once presented itself to her imagination; she had never calculated on the possibility that her alliance should be declined by any individual of a family less than sovereign. She possessed, however, pride of character superior to her pride of rank, and strength of mind suited to the loftiness of her ambition. With dignity in her air and countenance, after a pause of reflection, she replied, "Count Albert Altenberg is, I find, equal to the high character I have heard of him: deserving of my esteem and confidence, by that which can alone command esteem and merit confidence—sincerity. His example has recalled me to my nobler self, and he has, in this moment, rescued me from the labyrinth of a diplomatist. Count Albert's sincerity I—little accustomed to imitation, but proud to follow in what is good and great—shall imitate. Know then, sir, that my heart, like your own, is engaged: and that you may be convinced I do not mock your ear with the semblance of confidence, I shall, at whatever hazard to myself, trust to you my secret. My affections have a high object—are fixed upon him, whose friend and favourite Count Albert Altenberg deservedly is. I should scorn myself—no throne upon earth could raise me in my own opinion, if I could deceive or betray the man who has treated me with such sincerity."

Relieved at once by this explanation, and admiring the manner in which it was made, mingled joy and admiration were manifest in his countenance; and the lady forgave him the joy, in consideration of the tribute he paid to her superiority. Admiration was a tribute he was most willing to yield at this moment, when released from that engagement to love, which it had been impossible for him to fulfil.

The Countess recalled his attention to her affairs and to his own. Without his making any inquiry, she told him all that had been done, and all that yet remained to be done, for the accomplishment of her hopes: she had been assured, she said, by one now in the favour and private confidence of the hereditary prince, that his inclination for her was—painfully and with struggles, which, in her eyes, made his royal heart worthy her conquest—suppressed by a sense of honour to his friend.

"This conflict would now cease," Count Albert said. "It should be his immediate care to relieve his Prince from all difficulty on his account."

"By what means?" the Countess asked.

"Simply by informing him of the truth—as far as I am concerned. Your secret, madam, is safe—your confidence sacred. Of all that concerns myself—my own attachment, and the resignation of any pretensions that might interfere with his, he shall immediately be acquainted with the whole truth."

The Countess coloured, and repeating the words, "the whole truth," looked disconcerted, and in great perplexity replied, that Count Albert's speaking to the Prince directly—his immediate resignation of his pretensions—would, perhaps, defeat her plans. This was not the course she had intended to pursue— far from that which M. de Tourville had pointed out. After some moments' reflection, she said, "I abide by the truth—speak to the prince—be it so: I trust to your honour and discretion to speak to him in such terms as not to implicate me, to commit my delicacy, or to derogate from my dignity. We shall see then whether he loves me as I desire to be loved. If he does, he will free me, at once, from all difficulty with my friends, for he will speak en prince—and not speak in vain; if he loves me not, I need not tell you, sir, that you are equally free. My friends shall be convinced that I will never be the bride of any other man."

After the explanation with the Lady Christina, Count Albert lost no time; he went instantly to the palace. In his way thither, he was met by one of the pages, who told him the Prince desired to see him immediately. He found the Prince alone. Advancing to meet him, with great effort in his manner to command his emotion, the Prince said, "I have sent for you, Count Albert, to give you a proof that the friendship of Princes is not, in every instance, so vain a thing as it is commonly believed to be. Mine for you has withstood strong temptation:—you come from the Countess Christina, I believe, and can measure, better than any one, the force of that temptation. Know, that in your absence it has been my misfortune to become passionately enamoured of your destined bride; but I have never, either by word or look, directly or indirectly, infringed on what I felt to be due to your friendship and to my own honour. Never did I give her the slightest intimation of my passion, never attempted to take any of the advantages which my situation might be supposed to give."

Count Albert had just received the most convincing testimony corroborating these assertions—he was going to express his sense of the conduct of his Prince, and to explain his own situation, but the Prince went on speaking with the eagerness of one who fears his own resolution, who has to say something which he dreads that he should not be able to resume or finish, if his feelings should meet with any interruption.

"And now let me, as your friend and prince, congratulate you, Count Albert, on your happiness; and, with the same sincerity, I request that your marriage may not be delayed, and that you will take your bride immediately away from my father's court. Time will, I hope, render her presence less dangerous; time will, I hope, enable me to enjoy your society in safety; and when it shall become my duty to govern this state, I shall hope for the assistance of your talents and integrity, and shall have deserved, in some degree, your attachment."

The Count, in the strongest manner, expressed his gratitude to his Prince for these proofs of his regard, given under circumstances the most trying to the human heart. He felt, at this instant, exquisite pleasure in revealing to his highness the truth, in showing him that the sacrifice he had so honourably, so generously determined to make, was not requisite, that their affections were fixed on different objects, that before Count Albert had any idea of the prince's attachment to the Lady Christina, it had been his ardent wish, his determination, at all hazards, to break off engagements which he could not fulfil.

The Prince was in rapturous joy—all his ease of manner towards his friend returned instantly, his affection and confidence flowed in full tide. Proud of himself, and happy in the sense of the imminent danger from which he had escaped, he now described the late conflicts his heart had endured with the eloquence of self-complacency, and with that sense of relief which is felt in speaking on the most interesting of all subjects to a faithful friend from whom a secret has been painfully concealed. The Prince now threw open every thought, every feeling of his mind. Count Altenberg rose higher than ever in his favour: not the temporary favourite of the moment—the companion of pleasures—the flatterer of present passion or caprice; but the friend in whom there is certainty of sympathy, and security of counsel. The Prince, confiding in Count Albert's zeal and superior powers, now took advice from him, and made a confidant no longer of M. de Tourville. The very means which that intriguing courtier had taken to undermine the Count thus eventually proved the cause of establishing more firmly his credit. The plain sincerity of the Count, and the generous magnanimity of the lady, at once disconcerted and destroyed the artful plan of the diplomatist. M. de Tourville's disappointment when he heard from the Countess Christina the result of her interview with Count Albert, and the reproaches which in that moment of vexation he could not refrain from uttering against the lady for having departed from their plan, and having trusted to the Count, unveiled to her the meanness of his character and the baseness of his designs. She plainly saw that his object had been not to assist her love, but to gratify his own hate: not merely to advance his own fortune—that, she knew, must be the first object of every courtier—but "to rise upon the ruins of another's fame;" and this, she determined, should never be accomplished by her assistance, or with her connivance. She put Count Albert on his guard against this insidious enemy.

The Count, grateful to the lady, yet biassed neither by hope of her future favour nor by present desire to please, firm in honour and loyalty to the Prince who asked his counsel, carefully studied the character of the Countess Christina, to determine whether she possessed the qualities fit for the high station to which love was impatient that she should be elevated. When he was convinced that her character was such as was requisite to ensure the private happiness of the prince, to excite him to the attainment of true glory—then, and not till then, he decidedly advised the marriage, and zealously offered any assistance in his power to promote the union. The hereditary Prince about this time became, by the death of his father, sole master of his actions; but it was not prudent to begin his government with an act in open defiance of the prejudices or customs of his country. By these customs, he could not marry any woman under the rank of a Princess; and the Emperor had been known to refuse conferring this rank, even on favourites of powerful potentates, by whom he had been in the most urgent manner solicited. Count Albert Altenberg stood high in the esteem of the Emperor, at whose court he had spent some time; and his prince now commissioned him to go to Vienna, and endeavour to move the Emperor to concede this point in his favour. This embassy was a new and terrible delay to the Count's anxious desire of returning to England. But he had offered his services, and he gave them generously. He repaired to Vienna, and persevering through many difficulties, at length succeeded in obtaining for the Countess the rank of Princess. The attachment of the Prince was then publicly declared—the marriage was solemnized—all approved of the Prince's choice—all—except the envious, who never approve of the happy. Count Albert received, both from the Prince and Princess, the highest marks of esteem and favour. M. de Tourville, detected and despised, retired from court in disgrace and in despair.

Immediately after his marriage, the Prince declared his intention of appointing Count Albert Altenberg his prime minister; but before he entered on the duties of his office and the very moment that he could be spared by his Prince, he asked and obtained permission to return to England, to the lady on whom his affections were fixed. The old Count, his father, satisfied with the turn which affairs had taken, and gratified in his utmost ambition by seeing his son minister of state, now willingly permitted him to follow his own inclination in the choice of a wife. "And," concluded Count Albert, "my father rejoices that my heart is devoted to an Englishwoman: having himself married an English lady, he knows, from experience, how to appreciate the domestic merits of the ladies of England; he is prepossessed in their favour. He agrees, indeed, with foreigners of every nation, who have had opportunities of judging, and who all allow that—next to their own countrywomen—the English are the most charming and the most amiable women in the world."

When the Count had finished, and had pronounced this panegyric of a nation, while he thought only of an individual, he paused, anxious to know what effect his narrative had produced on Mr. and Mrs. Percy.

He was gratified both by their words and looks, which gave him full assurance of their entire satisfaction.

"And since he had done them the honour of appealing to their opinion, they might be permitted to add their complete approbation of every part of his conduct, in the difficult circumstances in which he had been placed. They were fully sensible of the high honour that such a man as Count Altenberg conferred on their daughter by his preference. As to the rest, they must refer him to Caroline herself." Mr. Percy said with a grave voice, but with a smile from which the Count augured well, "that even for the most advantageous and, in his opinion, desirable connexion, he would not influence his daughter's inclination.—Caroline must decide."

The Count, with all the persuasive tenderness and energy of truth and love, pleaded his own cause, and was heard by Caroline with a modest, dignified, ingenuous sensibility, which increased his passion. Her partiality was now heightened by her conviction of the strength and steadiness of his attachment; but whilst she acknowledged how high he stood in her esteem, and did not attempt to conceal the impression he had made on her heart, yet he saw that she dreaded to yield to the passion which must at last require from her the sacrifice of her home, country, friends, and parents. As long as the idea of being united to him was faint and distant, so was the fear of the sacrifices that union might demand; but now, the hope, the fear, the certainty, at once pressed on her heart with the most agitating urgency. The Count as far as possible relieved her mind by the assurance, that though his duty to his Prince and his father, that though all his private and public connexions and interests obliged him to reside some time in Germany, yet that he could occasionally visit England, that he should seize every opportunity of visiting a country he preferred to all others; and, for his own sake, he should cultivate the friendship of her family, as each individual was in different ways suited to his taste and stood high in his esteem.

Caroline listened with fond anxiety to these hopes: she was willing to believe in promises which she was convinced were made with entire sincerity; and when her affections had been wrought to this point, when her resolution was once determined, she never afterwards tormented the man to whom she was attached, with wavering doubts and scruples.

Count Altenberg's promise to his prince obliged him to return at an appointed time. Caroline wished that time had been more distant; she would have delighted in spending the spring-time of love in the midst of those who had formed till now all the happiness of her life—with her parents, to whom she owed every thing, to whom her gratitude was as warm, as strong, as her affection—with her beloved sister, who had sympathized so tenderly in all her sorrow, and who ardently wished to have some time allowed to enjoy her happiness. Caroline felt all this, but she felt too deeply to display feeling: sensible of what the duty and honour of Count Altenberg demanded, she asked for no delay.

The first letters that were written to announce her intended marriage were to Mrs. Hungerford and to Lady Jane Granville. And it may be recorded as a fact rather unusual, that Caroline was so fortunate as to satisfy all her friends: not to offend one of her relations, by telling any too soon, or too late, of her intentions. In fact, she made no secret, no mystery, where none was required by good sense or propriety. Nor did she communicate it under a strict injunction of secrecy to twenty friends, who were afterwards each to be angry with the other for having, or not having, told that of which they were forbidden to speak. The order of precedency in Caroline's confidential communications was approved of even by all the parties concerned.

Mrs. Hungerford was at Pembroke with her nieces when she received Caroline's letter: her answer was as follows:

"MY DEAR CHILD,

"I am ten years younger since I read your letter, therefore do not be surprised at the quickness of my motions—I shall be with you at the Hills, in town, or wherever you are, as soon as it is possible, after you let me know when and where I can embrace you and our dear Count. At the marriage of my niece, Lady Mary Barclay, your mother will remember that I prayed to Heaven I might live to see my beloved Caroline united to the man of her choice—I am grateful that this blessing, this completion of all my earthly hopes and happiness, has been granted to me.

"M. ELIZABETH HUNGERFORD."
The answer of Lady Jane Granville came next.

"Confidential.

"This is the last confidential letter I shall ever be able to write to you—for a married woman's letters, you know, or you will soon know, become, like all the rest of her property, subject to her husband—excepting always the secrets of which she was possessed before marriage, which do not go into the common stock, if she be a woman of honour—so I am safe with you, Caroline; and any erroneous opinion I might have formed, or any hasty expressions I may have let drop, about a certain Count, you will bury in oblivion, and never let me see you look even as if you recollected to have heard them.

"You were right, my dear, in that whole business—I was wrong; and all I can say for myself is, that I was wrong with the best possible intentions. I now congratulate you with as sincere joy, as if this charming match had been made by my advice, under my chaperonage, and by favour of that patronage of fashion, of which I know your father thinks that both my head and heart are full; there he is only half right, after all: so do not let him be too proud. I will not allow that my heart is ever wrong, certainly not where you are concerned.

"I am impatient, my dear Caroline, to see your Count Altenberg. I heard him most highly spoken of yesterday by a Polish nobleman, whom I met at dinner at the Duke of Greenwich's. Is it true, that the Count is to be prime minister of the Prince of —? the Duke of Greenwich asked me this question, and I promised I would let his grace know from the best possible authority—but I did not commit you.

"And now, my dear, for my own interest. If you have really and cordially forgiven me, for having so rashly said, upon a late occasion, that I would never forgive you, prove to me your placability and your sincerity—use your all-powerful influence to obtain for me a favour on which I have set my heart. Will you prevail on all your house to come up to town directly, and take possession of mine?—Count Altenberg, you say, has business to transact with ministers: whilst this is going on, and whilst the lawyers are settling preliminaries, where can you all be better than with me? I hope I shall be able to make Mr. and Mrs. Percy feel as much at home, in one hour's time, as I found myself the first evening after my arrival at the Hills some years ago.

"I know the Hungerfords will press you to go to them, and Alfred and Mrs. A. Percy will plead nearest of kin—I can only throw myself upon your generosity. The more inducements you have to go to other friends, the more I shall feel gratified and obliged, if you favour me with this proof of your preference and affection. Indulge me, my dear Caroline, perhaps for the last time, with your company, of which, believe me, I have, though a woman of the world, sense and feeling sufficient fully to appreciate the value. Yours (at all events), ever and affectionately,

"J. GRANVILLE.
"Spring Gardens—Tuesday.

"P. S.—I hope your father is of my opinion, that weddings, especially among persona of a certain rank of life, ought always to be public,—attended by the friends and connexions of the families, and conducted with something of the good old aristocratic formality, pomp, and state, of former times."

Lady Jane Granville's polite and urgent request was granted. Caroline and all her family had pleasure in showing Lady Jane that they felt grateful for her kindness.

Mr. Temple obtained permission from Lord Oldborough to accompany the Percys to town; and it was settled that Rosamond and Caroline should be married on the same day.

But the morning after their arrival in London, Mr. Temple appeared with a countenance very unlike that which had been seen the night before—Hope and joy had fled.—All pale and in consternation!—Rosamond was ready to die with terror. She was relieved when he declared that the evil related only to his fortune. The place that had been promised to him was given; indeed—the word of promise was kept to the ear—but by some management, either of Lord Skreene's or Lord Skrimpshire's, the place had been saddled with a pension to the widow of the gentleman by whom it had been previously held, and the amount of this pension was such as to reduce the profits of the place to an annual income by no means sufficient to secure independence, or even competence, to a married man. Mr. Temple knew that when the facts were stated to Lord Oldborough, his lordship would, by his representations to the highest authority, obtain redress; but the secretary was unwilling to implicate him in this disagreeable affair, unwilling to trouble his tranquillity again with court intrigues, especially, as Mr. Temple said, where his own personal interest alone was concerned—at any rate this business must delay his marriage. Count Altenberg could not possibly defer the day named for his wedding—despatches from the continent pressed the absolute necessity of his return. Revolutionary symptoms had again appeared in the city—his prince could not dispense with his services. His honour was at stake.

Mr. Temple did not attempt or pretend to bear his disappointment like a philosopher: he bore it like a lover, that is to say, very ill. Rosamond, poor Rosamond, rallied him with as much gaiety as she could command with a very heavy heart.

After a little time for reflection, her good sense, which, when called upon to act, never failed to guide her conduct, induced her to exert decisive influence to prevent Mr. Temple from breaking out into violent complaints against those in power, by whom he had been ill-treated.

The idea of being married on the same day with her sister, she said, after all, was a mere childish fancy, for which no solid advantage should be hazarded; therefore she conjured her lover, not in heat of passion to precipitate things, but patiently to wait—to return and apply to Lord Oldborough, if he should find that the representations he had already made to Lord Skrimpshire failed of effect. With much reluctance, Mr. Temple submitted to postpone the day promised for his marriage; but both Mr. and Mrs. Percy so strongly supported Rosamond's arguments, that he was compelled to be prudent. Rosamond now thought only of her sister's approaching nuptials. Mrs. Hungerford and Mrs. Mortimer arrived in town, and all Mr. and Mrs. Percy's troops of friends gathered round them for this joyful occasion.

Lady Jane Granville was peculiarly happy in finding that Mr. Percy agreed with her in opinion that marriages ought to be publicly solemnized; and rejoiced that, when Caroline should be led to the altar by the man of her choice, she would feel that choice sanctioned by the approbation of her assembled family and friends. Lady Jane justly observed, that it was advantageous to mark as strongly as possible the difference between marriages with consent of friends, and clandestine unions, which from their very nature must always be as private as possible.

If some little love of show, and some aristocratic pride of family, mixed with Lady Jane's good sense upon this as upon most other occasions, the truly philosophic will be inclined to pardon her; for they best know how much of all the principles which form the strength and happiness of society, depends upon mixed motives.

Mr. and Mrs. Percy, grateful to Lady Jane, and willing to indulge her affection in its own way, gratified her with permission to arrange the whole ceremonial of the wedding.

Now that Rosamond's marriage was postponed, she claimed first right to be her sister's bridemaid; Lady Florence Pembroke, Mrs. Hungerford's niece, had made her request, and obtained Caroline's promise, to be the second; and these were all that Caroline desired to have: but Lady Jane Granville evidently wished for the honour and glory of Lady Frances Arlington for a third, because she was niece to the Duke of Greenwich; and besides, as Lady Jane pleaded, "though a little selfish, she really would have been generous, if she had not been spoiled: to be sure, she cared in general for no one but herself; yet she absolutely showed particular interest about Caroline. Besides, her ladyship had set her heart upon the matter, and never would forgive a disappointment of a fancy." Her ladyship's request was granted. Further than this affair of the three bridemaids we know not—there is no record concerning who were the bride-men. But before we come to the wedding-day, we think it necessary to mention, for the satisfaction of the prudent part of the world, that the settlements were duly signed, sealed, and delivered, in the presence of proper witnesses.

At the moment of recording this fact, we are well aware that as much as we shall gain in the esteem of the old, we shall lose in the opinion of the young. We must therefore be satisfied with the nod of approbation from parents, and must endure the smile of scorn from lovers. We know that

"Jointure, portion, gold, estate,
Houses, household-stuff, or land,
The low conveniences of fate,
Are Greek, no lovers understand."

We regret that we cannot gratify some of our courteous readers with a detailed account of the marriage of Caroline and Count Altenberg, with a description of the wedding-dresses, or a list of the company, who, after the ceremony, partook of an elegant collation at Lady Jane Granville's house in Spring-Gardens. We lament that we cannot even furnish a paragraph in honour of Count Altenberg's equipage.

After all their other friends had made their congratulations, had taken leave of Caroline, and had departed, Mrs. Hungerford and Mrs. Mortimer still lingered.

"I know, my love," said Mrs. Hungerford, "I ought to resign you, in these last moments, to your parents, your brothers, your own Rosamond; yet I have some excuse for my selfishness—they will see you again, it is to be hoped, often—But I!—that is not in the course of nature: the blessing I scarcely could have expected to live to enjoy has been granted to me. And now that I have seen you united to one worthy of you, one who knows your value, I am content—I am grateful. Farewell, again and again, my beloved Caroline, may every—"

Tears spoke the rest. Turning from Caroline, she leaned on Count Altenberg's arm; as he conducted her to her carriage, "You are a happy man, Count Altenberg," said she: "forgive me, if I am not able to congratulate you as I ought—Daughter Mortimer, you know my heart—speak for me, if you can."

Count Altenberg was more touched by this strong affection for Caroline than he could have been by any congratulatory compliments to himself. After the departure of Mrs. Hungerford and Mrs. Mortimer, came the separation so much dreaded by all the family, for which all stood prepared. Despising and detesting the display of sensibility, they had fortified themselves for this moment with all their resolution, and each struggled to repress their own feelings.

Count Altenberg had delayed till the last moment. It was now necessary that they should set out. Caroline, flushed crimson to the very temples one instant, and pale the next, commanded with the utmost effort her emotion; Rosamond, unable to repress hers, clung to her sister weeping. Caroline's lips quivered with a vain attempt to speak—she could only embrace Rosamond repeatedly, and then her mother. Her father pressed her to his bosom—blessed her—and then drawing her arm within his, led her to her husband.

As they passed through the hall, the faithful housekeeper, and the old steward, who had come from the country to the marriage, pressed forward, in hopes of a last look. Caroline stopped, and took leave of each. She was able, though with difficulty, to speak, and she thanked them for all the services and kindness she had received from them from childhood to this hour: then her father led her to the carriage.

"It is the order of nature, my dear child," said he; "we are fond but not selfish parents; your happiness is gained by the sacrifice, and we can part with you."

CHAPTER XL

Some sage moralist has observed, that even in the accomplishment of our most ardent wishes in this world, there is always some circumstance that disappoints our expectations, or mixes somewhat of pain with the joy. "This is perfectly true," thought Rosamond. "How often have I wished for Caroline's marriage with Count Altenberg—and now she is married—really married—and gone!"

It had passed with the rapidity of a dream: the hurry of joy, the congratulations—all, all was over; and in sad silence, Rosamond felt the reality of her loss—by Rosamond doubly felt at this moment, when all her own affairs were in great uncertainty. Mr. Temple was still unable to obtain the performance of the promise which had been made him of remuneration and competent provision. He had gone through, in compliance with the advice of his friends, the mortification of reiterating vain memorials and applications to the Duke of Greenwich, Lord Skrimpshire, Lord Skreene, and Mr. Secretary Cope. The only thing which Mr. Temple refused to do, was to implicate Lord Oldborough, or to disturb him on the subject. He had spent some weeks with his old master in his retirement without once adverting to his own difficulties, still hoping that on his return to town a promise would be fulfilled, which Lord Skreene had given him, that "the affair should in his absence be settled to his satisfaction." But on his return to town, his lordship found means of evasion and delay, and threw the blame on others; the course of memorials and representations was to be recommenced. Mr. Temple's pride revolted, his love was in despair—and frequently, in the bitterness of disappointment, he reiterated to his friend Alfred his exclamations of regret and self-reproach, for having quitted, from pique and impatience of spirit, a profession where his own perseverance and exertions would infallibly have rendered him by this time independent. Rosamond saw with sympathy and anguish the effect which these feelings of self-reproach, and hope delayed, produced on Mr. Temple's spirits and health. His sensibility, naturally quick, and rendered more acute by disappointment, seemed now continually to draw from all characters and events, and even from every book he opened, a moral against himself, some new illustration or example, which convinced him more and more of the folly of being a dependant on the great. He was just in this repentant mood, when one morning, at Mrs. Alfred Percy's, Rosamond heard him sigh deeply several times, as he was reading with great attention. She could not forbear asking what it was that touched him so much. He put the book into her hands, pointing to the following passage. "The whole of this letter(1)," said he, "is applicable to me and excellent; but this really seems as if it had been written for me or by me."

(Footnote 1: Letter from Mr. Williams, secretary to Lord Chancellor West, to Mrs. Williams)

She read,

"I was a young man, and did not think that men were to die, or to be turned out . . . What was to be done now?—No money, my former patron in disgrace! friends that were in favour not able to serve me, or not willing; that is, cold, timid, careful of themselves, and indifferent to a man whose disappointments made him less agreeable . . . I languished on for three long melancholy years, sometimes a little elated; a smile, a kind hint, a downright promise, dealt out to me from those in whom I had placed some silly hopes, now and then brought a little refreshment, but that never lasted long; and to say nothing of the agony of being reduced to talk of one's own misfortunes and one's wants, and that basest and lowest of all conditions, the slavery of borrowing, to support an idle useless being—my time, for those three years, was unhappy beyond description. What would I have given then for a profession! . . . any useful profession is infinitely better than a thousand patrons."

To this Rosamond entirely acceded, and admired the strong good sense of the whole letter; but she observed to Mr. Temple, that it was very unjust, not only to himself, but what was of much more consequence, to her, to say that all this applied exactly to his case. "Did Mr. Temple," she asked, "mean to assert that she could esteem a man who was an idle useless being, a mere dependant on great men, a follower of courts? Could such a man have recommended himself to her father? Could such a man ever have been the chosen friend of her brother Alfred?

"It was true," she acknowledged, "that this friend of her brother had made one mistake in early life; but who is there that can say that he has not in youth or age committed a single error? Mr. Temple had done one silly thing, to be sure, in quarrelling with his profession; but he had suffered, and had made amends for this afterwards, by persevering application to literature. There he had obtained the success he deserved. Gentlemen might sigh and shake their heads, but could any gentleman deny this? Could it be denied that Mr. Temple had distinguished himself in literature? Could any person deny that a political pamphlet of his recommended him to the notice of Lord Oldborough, one of the ablest statesmen in England, who made him his secretary, and whose esteem and confidence he afterwards acquired by his merit, and continued, in place and out, to enjoy?—Will any gentleman deny this?" Rosamond added, that, "in defence of her brother's friend, she could not help observing, that a man who had obtained the esteem of some of the first persons of their day, who had filled an employment of trust, that of secretary to a minister, with fidelity and credit, who had published three celebrated political pamphlets, and two volumes of moral and philosophical disquisitions, which, as she had heard the bookseller say, were become stock books, could not deserve to be called an idle useless being. To be born and die would not make all his history—no, such a man would at least be secure of honourable mention in the Biographia Britannica as a writer—moral—political—metaphysical."

But while Rosamond thus did her utmost to support the spirits of her lover, her own began to fail; her vivacity was no longer natural: she felt every day more and more the want of her sister's sympathy and strength of mind.

Letters from abroad gave no hope of Caroline's return—delay after delay occurred. No sooner had quiet been restored to the country, than Count Altenberg's father was taken ill, and his illness, after long uncertainty, terminated fatally.

After the death of his father, the Count was involved in a variety of domestic business, which respect for the memory of his parent, and affection for surviving relations, could not allow him to leave. When all this had been arranged, and when all seemed preparing for their return to England, just when Rosamond hoped that the very next letter would announce the day when they would set out, the French declared war, the French troops were actually in motion—invasion was hourly expected—it was necessary to prepare for the defence of the country. At such a moment the Count could not quit his country or his Prince. And there was Caroline, in the midst of a country torn by civil war, and in the midst of all the horrors of revolution.

About this time, to increase the anxiety of the Percy family, they learned that Godfrey was taken prisoner on his way home from the West Indies. The transport, in which his division of the regiment had embarked had been separated from her convoy by a gale of wind in the night, and it was apprehended that she had been taken by the enemy. Godfrey's family hoped for a moment that this might be a false alarm; but after enduring the misery of reading contradictory paragraphs and contests of the newspaper writers with each other for several successive days, it was at last too clearly established and confirmed, by official intelligence, that the transport was taken by a Dutch ship.

In the midst of these accumulating causes of anxiety, trials of another kind were preparing for this family, as if Fortune was determined to do her utmost to ruin and humble those who had despised her worshippers, struggled against her influence, and risen in the world in defiance of her power. To explain the danger which now awaited them, we must return to their old family enemy, Sir Robert Percy. Master of Percy-hall, and of all that wealth could give, he could not enjoy his prosperity, but was continually brooding on plans of avarice and malice.

Since his marriage with Miss Falconer, Sir Robert Percy's establishment had become so expensive as to fret his temper continually. His tenants had had more and more reason to complain of their landlord, who, when any of his farms were out of lease, raised his rents exorbitantly, to make himself amends, as he said, for the extravagance of his wife. The tenants, who had ever disliked him as the successor and enemy of their own good and beloved landlord, now could not and attempted not to conceal their aversion. This renewed and increased the virulence of his dislike to our branch of the Percys, who, as he knew, were always compared with him and his, and seemed to be for ever present to the provoking memories of these tenants.

Sir Robert was disappointed hitherto in the hope for which he married, the hope of an heir, who should prevent the estate from returning to those from whom it had been wrested by his arts. Envy at seeing the rising and prosperous state of those Percys, who, in spite of their loss of fortune, had made their way up again through all obstacles, combined to increase his antipathy to his relations. His envy had been exasperated by the marriage of Caroline to Count Altenberg, and by the high reputation of her brother. He heard their praises till his soul sickened; and he was determined to be their destruction. He found a willing and able assistant in Sharpe the attorney, and they soon devised a plan worthy of their conjoined malice. At the time when Sir Robert had come into possession of Percy-hall, after the suit had been decided in his favour, he had given up all claim to the rents which Mr. Percy had received during the years which he had held the estate, and had accepted in lieu of them the improvements which Mr. Percy had made on the estate, and a considerable quantity of family plate and a collection of pictures. But now Sir Robert wrote to Mr. Percy without adverting to this agreement, and demanding from him the amount of all the rents which he had received, deducting only a certain sum on his own valuation for improvements. The plate and pictures, which he had left at Percy-hall, Sir Robert said he was willing to take in lieu of the debt; but an immense balance against Mr. Percy remained. In technical phrase, we believe, he warned Mr. Percy that Sharpe his attorney had directions to commence a suit against him for the mesne rents. The amount of the claim was such as it was absolutely impossible that Mr. Percy could pay, even by the sale of every thing he possessed in the world. If this claim were established, his family would be reduced to beggary, he must end his days in a prison, or fly his country, and take refuge in some foreign land. To this last extremity Sir Robert hoped to reduce him. In reply, however, to his insolent letter, he was surprised, by receiving from Mr. Percy a calm and short reply, simply saying that his son Alfred would take the proper steps to bring the affair to trial, and that he must submit to the decision of the law, whatever that might be. Sir Robert was mortified to the quick by finding that he could not extort from his victim one concession or complaint, nor one intemperate expression.

But however calm and dignified was Mr. Percy's conduct, it could not be without the greatest anxiety that he awaited the event of the trial which was to decide his future fate and that of his whole family.

The length of time which must elapse before the trial could come on was dreadful. Suspense was the evil they found most difficult to endure. Suspense may be easily borne by persons of an indolent character, who never expect to rule their destiny by their own genius; but to those who feel themselves possessed of energy and abilities to surmount obstacles and to brave dangers, it is torture to remain passive—to feel that prudence, virtue, genius avail them not—that while rapid ideas pass in their imagination, time moves with an unaltered pace, and compels them to wait, along with the herd of vulgar mortals, for knowledge of futurity.

CHAPTER XLI

What has become all this time of the Falconer family?

Since the marriage of Miss Falconer with Sir Robert Percy, all intercourse between the Falconers and our branch of the Percy family had ceased; but one morning, when Alfred was alone, intently considering his father's case, and the legal difficulties which threatened him, he was surprised by a visit from Commissioner Falconer. The commissioner looked thin, pale, and wretched. He began by condoling with Alfred on their mutual family misfortunes. Alfred received this condolence with politeness, but with a proud consciousness that, notwithstanding his father's present difficulties, and the total loss of fortune with which he was threatened, neither his father, nor any individual in his family, would change places with any one of the Falconers; since nothing dishonourable could be imputed to Mr. Percy, and since none of his misfortunes had been occasioned by any imprudence of his own.

A deep sigh from the commissioner, at the moment these thoughts were passing in Alfred's mind, excited his compassion, for he perceived that the same reflections had occurred to him.

After taking an immoderate quantity of snuff, the commissioner went on, and disclaimed, in strong terms, all knowledge of his son-in-law Sir Robert's cruel conduct to his cousin. The commissioner said that Sir Robert Percy had, since his marriage with Bell Falconer, behaved very ill, and had made his wife show great ingratitude to her own family—that in Mrs. Falconer's distress, when she and Georgiana were most anxious to retire from town for a short time, and when Mrs. Falconer had naturally looked to the house of her married daughter as a sure asylum, the doors of Percy-hall had been actually shut against her; Sir Robert declaring, that he would not be involved in the difficulties and disgrace of a family who had taken him in to marry a girl without any fortune.

Alfred was perfectly convinced, both from the cordial hatred with which the commissioner now spoke of his son-in-law, and from Mr. Falconer's disposition, that he had nothing to do with the cruel measures which Sir Robert had taken against his father. Commissioner Falconer was not a malevolent, but a weak man—incapable of being a disinterested friend—equally incapable of becoming a malicious enemy. The commissioner now proceeded to his own affairs, and to the business of his visit. He said that he had been disappointed in all his hopes from the Greenwich party—that when that sad business of Mrs. Falconer's came out, they had seized this as a pretence for dropping him altogether—that when they had, by Lord Oldborough's retreat from office, obtained every thing they wanted, and had no more occasion for assistance or information, they had shamefully forgotten, or disowned, all their former promises to Cunningham. They had refused to accredit him at the court of Denmark, refused even to defray the expenses of his journey thither, which, in the style he had thought it necessary for an ambassador to travel in, had been considerable. Upon the hopes held out, he had taken a splendid house in Copenhagen, and had every day, for some weeks, been in expectation of the arrival of his credentials. When it was publicly known that another ambassador was appointed, Cunningham's creditors became clamorous; he contrived to escape from Copenhagen in the night, and was proceeding incog. in his journey homewards, when he was stopped at one of the small frontier towns, and was there actually detained in prison for his debts.

The poor commissioner produced his son's letter, giving an account of his detention, and stating that, unless the money he had raised in Copenhagen was paid, there was no hope of his being liberated—he must perish in a foreign jail.

We spare the reader the just reproaches which the unhappy father, at this moment, uttered against the son's duplicity. It was his fate, he said, to be ruined by those for whom he had been labouring and planning, night and day, for so many years. "And now," concluded Mr. Falconer, "here am I, reduced to sell almost the last acre of my paternal estate—I shall literally have nothing left but Falconer-court, and my annuity!—Nothing!—But it must be done, ill as he has used me, and impossible as it is, ever, even at this crisis, to get the truth from him—I must pay the money: he is in jail, and cannot be liberated without this sum. I have here, you see, under the hand of the chief magistrate, sufficient proof—I will not, however, trouble you, my dear sir, with showing more of these letters—only it is a comfort to me to speak to one who will listen with some sympathy—Ah! sir, when out of place!—out of favour!—selling one's estate!—how people change!—But I am taking up your time. Since these lands are to be sold, the sooner the better. Your father, you know, is trustee to my marriage-settlements, and, I believe, his consent, his signature, will be necessary—will it not?—I am no lawyer—I really am not clear what is necessary—and my solicitor, Mr. Sharpe, I have dismissed: perhaps you will allow me to put the business into your hands?"

Alfred undertook it, and kindly told the commissioner that if he would send him his papers, he would, without putting him to any expense, look them over carefully—have all the necessary releases drawn—and make his title clear to any purchaser who should apply.

The commissioner was full of gratitude for this friendly offer, and immediately begged that he might leave his title-deeds. Accordingly the servant was desired to bring in the box which he had left in the carriage. The commissioner then rose to take leave, but Alfred begged he would stay till he had written a list of the deeds, as he made it a rule never to take charge of any papers, without giving a receipt for them. The commissioner thought this "a superfluous delicacy between friends and relatives;" but Alfred observed that relations would, perhaps, oftener continue friends, if in matters of business, they took care always to be as exact as if they were strangers.

The commissioner looked at his watch—said he was in haste—he was going to wait upon Lord Somebody, from whom, in spite of all his experience, he expected something.

"You will find a list of the deeds, I have a notion," said he, "in the box, Mr. Alfred Percy, and you need only sign it—that will be quite sufficient."

"When I have compared the papers with the list, I will sign it," said Alfred: "my clerk and I will do it as quickly as possible. Believe me, you cannot be in greater haste than I am."

The commissioner, secretly cursing Alfred's accuracy, and muttering something of the necessity for his own punctuality, was obliged to submit. He sat down—the clerk was sent for—the box was opened. The list of the papers was, as Alfred found, drawn out by Buckhurst Falconer; and the commissioner now recollected the time. "Just when poor Buckhurst," said the father, with a sigh, "was arguing with me against going into the church—at that time. I remember, he was desperately in love with your sister Caroline."

"Why, in truth," said Alfred, smiling, as he read over the scrawled list, "this looks a little as if it were written by a man in love—here's another reason for our comparing the papers and the list."

"Well, well, I took it all upon trust—I am no lawyer—I never looked at them—never opened the box, and am very sorry to be obliged to do it now."

The essential care, either of papers or estate, the commissioner had evermore neglected, while he had all his life been castle-building, or pursuing some phantom of fortune at court. Whilst Alfred was comparing the papers and the list, the commissioner went on talking of the marriage of Caroline with Count Altenberg, asking when they expected them to return. It was possible that Count Altenberg might be moved to make some remonstrance in favour of Cunningham; and a word or two from him to the Duke of Greenwich would do the business. The commissioner longed to hint this to Alfred, but he was so intent upon these bundles of parchment, that till every one of them was counted, it would be in vain to make that attempt: so the commissioner impatiently stood by, while the clerk went on calling over the papers, and Alfred, in equal strains, replying. "Thank Heaven!" said he to himself, "they have got to the last bundle."

"Bundle eighteen," cried the clerk.

"Bundle eighteen," replied Alfred. "How many numbers does it contain?"

"Six," said the clerk.

"Six!—no, seven, if you please," said Alfred.

"But six in the list, sir."

"I will read them over," said Alfred. "No. 1. Deed of assignment to Filmer Griffin, Esq. No. 2. Deed of mortgage to Margaret Simpson, widow. No. 3. Deed of lease and release. No. 4. Lease for a year—"

"No. 4. no such thing—stop, sir—Deed!"

Alfred gave one look at the paper, and starting up, snatched it from the hands of his clerk, with an exclamation of joy, signed the receipt for the commissioner, put it into his hands, locked the box, and sat down to write a letter, all with such rapidity that the commissioner was struck with astonishment and curiosity. Notwithstanding all his impatience to be punctual to his own engagement, he now stood fixed to the spot, and at last began with "My dear Mr. Alfred Percy, may I ask what has happened?"

"My dear commissioner, I have found it—I have found it—the long-lost deed, and I am writing to my father, to tell him. Excuse me—excuse me if I am not able to explain farther at this moment."

The commissioner understood it all too quickly. He saw how it had happened through Buckhurst's carelessness. At the time Buckhurst had been packing up these papers, some of Mr. Percy's had been lying on the table—Buckhurst had been charged not to mix them with his father's; but he was in love, and did not know what he was doing.

The commissioner began three sentences, and left them all unfinished, while Alfred did not hear one word of them: the first was an apology for Buckhurst, the second a congratulation for his good cousin Percy, the third was an exclamation that came from his heart. "Good Heavens! but what will become of my daughter Bell and Sir Robert? I do not comprehend quite, my dear sir."

Perceiving that he was not heard by Alfred, the commissioner took up his hat and departed, determining that he would inquire farther from Sir Robert's solicitor concerning the probable consequences of the recovery of this deed.

Alfred had no sooner finished his joyful letter to his father than he wrote to Sir Robert Percy, informing him of the recovery of the deed, and letting him know that he was ready to show it to whomsoever Sir Robert would send to his house to examine it. He made this offer to put an end at once to all doubts. He trusted, he said, that when Sir Robert should be satisfied of the existence and identity of the deed, he would stop his present proceedings for the recovery of the mesne rents, and that he would, without obliging his father to have farther recourse to law, restore to him the Percy estate.

To this letter no answer was received for some time. At length Mr. Sharpe called on Alfred, and begged to see the deed. He was permitted to examine it in Alfred's presence. He noted down the date, names of the witnesses, and some other particulars, of which, he observed, it was necessary he should inform Sir Robert, before he could be satisfied as to the identity of the conveyance. Sharpe was particularly close and guarded in his looks and words during this interview; would neither admit nor deny that he was satisfied, and went away leaving nothing certain, but that he would write to Sir Robert. Alfred thought he saw that they meant to avoid giving an answer, in order to keep possession some months longer, till another term. He took all the necessary steps to bring the matter to trial immediately, without waiting for any answer from Sir Robert. No letter came from him, but Alfred received from his solicitor the following note:

"Sir,

"I am directed by Sir Robert Percy to acquaint you, in reply to yours of the 20th instant, that conceiving his title to the Percy estate to be no way affected by the instrument to which you allude therein, he cannot withdraw his present suit for the mesne rents that had been already received, if you proceed in an ejectment for the recovery of the aforesaid estate.

"I am, sir,

"Your humble servant,

"A. Sharpe.

"Wednesday."

Alfred was surprised and alarmed by this letter. It had never occurred to him as possible, that Sir Robert and his counsel would attempt to stand a new trial in the face of this recovered deed; this was beyond all he could have conceived even from their effrontery and villany. He consulted Mr. Friend, who, after considering Sharpe's letter, could not devise what defence they intended to make, as the deed, upon most accurate examination, appeared duly executed, according to the provision of the statute of frauds. Upon the whole, Mr. Friend was of opinion that the letter was meant merely to alarm the plaintiffs, and to bring them to offer or consent to a compromise. In this opinion Alfred was confirmed the next day, by an interview with Sharpe, accidental on Alfred's part, but designed and prepared by the solicitor, who watched Alfred as he was coming out of the courts, and dogged him till he parted from some gentlemen with whom he was walking—then joining him, he said, in a voice which Mr. Allscrip might have envied for its power of setting sense at defiance, "I am happy, Mr. Alfred Percy, to chance to see you to-day; for, with a view to put an end to litigation and difficulties, I had a few words to suggest—premising that I do not act or speak now, in any wise, as or for Sir Robert Percy, or with reference to his being my client, or as a solicitor in this cause, be it understood, but merely and solely as one gentleman to another, upon honour—and not bringing forward any idea to be taken advantage of hereafter, as tending to any thing in the shape of an offer to compromise, which, in a legal point of view, you know, sir, I could not be warranted to hazard for my client, and of consequence, which I hereby declare, I do not in any degree mean."

"Would you be so good, Mr. Sharpe, to state at once what you do mean? for I confess I do not, in any degree, understand you."

"Why, then, sir, what I mean is, simply, and candidly, and frankly, this: that if I could, without compromising the interest of my client, which, as an honest man, I am bound not to do or appear to do, I should wish to put an end to this litigation between relations; and though your father thinks me his enemy, would convince him to the contrary, if he would allow me, and could point out the means of shortening this difference between relations, which has occasioned so much scandal; and moreover, could devise an accommodation, which might be agreeable to both parties, and save you a vast deal of trouble and vexation; possession," added he, laughing, "being nine points of the law."

Mr. Sharpe paused, as if hoping that something would now be said by Alfred, that might direct him whether to advance or recede; but Alfred only observed, that probably the end Mr. Sharpe proposed to himself by speaking was to make himself understood, and that this desirable end he had not yet attained.

"Why, sir, in some cases, one cannot venture to make one's self understood any way, but by inuendoes."

"Then, good morning to you, sir—you and I can never understand one another."

"Pardon me, sir, unless you are in a hurry," cried Mr. Sharpe, catching Alfred by the button, "which (when so large an estate, to which you might eventually succeed, is in question) you are too much a man of business to be—in one word, then, for I won't detain you another moment, and I throw myself open, and trust to your honour—"

"You do me honour."

"Put a parallel case. You, plaintiff A—, I, defendant B—. I should, if I were A—, but no way advising it, being B—, offer to divide the whole property, the claim for the mesne rents being wholly given up; and that the offer would be accepted, I'd engage upon my honour, supposing myself witnessing the transaction, only just as a gentleman."

"Impossible, sir," cried Alfred, with indignation. "Do you take me for a fool? Do you think I would give up half my father's estate, knowing that he has a right to the whole?"

"Pardon me, sir—I only suggested an A. B. case. But one word more, sir," cried Mr. Sharpe, holding Alfred, who was breaking from him, "for your own—your father's interest: you see this thing quite in a wrong point of view; when you talk of a few months' more or less delay of getting possession, being all there is between us—depend upon it, if it goes to trial you will never get possession."

"Then, sir, if you think so, you are betraying the interest of your client, in advising me not to let it go to trial."

"Good God! sir: but that is between you and me only."

"Pardon me, sir, it is between you and your conscience."

"Oh! if that's all—my conscience is at ease, when I'm trying to prevent the scandal of litigation between relations: therefore, just let me mention to you for your private information, what I know Sir Robert would not wish to come out before the trial."

"Don't tell it to me, sir—I will not hear it," cried Alfred, breaking from him, and walking on very fast.

Faster still Sharpe pursued. "You'll remember, sir, at all events, that what has been said is not to go further—you'll not forget."

"I shall never forget that I am a man of honour, sir," said Alfred.

Sharpe parted from him, muttering, "that if he lived to the day of trial, he would repent this."

"And if I live till the day of judgment, I shall never repent it," thought Alfred.

Now fully convinced that Sir Robert desired a compromise, and wanted only to secure, while in possession, some portion of that property, which he knew the law would ultimately force him to relinquish, Alfred persevered in his course, relieved from the alarm into which he had at first been thrown, when he learned that his opponents intended to make a defence. Alfred felt assured that they would never let the matter come to trial; but time passed on, and they still persisted. Many of his brother lawyers were not only doubtful, but more inclined to despond than to encourage him as to the event of the trial; several regretted that he had not accepted of Mr. Sharpe's offered compromise. "Half the estate certain, and his father's release from all difficulties, they thought too good offers to have been rejected. He might, as Sharpe had prophesied, have to repent his rejection of that proposal."

Others observed, that though Mr. Alfred Percy was certainly a young man of great talents, and had been successful at the bar, still he was a young lawyer; and it was a bold and hazardous, not to say rash thing, to take upon himself the conduct of a suit against such opponents as Mr. Sharpe and Sir Robert Percy, practised in law, hardened in iniquity, and now driven to desperation.

Mr. Friend was the only man who stood steadily by Alfred, and never wavered in his opinion. "Trust to truth and justice," said he; "you did right not to compromise—be firm. If you fail, you will have this consolation—you will have done all that man could do to deserve success."

The day of trial approached. Mr. Friend had hoped, till very late in the business, that the object of their adversaries was only to intimidate, and that they would never let it go to trial: now it was plain they would. But on what grounds? Again and again Mr. Friend and Alfred perused and reperused Sir John Percy's deed, and examined the opinions of counsel of the first eminence. Both law and right appeared to be clearly on their side; but it was not likely that their experienced opponents should persist without having some strong resource.

A dread silence was preserved by Sir Robert Percy and by Mr. Solicitor Sharpe. They must have some deep design: what it could be, remained to be discovered even till the day of trial.

CHAPTER XLII

The day of trial arrived—Mr. Percy came up to town, and brought Mrs. Percy and Rosamond with him to his son Alfred's, that they might all be together, and hear as soon as possible their fate.

The trial came on about three o'clock in the afternoon. The court was uncommonly crowded. Mr. Percy, his son Erasmus, and all his friends, and Sir Robert and his adherents, appeared on opposite sides of the galleries.

The excellent countenance and gentlemanlike demeanour of Mr. Percy were contrasted with the dark, inauspicious physiognomy of Sir Robert, who sat opposite to him, and who was never tranquil one second, but was continually throwing notes to his counsel, beckoning or whispering to his attorney—while convulsive twitches of face and head, snuff-taking, and handkerchief spread frequently to conceal the expression of his countenance, betrayed the malignant flurry of his spirits.

Alfred conducted his father's cause in the most judicious and temperate manner. An attempt had been made by Sir Robert to prejudice the public against Mr. Percy, by representing him as the descendant of a younger brother, who was endeavouring to dispossess the heir of the elder branch of the family of that estate, which belonged to him by right of inheritance. Alfred's fast care was to put the court and the jury in full possession of the facts. He stated that "His father, Lewis Percy, plaintiff in this cause, and Robert Percy, Bart. defendant, both descended from Sir John Percy, who was their grandfather. Sir John outlived both his sons, who left him two grandsons, Robert was the son of his eldest, and Lewis of his youngest son. Sir John had two estates, one of them paternal, which went in the ordinary course of descent to the representative of the eldest son, being the present Sir Robert Percy. Sir John's other estate, in Hampshire, which came to him by his wife, he conveyed, a short time before his death, to his youngest grandson, the present Lewis Percy, who had held undisturbed possession of it for many years. But, in process of time, Sir Robert Percy ruined himself by play, and having frequent intercourse with Sharpe, the solicitor, upon some great emergency inquired whether it was not possible to shake the title of his cousin Mr. Percy's estate. He suggested that the conveyance might not be forthcoming; but Sir Robert assured him that both his grandfather and the present Mr. Percy were men of business, and that there was little likelihood either that the deeds should be lost, or that there should be any flaw in the title. Afterwards a fire broke out at Percy-hall, which consumed that wing of the house in which were Mr. Percy's papers—the papers were all saved except this deed of conveyance. Mr. Sharpe being accidentally apprized of the loss, conveyed the intelligence to Sir Robert. He immediately commenced a suit against his cousin, and had finally succeeded in obtaining a verdict in his own favour, and possession of the Hampshire estate. At the time when Mr. Percy delivered up possession and quitted Percy-hall, in consideration of the extensive improvements which he had made, and in consideration of his giving up to Sir Robert plate, furniture, wine, horses, and equipages, Sir Robert had promised to forego whatever claim he might have upon Mr. Percy for the rents which he had received during the time he had held the estate; but, afterwards, Sir Robert repented of having made this agreement, broke his promise, and took out a writ against his cousin for the mesne rents. They amounted to an immense sum, which Mr. Percy was utterly unable to pay, and he could have had no hope of avoiding ruin, had the claim been by law decided against him. By fortunate circumstances, however, he had, while this cause was pending, recovered that lost conveyance, which proved his right to the Hampshire estate. Of this he had apprized Sir Robert, who had persisted, nevertheless, in holding possession, and in his claim for the mesne rents. The present action was brought by Mr. Percy in resistance of this unjust claim, and for the recovery of his property."

Not one word of invective, of eloquence, of ornament, or of any attempt at pathos, did our barrister mix with this statement. It was his object to put the jury and the court clearly in possession of facts, which, unadorned, he knew would appear stronger than if encumbered by any flowers of oratory.

Having produced the deed, conveying the Hampshire estate to his father, Alfred called evidence to prove the signature of Sir John Percy, and the handwriting of the witnesses. He farther proved that this conveyance had been formerly seen among his father's papers at Percy-hall, showed it had been recently recovered from Mr. Falconer's box of papers, and explained how it had been put there by mistake, and he supported this fact by the evidence of Commissioner Falconer, father-in-law to the defendant.—Alfred rested his cause on these proofs, and waited, anxious to know what defence the defendant was prepared to make.

To his astonishment and consternation, Sir Robert's counsel produced another deed of Sir John Percy's, revoking the deed by which Sir John had made over his Hampshire estate to his younger grandson, Mr. Percy; it appearing by a clause in the original deed that a power for this purpose had been therein reserved. This deed of revocation was handed to the judge and to the jury, that it might be examined. The two deeds were carefully compared. The nicest inspection could not discover any difference in the signature or seal. When Mr. Friend examined them, he was in dismay. The instrument appeared perfect. Whilst the jury were occupied in this examination, Mr. Friend and Alfred had a moment to consult together.

"We are undone," whispered Mr. Friend, "if they establish this deed of revocation—it sets us aside for ever."

Neither Mr. Friend nor Alfred had any doubt of its being a forgery, but those, who had plunged thus desperately in guilt, would probably be provided with perjury sufficient to support their iniquity.

"If we had been prepared!" said Mr. Friend: "but how could we be prepared for such a stroke? Even now, if we had time, we could summon witnesses who would discredit theirs, but—"

"Do not despair," said Alfred: "still we have a chance that their own witnesses may cross each other, or contradict themselves. Falsehood, with all its caution, is seldom consistent."

The trial proceeded. Alfred, in the midst of the fears and sighs of his friends, and of the triumphant smiles and anticipating congratulations of his enemies, continued to keep both his temper and his understanding cool. His attention was fixed upon the evidence produced, regardless of the various suggestions whispered or written to him by ignorant or learned advisers.

William Clerke, the only surviving witness to the deed of revocation produced by Sir Robert, was the person on whose evidence this cause principally rested. He was now summoned to appear, and room was made for him. He was upwards of eighty years of age: he came slowly into court, and stood supporting himself upon his staff, his head covered with thin gray hairs, his countenance placid and smiling, and his whole appearance so respectable, so venerable, as to prepossess, immediately, the jury and the court in his favour.

Alfred Percy could scarcely believe it possible, that such a man as this could be the person suborned to support a forgery. After being sworn, he was desired to sit down, which he did, bowing respectfully to the court. Sir Robert Percy's counsel proceeded to examine him as to the points they desired to establish.

"Your name, sir, is William Clerke, is it not?"

"My name is William Clerke," answered the old man, in a feeble voice.

"Did you ever see this paper before?" showing him the deed.

"I did—I was present when Sir John Percy signed it—he bid me witness it, that is, write my name at the bottom, which I did, and then he said, 'Take notice, William Clerke, this is a deed, revoking the deed by which I made over my Hampshire estate to my youngest grandson, Lewis Percy.'"

The witness was going on, but the counsel interrupted.

"You saw Sir John Percy sign this deed—you are sure of that?"

"I am sure of that."

"Is this Sir John Percy's signature?"

"It is—the very same I saw him write; and here is my own name, that he bid me put just there."

"You can swear that this is your handwriting?"

"I can—I do."

"Do you recollect what time Sir John Percy signed this deed?"

"Yes; about three or four days before his death."

"Very well, that is all we want of you, Mr. Clerke."

Alfred Percy desired that Clerke should be detained in court, that he might cross-examine him. The defendants went on, produced their evidence, examined all their witnesses, and established all they desired.

Then it came to Alfred's turn to cross-examine the witnesses that had been produced by his adversary. When William Clerke re-appeared, Alfred regarding him stedfastly, the old man's countenance changed a little; but still he looked prepared to stand a cross-examination. In spite of all his efforts, however, he trembled.

"Oh! you are trembling on the brink of the grave!" said Alfred, addressing him in a low, solemn tone: "pause, and reflect, whilst you are allowed a moment's time. A few years must be all you have to spend in this world. A few moments may take you to another, to appear before a higher tribunal—before that Judge, who knows our hearts, who sees into yours at this instant."

The staff in the old man's hand shook violently.

Sir Robert Percy's counsel interrupted—said that the witness should not be intimidated, and appealed to the court. The judge was silent, and Alfred proceeded, "You know that you are upon your oath—these are possibly the last words you may ever utter—look that they be true. You know that men have been struck dead whilst uttering falsehoods. You are upon your oath—did you see Sir John Percy sign this deed?"

The old man attempted in vain to articulate.

"Give him time to recollect," cried the counsel on the opposite side: "give him leave to see the writing now he has his spectacles."

He looked at the writing twice—his head and hands shaking so that he could not fix his spectacles. The question was repeated by the judge. The old man grew pale as death. Sir Robert Percy, just opposite to him, cleared his throat to catch the witness's attention, then darted at him such a look as only he could give.

"Did I see Sir John Percy sign this deed?" repeated William Clerke: "yes, I did."

"You hear, my lord, you hear," cried Sir Robert's counsel, "the witness says he did—there is no occasion farther to intimidate this poor old man. He is not used to speak before such an audience. There is no need of eloquence—all we want is truth. The evidence is positive. My lord, with your lordship's leave, I fancy we may dismiss him."

They were going to hurry him away, but Alfred Percy said that, with the permission of the court, he must cross-examine that witness farther, as the whole event of the trial depended upon the degree of credit that might be given to his evidence.

By this time the old man had somewhat recovered himself; he saw that his age and reverend appearance still prepossessed the jury in his favour, and from their looks, and from the whispers near him, he learned that his tremor and hesitation had not created any suspicion of guilt, but had been attributed rather to the sensibility of virtue, and the weakness of age. And, now that the momentary emotion which eloquence had produced on his mind had subsided, he recollected the bribe that had been promised to him. He was aware that he had already sworn what, if he contradicted, might subject him to be prosecuted for perjury. He now stood obstinately resolved to persevere in his iniquity. The first falsehoods pronounced and believed, the next would be easy.

"Your name is William Clerke, and this," said Alfred (pointing to the witness's signature), "is your handwriting?"

"Yes, I say it is."

"You can write then?" (putting a pen into his hand) "be so good as to write a few words in the presence of the court." He took the pen, but after making some fruitless attempts, replied, "I am too old to write—I have not been able to write my name these many years—Indeed! sir, indeed! you are too hard upon one like me. God knows," said he, looking up to Heaven, some thought with feeling, some suspected with hypocrisy—"God knows, sir, I speak the truth, and nothing but the truth. Have you any more questions to put to me? I am ready to tell all I know. What interest have I to conceal any thing?" continued he, his voice gaining strength and confidence as he went on repeating the lesson which he had been taught.

"It was long, a long while ago," he said, "since it had all happened; but thank Heaven, his memory had been spared him, and he remembered all that had passed, the same as if it was but yesterday. He recollected how Sir John looked, where he sat, what he said when he signed this deed; and, moreover, he had often before heard of a dislike Sir John had taken to his younger grandson—ay, to that young gentleman's father," looking at Alfred; "and I was very sorry to hear it—very sorry there should be any dispute in the family, for I loved them all," said he, wiping his eyes—"ay, I loved 'em all, and all alike, from the time they were in their cradles. I remember too, once, Sir John said to me, 'William Clerke,' says he, 'you are a faithful lad'—for I was a lad once—"

Alfred had judiciously allowed the witness to go on as far as he pleased with his story, in the expectation that some exaggeration and contradiction would appear; but the judge now interrupted the old man, observing that this was nothing to the purpose—that he must not take up the time of the court with idle tales, but that if he had any thing more to give in evidence respecting the deed, he should relate it.

The judge was thought to be severe; and the old man, after glancing his eye on the jury, bowed with an air of resignation, and an appearance of difficulty, which excited their compassion.

"We may let him go now, my lord, may not we?" said Sir Robert Percy's counsel.

"With the permission of his lordship, I will ask one other question," said Alfred.

Now it should be observed, that after the first examination of this witness, Alfred had heard him say to Mr. Sharpe, "They forgot to bring out what I had to say about the seal." To which Sharpe had replied, "Enough without it." Alfred had examined the seal, and had observed that there was something underneath it—through a small hole in the parchment he saw something between the parchment and the sealing-wax.

"You were present, I think you say, Mr. Clerke, not only when this deed was signed, but when it was sealed?"

"I was, sir," cried Clerke, eager to bring out this part of the evidence, as it had been prepared for him by Sir Robert; "I surely was; and I remember it particularly, because of a little remarkable circumstance: Sir John, God bless him!—I think I see him now—My lord, under this seal," continued the old man, addressing himself to the judge, and putting his shrivelled finger upon the seal, "under this very seal Sir John put a sixpence—and he called upon me to observe him doing it—for, my lord, it is my opinion, he thought then of what might come to pass—he had a sort of a foreboding of this day. And now, my lord, order them, if you please, to break the seal—break it before them all,—and if there is not the sixpence under it, why this deed is not Sir John's, and this is none of my writing, and," cried he, lifting up his hands and eyes, "I am a liar, and perjured."

There was a profound silence. The seal was broken. The sixpence appeared. It was handed in triumph, by Sir Robert Percy's counsel, to the jury and to the judge. There seemed to be no longer a doubt remaining in the minds of the jury—and a murmur of congratulation among the partisans of Sir Robert seemed to anticipate the verdict.

"'Tis all over, I fear," whispered Friend to Alfred. "Alfred, you have done all that could be done, but they have sworn through every thing—it is over with us."

"Not yet," said Alfred. Every eye turned upon him, some from pity, some from curiosity, to see how he bore his defeat. At length, when there was silence, he begged to be permitted to look at the sixpence. The judge ordered that it should be shown to him. He held it to the light to examine the date of the coin; he discovered a faint impression of a head on the sixpence, and, upon closer inspection, he made out the date, and showed clearly that the date of the coin was later than the date of the deed: so that there was an absolute impossibility that this sixpence could have been put under the seal of the deed by Sir John.

The moment Alfred stated this fact, the counsel on the opposite side took the sixpence, examined it, threw down his brief, and left the court. People looked at each other in astonishment. The judge ordered that William Clerke should be detained, that he might be prosecuted by the crown for perjury.

The old man fell back senseless. Mr. Sharpe and Sir Robert Percy pushed their way together out of court, disclaimed by all who had till now appeared as their friends. No farther evidence was offered, so that here the trial closed. The judge gave a short, impressive charge to the jury, who, without withdrawing, instantly gave their verdict in favour of the plaintiff, Lewis Percy—a verdict that was received with loud acclamations, which not even respect to the court could restrain.

Mr. Percy and Alfred hastily shook hands with their friends, and in the midst of universal applause hurried away to carry the good news to Mrs. Percy and Rosamond, who were at Alfred's house, waiting to hear the event of the trial.

Neither Alfred nor Mr. Percy had occasion to speak—the moment Mrs. Percy and Rosamond saw them they knew the event.

"Yes," said Mr. Percy, "our fortune is restored; and doubly happy we are, in having regained it, in a great measure, by the presence of mind and ability of my son."

His mother and sister embraced Alfred with tears of delight. For some moments a spectator might have imagined that he beheld a family in deep affliction. But soon through these tears appeared on the countenance of each individual the radiance of joy, smiles of affection, tenderness, gratitude, and every delightful benignant feeling of the human heart.

"Has any body sent to Mrs. Hungerford and to Lady Jane Granville?" said Mr. Percy.

"Yes, yes, messengers were sent off the moment the verdict was given," said Erasmus: "I took care of that."

"It is a pity," said Rosamond, "that Caroline is not here at this moment, and Godfrey."

"It is best as it is," said Mrs. Percy: "we have that pleasure still in store."

"And now, my beloved children," said Mr. Percy, "after having returned thanks to Providence, let me here, in the midst of all of you to whom I owe so large a share of my happiness, sit down quietly for a few minutes to enjoy 'the sober certainty of waking bliss.'"

CHAPTER XLIII

The day after the trial brought several happy letters to the Percys. Rosamond called it the day of happy letters, and by that name it was ever after recorded in the family. The first of these letters was from Godfrey, as follows:

"Dear father, mother, brothers, and sisters all! I hope you are not under any anxiety about me, for here I am, safe and sound, and in excellent quarters, at the house of Mynheers Grinderweld, Groensveld, and Slidderschild, Amsterdam, the Dutch merchants who were shipwrecked on our coast years ago! If it had happened yesterday, the thing could not be fresher in their memories. My dear Rosamond, when we laughed at their strange names, square figures, and formal advice to us, if ever we should, by the changes and chances of human events, be reduced to distress, we little thought that I, a prisoner, should literally come to seek shelter at their door. And most hospitably have I been received. National prejudices, which I early acquired, I don't know how, against the Dutch, made me fancy that a Dutchman could think only of himself, and would give nothing for nothing: I can only say from experience, I have been as hospitably treated in Amsterdam as ever I was in London. These honest merchants have overwhelmed me with civilities and substantial services, and still they seem to think they can never do enough for me. I wish I may ever see them on English ground again. But we have no Percy-hall to receive them in now; and as well as I remember the Hills, we could not conveniently stow more than one at a time. Side by side, as they stood after breakfast, I recollect, at Percy-hall, they would completely fill up the parlour at the Hills.

"I may well be in high spirits to-day; for these good people have just been telling me, that the measures they have been taking to get my exchange effected, have so far succeeded, they have reason to believe that in a week, or a fortnight at farthest, I shall be under weigh for England.

"In the mean time, you will wonder perhaps how I got here; for I perceive that I have subjected myself to Rosamond's old reproach of never beginning my story at the beginning. My father used to say, half the mistakes in human affairs arise from our taking for granted; but I think I may take it for granted, that either from the newspapers or from Gascoigne, who must be in England by this time, you have learned that the transport I was on board, with my division of the regiment, parted convoy in the storm of the 18th, in the night, and at daybreak fell in with two Dutchmen. Our brave boys fought as Englishmen always do; but all that is over now, so it does not signify prosing about it. Two to one was too much—we were captured. I had not been five minutes on the Dutchman's deck, when I observed one of the sailors eyeing me very attentively. Presently he came up and asked if my name was not Percy, and if I did not recollect to have seen him before? He put me in mind of the shipwreck, and told me he was one of the sailors who were harboured in one of my father's outhouses whilst they were repairing the wreck. I asked him what had become of the drunken carpenter, and told him the disaster that ensued in consequence of that rascal's carelessness. My sailor was excessively shocked at the account of the fire at Percy-hall: he thumped his breast till I thought he would have broken his breast-bone; and after relieving his mind by cursing and swearing in high Dutch, low Dutch, and English, against the drunken carpenter, he told me there was no use in saying any more, for that he had punished himself.—He was found dead one morning behind a barrel, from which in the night he had been drinking spirits surreptitiously through a straw. Pray tell this to old John, who used always to prophesy that this fellow would come to no good: assure him, however, at the same time, that all the Dutch sailors do not deserve his maledictions. Tell him, I can answer for the poor fellow who recognized me, and who, during the whole passage, never failed to show me and my fellow-prisoners every little attention in his power. When we got to Amsterdam, it was he reminded me of the Dutch merchants, told me their names, which, without his assistance, I might have perished before I could ever have recollected, and showed me the way to their house, and never rested till he saw me well settled.

"You will expect from me some account of this place. You need not expect any, for just as I had got to this line in my letter appeared one who has put all the lions of Amsterdam fairly out of my head—Mr.

Gresham! He has been for some weeks in the country, and has just returned. The Dutch merchants, not knowing of his being acquainted with my family, never mentioned him to me, nor me to him: so our surprise at meeting was great. What pleasure it is in a foreign country, and to a poor prisoner, to see any one from dear England, and one who knows our own friends! I had never seen Mr. Gresham myself, but you have all by your letters made me well acquainted with him. I like him prodigiously, to use a lady's word (not yours, Rosamond). Letters from Mr. Henry were waiting for him here; he has just opened them, and the first news he tells me is, that Caroline is going to be married! Is it possible? Count Altenberg! The last time I heard from you, you mentioned nothing of all this. Some of your letters must have been lost. Pray write again immediately, and do not take it for granted that I shall be at home before a letter reaches me; but give me a full history of every thing up to the present moment. Groensveld is sealing his letters for London, and must have mine now or never. Adieu! Pray write fully: you cannot be too minute for a poor prisoner.

"Yours affectionately,

"burning with curiosity,

"GODFREY PERCY."

A letter from Mr. Gresham to Mr. Henry farther informed them, that Godfrey's exchange was actually effected, and that he had secured his passage on board a vessel just ready to sail for England.

Next came letters from Count Altenberg. Briefly, in the laconic style of a man pressed at once by sudden events and strong feelings, he related that at the siege of the city of — by the French, early in the morning of the day on which it was expected that the enemy would attempt to storm the place, his prince, while inspecting the fortifications, was killed by a cannon-ball, on the very spot where the Count had been standing but a moment before. All public affairs were changed in his country by the death of the prince. His successor, of a weak character, was willing to purchase present ease, and to secure his low pleasures, at any price—ready to give up the honour of his country, and submit to the conqueror— that he had been secretly intriguing with the enemy, had been suspected, and this suspicion was confirmed by his dastardly capitulation when the means of defence were in his power and the spirit of his people eager for resistance.

With indignation, heightened by grief, contrast, and despairing patriotism, Count Altenberg had remonstrated in vain—had refused, as minister, to put his signature to the capitulation—had been solicited urgently to concede—offers of wealth and dignities pressed upon him: these he rejected with scorn. Released from all his public engagements by the death of the prince, and by the retiring of the princess from court, Count Altenberg refused to act as minister under his successor; and seeing that, under such a successor to the government, no means of serving or saving the country remained, he at once determined to quit it for ever: resolved to live in a free country, already his own, half by birth and wholly by inclination, where he had property sufficient to secure him independence, sufficient for his own wishes, and for those of his beloved Caroline—a country where he could enjoy better than on any other spot in the whole compass of the civilized world, the blessings of real liberty and of domestic tranquillity and happiness.

His decision made, it was promptly executed. He left to a friend the transacting the sale of his German property, and Caroline concluded his letter with

"MY DEAR FRIENDS,

"Passports are obtained, every thing ready. Early next week we set out for England; by the first of next month we shall be at HOME."

Then came a letter from Lord Oldborough. Some time previously to the trial, surprised at neither seeing Mr. Temple nor hearing of his marriage, his lordship had written to inquire what delayed his promised return. Taking it for granted that he was married, his lordship in the most polite manner begged that he would prevail upon his bride to enliven the retirement of an old statesman by her sprightly company. As the friend of her father he made this request, with a confidence in her hereditary disposition to show him kindness.

In reply to this letter, Mr. Temple told his friend and master what had delayed his marriage, and why he had hitherto forborne to trouble him on the subject. Lord Oldborough, astonished and indignant, uttered once and but once contemptuous exclamations against the "inconceivable meanness of Lord Skrimpshire," and the "infinitely small mind of his grace of Greenwich;" then, without condescending to any communication with inferior powers, his lordship applied directly to the highest authority. The consequence was that a place double the value of that which had been promised was given to Mr. Temple, and it was to announce his appointment to it that occasioned the present letter from Lord Oldborough, enclosing one from Mr. Secretary Cope, who "had it in command to assure his lordship that the delay had arisen solely from the anxious desire of his majesty's ministers to mark their respect for his lordship's recommendation, and their sense of Mr. Temple's merit, by doing more than had been originally proposed. An opportunity, for which they had impatiently waited, had now put it into their power to evince the sincerity of their intentions in a mode which they trusted would prove to the entire satisfaction of his lordship."

The greatest care was taken both in substance and manner to gratify Lord Oldborough, whose loss had been felt, and whose value had, upon comparison, increased in estimation.

Rosamond was rewarded by seeing the happiness of the man she loved, and hearing him declare that he owed it to her prudence.

"Rosamond's prudence!—Whoever expected to hear this?" Mr. Percy exclaimed. "And yet the praise is just. So, henceforward, none need ever despair of grafting prudence upon generosity of disposition and vivacity of temper."

Mr. Temple obtained from Rosamond a promise to be his, as soon as her sister Caroline and her brother should arrive.

Lady Jane Granville, who felt the warmest interest in their prosperity, was the first to whom they communicated all this joyful intelligence. Her ladyship's horses had indeed reason to rue this day; for they did more work this day than London horses ever accomplished before in the same number of hours, not excepting even those of the merciless Mrs. John Prevost; for Lady Jane found it necessary to drive about to her thousand acquaintance to spread the news of the triumph and felicity of the Percy family.

In the midst of this tumult of joy, Mr. Percy wrote two letters: one was to his faithful old steward, John Nelson, who deserved from his master this mark of regard; the other was to Commissioner Falconer, to make him some friendly offers of assistance in his own affairs, and to beg that, through him, his daughter, the unhappy and deserted lady of Sir Robert Percy, might be assured that neither Mr. Percy nor any of his family wished to put her to inconvenience; and that far from being in haste to return to Percy-hall, they particularly wished to wait in town for the arrival of Caroline and Count Altenberg; and they therefore requested that she would not hasten her removal, from any false idea of their impatience. We said the deserted lady of Sir Robert Percy, for Sir Robert had fled from the country. On quitting the court after the trial, he took all the ready money he had previously collected from his tenants, and set out for the continent, leaving a note for his wife, apprizing her "that she would never see him more, and that she had better return to her father and mother, as he had no means left to support her extravagance."

Commissioner Falconer was at this time at Falconer-court, where he had been obliged to go to settle some business with his tenantry, previously to the sale of his land for the redemption of Cunningham. The Commissioner's answer to Mr. Percy's letter was as follows:

"I cannot tell you, my dear sir, how much I was touched by the kindness of your letter and conduct—so different from what I have met with from others. I will not cloud your happiness—in which, believe me, I heartily rejoice—by the melancholy detail of all my own sorrows and disappointments; but only answer briefly to your friendly inquiries respecting my affairs.

"And first, for my unfortunate married daughter, who has been in this terrible manner returned upon our hands. She thanks you for your indulgence, on which she will not encroach. Before you receive this, she will have left Percy-hall. She is going to live with a Miss Clapham, a great heiress, who wants a fashionable companion and chaperon. Mrs. Falconer became acquainted with her at Tunbridge, and has devised this plan for Arabella. I fear Bell's disposition will not suit such a situation, but she has no other resource.

"Mrs. Falconer and Georgiana have so over-managed matters with respect to Petcalf, that it has ended, as I long since feared it would, in his breaking off. If Mrs. Falconer had taken my advice, Georgiana might now be completely settled; instead of which she is fitting out for India. She is going, to be sure, in good company; but in my opinion the expense (which, Heaven knows, I can ill afford) will be thrown away like all the rest—for Georgiana has been much worn by late hours, and though still young, has, I fear, lost her bloom, and looks rather old for India.

"I am truly obliged to you, my dear sir, for your friendly offer with respect to Falconer-court, and have in consequence stopped the sale of the furniture. I shall rejoice to have such a good tenant as Mr. Temple. It is indeed much more agreeable to me to let than to sell. The accommodation, as you propose, will put it in my power to release Cunningham, which is my most pressing difficulty.

"As you are the only person in the world now who takes an interest in my affairs, or to whom I can safely unburden my mind, I must, though I know complaint to be useless, relieve my heart by it for a moment. I can safely say, that for the last ten years of my life I have never spent a day for myself. I have been continually planning and toiling to advance my family,—not an opportunity has been neglected; and yet from this very family springs all my unhappiness. Even Mrs. Falconer blames me as the cause of that sad business, which has disgraced us for ever, and deprived us of all our friends—and has afforded an excuse for breaking all promises. There are many, whom I will not name, but they are persons now high in office, who have—I may venture to say it to you—used me shamefully ill.

"Many an honest tradesman and manufacturer, to say nothing of men of talents in the liberal professions, I have seen in the course of the last forty years make their own fortunes, and large fortunes, while I have ended worse than I began—have literally been working all my life for others, not only without reward, but without thanks. If I were to begin life again, I certainly should follow your principles, my dear sir, and depend more upon myself and less upon others, than I have done—But now all is over. Let me assure you, that in the midst of my own misfortunes, I rejoice in your prosperity, and in the esteem and respect with which I hear you and yours spoken of by all.

"Present my affectionate regards and congratulations to Mrs. Percy, and to all your amiable and happy circle. Propriety and feeling for my poor daughter, Lady Percy, must prevent my paying at present my personal congratulations to you at Percy-hall; but I trust you will not the less believe in the sincerity of my attachment.

"I am, my dear sir,

"Your obliged and faithful

"Friend and servant,

"T. FALCONER.

"P.S.—I have just learnt that the little place I mentioned to Mr. Alfred Percy, when we last met, is not disposed of. Lord Oldborough's influence, as Mr. Temple well knows, is still all-powerful; and your interest with his lordship, you must be sensible, is greater than that of any other person living, without exception. A word from you would do the business for me. It is but a trifle, which I should once have been ashamed to ask: but it is now a matter of necessity."

The event of the trial, and the restoration of the Percy family to their property, were heard with transports of joy by the old tenantry. They had not needed the effect of contrast, to make them love and feel the value of their good landlord; but certainly Sir Robert Percy's tyranny, and all that he had made them suffer for their obstinate fidelity to the old branch, had heightened and fortified their attachment. It was now their turn to glory in that honest obstinacy, and with the strong English sense of justice, they triumphed in having the rightful owners restored to their estate, and to the seat of their ancestors.

As the Percy family crossed the well-known bridge at the end of the village, those bells, which had sounded so mournfully, which had been muffled when they quitted their home, now rang out a merry triumphant peal—and it was rung by the hands of the very same persons who had formerly given that proof of attachment to him in his adversity.—Emotion as strong now seized Mr. Percy's heart. At the same spot he jumped out of the carriage, and by the same path along which he had hastened to stop the bell-ringers, lest they should ruin themselves with Sir Robert, he now hastened to see and thank these honest, courageous people. In passing through the village, which had been freshly swept and garnished the people, whom, he remembered to have seen in tears following the carriage at their departure, were now crowding to their doors with faces bright with smiles. Hats that had never stirred, and backs that had never bent for the usurper, were now eager with low bows to mark their proud respect to the true man. There were no noisy acclamations, for all were touched. The voices of the young children, however, were heard, who, as their mothers held them up in their arms, to see the landlord, of whom they had heard so much, offered their little nosegays as the open carriage passed, and repeated blessings on those, on whom from their cradles, they had heard blessings bestowed by their parents.

The old steward stood ready at the park-gate to open it for his master. His master and the ladies put their hands out of the carriage to shake hands with him, but he could not stand it. He just touched his master's hand. Tears streamed down his face, and turning away without being able to say one word, he hid himself in the porter's lodge.

As they drove up to the house, they saw standing on the steps waiting—and long had he been waiting there, for the first sound of the carriage—Johnson, the butler, who had followed the family to the Hills, and had served them in their fallen fortunes—Johnson was now himself. Before the hall-door, wide open to receive them, he stood, with the livery-servants in due order.

Mrs. Harte, the good old housekeeper, had been sent down to prepare for the reception of the family, and a world of trouble she had had; but all was now right and proper, and she was as active and alert as the youngest of her maidens could have been, in conducting the ladies to their apartments, in showing all the old places, and doing what she called the honours of the re-installation. She could have wished to have vented a little of her indignation, and to have told how some things had been left; but her better taste and judgment, and her sense of what would be pleasing to her master and mistress, repressed all recrimination. By the help of frequent recurrence to her snuff-box, in difficulties great, together with much rubbing of her hands, and some bridling of her head, she got through it, without naming those, who should not be thought of, as she observed, on this joyful day.

The happiness of the Percy family was completed by the return of Godfrey, of Caroline, and Count Altenberg. Godfrey arrived just as his family were settled at Percy-hall. After his long absence from his home and country, he doubly enjoyed this scene of domestic prosperity. Beloved as Rosamond was by rich and poor in the neighbourhood, and the general favourite of her family, her approaching marriage spread new and universal joy. It is impossible to give an idea of the congratulations, and of the bustle of the various preparations, which were going on at this time at Percy-hall, especially in the lower regions. Even Mrs. Harte's all-regulating genius was insufficient for the exigencies of the times. Indeed, her head and her heart were now at perpetual variance, continually counteracting and contradicting each other. One moment delighted with the joy and affection of the world below, she would come up to boast of it to her mistress and her young ladies; the next moment she would scold all the people for being out of their wits, and for not minding or knowing a single thing they were doing, or ordered to do, "no more than the babes in the wood;" then proving the next minute and acknowledging that she was "really quite as bad as themselves. And no wonder, for the thoughts of Miss Rosamond's marriage had turned her head entirely upside down—for she had been at Miss Rosamond's christening, held her by proxy, and considered her always as her particular own child, and well she might, for a better, except, perhaps, Miss Caroline—I should say the countess—never breathed."

The making a desert island for Miss Rosamond's wedding-dinner was the object which had taken such forcible possession of Mrs. Harte's imagination, that till it was accomplished it was in vain to hope that any other could, in her eyes, appear in any kind of proportion. In the midst of all the sentimental joy above stairs, and in the midst of all the important business of settlements and lawyers, Mrs. Harte was pursuing the settled purpose of her soul, constructing with infinite care, as directed by her complete English Housekeeper, a desert island for a wedding, in a deep china dish, with a mount in the middle, two figures upon the mount, with crowns on their heads, a knot of rock-candy at their feet, and gravel-walks of shot comfits, judiciously intersecting in every direction their dominions.

CHAPTER XLIV

As soon as it was possible, after his return to Percy-hall, Mr. Percy went to pay his respects to Lord Oldborough. He found this great statesman happy in retirement, without any affectation of happiness. There were proofs in every thing about him that his mind had unbent itself agreeably; his powers had expanded upon different objects, building, planting, improving the soil and the people.

He had many tastes, which had long lain dormant, or rather which had been held in subjugation by one tyrant passion. That passion vanquished, the former tastes resumed their activity. The superior strength of his character was shown in his never recurring to ambition. Its vigour was displayed in the means by which he supplied himself, not only with variety of occupation, but with variety of motive. Those, who best know the human mind must be aware of the difficulty of supplying motive for one accustomed to stimulus of so high a kind, as that to which Lord Oldborough had been habituated. For one who had been at the head of the government of a great nation, to make for himself objects in the stillness and privacy of a country life, required no common talent and energy of soul. The difficulty was increased to Lord Oldborough, for to him the vast resource of a taste for literature was wanting.

The biographer of Sir Robert Walpole tells us, that though he had not forgotten his classical attainments, he had little taste for literary occupations. Sir Robert once expressed his regret on this subject to Mr. Fox, in the library at Houghton. "I wish," he said, "I took as much delight in reading as you do; it would be the means of alleviating many tedious hours in my present retirement. But, to my misfortune, I derive no pleasure from such pursuits."

Lord Oldborough felt, but never condescended to complain of that deficiency of general literature, which was caused in him, partly by his not having had time for the attainment, and partly by his having formed too low an estimate of the influence and power of literature in the political world. But he now took peculiar delight in recalling the classical studies in which he had in his youth excelled; as Mr. Percy sympathized with him in this taste, there was another point in which they coalesced. Mr. Percy stayed with his old friend some days, for he was anxious to give him this proof of attachment, and felt interested in seeing his character develope itself in a new direction, displaying fresh life and strength, and unexpected resource in circumstances, in which statesmen of the most vigorous minds, and of the highest spirit, have been seen to "droop and drowse," to sink into indolence, sensuality, or the horrors of hypochondriacism and superstition.

Lord Oldborough, on his first retiring to Clermont-park, had informed Mr. Percy that he should wish to see him as soon as he had arranged certain papers. He now reminded his lordship of it, and Lord Oldborough put into his hands a sketch, which he had been drawing out, of the principal transactions in which he had been engaged during his political career, with copies of his letters to the first public characters of the day in our own and in foreign countries. Even by those who had felt no regard for the man, the letters of such a minister would have been read with avidity; but Mr. Percy perused them with a stronger interest than any which could be created by mere political or philosophical curiosity. He read them with a pleasure which a generous mind takes in admiring that which is good and great, with the delight which a true friend feels in seeing proofs that justify all the esteem he had previously felt. He saw in these original documents, in this history of Lord Oldborough's political life, the most perfect consistency and integrity, the most disinterested and enlightened patriotism. When Mr. Percy returned the manuscript to his lordship, he spoke of the satisfaction he must experience in looking back upon this record of a life spent in the service of his country, and observed that he was not surprised that, with such a solid source of self-approbation, such indefeasible claims to the gratitude of his countrymen, and such well-earned fame, he should be, as he appeared, happy in retirement.

"I am happy, and, I believe, principally from the cause you have mentioned," said Lord Oldborough, who had a mind too great for the affectation of humility. "So far I am happy."

"Yet," added he, after a considerable pause, "I have, I feel, a greater capability of happiness, for which I have been prevented from making any provision, partly by the course of life of which I made choice, and partly by circumstances over which I had no control."

He paused again; and, turning the conversation, spoke of his sister, an elderly lady, who had come to pass some time with him. They had lived separate almost all their lives; she in Scotland with her husband, a Scottish nobleman, who having died about the time when Lord Oldborough had resigned his ministerial situation, she had accepted his lordship's invitation to visit him in his retirement. The early attachment he had had for this sister seemed to revive in his mind when they met; and, as if glad to have some object for his affections, they were poured out upon her. Mr. Percy observed a tenderness in his manner and voice when he spoke to her, a thousand little attentions, which no one would have expected from the apparently stern Lord Oldborough, a man who had been engrossed all his life by politics.

On the morning of the last day which Mr. Percy meant to spend at Clermont-park, his lordship, as they were sitting together in his study, expressed more than common regret at the necessity for his friend's departure, but said, "I have no right to detain you from your family." Then, after a pause, he added, "Mr. Percy, you first gave me the idea that a private life is the happiest."

"My lord, in most cases I believe it is; but I never meant to assert that a public life spent in noble exertion, and with the consciousness of superior talent and utility, is not more desirable than the life of any obscure individual can possibly be, even though he possess the pleasure of domestic ease and tranquillity. There are men of eminent abilities, capable of extraordinary exertions, inspired by exalted patriotism. I believe, notwithstanding the corruption of so many has weakened all faith in public virtue, I believe in the existence of such men, men who devote themselves to the service of their country: when the time for their relinquishing the toils of public life arrives, honour and self-approbation follow them in retirement."

"It is true, I am happy," repeated Lord Oldborough; "but to go on with what I began to say to you yesterday—I feel that some addition might be made to my happiness. The sense of having, to the best of my ability, done my duty, is satisfactory. I do not require applause—I disdain adulation—I have sustained my public life without sympathy—I could seldom meet with it—where I could, I have enjoyed it—and could now enjoy it—exquisitely—as you do, Mr. Percy—surrounded by a happy family. Domestic life requires domestic pleasures—objects for the affections."

Mr. Percy felt the truth of this, and could answer only by suggesting the idea of Mr. Temple, who was firmly and warmly attached to Lord Oldborough, and for whom his lordship had a strong regard.

"Mr. Temple, and my daughter Rosamond, whom your lordship honoured with so kind an invitation, propose, I know, paying their respects to you next week. Though I am her father, I may venture to say that Rosamond's sprightliness is so mixed with solid information and good sense, that her society will become agreeable to your lordship."

"I shall rejoice to see Mrs. Temple here. As the daughter of one friend, and the wife of another, she has a double claim to my regard. And (to say nothing of hereditary genius or dispositions—in which you do not believe, and I do), there can be no doubt that the society of a lady, educated as your daughter has been, must suit my taste. The danger is, that her society should become necessary to me. For Mr. Temple I already feel a degree of affection, which I must repress, rather than indulge."

"Repress!—Why so, my lord? You esteem him—you believe in the sincerity of his attachment?"

"I do."

"Then why with stoicism—pardon me, my dear lord—why repress affection?"

"Lest I should become dependent for my daily happiness on one, whose happiness is independent of mine—in some degree incompatible with mine. Even if his society were given to me, his heart must be at his home, and with his family. You see I am no proud stoic, but a man who dares to look at life—the decline of life, such as it is—as it must be. Different, Mr. Percy, in your situation—and in mine."

The conversation was here interrupted by the arrival of a carriage.

Lord Oldborough looked out of the window as it passed—then smiled, and observed how altered the times were, since Clermont-park used to be crowded with visitors and carriages—now the arrival of one is an event.

The servant announced a foreign name, a Neapolitan abbé, who had come over in the train of a new ambassador: he had just arrived in England, and had letters from the Cardinal . . ., his uncle, which he was desired to deliver into Lord Oldborough's own hand. The abbé was, it appeared, personally a stranger to him, but there had been some ministerial intercourse between his lordship and the cardinal. Lord Oldborough received these political letters with an air of composure and indifference which proved that he ceased to have an interest in the game.

"He supposed," he said, "that the abbé had been apprized that he was no longer one of his majesty's ministers—that he had resigned his official situation—had retired—and that he took no part whatever in public affairs."

The abbé replied that he had been apprized that Lord Oldborough had retired from the public office; but his uncle, he added, with a significant smile, was aware that Lord Oldborough's influence was as great still as it had ever been, and greater than that of any ostensible minister.

This Lord Oldborough disclaimed—coolly observing that his influence, whatever it might be, could not be known even to himself, as it was never exerted; and that, as he had determined nevermore to interfere in public business, he could not be of the least political service to the cardinal. The Duke of Greenwich was now the person to whom on such subjects all applications should be addressed.

The abbé, however, repeated, that his instructions from the cardinal were positive and peremptory, to deliver these letters into no hands but those of Lord Oldborough—that in consequence of this strict injunction he had come purposely to present them. He was instructed to request his lordship would not put the letters into the hands of any secretary, but would have the goodness to examine them himself, and give his counsel how to proceed, and to whom they should, in case of his lordship's declining to interfere, be addressed.

"Mr. Percy!" said Lord Oldborough, recalling Mr. Percy, who had risen to quit the room, "you will not leave me—Whatever you may wish to say, M. l'abbé, may be said before this gentleman—my friend."

His lordship then opened the packet, examined the letters—read and re-directed some to the Duke of Greenwich, others to the king: the abbé, all the time, descanting vehemently on Neapolitan politics—regretting Lord Oldborough's resignation—adverting still to his lordship's powerful influence—and pressing some point in negotiation, for which his uncle, the cardinal, was most anxious.

Among the letters, there was one which Lord Oldborough did not open: he laid it on the table with the direction downwards, leaned his elbow upon it, and sat as if calmly listening to the abbé; but Mr. Percy, knowing his countenance, saw signs of extraordinary emotion, with difficulty repressed.

At length the gesticulating abbé finished, and waited his lordship's instructions.

They were given in few words. The letters re-directed to the king and the Duke of Greenwich were returned to him. He thanked his lordship with many Italian superlatives—declined his lordship's invitation to stay till the next day at Clermont-park—said he was pressed in point of time—that it was indispensably necessary for him to be in London, to deliver these papers, as soon as possible. His eye glanced on the unopened letter.

"Private, sir," said Lord Oldborough, in a stern voice, without moving his elbow from the paper: "whatever answer it may require, I shall have the honour to transmit to you—for the cardinal."

The abbé bowed low, left his address, and took leave. Lord Oldborough, after attending him to the door, and seeing him depart, returned, took out his watch, and said to Mr. Percy "Come to me, in my cabinet, in five minutes."

Seeing his sister on the walk approaching his house, he added, "Let none follow me."

When the five minutes were over, Mr. Percy went to Lord Oldborough's cabinet—knocked—no answer—knocked again—louder—all was silent—he entered—and saw Lord Oldborough seated, but in the attitude of one just going to rise; he looked more like a statue than a living person: there was a stiffness in his muscles, and over his face and hands a deathlike colour. His eyes were fixed, and directed towards the door—but they never moved when Mr. Percy entered, nor did Lord Oldborough stir at his approach. From one hand, which hung over the arm of his chair, his spectacles had dropped; his other hand grasped an open letter.

"My dear lord!" cried Mr. Percy.

He neither heard nor answered. Mr. Percy opened the window and let down the blind. Then attempting to raise the hand which hung down, he perceived it was fixed in all the rigidity of catalepsy. In hopes of recalling his senses or his power of motion, Mr. Percy determined to try to draw the letter from his grasp; the moment the letter was touched, Lord Oldborough started—his eyes darting fiercely upon him.

"Who dares? Who are you, sir?" cried he.

"Your friend, Percy—my lord."

Lord Oldborough pointed to a chair—Mr. Percy sat down. His lordship recovered gradually from the species of trance into which he had fallen. The cataleptic rigidity of his figure relaxed—the colour of life returned—the body regained its functions—the soul resumed at once her powers. Without seeming sensible of any interruption or intermission of feeling or thought, Lord Oldborough went on speaking to Mr. Percy.

"The letter which I now hold in my hand is from that Italian lady of transcendent beauty, in whose company you once saw me when we first met at Naples. She was of high rank—high endowments. I loved her; how well—I need not—cannot say. We married secretly. I was induced—no matter how—to suspect her fidelity—pass over these circumstances—I cannot speak or think of them. We parted—I never saw her more. She retired to a convent, and died shortly after: nor did I, till I received this letter, written on her death-bed, know that she had given me a son. The proofs that I wronged her are irresistible. Would that they had been given to me when I could have repaired my injustice!—But her pride prevented their being sent till the hour of her death."

On the first reading of her letter, Lord Oldborough had been so struck by the idea of the injustice he had done the mother, that he seemed scarcely to advert to the idea of his having a son. Absorbed in the past, he was at first insensible both to the present and the future. Early associations, long dormant, were suddenly wakened; he was carried back with irresistible force to the days of his youth, and something of likeness in air and voice to the Lord Oldborough he had formerly known appeared to Mr. Percy. As the tumult of passionate recollections subsided, as this enthusiastic reminiscence faded, and the memory of the past gave way to the sense of the present, Lord Oldborough resumed his habitual look and manner. His thoughts turned upon his son, that unknown being who belonged to him, who had claims upon him, who might form a great addition to the happiness or misery of his life. He took up the letter again, looked for the passage that related to his son, and read it anxiously to himself, then to Mr. Percy—observing, "that the directions were so vague, that it would be difficult to act upon them."

"The boy was sent when three years old to England or Ireland, under the care of an Irish priest, who delivered him to a merchant, recommended by the Hamburg banker, &c."

"I shall have difficulty in tracing this—great danger of being mistaken or deceived," said Lord Oldborough, pausing with a look of anxiety. "Would to God that I had means of knowing with certainty where, and above all, what, he is, or that I had never heard of his existence!"

"My lord, are there any more particulars?" inquired Mr. Percy, eagerly.

Lord Oldborough continued to read, "Four hundred pounds of your English money have been remitted to him annually, by means of these Hamburg bankers. To them we must apply in the first instance," said Lord Oldborough, "and I will write this moment."

"I think, my lord, I can save you the trouble," said Mr. Percy: "I know the man."

Lord Oldborough put down his pen, and looked at Mr. Percy with astonishment.

"Yes, my lord, however extraordinary it may appear, I repeat it—I believe I know your son; and if he be the man I imagine him to be, I congratulate you—you have reason to rejoice."

"The facts, my dear sir," cried Lord Oldborough: "do not raise my hopes."

Mr. Percy repeated all that he had heard from Godfrey of Mr. Henry—related every circumstance from the first commencement of them—the impertinence and insult to which the mystery that hung over his birth had subjected him in the regiment—the quarrels in the regiment—the goodness of Major Gascoigne—the gratitude of Mr. Henry—the attachment between him and Godfrey—his selling out of the regiment after Godfrey's ineffectual journey to London—his wishing to go into a mercantile house— the letter which Godfrey then wrote, begging his father to recommend Mr. Henry to Mr. Gresham, disclosing to Mr. Percy, with Mr. Henry's permission, all that he knew of his birth.

"I have that letter at home," said Mr. Percy: "your lordship shall see it. I perfectly recollect the circumstances of Mr. Henry's having been brought up in Ireland by a Dublin merchant, and having received constantly a remittance in quarterly payments of four hundred pounds a year, from a banker in Cork."

"Did he inquire why, or from whom?" said Lord Oldborough; "and does he know his mother?"

"Certainly not: the answer to his first inquiries prevented all further questions. He was told by the bankers that they had directions to stop payment of the remittance if any questions were asked."

Lord Oldborough listened with profound attention as Mr. Percy went on with the history of Mr. Henry, relating all the circumstances of his honourable conduct with respect to Miss Panton—his disinterestedness, decision, and energy of affection.

Lord Oldborough's emotion increased—he seemed to recognize some traits of his own character.

"I hope this youth is my son," said his lordship, in a low suppressed voice.

"He deserves to be yours, my lord," said Mr. Percy.

"To have a son might be the greatest of evils—to have such a son must be the greatest of blessings," said his lordship. He was lost in thought for a moment, then exclaimed, "I must see the letter—I must see the man."

"My lord, he is at my house."

Lord Oldborough started from his seat—"Let me see him instantly."

"To-morrow, my lord," said Mr. Percy, in a calm tone, for it was necessary to calm his impetuosity—"to-morrow. Mr. Henry could not be brought here to-night without alarming him, or without betraying to him the cause of our anxiety."

"To-morrow, let it be—you are right, my dear friend. Let me see him without his suspecting that I am any thing to him, or he to me—you will let me have the letter to-night."

"Certainly, my lord."

Mr. Percy sympathized with his impatience, and gratified it with all the celerity of a friend: the letter was sent that night to Lord Oldborough. In questioning his sons more particularly concerning Mr. Henry, Mr. Percy learnt from Erasmus a fresh and strong corroborating circumstance. Dr. Percy had been lately attending Mr. Gresham's porter, O'Brien, the Irishman; who had been so ill, that, imagining himself dying, he had sent for a priest. Mr. Henry was standing by the poor fellow's bedside when the priest arrived, who was so much struck by the sight of him, that for some time his attention could scarcely be fixed on the sick man. The priest, after he had performed his official duties, returned to Mr. Henry, begged pardon for having looked at him with so much earnestness, but said that Mr. Henry strongly reminded him of the features of an Italian lady who had committed a child to his care many years ago. This led to farther explanation, and upon comparing dates and circumstances, Mr. Henry was convinced that this was the very priest who had carried him over to Ireland—the priest recognized him to be the child of whom he had taken charge; but farther, all was darkness. The priest knew nothing more—not even the name of the lady from whom he had received the child. He knew only that he had been handsomely rewarded by the Dublin merchant, to whom he had delivered the boy—and he had heard that this merchant had since become bankrupt, and had fled to America. This promise of a discovery, and sudden stop to his hopes, had only mortified poor Mr. Henry, and had irritated that curiosity which he had endeavoured to lull to repose.

Mr. Percy was careful, both for Mr. Henry's sake and for Lord Oldborough's, not to excite hopes which might not ultimately be accomplished. He took precautions to prevent him from suspecting any thing extraordinary in the intended introduction to Lord Oldborough.

There had been some dispute between the present minister and some London merchant, about the terms of a loan which had been made by Lord Oldborough—Mr. Gresham's house had some concern in this transaction; and it was now settled between Mr. Percy and Lord Oldborough, that his lordship should write to desire to see Mr. Henry, who, as Mr. Gresham's partner, could give every necessary information. Mr. Henry accordingly was summoned to Clermont-park, and accompanied Mr. Percy, with his mind intent upon this business.

Mr. Henry, in common with all who were capable of estimating a great public character, had conceived high admiration for Lord Oldborough; he had seen him only in public, and at a distance—and it was not without awe that he now thought of being introduced to him, and of hearing and speaking to him in private.

Lord Oldborough, meanwhile, who had been satisfied by the perusal of the letter, and by Mr. Percy's information, waited for his arrival with extreme impatience. He was walking up and down his room, and looking frequently at his watch, which he believed more than once to have stopped. At length the door opened.

"Mr. Percy, and Mr. Henry, my lord."

Lord Oldborough's eye darted upon Henry. Struck instantly with the resemblance to the mother, Lord Oldborough rushed forward, and clasping him in his arms, exclaimed, "My son!"

Tenderness, excessive tenderness, was in his look, voice, soul, as if he wished to repair in a moment the injustice of years.

"Yes," said Lord Oldborough, "now I am happy—now, I also, Mr. Percy, may be proud of a son—I too shall know the pleasures of domestic life. Now I am happy!" repeated he,

"And, pleased, resigned
To tender passions all his mighty mind."

March 26th, 1813.

Maria Edgeworth – A Short Biography

Maria Edgeworth was born at Black Bourton, Oxfordshire on January 1st 1768, the second child of Richard Lovell Edgeworth and Anna Maria Edgeworth (née Elers).

Her early years were with her mother's family in England. Sadly, her mother died when Maria was only five. When her father married his second wife, Honora Sneyd, in 1773, the family went to live at his estate, Edgeworthstown, in County Longford, Ireland.

Maria was later sent to Mrs. Lattafière's school in Derby after Honora fell ill in 1775. There she studied dancing, French and other subjects. After Honora died in 1780 Maria's father married Honora's sister, Elizabeth, causing much social disapproved.

Maria transferred to Mrs. Devis's school in Upper Wimpole Street, London. Her father began to focus more attention on Maria in 1781 when she nearly lost her sight to an eye infection.

She returned home to Ireland at 14, and took charge of her younger siblings. She herself was home-tutored by her father in Irish economics and politics, science, literature and law. Despite her youth literature was in her blood.

She became her father's assistant in managing the Edgeworthstown estate, which had become run-down during the family's absence. Maria would now live and write there for the rest of her life.

With her father she began a lifelong academic collaboration. She meticulously detailed daily Irish life; a valuable lodestone of references for later use in her novels. Maria mixed with the Anglo-Irish gentry, and her aunt, Margaret Ruxton of Blackcastle, supplied her with the novels of Anne Radcliffe and William Godwin and encouraged her ambition to write.

Edgeworth's first published work in 1795 was 'Letters for Literary Ladies'. That same year 'An Essay on the Noble Science of Self-Justification', written for a female audience, states that the fair sex is endowed with an art of self-justification and women should use their gifts to continually challenge the force and power of men, especially their husbands, with wit and intelligence.

In 1796 her first children's book, 'The Parent's Assistant', which included the much loved short story 'The Purple Jar' was published.

In 1798 her father married for the fourth and last time, this time to Frances Beaufort. Frances was a year younger than Maria and they quickly became close.

'Practical Education' (1798) is a progressive work on education that combines the ideas of Locke and Rousseau with scientific inquiry. Edgeworth believed that "learning should be a positive experience and that the discipline of education is more important during the formative years than the acquisition of knowledge." The ultimate goal of Edgeworth's system was to create an independent thinker who understands the consequences of his or her actions.

Her first novel, 'Castle Rackrent' (1800) was published anonymously without her father's knowledge. It was an immediate success and firmly established Maria's appeal to the public.

'Belinda' (1801), was her first full-length novel. It dealt with love, courtship, and marriage, and she examined these as conflicts within her "own personality and environment; conflicts between reason and feeling, restraint and individual freedom, and society and free spirit." Startlingly, 'Belinda' also included a depiction of interracial marriage between an African servant and an English farm-girl. Later editions of the novel, in line with unforgiving times, removed these sections.

Frances also pushed the family to travel more first London (1800), the Midlands (1802) and later the continent; first to Brussels and then to France. They met all the notables, with Maria even receiving a proposal of marriage from a Swedish courtier.

'Tales of Fashionable Life' (1809 and 1812) is a 2-series collection of short stories that often had its focus on the life of women. The second series was so successful that she was now the most commercially successful novelist of her age and ranked alongside her contemporaries Jane Austen and Sir Walter Scott.

On a visit to London in 1813, she met many notables including Lord Byron. She entered into a long correspondence with Sir Walter Scott after the publication of 'Waverley' in 1814, in which he acknowledged her influence, and they formed a lasting friendship. She visited him in Scotland at Abbotsford House in 1823 and the following year he visited Edgeworthstown.

After debating the issue with the economist David Ricardo, Maria came to believe that better management and the further use of science in agriculture would raise food production and help to lower prices. They were both in favour of Catholic Emancipation, enfranchisement for Catholics without property restrictions, agricultural reform and increased educational opportunities for women.

She worked particularly hard to improve the living standards of the poor in Edgeworthstown and to provide schools for the local children whatever their denomination.

After her father's death in 1817 she edited his memoirs, and extended them with her biographical addenda. Her father had married 4 times and sired 22 children. At the height of her creative endeavours, Maria had written, "Seriously it was to please my Father I first exerted myself to write, to please him I continued."

Maria worked for the relief of the famine-stricken Irish peasants during the Irish Potato Famine. She wrote 'Orlandino' and gave the proceeds to the Relieve Fund. However, during the famine her 'business head' insisted that only those tenants who had paid their full rent would receive any relief. She also punished any tenants who voted against her Tory preferences.

'Helen' (1834) is Maria Edgeworth's final novel, the only one she wrote after her father's death. Here the focus was on characters and situation and not moral lessons.

William Rowan Hamilton was elected president of the Royal Irish Academy and Maria's advice was constantly sought especially regarding literature in Ireland. She suggested that women should be allowed to participate in Academy events. Hamilton made Maria an honorary member in 1837.

After a visit to see her relations Maria was struck with severe chest pains and died suddenly of a heart attack in Edgeworthstown on 22nd May 1849. She was 81.

Maria Edgeworth is buried in the family tomb at St. John's Church, Edgeworthstown, Longford, Ireland.

Maria Edgeworth – A Concise Bibliography

Letters for Literary Ladies (1795) Second Edition (1798)
An Essay on the Noble Science of Self-Justification (1795)
The Parent's Assistant (1796)
Practical Education (1798) (2 Vols; collaborated with her father and step-mother)
Castle Rackrent (1800) Novel
Early Lessons (1801)
Moral Tales (1801)
Belinda (1801) Novel
The Mental Thermometer (1801)
Essay on Irish Bulls (1802)
Popular Tales (1804)
The Modern Griselda (1804)
Moral Tales for Young People (1805) (6 Vols)
Leonora (1806)
Essays in Professional Education (1809)
Tales of Fashionable Life (1809)
Ennui (1809) Novel
The Absentee (1812) Novel
Patronage (1814) Novel
Harrington (1817) Novel
Ormond (1817) Novel
Comic Dramas (1817)
Memoirs of Richard Lovell Edgeworth (1820) Editor
Rosamond: A Sequel to Early Lessons (1821)
Frank: A Sequel to Frank in Early Lessons (1822)
Tomorrow (1823) Novel
Helen (1834) novel

Orlandino (1848) Temperance novel

Made in the USA
Columbia, SC
12 March 2021

34377829R00238